survive and grow in difficult times

julia cutmore and jack **stuart**

For Stonewall

Julia T. Cutmore

sketty books and workshops
swansea

published by *Sketty Books and Workshops*
a limited company

sketty books and workshops
is a publishing, educational and personal growth institute
based in south Wales, UK

we run workshops and give talks in a variety of locations
across the UK

contact us at

email:	skettybooksandworkshops@btconnect.com
post:	PO Box 680, Swansea, SA1 9NU
web:	www.skettybooksandworkshops.co.uk
	facebook.com/Sketty Books and Workshops
	http://twitter.com/Sketty Books

ISBN 978-0-9575918-0-6

Printed and bound in the UK by
Cambrian Printers, Llanbadarn Road, Aberystwyth, Ceredigion, Wales, SY23 3TN

the background for the book-cover and website is from an original
painting by jack stuart (2011) *level crossing ahead* acrylic on canvas –
www.jackstuart.net

we dedicate the book to Frances (1925-2013) who gave us loving support
and encouragement throughout the project and to Tesni, who gave us
fantastic backup during the writing of the book and for whom
(as well as for ourselves and all who might value it)
we wrote it

acknowledgements

to all those in our bibliography pages whose ideas have helped us
understand more about the world and through whom we've felt inspired
to put our own thoughts and feelings into print

thanks too to parents, siblings, friends, lovers, spouses, colleagues,
clients, therapists, students, government officials, doctors, teachers,
neighbours, shop-keepers, book-club members, international call-centre
staff and others from whom we've learned so much

biographical notes

Julia

I grew up in south-east London, the eldest daughter of a dad who ran a small successful freelance business all his life, was an inventor, and was related distantly to the Beecham family (both the 'Pill' man and the conductor). As a young man, my father set up a pirate radio station to play dance and big band music, and when I was growing up, we always had a huge aerial in the garden towering above the house for his amateur radio activities. My mother worked in Fleet Street as a senior secretary and had a lot of champagne lunches. One grandfather was a freethinker, a trade unionist and a pioneer in the temperance movement, whilst the other grandfather was an hotelier and publican. I had a brother who died of cancer who was a saxophonist, composer and jazz critic based in Liverpool. Most of my family is dead now, but I still have a younger brother who is currently in the property development field and a sister who is a wonderful cook and glass-maker.

I got through the 11-plus and went to a girls' grammar school in London where I refined my accent and developed my singing voice through annual performances of the Messiah. Although the schooling was probably designed as a training for Oxbridge, I chose instead the freedoms of the local technical college and then started my first proper job as a clerk in the British Library in Bloomsbury. Then, in search of something more emotionally meaningful, I went first into psychiatric nursing and then to Goldsmiths' College which I chose because of its community outreach and artistic flavour, soldiering through a disappointingly dull and scientifically-oriented degree in psychology and doing secretarial work on newspapers and magazines in the breaks.

At the age of 26, I landed a temporary lectureship which proved to mark the beginning of 30 full-time years of university teaching and academic politics. I spent the first decade teaching applied psychology to professionals including people from banking, business, engineering and social work; the second decade heading up a national social work training and accreditation consortium; and the third decade teaching social science in a medical school. Along the way I've completed a number of small projects in the fields of sexuality, counselling, equality and creativity - some I've submitted for Masters degrees (of which I have two) and some I've done as consultancy work.

Although having had a left-wing approach to life and the world for the last 40 years, I originally grew up in a traditional Tory home and trained in public speaking at Conservative Central Office when I was 15. As I moved away from the influences of home I started critiquing my upbringing, both politically and psychologically. In London in the 1970s and 80s, I was active in feminist politics and in teaching women's studies, including exploring the emerging field of men and masculinity at a time when issues like 'political lesbianism' and 'women's therapy' were high on the agenda. Over the years I've continued to be involved in gender and race equality matters and in trade union activism.

Brought up within a kind of context-less secular Christianity, I've linked to people who've been on a variety of spiritual, psychological and existential/atheistic journeys. It's likely that I have some Jewish connections in my family history but post-second World War, the line is broken.

I've had many challenges to face in my life, including the death of my second husband and several other significant emotional losses and financial struggles. I've had a lot of experience in the counselling and therapy field - as client, student, practitioner, supervisor, supervisee and teacher. Although there's much to critique about psychoanalysis, I still find it interesting and helpful, and currently drive out each week into Welsh valley communities to teach this kind of material to people who want to develop through formal learning.

I recently married Jack, whom I met via an internet dating site in 2010. Jack invites me constantly to give full attention to the business of 'relating', something which in the past I've found hard to prioritise. We now live very happily with our teenage daughter and two cats.

Jack

I come from a family of entrepreneurs, artists and academics and I have relatives in Ireland and Scotland. My grandad was an unacknowledged war hero in the First World War. In the Irish branch of the family, according to legend, there were millionaire circus owners. My dad became a writer. Also on my dad's side was the inventor of a trouser press in the 1930s. My mother's grandad was a successful Victorian greengrocer who sold his land eventually to Halifax Rugby Club and in her family there were also a couple who started an ice-rink in Glasgow in the 1920s.

I've got 4 degrees including one in psychology and 2 MAs including one from the Royal College of Art. I had a breakdown as a student at the RCA (serious but 'neurotic') and I pieced my life together, learnt psychology, married a psychologist and became a therapist. I've also worked in the addiction field for 7 years in a voluntary sector organisation. Now, as well as writing and painting, I design and hand-build a wide range of wood furniture.

Events in my life have given me a lifelong interest in personal growth and psychology. I had blood vessels burst in my lung in 1988 resulting in an emergency admission to hospital. I was given an additional serious health condition during the operation to fix my lung problem and have had other health issues, such as diabetes, develop since. I think my experience of healthcare has taught me a lot – at last now I get on OK with doctors as an equal and as a person, as I've refused to be put into the patient 'box'. A lot of the more 'therapeutic' ideas in this book come from not only a wide knowledge of the therapy world but also from experience of what actually works in practice.

contents

introduction

Surviving the 'difficult' times on an individual level and deciding what can be done.

We're uniquely living in a time of uncertainty with serious economic, political, social and environmental issues which are hard to deal with and which cause stress and unhappiness. This is what we call *difficult times*. Reporting of these is often distorted through the media, so we're misinformed. Problems exist now in the world that are *new* - they affect everyone and they need thinking about.

What this book is about is:

---

psychological survival
- looking after ourselves and *our relationships* and
developing an understanding of the processes going on in the world today

personal growth
– developing our inner lives and *becoming more effective in our contributions to social change*

We're very aware of the fears that can stalk us as we think about the future – and about the present – whether we can pay our bills, earn enough money, feed our family, or replace a home computer or the car if they break down; whether the government's measures will destroy our working life or affect the charity upon which we've come to depend; whether there will be widespread poverty and anarchy on the streets or daily suffering as volcanic dust covers half the planet or floods engulf countryside and cities. Stress itself can ruin our emotional and physical health as we worry.

In this book, we aim to stimulate thinking about the stress in our lives and how we might manage it, because our long-term survival will depend on staying as well and happy as possible. In this book, we offer ideas to turn fear into something positive, largely by understanding things around us and the social and political processes that affect us so that we can work out what response we want to make, stop living in confusion and puzzlement and anger or sadness, and take our share of responsibility for the state of our lives and of the planet.

Ourselves and the world

The issue that concerns us most is the *link between* our own individual experience and wider social processes – for example, how very often we're unaware of the real agendas behind what is happening to us at a personal level, or we're bombarded with info which makes us feel powerless without understanding why. We're also concerned about the range of responses people can have – such as over-conformity, passivity, miscommunication, aggression, denial - and how to turn these into things like informed awareness, personal autonomy, clear transactions, kindness and social action.

One of the key dilemmas for us is the polarity between the individual enterprise of 'personal growth' and the collective enterprises of community action and political struggle. For example, this has often meant that people in political life deny the value of therapy because it can focus the blame for problems on the individual (or their parents) and is mostly rooted in middle-class culture, whilst entrepreneurs, psychologically-minded people, and careerists eschew the political process because they're too busy making their own lives work out to worry about economics and climate change or social revolution.

However, such stereotypes are out of date – and in this book, we aim to encourage greater fluidity in ideas so that it's possible to see one's own development and growth *as synonymous with* being more able to engage with issues in the wider world and so that people engaged in social action, public works and business development can recognise that their mental and physical health and the state of their relationships has a tremendous effect on the kind of outcomes they produce. For those of us who are struggling to make ends meet or to get out of the house because of ill-health, there are ideas here about the world that may enable us to understand what has happened to us and free us up to be more articulate if not more active.

Like a lot of our generation, we've lived through different traditions – the humanistic personal growth agenda of the 1960s and the emphasis on civil and human rights, and the social control and surveillance agenda and emphasis on scientific-technological-rational thinking of subsequent years which has been coupled with engaging as many people as possible in the mad race for economic growth, regardless of the human, ecological - and economic - consequences.

We're still working on a creative reconciliation of these different traditions and we suspect that there is a trade-off between them – for example, it looks as if with economic growth as a goal, there are inevitable cutbacks in human happiness, freedom and integrity despite the compensation of material goods and the rhetoric about democracy. We argue for a more humane – and rational – way forward.

This balancing is evident in the way we have tackled different topics in the book, and we can't guarantee that our position is the same in every aspect of life. Most of us are full of contradictions and few of us are constant in all domains of life, and this is true for us too. We believe that a lot of life's journey is about becoming ever more consistent and 'worked-out' but it can take a lifetime to get to that point if at all. If we waited till we had the answers to all of it, this book would never have got finished, but it does not represent our last word on anything. We look forward to dialogue with many of our readers.

This kind of struggle is evident in the way in which our psychology is understood, some theorists like Sigmund Freud focusing more on the individual and others like Donald Winnicott emphasising the interaction with others as central to the way we develop as human beings. It's not in our view a question of who is right; rather, what's important is to recognise that there is a *dialectic* between these positions, that we all struggle between wanting to be unique, autonomous individuals *and* recognising that we're deeply attached to others through close relationships

13

and interaction with the institutional structures around us. Sometimes we think we're 'free' *and* sometimes we realise we're not. Sometimes freedom feels great *and* sometimes it's a bit lonely or hard. Sometimes we glow with the security of being connected to others or recognised for our good work *and* sometimes we feel trapped and resentful. The dialectical relationship happens when these positions go back and forth, influencing each other.

The more we all read of history the more we may realise that we're members of populations and treated as numbers who can be raised up or shot down (sometimes literally), whilst our creative or spiritual activity may encourage us to think of ourselves as separate beings capable of taking responsibility for our actions.

This question of *responsibility* is a key theme in the book – we hope that you will find in it much support for the concept of taking responsibility for your own life, however much you feel embedded in systems or in contrast, have found yourself detached from others. We also criticise those who have had responsibility in a big way for financial management and wealth creation, for looking after the planet, for looking after our health, for informing us through the media etc. where we think this is justified.

Intellectual, emotional, physical, spiritual, creative, political etc.

In this book, we're explicitly challenging the cognitive and scientific-rational mind-set that has been dominant in our society for far too long in our view. We value and use our intellect in the book and of course use formal (and informal) language here to express our views, but we also argue for *other ways of knowing* – for example, through our *emotional* and *bodily* responses, and we value our *unconscious processing mechanisms* in relation to the mass of knowledge (intellectual, emotional, sensory, etc) and memory that we carry in us at all times.

Thus we suggest that taking this book on as an intellectual challenge won't work so well – we suggest instead that you allow your personal experience of relationships, of sex, of illness, of money management, of conflicts at work, of psychological disturbance, of stress and the way you've handled it, of creative activity or the avoidance of it, of spiritual experience or disappointment, of political struggle or complacency, of business success and failure, etc. to infuse your responses to the material.

We're not setting out to persuade you to change your views nor to break down your habitual forms of defence, but rather to offer you *more* defence mechanisms, *more* strategies for surviving, *more* ways to understand your own psychological mechanisms and make them healthier and stronger. We offer you ideas and resources and aim to encourage you to look at both yourself and the world as you relate to it.

We anticipate that you may not automatically find this an easy read. Much of the book is likely to produce *'cognitive dissonance'* (a term originally coined by the psychologist Leon Festinger), a feeling of mental discomfort that can often only be resolved by shifting the way we think. But (like the academic Klaus Riegel) we recognise too that holding contrasting views and perceptions *at the same time* can be an important skill to develop in a world of such complexity and with so many stakeholders. Easy resolution is rarely possible and by not foreclosing too early on difficult dilemmas, we have the possibility of finding fairer, more balanced outcomes or developing new creative approaches.

It's our view that an over-reliance on the scientific-mind-set has led us towards a path that discounts other ways of knowing that are more mysterious, less amenable to measurement, and are not easily observable or demonstrable. Whilst science and logic have helped us with many significant developments that have improved lives, reducing everything in life to 'evidence' and falsifiability is an intolerable limitation on human experience and the neglect of other factors such as unpredictability, power-mongering, greed and ego, corruption, love, hate and sexual passion, rivalry and competition, and financial 'imperatives' in the scientific equation mean that what is purported to be scientific, rational and logical is often nothing of the sort, and can in fact be the antithesis of the logical objectivity claimed.

The philosopher, Jean François Lyotard has pointed out that the 'grand narratives' of the modern world are not working – for example, 'progress' and 'justice' cannot be relied upon, and Jean Baudrillard has questioned even the idea that there's an end to history, suggesting that we're constantly re-making history to suit us. So the 'promised land' myth has turned into a reality more akin to a monster which is out of control. This is the basic premise underpinning much of what we have to say.

How to relate to this book

We believe that people come from different perspectives depending on their own dominant 'domain' – for example, for some people, *emotional* experience has been so painful that they tend to ignore or discount emotions as a way of knowing and experience the world through academic prowess, or physical agility and potency; for others, because of difficulties with *language* as in dyslexia or with numbers as in dyscalculia, or through having communication difficulties (eg. of an autistic kind), cognitive-logical processing may not be their dominant mode of experiencing the world and they may go more on their *instincts, non-verbal and physical/tactile relating*, or have well-developed avenues of *creative expression* like art or music. Some people who choose a therapeutic career are good at reading their own emotions and some are actually good at not reading them but are nevertheless able to articulate sensible ideas about feelings and interpersonal relating that get them by with clients. Some people are so embedded in a *cognitive way of processing feelings* and in a *practical way of tackling problems in life* or are so caught up in scientific-rational thinking that the notion of spirituality seems to them to be nonsense. Love for some is a system of exchange whilst for others it can be a neurotic over-investment in others instead of taking responsibility for one's own life. On the other hand, for yet another group of people, love may be a *'spiritual' or ethical activity*, expressed not only in care and support for others including social action or politics, but also in care for their own health and self-esteem.

The point is that there are many ways of relating to the world, and to this book. We hope you enjoy whatever it evokes in you and

16

that you feel empowered to use ideas and stimuli within the book for good in your own life.

We see the book as a resource that you can return to again and again, often seeing new things or reminding yourself about something you now see more clearly or differently.

How we wrote the book

We met through internet dating in 2010, Jack having been ill for quite a while and Julia having been widowed. We were both living in south Wales at the time.

We started talking about our interests and the idea of developing workshops together emerged as a possibility because of our overlapping knowledges and skills. We discovered that we'd both taken the same Psychology degree course at Goldsmiths College in south London at the end of the 1970s/early 1980s, though not in the same cohort. Through an ongoing conversation, we came to make profound life-changes including Julia leaving university life after 30 years, Jack selling his flat and both of us deciding to get married to each other. Having gone freelance ourselves, we also decided to offer a freelance education to our daughter/step-daughter and left school behind. To move out of institutional structures has felt at times like launching ourselves onto a choppy sea with only a raft and basic provisions. Exhilarating!

We realised that we needed to clarify and document what we thought as a preparation for the workshops and that by writing everything down we would be developing a resource for people coming to the workshops. Being in touch with the fragility of life and life structures, we also responded to the sense we had of wanting to leave a document behind which contained much of our thinking and processing about the life experiences we've had.

Initially our thinking was primarily about *psychological* skills – dealing with relationships, sexuality, tapping into the resources of our unconscious memory etc. Jack has worked as a psychotherapist and social worker whilst Julia has studied sociology and anthropology (as well as psychology) and taught in

17

departments of social work and medicine as well as in the field of counselling. We've also both been involved in *art* in different ways. Then we did some work on *spirituality* which involved a lot of processing and discussion because we'd had different spiritual journeys. Julia was adamant that we had to locate what we were saying in psychology and spirituality within the larger setting of *social and political change*, the *process of history*, and *different ideologies*. Chance encounters with friends got us engaged with thinking about the wider *economic and environmental context* of our work, and the book started to become more comprehensive and rounded than we had originally envisaged. We also discovered *RT* – a TV news channel that gave us a whole new perspective on current events.

The book grew larger in scope as we became more and more aware of the many processes going on in the world which ultimately affect people both personally and on a daily basis. There are so many interconnecting factors and so many factors which are presented to us as distinct and separate – when they're not.

Another starting point was our discomfort, not only with the complexity of the 'crisis we're in' which makes it hard to understand but also with the speed of change which is breath-taking. At the same time, official mind-sets are changing and new policies emerging. Due to being trained in conformity through the inculcation of fear, many of us are 'adjusting' our lives and our personalities - often unconsciously - in an attempt to 'keep up', and we feel that the directions of that conformity may not be the best ones for ourselves or for the world. **Thinking for ourselves** and **taking responsibility** seem to us to be key skills to strengthen.

The personal and the political

We need both to develop our own *personal psychological survival and growth strategies* and to decide what we *want* to do or *can* do on *a wider, social level*.

We've tried to make links throughout between the personal and the political remembering that watch-phrase 'the personal *is* political'. We've tried to show how things that we may believe are purely individual or psychological are actually the result of much wider and historical processes, and to stimulate thinking about how we can respond to our own ways of processing the pressures upon us. This for example is particularly clear in our chapters on stress, the body, and sexuality. We've also spent some time on how to understand 'the self'.

When we get on to what's happening in the political, academic, media and economic power systems we focus on the skills of 'deconstruction' so that we can work out the motives of key players and discern connections between events, thus equipping ourselves for making decisions about our own energy, commitments and lifestyles.

This book is for people who want to give attention to their self-awareness, emotional and physical health and relationships and to personal growth in terms of making psychological, social, creative, spiritual and political responses to the world.

The practical aspect of getting the book off the ground

It's important to stress that it wasn't easy to create the time and space to write the book. Julia gave up her job after more than 30 years of full-time work and used her 'lump sum' on food, rent, books and catfood to keep us all going (including the cats). Jack sold his flat and used that money to keep us afloat as the project had taken much longer than we had anticipated, and to pay for initial printing and advertising outlays. During the process, Jack was hospitalised three times, Julia's aunt fell and broke her hip, and our teenage daughter needed our ongoing commitment to her education and wellbeing. The cats kept us entertained throughout, and our daughter took on a major share in the household tasks. We decided against waiting for a publisher to accept the book but by the time we'd finished the project, found that we had little money left over for publishing and marketing it ourselves. We had no contacts in the publishing or celebrity world upon whom we could call, and no experience of going it alone. Doing it yourself is

19

clearly not for the fainthearted. We have little idea how the book will be received and whether we will sell it to more than our friends and foes – we only know that it was a project we had to do.

What our book is

Books on 'change', or 'the state of the planet', or which tell us what to do, are usually primarily written from within a single discipline. Ours is more multidisciplinary. In addition, many of the debates about the environmental challenges that face us have taken place without reference to spiritual or social science perspectives; we try to integrate these.

Usually authors go round and round a single point of argument – we don't. We present a range of ideas as they occurred to us.

We've deliberately chosen a 'journalistic style' as we want to connect to you as readers. We've avoided producing a stodgy academic book and the most important reasons for our personal approach are:

1. a belief that bias is there anyway – there's a pretence of balance, objectivity and proof in the academic world but in reality, academics are usually squabbling and involved in 'turf wars'

2. we're expressing views we feel about, care about, and are being honest about – we're not being paid to say them

3. we're suspicious of the expert power involved in the formal academic world – for example, the mystification and obfuscation of things which are really quite simple which can make it seem as if they are difficult to grasp and need a specially trained mind, when they don't

4. unlike much of the university and publishing system, where there is significant gatekeeping, we want to make our ideas accessible to all

We find ourselves in an 'emperor's new clothes' situation, in that we have many 'experts' about but wisdom is hard to find.

We're not arguing a case or trying to persuade you. A lot of the content is about raising awareness of issues and of practical things you can do so that you can decide for yourself.

We're not suggesting that change is quick and easy, much of the time it is NOT; sometimes it is, but quick and easy change is more for the pop psychology world.

We're seeing the book as promoting a creative process of change for the better.

We see the book as getting people thinking and developing their awareness.

What the book is not

Although we've studied and learned about many things over the years, we not only renounce the expert position but also the guru position (a charismatic expert position) because we believe strongly in the OK-OK position - which we write about in later chapters.

Throughout our lives, we've struggled to adapt in the world ourselves and we speak from our experience. We're happy to share our ideas with you and look forward to getting ideas back from you.

We're not promising solutions for you personally or to solve the 'crisis we're in' but hope we can contribute to a more holistic and creative solution.

key messages

Some key themes and messages from the book are that we think it's a good idea to:

- stand back from the crowd, not conform blindly, decide for ourselves what is best

- not be naïve, read the small print, recognise media presentation (including films) for the propaganda it is

- start recognising that policy (political, social, economic etc) is not 'rational' – it emerges from vested interests, emotions, psychopathology, etc. and that more than a good rationale is needed to bring about change

- face up to the structural aspects of life including the idea of 'élites' - bankers, aristocrats, business leaders, politicians, sports and arts celebrities and some professional groups like lawyers, architects and doctors as being in a different position from the average working (or non-working) person, many of whom round the globe live in abject poverty and some of whom are enslaved or mistreated or killed by disease or war

- accept that the élites might have been ignoring the 'green' lobby for a reason i.e. that in many cases they may have decided to 'milk' the earth for what they can get before it all runs out

- see that commerce largely depends on brainwashing us that endless consumption is necessary, that the deliberately created idea of novelty fuels our dependence on buying; start recognising that a focus on old, second-hand, reclaimed, restored, repaired, modified and recycled goods - *valuing what has already been produced* - and on items that *we produce ourselves* may be what's needed

- recognise that we've all been seduced by technology which is often produced on the backs of slave labour elsewhere in the world, technologies which have created problems of their own (eg. waste disposal, repetitive strain injury, toxins, information overload etc) and that there's a crisis in resource depletion which will force changes on all of us

- accept that personal (and institutional) *status* is the first thing to drop if we're to develop a sustainable economy

- give thought to how our children are influenced by the school, college, media and advertising systems and pressured by society to conform to particular systems and values which are not necessarily designed to help them face the life in the future that is now coming (but are instead meeting needs for the economy, for social control, for company profits etc); we might for example ask searching questions about the value of university education and about how we can encourage commitment to personal values and ethics in young people

- recognise that most people across the world can now never have what people in the West have had and face up to the fact that the élites plus some of the middle classes, have had as much of the cake as they can have before it disappears

- recognise the ruthless competitive nature of nations which have often dumped significant aspects of their cultures in the race to get the best material spoils

- counter the downward reach of élite attitudes which discredit people lower down in society to mask the reality of inequality; challenge stereotypes and look at each person as a unique human being

- take responsibility and not leave the running of our lives to the 'authorities' – we need to be active and in charge

- realise that Western life has emphasised comfort which has resulted in passivity and that this is NOT the norm for most people across the globe; accept that facing challenges and obstacles is not only likely to become necessary for all of us but may actually be good for us

- learn and change – for the first time in history we can access information and knowledge on an unprecedented scale – we have the means to inform ourselves to make the changes we need

- challenge our internal 'vultures' – we've had years of training to conform and we need to retrain our minds to turn off the negative messages that assail us when we take the risk of not conforming

- seriously question and challenge the old mind-set of 'selfish' individualism, 'value-free' science, free-market capitalism and materialist values

- anticipate possible resistance from family and friends if/when we start to change - and switch it off

- find the courage to speak out about things we're concerned about and develop networks of support for doing so

In much of the world, we've become bankrupt in values and spirituality, with an overdose of individualism, egoism and consumption, rather than being committed to a social world that is caring and values-driven. Surprisingly perhaps, in a book written by *economists* - the 30-year update to their watershed book *Limits to Growth,* Donnella Meadows and colleagues say we need *love* to save the world.

Furthermore, we need to face up to the interpretations available –

- that there's no choice because it's too late or almost too late
  or
- that we can go on as we are and the doomsayers are wrong
  or
- that we can go on as we are, responding to those problems of decline that become too obvious to ignore, as they occur, with piecemeal solutions
  or
- that there *is* just enough time to turn things around if we wake up now

Colin Feltham, in his 2007 book *What's Wrong with Us?* is pessimistic about our capacity as a species to transcend our own dysfunctional psychology. Mike Hulme, in his book *Why we Disagree About Climate Change* explores how we struggle with a wide range of diverse perspectives on one of the most important and urgent issues of our age.

The world is in a crisis. You may choose to read our final chapter about this early on. There are no rules about the order in which you might read chapters – it's intended as a resource book that you might dip into again and again, finding different things of use to you each time.

This is a book about change, about taking control of our lives, and becoming more active, responsible, self-aware and aware of others.

We have to inform ourselves and make choices about *our own interpretation* of the state of the world and *how we want to spend our lives* in the light of it.

The approach in this book

We've thought carefully about you, the reader, believing your time to be important and that you deserve a clear writing style. We have different writing styles and you'll find some sections labelled clearly 'Jack' or 'Julia' while much of the book is presented jointly. Jack's style is very to the point, identifying the 'gist' of arguments clearly and often being practical whilst Julia (with a long teaching background) tends to explain things more fully.

This book has a psychological and social bias which reflects our backgrounds and interest. Some subjects we know a lot about, particularly the psychological ones, but in some subjects – like economics and climate change and philosophy, we've had to catch up with both old and current thinking. The book developed organically and we've reached out again and again to different writers and resources to clarify issues, realising that for us, one discipline was not enough to get a grasp on things. We do believe however that there's something in this book for everyone – there will be things here that you've not come across before or not really investigated before, and in that sense you'll be treading along the same steps we took ourselves to discover things as we wrote the book. It's a wonderful treasure trove of material and will equip you with a good knowledge of the range of available literature in relation to a number of topics.

Some of the information contained in the book has been hard to find, some is original, and most is linked up to other books and websites etc., details of which we've collated so that you can choose to follow up on what interests you. Every chapter has its own reference list as well as the whole book having a full bibliography.

The book is a 'personal take' on a number of topics, and we hope that you find our perceptions interesting and refreshing. It's unlikely that anybody will like everything in here – the book is full of ideas and 'angles' on things that we hope will make you think or review your own. Sometimes we do give advice, but our overall aim is to stimulate thinking and offer possibilities for problem-solving in your life.

We've not tried to undertake a systematic analysis of each topic – we've put in material that we find useful or think you will – so it's likely that you may wish we'd included something that we haven't. We welcome feedback which can influence us for a second edition or a new volume. Chapters vary in their length – some are quite short and others substantial, depending on where we intuitively felt our direction lay for this particular book. Sometimes we've reached conclusions; sometimes we're still thinking ourselves about where to go with issues.

We haven't written this book neatly packaged like a textbook – it's lively and interesting and you can dip into it wherever you like if there's something you're struggling with or want inspiration. We've varied the way we've tackled topics - in some chapters, we've felt there was a personal story to tell to clarify what we mean; sometimes, things get quite technical or interesting detail is included. Always, we've aimed for clarity and being as concise as possible.

We're not professional journalists but have aimed for a journalistic approach. We both have teaching and therapy backgrounds and this no doubt shows in how we communicate, hopefully in a warm and human way, recognising our mutual humanity with you, the reader.

We've been careful to abide by what we understand to be copyright and libel law - if we've made mistakes with regard to legalities, these are not intentional and can be rectified. It's always a challenge to raise issues, express views and to voice dissent - we look forward to feedback from you on a variety of issues.

We plan a number of workshops based on themes in the book and hope that you will feel moved to come to one or more, where we hope you'll enjoy meeting others who are also thinking about these issues.

Resources

In this book, we've chosen to offer a wide range of resources – books, papers, websites and films -which you can follow up on because we believe that the power to inform ourselves is an important strategy for survival. We make no apology for the range of material from the 1950s to present-day – where there's a current version of a book we've aimed to include it (though new versions of books are undoubtedly emerging as we go to print such is the speed of modern publishing) but there are also many classic texts which still have value today.

There's a specialist resource list at the end of every chapter and a full list of references at the end of the book.

Books and papers for the introduction

Jean Baudrillard (1994) *The Illusion of the End* Polity Press

Alain de Botton (2004) *Status Anxiety* London: Penguin Books

Colin Feltham (2007) *What's Wrong With Us? The Anthropathology Thesis* Wiley-Blackwell

Leon Festinger (1970) *A Theory of Cognitive Dissonance* Stanford University Press

Richard Heinberg (2011) *The End of Growth: Adapting to Our New Economic Reality* Forest Row: Clairview

Mike Hulme (2009) *Why We Disagree About Climate Change* Cambridge University Press

Tim Jackson (2009) *Prosperity without Growth: Economics for a Finite Planet* London: Earthscan

Oliver James (updated 2007) *Affluenza* Vermilion

Christopher Lasch (1995) *Revolt of the Elites and the Betrayal of Democracy* New York: W W Norton & Co

Simon Malpas (2003) *Jean-François Lyotard* London: Routledge

Donella Meadows, Jorgen Randers and Dennis Meadows (2004) *Limits to Growth: the 30 year Update* London: Earthscan

Adam Phillips (1997) *Winnicott* Fontana Modern Masters

Klaus F Riegel *The dialectics of human development* American Psychologist, Vol 31(10), Oct 1976, 689-700.

Anthony Storr (2001) *Freud: a very short introduction* Oxford paperbacks

1   becoming our self

In this chapter, we explore the question of how we become ourselves and go on developing throughout life. One of the important issues is the question of autonomy – do we belong to ourselves, to our families, to our communities or to the state? In early life and young adulthood, despite appearances, most of us still live the lives that others expect or require of us. As we come into mid-life, events have usually conspired to present us with the challenge to 'individuate' – to integrate different aspects of ourselves and to become fully-fledged human beings in our own right, taking charge of our own lives and destinies. We will have internalised the voices of many people we have encountered through our life and we may need to challenge these voices as well as the pressures all around us to conform to 'norms' set by others. At the same time, we need to balance the needs of others we care about – our children, our parents, our partners, sometimes our friends, whose needs may compete with our own for attention, particularly during crises such as illness and at critical points in their personal development. Considering a way of 'being' rather than one of 'having', rebutting an approach to living that is about material accumulation which can ultimately imprison us in a context from which it is hard to escape, and finding a path that is authentic, flexible and true to our personal values and needs is likely to be the most rewarding path in our journey to the end of our life.

Most of this chapter is written by Julia, with contribution from Jack in the second part.

Do we belong to ourselves?

The first question to look at is that of 'ownership' of the self – a precursor to the question of 'self-awareness'.

Under the mandate of votes and laws, in peacetime, governments can put us in prison if we don't send our children to school; in wartime, they assert the right to conscript us and to punish us if we refuse to comply; in serious economic circumstances, they can impose measures like rationing and shorter working hours, and in times of extreme political disorder, they can teargas crowds, use batons and taser guns and in some countries, firepower, and arrest people as well as imposing curfews and other restrictions.

In contrast, belief in human rights and individual fulfilment asserts 'ownership' of the self by ourselves and sees government actions as intrusion into our natural freedoms. However, in a 'healthy' system, some kind of positive social contract exists, whereby extreme government measures are only taken against people who are themselves 'extreme' or anti-social and dangerous. Obviously where the lines are drawn depends on your particular political viewpoint. But the point here is that all the talk of developing ourselves and aiming for personally fulfilling lives can seem to be at odds with the current rhetoric of 'work harder and put up with less' (less pension, less pay, lower bonuses, fewer bank holidays, more charges and fees, lower compensation payments, higher fuel and energy costs etc. etc). There's a tussle between the needs of the economic machine (as defined by the boundaries of a country – and wider) – and the desires of individuals.

I'm coming from the view point that autonomous people are able to be critical of those in power and authority, and have the courage to challenge when necessary. If you don't want to be that kind of person, there may not be much point in reading this book. I believe that only when there is a critical mass of such healthy people can we have a healthy society – one where governments are not afraid of dissent, where the will of the people determines government policy, and where people are not afraid to express their views.

In order to be an autonomous person, we have to understand the nature of self and how to 'take ownership' of ourselves. This has to begin with taking charge of ourselves as distinct from our family of origin, even whilst we may choose to remain in loving connection with them. It's important to recognise that society is organised to manage and control us through various institutions such as the family, school, the workplace, the health system and the banking system. This chapter looks at our relationship with the family and how we come to know our self.

What do we bring with us into life?

My mother was adamant that we are born with *'a blank slate'* whilst I consume history books avidly, convinced that we are the product of our past and of the inheritance of previous generations. I not only believe this for us as individuals, but also for us collectively. This means for example that I believe European countries are still struggling with their psychology following second world war trauma (– it seems to me that the proliferation of TV dramas and documentaries about the war testify to this) – such as the struggle with eating disorders and obesity in the West, following years of starvation and rationing, and the way in which recent generations have been brought up by parents who lived through the horrors of the war. Collective effects are nevertheless not universal – it depends how you experienced the past – for example, even fifty years after the war, those who were involved in resistance activity at the time have reported less long-term traumatic effects than those who experienced helplessness and persecution. There are apparently people, who (like my mother) having been evacuated out of London as children during the war and away from their parents, have suffered attachment problems for the rest of their lives which will in turn have affected *their* parenting styles.

But in fact, why stop with the Second World War? The power of history to affect us through the centuries is still there, and as I walk round certain cities in the UK, looking at the Victorian architecture and the grand parkland, I recognise that they are the heritage of slavery from which we are still benefiting. Attitudes towards different nationalities and between different groups have been scored into our consciousness from decades and centuries of warfare and conflict. This doesn't mean we shouldn't try to change, forgive, repair, compensate, move forward etc. – whatever we feel is right – but it does mean that we don't start life as if nothing has already happened.

Proponents of the *'tabula rasa'/'blank slate'* idea, including Aristotle and Avicenna, and later John Locke, suggested that we come into the world without any 'pre-programming', but research in recent decades in neuroscience, evolutionary biology and cognitive science of course challenges this, including theories that we are pre-programmed to pick up spoken language structures such as that by Noam Chomsky, studies of twins who though brought up under different circumstances from each other demonstrate similar characteristics and a range of evidence that qualities, tendencies and disorders are genetically transmitted. It seems that even when we believe that much is socially constructed through the influences and experiences of childhood and beyond, there must be something there in us (eg. genetic pre-programming) that pre-disposes us to learn from these.

Those first feelings of being a person in our own right are not automatic and can get confused

Donald Winnicott, paediatrician and leading proponent of the *'object relations'* school of psychoanalysis, wrote about the mother-infant 'dyad' or pair, and the process that babies go through to begin to exist as separate individuals in their own right. In early stages, parent-figures meet our every need with varying degrees of consistency and love, depending on their own capacities and intentions. The 'dance' between caregiver and infant is very significant in this process with a sensitive *'good-enough'* mother or mother-substitute being able to bring about an effective distinction between what is the self and what is *'not-me'*. The way in which a parent is able not only to physically hold the baby but also to *'hold the baby in mind'* when absent is a feature of being *'good enough'* – a caregiver who does this kind of *'holding'* effectively helps the infant to grow in the safety of a sense of reliability, predictability and continuity. (And as we go on through life, this kind of *'internalising'* of people we love becomes very important, especially when we have to experience separation – eg. when someone is at work or college, away travelling, in prison, in hospital, fighting in a war, or on a spiritual retreat).

If at this early stage, parenting is not so good – being for example unreliable, erratic, selfish, insensitive to the infant's needs or offering frequent *'impingements'* of the baby's delicate psychological being (for example, trying to get the infant to do things before he/she is ready), we're likely to develop protective

32

defences in the form of a *'false self'* – see Jack's work on *'persona'* later in the chapter. The psychoanalyst Masud Kahn (a charismatic character – see Linda Hopkins' new biography) suggests that this kind of parenting – a kind of *'over-stimulation'* before the child is ready to cope with it - can produce *'cumulative trauma'* over time so that we become overly concerned with the mood and state of our parents and crave their attention in ways that are no longer appropriate for our age. The main way to overcome this is to return to that earlier stage of dependency within a safe relationship – such as that with a good therapist or a loving partner – and allow a truer self to emerge.

However, if instead, we are able to feel *rage* in the face of impingement or frustration, this is a healthy response and may protect us from later problems, so long as we can cope with the guilt about our feelings of anger against our ('loving') caregivers and any feelings that we might have harmed them. Essentially our fury is about getting in touch with the pain of our *dependence* on our caregivers and an inability to get from them what we so desperately want, for example, when they are not there. (There are echoes of this in old age when we can become angry at those upon whom we depend for help). In fact, once the child begins to express anger at the parent and the parent survives the attacks, the child begins to realise that the parent is a separate being from him/herself – it's through aggression that the child learns to differentiate itself from the parent. If the parent attacks back however, the child may decide to inhibit his aggression or to allow the parent to hurt her/him – it's important that the parent – and anyone we love – can handle our anger with maturity and recognise that hurt has occurred, and attend to the long haul of relating rather than attacking back or cutting off in the short-term. If you'd like to explore these kinds of ideas, the work of the psychoanalyst Melanie Klein is relevant.

It's important to recognise too that Donald Winnicott believed that our 'self' resides *in the body*. It's through our physical relationship with the mother or caregiver that we first learn an awareness of our self. There is more about this in the chapter on *'the body, health and illness'*.

33

Finding out who we are from others

The psychoanalyst, Jacques Lacan, described his concept of the *'mirror stage'* in childhood, when as children, we first see ourselves reflected back as others might see us – eg through what they say to us and how they behave towards us as much as from seeing ourselves in actual mirrors, marking the early development of this process of separation from the parents – of seeing ourselves as distinct beings and operating from our own autonomous core. It's interesting that modern personnel development often involves getting '360 degree' feedback – from seniors, juniors, peers, customers and external bodies in the belief that it is helpful for key personnel to find out how they are perceived before they can set goals for change.

There's no longer the trust that we can effectively 'know ourselves' simply by keeping a watch on our inner experiences. In many fields of therapy work, it's a requirement that therapists see their own therapist and supervisor or supervision group regularly so that they remain aware of any distortion and false beliefs about themselves and can aim to relate authentically to clients. However, none of this should blind us to the fact that everyone has an 'agenda' – there are no ideal saints out there, and we should view all feedback with a curious scepticism, asking ourselves questions about the pressures on people and what motives and experiences affect their perceptions and the kind of feedback they give.

During my teaching career, student feedback became so important to one university hierarchy that they decided to move towards incorporating it in staff appraisal. Every week, as 'faculty', we were expected to sit round a table and scrutinise student comments, taking them on the chin and responding – first by accounting to our colleagues, then by commenting back to the students publicly, and then by adjusting our teaching. However, although there was often useful comment and ideas that made us think, and sometimes relevant criticism, it seemed to me that students could be favouring staff who had power over their assessments and discipline; they would criticise subjects that didn't seem to them to be mainstream and whose relevance they couldn't yet understand; they hated material that was difficult to grasp and complained bitterly about teachers who couldn't make it easy for them; they enjoyed subjects that were practical and clear-cut. Furthermore, since the vast majority of students didn't bother with feedback, it was impossible to know whether the students who did contribute were the most committed or ones who thought you could change things by complaining rather than by doing the hard graft.

Ultimately, whichever category they might be in, the feedback raised the question of whether we –the teachers - were right to insist on things like intellectual rigour because it's important (or because we enjoyed it!) or whether we should be responding more fully to the preferences and perhaps foresight of our student 'customers'.

Feedback and complaints systems must be used with care – they are at the cutting edge of the power balance between suppliers and consumers.

The point here is to look with interest at all feedback, to respond where it seems fair and justified, but also to examine *what it tells you about the person or people giving it*, too.

Exercise on messages from childhood
– gather together some of the messages that stick in your mind from early on in life

From parents and/ or primary caregivers	From siblings and peers	From teachers	From results of efforts eg. in sports, academia, the arts	From other sources like health, religious or creative environmts
Name someone:	*Name someone:*	*Name someone:*	*Identify an achievement or name a person who commented:*	*Name someone:*
What was the message?	*What was the message?*	*What was the message?*	*What was the message?*	*What was the message?*
What was their perspective /'agenda'? (altruistic/ loving/ genuine /self-interested/ meeting the needs of the family etc?)	*What was their perspective /'agenda'? (loving/ genuine/self -interested/ from a particular perspective etc?)*	*What was their perspective /'agenda'? (intended to be helpful/ genuine/ self-interested/ meeting the needs of the school etc?)*	*What was their perspective /'agenda'? (intended to be helpful/ genuine/self-interested/ meeting the needs of the institution/ from a particular perspective etc?)*	*What was their perspective /'agenda'? (intended to be helpful/ genuine/ self-interested/ meeting the needs of the institution/ from a particular perspective etc?)*

Exercise on messages as we get older

		From events in life eg. business failure, accidents, new jobs, awards, work promotions	From health professionals/ sports/gym trainers/ clothes shops etc. re: our body
From partner(s)	*From employer/ funders etc.*		
Message	Message	Message	Message
Agenda of person(s) giving message	Agenda of person(s) giving message	Agenda of person(s) giving message	Agenda of person(s) giving message
From customers/ pupils/ patients etc.	*From friends*	*From different environments/ neighbourhoods etc*	*From any other sources eg. colleagues, fellow hobbyists, community or group members*
Message	Message	Message	Message
Agenda of person(s) giving message	Agenda of person(s) giving message	Agenda of person(s) giving message	Agenda of person(s) giving message

Have a look at the messages you've received and remembered during your life to date and think about how you've responded to them. Have you:

- rejected them?
- ignored them?
- taken them to heart?
- made changes to make them less true?
- been hurt by them?
- found them useful?
- laughed at them?
- recognised that they say more about the other person than about you?
- shelved them – to think about one day in the future?
- changed reluctantly under pressure?
- welcomed them?
- seen them as a sign of love or genuine concern?
- been offended by them?
- understood the perspective from which they were given and found that useful?

Your response to different messages is likely to vary.

By doing the exercise you may be able to discover (if you don't know already) which sources have affected you the most. Parental messages may get listened to or dis-counted. I remember my mother blurting out in frustration: *'but that's what I've been telling you for years!!'* when I recounted to her something I'd responded to in someone's message to me. Sometimes it's not the message itself - it's the *credibility* of the person giving it. Sometimes it's *our readiness* to hear it – at certain times in our life particular messages are not welcome – years later, they come back to us in another form (eg. through someone else's words or in a book) and we can act on them.

Separating from parents

As we get older, we usually want to separate from the symbiotic relationship with our parents. This doesn't necessarily mean that we shouldn't remain close to them throughout our life, but it's important that we come to belong to ourselves and take responsibility for the person that we are. If we don't 'get on' with our parents, it may seem easier to break away emotionally, but in fact, 'in rebellion' we may be just as connected in a negative sense. We can be as bonded to a parent through painful arguments and disagreements as we would be by being loving and companionable, sometimes more so, as illustrated by the Biblical story of the 'Prodigal Son' – the wayward child being the one celebrated over the dutiful one who had stayed at home and helped. The idea of life 'scripts' within Transactional Analysis is relevant here (see our chapters on *Therapy* and *Dependencies*), developed in the work of Claude Steiner.

It might be that it's only when we find a peace balancing the good and the bad in our upbringing that we can really claim to have come into our own true adulthood, and to truly establish things like a mature relationship, a creative life-path and a home in which we feel happy.

On the other hand, psychologist Alice Miller takes a different view in cases where we've been subject to *'poisonous pedagogy'* – she believes that unless we speak out about abuses and neglect and unkindness in the parenting we've received we will experience physical illness, depression and fatigue in the effort to suppress these memories and deny them. Alice Miller spent her life campaigning about this, arguing that traditional psychoanalysts had usually failed to challenge the parenting they had received themselves and that they could therefore only lead people towards 'forgiving and forgetting' instead of 'naming and shaming'. Her work is passionate and articulate and flies in the face of much of the usual measured approaches to childhood trauma. One of the key features in her thinking is that we need a witness or companion who believes us about what we have endured and what has been done to us in order to heal – 'neutrality' is no good to us. References to her work are given at the end of this chapter if you want to follow it up.

Growing up and away from our parents

As we grow up, alternative supports emerge in the shape of teachers, priests, youth leaders, sports coaches, musicians, shopkeepers and café owners, peers and friends. Connecting to trade unionism, student politics, rap, punk or rock, extreme sports like snowboarding and surfing, football, the Church of England or Goth subculture – there are many places that become an alternative world from home. For me, it was initially feminist thinking that helped me to critique my background and reject the expectations my parents had for me to use my looks and skills to charm my way into a high-status marriage. However, recent decades have revealed to us that many of the adults outside our home are not to be trusted – it's no good idealising them as automatic safe havens from bad parents in a world where priests and TV celebrities have abused children, policemen have accepted bribes, lied about their own crimes, killed innocent people and nurses have been found to abuse, neglect or even kill their patients. We have to learn to be streetwise; in a 'good' home, parents help us to develop the skills to discern the people who are helpful and safe even if they help us to separate from those same parents. 'Good enough' parents recognise that we have to find our own path and that we'll need to explore and take risks and they give us their best support and advice, whilst facing the fact that we'll eventually live separate lives from them.

Developing interests helps us make connections through the links we build with other like-minded people. Eventually, as we find ourselves attracted to partners, we make the break, but this isn't automatic for everyone, and depends on a number of factors, including our psychological readiness for intimacy and our capacity to attract people who like us. In our chapter on *Close Relationships*, we include a typology of relationships – *live, fixed* etc. which helps us to recognise what's happening in our relationships at any time.

Career aspirations and access to job opportunities are of course common reasons for moving away, but lack of finance is one of the bulwarks against becoming independent in the modern world, and many of us nowadays find ourselves having to rely on parents for housing – either living with them or having our home paid for – partially or totally - by them. In some cases, we may feel obligated towards our parents or other family members which may militate against setting up separate or distant housing arrangements. For others, there's a cultural environment in which the idea of living close to family, with the possibilities of mutual support and connection, is highly prized and difficult to break away from. Within some religious cultures, to leave home and set up home with a sexual partner is to court ostracism and ex-communication. Conversely, for others, especially if the result of migration, bereavement, family breakdown or family dispute, there's little question of being near to family – we are on our own.

The point is to recognise that our own situation (whatever it is) is *not the only model* – there are communities and families where the beliefs are different. Being in charge of our lives is about **not conforming** to what others want for us or of us (*unless of course we truly want to*).

Exercise
– try completing the following:

What my family expects of me	What I really want to do/ How I really want to live	What are the blocks in my path? In myself? In my family system? In the external world?	What am I going to do about it?

Once we've got in touch with what we want, then is the time for negotiation.

If negotiation is ultimately not possible, then we have choices about whether we simply break away or take a break from the family situation, or if we want to give in, with the chance that we might face a breakdown, a relationship separation or some kind of self-sabotage like business failure or debt or illness much later on.

We're more likely to take a strong negotiating position if we have an ally or a bolthole lined up. In relationship breakdown, by the time people start arguing, the partner or son/daughter has often already got someone else *in situ* or a place to move to organised - and negotiation is somewhat fruitless for the person being left – this is often about turning the tables on someone who has up to then seemed to dominate. Nevertheless, even if at a later point, we reflect that breakdown of communication and commitment was due to factors in both sides, the idea of having a *confidante* in place is very much in line with Alice Miller's thinking that we need someone who listens to us and believes in us in order to stand in our own space and carve out our own life.

Sometimes it's not *'make or break'* – it's about negotiating some kind of compromise – getting our family (or partner) to accept we are *not* what they want us to be – we're our own person - and getting *some* agreed steps towards what we want, perhaps experimenting with some new patterns of living etc., trying out some changes, getting everybody used to the fact that *'things ain't wot they used to be'*. We have to decide if our family's wishes are really 'for *our* good' or if they are for *'their* good'. We may need to be sensitive to the fact that our separating from them is painful for all concerned whilst not giving in to emotional pressure.

Developing relationships with others

Leaving home, if we manage this, does not necessarily mean that we *are* psychologically separate from our parents.

We may think that sex (and the bond we seek through it with a partner) is the route to separation from our family of origin but it really isn't as simple as that.

It's quite hard to develop an authentic relationship with another person when we're young, for all sorts of reasons:

- because we're projecting parental figures onto partners
- because we're often not fully in charge of ourselves.
- because the way in which we relate may be modelled on our parents and not the result of our own choice or experience
- because there are so many things we're trying to sort out including life direction and when and whether to have children
- because we may not have the right space, perhaps not having our own home etc.
- because we may not be sure about how permanent we want to be, we may be unable to commit our futures with any certainty
- because we're relatively new to sex and its power clouds our more rational judgement
- because we may have 'rules' about things like fidelity and behaviour and feel that any infringement is an attack on our self-worth
- because we may lack skills in conflict resolution and compromise
- because we may believe that it's easy to find a new person with whom it will all work out better than the person we currently relate to
- because we lack support, or conversely because we have too much support and can't clarify our own true feelings

etc.

Even if we get over all that, we may hear parental messages echoing in our heads. Having faith in our judgements and our own ability to relate to others can take some energy to develop.

Erik Erikson's model of life development outlines a dilemma to resolve at each 'stage' of life, suggesting that in the teenage years we have to *forge our identity* from a variety of role opportunities, and that we have to move on to the challenge of *becoming intimate with another person* and breaking out of our own individual world, no longer staying within the cocoon of self. If we aren't able to do

43

these things, he believed we run the risk of continuing to feel fragmented and uncertain about our life-path and lonely. However, contemporary models of life development are less prescriptive about the idea of settling on a 'career path' or settling into a marital situation – there is an acceptance that life is more fluid and varied than it used to be, as well as support for the value of solitude. Eric Klinenberg, New York sociologist, reports that in countries where people can choose how to live, more people than ever before are choosing to live alone, with perhaps more than half households in many western countries being solo; people who can afford it preferring (in his view) to have privacy and personal space. Older people (if they have the choice) tend to prefer their own independence to living with family or in residential care. Interestingly, it appears that people who live alone frequently have richer social lives and internet connection with others than do people in families. With regard to working lives, people no longer expect to have 'linear' careers or single employers – the emphasis has shifted to 'employability' and 'intelligent careers' – people have to be able to adapt themselves to shifting work opportunities and to develop 'transferable' skills, the responsibility for their 'careers' resting with them and not with specific organisations.

Sigmund Freud's model of sexual development describes the change that needs to be made from sexuality that is focused on one's own body in childhood and adolescence, breaking away from the connection to the mother in infancy through to the sharing of physicality with another as we grow into adulthood. Religious and medical collusion in issuing dire warnings against masturbation in the late nineteenth and early twentieth centuries couldn't have helped people to develop a sense of their own autonomy and coupled with ideas about compulsory heterosexuality and sex-for-procreation-only, led to a very conservative set of life choices. Yet now, in Western culture, with more openness and the developments of contraception and protection from diseases, the pressure to move into sexual relating is strong for teenagers, and there can be a temptation for all of us to do this before we're clear about our relationship with our selves. We can be torn between the wish to conform and not stick out from our peers and the feeling that we're special and want to have a distinctive identity and life. In an era when work opportunities

44

for young people are contracting, there's a need for ways of defining the self that don't depend on work identity. It's likely that young people will take the lead in defining themselves as *'people'* rather than through occupational roles such as *'nurse'*, *'postman'*, *'manager'*.

Stock-taking

At various points in life, there can be a need to review what has happened and determine what resources we have or need to have before moving forward. Mid-life for many people is one of those points. The analytical psychologist Carl Jung understood *individuation* to be the outcome of years of self-development as we integrate the different elements of our self into a whole. He thought that individuation was a process that continued throughout life but was especially significant in middle age.

Individuation

As we move towards the middle of our life, the developmental focus of our growth becomes *individuation.* It's an internal process of self-development that happens over time. The most significant features of this process are that of **reconciling opposites** and **bringing the conscious and unconscious into connection with one another** eg. through dreams, memories and creative work.

Important aspects of this process include:

- engaging with the quest for **meaning** in our life. The 'Self' is the *organising* part of the personality in Jung's view, and the task of finding meaning is fundamentally a spiritual one. It may mean engaging with the deeper questions of existence, it may mean exploring how we live our lives and asking questions about our activities, values, occupations, ways of relating to others, and our journey through life.

- accepting our **sexual self** – coming to terms with our needs and desires and bringing our life into harmony with them – this might involve reaching out for the kind of sex

45

we really want, recognising when emotions and sexuality are out of synch, expressing ourselves more fully sexually and sensually – in some cases, this new acceptance of our selves and who we are cannot be reconciled within an existing partnership leading into new explorations and resulting in emotional challenges; in other cases we may not have a partner with whom we can explore sexuality and we have to be creative about this, perhaps developing interests in erotic art or architecture, surrounding ourselves with textures, fabrics, foods, music etc. that express our sensual awareness and so on; for a couple who are able to move forward in their sexual relationship there can be new challenges of enjoying sex and making time for it, developing their sexual relationship and allowing each person to play out their fantasies and desires and to be vulnerable to each other, perhaps new ways of dressing and behaving in general life, as well as the testing of the meaning of fidelity and commitment.

- accepting our **shadow side** – dealing with those aspects of ourselves we find it difficult to admit to – perceived shortcomings like jealousy, cruel intentions, laziness, anger, cowardice, materialism, carelessness - usually feelings and behaviours that we are ashamed of. Carl Jung's idea was that in response to the pressures to be 'civilised' we bury certain feelings and behaviours in our shadow side. It can be important to stop idealising ourselves and much more interesting in relating to others if we let go of always taking the moral high ground and believing that we're in the right, if we talk over feelings of doubt and uncertainty and hurt and desire with others in a way that isn't destructive. We're more likely to be trusted (and liked) if we're able to be open about our shortcomings than if we hide them behind a façade or *persona* (see below). This is true for professionals where there can be a strong pressure to present as ethical and sorted-out, never prejudiced, always fair and compassionate etc – whilst in early career stages, we're still learning the rules, as we approach mid-life and late working-life, we may find ourselves becoming more

46

'real', admitting to mistakes and doubts, and being able to laugh about ourselves as imperfect. It's also possible that, as Carl Jung thought, we can find possibilities for transformation within our shadow side (see for example Mark Vernon's article referenced at the end of this chapter).

- the bringing together of our **female and male energies** – what Carl Jung called the *anima* – the feminine principle in men (tenderness, sensitivity to nature, receptiveness, patience) and *animus* – the masculine principle in women (assertiveness, desire for mastery and control, energy to fight) in Jungian terms. If we've lived in predominantly male or female roles, we'll find ourselves seeking greater balance and questioning the way we've tended to treat the other sex. For example, if we've always been rather cautious about the other sex, seeing them almost as a different species, in individuation, we may come to see them as less idealised, as capable of equal partnership with us, and as 'equally flawed'.

In what ways can I accept the masculine or feminine more fully into my being?

But gender isn't as simple as this!

Although Carl Jung's work is well-established and he has many followers, there are nevertheless also a number of critics of Carl Jung's approach. Perhaps one of the most contentious aspects of his work (aside from the question of archetypes in general) is that of the *anima* and *animus* and their part in fixing idealised or

47

traditional notions of gender-role. For those of us who are gay, bisexual or transsexual, the ideas can be complex to apply – because originally written for the heterosexual 'norm' - and are consequently rejected entirely by some.

The main idea in gay texts that do work with Carl Jung's ideas is that *'coming out'* **is central to individuation** – becoming fully who we are, particularly in relation to accepting our sexuality, is the *fulfilment of individuation* in Jung's terms.

Some writers have worked hard to make more nuanced links including Alexandre Beliaev who comments on the movement within male gay culture from the emphasis on *negative anima* – focusing on 'divas' as cultural icons such as Mae West and the character of Scarlett O-Hara in *'Gone with the Wind'* who play to muted, beautiful but dominated males – at a time when gay men were aligned with the feminine, to *positive anima* in more recent times (post-Stonewall), when gay men have been able to embrace the masculine, and the *anima* as being represented by the *'spiritual mother'*. Beliaev writes movingly about gay men's struggle to be authentic as a prerequisite to the capacity for relationship, suggesting that prior to the Stonewall riots in New York City when the gay rights movement is credited as starting (1969), gay men had to *act/perform* rather than *being real* - for example, by taking on a 'camp' *persona* or hiding who they were.

The philosopher Judith Butler who introduced us to some of the key ideas in what is known as *'queer theory'* sees gender as *behaviour* – as a *performance* – rather than as a *fixed status;* as a verb rather than as a noun. This idea explodes traditional notions of male and female and what it's appropriate for 'men' and 'women', 'boys' and 'girls' to do, and helps us to see that we *perform* our masculinity and femininity every day in the way we walk, talk, dress, move, gesture, eat, work, dance etc. and according to the contexts we're in. Someone might behave differently in a gay club than in the council offices where they work, or in the working men's club to being at home with 'the wife' etc. We make numerous decisions all the time, probably mostly below consciousness, about how we want to present to the world. Schools are arenas where, as children and young people, we

48

are made acutely aware of the expectations from teachers and our peers in relation to gender behaviour, little knowing that in fact our gender status may not be as fixed as we imagine. Our genetic makeup may not be the 100% male or female that we like to imagine – some males may have more female material than others in them, some females the reverse. And there's no question that we all receive different kinds of training at home about how we should perform our gender roles. Neither are our physical credentials always exactly male or female – the proliferation in the West of 'corrective' surgery to 'normalise' people with indeterminate or ambiguous genitalia and other sexual characteristics – operations to augment breasts or enhance 'six-packs' testify to this.

The important thing is to feel our way towards what seems right for us – to be as male and female as suits our life and our relationships with people we love, and to challenge the pressures to conform to narrow definitions of gender role and behaviour and narrow perceptions of how fixed these need to be, as well as of course extending this openness to others and what they choose.

Life events that provoke shifts in us

In order to develop as a mature human being with an integrated sense of self, we have to face up to things about ourselves. Typically, in later mid-life, most of us will have experienced life events that may tip us into the process of reaching more deeply into our unconscious mind to explore and understand things. Triggers might include a confrontation with a partner or relative, bereavement, business loss, conflict at work, children leaving home, a moral/ethical crisis – things which may give us uncomfortable feedback or awareness about ourselves. We're faced with the question – *do I let myself make a mess of this, or do I want to survive and come through it?*

Martin Seligman, the American psychologist who is one of the pioneers of 'positive psychology' and 'authentic happiness' tells us (as do many others) that we can turn trauma into an opportunity for growth.

In order to 'flourish' he says we need to develop optimism, engage meaningfully and effectively in our lives and create positive relationships.

He stresses the fact that traumatic events can challenge our beliefs about our self, others and the future and that we have to find a way of balancing the positive things that emerge as well as the bad things, finally developing and expressing life principles that are 'more robust' than the ones we held before.

You can follow up Martin Seligman's work in his latest book *'Flourish'*, in which he writes about his life and experience as well as explaining the life strategies he teaches.

One winter recently, in the early morning, I had a car accident in which I pulled up at traffic lights on a fast road after it had been raining, put on the handbrake, and looked in the mirror. To my horror, I saw that a large lorry behind me was attempting to stop and was right behind me. I knew there was nothing I could do – my daughter (aged 13) beside me said I screamed out – and we were shunted several yards and the whole of the back of the car was smashed in. I briefly lost consciousness. My own seat – when I later looked at it, was completely flattened and broken on the floor behind me indicating that I must have gone backwards with a huge force before bouncing back upwards. Miraculously, my daughter and I got out of the car seemingly OK and the driver of the lorry came towards us with his arms open to hug us saying 'thank God!' In practice, several months later I was still struggling with back and neck pains and anxiety when driving. I was referred for cranio-sacral therapy.

To my surprise, I found myself talking about the damage to my sense of competence – that somehow my sense of myself as a person who could do things and who could be relied upon to look after people safely, was shaken. Suddenly I started to feel old and that I was in touch with the idea that I could not always go on thinking I was in charge or that it was completely up to me to look after everyone or to keep them safe. In fact, I suddenly realised I couldn't look after the world – I think up to then I had imagined somehow I could keep the world OK if I just remained vigilant and kept working hard to be good. I started to let go of an old and inappropriate belief about myself gleaned from childhood – everything doesn't depend on me, and I can't make the world safe.

Developing our spiritual self

Carl Jung was explicit about the possibility of developing our ethical and spiritual life in mid-life – there is something akin to a 'new door' into the realm of something bigger than our everyday concerns. There's much more on this topic in the chapter on 'spirituality', but suffice it to say here that 'spirituality' does not mean the same as 'religious' or being part of a 'religious institution'.

In later life, there's a real opportunity to connect up to a wider vision of life and the world than ever before, because the detail of how to live and what to do has already been engaged with – we have experience of life and we have a chance to gain perspective on the choices we made and others have made, we've seen political figures as well as colleagues, neighbours, friends, relatives etc. come and go – people have died or moved on and new people have been born or have entered our world – and organically, we seem to have the capacity to look with a wider and more measured view at the world than through the smaller lens of youth.

There's also a chance to move from *material* matter in our life to something that is perhaps more *ethereal or difficult to define* but nevertheless more lasting – a sense of life beyond the everyday, beyond the actual people we know and speak to, beyond the everyday dross of our lives, beyond the relationships and commitments we currently have – we start to realise that something of our self might be left behind after we are dead. For me, this is the idea that we 'live on' in the memories of people we have known – and indeed, we already do exist in the memories of people we have known whilst we are alive too – but there are a variety of ways of intentionally or unintentionally leaving our mark on the world.

Time with our selves

One of the main challenges for our relationship with our self is how we feel when alone.

The quality of our alone-time is important. If it's not good, we may need to look at our life and find what is wrong.

For those of us who've lost ourselves in *'over-adapting'* to the needs of others, returning to solitude can help us regain a sense of control and renewed familiarity with our own self and needs. Nothing is more inclined to reduce us to a sense of pointlessness and misery than losing touch with our own needs and interests, and giving up too many of these in the service of others is not good for us. Try the following questions:

Do I enjoy being alone?

How much time have I spent on my own in the last 3 months?

How alone do I feel when I'm in the presence of others – do I have an inner dialogue that keeps me company or do I forget myself and enter the world of others?

What do I do when I'm alone? Do I drink/smoke/eat? Meditate? Walk? Read? Play music? Knit? Do woodwork? Ring a friend? Housework? Watch TV? Get on with work from work? Am I productive or dissipated?

Do I consider the time 'quality time' or do I rush to fill it so that it passes quickly?

Do I dread being left alone by partners or children or long for it?

Am I bored – do I look forward to the return of people so I can escape from boredom?

Is time alone full of worry, memory, grieving, hurt?

Does being alone remind me of times when I was alone as a child, perhaps feeling abandoned or frightened or neglected?

What's getting in the way of enjoying my time alone?

What other reflections do I have on aloneness?

Anthony Storr, along with Donald Winnicott, felt that *the capacity to be alone* should be considered to be a sign of emotional maturity of equal worth to *the capacity for interpersonal relating.* He came to feel that we may need both capacities for the best chance at fulfilment in life, but felt that either route could allow us to get through life effectively. We're not all the same and our particular psychological makeup and our childhood experiences will usually determine whether we're inclined towards others or whether we prefer to generally withdraw from social contact and invest in work that we can do on our own. Unconsciously or consciously, we choose different roles in life that fit our personality structure – for example, being a lone researcher who spends hours at a computer generating ideas, applying formulas and making calculations and projections is different from being a public relations person who loves organising parties and liaising with a variety of people or from being a florist who does solitary creative work with flowers but also sensitively discusses requirements for weddings and funerals with customers and goes to the market to negotiate the best prices for the goods needed.

Donald Winnicott was clear that the child can only develop the ability to be alone *in the presence of caring others* (and initially, usually the mother). When we're alone, we need to feel connected to someone – perhaps they're far away, or back in our history – our aloneness is made bearable by the sense that we're connected to others. If we're doing creative work, we're preparing it for an imagined audience to whom we are communicating – even if that's an audience of one person, and even if they're no longer alive.

If our early years weren't marked by consistent and loving care from parents or care-givers, we're more likely to be ill at ease with ourselves and out of touch with our own needs and wants. Building a relationship with a therapist who effectively '*re-parents'* us is one way to recover, as is finding a partner or friend who allows us to work through what we need to with them. This is one reason why we so often feel a longing for a partner – it's the need to find a loving person who can allow us to practise being who we are authentically. In reality, few partners measure up to the idealised perfect loving parent and we have to take on *their* needs, *their* 'shit' as well as trying to be ourselves. We have to trust that they are genuinely loving and not trying to meet their own needs in a distorted way by pretending to facilitate our growth.

Being alone is another route to getting in touch with our self and *can* be more readily trustworthy than time with another person, unless we happen to have lots of distortions in our own psychology from our past, which another person can reflect back to us. If we constantly avoid being alone, we can miss finding out about what we need or who we are.

Solitude and creativity

The psychiatrist, Anthony Storr, writing about depression and tapping into the biographies of a number of poets and other creative people, suggested that creative activity such as painting and writing often helps. He believes it enables us to overcome feelings of helplessness and the possibility of being overwhelmed by depression, and that creative activity is often a way of putting order onto a morass of emotions and onto a catalogue of life experiences, helping us to feel in charge of ourselves again. Creative work can provide the integrating factor for the personality – Storr is clear that integration of ourselves – individuation – does not *have* to come from interpersonal relating if we're the sort of person who seeks to avoid human contact or for one reason or another cannot tolerate much intimacy, or if in psychiatric terms, we're 'schizoid' in nature. This is important because there's general pressure on us all to feel that unless we're out there relating to others, there's something wrong with us, and in a world where we've become suspicious of each other (and are encouraged to inform on one another) loners are often treated with derision and feared. But making it clear that we're engaged in positive activity, have a sense of something bigger than ourselves (like spirituality or human compassion or environmental politics), accomplishing outcomes and completing projects etc. can help to reduce this kind of attitude – promoting our own value without being egotistical can break down prejudice.

Anthony Storr thought that *we need connection with others in order to be able to make the most of solitude for creative production* – people whom we've internalised, rather than their actual presence. He believes that for some of us, creative activity is a way of developing ourselves through *the search for coherence*, as an alternative to doing so through our relationships with others. This is not a prescription for being alone, but it does allow us to think positively about solitude as a lifestyle choice, about engaging in specifically creative activity as a satisfying way to live, with the potential for self-healing. No stranger to mental anguish himself, he understood that much creativity can emerge from mental suffering, and that creative and intellectual engagement can be a healing activity.

Anthony Storr also believed that the capacity for solitude was as important in judging mental health as the capacity for social interaction.

Do we have interests and passions that fulfil us without the need for others, and if not, should we be developing them?

Interests can include:

- Creative activity or appreciation
- Intellectual study and productivity
- Spiritual life
- Sport
- Music
- Politics
- Environmental engagement or an interest in nature
- Relating to or protecting animals

Some activities can be followed and developed completely on our own (though reading up on our subject for example does involve engagement with the *ideas* of other people), others may involve being with others but can be enhanced by skill development or personal practice on our own.

In the end, it may not be so much about *what* we do as the fact that we do *something* that helps us be a person in our own right. We may need to take on the mantle of different identities and organisations for a while before we find what is right for us – it's important to listen to our own inner voice and honour its truth. On the other hand, it's good to just 'be' – we don't have to do something at all – we may just need to be *happy with who we are*.

If we're simply finding it all a bit of an effort and would rather go home and curl up in front of the TV, we might need to analyse what's true for us.

- is it that we're not articulating clearly enough how we see things and thus just going along with how other people want to do things (–ultimately not very fulfilling)?
- is it that we need to dig in deeper and learn more about the thing we're trying out?
- how lazy are we?
- how much determination do we have to become a 'whole' human being?
- is something blocking our development like unprocessed emotional baggage from the past?

Being able to find fulfilment in something will allow us to be better partners and friends because we won't need to seek the satisfaction of our needs entirely from another human being and can leave others the space to do what they need to do. We'll also be fulfilled in our interests and have a sense of competence which helps when we engage with the question of sustaining ourselves economically as well as making us a more rewarding person to know.

It's not simply a matter of going through the motions of developing a leisure interest so that we 'have' something to talk about – it's about *how* we do it. It's about engaging fully in what we do -

- setting aside proper time
- finding out about things
- defending our new interest from intrusion or ridicule
- understanding its roots and its meaning and its history
- gathering equipment or data or materials

- creating a personal workspace
- talking to people who have experience in it
- disseminating the products of our efforts – entering an exhibition or competition, framing something and putting it on the wall, reading out our poems, telling people about what we do, taking people to where we do what we do etc.

If you're going to go for something, go for it properly. Make your involvement something you're proud of. Satisfaction often comes from a sense of mastery and competence or understanding, from deep immersion in something regardless of what it is. This is similar to what Martin Seligman calls 'engagement' and is a factor in 'wellbeing' – it's about getting lost in something because you enjoy it. This isn't a charter for obsession, but it *is* a caution against being too superficial and just playing at things in order to have the social status of *being seen* to do something. Real satisfaction will only come through the effort of *actually* doing something.

Who's inside our head?

Our internalisation of early figures in our life shapes the way we live. Watch Russell Crowe in the film *A Beautiful Mind* for a dramatic example of how 'voices' and perhaps 'figures' can live within us, and how we may need to struggle to exorcise them or turn them into something positive. In the film, of course, the Nobel Laureate John Nash depicted has a herculean battle through his life with visual and auditory hallucinations. Nevertheless, for most of us there are messages in our heads that may or may not be useful.

Sigmund Freud talked of the *'id'* – the powerful energy for life and the instinctual, pushing self, and conversely the *'super-ego'*, the voice of conscience and self-discipline, making us aware of the needs of others and restraining our instinctive self-expression. Later psychoanalysts who were part of the 'object relations' school (like Donald Winnicott and Harry Guntrip) wrote of the way in which we might have to referee between *'facilitating'* objects and *'persecutory'* objects in our inner worlds (such as a lax, 'maternal' parent and a strict parent).

We're not all the same on this. Some of us have stronger *'free child'* (in Transactional Analysis terms) and are able to play and enjoy life, expressing ourselves honestly and directly without anxiety. Others of us have more *'adapted child'*, and are inhibited by the need to be sensitive to others and to conform to rules and regulations and moral prescriptions on behaviour. Both forms of personality in their pure forms can be a nightmare to live with.

Somewhere in all this, we each have to find our way, and there may be a time in life where we have to make changes, realising perhaps that we have been too *'adapted'* and controlled by our *'superego'* – that suppressing our deepest wishes and longings is messing up our life and making us unhappy.

Conversely, it may be that we've been rather too selfish and self-centred, our *'free child'* completely unfettered, and need to take on board more about others' needs if we are to sustain relationships and work roles. Having *any* restriction on us can be irritating, yet if we're to remain in a deep relationship or survive in an institutional role, there are inevitably limits to our freedom.

These kinds of ideas are central to the question of our relationship to the powerful institutions in our world – and how we respond to laws, rules, sanctions and expectations. We will have found ways of relating to control systems at home and school – *obedience, rebellion, subterfuge, avoidance, keeping our head down, running away, finding alternative places to spend time in with different regimes etc.*

We may revisit these patterns as we go through life.

Conforming and not conforming

The driving force for many of us is the desire to conform that we first felt at home or in primary school, to please or appease, to avoid the discomfort of an authority figure being angry with us, usually our parents and teachers. From the way we're toilet-trained to the way we move round the school building to bells or buzzers, from the expectations that we turn up on time for appointments and lessons and meetings and employment to the control systems around us – surveillance cameras, the police, penalty clauses in contracts, courts and prisons, sanctions like school exclusion and workplace disciplinary procedures, and charges for overdue payments, library books and DVDs, and overdrawn accounts – there's no end to the ways in which we're shaped into well-behaved citizens. In the West, curricula have been watered down so that the youth of today concentrate on how to be effective consumers and how to contribute to the capitalist machine – they're no longer being taught radical ideas that help them to critique what they're being told, and they're being weighed down with student loan debt so that they're likely to be a bit too busy working to pay it all back and avoid bankruptcy to have time to be future revolutionaries. Susan Jeffers in her 1987 book *Feel the Fear and Do It Anyway* identified fear as a key element in the way most of us live life, as well as offering ways of cutting through fear by *doing things anyway.* This is still a bestselling book 25 years later. Perhaps the important message is that feeling fear is natural but we don't have to let it paralyse us, and indeed, *acting* on our situation may be the best antidote to the discomfort of feeling fear.

The psychologist Alice Miller looks at the biographies of a number of celebrated artists, writers, philosophers, and politicians and traces the roots of their work (which in Hitler's case was horrific) to the failure to recognise and name the system in which they had been brought up – identifying with their own weakness and failing to respond to bullying adults themselves. Some, like Frederic Nietzsche, were able to critique systems - like Christianity - but were unable to actually challenge the family members who brought them up in a crushing emotional regime – in his case, one justified by 'Christian' morality. When we grow up in situations where our tender roots have been crushed by authoritarian parenting, we often repress the memories into our unconscious mind or remember but cannot bring ourselves to face up to our oppressors – the actual ones or their replacements in the workplace or wider world. We may be drawn again and again to 'repeat' the experience by moving into situations where we can't protect ourselves, as if in replay we have another chance to get things right. But without proper understanding and support, we may be doomed to repeat our own victimisation.

59

Psychologists like Philip Zimbardo and Stanley Milgram famously undertook studies of conformity and obedience after the Second World War when everyone wanted to understand how people could have gone along with destructive regimes in Germany and the Soviet Union, as well as of course driven by the desire to understand such processes for military training relevant to the Korean and Vietnam wars.

Philip Zimbardo was able to show that students who had agreed to act as prisoners and prison guards behaved according to role, and that those in the guard roles were willing to become cruel under the authority of the experimenter. Stanley Milgram was able to show that people were willing to administer electric shocks to levels of severity that were 'fatal' to the subjects of learning experiments under the instructions of the psychologist. Stanley Milgram wrote in 1974 of his horror at the results (replicated many times on different groups of people in America), indicating that not even the cries of victims or their apparent (faked) death were sufficient to stop people conforming to the rules of the experiment and obeying the authority of the psychologist in charge. So long as we believe commands come from a 'legitimate authority', we're trained throughout our lives to obey and find it very difficult to refuse to do so.

This is why it's so important that we get in touch with our inner self, with our feelings, our intuitions, our unconscious mind, our bodily sensations, and our deeper morality. These will guide us to assess whether what's required of us by employers, governments, even partners, is right and fair and ethical, or whether we should in all conscience, disobey. Carl Rogers, the pioneer of person-centred therapy, wrote eloquently about the need to be in touch with our deep, authentic, 'organismic' self rather than relying on the self-concept that is constructed as we grow up under the 'conditions of worth' in our childhood – ie. the way in which we've learned to value ourselves.

This is also why it's important not to assume that those who claim legitimate authority do in fact have it. We should always check out the validity of their commands and expectations and test their competence against our own knowledge, beliefs and values. It's worth reminding ourselves sometimes that people are in particular roles not because they're the best person for the job but because they happened to be in the right place at the time, or because no-one better was around to apply, or because they had the right connections, or because the person who would have been good in the role fell ill, or because no-one else wanted to do the job, or because they were the only one prepared to do the job at the price offered etc. etc.

As we emerged from the preoccupation with studies of obedience, and a culture that had schooling and parenting methods that included corporal punishment, a criminal justice system that included hanging and electrocution, a political and espionage system that included torture, a medical system that punished masturbation and homosexuality, and a social system that deterred infidelity, divorce, premarital sex and unmarried parenting, the Western world exploded into an era of youth rebellion in the 1960s that threatened to overthrow their governments and change the international landscape. Benjamin Spock, the doctor who had advocated parenting that met the needs of each individual child in his 1946 book, was often blamed for bringing about the revolution that led to more permissive childrearing and less obedient, rebellious young people, particularly those who opposed the Vietnam war as he did.

The point about conformity and unquestioning obedience is that it has a number of negative consequences, including:

- we can become like automatons and go through the motions of things, not living authentically and not relating in a real way
- we have no motivation or vitality
- we can impose on others without compassion or empathy regulations and procedures (and whether or not we actually believe in them)
- we can wreck our own lives by going along with decisions that are not in keeping with our own real needs like marrying a person with the right credentials rather than someone we love, training for a profession our heart is not

in, committing to a way of life that destroys our hopes for creative activity

- we become insensitive to others, believing that they too should conform and keep up with unwritten rules of social living like dinner parties, home improvements, monogamy, looking good, keeping slim, having a new car every year etc – things that we ourselves struggle to maintain
- we distance ourselves from people who don't 'fit', missing out on the richness of diversity, narrowing down our circle of contacts, reducing the information we allow into our lives, believing our own story and becoming less and less interesting as a person
- we become more cautious, saying only what is acceptable among our associates, and avoiding making any challenges to what is said or done, even when we know it is unfair or mean or risky
- we allow bad things to happen to other people without speaking out or trying to stop them
- we live with internalised guilt and shame that though unconscious, corrodes our life energy

Breaking the habit of conforming on the other hand can bring us the opposite:

- we can feel alive and authentic
- we can feel connected to others through challenging wrongs and determining what should be done
- we can take action on things that have meaning for us
- we can develop a critique about things we observe
- we can become more sensitive to those around us
- we can stop blindly carrying out orders and policies and behaving as others expect us to do
- we take charge of our own life
- we feel empowered and vital

However of course *conformity* is often rewarded with external benefits such as stable employment, promotion at work, social inclusion, praise and reassurance, and *non-conformity* is often (but not always) met with punishment, disapproval and ostracism.

Sometimes conforming without questioning the framework and aims of the institution we're in can be really boring. Sometimes standing up for things brings us surprising new connections with people who are grateful or who want to link up.

Erich Fromm, the psychoanalytical writer, believed that we conform largely because we fear being outcasts, that we hate being marginalised and stigmatised 'more even than dying', and that this is one of the reasons we conform – to belong to the herd. If we can free ourselves from this fear and start believing in ourselves, we have a chance to stop conforming, to stop doing things because others expect them of us, to doing things because we just can't say no.

What are the steps we need to make to move out of 'conformity'?

To stop conforming and *live our own life*, we need to:

- *get* angry
- *decide* to be ourselves
- *find out* who we are, including doing a 'stock-take' on our qualities and personal resources
- *enjoy* who we are and what we believe
- *learn* why we believe as we do and know the reasons why we have stepped away from orthodoxies we grew up with or were surrounded by at school or work or in our community of friends, neighbours and peers
- *detach* ourselves from fear of social ostracism and keep away from critics and those who mock or sneer
- *be courageous* and get ready for some losses as people pull away from us
- *find* allies and people who believe in us
- *invest* in some things we can do alone, without the need for social connection
- *find* like-minded people, even if they are across the globe – we may be surprised how near to us geographically some are
- *take real steps* to live more fully how we want to live eg. in harmony with nature, more truthfully, more

emotionally, more organically, more sober, more solvent etc.

- *get in touch with feeling* alive and authentic every day
- *link up* with thinking about something bigger than our self, something where we can agree with certain principles that guide us into the long-term and beyond the everyday
- *pursue* our own freedom and/or the freedom of others

Note some of the verbs:

decide   find out   enjoy   learn   detach   be courageous   find   invest   take real steps   get in touch with feeling   link up

Exercise – take each one of these verbs and **apply it to yourself** as a way of making a plan for change
eg.
Enjoy – what?
Detach from – who or what?
Get in touch with feeling – feeling about what?   which feeling?
Invest in – what?

Alice Miller, who was writing over the last 25 years, believed that young people (in every generation) ought to be rebelling against war, against the sacrifice of their lives and safety for the war-mongering of their elders – she believed that confronting the hurt in our upbringing is the key to challenging the parental generation. However, she's clear that for many of us, the knowledge of that hurt is hidden from view, locked in our unconscious memory, encoded in our body in the form of aches, pains and illness, and furthermore that we're brought up to believe that we must always honour our parents and never directly confront the emotional scarring that they have caused us. Central to her thesis is the idea that we need someone who believes us, who can be a witness to our suffering, someone who loves us - without that, we are doomed to repeat unconsciously what has happened to us or to turn inward with destructive health patterns. Once we've found someone who takes our side, we have a chance of being freed to challenge the parenting we had and ultimately the things around us which aren't right.

The important thing is to *decide what's best for us* – whether to live as someone else wants us to live or whether to *take charge*. Whether we're struggling with whom our family or partner wants us to be or whether it's the replacement figures in the form of institutional authorities or governments who try to coerce us into particular ways of being, remember that there's a big question about *'whose life is it'*? Do you believe that you belong to the state or your family or *is your life your own*?

Getting on with things and our responsibilities

It's important to assess how much we need to do what *we* need to do and how much we need to *look after others*. This is particularly tricky for women who are more often (but not exclusively) having to balance caring for children, partners and parents, (not to mention going to work), than men.

In the end, it's important that we learn to live with our selves, to be able to sleep at night, peacefully, happy with our choices.

We may feel it's a moral tussle and that living life *for ourselves* is 'selfish'. There is plenty written about this dilemma, including novels. In the end, we have to face up to the stark reality that life is limited and that we have to make the most of the time we have. We have to balance the personal and the political, the personal and the creative, the personal and the social – determining how much energy and time to give to our personal worlds – to people we love, and how much to other concerns that matter to us. There are no guidelines on this, but *failing to look after our bodies, our minds, our health, our money, and the key people in our life is likely to lead to us running out of steam at some point in our journey.*

It's important too to be completely honest with ourselves and know that the wider causes we feel drawn to really do matter to us – do we believe in them for their own sake, are they distractions from things we really should be doing, are they opportunities for seeking power or status, are they escapes from painful home situations, a route to meeting people or an opportunity to be with people we care about? The important thing is to be clear with ourselves. Perhaps decisions can be revised at a later point, but if investing in external activities, projects or organisations ultimately leads to personal relationship breakdown, our children going stray or business failure etc. we need to be sure that that is what we were willing to risk. Women who set up camp at Greenham Common in 1981 to protest about nuclear warfare no doubt included some who 'found themselves' through new lesbian relationships and feminist politics, some who wanted to get away from their marriages, some who believed that the sacrifice of daily engagement with husband and children was worth the wider aim of saving them from nuclear warfare, some for whom engaging actively with the world gave them a new sense of inner strength and independence etc. and some no doubt who chose to give up and go home. *Know yourself* and use your imagination fully to envisage the long-term implications of your choices.

Is there an ongoing 'core of self'?

Referring to poems by Stanley Kunitz and Naomi Shihab Nye included in his collection *poems to set you free*, Roger Housden points to the *continuing sense of self* that is so difficult for us to get hold of. First of all, what is that self that we have to create and that remains after everything in life has been lost and left behind, and is there anything that is an essential *'principle of being'* that we can point to as indicative of our *'self'*?

Paul Tillich, the existentialist theologian, writes about the problem of thinking about God as subject or object, as an all-knowing Being in comparison with whom we are lacking and predetermined. Instead, Tillich sees God as *the ground of all Being*, the ground which precedes the subject-object divide. He talks about an essential vitality which resists despair and that *we can only experience despair <u>because we have</u> that essential vitality*. Perhaps it's that 'essential energy' that we can point to as our *'self'*, when all the chips are down and we still have the will to go on and to survive.

Roger Housden talks of the fact that we can have no control over our lives – that people and things close to us will ebb and flow, come and go, that it's inevitable that those we love will go from us or we them, even if that is through death. He talks of the fact that happiness can come at any moment and that we should be ready to feel it, to *notice* it, even (or even particularly) at moments of transition or when travelling between places. It's not to be found in material solidity, even though many of us have been persuaded that the investment in material goods and the pleasure of shopping is akin to happiness.

Neither does happiness depend absolutely on *relationship* which is also vulnerable to the ravages of time.

I've found in a number of people of my acquaintance that they seem to have their houses (particularly kitchens!) refurbished at points when their relationships are deemed to be very secure and long-established – almost like a sign that this is so - they would be astonished if it was suggested to them that 'refurbishing' their relationship ought to be their priority, since they feel confident about the assumptions they have long been making about life with their partners. Yet relationships and the happiness they can bring are not synonymous with having showcase homes.

In the UK, divorce is beginning to increase with more widespread economic pressure, and is highest among men and women in their early 40s, just at that point when commitment might be expected to be strong but the financial burden on families (including the need for refurbishments) is often heavy with the weight of accumulation and time having passed. At such points, what's our relationship to our self and our happiness and could we feel a sense of continuity even if everything around us were to fall away?

Something that is a *'principle of being'*, that takes us through our life beyond current relationships, friendships, homes, roles – could be seen as the essential core of 'self'. We may not be able to define it but when we finally return to it, we might recognise it as a familiar *psychological home*.

When we're uncomfortable with ourselves, for example, having internalised negative messages from others and from the evidence of our life, believing we're full of faults and inadequacies, it can be more difficult to survive unwanted or unexpected change. As we slowly come to terms with what has happened in our life – a partner or friend who's chosen someone else, a sibling or parent who's died or fallen out with us, a job that hasn't worked out or an ethical crisis where we didn't find enough courage – we start to accept the range of self-perceptions we have and integrate the values we think we *should* have with the capacity for moral behaviour we *actually* have. We start to become more comfortable in our own shoes, and even though we might be bereft or lonely, we start to experience the joy of *knowing* ourselves as an OK-person - not perfect, but *OK*. We're not the same as we were, but we do have a continuing inner core or principle that defines us.

The project of happiness

The idea that meeting all our wishes for material goods and activities will make us happy is misguided. Even when all our desires are met, there are a number of negative consequences that can follow:

- new longings can arise
- we can find ourselves in competition with others, especially if others seem to put us down or have something better
- we can worry about losing what we've gained, and the security of our 'stuff' becomes an overriding preoccupation (– burglar alarms, not leaving the house, watching every other man or woman and how they behave with our partner, varying our routines etc)
- we can find that we lack someone to share it all with
- we can become aware of others who don't have what we have and feel guilty or ashamed
- we can find that the price of meeting all our desires is too high – perhaps carrying anxieties, experiencing conflict, or having to work long hours or be away from those we care about

- the fulfilment of our desires may not give us the promised sense of wellbeing – as we look round at what we have we can feel a sense of emptiness and boredom

Radical hedonism, as described by Erich Fromm, in *To Have or To Be?* – the idea that we should live our lives trying to meet any subjective need we feel has, in his words, always been practised by 'the rich' throughout history, and since the industrial revolution and after the two World Wars, the aim has been to extend this approach to life to the middle classes.

The Great Promise of Progress - unlimited production, absolute freedom and unrestricted happiness – has been recognised as a failure for several decades, as we've come to appreciate that the world's resources and ecosystems are becoming depleted and damaged, a lot of human misery has resulted from the bureaucratisation and technologising of work and social systems like healthcare, and inequality across the globe has widened. As a population, we're not generally happy – we're depressed, stressed, lonely, self-destructive, violent, chronically ill, etc.

Erich Fromm writes about the concept of *'having'* as having developed in today's consumer society and identifies the problem as our desire to *'have'* so that it [whatever we want to have] cannot be taken away, whilst at the same time needing more and more to assuage our suppressed feelings, a kind of addiction to consumerism that can never ultimately be satisfied. Travel and education have become commodities that we cannot lose because once we've had the holiday of a lifetime or got that postgraduate diploma, it's (generally) there as a fact forever. We see in celebrity lifestyles that they can't stop accumulating accolades, more championships, more prizes, more television appearances, more transfer deals, more media exposure – they find it hard to step off the rollercoaster that makes them feel secure and valued, even though they already have the means in many cases to sustain themselves comfortably without ever working again.

People who **'have'** bolster their self-presentations with the details of their homes, social positions, jobs and promotions, children's careers, cars, holidays, study-courses and qualifications, etc. as well as the distinctions between themselves and those they see as different – *'my' patients, the new people in the neighbourhood, the 'undesirables', 'my' pupils, 'my' customers', benefits claimants, teenagers, unmarried mothers, gay people, students etc.* If they can add a possessive pronoun, so much the better – it really boosts their status as someone with ownership or power.

People who **'are'** don't need to exchange commodities or knowledge or information, nor do they need to be right. It's akin to James Fowler's later stages of faith development, in which people are able to be open to one another and don't need to insist on the rightness of their own beliefs. *'Being'* becomes ultimately something spiritual, something that flows, something that is more open to the richness of human connection rather than the locked-in-ness of egocentric self-promotion and reinforcing of who one is by *'having'*. *'Being'* means that we understand the flow of life, understand that each moment counts, understand that all of us, as we look one another in the eye, are going to die, and that one day one or other of us will no longer be here. With that in mind, we're able to engage in exploring the nature of the other person and our interaction with them in a loving and respectful way, and our talk of others in our lives will reflect our valuing of other human beings and their efforts to survive in this world. *'Being'* means that (except in very extreme circumstances such as brainwashing and torture), key elements of our existence can't be taken from us – we are what we are regardless of any employment, any level of income, any stressors, or even whether or not someone loves us.

Paradoxically, when rooted in our being, we're more likely to be loved because we exist as real human beings, able to be responsive and spontaneous, loving and compassionate, non-possessive and altruistic without needing to feed our own needs in the process.

Being grounded in ourselves should nevertheless be a fluid process, with the flexibility to change as we go through life. The accumulation of things around us can 'fix' us more than we think, so that we become unwilling to make life changes – our furniture for example can be a heavy weight on our freedom. Looking around our home – wardrobes, dressing-tables, beds, sofas, dressers, tables, desks, chairs, fridges, chests of drawers, washing-machines etc., we can feel overwhelmed with the fixed 'reality' of our life and believe it to be more immutable than it actually is. An earthquake or tsunami would soon change our feelings about it all – we would suddenly realise that what matters is entirely portable, and that although we have a core self, its priorities can shift according to what is happening around us and as we live through different life events. Sometimes 're-framing' happens naturally as new contexts and situations make us aware of different things.

Self-belief

During the 1960s and 1970s, there was an emphasis on developing self-esteem as a good thing for doing well in life. It IS important that we feel good about ourselves and relate to others on an OK-OK basis (see chapter on *Effective relating* and also our chapter on *Positive Thinking*). However, it's important that we don't over-estimate our abilities or radiate over-confidence. Jean Twenge's work shows that for people with narcissistic personalities, when outcomes (business investment, exam grades, job applications etc) don't match up to over-inflated expectations we can become extremely upset and aggressive to others. Although no-one can demonstrate causation there's a possibility that some violent crimes have been committed by people not long after experiencing feedback that damages their self-esteem in this way. (See also our notes on narcissism in our chapter on *Emotional health*).

Jean Twenge and Keith Campbell also believe that young people are being pushed to project themselves in ways that help them get to know people but are not necessarily enabled to develop qualities that are needed to sustain relationships. It's no good developing a *persona* of success that we can't actually deliver on (because we're deluded about ourselves) or that alienates people we're getting to know because it's insensitive to how they might feel about themselves.

Jack contributes:

Ego

A lot of problems in talking about 'ego' are about are about its definition and who's defining it.

The *'ego'* as part of psychological theory started with Sigmund Freud who saw it as an executive reality-focussed part of the personality mediating between the *'id'* (unconscious drives) and the *'superego'* (introjected parental values).

The *'ego'* then to Sigmund Freud is essential for balance of energy in the personality and dealing with reality and is therefore a good thing and essential.

The adult *'ego state'* as suggested in Transactional Analysis is similar but different from the *'ego'* in Freudian theory. Its role is usually seen as positive and mainly to do with reality assessment. Intuition in TA theory is seen as the adult in the child – ie. before a full Adult *'ego-state'* is developed.

In everyday use, *'ego'* describes excessive and distorted preoccupation with self-importance (grandiosity), status, power, money. There's a link to pathology, especially to narcissism suggested here (see our chapter on *Emotional health*).

'Ego' in spiritual terms as indicated by various religions is not thought of as desirable as it is seen as for example, as:

- over-preoccupation with worldly issues
- out of balance for example, greediness
- individualistic vs loving/social
- related to selfish vs spiritual goals

etc.

The Buddhists see the *'ego'* as a source of 'grasping' of worldly things ie, attachment an attempt to 'have' them. Reduction of *'ego'* is a main aim of most spiritual endeavour whether inside religion or as part of a personal spiritual quest. It's easy to see that there's an enormous clash between spiritual values and materialism.

The way I've found of dealing with *'ego'* is to say whether I am talking or thinking about the psychological or everyday or spiritual use of the word.

In the context of this book, I'm referring to the everyday and spiritual use of *'ego'* unless I state otherwise and I'm talking about the negative qualities of *'ego'*

Persona – the 'social self'

Back to Carl Jung, briefly - he called the way people present themselves socially was through the use of a *'persona'* - the word coming from Latin, means *'mask'*.

Although it's an important matter - and particularly in the current age of 'presentation' - there is a lot *not* said in Jung's explanation.

Throughout history, people have been presenting only parts of themselves socially. Carl Jung's idea is that this part of the personality is necessary to enable us to get around in the world - for example, having 'good manners' or presenting a 'readable front' to the world. However, its usefulness can be offset by a host of problems which arise. These are:

- what if the *persona* doesn't 'say' much, or is just a front?
- what is the relationship of *persona* with status, image, social class presentation etc?
- what about the 'best' *persona* in different cultures – eg. the best *persona* in the Wild West would be different from that in a Buddhist monastery ie. is it changeable according to circumstances?
- how does it overlap with role?
- is it a defence or designed for personal advantage?
- what if a *persona* is too fixed/narrow?
- how does *persona* relate to 'reputation'
- what if people believe their *persona* is their real self?
- what is the difference with OK-ness?

- how does *persona* relate to equality?
- where does *persona* come from?
- can you have a healthy *persona* in a distorted society?

I think there are far more questions than answers.

How development can affect *persona*

If you are 'formed' by upbringing to be *over-conscious* of your social self, making a 'social self' can have more significance.

In babyhood, according to paediatrician and psychoanalyst Donald Winnicott, we can create *'false selves'* to protect our real selves. Carl Rogers, person-centred therapist described the gap between the deeper, natural *'organismic self'* and the *self-concept*, which is created by internalising messages from people around us as we grow up and through life.

The theory goes: ....to a very young child, acceptance/rejection can be a survival issue and a baby may make a *'false self'* to protect its *'real self'*. *'False self'* is essentially a layer of acceptable behaviours presented to caretakers to get needs met, and over time, it can become ingrained. 'False self' is not adapting to another person, it is *'over-adaptation'* – see work on this within Transactional Analysis - such as that by Ian Stewart and Vann Joines.

At later ages, also, all kinds of programming can affect the *persona*. To be brought up with an excessive focus on being a well-behaved good girl or boy or being expected to please, or to be brought up in a family where status and competition has been overly emphasised, when this later 'scripting' is superimposed on earlier issues, it becomes even more ingrained. Then there is the social pressure, a drive toward conformity, 'presentation' etc. as well as the range of pressures relating to class, race, status, role etc. Then there is sex-role pressure to appear as the most acceptable male or female etc. etc. not to mention ideas about age-appropriate behaviours. Jenny Joseph's poem *'Warning: when I am old I shall wear purple'* addresses some of this.

More about *'persona'*

Persona includes a vast range of behaviours both verbal and non-verbal. It includes accents, types of conversation, status objects, etc. Also *persona* is the producer of *'presentation'*. *'Presentation'* however is beyond *persona* – it's a further step to include the wider world of larger influence than personal or everyday encounters or work contacts for most people. The presentation or image bar though has been lowered in society so people seem more pressured into constructing their social image when they are 'everyday people' not celebrities. This could be seen in Alexander Lowen's terms as an effect of *'narcissistic over-concern with'* appearance/status/presentation entering the culture.

Also I think the 'respectability' bar has been raised so that for example, the middle classes (especially in certain countries) are trying to present 'squeaky-clean' sanitised images which don't map exactly onto the reality of their complex and messy lives and can hide the real struggles that they are having to 'keep up', causing serious stress and ultimately all the problems that can ensue from stress.

Another fashion in the current use of *persona* is to present lifestyle signals and information that show you are trying to live up to the ideals of your social group – ideals that in fact are nothing to do with the reality.

So *persona* isn't just a useful front or about socially getting around (as Jung thought) - it can be:

- very false
- constructed with intent (towards 'presentation')
- competitive and destructive of real relating
- manipulative
- designed to make self OK others not (status)
- discordant - not reflecting your real self
- confused with role
- to do with power
- idealised

- about projecting an 'ideal' self in pursuit of idealised goals, neither of which is real
- about appearance vs substance
- so distorted and over-emphasised it reflects underlying psychological issues
- very conformist – in an extreme, everyone could end up with the same *persona*
- a 'game'
- based on fear, for example, of not fitting in or of more serious exclusion
- like an advert for a product – the 'commodification' of self
- damaging to close relationships because *persona* can become more important than being authentic
- emotions that don't fit with the *persona* can get suppressed or edited out and you can get angry about demands to relate outside of your *persona*

Apart from all these issues, some people start to believe their projected image is actually their real self (check the psychopathology section).

Another issue with *persona* is that people sometimes have one which is too fixed, making it more difficult to make life-changes (even subtle ones), or to respond to new demands in a changing situation such as a new role.

Internet dating is one arena where people are more or less invited to develop a 'persona', to market themselves as products, and where they have the opportunity with perfect strangers to try to 'be' their *personas*. However, this is unlikely to be successful as a strategy for people who want to develop long-term relationships where 'real life' challenges threaten to crack open the *persona*.

Good news

As you get older, you can get more relaxed, be more real, and less worried about what people think, and can potentially let go of a narrow *persona*.

76

More good news

You can decide if you need to manage your 'image' like a celebrity and ask questions about why celebrities bother.

The less you conform the more relaxed you'll be about your *persona.*

I find it best just to 'be myself' and have a *persona* which is to do with *being my real self* as much as possible.

I think it's useful to see where people are coming from and try and figure out what is their *real self* and what is a projected image.

Also as people can have very rigid ideas about your *persona*, let them know clearly that you're <u>important</u> and insist on OK-OK/equal relating and be clear about things they need to know to understand you.

Don't though depend on your *persona* to get you through. They will need to know something about the *real* you, so be bigger than your *persona* - or theirs.

The *persona* or social self is what a person creates to 'get around' in the world: it reduces conflict, lubricates relating, is defensive (nothing too personal is revealed) and it's a quick way of being understood and 'read'.

Also it's a shorthand way of relating and includes useful things like good manners.

The *persona* is also full of problems, many of which have been mentioned.

There's also a growing trend towards the development of *persona,* - which is for everyday use - into what I would call *presentation* (of an image) which is for wider influence than everyday use and for the purpose of demonstrating power or persuasion.

Some of the main problems with the use of *personae* are:

- having one that's too rigid
- having a 'conformist' one – developing a self-seeking and idealised lifestyle, neither of which actually exists
- having one which is too 'respectable'
- overdoing the whole thing and creating a celebrity image for everyday life

We're living in an era which gives a lot of emphasis to 'packaging' – whether of goods in the supermarket , to important things like sex, or to messages like the news on TV, where newscasters spend significant budgets on their clothes and hair in order to look good and 'sell' the success of the western ideal to the public, conveying an air that all is well and that the situation is stable, 'normal' and indeed, thriving, regardless of how catastrophic the actual substance of the news is.

We need to be careful that we don't spend more money and time on our *'packaging'* than on the *substance* of ourselves and our lives, and also to aim to find consistency between our *persona* and our *real* selves.

Issues in general concerning *persona* are:

- substance vs presentation
- believing it's the 'real' you
- competition – through status and all the effort, stress and costs of it all
- it's much better to have a simple one that's close to the real you.

Additional note from Julia

For some roles, it seems important to present in a certain way. For example, doctors feel that they have to present as confidant and competent in order that patients feel able to trust them with their bodies; bankers – (though beginning to be woefully inadequate!) have to come across as successful and capable in order that their clients feel ready to trust them with their money etc. A patient has

78

to present as sick or well if they want a sick or fitness note; a student as distressed if they want deferment of a deadline etc. It's clear that professionals across the board have gone far too far in this direction, hoodwinking people and preventing consumers from being able to make proper assessments. There's an important balance to get right between being authentic and true to yourself and to people you have to relate to and varying your presentation to suit the situation.

The character Marjorie Dawes who runs the *Fatfighters* group in the comedy programme *Little Britain* is an example of a character demonstrating a comedy *persona* – exaggerating her words and her non-verbal behaviours.

> At one time, in my 30s, whilst during a postgraduate course, I was doing a number of part-time teaching jobs. When I was teaching bankers, I went out in a black jacket and skirt, then I would rush home at lunchtime to emerge in something colourful and unusual for meeting the art students, then home again for a change into soft trousers and a simple top for my group of counselling students in the evening. It was a clear sign to me that I was amending my style to meet my own image of students' needs. I taught the bankers how to manage staff, the art students how to be creative, and the counsellors hold to look after themselves and other people – I had a different *'persona'* in each case, and thought nothing of moving from one to the other. Looking back, I wonder if I could have been more *'real'* – turning up in the same outfit to all groups and saying similar things to them all…….at the time I was more fragmented (and much younger), and hadn't yet come to terms with the inconsistencies between teaching these different groups and each group's values, and I was able to hold parts of my 'self' in different compartments – something that at nearly 60, I am no longer able or willing to do.

Final points

Important things include:

- deciding how real we want to be with people and take the litmus test of whether or not we enjoy spending time with ourselves to find out how much we're at peace with ourselves.

79

- cultivating an ability to enjoy solitude

- getting ourselves *fit for purpose* may require going for personal counselling or psychotherapy (but pick the right therapist), getting fit and healthy, and investing in our own growth.

- not being afraid to look back and face up to our 'demons', clarifying with parents and caregivers what happened in the past, and working out our feelings about it all with someone in our present life

- always setting ourselves in context – getting a perspective on things and identifying how well our personality and self match the prevailing ideas about how people should be. Checking how unusual we are by looking at statistics.

- finding at least one ally especially if we've had bad experiences earlier in our life or if we want to make changes or to speak out about injustice.

- preparing for loss and censure in our lives if we decide to 'be ourselves' and free ourselves from pressures and expectations from others. Examine others' agendas.

- treating *solving problems* as a way of life.

We can be dedicated to growing and changing and remain tuned in to changes in ourselves.

We can think positively and visualise the freedoms and opportunities we will have as we move into a more authentic, fluid and creative phase of our lives.

Books and papers

Alexander Beliaev (22nd September 2003) *Gay Men and the Anima Function* www.cgjungpage.org

Noam Chomsky (1998) *On Language* The New Press

Erik Erikson (1994 edition) *Identity and the Life Cycle* W W Norton

Erich Fromm (1969) *To Have or To Be?* Abacus Books

Robert H. Hopcke, Karin Lofthus Carrington, and Scott Wirth (eds) (1993) *Same-Sex Love and the Path to Wholeness* Shambhala

Linda Hopkins (2006) *False Self: A Life of Masud Khan* Other Press

Roger Housden (2003) *ten poems to set you free* New York: Random House Crown Publishing/ Harmony Books

Susan Jeffers (1987) *Feel the Fear and Do It Anyway* Century Hutchinson

Jenny Joseph (1997) *Warning: when I am old I shall wear purple* Souvenir Press Ltd.

Melanie Klein (1975) *Envy and Gratitude and Other Works 1946-1963 (The Writings of Melanie Klein, Volume 3)* Karnac Books / Vintage books

Eric Klinenberg (2013) *Going Solo* Gerald Duckworth & Co.Ltd

Darian Leader and Judy Groves (2010 revised ed) *Lacan: A Graphic Guide* Icon Books

John Locke (1690) *An Essay Concerning Human(e)Understanding Works, Vol 1*. London: Taylor 1722

Susan Rowland (2001) *Jung: a Feminist Revision* Polity Press

Adam Phillips (2007) *Winnicott* Penguin Books

Carl Rogers (1961) *On Becoming a Person* Constable

Martin Seligman (2011) *Flourish* London: Nicholas Brealey Publishing

Benjamin Spock (1946) (original ed); Benjamin Spock and Steven Parker (1998) (7th ed) *The Common Sense Book of Baby and Child Care* Pocket Books

Claude Steiner (1974) (1990 edition) *Scripts People Live* Grove Press

Ian Stewart and Vann Joines (1987) *TA Today: A New Introduction to Transactional Analysis* Life Space Publishing

Anthony Storr (1988) *Solitude* Collins: Fontana Books/Flamingo

Paul Tillich (1952) *The Courage To Be* Collins: Fount Paperbacks

Jean Twenge (2012)_*The Revenge of the Insulted Narcissist* Psychology Today 25 July, 2012 (online)
http://www.psychologytoday.com/blog/the-narcissism-epidemic/201207/the-revenge-the-insulted-narcissist
Marc Vernon *Carl Jung part 8: Religion and the search for meaning* Guardian.co.uk Monday 18 July 2011
http://www.guardian.co.uk/commentisfree/belief/2011/jul/18/how-to-believe-jung-religion
Philip Zimbardo and Stanley Milgram (2010) *Obedience to Authority: An Experimental* View
Pinter and Martin Ltd.
http://www.telegraph.co.uk/technology/news/9182464/Working-from-home-more-productive.html
The Holy Bible *Parable of the Prodigal Son* Luke 15:11-32

TV
Matt Lucas and David Walliams (2003-2006) *Little Britain* BBC

2 effective relating to other people (getting on with the world)

In this chapter we tackle the tricky area of everyday interactions within our consumer culture, with an emphasis on OK-OK transactions between people. We look at ways of remaining aware of how we feel about ourselves whilst we're in the middle of difficult interactions, and explore issues such as organisational role-playing, being clear and sincere about our needs, being creative and flexible around communication, being pragmatic, being committed to equality, dealing with cultural scripts, handling envy, how we might use swearing, feeling free to 'do the opposite' of what is expected of us and the important skill of *humanising* interchanges.

The first part of this chapter is written by Jack and the second part by Julia.

Summary

As I see it, there are three kinds of relating:

- relating to ourselves, particularly *taking care* of ourselves
- having close relationships - *growing within and nurturing* close relationships
- effective relating to other people - getting on with the world

This chapter offers ideas relevant to all three kinds of relating, but is targeted particularly at the third kind of relating – everyday transactions within roles eg. as consumers, patients, clients, employees, colleagues, students, committee members etc. If we're in the 'senior' role eg. as chair of a committee, company director, head of a medical team etc. we can still feel trampled on or struggle to get our voice heard, so the chapter is relevant to anyone who wants to relate at an OK-OK level.

The method can be used in 'personal' situations including close relationships, at work and in dealing with organisations (eg. as a consumer or citizen) but bear in mind that these domains won't all be equally easy to tackle or to stand our ground in. We need to be persistent and accept that change takes time. It's no good expecting to change a multinational company's policy with one complaint call – (though this is possible!).

I envisaged this method as a way of handling transactions with *non-close others*, and it does that very well but there is some overlap with *close relationships*. The emphasis in the *Close Relationships* chapter is mainly on the *quality and design* of close relationships; the main emphasis in this chapter is on *the effectiveness of actual transactions* and the method can also be used in transactions in close relationships.

I've developed this method over many years, having learned assertiveness techniques and a lot of theory and practice in psychology, and then doing a mix-and-match and a fine-tuning based on personal experience.

I've used it in a variety of critical situations - in medical emergencies, in various crises and in personal relationships.

This section is about *getting across to other people, being clear and getting what we want*. Also it's about *making sure our rights are not trampled on*.

The method I'm describing is designed particularly for relating where there are problems, such as:

- people treating us in a dismissive way
- people trying to unduly influence us
- people misusing power and so on.

It's about *not conforming* to the wishes of others and/or organisations and bureaucracy, but *following our own needs and process*.

Basically I'm making a case for **more direct, more honest and open relating.**

The importance of awareness

Awareness is central to the method whether this is:

- self-awareness
- awareness of the situation
- awareness of others and their roles
- awareness of constraints on others (eg. organisational, personal, legal, financial, fear of loss of their jobs etc.)

It's important therefore to be in touch with our own inner needs and wishes –our chapters on *The Self*, *Values* and *Sexuality* can be helpful on this.

We need to develop our skills in things like:

- tuning in to our instincts – eg. picking up quickly on inner feelings of unease or feeling putdown etc.
- identifying and articulating our own preferences rather than being unclear and confused about them
- recognising *body signs* like tension, nervousness, headaches, stuttering and *mental signs* like memory blocks, going blank, feeling hopeless etc. as clues to how we're doing
- continually referring to our own values as a guide (and amending them if they're not working or we're changing)
- recognising when old material is being triggered, patterns from our pasts like the way we were treated when we were small, knowing that *we can react differently now*

Introduction to the method

This method is flexible and can be constructed and built on to make it individual for you.

The aim is to foster healthy and equal relationships and not to be hampered by the usual junk in relating eg. pleasing, vagueness, coercion etc. My hope is that people develop more warmth and humanity and creativity in relating rather than relating like robots.

85

Whilst it was originally designed for relating to professionals and in consumer transactions the method can also be used in close relationships.

Don't panic and think that all the sophisticated diplomatic relating and skilful social skills are redundant; think of this method as a much-needed *addition* to the diplomacy tool chest that is usually missing and is important in problem-solving situations.

In this section I mention *power* in transactions, but have not dwelt on 'dominance', which I cannot just envisage as belonging solely to the 'animal kingdom'. I think humans engage in trying to dominate by tone and loudness of their voices, 'pushing in' to conversations and in a host of other non-verbal behaviours, including how they dress and which cars they drive. I am not a fan of people pulling status on each other.

For the last forty years, there's been an interest in 'assertiveness', which (briefly) means *standing up for your rights*. Books like those by Robert J Alberti and Manuel J Smith brought these techniques into the public domain in the 1980s.

At its crudest, this involved simple behavioural techniques like *broken record* (steamrolling other people) and *fogging* (finding something to agree with in the other person's presentation) as described in Manuel Smith's book; slightly improved, it meant adjusting your transactions with ideas of *parent, adult* and *child* ego-states eg. through the use of *transactional analysis* (as pioneered by Eric Berne). Even more improved versions may include *reading non-verbal language* and *affording rights to others.*

There are some problems though with all these methods, including:

- they missed the bigger picture
- they were usually not coordinated
- they were fairly simple
- they missed a lot of situational information

This method is based loosely on the notion that relating has become affected by people's *egos* (see section in our chapter on *The Self* on *'ego'*) and that power and competition has affected relationships. In other words, don't expect that fairness, honesty etc will *automatically* be there in most relating unless we put it there and **figure out what is our - and the other person's - motivation for relating:** are they trying to 'chat us up' or sell a product? are we trying to get recognition, impress them etc?

Turning our mistakes around

We often don't relate as effectively as we could and we tend to make mistakes which include:

- *being **not OK** – behaving as one-down, that there's something wrong with us and feeling that we're unequal and don't have rights*
- *being unaware*
- *conforming to what the other(s) want(s) and not setting our own agenda - this often means having our rights and wishes compromised*
- *'moving forward' with relating when we feel intuitively that something is wrong and the situation is not right for 'moving forward'*
- *being fearful of outcomes and avoiding conflict or adult disagreement*

This method is for relating to the world in such a way that *we don't lose out, don't adjust to others' agendas too much,* and *have more chance of getting what we want.*

When to use this method

The model I'm presenting here works **most of the time** and can be developed to meet an individual's needs or a wide range of situations.

There are more issues to consider when using the model:

- it needs practice and development to suit our needs
- it depends on self-awareness and awareness of the situation
- it needs to be used flexibly
- it depends on learning about ourselves and the situation
- it can be very helpful in an emergency when we're not getting the responses we want

I would call it a *method* rather than a technique as it involves several techniques and is *'process'*-based, which means it's based on our *interaction with the world and with ourselves.*

'Process' is a term borrowed from group-work but I've expanded it to include *an individual's process.*

To see what this means, I will give an example.

When I wake up in the morning, it's gradual. My *process* is a gradual awakening during which I want coffee, no phone calls, and no reading of letters until I'm fully awake; having to answer the phone would be interfering with my gradual awakening, which is my *process* in the morning.

The idea of an OK-OK and not-OK process.

In my **'OK' process**, I'm in the healthy self-regulating side of myself. *I know what I want, what I don't want, etc.* and *how I feel when someone stands on my foot* or *bullies me to buy a product.*

In my **'not-OK' process** (usually historical), I may remember *not feeling I had rights, feeling I had to do what other people wanted, I had to please other people* - the last two behaviours I will call over-adapting. Not-OK events inside ourselves usually come from childhood experiences and earlier decisions made before we had enough information.

Why all this preamble?

Because although the model is straightforward and simple, it needs to be learnt thoroughly and understood, then it can be built on. So far I have looked at our *individual process* which has a not-OK part and an OK part, here's the diagram for that:

Internal not-OK process		Internal OK process

diagram 1
individual process

The next thing to insert into the diagram is the other person but first I would like to comment on **not-OK** and **OK** internal individual process.

In this model, the idea is that we **don't respond** to what's coming at us in ways based on past habits, feeling bad from fear or because we're conforming or over-adapting to what we 'should' do or because of how we were taught to respond as children.

Exercise
List all the ways you 'adjust' to others in a **not-OK** way and be aware of how you may do this in the present.
....
....
....
....
....

Instead, the idea is that we **react as OK-individuals with rights**, in a powerful and clear way and if necessary, block people trying to get us to adjust and interrupt our own OK equilibrium.

The other person or persons

To return to the developing diagram: on the left there is YOU with your **OK-self** and process and your **Not-OK self** and process. Now I'm putting in the *other* person or people:

YOU Not-OK process | OK process	OTHER PERSON(S) Not-OK process | OK process

diagram 2
two individual people

The division between the two parts of self is important to maintain.

Don't get into your **not-OK self** or if you do (temporarily), get out of it by being aware and switching to your **OK-self.**

It's quite easy to recognise the two parts (and no, it's not quite the same as *ego states* in *Transactional Analysis*). Remember that our **not-OK sides** are likely to have been formed in childhood or even babyhood – they've been with us a long time and are familiar. Coming into our **OK-self** may seem scary and take time and practice.

General features of not-OK and an OK self

Not-OK self	OK self
is historical, links to early experience	is 'mature'
feels familiar	has rights
is scared	is assertive
is likely to:	can perceive what's truly
conform	going on
please	can use discomfort
over-adapt	experienced by transactions to respond
give in etc.	is more powerful, less scared than not-OK self
has 'wonky' beliefs	can express feelings eg. *anger*
like *I have to be nice*	in a controlled and adult way
can't express feelings	can be upfront and clear….
is likely to believe people can guess what we feel/want	
likely to be shaped by history	is in the present
can have naïve or 'magical' ideas	
can be distorted or grandiose	is not naïve or distorted

Transactional Analysis overlaps

If you're not familiar with TA, try the books by Eric Berne and Ian Stewart and Vann Joines.

If you are familiar with TA, the **not-OK self** is likely to be in *Negative Critical Parent* and *Adapted Child* or 'dry' or boring *Adult* (excluding or excluded) and the **OK-self** will be flexible in ego states and be particularly good at *Free Child, Positive Nurturing* and *Critical Parent* and an uncluttered *Adult*.

In both an **OK-self** and **not-OK self** you can use intuition.

nb. The **OK-self** and **not-OK self** here is 'functional' and I think TA has built-in confusion re: function and structure. If we look at the other person (or more than one person) we're relating to, they also have an **OK (current) self** and a **not-OK (learned) self.**

One criticism here is that it's not clear how any of us decide what is OK and what is not, in ourselves or others.

Generally **OK-self** is *propelled towards growth in self and others, is 'healthy' psychologically and is good at relating in fair, reasonable ways in an engaged, non-superficial way.*

A **not-OK self** *feels robotic, conformist, shallow, uninterested in the other, treats others like objects, lacks humanity or empathy and is rigid.*

Also someone in **not-OK self** is *more likely to **be unable to rise above their role**
- in an organisation they may be rigid, bullying, narrow etc.*

Role-bound behaviour is also for unconfident, inexperienced professionals or experts
to hide behind; a role can therefore be rigid if it is a defence.

More on roles

In everyday transactions, we meet many people who are in their roles, doing their jobs and this will be the deciding factor in how they relate to us. However, most people define their roles too strictly and they 'become their role'; possibly for many, this involves convincing themselves psychologically that what they do is OK morally, socially etc. and identifying strongly with their roles.

I have a different view of a role: it's possible to have a broad view of a role, humanise the role, and to realise that it's not *you* as a person - it's a set of *behaviours* that you happen to be putting into action.

Given all of that, if we're in a role there are such things as *professional standards* to which we're supposed to adhere: these are actually an ideal, but many people now in my view are not only unaware of what their roles are meant to be, but are also unaware of the relevant professional standards, let alone know the difference between competence and incompetence. Also unfortunately, the organisations we work for may claim to be 'value-free' – but 'value-free' can often mask corruption and scandal, and the real values – often profit or dominance – are simply hidden from view. See our chapter on *The crisis we're in* for more on this.

Transactions between ourselves and another person: roles

We're up to diagram 2 now and have added the fact that the other person or people may be in a role and may represent an organisation.

When applying this method to *personal relationships*, remember that the other person is not necessarily in a role. In personal relationships, the other person may have internalised a value from their family or social conditioning which is not able to be easily updated - for example, ideas about men, women, politics, gay people, 'kids nowadays' – *anything* in fact.

People in roles will also probably have internalised values and ideas about their role which they've not questioned or updated.

People acting in roles or in organisations tend to put the organisational needs or recent instructions beyond everything and can seem driven by them, and they will attempt to get us to conform to their organisational, professional or role-driven demands.

Roles and culture

It's worth mentioning that we're in the culture and country we happen to be in and the other party will have ideas derived from the setting about how people should behave and what the public can demand. In the UK for example, so I have been told by a Czech, we are:

- a subject nation (having a monarchy and being 'subjects', not citizens with rights)
- a Protestant nation (no fun)
- an island nation (small minded, xenophobic and piratical ie. formerly pirates).

I would add to this that in the UK we are against public expression of feelings, are not direct/upfront, have a high tolerance of incompetence, and put up with being treated badly without complaining.

You may have a different view of things, depending on your own history.

OK, we've considered the country, what next?

Other information we need to be aware of include: which *culture* are we dealing with? Is it middle class/ 'toffs'/working-class, self-employed, Anglican/ Catholic/ Evangelical, military/ex-military, marrieds/singles/gays, students, swingers, drug users, or collectors and restorers of 1930s buses? In other words, there are cultural rules in any society, depending with which group within that society we're 'doing business' - we need to be aware that cultural norms will have been internalised.

Different groups act differently and have different expectations of different events. In one culture, people wear black at funerals and stand around a coffin, in another there may be a wake, in another there is a communal festival with flowers and fruits and sizzling meats and ritual dances. What is important is that the 'sense of occasion' is not disrespected, and actually we can ask what we should do so as not to offend or break any group norms or traditions.

At last - getting back to the diagram

diagram 3
relating between the two people

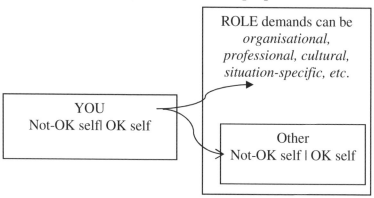

Remember in the **OK-selves** and **not-OK selves** of both *you* and the *other person(s),* there may be internalised values and attitudes which are like loops of tape telling people what to do.

The demands on someone can apply from organisational demands as talked about already but different organisations can be <u>very</u> different about how they treat customers and we need to be aware of how they try and make us feel **not-OK**, for example: *'nobody else has complained'.*

Some organisations and their staff can be short-sighted or too defended to realise that customer feedback helps them improve and they may also turn complaints into stuffy procedures that frighten their staff.

A simple rule

If you're having trouble, *go higher* in the organisation with any issues. Ask for the supervisor, the manager, the director, the headmaster/mistress, the boss, the owner, the proprietor, the chief executive, the head of operations, the chief engineer, the senior scientist, the project leader etc. Work *with* the hierarchy that exists.

Don't forget we will have *our* agenda. We should remain careful and aware – we need to make sure for example that we don't take out our old stuff - for example, about teachers and schools - on our child's teacher. We can also remain aware of being stressed, pushy, grabbing, insensitive etc. and take a step back before proceeding.

It's important that we always try to treat people as we'd like to be treated and respect others' rights etc. We can decide for example that we're not trying to get someone sacked or destroy their self-esteem; we're simply trying to get proper service or decent attention. We can recognise that someone is following an organisational 'script' but if they won't speak to us as a human being, then it's appropriate to find someone who will.

Power and misunderstanding

The central problem in any relationship or interchange is often to do with power or misunderstanding and power is usually first on the list.

Misuse of power

The feeling we get when we know something is really wrong in a relationship is when our rights are trampled on - it's unfair, insensitive, or unequal and we can feel not-OK.

I think a lot of problems boil down to a misuse of power; however, if we're in an OK position and are sure of our rights, we can usually stand our ground.

Misunderstandings

There are clearly 'cultural' mix-ups and it helps if we ask questions to clarify and sometimes self-disclose important information, for example, *'I'm ill, can you help or not?'*

I think we should also enquire as to whether we're getting accurate information and not assume that companies, governments and people are not being devious. A lie is a lie if it's not the whole truth. We shouldn't be naïve; we can look up the 'real' context on Google.

> Much of modern technology is driven by needs which are not fully articulated. For example, car clutches have been changed partly because of the problem of asbestos which was hazardous to mechanics. Modern clutches need to be managed differently by drivers but garages and manufacturers don't make this clear – they put problems down to 'driver error'. Computer packages are upgraded with the presentation that every new upgrade is better than the last – in fact, quite often they represent a drop in quality and stability.

We can get ourselves with practice to be aware of our own and others' OK and not-OK processes and 'loops' and to be aware of where the other is coming from. A lot of this awareness and information flows from the discomfort or ease of the transactions between people. The next part of this method is dealing with the actual interaction and making that effective and creative.

Effective transactions

I will mention what has worked for me but first recap on the diagram.

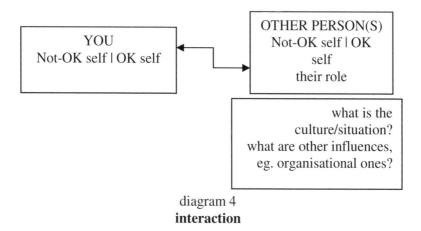

diagram 4
interaction

Steps:

- be aware of your OK and not-OK process
- be aware of other's OK and not-OK process if possible
- check roles, the 'culture' and situation
- check other influences
- be aware of the 'feel' of the interaction as well as the verbal content

This may seem like a lot to be aware of but with practice it comes easily. There are also some more things that are well worth utilising.

Intuition, the unconscious and non-verbal behaviour

Starting with non-verbal behaviour, a psychologist called Michael Argyle came to the conclusion that most communication was non-verbal. This is slightly misleading as words are often used to finally decide interactions in our culture. However, it does suggest that people relate in ways other than the verbal and that these levels are very powerful and must be considered.

Included in non-verbal behaviour would be eye contact, body posture, speed, loudness and clarity of speech; also I would add accent, repetition of words for effect etc.

Non-verbal behaviour exists even on the telephone – is your tone and overall effect clear, assertive, honest, direct or are you using strategies; are you 'hoping' for a particular response?

I give compliments freely when people do their jobs, are helpful etc. as well as disclosing important information about myself (with some caution), criticising what needs criticising and stating the obvious, going back and re-stating the obvious if needed.

For **intuition and the unconscious** see other sections of the book including our chapter on *The Unconscious.*

I trust my intuition and unconscious mind in my relating – this doesn't mean that these are always right but we can exclude a lot of our perception if we don't use them, for example we may pick up that something feels 'wrong' but may not quite know what is wrong in our 'rational mind'

We can be aware of any discrepancies between the feel of the interaction and the strictly verbal/or information content.

If we do have an intuitive hunch, we need to *register* it – we can always refine our perception later as 'more factual' info comes to light.

Ways of relating that work

Awareness includes:

Checking out sincerity and reliability - can we trust this relationship or person?

Use all our skills....including intuition

I'm putting in a quick note here that is important. As a lot of relating is about trust and clarity it's very important to not only figure out what someone's agenda, role, organisational influences are if relevant but please remember that a lot of good relating is based on a basic feeling that we need to be safe and trust people and trust is often what is manipulated.

So use this method and also your intuition to find out:

- Are they reliable?
- Do they mean what they say - many people are pretty sloppy with how they express things or they don't mean what they say or they are not 'congruent' (what I say is not what I do or what I am)
  [An example of blinkered non-congruence is saying you love wild animals and hunting foxes with dogs, saying you're a writer when you wrote half a chapter in 1987 etc.]
- Personally I do not feel I can rely on things said to overly influence or impress others, to present an image, or for people to present a 'social self'.

- Another problem can be people agreeing with you to 'keep you happy' - this simply doesn't work it's short-lived and is a way of avoiding difference and healthy disagreement - it's not 'grown up' relating

Being in our OK-self

In an OK-self, we are equal with others, it doesn't matter if *they think* they're more important than us, they are *not* – we're *all* equally important.

In our OK-self, we're not over-impressed with status, wealth, complex arguments, etc.

In our OK-self, we're free and we have power and are operating far less from fear. In the worst, we need to be willing to *not* get what we're trying for; if we don't take some risk, we'd never leave our house.

In our OK-self, it's important we're treated with respect and not treated dismissively.

Yes, we can be patient and understanding if they explain all the usual nonsense about why their behaviour, system or organisation doesn't work, but remember your own priorities and be careful. Some people we're dealing with will stop being helpful the minute we appear to give in, so I would be tempted to adopt high standards, expect them to continue and chase things up that are promised and don't appear or are not done.

Always be ready to go higher up if dealing with organisations and professionals and keep records, particularly of mistakes - as a *'victim'*, we have real power (see Foucault).

If people we're dealing with can be brought round to being decent, helpful and not dismissive and trying a power trip on us, fine, we may 'do business' but expect to keep on and keep up the pressure.

What we're talking about here is stopping bad treatment of *us*, not flipping into dismissing *them* or *their* rights.

If we can maintain detachment or get into a spiritual state, then we should do that – it will help a lot.

Also, we can employ our unconscious mind, generally trust it, and use creativity or techniques like visualisation.

I've mentioned roles and the influence of the culture and situation without going into detail yet about the actual interchange/interaction.

If we're dealing with different organisations, they may put their employees under very different pressures or constraints or their employees may be unmotivated to do a good job and settle for poor standards, treating the public as a nuisance, etc. Also, the actual competence of anyone is worth looking at and this includes everyone - every professional and every government department.

Questions to ask are:

- are they doing their job properly?
- are they explaining what they're doing?
- do I feel that I'm being asked to do all the work etc.?
- am I asking clearly for something or informing them clearly – they can't 'mind-read'

A last consideration before talking about handling the interaction is that it's important to be aware of whether we're entering a long 'relationship' or whether it's a one-off interchange, as well as the significance of the transaction – what's at stake. In addition, it really does help if there is some structure designed to help us - for example, a professional body, a head office, a complaints department - unless these are just cosmetic.

Handling interactions

So far, the diagram looks like this:

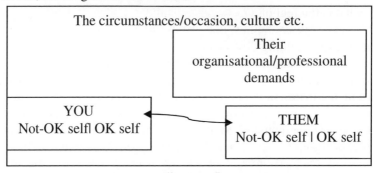

diagram 5
transactions
(relating between you and others)

questions, one-off transactions or ongoing
eg. with work colleagues

significance of transactions – (eg. is it a life or death
situation?, do the possible outcomes really matter?)
have a plan B – think what's the worst that can happen and
what would I do if it did?

Yes, at last we are on to the juicy bit which is *the actual transaction*, which may be by phone, letter or in person. As mentioned before, non-verbal behaviour applies on the phone with tone, loudness, clarity and yes, status (usually social class in the UK) - although this isn't always clear-cut as the 'classless' accent may be subject to less prejudice and achieves more cooperation.

What's the feel of the interaction?

Do we feel treated like a cog in their machine, are they pushy or dismissive or aggressive or superior? Whatever the actual words used, we should 'listen' to our reaction and be sensitive to the whole tone of their approach. If we're doing this, we should be picking up what their style and their organisational style is; possibly also what their agenda is.

So, what *is* the feel of it?

Is it an expert talking down to us, an interrogation, an interchange designed to intimidate or a dialogue etc.? What is the speed, the tone and if in person, what are the rituals and body language, what does their 'office' say, their clothes and their receptionist? Do they expect us to 'just conform'? Are they coming from an expert position or a partnership position (which is more equal than the expert position)?

Interactions

Whilst interactions are complex, there is a beautiful simplicity to the 'difficult' ones.

1. The interactions are about power
2. You are *meant* to adjust
3. Usually the other party is following an agenda which suits them and is secret or semi-secret
4. In any event, important information is not easily available to you

The beautifully simple main response is:

> – don't adjust, ***do something different or do the opposite***

In psychological terms, the interactions are usually designed to get you to 'over-adapt' and deny you your rights, so they are trying to get you to conform. The reason that this is so powerful is that we have all spent many years conforming and being trained to conform to authority both in formal and informal situations, which has created codes of behaviour which people often follow out of fear or of being left out or excluded or punished.

Is that all there is to it?

No.

'Doing the opposite' is included in 'doing something different'

I think it's best to use a package of approaches for being more in charge of interactions. They are not grouped 'perfectly', but putting them into groups may be useful.

Here are the subheadings I can think of under the heading of 'doing something different'

- stopping the interaction or commenting on it
- being active
- clarity and confrontation

Then there is…

- doing the opposite
- other approaches ……. or ones you decide on for yourself
- optional: learn about psychopathology - different 'types' of personality (gaining knowledge about 'pathology' is covered elsewhere in this book eg. sections on *narcissism* and *psychopathy* in our chapter on *Emotional health*).

As well as concentrating on relating, remember also to remain aware of and collect information on:

- your and the other person's OK/not-OK self
- roles
- anything else like organisational shape/demands etc
- the *significance* of the transactions
- other options.

Stopping the interaction or commenting on it

If, for example, someone is rushing things and bombarding us with questions, we have the option of simply stopping them - for example:

'You're asking too many questions too fast - how about you slow down and give me time to think'

'You're asking too many questions, it feels like being interrogated and it's making me feel uncomfortable'

'I've got a question for <u>you</u> now'

'I find your questioning aggressive and relentless'

The point here is that you can slow down, stop or comment on the interaction including how the interaction looks and feels to you and you can suggest ways that it may suit you better. I often ask people to speak more loudly and clearly on the phone if I can't hear them well.

Being active

This is very important and generally means being organised and being in charge and not expecting others to do what we think they may or should do, or to think like us, or to have our values or to follow high standards, or indeed, *any* standards.

The message we're conveying is *'I'm no-nonsense, informed, organised, active, and ask intelligent questions or make intelligent perceptive comments'* and in brackets *'I ask the same of you'*. At its best, *being active* can get people adjusting to <u>us</u>, doing their jobs and bringing out the best in them.

It includes:

- going elsewhere or higher up to get a service
- doing research, learning in advance (a move to being our own expert) and having questions prepared
- utilising their mistakes or any of their obnoxious behaviour for our benefit *(see for example, Foucault's work on the power of the victim which includes reconceptualising things so that they work in our interest)*
- getting the names of people we talk to, getting as much as possible in email or in writing, making a written record of the contents of calls to send to them.
- trying to get a named person to whom we can relate and getting their phone number and email address

105

- finding out the other party's routines and procedures and timescales
- chasing up things and people

Clarity and confrontation

- refusing and challenging their negative views and/or labelling of us and trusting our OK-self-definition and perceptions
- getting them to listen to us
- being clear and concise instead of waffling and overdetailing
- being ruthless and pointing out any changes of rules, procedures, promises we experience - known in the UK as 'changing the goalposts'
- refusing their explanations unless they're sincere, as these are often really descriptions of their ineffective systems

'Doing the opposite'

- **humanising the interchange** - this is to combat robotic, bureaucratic approaches to us. Making things colourful and personal vastly reduces attempts to treat us as objects or as any one-down kind of person so it's a good idea take an interest in the other person and ask them questions about their work, life, location etc. In recent times, I've learned quite a lot from call centre staff about the geography of Scotland, the economic boom in India, and the state of British Telecom - by finding out about the person I'm talking to and their context.

- **equalising the interaction**. I've already mentioned *accent* in talking as part of non-verbal behaviour - in a lot of transactions in the UK (which is an unequal society), people usually try to be 'more equal' with middle class accents. Be aware of social status.

  The best way to handle inequality is to **believe in equality and act as though people are equal**, this means valuing ourselves and not being too accommodating - this may involve bringing it out in the open by commenting eg. *'I feel you're not treating me as an equal, stop that and treat me as equal'*

- **being an exception -** we need to be comfortable doing this wherever we can to stop being treated as routine

- **introducing feelings into the conversation** - it can be extremely important to let people know how we *feel*, so they know more about us and where they stand in relation to us

Yes, we need to have some discretion about how much feeling we reveal to whom, but actually most people flatten the feeling out of so much of their relating, their words no longer convey any feelings or their true positions.

To counteract this we can add to our words a description of how we feel eg. *'I've already spoken to two different opticians, **wasted a lot of my time**, it's **annoying.** I want to get the right type of contact lenses - it's important to me because I need to see properly to drive and **I'm frightened about this.** Can you fix the problem or not?'* (said in an exasperated way, with energy and a no-nonsense expression). Or *'I'm really **worried and anxious** about my eyes and **I need your reassurance** that we can sort something out and that I haven't got an intractable sight problem'.*

Expressing feeling doesn't mean getting stuck in the actual feeling, though if we do get stuck in it it's unlikely to be the end of the world. It often means letting people know how we feel both in words *and* non-verbally *and/or* with our energy pointing to our feelings. A feeling can be anything - anger, frustration, jealousy, joy, disappointment, worry, fear etc.

- **stopping pussyfooting** I think being 'careful' is usually being fearful and being fearful is encouraged by organisations, social groups, governments. As well as having options lined up and an idea of the importance of any transaction, it's important to stop avoiding risk; *nothing progresses without risk.* If we make a mistake, we can always apologise - that costs nothing and seems fair.

- **introducing humour -** life is very dry and over-serious without it

- **introducing flexibility -** most routines we're expected to fit into are inflexible but can usually be made more flexible to suit us – with a bit of assertiveness on our part

- **introducing equal 'partnership'** versus the 'expert' and *passive recipient* position. However, partnership does involve us in being active and responsible.

- **getting people to give us a simple layperson's version -** most complexity and *jargonese* can be cut through so if this can't be done, there's something wrong.

Summary
- *practise*
- *it will make a difference being in charge and being aware of what's going on*
- *fear means 'no risk' relating so ditch it*
- *be an exception*
- *give them instructions*
- *make it your own style*
- *make it fun and flexi*
- *don't be afraid to stop an interaction or comment on it*
- *be active instead of leaving it to others*
- *utilise their mistakes or obnoxious behaviour (Foucault's 'power of the victim') for your benefit, eg. by justifying a complaint by you or requiring an adjustment to the normal process from them etc.*
- *be willing to go elsewhere or go higher up to get a service*

- *do research and learn in advance (being your own expert) – have questions prepared*
- *refuse and challenge their negative views and labelling of you, and trust your OK-self-definition and perception*
- *keep things crisp and clear and SIMPLE - usually the issues <u>are</u> simple – it's the strategies, manipulations, procedures etc. which are complex*
- *get names, give and get as much in writing as possible, record phone talks in writing etc.*

Julia's comments

I've been embroiled in public sector institutional life for decades, whilst Jack's been more involved in voluntary sector and freelance activity. I've found Jack's material totally refreshing. Having his ideas at the forefront of my mind is helping me to become more assertive and more articulate about my feelings and to stand up for myself in situations where before I would have let people get away with putting me down or requiring me to fit in to their system, sometimes without even noticing. I've always been quite assertive *as a consumer* but using the techniques in relation to *people I know* is more of a challenge I find; looking at this field has started to transform a number of my relationships - some friendships and colleague relationships have foundered, some have strengthened, and not necessarily the ones I had expected. I believe I'd got into some long-established dynamics with some people that needed shaking up and my relationship with *myself* definitely needed an overhaul.

Human rights

Standing up for human rights is important if we're not to lose many of the rights that others have fought and often died for. As I've got older, I've found more courage to do this than before, particularly as an advocate for colleagues and students, but also in relation to wider issues as well as with people close to me. There have been occasions in my life when I've failed to stand up for people, because I was frightened for myself, physically, psychologically, economically, and of course I regret that. By failing to speak out or fight when we should, we can lose our self-respect and live with lifelong sorrow.

However, there are often 'bottom-lines' where the costs of engaging in battle seem more than we are prepared to pay at the time. It's a painful process of weighing up our own interests against those of others – and sometimes we can get it wrong, perhaps underestimating how badly we'll feel if we don't help or for how long we will carry the guilt, or failing to assess whether we have the right skills or experience to help, or not realising the toll it will take on us or those around us if we get involved in something we're not ready for etc. People who help others often have their own reasons for doing so and their own particular resources (money, support, expertise, knowledge, risk-assessment skills etc) – these are not always the same as our own and it's important to know what we can take on and what we can't.

Somehow these days it seems easier to stand up for *someone else's* rights, especially if they are far across the globe, than to say simply to someone near us that something isn't fair or right and that we are entitled to be considered and treated properly. The hardest challenge is usually right in front of us.

What Jack writes about in this chapter is particularly pertinent to standing up for our *own* rights, something that can sometimes be harder than standing up for someone else.

Self-belief

When I first watched *'The X-factor'* in its early days, I remember being amazed that some people were turned down because although they were quite good at singing, they lacked 'self-belief'. I didn't really understand the concept, perhaps because I've always lacked some. I knew I was qualified and was conversant with my subject area and I had no difficulty in teaching it. But I've frequently worked in roles where I've been the lone psychologist/sociologist and have had to challenge or advise professionals (eg. in banking, social work, medicine) who've questioned my credibility. And maybe sometimes I *have* hesitated in discussions, daunted by others' belligerent self-presentations. I always used to *believe* people's self-presentations. Now I realise that we live in an era when presentation is supposed to validate people more than whether or not they know what they're actually talking about!

Keeping going against all manner of opposition and prejudice is a sign that we do have self-belief - just because it's difficult doesn't mean we have no self-belief.

The point is that some of us have found ourselves in situations where we are well-supported for our role – and *some of us have not*. And as the psychologist Alice Miller once wrote, we need an ally or someone who believes us, and I guess, believes *in* us.

There may come times in life where we are called upon to push ahead – we might have outgrown systems, we might have become critical of the situation we're in and the way things are done, we might have begun to have our own ideas about things and become tired of waiting to put them into practice etc. If we're to stand up as adult human beings, we have to believe in ourselves and think we're worth taking a chance on.

Nearly 30 years ago, I was talking to the poet and speaker, Roger Housden, who, along with others, was sitting in my dining-room and I must have been talking about my upset that the college I worked for wouldn't support me for further training. *'Ah'*, he said, *'have you thought of investing in yourself?'* It was a salutary moment because it's a sentence I've never forgotten, and one that at the time led to me funding myself through a Master's degree which changed the course of the next few years for me.

We have to have belief in ourselves and *invest* in ourselves, put money and time behind our own projects, take risks, step into the unknown. We have to stop waiting for others to invest in us – employers, partners, parents, banks etc. We need to do it ourselves. Once we honour this sense of our being *worth* investing in – once *we* believe it – it will come across to others, and will infuse our transactions with confidence.

We need of course to be realistic and make sure that we have a reasonable basis on which to believe in ourselves. It's probably no good going for the *X-factor* if we've never sung anything or been in a band – if we've already come along a road and we know that we do have something to offer, then we need to support that confidence with energy. We should radiate self-belief. Quietly. Firmly. Or noisily. Whatever is our style.

Pragmatism

Jack's style calls us to be upfront and direct, honest, warm, clear. It sounds good, but for me it's been difficult to be like that. In a lifetime of organisational and personal roles, I've learned to be pragmatic and strategic. My colleagues would call me 'diplomatic', Jack would call my behaviour a number of unflattering things. He doesn't think we should smile and be placatory if that's not the truth of the matter, he doesn't believe we should hide our true feelings, he doesn't believe we should be devious, he doesn't think we should avoid conflict. Yet I've spent a lifetime doing all these things. In fact, I used to be proud of the fact that I could handle meetings with a po-face, conveying neutrality from the chair-person's seat even when I actually had a strong view on the matter, and that in tricky situations, I could rally up support with a series of phone-calls behind the scenes. It's because of this long experience that I can now watch news bulletins and work out what I think the government are up to – when we're just being told things to keep us quiet, to spread propaganda to the external world, to discredit dissenters, etc. I've seen and done it all (been discredited), been there, got the tea-set and T-shirt. What's mattered in my working life has been 'delivering outcomes' and surviving in complex institutions, not being an upfront, direct human being. Now I'm committed to finding a way of making these consistent with each other.

Conflict

In 1976, a psychiatrist called Jean Baker Miller in her book on women's psychology identified a problem that I'd been struggling with as a psychology student and as a feminist. She said: *'women are **not creating conflict**, they are **exposing the conflict that**

112

exists'. In that idea, I realised that the conflicts I was engaging in – whether or not they had anything to do with gender - were reflections of power dynamics that I was *disturbing*, not *generating*, and this has helped me a great deal.

Recognising that we are tapping into issues that are buried beneath the surface of human interactions – usually involving people who have comfortable niches or significant power in their hands – allows us to understand why they are getting angry, ignoring us, rubbishing our ideas, or going behind our backs to sabotage our efforts. They don't want to be knocked off their perch. They don't want us to have a bigger slice of the cake. And what's more, if at all possible [and this is VERY IMPORTANT] ***they would prefer it if we didn't realise this***, *and didn't realise that it's a cake we could or should have a slice of.*

Standing up for our rights can evoke strong responses. Women in violent relationships, black people in segregated townships, *'Olivers'* in orphanages, etc. have had to face the outrage that people in dominant positions – men, white people, the dispensers of charity etc. can feel when the question of equal rights comes up, as well as sometimes the indifference that people around have felt when they hear the screams of anguish, indifference that is often feigned because of their own fear of what is happening. Personally, I think we have to consider the timing of our interactions carefully and strike only when we have the right information about our opponents, are strong enough and have support. Ideally, this takes preparation, discussion with allies, and careful thought.

But sometimes it's an emergency. Situations arise suddenly in front of us. We don't have any backup or preparation. That's where knowing Jack's techniques by heart can come in particularly handy.

I remember working on *The Times* in Holborn in my 20s, as the industrial dispute that was to close the paper down was gathering force. I had just returned from a union meeting where all of us secretaries had been instructed 'not to cover for holidays or sickness' when the head of the department summoned me into his

113

office and asked me to cover for his secretary whilst she went off for a 2-week holiday. *'No'* I said, *'I support the claim for better pay and conditions of all secretaries and I won't do this'*. *'What did you say to him?'* asked two young clerks, *'his face went very dark'*. *'Don't know'*, I said, *'I was so scared I didn't notice what his face looked like'*. Over the next week or two, I was put under a lot pressure to do it from my own boss, but I didn't cave in. When a few months later I left to go to college, to my surprise, that man gave me a glowing testimonial to take with me. It was my first lesson in the idea that *confronting someone can earn their respect.*

Susan Jeffers' book *'Feel the fear and do it anyway'* was another breakthrough for me. When I read it (and anyway it's all there in the title), I stopped thinking that because I felt frightened I shouldn't do something. When now, as a consumer, I am facing up to the monoliths of gigantic corporations, I remind myself that anxiety is OK. When turning up to a protest meeting or to a tense gathering, (whatever side we're on), it's OK to have a nervous stomach or sweating brow. In fact, in many situations, anxiety is natural; rather like with 'stage fright' – we still go on.

Worrying about how we look

It's time to ditch any fears about how we might seem to others or to ourselves. It doesn't matter if we seem ugly or noisy or unattractive in the moment of conflict. As with sex, emotional expression can be chaotic and disturbing, but that doesn't make it wrong or something to be avoided. When our rights are restored, we can calm down again, exude the warmth we have in our heart, and comb through our hair (if we have any!). Direct communication doesn't always look pretty. It's often a bitter struggle, so it seems to me. A struggle for equality. For fair dos. For human rights.

We also have to ride through those moments when we see ourselves replicating behaviours and phrases we heard in adults around us as we grew up, and whom we may have decided not to emulate. When that first happens there may be little to do about it except perhaps to realise retrospectively that we may now be in touch with the way our parents, teachers, caregivers felt. Over

114

time we can modify our own style so that we find a way of getting angry or confronting someone that emerges from our own personality and not theirs. It is not inevitable that we become like others before us. We can be different.

Honesty

Who could argue against the ideal of honesty? Yet I know from my work with students struggling with medical ethics, that honesty is not a straightforward thing. Do you tell a patient they're dying? Could it hasten someone's demise to know that they are expected to die? Will it make the patient more difficult to manage? Will it distress the relatives? What do you do if the partner begs you not to tell the patient? What do you do if the patient tells you they know they're dying but not to tell the relatives?

When friends encouraged me into internet dating, I noticed that high on the list of desirable characteristics some people were searching for in a mate was *'faithfulness'*, often because people had been scarred by betrayal in a previous relationship. But although I do believe now that being honest and true and close to our partner is central to making a relationship work, people for whom 'fidelity' is the most important issue frighten me because to me, this conveys a sense of 'ownership' and obsession. When we look back at the history of homosexuality, it's clear that many people have had to choose to live without the comfort of congruence between their outer presentation and their inner feelings - and some still have to do this. There are sometimes times when we can't be transparent and that is very painful. Much of the struggle for acceptance and equal rights is for the right to live authentically and openly because hiding things is agonising.

Many of us live lives that are not ideal, or have phases in our lives when this is the case. Our work situations and our relationships are frequently not based on honest, direct communication – they may be unfulfilling and problematic, or they may appear to work but ultimately be inauthentic and let us down. Jack is offering us a way of moving out of these stultifying ways of living.

For me, the most important thing has always been to be honest with myself. Being honest with other people has been harder! Digging deep for what we want and sharing that with others is the path to a fulfilling life and to creative, rewarding relating. That path may be painful and at times, lonely. But the relationship with our self will be one of integrity and wholeness, and that means that we can be our own best companion through whatever life throws at us.

Not being afraid to lose what we've got

There are some things that are harder to lose than others. I was appalled recently to learn that Tibetan monks and nuns were setting fire to themselves rather than surrender to the Chinese authorities, and heard the journalist saying that *'perhaps they have come to the end of the road of non-violence'*. There is a long tradition of martyrdom in many cultures – including allowing ourselves to be arrested and imprisoned – to register protest. And of course we hope (even unconsciously) in such situations that our actions will inspire others, but sometimes all we face is a long, long process of being ignored or punished. Steve McQueen's film *Hunger* about Bobby Sands and the 1981 Irish hunger-strike highlights this kind of issue. Sometimes, even if it takes more than one generation, our mortification brings about change, but it depends how long we are prepared to wait, and the risk of losing *belief in a way of doing things* – such as non-violence - could be a tremendous loss. The dilemma can sometimes be the one of undermining our own belief in a *way of doing things* – in our own *process* - in order to get an outcome we want or holding to our *values-base* and not getting the outcome we want.

My mother used to say to me: *'the trouble with you, Julia, is that you're always afraid to lose what you've got'*. Having marriages, jobs, homes, friends, parents, relatives and youth go from me, I now have a lot of experience in losing what I've got. Overall, I do believe that adage *'when one door closes another one opens'* but there have been many times in my life when it's been hard to believe it, and in fact, too painful to believe it. There are times when we don't want another door to open, when things are too painful and we just need to go inside that pain and feel it. After several bereavements, apart from going to work, I essentially wore the same three dark items of clothing and lived largely in my study with the curtains closed for two years, finding in this 'hibernation' some kind of space where I could work things through.

Spending our time trying to hold onto what we've got is not guaranteed to bring us fulfilment, and because it is based on living fearfully, can result in a compromising of our standards and values. When we see that things in our life are in jeopardy, we are presented with choices such as:

- falling apart, getting ill, perhaps reaching out for help
- staying just as we are and hoping things will blow over or the situation will change (which sometimes it will)
- blaming others and fighting for everything we can get out of the situation
- renewing ourselves and being creative about our own lives
- getting out of the situation and moving into something else
- accepting change and having honest, open conversations with people who are moving on without us – partners who are thinking of leaving us, employers who are thinking of making us redundant, customers who are moving to new suppliers – and negotiating the way forward positively

What's certain is that *what we do WILL affect the situation.* We may not be able to stop things changing or change someone's mind, but the way we handle it all will leave an indelible mark on other people and on ourselves. Moving into acrimony and bitterness will be different from clear-cut confrontation and saying things how they are, or negotiating a peaceful and positive arrangement for the future where the door is kept open for new negotiations if ever wanted.

The point I think is about *negotiation.* We have to know our bottom line. Even if we accept we have to let go of a relationship, work or study situation, income or our home (and these might be difficult), there may be something that we feel we absolutely have to protect like access to our children or our good name and reputation. *Being clear about what we're fighting for* will help in any transaction.

117

Accepting equality often means that we can't expect that we will win *all* – it means everyone should get *something*. The nature of today's world is that ideas of endless progress and infinitely growing incomes are now in question for most people. We should no more automatically relinquish everything we've got any more than we should grab everything's that's available on the sinking ship.

Being good at transactions means that:

- we look at the problems with a human heart and work honestly with others to find solutions
- we remain in OK-OK position and stick up for our rights without treading on the rights of others.
- we're not overwhelmed by the general panic and argue clearly and calmly (and if necessary, repeatedly) for our needs to be addressed
- we hold to our belief in equality as *fair* to all, but not standardised, not 'the same' for everyone because everyone is not the same
- we're not put off by the general drift in quality of human interaction – we require that people treat us properly and put our point of view forward
- we recognise that others may be stuck in narrow role definitions and limited thinking and we offer solutions and ways out rather than leaving it to them
- we recognise the difference between our goals in a transaction (that which we would like to gain or keep) and our bottom line (that which we are not prepared to trade or lose)
- we insist that interactions are humanised and not robotic, that in fact, *'we're all in it together'* and *'OK-OK'*.
- we remember that in close relationships we need to be sensitive to not stepping on sensitive 'old' material in the other person

Equality

It's worth keeping up to date with equality legislation (and other forms of legislation) – the following are now seen as *'protected characteristics'* in UK law:

- age
- disability
- gender reassignment
- marriage and civil partnership
- pregnancy and maternity
- race
- religion or belief
- sex
- sexual orientation

It's important to recognise that equality is a complex phenomenon and that people across the globe debate and disagree about it in a multitude of ways. Much legislation is about 'fairness' and the idea of not discriminating against people because of 'protected characteristics', (which vary from nation to nation).

The idea of equal opportunities is often undermined by the fact that people do not usually have a level playing-field when they compete for jobs, prizes, courses etc.

For example, some people:

- went to public school or a 'good' university
- went to a 'rubbish' school
- had 'good looks'
- were disfigured
- had money to set themselves up with
- had no start-up resources
- had family around them
- were born into a culture that supported and taught them
- were on their own
- had contacts in relevant organisations
- knew no-one in the business
- had easy access to food and water and healthcare

- had to struggle for food and water and healthcare
- had to escape from brutal regimes
- were encouraged to speak out
- learned to keep quiet
- had disabilities and health conditions
- had good health

Conversely, once selection has been made, people whose background hasn't been supportive often struggle more than others to keep up, to make the most of opportunities etc. but this shouldn't be a basis on which to exclude them in the first place. *Facilitating equality requires ongoing commitment.*

One of the issues that upsets a number of people is the idea that those with plenty ought to share what they have in order to help balance things out – the kind of thinking that is currently been used to remind wealthy people that philanthropy might be the decent thing in times of general austerity. We shouldn't be afraid of pointing this out and making our claim for fair shares. Ultimately people are happier and healthier in fairer societies. When the rich start living in gated communities and employing bodyguards, we know we are in troubled territory and that there is a need for change – for all concerned. It's interesting that some employers have started suggesting that the better-paid staff forego annual increments and pay rises in order to have enough money to hold onto jobs and keep contract staff on the books. And in some cases, people with full-time jobs are steadily being replaced by part-time workers and job-sharers. Though these ideas don't sit well with traditional trade unionism, we all have to be more creative and think about sharing out the 'cake' if we're to have a sustainable and more equal future.

Letting go of things allows us to move forward, and even if we don't want the changes ahead, they are often inevitable and we must call upon all our resources to deal with them.

Cultural scripts

From Transactional Analysis, we get the idea of *cultural scripts,* whereby mind-sets can be passed on inter-generationally. Thus it's possible that current conflicts between Christian and Muslim nations (eg. via terrorism and the war against it) are still playing out old issues from the Crusades; and that battles between Catholics and Protestants in Northern Ireland or between Jews and Arabs in the Middle East hark back to previous generations. Sometimes things that seem personally vital are nevertheless linked to the wider groups of which we are a member. It's worth exploring our own history – family history, local history, national history, religious history, political history etc. in order to understand more clearly why we feel as we do about things and how it might be that we think differently from friends with different backgrounds from our own.

Envy

Many of us can fall prey to envy in our lives, longing for what others have and feeling bad about what we have or don't have - in a climate of economic decline, and within a materialistic framework, these feelings could get stronger.

> *I remember a time when I had recently lost my own home and my marriage had dissolved. I was living in a small, furnished flat on the edge of the city with my cat and I was fairly miserable. I went to visit a friend in a comfortable area of the city, near the sea, where she lived with her partner and children; her house was a huge Victorian property in a tree-lined road, every room seemed filled with colour, dressers full of ceramics, tapestries and hangings, beautiful drapes and cushions on sofas, stained glass windows on doors, large plants in burnished pots. She went to find her husband and put the kettle on – I RAN. I was so upset at the loveliness of it all I couldn't bear the pain. I decided after that that I couldn't see a number of people until I had got my own life more sorted and had found my own core again. It took a while.*

Feeling superior

We might criticise what others have and what they are like in order to hide even from ourselves our own envy of them, their easier advantages, their greater external success, their good fortune in love etc. A sense of superiority can obscure our own deeprooted feelings of inadequacy; some of us may encourage others to feel envious of us so that we forget our own envious feelings. People who have not been happily and reliably cared as infants may hide their pain inside a 'false self' (see for example the work of Donald Winnicott or Masud Khan), covering up their anguish in an 'enviable' self-presentation, showing off what they have and projecting a confident, successful image that may not match up to the reality of how they actually feel about their lives. It becomes impossible to experience truly equal relationships, vacillating between contempt and idealisation, instead of being able to take in the good from others and experiencing the happiness of intimacy.

Fear of being envied

Alternatively, we can get into a pattern of denigrating our own successes – however modest these seem – in order to avoid others being negative and covetous towards us, and even to punish ourselves for any feelings of envy that run deep within us. It can become a habit to hide our own strengths, sometimes even from ourselves.

Feeling afraid of others' envy can stop us from being ourselves, and from thinking that it is OK to *be* OK. If we feel afraid to move forward or to speak out, it could be worth considering if we're worried about going beyond the achievements of someone close to us, a parent perhaps, or a friend. Jeremy Hazell (1989), object relations therapist, spoke of this in his work on students who plagiarised or failed their exams. It may be true that others envy us for our good fortune or our courage to break through difficulty, but that doesn't have to stop us. In this situation, even if we move forward, suffering another's envy (even if only in our imagination) can seem too stressful and we find ourselves sabotaging our new steps, unconsciously making ourselves ill, or turning up late to appointments in a new job and irritating the new boss. Or it may be that we transfer our anxieties onto others – neighbours, fellow students, or workmates – imagining that they too will envy us – we minimise our achievements and underplay what we can do. Of course there are times when it's sensible for security reasons or just from sensitivity to what others lack, to be modest about what we have but we need to check out whether this has become too much of a habit.

So in order to have OK-OK transactions, it's important to deal with these shadows from our own history. A voice on a telephone or the way someone talks to us in the shop can trigger deep-seated ideas about our own worth and where we see ourselves in society. Nowhere is this more true than in relation to social status, and we can give ourselves infinite trouble if we run around trying to present ourselves as important or high status in the way that we dress, what we drive, where we go for holidays, or pretending that charity clothes hide our educational background. *Give yourself a break and be what you need to be.*

How we can use envy

Envy can be a sign of hope because the idea of what we want is still alive in us. Our dreams and fantasies have not been completely quashed.

Our lives will be restricted if we are too fearful of others' envy. It's important to recognise that our fear of being envied can mean that we fail to celebrate and value what we have in our lives. In an age when economic success is more difficult to achieve, and therefore it is less likely that we can avoid our uncomfortable feelings, it will be helpful to really value the positive qualities and creative abilities in ourselves that we have. However, this doesn't mean parading the things we can (still?) afford to buy, it means rather finding the deeper things in ourselves and in our lives for which we can feel gratitude and appreciation.

Accepting our own envy will allow us to contact our sense of lack honestly and could fuel our energy to enter into life's battle to survive and to be equal contributors to the world – in effect, to go out there and get what we actually want for ourselves.
In interacting with others, we may need to really address this OK-OK relationship dynamic. Thinking that someone else is more OK than ourselves is a warning light that we are not being assertive enough in our lives to meet our own needs.

Race inequality

Race inequality exists across the globe, and in some cases, people feel that they've been made unequal even in their own home countries, for example, where local people can't afford to buy property, are forced to work in tourism industries where they service people (sometimes sexually) from much wealthier countries, find that their indigenous language and customs are under threat, experience themselves as suffering unfairly in the allocation of housing, health, education and job opportunities which they perceive as more competitive than before, or have to leave their homes to work for rich people away from their own partners and children, sometimes going into very questionable situations. See for example Barbara Ehrenreich and Arlie Hochschild's collection of papers about women round the globe in these kinds of situations. Although there are many positives about globalisation (particularly if we're well-heeled and can travel or we have an international business or we're able to buy goods from round the world), there are also some downsides at a human level, which mean that people are sometimes forced to leave their places of origin and their families in order to survive themselves or to provide for their relatives, or made to feel like second-class citizens in their own locality.

The weight of the history of empire and warfare is so great that there is much deep ambivalence in most countries about race equality, particularly where brutality and atrocities, genocide, ethnic cleansing and slavery have been involved (few of us have escaped this kind of issue in our history from one perspective or another). It's a good idea to inform ourselves of relevant history, especially if we're feeling unhappy about people from a particular ethnic group. History tends to unravel layers of injustice, human misery, territorial expansionism and power struggles, and can indeed show us how whole peoples can be led down paths that reflect the feelings of envy, grandiosity, and the wish for dominance in their leaders and ruling élites.

The point is that understanding the relationship between different races can be helpful to us when we ask ourselves the question why any set of people are here *now*, needing or requiring our help, working alongside us and supplying skills, spending money on tourism or receiving money to survive. The modern world is a melting pot of racial integration, mass migration, claims to regional autonomy, global business, international organisations, cultural interchange, and sadly, much warfare, often between religious and racial groups.

International migration is a huge factor to take on board – with more than 200 million people on the globe categorised as migrants currently. According to the International Organisation for Migration, one out of every 33 people on the earth is a migrant, whilst of these a certain proportion are refugees, others are different categories of economic migrant, some are 'irregular' – for example, staying beyond the length of visas, and some are 'trafficked'. Destination countries vary greatly on this – with Qatar apparently having nearly 90% of its population formed of 'migrants' and Indonesia less than 1%.

It can be a challenge in our transactions to take on facts about the fluid nature of the world population and to shape our communications to relate fairly and equally to people in a call centre on the other side of the world or someone who's just moved into our street from somewhere else.

Diversity

Countries have varied on how they've managed diversity agendas and the situations they've had to deal with – for example, how much control they've had over influxes of migrants (eg. sudden large numbers of refugees from war or much-needed and encouraged economic migrants) and whether they've been able to exercise any moral or legal control over inward migration in general. The British Prime Minister David Cameron's 2011 speech in Germany ignited debate when he suggested that multiculturalism in Britain had given licence to too much separatism and the risk of extremism, and argued for a stronger national identity. Will Kymlicka (2012) argues that we need to be cautious about assuming that 'multi-culturalism' is 'in retreat' (particularly in cases where countries may never really have embraced the idea), and suggests that it works best when there is a variety of cultures involved so that a country is benefiting from real diversity and where issues between support for human rights and anxieties over national security are resolved.

There's always an anxiety in the indigenous population that people who share a cultural identity different from the mainstream cultural group will become articulate in asserting their claims for rights and shares of the 'pie'. But it's not just a one-way deal. We can forget to count up the contributions that people who come from different cultures can make to a country – Jeremy Seabrook's work documenting the range of academic refugees who've come to Britain over the past 75 years is an example of this (– neither does he gloss over the contradictory receptions that they received). And there's the excitement and stimulation of 'fusion' in food, music, art, fashion etc. that emerges when different cultures absorb ideas from each other, whether these are completely fused into something new or represent a mix of more than one cultural idea which are nevertheless still recognisable. The translation of American hip-hop fashion into Asian cultures is one example, whilst the neck-rings of the Burmese Kayan tribe and shamanic decorations clearly infuse contemporary Western jewellery and dress designs. Urban restaurants in the West now often offer a range of foods from different cultures side by side.

Multiculturalism doesn't just work automatically – for example, care needs to be exerted over how different groups are expected to 'integrate' – in some cases, there have been compulsory requirements for learning language and acquiring knowledge about the 'host' country for 'incomers', as well as agreements about how different cultural ideas about things like marriage, divorce, self-presentation, approaches to religious practice and education can be handled, and rules for everyone about mutual respect and anti-racism. And institutions have sometimes found it difficult to accommodate to new challenges, becoming charged with 'institutional racism' that takes a long time to change.

Countries have varied in how 'coercive' they've been towards people of other races in respect of these kinds of requirements – sometimes requirements are easier for some groups than others to fulfil. Will Kymlicka describes the spectrum of 'civic integration' in Europe as running between *'prohibitive'* and *'enabling'*. Australian people believe in finding a balance between making demands of immigrants (such as their agreement to the primacy of national values) and giving them full citizenship. Some countries refuse to do this – for example by not allowing immigrants to move beyond 'guest-worker' status. Policies on funding community developments can be used to promote integration and collaboration but can also be used to support distinctive cultural heritage.

One of the distinctions between approaches to diversity is the extent to which each culture is given value and respect *rather than* or *as well as* assuming that immigrant cultural groups will – or should - assimilate into the host country's culture. Tariq Modood is one who has challenged *radical secularism*, the way in which secular states can promote policies which undermine religious practice and spiritual values.

Inter-cultural relating is a two-way process – some people believe that newbies should do all the running, whilst others feel that too much is asked of them as hosts. **Our position is that people from different cultures need to understand each other and that different races have equal rights, however these are organised.**

It's not a matter of developing superficial political correctness but feeling resentful or antipathetic behind closed doors. There's a lot of hidden resistance to change and integration which is why simply learning to say the right things doesn't quite cut it (though it may be better than saying the wrong things!). There are many books and papers on these kinds of issues and if they're pertinent to your relationship with others, it will be worth getting more informed.

Cross-cultural communication

There are also books and DVDs on *cross-cultural communication* that may be helpful, and we can spend time making ourselves familiar with the particular needs of cultural groups with whom we have to deal regularly. For example, in the medical school where I taught, it was clear to me that it would be good for students to understand the differing needs of Jewish, Muslim, Hindu, Christian, and other groups in relation to death and dying, where there are many cultural differences, such as the time that should elapse before burial or cremation, whether or not strangers or family members should touch the person's body and what should be done. Cecil Helman's work on medical anthropology is an excellent guide to understanding cross-cultural differences.

But it's no good operating as if there's a catalogue of answers. No individual or family lives exactly within the 'rules' of their race or culture (even if such rules were generally agreed upon which of course they're usually not), and can easily take offence if expected to do so. What's needed is a general awareness that each of us is unique and different and that we should not assume we know what people want done. An approach that recognises that *we have to enquire of others what would seem OK to them* and that *we have to explain why something matters to us* is the beginning of true cross-cultural communication.

It's also worth remembering that even within our own cultural group (whatever we deem that to be), each *family* (and indeed ultimately *each person*), has its own cultural rules and styles, so that racial equality ultimately comes down to human equality. Visiting someone else's home or office or 'church' always makes it clear how much we 'fit in' or 'adapt' to that person's/family's/ team's culture and how much we assert our own needs within it, even though it's not our own home or workplace or place of worship. Quite a lot of this book is about just such a dilemma – how much to be ourselves within a culture that has values we may not agree with.

Swearing

Although swearing itself isn't usually illegal (though it may depend on the country), if used in certain circumstances, it can be construed to be part of bullying, harassment, or causing distress to others. In particular, as with all language (including non-verbal language such as use of touch), it usually depends on the power relationship between the parties or whether it can be construed as part of abuse such as sexist, racist or homophobic abuse. If swearing and bad language is used to intimidate or upset another person, then there are sanctions available to police, employers, public bodies etc. on a variety of grounds other than purely the use of specific words. The issue to take hold of is the degree of warmth and simple humanity that is present in a communication and whether conversely, there is any bias, prejudice, hatred or cruelty in it. If people can hear that we are ourselves deeply frustrated, but basically trying to sort out a problem (or reacting to physical pain), this will come across differently from trying to deliberately denigrate or hurt someone. Swearing in a way which emphasises this point will come across differently from shouting out words which wound people in sexual or personal terms.

Overall message

Having successful transactions with people in our lives comes down to feeling OK with ourselves and having worked through some of those things in our inner world that might be undermining our communications (including a lack of knowledge about the external world). Learning to structure transactions, have clear aims and use skill in how we communicate can ensure that - rather like a pendulum or a homing pigeon - we constantly come back to a base of OK-ness in ourselves and an approach to others that is OK-OK.

Books

Michael Argyle and Peter Trower (1979) *Person to Person: Ways of Communicating* Harper and Row
Barbara Ehrenreich and Arlie Russell Hochschild (eds) (2003) *Global Woman: Nannies, Maids, and Sex Workers in the New Economy* Henry Holt and Co./ Metropolitan Books
Michel Foucault (1995) *Discipline and Punish: The Birth of the Prison* Vintage Books
Jeremy Hazell (1989) *Thoughts on the Pain of Self-Disclosure* Journal of the British Association of Psychotherapists no.20 July 1989
Cecil G Helman (2007) (5th ed) *Culture, Health and Illness* Hodder Arnold

Linda Hopkins (2006) *False Self: A Life of Masud Khan* Other Press

Roger Housden (2001) *ten poems to change your life* Harmony

Susan Jeffers (2012 25th anniversary edition) *Feel the Fear and Do It Anyway* Vermilion

Will Kymlicka (2012) *Multiculturalism: Success, Failure, and the Future* Queen's University, Canada February 2012 Migration Policy Institute of Europe

Alice Miller (2008 3rd edition) *The Drama of the Gifted Child* Basic Books

Jean Baker Miller (1977) *Toward a new psychology of women* Beacon Press

Tariq Modood (2013) *Multiculturalism* Polity Press

Adam Phillips (1997) *Winnicott* Fontana Modern Masters

Jeremy Seabrook (2009) *The Refuge and the Fortress: Britain and the flight from tyranny* Palgrave Macmillan

Richard Stephens, John Atkins, and Andrew Kingston (2009) *Swearing as a Response to Pain* Neuroreport **20** (12): 1056–60.

Ian Stewart and Vann Joines (1987) *TA Today: A New Introduction to Transactional Analysis* Life Space Publishing

TV
Simon Cowell *The X-factor* SYCOtv

3   close relationships

In this chapter, we cover a range of issues related to maintaining close relationships including getting good at emotional problem-solving, getting in touch with material from our infancy that is affecting our adult relating, being honest about why we choose or have chosen our partner, deciding on priorities like making time for sex and being aware of each other's sensitivities, how we manage questions of freedom within intimate relationships including the freedom for self-development as well as sexual freedom, how we handle criticisms and putdowns about the relationship we've chosen, and how economic pressures in today's world may be affecting the way we relate and the kinds of deals we strike with intimate partners for survival and growth under today's difficult conditions. Close relationships involve facing up to painful issues as well as to pleasure and love, and it's important to keep them vibrant, facilitating each other's growth, and concentrating on good communication.

The first part of this chapter is written by Jack and the second part by Julia.

Jack:

In this chapter, we'll be talking about *close* relationships, the various issues and problems they bring up and how they can work well and bring joy and creativity and happiness. We're talking about *any* close relationships – partners, relatives, friends, etc. and attempting to separate out 'partnerships' from other types of relationships.   Most of the material though applies to all relationships.

In the subsequent chapter, we talk about letting go of relationships, what can go wrong and with loss and the process of grieving.

It's useful to discuss the kind of close relationship you have in your life with one another to clarify what you both think is going on - if for example, you see a colleague as both a colleague and a close friend and they see you as a colleague only or if you're married or just friends – have you each got the same idea of the marriage or friendship? It's worth checking out your ideas to avoid misunderstandings.

Why is there so much confusion about close relationships?

Close relating is something people do, they've always done and probably always will do. Close relationships are affected by social change, people's attitudes, circumstances, etc.

As a lot of relating is done intuitively and unconsciously, people are able to relate without experts, theories, analysis and so on. This is just as well because whilst you can boil relationships down to key features, they are complex and can normally only be processed unconsciously. When there is a need to look at relationships, it's usually when problems arise within them and at that point it's useful to (re)solve any problems – but this is usually what people are not so good at. I would go so far as to say that *good problem-solving* is one of the most important aspects in close relationships.

Important features of good relationships

Here's a list of some of the important features of relationships that seem to work well – they include:

- love
- problem-solving
- attachment
- communicating
- being yourself
- growing/developing
- freedom
- trust
- equality

However, when people get together they often look at things like:

- stereotypical attractiveness
- capacity for worldly survival (– millionaires get a lot of points on this)

132

- having worldly 'extras' like being well-connected, having a high-status position etc.
- capacity for meeting surface emotional needs like the need for flattery or sharing fun

Love – what is it?

Answer – a BIG topic - here's a start......

Love is a complicated thing to talk about but it's possible to find some useful keys.

One key is *conditional* versus *unconditional* love; if you are loved for example, for how well you perform, that is *conditional*. A lot of love in this society is conditional. *Unconditional* love is being loved for who you are and this kind of love is more likely (though not always) to be found in a parent-child relationship. See for example Ian Stewart and Vann Joines on this.

There's another kind of unconditional love which is *spiritual love* and this should not be affected by anything 'worldly'.

Carl Rogers' work on *person-centred therapy/client-centered therapy* focuses on the way in which our self-worth is governed by the conditions under which we grow and develop, and his work is worth perusal if this is something you struggle with.

Love can be conceptualised as an *upward spiral*, by which we continually stretch ourselves to break through the conditionality of love and become more open and generous in our loving, more *unconditional* about the love we offer.

Love has many features which include caring, giving people equality and freedom and respect and being interested in their development; also, it can grow in an unlimited way instead of being rationed or having limits placed on it.

People can love themselves or have a notion of being loved spiritually. If people truly do love themselves it may fill gaps that are currently filled by consumerism and relationships.

Exercise:

> ### *What do you* **love/not love** *re yourself?*

Although not exclusively, this exercise tends to give an idea of internalised messages and decisions from childhood.

Allied to love are *strokes* which in TA are defined as 'units of recognition'. People need different strokes. *Positive strokes* are things like praising people, saying that you love them, giving them money. *Negative strokes* are things like saying what you don't like about people, taking something from them, etc. Strokes can be used manipulatively. Touch and holding are physical strokes that the research and experience tells us, are very powerful.

TA is an incomplete but very valuable psychology designed to be understandable and can be used in all aspects of your life. The problem is that in TA, as most therapy schools, they see themselves as having *all* the answers to life, which is far from true. It's helpful to see it in wider psychological context which includes behaviourism, psychoanalysis, Jungian psychology, etc. – reading about the field will be useful to you.

There's a wealth of information on strokes in *Transactional Analysis* and see as well 'the stroke economy' developed by Hogie Wyckoff and Claude Steiner in the early 1970s.

For some, the Baptist pastor and marriage counsellor, Gary Chapman, has written a bestseller called *The Five Love Languages* which explores the ways in which couples can learn to understand their own profiles for relating including how they exchange resources such as doing things to help each other and valuing quality time together.

See more about love from Julia in our chapter on *Values.*

Problem-solving

Part of problem-solving in relationships is to try to identify non-judgmentally where the problem arises from. Often the things that upset people most are buried deep in their minds and involve past hurts.

An example: if one person in a partnership doesn't give enough praise, the other person may ratc this as a 8/10 problem (ie. highly significant) and may have the awareness that that is what their parents did *and* know that they want more praise than this.

More difficult examples to figure out consciously are when there is no conscious memory but only a physical/body and unconscious memory eg. issues from babyhood, often issues that involve basic bonding like trust, safety, responsiveness etc.

I'm not suggesting doing Do-It-Yourself therapy in problem-solving but suggesting that historical problems, not just from the distant past but also from previous partners or friends, may have created sensitivity.

Of course, not all problems are from the past but most involve what Ken Mellor and Aaron Schiff called '*discounting*'.

It can be problematic if things are allowed to become routine and out of awareness rather than being explored and stated.

When exploring sensitive areas other issues can emerge where there is a difference between the partners eg. different ideas around sex, money, values etc.

Keys to problem-solving:

- identify the problem.
- if possible, find out where it comes from.
- rate the importance of it 1-10.
- don't judge anyone.
- try and negotiate a way to be aware of it now/in future and look for solutions if everyone is willing and able.

More of the same

'More of the same' as a solution is an idea from the world of Steve de Shazer's approach to *Brief Therapy*. Here the problem is chronic and made worse by the solutions that have been tried. The idea is to find novel solutions that do not cause the same or further problems.

I think it's impossible to overestimate the value of a problem-solving, caring and creative approach to close relationships and I think it is worth building this in from the start. Problems that are allowed to go on may be OK but they may be harder to sort out later.

It's worth communicating well from the start as this can avoid problems.

Communication

I'm not just talking about the *quantity* of communication here. If people are clear and concise, it helps, instead of meandering. Most people are not mind-readers; some may be, but it is worth stating the obvious.

It's also worth being aware of what you want and don't want and asking for *what you want* or for *less of what you don't want.*

A lot of the material in the *Transactions* chapter relates to close relationships as well as to not-so-close ones.

What doesn't work in communication is hinting, pleasing, nagging, expecting others to guess, being unclear or not being upfront.

Remember though that a huge amount of communication is non-verbal and/or unconsciously understood.

What you are *not* talking about can be a clue to areas that can cause problems, so a possible exercise is to look at what you *are* talking about (eg. your child's education) and what you are *not* talking about (eg. sex). You may find that different contexts set off different kinds of conversations and that in order to discuss a particular subject, you need to arrange to be together in a particular setting. You might also find that going to the supermarket stimulates talk about money when in fact it might be better to arrange some time to sit and talk about this under less pressure. You may find that you're avoiding talking about sex in bed, and are discussing everything else under the sun there instead.

Location of talking	Topics I and my partner have talked about this week	Topics I and my partner have **not** talked about this week
In bed		
Over meals		
On the telephone		
In the park		
Collecting the children from school		
At the doctor's surgery		
Out shopping		

Attachment

Attachment is fostered by behaviours such as honesty, reliability, working on mutual projects, co-operation, thoughtfulness, and caring but for many people it is a deeper unconscious process that dates back to early bonding in attachments to parents, caretakers etc. The idea here is that people will 'refer' back to what very

137

survive and grow in difficult times – close relationships

early attachments were like in their current emotionally-significant relationships.

As mentioned in other parts of the book, very early experience is usually stored in memory in the unconscious and is only retrievable through routes such as dreams, body therapy or checking for catastrophic or black-and-white thinking or relational processes like *splitting* or *symbiosis* as described for example in psychoanalysis.

Sometimes it's worth making conscious or becoming consciously aware of early experience or making a best guess of it if it's important in a relationship or in general.

An example from my own life is that as a baby I was in hospital twice from around the age of 1 year without my mother and this has led to a desire for a stable environment, which I cannot always have and a partner with whom I can, if needed, be in touch with quickly.

Being yourself

If you cannot do this in a close relationship, where can you be yourself?

It means expressing yourself as you really are, faults and all.

What gets in the way of being yourself is putting on a front or making 'social' *adaptations* (see *persona* in the *Self* chapter), fear of rejection, pleasing others (*'over-adapting'*)– see Mellor and Schiff, 1975).

What aids the process is being in *Free Child* in TA terms, getting in touch with your unconscious and feeling and body 'selves', and being able to 'play' rather than conforming to rules or expectations.

I think the old wisdom of *'just be yourself'* is true.

138

Growing and developing

This is a lifelong process and people develop throughout their lives, or try and stay the same, or seem stuck and some seem to go backwards or 'regress' in psycho-speak. In fact, we are changing all the time and people can grow and develop psychologically, morally (see Lawrence Kohlberg), and spiritually (see James Fowler and Morgan Scott Peck's work).

There's the point of view, which goes against Western notions of comfort, that *facing adversity* aids growth and though this isn't always true, this wisdom from the spiritual growth world suggests it can lead to a reduction of *ego* and to spiritual development. Also there are the old wisdoms *that 'adversity is the mother of invention'* and *'every cloud has a silver lining'*.

According to Carl Jung, there's a lifelong process of development going on called *individuation* (see the *Self* chapter) which is particularly in focus in middle age.

Intimacy – what it is

Intimacy is a kind of safe closeness. I think it *usually happens in a climate of caring* and includes *a lack of 'censorship', spontaneity* and *trust.* That's a list of **major *useful* things in relationships** – there's a few more in the chart further on with the opposites.
Another example of a possible disturbance in attachment may be whilst a couple may have a deal to have affairs as long as they tell each other; somehow when it happens this may not be accepted as it disturbs an older, historical notion of attachment in the unconscious mind of one person (or both) and evokes feelings of abandonment or distrust.

Here's a list of important *non-useful* things (but see list later on as well)**:**

Firstly, people tend to have 'ideals' of relating which are unreal, for example, wanting the perfect partner. See elsewhere in the book as well for notions of perfection getting in the way for example, *my perfect house, job, lifestyle.* There's a difference between pursuing an ideal like honesty and creating often fantastic or unachievable ideal lives, partners, jobs etc. The difference is that a goal like *honesty* is largely achievable.

Other non-useful issues in relationships include: a lack of depth, ie. a lack of useful things like love, attachment and intimacy. Some people are known to have problems in relating (see our chapter on *Emotional health*) and achieving depth is something that they will have to work at or may never achieve.

Within the type of relationship you think you have, it's worth checking as well that you both agree about the nature of your relationship. People tend to think that others are like themselves. If you are very involved emotionally, you may think that the other person is too – this is worth checking out.

People in relationships may also find their *egos* or *personas* (social selves) get in the way.

Here's a chart with useful and non-useful aspects of relationships:

What works	What doesn't work
Love	Little depth/emotional shallowness
Attachment	as above
Intimacy	as above
Less *ego* (see *Self* chapter)	More *ego*
More communication	Less communication
Problem-solving	Unsolved or unidentified problems
Being yourself	Over-adjusting, being 'careful'
Less social self or *persona* (see *Self* chapter)	More *persona*
Less conditional love	More conditional love
Being 'important'	Not valuing yourself
Being assertive	Being 'nice'
Honesty	Deviousness, manipulativeness
Being direct	Being unclear
Updating the relationship	Ignoring it or not
Keeping it vibrant	Letting things drift

Nurturing your partner and relationship	Neglect
Equality	Power plays or unfair balance
Stating the obvious	Not stating the obvious
Trust	Suspicion
Putting growth and development at the top of your agenda	Giving growth a backseat
Awareness	Ignoring issues
Being aware and sensitive to old stuff (yours or theirs) and having deals about these	Treading on 'old stuff'
Love being selfless	Me me, more more
Not leaving sex to chance	Hoping for the best
Being spiritual	Being materialistic/worldly
Stating the obvious	Mindreading
Asking	Not asking
Having things defined clearly	Vagueness
Tolerance and forgiveness	None or less; judgement
Communicating 'as you go'	Leaving things unsaid
Assertiveness	Being a doormat
Freedom	Feeling unfree
Patience	Impatience
Respect and 'rights' – active attention on these	Leaving it to chance

Five 'types' of relationship

Each 'type' has different implications for the long-term:

LIVE
PROBLEMATIC
FIXED
DEAD
REVIVING/RETURNING (OLD FRIENDS)

141

A **LIVE** relationship is where both partners share fully their concerns, hopes, and feelings and attend to the process of relating between them

A **PROBLEMATIC** relationship – where there is an attempt to meet intimacy and happiness needs but problems such as issues from the past, childhood patterns, a significant imbalance of finance, education, power in the relationship, trauma or injury or disability, dynamics in the wider family network or material from previous relationships make things difficult – not solving problems can cause stress depending on factors like how big the problems are and how long they are sustained

A **FIXED** relationship – where the relationship meets a number of needs external to the inner soul such as the agreement to bring up children together, present a married or institutionalized front to the outside world, run a shared business or manage joint financial concerns, or develop a home-base, but where intimacy and personal happiness needs are met elsewhere or put on hold, and daily life becomes routinized. Often, relationships with relatives such as parent-adult child relations suffer from this fixedness, not facilitating each other's growth but meeting a number of practical and perhaps social needs. Sometimes hidden affairs are like this too, because they can only function within tight parameters and partners are enabled to stay in their life situations rather than growing.

A **DEAD** relationship where one or both partners come to accept that the relationship dynamics cannot be repaired, perhaps because of damage to the relationship through betrayal of trust, or because of despair that intimacy and happiness can ever be met with each other, or because one or both parties feel that they have never really been suited or attractive to one another. The situation becomes chronic and intractable. Things are 'going nowhere'.

A **REVIVING/RETURNING** relationship where a partner or friend from the past returns, often resulting in unexpected new feelings associated with both nostalgia and idealisation of the past, grief and regret, fantasies of what might have been, disillusionment with choices already made etc. so ongoing communication is particularly important in order to accommodate change.

Julia's further comments

Reading Jack's section has been fascinating to me because for the first time I can understand fully everything that drives him in his quest for good relating, and what he brings and expects in a relationship. I think every couple could benefit from spelling out on paper how they see 'relating'. I also see that I sometimes think somewhat differently.

Though we both did the same basic psychology degree at the same college (but not at the same time and before we met each other) ultimately we come from different traditions – Jack from *Transactional Analysis* and the 'growth' movement, and me from psychoanalysis and sociological and cultural analysis.

The human potential 'growth' movement emerged from California in the 1960s and included the work of people like Abraham Maslow, Carl Rogers, and Fritz Perls. The traditional power structures of psychoanalysis were challenged by advocates of client-centred therapy such as Rogers, who believed that people should be given *unconditional positive regard* in the light of which they would naturally grow towards *self-actualisation,* and that the relationship between client and counsellor was critical to the growth process. Much of the therapeutic work was done in encounter groups where people shared their inner feelings and challenged one another on how they related to each other, which later gave rise to models of training that focused on the *process* of relating rather than the *content*. Eric Berne launched the field of TA around the same time, following and moving on from Freudian psychoanalysis and building an entirely modern framework for analysing relationships including the idea of *parent, child* and *adult ego states*, giving *positive and negative strokes*, living *life scripts*, taking *life positions* (eg. based on *OK-ness*) and *game-playing*.

I've spent my life associated with *psychodynamic therapy* (derived from *psychoanalysis*) which primarily works with individuals (rather than in groups), slowly dissecting the material that lies below conscious awareness as the person learns to let it emerge through techniques such as *free association* of thoughts, *dream analysis* and *interpretation*. The therapist uses their model (in my case the *'object relations'* model) to explain early experience - for example ideas like the mother as a persecutory object because she has temporarily been absent and our infantile need to destroy the mother in retaliation. In such a case, it's important that the mother withstands the aggression of the child so that the child both recognises that their own fantasies are not the same as reality and that their feelings are not as destructive as they fear. In this way, for example, we learn to handle complex feelings like ambivalence.

The therapeutic relationship is important in object relations work because we can bring our patterning from early childhood into that relationship and a skilled therapist can reflect back to us our *transference* – eg. our sense of abandonment when the therapist takes a holiday as we must have felt when our parent was temporarily unavailable, and also how we get angry when a close partner, friend or relative appears to abandon us when in fact they are simply acting as autonomous human beings, rather than as our possessions. Key people in the object relations field include Donald Winnicott, Harry Guntrip and Melanie Klein – there are differences between all the theorists.

As well as psychoanalysis, I have also been profoundly influenced by the critiques of social and cultural analysis, which include new ways of looking at categorisations of gender, ethnicity and sexual identity and understanding how our social context influences the way we relate, particularly in terms of power differentials including social class and social roles like employer/employee.

What does all this mean for our approach to 'close relating'?

It means that as I see it, Jack requires that we are upfront about our feelings, perceptions, and observations in the here and now, that we are direct and clear, open and transparent, and work on the process of relating by giving feedback and solving problems together.

For me, this is rather daunting, as I tend to 'split off' from confrontation - I like to be very private and find it at times difficult to be open and transparent. I believe this comes from my upbringing where I was sometimes confronted by adult rages and behaviour which humiliated people and didn't have strong models of how to tackle this.

I recognise the enormous strengths that come into a relationship when we employ Jack's ideas and have seen in our family life the improvements that have come and the increase in closeness that has developed.

It also means that I recognise that I work with more fuzzy, less direct concepts, leaving people be, letting things emerge over time, making the links with infantile experience when the person is ready for it, and I tend to gloss over *process*, thinking rather more about the deeper issues that underlie puzzling behaviours rather than confronting them. I tend to be interested in how the person relates *to themselves* whereas Jack will be interested in how a person relates *to others* (and specifically to the person they are close to). I am more interested in the *history* of feelings and behaviours whereas Jack is more interested in the process we use *now*, though there is some overlap on this. I tend to be interested in the broad sweep of emotional working-through over time whilst Jack tends to be interested in the micro-analysis of what is happening in the room now.

Both of us look to early experience and how it is manifest in the adult person and in their patterns of relating; we both recognise the 'baby' material that gets evoked by careless and unconscious ways of relating in adult life. It's important to avoid treading on each other's areas of sensitivity in this regard.

I have found that doing bodywork in recent months has helped me to get in touch with how it might have been/must have been for me as a baby and the kind of psychological environment I came into as I was born and as I learned to relate to others in the early months. This is helping enormously in helping me to face fears about the world in my adult life.

145

What do we mean by *'close'*?

Just because any of us appear to be involved in a relationship that is structurally meant to be so, doesn't mean that we actually *are* close.

We may have idealised pictures of what we think our relationships should be like and these can get in the way of us enjoying them for what they *are*, and may push us to evaluate them negatively – for example, jettisoning a partnership which doesn't seem to be the romantic ideal. Yet learning to know our partner's *actual* body and the changes in it as they get older, or capturing our parents' fading memories and understanding their significance to them are examples of what closeness can be like, rather than fantasising about what we haven't got and being disappointed.

With today's technology and over-population, it can be tempting to feel that we can quickly replace people if they don't please us, but there are rewards in getting to know someone well and enjoying the stability of ongoing closeness, even when it involves (as it inevitably will) the ups and downs of conflict and change. Such rewards include:

- affection and intimacy 'on tap'– regular physical and verbal reassurance and support, listening to one another, signs of commitment and appreciation regularly exchanged
- companionship in life's journey and in relation to questions of direction, investment, and decision-making
- shared goals can be worked towards – these may be related to personal growth or they may be survival goals but together you can be stronger
- friendship – relying on each other through a variety of tribulations
- child-rearing can be done – continuity to children can be offered, and differences about how to do it can be worked through as a model to children of how to relate
- shared interests – there can be fun and a deepening of knowledge or skill tempered by individual perspectives and experience

- sexual fulfilment from the stability of knowing each other, growing confidence, and the opportunity to explore and change
- a commitment to each other's growth – encouragement, praise, appreciation of the difficulties of change etc., support for developmental activity etc.
- the opportunity to repair/heal earlier life hurt within the security of commitment to each other and promises not to repeat that hurt
- a deepening of shared values, tested in a variety of shared situations and experiences over time

However, all this depends on relationships being good, and sadly, we can find ourselves settling for relationships that are not that good.

Settling for less than closeness

We are more likely to do this if we choose people for:

- their social status – people we can 'show off' to others as high-status, wealthy or highly attractive

- their role as a social companion who is there for us whenever we go out to events and social gatherings, if we are ashamed of being alone or fearful of being ostracised without a partner

- their role as a representative of us being OK, where we have doubts about how others view us mentally or socially – eg. because we have a stigmatised identity such as having been ill or belong to an ethnic or professional group that people we know are suspicious of etc.

- their capacity to feed our ego needs or extract from us nourishment for their ego needs or to battle with us over ego needs, feeding our arrogance or theirs

- their ability to offer us guidance, influence, answers, protection - which turns into dominance and control, limiting our freedom and autonomy, and in worst cases, leading to violent or verbal abuse and 'discounting' of us as people

- their suitability for fitting into a social structure of which we are part, such as a family where marriage is expected of us to someone of equal rank or local geography etc. rather for love, or where they will be good co-parents or help with the family business or caring roles etc. – in other words, for instrumental reasons

- their money, property, solvency

- their immediate sexual attractiveness not set into the wider context of personality, emotionality and cultural context

- their sobriety – they don't appear to suffer from any of the 'weaknesses' that worry us (eg. because of previous experience) such as flirty behaviour or alcoholism

- their controllability – they won't give us any cause to wonder if they're being faithful and conform to our needs for 'possessiveness'

When choosing a partner, it's important to assert our own relationship needs and not to be overly influenced by others in that choice, particularly those who have different values from us. Because status is such a big issue in contemporary society, we may be tempted to choose people because they fit the bill on status requirements and turn away from people who might meet us on intellectual, spiritual, emotional levels and ultimately make a happier and more fulfilling relationship with us.

However, *if we are not aware of our emotional needs or do not honour them*, getting it right may be difficult.

Of course, everything we are saying is built on the Western premise that relationships should be personally fulfilling, and for people in some cultures, this is not the top priority. Nevertheless, it is hard to imagine that people would not look to find the greatest emotional satisfaction within the framework of any other constraints there are on partner choice.

Playing out early family dynamics in adult relationships

To what extent does our current relationship structure reflect patterns we are familiar with from our family background?

It will be likely that we've done this if we're drawn to familiar patterns that are 'pre-set' even though at surface levels we're selecting something very different. Get two people who are doing this and you have a relationship in which two people are operating with *'transference'* – playing out issues that went on/go on between their parents and between themselves and their parents/caregivers which they're still trying to make sense of.

Examples are likely to include things like:

- not feeling free or able to assert ourselves
- having to keep feelings or sexual behaviour hidden
- feeling afraid of living life on our own
- having powerful conflicts that damage trust and affection
- avoiding sex, being more like brother and sister

Often in these dynamics, each partner is playing a complementary role – so one is dominant the other unassertive, one is transparent and the other is secretive, one threatens to leave and the other fears being left etc. We can think we have freed ourselves from family influences but they will go on shaping us until we start to unravel them and understand them. The idea that it's our partner who is 'wrong' is never the whole truth.

As a gay person, there may be complexities particularly if both partners have taken on similar social conditioning (eg. to act like men or like women) rather than having complementary roles as are assumed in traditional heterosexual relationships. In practice of course, we are attempting to give license these days to men and women being more fluid about how they enact their gender role.

How to categorise what's going on

Some theorists have identified different kinds of love and different dimensions that make up love, such as Robert J Sternberg's dimensions based on *passion, intimacy* and *commitment,* from which he has calculated a typology, depending on which elements predominate. As well as each partner having their own package of elements, which may or may not match, there's also the question of time elapsing, during which needs may change. It's common to feel romantic or infatuated love early on which might evolve into companionship in later years, or one might find that a crisis turns a companionate marriage into something with deeper intimacy and passion later on as a couple learns to be more open, trusting and intimate with each other.

In his recent formulation (2013), Robert Sternberg states his belief that couples benefit from having compatibility in their 'stories' about love – such as that love can be created by both partners, or is a game, or is a mystery, or is predetermined. His analysis of what predicts the best chance of sustaining loving relationships incorporates a number of factors including stories, thinking styles and creativity, and is worthwhile studying.

Problem-solving again

One of the things to get right early on in relationships is the *ability to problem-solve* together.

Whenever something comes up that disturbs us, we need to think about how much it matters (significance) and what our options are. If it's worth making a stand, we should do so. We should avoid letting things wash over us, putting up with them, in case that pattern becomes a habit or we forget where and when it started to matter.

Sometimes we just can't work out what's wrong, we're shouting at each other, bored and listless, irritated about the other's behaviour or choices, or embarrassed or upset about something the other has said or done in the company of others etc.

Problem-solving means that we take time to try to work out what's going on, in the spirit of love and friendship. We both try to say how we see things. We whittle away until we get to the bottom of what the issue or situation is about. Very often it will be that something has triggered an unconscious or bodily memory, something from early years that frightens us – often it's about safety, stability, trust and confidence.

> *After decades of happy friendship, I found that a close friend and I suddenly fell out when we discovered that we had no experience of solving problems within our relationship. As we'd never quarrelled, so we'd never had to sort anything out between us before, and we had absolutely no idea what to do. We'd never faced up to the true differences between us in our thinking – it had always seemed more important to sweep these 'under the carpet' in order to enjoy our time together and enjoy the benefits of emotional security that our friendship gave us, but moving into our 50s, we could no longer do this. Being whom we needed to be had become essential and I guess, more important than holding together our relationship with each other.*
>
> *When we clashed, it was painful – we tried to talk about things but we were overwhelmed by feelings that could not be resolved. Aghast, we found that we didn't have the flexibility in our relationship to deal with things and that over the years, the balance of support around our friendship had changed. We probably needed to recognise that our friendship had given us both the confidence to reach out more effectively for what we needed in intimate partnerships but instead we both felt abandoned.*

Of course, this process of problem-solving can be painful and uneven – as feelings well up and old habits of dealing with them kick in. *We may have to return to the same kind of scenario again and again before there is a breakthrough.* In a long-term relationship, we can find the staying power to do that.

People who have had long periods of therapy are more familiar with the process of sticking with a feeling or a situation and gently trying to unravel things, peeling away layers, steadily analysing things, and generating hypotheses like:

- *'maybe it's because I used to do that with my former partner'*
- *'could it be that you felt I didn't really care what you felt?'*
- *'I guess the way you were behaving didn't match my fantasy of how I expected you to behave'*
- *'is the fact that I had once upon a time promised to love you unreservedly getting in the way of you realising that some things you do, do actually upset me?'*
- *'might it be that when I'm late and don't ring you it triggers a memory of the way your father used to behave?'*
- *'when you go over budget I think what upsets me, even though I know our situation is different, is that I remember when my parents over-spent and the family ended up in serious debt – I think I over-react'*
- *'I'm sorry I got angry – I think it might have been these new tablets I'm taking, I'd forgotten that they can make me feel extra-anxious'*

When we get to an answer that feels right - and it may take a few 'goes' at it to do so - we will need to develop ideas about how to change things in the future, how to avoid triggering those feelings again, and what to do if they are triggered. If we've been upset by our partner's behaviour, we need to discuss with them how we will not let it upset us so much next time, and ask them how they can be more sensitive to our feelings. We need to develop strategies *together* - if necessary, we can write them out and put them up on a noticeboard or in a notebook.

This really is at the heart of long-term relating – and it helps us to grow and change as people and ultimately to find more emotional happiness and greater intimacy and understanding with the key people in our lives.

A note on gender

There are plenty of books on the market which reinforce gender differences and tell us how we can fix relationship difficulties by understanding how 'men' and 'women' tick. The popular *'Men are from Mars and Women are from Venus'* by John Gray is one of the more successful of this genre, and helps us to understand generalities about things like men's tendency to retreat into their 'cave' in order to process things and women's more cyclical approach to feelings, as well as putting forward the idea that men and women count up emotional 'strokes' differently from one another and have different preferences about how they would like to be related to, men for example, apparently preferring direct requests from their partner rather than indirect hints which can suggest manipulation. If these books work for us (and 7 million have apparently bought this book), that's good. In the end we all have to find a language that speaks to us, and for some of us, applying the idea that it's our sex-role that determines our behaviour and feelings can be helpful.

Whilst there's now a history of psychoanalytic thought that constructs women's psychology as different from men's and the idea of motherhood as significant in how women view life in a way that may be different from men's, there is of course a more recent debate about whether or not we're doing ourselves any favours by emphasising gender difference.

As outlined in the chapter on the *Self,* contemporary thinking suggests that we may not be as firmly categorised as totally 'male' or totally 'female' as we've previously believed, either at the physical level or at the psychological level. We have grounds for understanding that there is diversity among people on genetic, physiological and anatomical levels, as well as all of us having different patterns of role-modelling and behaviours within our family systems and upbringing. In parts of the West, we also have cultural environments that support us in defining our sexual identity and sexual lifestyles more freely than in the past, and new ways of thinking (particularly the post-structuralist critique) which allow us to crack open the 'either-or' traditions of conceptualising things and look at language and process. Judith Butler's approach to gender is an example of this, inviting us to see gender as 'performance' rather than as something solid that never changes and is immutable.

We therefore have growing evidence and scientific/intellectual permission to move away from the 'binary' approach to gender and sexual identity, and in this sense, we can be creative around the way in which explore problems in our relationships without retreating into fixed ideas about how 'men' and 'women' should relate or 'perform' based on traditional models of heterosexuality and family life.

Freedom within a relationship

People are often frightened that freedom they took for granted when they were 'single' will be curtailed in a relationship. It's important to identify what that 'freedom' means in each case, and for each partner, so that we understand the terms we are negotiating. Is it:

- the freedom to play the music we like, as loudly as we like, when we want?
- the freedom to leave the house whenever we want to without explanation?
- the freedom to see friends whether or not our partner likes them?
- the freedom to express opinions that differ sharply from our partner's?
- the freedom to mix with a variety of people at a gathering, or to go out with friends rather than go everywhere with our partner?
- the freedom to not wear a wedding or partnership ring, or not to change our name?
- the freedom to have sexual relations with other people?
- the freedom to talk intimately with different people?
- the freedom to choose our work, travel in our work, move the family when we want to without resistance?
- the freedom to wear what we like or change our appearance without opposition?
- the freedom to change our sexual identity?

Where do you draw the line as a couple?

Sexual freedom

As Jack has outlined, sometimes one member of a couple will 'believe' in giving their partner freedom but not like the result. A partner may want to have the freedom to have sex with someone else and believe that they will nevertheless remain faithful at root to their original (and perhaps 'lifelong') partner, but find that feelings or demands overcome them, and that they have to break that agreement, wanting to spend their primary time with the other person. We can't always know what we can handle.

If the alternative person our partner wants to be with is loving and caring and aware of the devastation the situation might have on us, that situation will be very different from our partner falling in love with someone who is fundamentally cold and unempathic and doesn't care what we experience. It may be very important to find out whether the alternative partner is emotionally healthy or whether they're suffering from some kind of pathology which is damaging everyone (though of course in our upset and anger we might attribute worse characteristics to them than may actually be the case).

We should decide whether the freedom required is for *behaviour* or for *words* – i.e. if we have another relationship is it to be kept quiet – do we have a policy of not discussing things – or do we both promise openness? If the latter, do we keep to this, or do we keep things secret? Is the greatest betrayal *lack of truthfulness*, or is it the *behaviour*? For some couples, what they don't know about doesn't hurt them. For others, the deal is one of complete openness, so secrecy undermines everything.

Is there an equality about all this, or does one partner have more freedom than the other? Do we respect each other's integrity and trust our care for each other whatever is happening, or is there a sense that one partner is actually exploiting or badly treating the other?

We need to be careful what we sign up to and try to imagine what we can truly handle. We must recognise that needs and wants *change over time*, and that what we're prepared to put up with or really want at one point may be different at a later stage in our life. For example, 'faithfulness' might be more important in earlier years when it seems as if there are plenty of attractive alternatives around us, whilst 'continuity and stability' might be more important in later years when there are likely to be significant investments in property and children and there has been an expectation of staying together to the end. However, there can be no clear formula, and for some people, a powerful sexual relationship or a time for truth and faithfulness comes later in life, with the hindsight of the pain that alternatives can cause.

The book by Sarah Litvinoff, *Better Relationships,* adopted as the *Relate* book on relationship maintenance, gives quite a bit of advice about this area.

Freedom for self-development

Creating freedom on a day-by-day basis for a person to express themselves or live life in a fulfilling way is nevertheless one of the best ways to nourish our relationship.

We can:

- help our partner to create space for themselves within the home or outside the home – a workshop, a shed, a shrine-room, a study, a desk, a studio, a garage, a personal shelf-unit.
- maximise privacy for them – don't open their post or answer their calls - unless we are offering this as a service to protect them from intrusion and that's what they want.
- support nascent ideas about what they would like to develop or wish they had done in their lives.
- suggest trips to places that will help them engage – a specialist shop, a mountain, a college, a mosque, a museum, horses in a field, a football match, a political talk, seeing a particular person who can help them or who has similar interests.
- not over-enthuse, but let them know we are willing to accompany them *or not* in these early stages of development.

- get on with our own stuff so that we are not burdening them with the worry of attending to us and so that we are not envious of their work – we have our own
- negotiate what we need to be creative ourselves
- retain an enduring interest in our partner *and* do what we need to do to keep *ourselves* vibrant and interesting

Sacrifice deals

We shouldn't allow our partner to sacrifice too much of their own dreams for us to follow ours. For some people, making a lot of sacrifice can be an ultimate green light to a sense of entitlement to a clandestine relationship or activity, or it can mean that they will later come to resent us or us them. Making sure there is a similar deal in place to help them do something they want at a later point and giving attention to what they can do in parallel right now, like being with the children or concentrating on a leisure activity of their own can help offset feelings of being left behind or neglected. Understand why they feel like retreating into the background or getting on with their path whilst we 'grow', or vice versa.

The psychoanalyst, Susie Orbach, wrote about the idea that we seek to meet our own 'unmet' needs by attempting to meet the needs of someone else. This is not so different from the kind of mechanism that propels some people who have had challenging childhoods into caring roles in adulthood, as if they can heal things in themselves by doing it differently for others, and by getting the reward of gratitude or of watching someone fulfil themselves as a result of their efforts. We should give thought as to whether we are meeting our own needs effectively or masking them by over-giving to our partner or children or friends. *Ask ourselves why it suits us to help our partner and avoid fulfilling our own destiny (or they theirs).* It's important to ensure that both members of a couple talk about what the secondary gains might be for the partner who is doing the supporting.

Emotional sensitivity and empathy

Emotional intelligence

Daniel Goleman's work on *'emotional intelligence'* has identified the realm of relationship skills that go beyond intellectual intelligence which are essential in building good partnerships and friendships. These include recognising, understanding and managing our *own* feelings and coming to appreciate, understand and respond to the feelings of *others;* this underlines the importance of empathic sensitivity.

We can't respond to others' feelings accurately unless we have some connection to our own. Getting to know our own emotions can be helped through:

- keeping a journal or diary
- playing music, drawing and painting and sculpting, knitting and sewing, woodwork and metalwork and glasswork – these kinds of avenues for self-expression offer opportunities for a kind of meditative processing of feelings and perceptions that are unspoken and come from deep within the unconscious mind.
- going out into nature for a walk or run can also have this effect.
- finding a therapist, counsellor or group where we can explore our past and present, fears and hopes, can be full of insights and may also be cathartic.
- having a massage, singing, dancing, yoga, gymnastics, physiotherapy can all help to unravel feelings embedded in our body's structures.

Using the unconscious

It's important not to believe that everything is available to us through *conscious thought.* We need the stimuli of our senses – vision, hearing, touch, smell, even taste - to enhance the connection to things which are not expressible through words and to evoke memories and connections that are sometimes not immediately available to consciousness. There can be too much emphasis on the *cognitive* level of relating; we may benefit from letting go of analysing. We might need to take a week together as partners to let ideas and insights emerge. Keeping a running noticeboard of points as they emerge into consciousness may be helpful. The whole exercise doesn't have to be 'cognitive' – it can be done like a meditation, or if it suits us, with music, wine, or walking in a beautiful park etc. We need to make time for it and enjoy the process.

We may be surprised at how confused or unaware we are about what we are actually feeling, perhaps spending years being emotionally anaesthetized about experiences of hurt, abandonment, rejection, and betrayal in childhood and early adulthood which when replayed in later years don't seem to affect us, and then seem surprised when we feel bored, listless, physically ill, sleepless, irritable or addicted to alcohol.

For ideas about how to tap into unconscious material, see the chapter on *The Unconscious*.

Dealing with negative messages

Julia Cameron's work helping people to get in touch with their spiritual and creative energy makes it clear that it's important to set boundaries on letting people into our psyche, to protect ourselves from negative energy, jealousy, ill-informed criticism, and the dynamics of other people's needs taking us away from our own path. Sometimes these constitute 'put-downs', however subtle, and they need to be countered. They may come from our own partner or from people around the relationship who have their own reasons for undermining it or for questioning our choices and processes.

In the case of gay relationships, dealing with homophobia may be a struggle, including disapproval or rejection by family, the attitude of neighbours, and challenges in the workplace or with customers and the public. One partner may be happy with 'coming out' whilst the other partner may be more cautious about this (ie. not at the same stage as each other), or there may be differences about whether or not to go for a civil partnership or marriage. A key source of tension can be the individuals' own sense of sexual identity and whether they feel confident about themselves within a society where the messages are predominantly heterosexual, or whether there is any self-hatred, guilt, doubt, or questions about the validity of the relationship, especially if the relationship is not being supported by significant people around the couple or if the relationship is 'out' in some contexts and 'hidden' in others. There may be differences in the extent to which each partner is prepared to make a stand about things, for example, being given separate rooms as guests or reacting to jokes and offensive comments. Colleen Connolly's article (listed below) outlines many of the difficulties involved.

If you experience put-downs within a family, partnership or friendship context, here are a few strategies to deal with them:

- the first step is *recognising* them, picking up where you are being *'discounted'* as unimportant or subsidiary to someone else.

- the second is to show you're unafraid, to be confident, and to pull the interaction back into OK-OK behaviour.

- don't let early 'discounts' persist – *confront them when they begin.*

- use your ability to praise others for their strengths and to be nurturing – you don't have to return in kind something that was unkind or belittling.

- show your own strengths and behave in accord with your own valued self. You are important too; don't be afraid to flag up your own standing as a person and your own abilities. Require respect as a human being from others.

- set limits on other people's behaviour where it transgresses.

- comment on the **process** of relating –

  - *'I'm not sure why you're behaving like this'*
  - *'I'm uncomfortable with the way you seem to be putting me down in front of others – is there something bothering you?'*
  - *'Is there a problem between us?'*
  - *'I'm unhappy with what you've just said and I need to correct the perception you seem to have of me'.*
  - *'I care about you very much but I'm not getting many positive messages from you at the moment'.*
  - *'Could we just stop this conversation and find out how we're feeling about each other?'*
  - *'We have such a lovely relationship but tonight we seem to have hit some difficulties – do you agree?'*

- reach for the spiritual or humanistic level of relating – find something to say or do that steps out of ego and competition, that calls to respect and care for each other

- insist on equal rights and protect yourself from exploitation and discounting

Avoid:

- being overly modest or unassuming
- being 'nice' and failing to confront bad behaviour
- being too open with people who are not psychologically safe for you
- being so careful that nothing meaningful is exchanged
- conforming and adapting to others against your own needs

Whilst a confrontation may be painful or embarrassing, you will bring the relationship into an equal balance – OK-OK, by insisting on mutual respect. A relationship that depends on false communication, on 'niceness' concealing deep resentments or egoistic competitiveness is not ultimately worthwhile or rewarding, and if sustained, will be bad for the psyche.

The facilitating environment

The concept of the 'facilitating environment' was developed by the British paediatrician and psychoanalyst, Donald Winnicott, who was able to observe the benefits to children of mothers who allowed them to develop without intruding or 'impinging' on their world of fantasy and play. The child could be 'alone', yet in the presence of their mother (or an 'other') – someone whom they trust not to disturb them but who offers a calm, loving companionship.

This is a helpful concept to apply within any intimate relationship.

It's not necessary or even wise to interrupt one another regularly. Try cultivating the art of being with one another without speaking, or without interrupting the thinking or speaking of the other with new thoughts of your own. Make your relationship a facilitating environment for the *development of inner life* – cultivate peace, listen to one another, enjoy emotional and spiritual connection even when you are doing things or being busy. Let your partner express themselves through the choices they make, the way they move, the things they do and read their behaviour as a key to understanding them. This is what any therapist would do, although unlike a therapist, you have a stake in what the result of behaviours will be and therefore may have a personal imperative to challenge them.

Personal relationships within the capitalist economy

In a capitalist economy, we're drawn into being not only *consumers* but also *products and services*. Internet dating and friendship selection has grown phenomenally in recent years and finding life partners through this route is now common, including for 'niche' markets such as farmers, Indian nationals, academics, Christians etc. In this process, we're reminded that we put effort in (usually!) to present ourselves as attractive to the kinds of people we imagine we want to meet and relate to, displaying not only our physical appearance but also our possessions, our occupations and our consumer tastes, as if we ourselves are 'for sale'. Even if we're not using the internet, literature and the news attests to the

162

fact that many people choose partners (through whatever route) because of what they have or are in social and economic terms rather than because of their personal qualities. The 19th century novelist Jane Austen explicitly dissects the dynamics of the middle and upper classes in terms of the financial transactions that surround marriage. The existence of internet sites like *'Sugardaddy'* and *'Date a millionaire'* at the farther end of this spectrum are confirmation that this kind of thing goes on in contemporary life.

In many countries, suitors are assessed on the basis of the family's capacity to provide a dowry and a fabulous wedding. Across the globe there are calls for bans to dowries and expensive weddings (eg. in Nepal, Afghanistan, Tajikistan and parts of Northern India) by governments aware of the strain on family budgets. Many people in the West borrow massively to launch their married life, often plunging themselves or their parents into serious debt. Chrys Ingraham, in his exploration of 'white weddings' suggests that the state has encouraged weddings among the poor as a way of encouraging people out of welfare benefits, explicitly linking heterosexual marriage with upward social mobility and increased income. Marriage ties people into the 'dream' of getting a home and bringing up children thus 'fixing' them within the capitalist machine, as well as reinforcing heterosexuality as the dominant identity within the culture. (This is of course under challenge in countries like Britain where civil partnerships are already established and there's a strong lobby for gay marriage).

Close relationships and economic pressures

As the world economic crisis begins to affect our daily lives, couples will find themselves having to cope with less and will be under stress – working harder and longer and carrying anxiety about job security, welfare cuts, their capacity to sustain current living standards, and their ability to survive any situations of crisis such as illness or accident.

The pressure on us to see relationships as forms of *economic exchange* is likely to increase in conditions of financial pressure. There will be a tendency to choose partners for their economic potential rather than for love, and to opt out of relationships for a better catch in situations of economic anxiety. More and more of us may feel that we're offering ourselves as sexual partners (whatever gender we are) as a way of securing commitment and economic security – a strategy that's likely to create painful power dynamics within our relationships.

This tendency will only be offset by the hardship likely for individuals who separate, for example because joint resources are halved or because of the need to support ex-partners and children as well as new ones. Domestic violence is a risk factor in these situations as is alcohol and drug use, as we try to face up to reductions in our economic expectations, for which we may have little experience or practice, and to the 'deals' we've made to save ourselves from imagined deprivations.

Looking for saviours

In a time of economic and political uncertainty, we're more likely to feel insecure, uncertain of our own futures, finding it difficult to plan, and upset about potential cutbacks and possible hardship. Our assumptions about linear and upward progress in life may be shaken and we might be tempted to look to our partners for the ability to save us from discomfort and anxiety which they may be unable to give us. It's important to recognise that our anger and fear should be shared *with* our partners, not expressed *at* them, and that our feelings may go back to infancy when we first felt uncertainty or doubts about our safety. These kinds of feelings will be stronger if we've already experienced separation or loss of our parents and older caregivers, and thus may affect those of us in mid-life more strongly. If we're younger, it might be important to make sure that our parents don't undermine our relationship because they seem to be more financially secure than we are ourselves; however in many cases, the opposite will be true and our relationship may be put under pressure by the need to look after our elders.

Some of us will be faced with situations that may feel like wartime, losing our homes or our jobs or having to make choices that we're unhappy about. We will have to draw upon our inner

164

resources to continue to inspire our children and to enjoy life with our partners in a different landscape from the one which we may have envisaged.

For some people, sadly, the test of downshifting may be too much for the relationship to bear and we may find that we need someone more able to 'get stuck in' to changes in circumstances than our existing partner.

Economic decline and change nevertheless present opportunities for learning about our own personalities, our own strengths, our spirituality and morality, and our capacity for love.

Choices include:

- letting go of expectations about life and about our partner 'as saviour'
- embracing the idea of downshifting and being creative around it
- appreciating what we *have* rather than focusing on what we are losing
- loving our partner and confirming our commitment to them
- valuing non-material things in life like nature, friends, our children, animals, art and music
- developing new ideas for making money eg. through freelance enterprise and creative thinking about our work
- seeing opportunities for change rather than catastrophe
- retaining enthusiasm and morale, developing positive self-talk
- developing our inner life eg. through creative, emotional and spiritual activity
- enjoying reducing expenditure and getting organised with less
- detaching from mainstream consumer culture and developing more contact with alternative culture
- becoming more imaginative about everything, including clothes, food, household, entertainment
- looking around and helping others – letting go of a focus on ourselves

- joining campaigns to change things
- making things
- finding new peace and quiet time
- swapping time for money
- letting go of old habits like regretting and blaming, starting to value and enjoy things and people
- questioning our 'reference groups' – eg. comparing ourselves with people who have less rather than (or as well as) with people who have more
- giving new attention to neglected people in our landscape including our family

Looking at internal goals, not external ones

Examples of external goals	Examples of internal goals
making money	*making each other laugh, lightening the load*
building a career	*processing your early history with each other*
having a family	*tackling sexual issues with each other*
developing business projects	*listening to each other*
seeking scientific or creative breakthroughs	*learning from each other*
making a home together	*helping each other to become loving people*
helping to make the world a better place	*supporting the growth of confidence in each other and fostering life energy*

Because the pressures of modern life tend to force us into prioritising 'externally-focused' activity, we can find that we've let go of the internal goals. It may be important to take time as a couple to have another look at the quality of our personal, internal lives and whether we need to make more space for interacting with each other and knowing one another's internal worlds. Without some concentration on and nurturance of 'internal' factors (ie. internal to each of us *and* internal to the relationship), a relationship can ultimately run dry, even whilst the outward picture is one of practical functioning.

Being aware of external factors

Look at 'external' factors which exert pressure on the relationship. We can benefit from discussing together whether we both acknowledge the same ones or whether we see the emphases differently. It might be that one partner has 'missed' a particular external stressor, which, once brought into the picture, helps to make certain behaviours more explicable.

External factors	*You*	*Me*
Illness or surgery		
Parents under stress/life-changes/illness		
Bereavement		
Bullying at work		
Tensions in working role		
Loss of income/debt/financial pressure		
Pressure in relation to housing		
Worries about pregnancy/childrearing etc.		
Exams/project deadlines		
Relatives or friends too influential		

We can explore how any particular external stressor makes us both feel, and work out what we can do about it.

Autonomy and togetherness

For many couples, a key issue is the balancing of taking space for oneself *and* having time together, of needing to express ourselves and do what we like versus enjoying each other's company and being close, often but not always, through sex. This depends on our being able to at peace with ourselves, and being able to effectively assert our own thoughts and approaches without these being seen as threatening or overwhelming by our partner.

For many of us, this can be difficult. We can find ourselves *'over-adapting'* to our partner in order to keep the peace or to keep them close to us, yet later resenting the giving up of our own view or needs and running the risk of 'splitting off' – going elsewhere for sustenance, to activities, to our children, or to other people. Or we can be too conflictive, asserting our ego needs, sure that we're 'right' or 'in the right', finding it difficult to back down from positions taken in argument, afraid to compromise or yield to our partner less we lose their respect or our own self-respect. Either position can be too extreme – the trick is to find a balance and this can be an ongoing challenge in relationships where one or both partners struggle with this; however, *this is the nature of relating* and working through this kind of struggle can lead to greater closeness.

The fear of being overwhelmed is sometimes seen as a male thing – with Paul Morel in D H Lawrence's *Sons and Lovers* being an iconic example of a young man who cannot escape from the cloying love of his mother, a situation replicated in his relationship with a young woman called Miriam. Yet quite often it's women who are over-dominated by men who believe that they should be in charge or have superior judgement. As we find so often in this book, the important skill is to believe in ourselves, to trust our own intuition, to resist influence from elsewhere that we've not evaluated ourselves, to listen to our unconscious, to speak out about things that matter and to be willing to listen and negotiate when our partner has something of value to contribute.

Symbiosis and individuation

There may be times in our relationship where we want *symbiosis* – where we feel the joy of togetherness, going around together, consulting each other on everything, having an exclusive intimate relationship with each other, but there may come times where we need more individuation. We need to recognise these feelings as natural outcomes and accept the necessary distinctions between each other that emerge as signs of a healthy, dynamic relationship. Indeed, it's possible to envisage relationships as successful when they *do* foster that possibility for each partner to flourish separately but we can't help nostalgia for the days of symbiosis re-emerging at times.

The difficulty comes because we don't always feel that need for separateness at the same time, and we need to find courage and patience and trust and sensitivity during times of transition.

Perception and reality

How can we do something about the mismatch between 'perception' and 'reality'?

Julia says:
From time to time, Jack accuses me of not giving him enough 'strokes' and says he doesn't feel loved or cared for. Yet I spend loads of time shopping and cooking – making lovely meals for him, clearing up, supplying fresh coffee during the day, organising appointments, driving him to meetings, talking to him and listening to his concerns, making love when he wants to, telling him that I love him etc. To me, the 'reality' is that I do all this but nevertheless, for him, he sometimes feels alone and uncared for.

I have to spell out all that I have done so that he 'sees' it. I have to recognise that sometimes he can't feel it or see it.

I have to ask myself if all my actions are perhaps compulsive, almost dutiful, but that I might be omitting something fundamental – like reading his emotional state and simply sitting with him and hugging him when he feels lonely or sad.

We can't assume that how we express love will come across to the other if they have another language or form in which they need to hear it.

Accepting the person and letting the detail go

Are we able to overlook things? Whilst it's important to pick up on things which could cause trouble later on, or which are 'discounting' of basic respect, it's appropriate to treat small skirmishes with gentle humour or a brief thoughtful comment rather than heading into a big scene or using unkind sarcasm which could escalate things. We need to learn to distinguish between those things that are truly a problem and those things which simply represent aspects of our partner's style, personality, way of doing things that are not perfect but which at some level, endear them to us.

Relationships as good for us

Perhaps it's worth remembering that loving relationships can provide a protective function in life. Of course if we're emotionally healthy we're probably well equipped to sustain loving relationships whereas if we're struggling with emotional difficulty within ourselves, relating closely to another person may be more difficult and fraught with ups and downs. However difficult it is, knowing that someone loves us and that we love them is one of life's greatest joys and can sustain us through times of pain, sadness, intimidation, conflict, stress, war, imprisonment, illness, absence and bereavement.

There is evidence that positive relationships are good for our physical health, helping us to survive and manage illness – if we have loving partners, friends, neighbours, family etc. these constitute a significant part of our 'social capital'.

In general terms, 'men' and 'women' may differ on the benefits they accrue in this way, perhaps because women often do much of the daily caring and may find it difficult to withdraw their services when they themselves are ill, although they're apparently more likely than men to have a network of social contacts around them when relationships break down. It's helpful not to assume that women are always the carers or that they have a natural ability to do the caring - many men have a wonderful affinity for the caring role and some women may struggle with the projection by others onto them that they 'should' be good carers when in fact they find the role intolerable or difficult. Robert F Murphy, the anthropologist who documented his own journey into quadriplegia describes poignantly the changing dynamics within his marriage as a result of his increasing disability.

There's also some evidence that we live longer if we remain in established relationships, though that might not be true for couples who are unhappy. If people care about each other they will usually have a vested interest in keeping the other alive, so mutual care ought to follow. There are of course cases where we have had to let people die because of the severity of their illnesses, where love and care to the end is what is needed.

Sometimes we have to let the person we love go. This is explored in more depth in the next chapter *Letting go of people*.

Books and papers

Lisa Appignanesi (2011) *All About Love* Virago

Jane Austen (1811) (2011 ed) *Sense and Sensibility* Penguin Popular Classics

Judith Butler (2006) *Gender Trouble: Feminism and the Subversion of Identity* Routledge

Julia Cameron (1995) *The Artist's Way* Pan Books

Gary Chapman (2010) *The Five Love Languages* Moody Publishing

Colleen M Connolly (2004) *Clinical issues with same-sex couples* Journal of Couple and Relationship Therapy Vol 3 No 2/3 p.3-12 The Haworth Press

Luise Eichenbaum and Susie Orbach (2000 edition) *What Do Women Want?* Harper Collins

James W Fowler (1981) *Stages of Faith* Harper and Row

Daniel Goleman (1996) *Emotional Intelligence* Bloomsbury

John Gray (1992) *Men from Mars, Women are from Venus* Harper Collins/Thorsons

Thomas Harris (1995) *I'm OK, You're OK* Arrow Books

Chrys Ingraham (2008) *White Weddings: romancing heterosexuality in popular culture* Taylor and Francis

Oliver James (1998, 2010) *Britain on the Couch* London Random House/Vermilion

Lawrence Kohlberg (1981) *Essays on Moral Development* Vol I: *The Philosophy of Moral Development* San Francisco: Harper & Row.

Christopher Lasch (1979) (1991) *The Culture of Narcissism* W.W.Norton & Co.

David H Lawrence (1913) (1992 ed) *Sons and Lovers* Wordsworth editions

Annette Lawson (1988) *Adultery* Basil Blackwell

Darian Leader and David Corfield (2007) *Why People Get Ill* Hamish Hamilton

Sarah Litvinoff (1991) *Better relationships: practical ways to make your love last* Ebury Press/ Vermilion

Alexander Lowen (1984) (2004) *Narcissism: Denial of the True Self* Simon and Schuster

Ken Mellor and Eric Schiff *Discounting* Transactional Analysis Journal V.5, No.3, July, 1975, p 295-302

Robert F Murphy (1990) *The Body Silent: The Different World of the Disabled* W W Norton

Virginia Nicholson (2007) *Singled Out: How Two Million Women Survived Without Men after the First World War* London: Penguin Books

Fritz Perls (1964) *Games People Play* New York: Grove Press

Adam Phillips (1997) *Winnicott* Fontana Modern Masters

Harvey Ratner, Evan George and Chris Iveson (2012) *Solution-focused brief therapy: 100 key points and techniques* Routledge

Carl Rogers (1961) (2004 ed) *On becoming a person* London: Constable and Robinson Ltd.

Joseph Sandler (1991) *Freud's 'On Narcissism: an introduction'* Yale University Press

Maggie Scarf (1987) *Intimate Partners* Century

Lisa Schlessinger (2001) *Ten Stupid Things People Do to Mess Up Relationships* Harper Collins

Morgan Scott Peck (1978) *The Road Less Travelled* Arrow Books

Steve de Shazer (1985) *Keys to Solution in Brief Therapy.* New York: W W Norton & Company

Claude Steiner (1971) *The Stroke Economy* TAJ, 1(3), pp.9-15

Claude Steiner (1974) (1990 edition) *Scripts People Live* Grove Press

Robert J Sternberg, (1988) *The Triangle of Love: Intimacy, Passion, Commitment.* Basic Books

Robert J Sternberg (2013) *Searching for Love* The Psychologist vol 26:2 February 2013 98-101

Richard Templar (2009 and 2013) *The Rules of Love* Pearson

Hogie Wyckoff (1971) *The Stroke Economy in Women's Scripts TAJ I*, 3 pp 16-30

4   letting go of people

> This chapter emerged out of the previous one on close relationships and tackles some issues when relationships don't work out as we planned or hoped – including bereavement, the experience of grief, difficulties in separating – including how to move forward, the pain of intimate partner violence and facing up to being alone.

This chapter is written by Julia.

Relationships can hurt us

Whilst close relationships can bring us much joy, if not the *main* joy in life, let's not gloss over the damage that relationships can do to people and the pain that letting go can involve.

Letting go

It's obviously true that things depend on the quality of our relationships – for some of us, the grief of loss of a loved partner or relative can hasten our own decline or death, whilst for others of us, a new lease of life emerges as we recover from bereavement or we gain freedom from a relationship that was unhappy or stressful.

> Julia says:
>
> *In the autumn and winter of 2007/8, I experienced an unprecedented set of bereavements all within six months – which involved two interwoven sets of close connections - my uncle, my mother, and my brother - and my husband's brother, followed by my husband's lifelong mentor, and then my husband himself. In a short period, the landscape of my life was entirely changed. Sometimes it goes like that.*
>
> *Sometimes, as in these cases, one death follows another because people are closely connected. All these people were so affected by the death of people they loved that it is hard not to reach the conclusion that these losses brought forward their own deaths.*

> *I had an uphill battle not to follow them all to the grave. Sometimes, even with one death, there is a pull like that of gravity, to go as well, and a reluctance to face the challenges of reconnecting with one's own life energy. I had to find the will to go on. I found it mainly in the feeling that since my own death was now more clearly a certainty than I had previously felt it to be, every moment now had to count. Although I had many problems to tackle, including financial, single parenting, housing and work, I decided that doing what I really wanted to do in life was vital to save myself from the quagmire of that pull.*

Grief

Loving people can be a hazardous activity because when they die, we can feel bereft. There is evidence now that *people are more likely to die in the first year after a significant bereavement*, and that *the stress of loss can bring on a range of symptoms* including heart attacks, depression, increased alcohol intake, an exacerbation of pre-existing conditions or trigger latent health conditions. There is evidence that we may die of a 'broken heart', and for some of us, there is recurrent sadness, particularly on anniversaries and when doing the things we used to do with the person who has now died. Authors Darian Leader and David Corfield explore how illness can often reflect such feelings and events.

And starting again in a new relationship can also bring on painful feelings even when it's hoped that it might assuage the agony.

There is also much evidence that anxiety and depression are increasing in today's climate with a higher turnover of relationships and less community support, and the sense of despair that people can experience trying to match their ideals of sexual and emotional fulfilment, fuelled by media images of beautiful people and glamorous relationships, with the reality of real human beings and the pressures on everyday relating. Because we increasingly look to our intimate and close relationships for everything, there can be great pain when they don't deliver nirvana and there is grief in that, including self-blame and blame of our partner, and sometimes this can lead to suicide.

Many people make the effort to maintain normal functioning after loss, particularly in the light of expectations on them from employers, friends and community. According to psychologist George Bonnano, many people demonstrate a lot of resilience after bereavement. For some people, that desire to carry on as normal works for a while, but grief reactions kick in later on. For some of us, avoiding things which trigger memories can be an effective way of moving on while there is now some evidence that laughter and humour can help alleviate the pain of loss. The point here is that grief reactions are *individual* and will depend on the significance and quality of our relationship with the person who died. It's important to recognise that we may be subject to a lot of pressure to behave in certain ways and the old idea that we all need to go through stages of acceptance and working through pain may not be appropriate for everyone.

Psychiatric bodies are currently planning to bring in revisions to recommendations for doctors regarding how long is 'normal' for grief, the pressure being on to bounce back as fast as possible. The idea is that in an increasingly commodified society, why waste time grieving when you can find a new model on the internet quite quickly? In an increasingly pressurised world, how can we spend energy grieving when there's work to get on with? Can we insist on meeting our own needs rather than conforming to expectations?

Complicated grief

It's important to recognise that grief is frequently *not straightforward*. It is often complicated by ambivalent feelings and 'forbidden' feelings, such as relief and a new sense of freedom – feelings that a person may not feel it is appropriate to express. In some cases there is a sense of guilt if we feel there is more we could have done to keep the person alive longer, particular if they were suicidal or suffering from severe illness, or a sense of anger that they themselves didn't do more to stay alive. Sometimes we may be mourning the loss of someone kept out of the limelight in our life –a married colleague, a former partner, or a gay partner who was not recognised by our family etc. where feeling our loss is not 'permissible' or recognised, so-called *'disenfranchised grief'*. (See for example Charles Corr's article). In such cases, it is important to go somewhere with our grief, such as to a confidential counsellor, or to take time to have a private ritual – like visiting a significant place and 'saying goodbye' in our own way. Sometimes we want to expunge the person from our hearts or memories – perhaps because we loved them or because we hated them, but sometimes we need to allow them to live with us, physical death being only a change of form. In this sense, our spiritual beliefs or lack of them will profoundly affect how we experience the death of someone we have known.

In addition, bereavement often brings in its wake economic and practical changes in a person's life – sometimes there is inheritance or the final paying-off of a mortgage, but sometimes there is hardship as a person loses the benefits of their partner's income or the things that the partner used to do, such as housework, DIY, driving or paperwork, or it may be that a project or business activity or plan is suddenly thrown into a crisis situation by the death, or we have to preside over the sale of property or disposal of effects. We may not always be up to an immediate resolution of practical and financial matters and decisions may be taken that at a later point we may wish we had done differently. We have to balance whether it's best to get support to protect ourselves during a time of stress and defer decisions or whether it's more important to take decisions quickly and help ourselves out of the stressful situation.

New models of grieving such as that by Margaret Stroeb and Henk Schut suggest that we may oscillate between concentrating on what and whom we have lost and restoring our life – for example by accepting new roles and situations such as that of widow/er and moving home. There is no clear rule about how much time we spend on looking *back* or looking *forward*.

Time to grieve

Insisting on the time we need to process things is important as well as the way we do it. We should not be forced into behaving the way others want us to, not jollied or medicated into moving on before we are ready. There are of course cases where our grieving can be perceived as 'pathological' – it's important that our cultural context is taken into account – if for example we come from a social or family culture where it is expected that we spend a long time in mourning, it is no good being hurried along by a doctor or employer who is enthusiastic about us 'returning to normal', whilst sometimes we may have to battle against the cultural expectations around us to grieve or not grieve in our own way. Sometimes there are factors that slow down our path such as inquests, contested probate, court cases, complaints processes etc. and hold us in an emotional limbo. We might feel we have to hold onto our feelings so as to remember the trauma for when we are called upon to explain or describe them, whilst at the same time, needing to let go or feel free to engage with new relationships and activities in our life. Again, choosing our own way of saying goodbye or relating to the dead person can help regardless of the official calendar.

On the other hand, sometimes it's right that we listen to what others are saying and allow ourselves to be gently prodded out of states we've got stuck in and use their support to find the courage to re-invest in life.

After multiple bereavements, it seemed to me that I started to live with the curtains closed and wore the same dark clothing for a couple of years. I let the housework pile up and my paperwork went 'to pot'. Friends invited us for meals and helped sort out the financial mess – accepting that I needed their support was difficult. Although the reality is that I went out to work, gave lectures and met up with people, my general experience was that I lived in 'mourning', feeling that 'real life' was like a film that went by in front of me.

It took a long time to 'engage' – it's possible in fact that that sense of unreality went on for two or three years. After that I slowly started to tidy up my life, employing people to help shift the backlog of household junk and paperwork that had built up and filled rooms around me, and I faced up to the fact that I could no longer ignore health problems that had started to take root. Eventually I started changing my life, tackling my health, establishing a new intimate relationship, leaving the job I'd had for twenty years, getting married again, taking my daughter out of formal education, writing a book. I found that moments of real sadness were now able to break into consciousness in a way that I couldn't have allowed before.

Grief as we lose the person we knew

Sometimes it's not an absolute loss of a person – it's the loss of a person as they used to be (or even how we hoped they'd be). Dementia and Alzheimer's disease strip away much of a person's functioning, and indeed many illnesses change people so that they are no longer the same as before. A stroke can mean that someone is no longer able to do the things they used to, and perhaps is never able to relate emotionally to us again in the same way – made all the more poignant because it's happened suddenly without a goodbye. In our chapter on *Emotional health* we write about the agony of deciding whether or not to stay with someone with emotional and communication difficulties. Grief can come upon us as we watch someone slide more and more into dependency on drugs and alcohol. Sometimes we feel left behind when someone we love grows stronger and more independent. And sometimes we have to face the fact that someone we care about is never going to be the kind of person we hoped they'd be. It's important to acknowledge grief in ourselves even within ongoing relationships – even whilst someone is still near us.

Separation trauma

Grief is usually associated with bereavement, but of course for many of us, there's the grief of separation. Relationship breakdown is now a very common experience. Factors that are changing the landscape of personal relationships include the reduction in religious affiliation in the western world, a climate of commodification and easy disposability, the internet which offers us 'unlimited' access to a range of alternative potential partners, increased economic freedom for women (even if in hardship, women can nevertheless work, access welfare support and financial services as independent people), and a social world in which changing partners is socially sanctioned and accepted.

Within families and friendships, issues can arise which push us apart from each other, and many people live apart from their families, purchasing childcare from strangers instead of receiving support from grandparents, and making our homes in communities that have no link with our original background, so that we live like

178

migrants within our own land, exiled from the world we grew up in. Whilst it may be psychological difficulty or family arguments that create these separations, it is also the nature of contemporary life which puts pressure on adults to go where work is, the middle-class stress on higher education and career development and the desperation for a meaningful or independent life that propels some young people into the armed forces to escape poverty. None of this mitigates the fact that for many people there is a profound underlying sense of loss which is the backdrop for all their subsequent choices and relationships.

Additional elements in relationship breakdown as distinct from bereavement include the doubts about self and identity that can follow and traumatic disputes over things like property and residence, the reasons for the decision to separate, and care and control of children. All of this can mean that we have the hard work of coming to terms with our sense of self. Despite the 'official' social climate of multiple relationships and sexual obsession that is socially sanctioned through television and the internet as well as attitudes and opportunities in 'urban metro-land', for the millions of us who live in 'ordinary' communities there can nevertheless be many psychological challenges.

These can include:

- a sense of failure or stigma around us

- doubts about our decisions to overcome or deal with things

- the pain of dreams that will no longer come to fulfilment and the loss of shared plans

- the sense of a lucky escape and reflection on trauma if relating had become frightening or dramatic

- a new awareness of social status having changed and being related to in different ways by people we know

- anxieties about managing parenting roles with less everyday support or shared decision-making

- a lot more time alone, a sense of silence descending

- a sense of *anomie*, being disconnected from life, not knowing which choices to make

- doubts about our personality or ability to form and maintain relationships

All of these can be turned into positives if we work at it:

internal feeling-states

- recognising the strengths in ourselves for moving on and rebuilding life

- recognising our courage and developing it

- looking for the good things about the decisions we have taken and recognising that sometimes a decision is better than no decision at all

- recognising that the long-term outcome of decisions will take time to know and we will have time to influence the future and make those decisions work for us

- getting support for processing difficult emotions and trauma

- recognising that sometimes there are no perfect choices to make, we simply have to start walking forward - right *or* wrong

- dismissing negative thinking and inner voices from the past that bring us down, learning more about our own trauma

- rejecting regular messages from people in our life who find it difficult to see us as the person we are or are becoming or who have a vested interest in keeping us where we were

- accepting our new status and looking for the good in it

actions

- learning to enjoy solitude, developing creative, intellectual, practical and spiritual activities

- making new connections with neighbours, colleagues, members of our (new or newly perceived) community

- getting advice and researching issues and getting a better foundation for our own decision-making

- presenting ourselves clearly to the world in our new identity

- taking control of our social world, letting go if necessary of old friends and finding new people who will be part of our future

- giving new attention to our role as parents, enjoying the total attention we can sometimes give when there are fewer competing emotional demands on us and building new networks of inter-connecting support

- going for counselling or joining courses, workshops, retreats, groups to reflect on our own nature, personality and communication skills

- tackling health and body issues, accepting our own beauty and taking the opportunity to work with anything that bothers us such as weight or disfigurement or disability in new ways

- working in our own terms on any feedback we've had and developing strategies such as mindfulness, assertiveness, anger control etc. where we feel feedback has been justified *(it may be that feedback we've had has been mixed up with our partner's other feelings such as jealousy or insecurity or anger, but in our quieter, reflective moments there may be clues there to something we do need to work on)*

- bringing positive activities and relationships into our life, spending more time with people we do care about and less with people who are not helpful, learning to appreciate things like the natural world, developing new mastery of skills that brings a new sense of competence, new interest and peace of mind into our life

Injury and 'intimate partner violence'

Women's Aid estimate that 1 in 4 women in Britain will experience domestic violence in their lifetime and that 2 women per week are killed by a current or ex-partner. Home Office statistics indicate that 1 in 6 men experience violent abuse by a partner (notwithstanding that in a number of cases this begins as self-defence). *The Mankind Initiative* suggests that one man in every 17 days is killed by a partner/ex-partner in Britain. *Action on Elder Abuse* suggest that between 4% and 8% of older men and women experience abuse in their own home from carers - often relatives and partners – and we're probably only at the beginning of starting to look at this. Statistics from the *NSPCC* indicate that approximately 1 in 4 young adults in the UK were abused or neglected when they were children, and that approximately a quarter of young adults in the UK were sexually abused, mostly by people they know and often by close relatives. And so on.

Doubtless there are numerous debates about the precise numbers involved, how statistics are collated and what are the finer points of definition of abuse, but the key point is that **a tremendous number of people** are living their lives carrying the scars of abuse, neglect, and hurt from people who were in relationships with them in which they should have been able to expect care and love. People who escape from such relationships often suffer from post-traumatic stress. As well as looking down the trajectory of our own life, a significant number of the people we deal with in organisations - the electricity meter-reader, the catering assistant serving our lunch, the tax adviser or the doctor saving our life – any of them could have experienced trauma or abuse themselves.

All of the ideas in the grief and separation sections are relevant to people coming out of painful relationships. Even when things have been very painful there can be strong bonding, and our grief is no less than when things have gone swimmingly.

If we want to enter into a new relationship, it's a good idea to do so with a strong determination not to repeat the mistakes of the past, to have an early-warning system about mistreatment, to insist on OK-OK relating, to ensure that support remains around us, and to stop listening to people (even those in our families) who encourage us into situations which might seem externally a good idea (eg. because a potential partner has a good income or a great lifestyle) but who don't have any understanding of the psychological dynamics that might arise. Whilst we need to trust our own intuitions, if we have any doubts about the state of our own emotional radar it could be a good idea to check our feelings, doubts and perceptions with others, but not to sabotage ourselves by seeking advice from people with vested interests or particular biases. We can also check out evidence on signs and risk factors from relevant websites and books and keep in contact with support organisations. We can rid ourselves forever of the idea that *'it can't happen to me'*.

Being without close relationships

There are of course many examples of people who prefer living on their own or living life by themselves, as well as communities such as monasteries and convents where personal relationships of an intense nature might be discouraged and the key relationship is with God. In prison or in the armed services, in care homes or hospitals, getting too close to someone else may have its hazards – challenges of trust and the difficulties of someone disappearing at short notice. After the first world war, as so many young men had perished, many women had to face the possibility of life without a marriage partner. (See for example Virginia Nicholson's book on this). And after emerging from a coercive or conflictive relationship, many of us are understandably wary of entering a new one.

For whatever reason, close relationships might elude us, or having experienced an intense relationship, we may choose a period of solitude or grieving. Dealing with aloneness is something we address in the chapter on *The Self.* Anthony Storr's work on *Solitude* is useful and reassuring reading on this subject.

Final thoughts

Relating to people closely is a major challenge and is certainly not anything like the media represents it. It takes effort and skill and if we want a close relationship as the basis of our life, *we should spend our lives getting better at it.*

Sometimes that means moving on from one relationship to another until we start to learn the lessons of our life; sometimes we find a way of changing and growing within a long-term partnership. We shouldn't give up hope just because something is difficult and we make mistakes. Perhaps love involves sufficient commitment on both sides that the ups and downs of relating can be contained and lived with and forgiven and both parties are prepared to re-invest again and again.

Further reading

Any of the references in the previous chapter on *Close Relationships* may be relevant, but in addition, the following deal directly with loss and grief.

George A Bonnano (2009) *The Other Side of Sadness: What the New Science of Bereavement Tells Us About Life After Loss* Basic Books
Charles A Corr (1999) *Enhancing the Concept of Disenfranchised Grief* Journal of Death and Dying vol 38 no 1/1998/99 pp 1-20

Sheila Haugh (2010) *The Person-Centred Approach to Working with Loss and Bereavement* Sage
Virginia Ironside (1996) *'You'll Get Over It': The Rage of Bereavement* London: Penguin Books
Darian Leader and David Corfield (2007) *Why People Get Ill* Hamish Hamilton
C S Lewis (1961) *A Grief Observed* London: Faber and Faber
Virginia Nicholson (2007) *Singled Out: How Two Million Women Survived Without Men after the First World War* London: Penguin Books
Anthony Storr (1988) *Solitude* Collins: Fontana Books/Flamingo
Margaret Stroebe, Robert O Hanson, Wolfgang Stroebe and Henk Schut (eds) (2001) *Handbook of Bereavement Research: Consequences, Coping and Care* Washington DC: American Psychological Association
Irvin D Yalom (2008) *Staring at the Sun: Overcoming the Dread of Death* Piatkus

5   therapy and counselling

In this chapter, we share some of our own experience in the therapy world including as clients, therapists/counsellors and teachers. We discuss who offers what and how to decide if you actually need or want therapy. We don't believe that you should go into therapy naively, and outline a number of critiques, ideas and learnings that may be helpful to you in your journey, including questions around power, labelling, effectiveness, expectations, different perspectives and schools, the idea of non-impingement, the importance of boundaries, and the way in which we can project experiences of other important figures in our life history onto the therapist. Therapists are not saints and you need to go into the therapy marketplace with as much care as you would any other field of consumerism.

The first part is mostly by Jack and the second part by Julia.

Therapy and counselling overlap and there's a debate about the terms – therefore I will call them both 'therapy'.

Rough guide to people involved in mental health

The different professions have claimed different parts of the territory of the mind as their own and they have disagreements, turf wars, etc.

A rough categorisation of helping professionals in the territory of the mind in slight caricature form would be as follows:

psychiatrists   psychiatrists are doctors and psychiatry is thought of as a Cinderella branch of medicine by other doctors. They are concerned with diagnosing people, prescribing drugs, and often have a miserable view of change, and are often content with containment and amelioration of symptoms. They work with 'difficult' problems including psychosis, people diagnosed as having personality disorder, and for example, brain conditions.

Occasionally they know about psychotherapy. They also work with psychological traumas of various types.

psychologists
psychologists work in various fields, for example, in industry, in education, etc. The ones concerned with the adult mind are clinical psychologists. They tend to work with specialised 'conditions', for example, phobias, obsessional-compulsive behaviour, learning problems, rehabilitation after strokes, dementia etc. They are usually employed in public health but can also be found working privately, occasionally they are also psychotherapists.

counsellors
these are usually working towards clients' goals, do not usually diagnose people and are not overtly working with babyhood or childhood issues that may hamper people

psychotherapists
psychotherapists may work with diagnosis or not and are usually less client-led than counsellors. A lot of them are interested in childhood and babyhood issues that are still affecting people.

other
this would include some doctors, the clergy who have a counselling role, in fact, anyone with a counselling or therapeutic component in their work, for example, probation officers.

The difference between psychotherapy and counselling is that these communities may have different takes on expertness and power and diagnosis, but they are similar in that they cannot figure out how they are different from each other – however, most therapists think that they are superior to counsellors.

Approaches to the world of the mind

These are approaches apart from the purely medical and since psychotherapy began, a number of schools of therapy/counselling have emerged and here is a short list.

Please remember that both counselling and therapy may operate from a 'school' ie. one approach which dominates.

Some of the schools are:

- behavioural or cognitive-behavioural
- cognitive
- acceptance and commitment therapy
- psychoanalytic
- transactional analysis
- person-centred counselling
- addiction counselling
- gestalt
- existential
- psycho-synthesis
- transpersonal
- narrative
- couples and family system work
- body-work *(as mentioned elsewhere in the book, very early memories can be stored in the body releasing these can promote regression so bodywork needs to be in the hands of a skilled therapist)* – can be further divided into Reichian, neo-Reichian etc.

There are also other approaches to therapy that are not focused so directly on the *psychological* domain.

- wilderness and outward bound therapies
- mindfulness (derived from meditation techniques) (although a number of psychological therapies incorporate *mindfulness* such as Paul Gilbert's compassion-focused therapy)

Different schools disagree about concepts like *transference*, the *unconscious,* etc and most of them believe they have the truth/can define everyone in their terms. Whatever criticisms can be made of them, Sigmund Freud did acknowledge the existence of the unconscious mind and Carl Jung did emphasise spirituality.

Therapy and spirituality

Some schools (brands) of therapy acknowledge a spiritual life eg. Jungian analytical psychology and Psycho-synthesis; most don't or they just tolerate spirituality as wacky non-scientific belief, which is insulting to those who are aware of their spiritual life.

Carl Rogers, who pioneered *client-centred therapy*, moved away from his Christian origins but came later in life to wonder about spirituality in his work, a theme later taken up by UK person-centred therapist, writer and Lay Canon at Norwich Cathedral, Brian Thorne.

Robert Assagioli, who owed a lot of his inspiration to both Sigmund Freud and Carl Jung, was not a great fan of the idea of pathology, and was closer in this sense to the humanistic therapists like Carl Rogers, seeing the human psyche as essentially healthy though often beset with temporary problems. Assagioli divided the unconscious into different levels with more primitive and painful feelings in the lower level, more automated functions and skills in the middle, and the 'higher self' linked to things like creativity, philanthropy, purpose and meaning in life, and spirituality.

Emmy van Deurzen in Britain and Irvin Yalom in the USA have developed existential therapy, which is based more on philosophical principles rather than on psychopathology or problem-fixing. Clients are helped to develop a philosophy of living, working with the therapist to make sense of their lives and to find meaning in being alive; it's founded on the assumption that a person's life can be made intelligible however confused it seems at the start of therapy.

189

Eclectic/integrative approaches

There are various ways of integrating therapies such as the *'common factors'* approach which is intended to find elements common to several such as the power of the therapeutic relationship, and *'assimilative eclecticism'* where a therapist keeps to one core therapy but uses elements from others. Norcross and Goldfried (2005) looked at the variety of ways that people combine different therapies.

Bruce Wampold (2001) concluded that psychotherapy works more or less **regardless of the type of method employed**, its efficacy being derived mainly from the *personality* of the therapist and the *strength of their belief in their method*, as well as the establishment of *a positive therapeutic relationship* between therapist and client to work towards change, and he reiterates this view more elaborately in his 2009 books with co-authors who support the *'common factors'* approach to psychotherapy. This is the idea that there are some common factors in any successful therapy including the *positive therapeutic relationship.*

Fashions in therapy

Fashions change:

- Sigmund Freud and his camp followers have been heavily criticised over the decades.
- Carl Jung's collective archetypes may be less popular now than they used to be
- aggressive Synanon-style confrontational treatments for addictions were stopped in the UK – they didn't work as a caring relationship had not been established as an essential basis for therapy. Therapists cannot just use techniques.
- doctors genitally massaged their female hysteric patients to orgasm as a treatment for hysteria in the mid-19th century (probably at medical seminars as well as in surgery), which nowadays would not only be seen as outrageous but perhaps criminal. (See for example Rachel Maines' book and the film *Hysteria*).

- tranquillisers like *Valium* were heavily over-prescribed in the 1970s – huge numbers of people became addicted and were treated as not-OK by doctors.
- although one estimate is that one-tenth of the world is gay, gayness has until recently been regarded as deviant or abnormal and still is in parts of the world and so-called 'conversion therapy' which has at times included 'aversive treatments' like electric shocks and chemicals to 'reorient' sexual preference, has been used. There's been a recent resurgence of interest in this.
- an interesting event has been that with developments in modern electronic brain-scanning, both the unconscious and the criminal mind seem back in fashion with science.

How accessible is therapy?

It's worth remembering that psychiatry, psychology and psychotherapy have been made very inaccessible to the public. The French philosopher Michel Foucault has described the acquisition of power in the middle classes by expert knowledge and argued that this was done first in psychiatry through the medical psychological classification of people. Power has also been acquired in other fields like the law, the priesthood and academia.

There was a huge growth in counselling and psychotherapy training from the mid-1980s onwards so being a therapist is/was different from what it was in the Wild West era before then. Now professionalism, expertness, and pompousness is in fashion. One good side of the pre-1980s time is that therapists seemed to have all the idealism/commitment and sincerity of pioneers. The downside was the lack of external regulation.

The recent over-training has probably created problems if therapists are freelance in that the number of people wanting to see them hasn't grown to accommodate all the therapists so we are probably looking at a buyers' market now.

Do we think like babies?

Psychoanalytic theory and practice such as that by Donald Winnicott or Melanie Klein (both object relations psychoanalysts) has concerned itself with babyhood and how babies behave, think etc. and what can impede healthy development. A main issue in therapy is how to work in a practical way with problems that started very early in life. Experience from babyhood or very early childhood is of a different type than the more easily-remembered issues from later childhood. These very early memories are pre-verbal. The memories are stored as body memories and baby thinking. Baby thinking can be grandiose (exaggerated), catastrophic, black and white, etc. and has to be worked out for each individual like a detective story.

An example of baby experience from my life that I still carry with me is an unrealistic desire for stability, including stability in a partner. This comes from a time before I was one-year-old and was hospitalised twice without my mother – which was the stupid 'expert' policy then despite new knowledge emerging about *maternal deprivation* by people like John Bowlby and James Robertson in the early 1950s. As a confirmation of the powerful effect this early experience had on me, I have re-lived in therapy the scary surgery I had as a baby which I had retained as a body memory.

Problems with 'therapy'

A lot of issues and problems with therapy have been well-explored by people like Jeffrey Masson and Colin Feltham. It's a good idea to read up on critiques before entering into the field as client or trainee.

Problems mainly involve *power issues* but include the *expertness of the helpers, rigidity of the types and schools of therapy, abuse of clients, confidentiality, psycho-diagnosis*, and *notions around normality*. I think that there are other problems with therapy, not always discussed. These are:

1. there's a tendency towards talking therapies being popular, but if people are working with strong feelings they may for example be *noisy* and this is inconvenient in institutional settings (for example, in a GP surgery), so types of therapy dealing with feelings such as gestalt or bodywork tend to be found with therapists working privately.

2. big egos. Apart from turf wars already mentioned in the therapy world which roughly speaking are to do with who does what and who is higher up in the pecking order of helpers, there is also the problem of big egos. See for example, Sigmund Freud, Fritz Perls, Eric Berne etc.

3. there's in-fighting *between* schools or approaches to therapy and in some schools there's *intra*-school fighting.

4. the sheer confusion and complexity in the way the world of the mind has been colonised. Basically it IS complicated and there's also an overload of often fairly useless information

5. problems stemming from babyhood are claimed to have been solved by parts of the therapy world rather than the counselling world. This may include a lot of diagnostic categories, some eating issues etc.

6. a big issue is that we can't really call our society 'normal' so the idea that people are adjusting to our society and being 'normal' in it is problematic.

7. the world of the mind is still dominated by middle-class values. Subscribing to these may neither work nor fit your value-system, for example do you want to accept values that are pro-materialism, pro-competition etc?

8. there's a general drift in therapy towards science and understanding how people tick, which leaves out a lot of mystery about the unconscious, growth, love, human relating etc.

9. apart from Jung and psycho-synthesis or overtly spiritual practitioners, and the interesting fact that Carl Rogers became more spiritual in his later thinking, most of the theory or practice leaves out the spiritual.

Types of experiencing

My position is that there isn't a 'normal' person and that to some degree we are all neurotic. The old-fashioned division of level of problem was that psychotic problems are more serious and difficult to solve than neurotic problems although some therapists do work with psychosis, notably the Schiffs and recently, Margaret Warner with her concept of *'fragile process'*.

The psychiatrist Paul Ware suggested that people were predominantly *thinking, feeling* or *doing* as a main way of being, some therapies eg. cognitive-behavioural are more about *thinking* and *doing* and leave out *feelings*; other types for example Gestalt would seem to suit *feelers*, although there is a case to be made for *thinkers* doing more *feeling* work and *feelers* doing more *thinking* work.

The TA idea of 'scripts', first introduced by Eric Berne in 1961, as part of learning about why people live certain lives and how they take on a particular perceptual filter is a very useful way to chart your childhood and check out any early messages, decisions, or parenting that may be helping or hindering you. Done by a skilled person, this can be a very powerful tool. One problem with TA scripts is that they may miss deeper experiences, for example, from babyhood, not in conscious or verbal memory.

When do we need therapy and what's it for?

Therapy is for several purposes which include:

-   when you're changing something in your life

-   when you and your friends and family cannot fix a problem

- for support with events like bereavement or trauma

- as part of support with a job – professional mentoring/counselling eg, time management, stress management, what works with clients etc.

- for personal development

- for general knowledge or training about psychology

Good news

You CAN find reasonable therapists and counsellors and it can help a lot to be informed.

Why change and when to change

My position on change is that people are changing anyway throughout their lives (not always in a positive direction) and that life events including difficult ones can foster positive change. Carl Jung called the process of psychological/spiritual development *individuation* and thought the process of individuation runs throughout someone's life. (See more on this in our chapter on *The Self*).

My view is that we need to learn to understand and manage our personality and that we're always changing anyway and developing (though sometimes that development has halted or got blocked). Some therapists however say that their therapy will change your personality completely and not only that, but they'll do it quickly, and not only that but you don't have to bother about what your personality is in the first place. This is to miss all the richness of what is you.

There is research about the idea of *'spontaneous remission'* which can be worth considering. For example, it's possible that people who are going to recover from depression *anyway* (though they may have further episodes at later points), regardless of whether or not they have therapy, are less likely to seek therapy help, so those who do go for help might have more complicated or deeprooted issues to sort out and may take longer to improve than those who don't go for therapy. But there is a risk that leaving conditions like depression 'untreated' could mean a longer time of not being able to function very well than might have been the case if they *had* gone for therapeutic help. It's not always clear what is best and the outcome may depend on whether or not you are able to find a therapist whom you trust and can work with well. And what alternatives you put in place instead of therapy!

I also think that people can change and develop their spiritual selves with or without genuine or phoney spiritual gurus and with or without belonging to an organized religion or church.

Julia and I have different experiences of therapy and have different things to say about it.

What I would look for in the non-existent ideal therapist

What I would look for would be that they were honest, value-for-money if that applies, that they are mature, competent and experienced. Other things would be that they have more than one theory / technique to offer, relate as an equal and treat me as OK and as an individual. I would also want them to be a bit wise and be very warm and bright and qualified – but not qualified just to impress people
or
at least….. honest, competent, broad, and coming from an OK-OK human place

Extra thoughts about the field of therapy

In this section I want to mention some of the things that usually go unsaid by people in the counselling and therapy field as well as mentioning some of the pitfalls and issues.

The important thing to realise is that there's a turf war between different practitioners, who vie for control over various groups of patients and for their own professional survival.

Training in psychotherapy is good job creation for trainers, it's hierarchical, and it recreates the power imbalance between 'client' (often a euphemism for someone seen as not-OK) and therapist, between trainer/supervisor and trainee.

My experience of the therapy world

As mentioned, therapists are flawed and are similar to people in other professions, and this is unexpected by clients who want to view them as nice, even as parental, even saint-like. I think that people attracted to therapy careers have often been in therapy themselves and are 'sorted out' with varying degrees of success.

My own experience of having therapy and being a therapist and a counsellor is as follows.

I had ten years of therapy after a big neurotic-level breakdown when I was 24. This breakdown was paralyzing and involved regression and very high levels of anxiety. For me, therapy wasn't optional - it was essential for me to function and slowly get my life together. I found travelling difficult and would have been labelled 'agoraphobic'. In any event, for some years I had to be on the phone to a therapist when I was panicking; as this problem decreased gradually, I realized that a lot (not all) of my parenting/preparation for life was wonky or damaging and my babyhood included trauma, both of which needed understanding and fixing. I found support from therapists but not much real understanding; instead it was more a question of which of their boxes I might fit into.

I realized that it would take a huge effort to fix myself with whatever help was there and made it my goal to get mended and I've made a lot of changes.

I got through four main 'talking' therapists one of whom I worked with on a single issue and one of whom was mediocre. I also had subsidiary help or short input from eight more and went to four bodywork therapists but only one of these helped. Also I went to many workshops and training events. In the end I became a 'therapy addict' and no, I didn't go to a therapist to sort this out.

I've worked as a therapist for more than 20 years including 7 years as a drug/alcohol counsellor. I've met a lot of people in the therapy world.

After all that I realized something was missing, that nobody had even mentioned spiritual development so I set about developing my spiritual life.

When to get involved in therapy

I identified some reasons earlier in the chapter for deciding to get involved in therapy, but a key issue is *when you and/or the people you know can't fix a problem or issue and need outside input.*

People's expectations of therapy may include completely fixing 'old stuff' and becoming a magically- transformed super-person - these outcomes are unlikely to happen; also, therapists don't love you and are flawed like everyone else. They have an unusual role - they can be fairly involved and caring but are not close like friends and often they are paid directly by the client, so that there is a business relationship.

Having therapy is useful when you want to learn skills in therapy or generally learn about psychology in practice, or do some personal growth or get support, or recover from trauma, or for specialized issues such as phobias, addictions, couples issues etc. Therapy can bring about big changes and it can help you understand very deep issues.

How many therapists are needed to change a light-bulb?

The usual answer is *the light bulb has to want to change*, no, I think it's more common that people who go to therapy may unconsciously not feel safe to change at that time or with that therapist .... I have seen people work on issues they didn't expect to come up and solve them with powerful competent therapists.

Questions to ask therapists

Forget gimmicks; forget 'front', including expertness.

Ask:
- what is your 'old stuff' and how is it going to affect my therapy?
- are you part of a healthy team and organization?
- what exactly is your experience?
- do you talk in psychobabble?

Problems with counselling and psychotherapy

I think the main problem areas of therapy could be summarised as *aims, equality/rights* and *values.*

Also as mentioned, there are different schools (flavours) of therapy which influence counselling as well, so for example you can get psychodynamic *psychotherapy* (what a mouthful), or psychodynamic *counselling.*

Aims of counselling and psychotherapy – who sets them?

I think counselling should be *client-centred* and people should *set their own goals.*

The underpinnings of *counselling* are usually that the process is driven by the client, and it's more about growth and support than most *psychotherapy* which is more likely to define people, fit them into boxes, impose more and have 'recipes' for treatment. However much *therapists* try to present themselves as user-friendly I've only met a small number who treat their clients as self-directing and OK; *counsellors* are generally less in their expert egos and are nicer to be with though I have had counsellors trying to impose their goals on me. *Therapists* tend to work more with history and educated guesses about a person's childhood development.

The changes to people's personalities proposed by some *therapy* schools and their neat 'treatment plans' approach comedy and are just not in reality. I like Carl Rogers on *counselling* who is refreshingly human and unpretentious, though waffly.

Equality, rights and diagnosis

There's more on this topic in our chapter on *Emotional and mental health*.

'Professional 'or 'expert' power is a problem in various fields in terms of its potential for manipulation and abuse and this equally applies to therapy. Here I am talking particularly about *diagnosis*, which is part of the equality picture, though abuse of power also happens in relation to the *process* of therapy. The problem with therapy is that people seeking it may be more vulnerable and trusting and into building a significant relationship with the professional than say they would be with a lawyer.

The first category people are put in is *client, patient, student, trainee* which means a status of less rights but which does carry some protection.

Is labelling good or bad?

Psycho-diagnosis, diagnosis, psychopathology are all terms that relate to the same thing- I will call them *labelling*.

The answer to whether it's good or bad depends on *who is doing it, why it's done and how it's done*.

The idea is that childhood problems at certain ages produce certain personality types. For example, *paranoid, hysteric/histrionic, narcissistic* etc - there is an endless list in the current diagnostic and statistical manual of the American Psychiatric Association.

I am not anti-diagnosis but think it should only be used as a best guess, then be individualized, then only used to benefit people and should have proper explanations. *The trouble is that it's not used like this.*

Instead, often people are categorised/labelled, made not-OK and put in a league table of labelled people which parodied, looks like this: *neurotic-level hysterics, though similar to paranoids are somehow more 'successful' and both are infinitely better than drug addicts or people with a psychotic problem.* All of this is similar to the pecking-order of helping professionals already mentioned, with doctors at the top.

Even if diagnosis is used in a helpful way there is very large individual variation in each category.

Psycho-diagnosis is not rocket science, though psychiatry likes to keep it to itself.

Fighting stigmatising conditions is officially on the agenda of organisations like the UK Royal College of Psychiatrists and the voluntary agencies like MIND and SANE. Increasingly politicians and others in the public eye are 'coming out' with stories about their own struggles, a process that was perhaps kicked off by Princess Diana being open with the public about her struggles with *bulimia*.

With so much that has been developed pharmacologically, the symptoms of many disorders are more controlled than ever before (and are thus less florid and less evident to others), whilst the dramatic stories of individual patients being a risk to the public are offset by the statistics indicating that care in the community is generally successful (though sometimes a sad and isolating option for those who would have felt more included within a hospital environment in years gone by).

Involuntary treatment

Sadly, there are people who find that once they come into contact with psychiatric services that they cannot retreat from labels, treatments and detentions which they may regard as contravening their human rights. In addition, anti-psychiatry groups have long argued that psychiatry exercises medical control over political dissidents and those who are socially 'deviant'.

The psychiatrist and academic Thomas Szasz wrote his book *The Myth of Mental Illness* in 1960, challenging the idea of symptoms, preferring the idea of 'problems in living' and being opposed to the arbitrary power of psychiatrists to detain people in institutions. He felt that doctors were defining *behaviour that was problematic for others* as *'disease'*, medicalising something that was not in fact ill-health, and practising psychiatry as a 'pseudo-science'.

One of the boundaries that has got blurred is that between *disease* (a model which Szasz resists) and *deviance* – whereby behaviour challenges social norms. Szasz would argue that controlling 'deviance' is not (or should not be) within the remit of medicine and that claiming that deviant people are 'ill' is morally wrong.

One of the debates about diagnosis has been the question of the *right to be sane*, pleaded by the Norwegian Anders Behring Breivik, after he had killed more than 70 people, pleading far-right militant ideology, who preferred to be jailed for political activity than to be put into a mental asylum for the rest of his life.

Other critics of psychiatry's role in social control of people include the philosopher Michel Foucault and the sociologist Erving Goffman.

Mind Freedom International supports people who are having or have had involuntary psychiatric detention or treatment which they don't want, so-called *'psychiatric survivors'*. The *Church of Scientology* has also strongly questioned the idea of 'mental illness' across the globe and has viewed enforced psychiatric treatment as 'torture'.

In the UK, *MIND* and *Rethink* are two key charities that aim to fight for the rights of mental health service users.

As with any organisation, it's always worth checking out the culture and background of the organisation we turn to for help.

Values

As already said, the predominant values of therapists and other helpers are bourgeois/middle-class. These values tend towards conformity, narrowness and unlike 'old-fashioned values', tend to be self-serving, and for convenience. In the worst, therapists use their values to judge others, not themselves, and they are certainly not usually spiritual. I think one problem here is that a lot of people are using values that are not coming from within but referring also instead to socially-made codes and structures.

Why are values important in therapy?

Because the minute we decide that adjustment to *'normality'* is a goal of helping then it's important to define normal behaviour and normal values. At present 'normal' is often about being greedy, conformist, manipulative, dishonest, and destructive, which is a problem for therapists who have to decide where to go in encouraging competitive and ruthless behaviour or supporting clients to go against mainstream culture.

Are helpers trying to fit people into a very narrow/ middleclass /conformist value system world-view or value system? If so, this will not help ethnic minorities, creative people, spiritual people, gay people, alternative people, people with gender and sexuality issues, people from a different social class, and people with different material circumstances.

In summary, I've learned a tremendous amount from being in counselling and therapy. It was mixed, but on balance, it was mostly supportive.

Julia

My experience

My path through counselling and therapy has been different from Jack's, and in particular, I've mostly had long-term counselling relationships over 4 years or so at a time, where I saw the counsellor/therapist weekly or fortnightly for an hour each time.

As I set about describing my therapeutic journey for this book, I found that each period of therapeutic work generated particular insights about the process, so I've decided to narrate the journey through a series of issues of interest about the therapy process which I hope might be helpful.

My grounding has always been in psychoanalytic counselling (particularly what is called the 'object relations' approach), but you will see that I also have some insight into other approaches. In the chapter on *Close relationships*, I say a bit more about the differences between Jack's therapeutic orientation and my own.

Counselling has often been essential to my life, providing support and an independent perspective as I've faced changes in relationships, homes, jobs, becoming a parent, etc. for example, or had to tackle issues of being discriminated against, being bullied, being overlooked, being excluded, being hurt or when events in my life have been overwhelming such as relationship breakdown, bereavement, financial fallout, and stress.

After many years of therapy during my adult life, I believe I now benefit from a level of mental and emotional health that has enabled me to cope with trauma and difficulty (and cumulative difficulty) in my life and survive. I can now understand much more clearly the dynamics in my family and how they affected me in my life – years ago, I did not have those insights and found my life-course much more puzzling.

However, a key theme for me in my work – and in this book – is to link the psychological with the social and political, and I say more about this at the end of this section.

Knowing your counsellor and knowing the client. I started having counselling when I broke up with first main partner towards the end of my first degree. The college counsellor suggested I approach my parents for help during the final stages of my degree and in the aftermath of the relationship break-up, and despite my reservations about the likely outcome, we 'rehearsed' the dialogue I would have with them. It was the most devastating encounter with my parents I've ever had. The point though was that the therapist – who didn't know me well – set me up for an encounter that has stayed in my mind (and that of my parents) as a puzzle for the rest of my life. It was a quick, intense early lesson in the power of therapy, ripping open the surface dynamics of my family situation to reveal underlying issues which I had failed to understand before. Sadly, it was many years before I felt like speaking to my parents again. In retrospect, I might have wished for something prepared for more carefully, but I expect at the time, things were intense with my final examinations imminent and no time to prevaricate. The counsellor projected onto me her values about parental support – she did not have a true appreciation of the diffcrent cultural values in my family home that were that children should be independent once they had left home.

Ethics and morality as a basis of counselling. After my first degree and my first post-degree job, I moved city and decided to go for some more counselling. I went to a woman counsellor on someone's recommendation – she specialized in counselling nuns and there was a spiritual and moral flavour to her approach, which I found supportive and peaceful. In the end she felt *I* was too hung up on the morality of my own actions, and coming from her, I felt able to free myself up to take necessary actions in my life about which I was hesitating. One view of therapists is as 'secular priests' (see for example Halmos' work). There can be a sense of the confessional and a desire for forgiveness or release or decisions about actions to repair things, the need to question the ethics of our behaviour without the judgement found in many religious contexts. Or we might be on the search for meaning in our life, perhaps beginning to critique the choices we have made and the foundations of institutions to which we are giving our energy. I didn't question this woman on her faith or her ideas very much – her compassionate and thoughtful manner seemed enough for me at the time. Whatever we are involved in, we can all benefit from a space that does not attempt to influence us, but where someone listens and encourages us to be courageous in terms of what we need to do.

Non-impingement and the idea of love. Being involved in the teaching of human relations skills as I was in the 1980s, I decided to embark on a counselling training at the end of which I was assessed by a psychoanalytic counsellor of some repute. I decided to go to him for a long period of counselling and stayed initially for 4 or 5 years, seeing him fortnightly. Years later I returned for another 3 years. We often sat in silence until I began - he was committed to *'non-impingement'* of the psyche and never tried to influence or shape the content of the sessions. Once I talked about 'working' on things – he questioned even that – perhaps 'play' or 'free space' was more appropriate he thought. Nothing was required. He thought that that 'non-demand' was essential to healthy psychological development. He was an *'object relations'* therapist, and taught me about Donald Winnicott's idea of *'the facilitating environment'* in which a baby flourishes when *'alone in the presence of the mother'*. I learned that I needed my own space, not to be interrupted psychologically when doing my creative or intellectual work, and from reading Anthony Storr's work on solitude, I came to understand that we need connection to internalised others in our life in order to be at our most creatively productive. Through this therapist, I learned that it was fruitless and unhelpful to try to manipulate love. Learning that love would exist *or not*, as a free energy, has been one of the most important and releasing lessons of my life. I don't have to seduce or be strategic or pleasing etc. to get love. It makes no difference. I can be me. Someone will love me, *or not*.

Finding a focus When I began teaching counselling and running a small supervision practice, I went to a counsellor (a clinical psychologist who happened to specialise in child sexual abuse) for exploring my own life material and to a supervisor (who happened to be a forensic psychoanalyst) for my work with practising counsellors - the work with both lasted for 4 or 5 years. One of the main memories I had from going to see the psychologist was the challenge it felt to me to choose something to talk about - there were so many things going on in my mind and my life and I didn't want to waste the session or pick the wrong thing. I took to producing on paper a diagram with a stick person representing me in the middle and all the different issues going on at the time ranged around me – something like the picture below (although not necessarily those particular issues!):

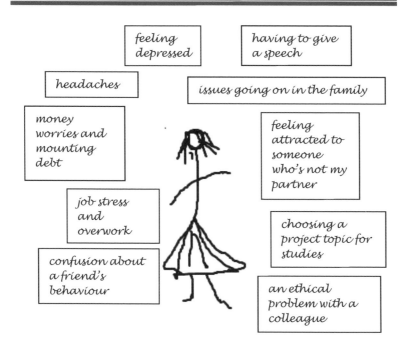

What I was then able to focus on was the issue of the fragmentation of myself and the themes that could link up all these things to an integrated sense of self. For example: *Was I dissatisfied with my job or my partner and investing in the other in order to cope? Did I need to say no to demands in my life? Was I living out my mother's wishes or in charge of my own choices?* Although sometimes it all gave rise to an equally complex set of questions, sometimes I was able to leave the session much calmer, much less fragmented, much more focused again on the priorities in my life.

Finding a path Over the years I went to various workshops including behavioural psychotherapy training, Reichian bodywork, Tibetan Buddhist meditation teachings, American Indian workshops and sweat lodges, Quaker retreats, assertiveness courses, a psychodrama workshop, a feminist self-help health group, women's therapy centre workshops, voice dialogue weekends, a negotiation skills course, and constellation therapy work based on Bert Hellinger's ideas. I studied counselling further and wrote a dissertation about intimacy and early dynamics that

207

involved interviewing my parents in depth. I developed courses in which I explored the ideas of different psychoanalysts, and of the cognitive-behaviourists, the humanistic client-centred counsellors, and the existentialists.

All of these experiences enriched my knowledge and gave me learnings about myself and others and the limits and potential of therapy. I was careful however not to get caught up overmuch in any one, and remained fundamentally 'loyal' to the psychoanalytic path. This I think kept me 'on course' and stopped me from being pulled too much in one direction or another. Some people may benefit from being freer – for me, that was my safety but it also meant I was perhaps more conservative and cautious and some might think I have held back from fuller engagement and transformation through more adventurous paths. In the end, I have found that it is sociological thinking through feminism and a left-wing perspective (reinforced through my experience in trade unionism) that gave me the tools I needed to transform my perceptions of the world, but it is therapy that gave me the power to stand alone and make up my own mind about things.

Anonymity of the therapist. Later I saw another therapist who had an academic background and an interest in writing and the arts, and as she said *'in another life, we might have been friends'*. She supported me through a raft of sad and challenging events in my life and when I needed it, encouraged me to keep going with the MSc that I was trying to complete. This was different from the friends in my life who in the main thought I should give it up in order to cope with the emotional, practical and financial fallout of my life. I stayed in therapy with her for about 4 years and after a gap of some years, there's now the possibility of starting to get to know her. This represents a big shift for me as having had years of therapy experience, I no longer find a relationship founded on the complete anonymity of the therapist and the complete exposure of the client an acceptable way to proceed.

Equality. When I went freelance in my late 50s, I chose to see a woman I already knew and valued, for three sessions, in order to release some of the feelings about leaving the academic life, and my fears and hopes for my new life working with my creativity. I insisted on an open, informal way of relating, and we sat down and had tea together and talked – she fed in elements of her life to the conversation as needed. I no longer want the traditional therapist OK-client not OK model and am reaching for something else now. When I was younger I needed to feel that I was paying for the therapist not to impinge, for me not to care what they were living through, for the focus to be just on me. I find not knowing anything about them and their silence impossible now to tolerate for long. I need the equality. I would however keep my eyes open if I were going to a new or inexperienced counsellor to ensure that they were clear about 'boundaries'. And what I want now may only 'work' because of my long experience in counselling.

(I'm not talking here about co-counselling - this was a model which allowed two people to offer reciprocal counselling to each other. You clearly have to be well-matched in experience and skill to do this well).

Boundaries are that element protected by keeping fairly strictly to the time parameters of the session and the behaviour (eg. no touching, no joking or sarcasm) and perhaps non-intrusiveness, which are all different from a mature counsellor attempting to help you explore something or finding a nugget of life experience that they think will be helpful. Codes of ethics generally prevent a counsellor from sharing too much of their own stuff with you, arguing that the session is about *you* not the therapist, and that there can be a danger of the therapist thinking that their experience is the same as yours and forgetting to look properly at the uniqueness of *your* response to situations and events. If you are beginning a counselling or therapy relationship, you may find the exposure of yourself difficult to handle – the therapist's dogged silence about their own life can feel cold or harsh, but it is designed to ensure that you experience you as *you*, unshaped by the therapist, and to allow you to find your own voice, hear your own story, however long it takes you to tell it (and it might take weeks or months or years). Therapists who spend a lot of time telling you their story or expressing their needs are usually going beyond their brief and should be avoided. Therapists who want to turn you into a friend or lover are a complete no-no. Most of us choose therapy because people or events in our life have overwhelmed us or evade understanding or resolution. We don't benefit from a therapist whose own life needs are so urgent or unresolved that they abuse us. Our understanding from numerous histories is that the powerful usually exploit the weak – it's vital to find a therapist where you feel that they won't exploit you. You may need to sort out how much of those feelings are real scepticism about a therapist's position and attitude and how much of them are from your own childhood scripting whereby adults abused you.

Transference is the idea that we replay relationships from our life in the therapist-client relationship. If you find yourself attracted to or fantasizing about the therapist (and that's often easier to do if we don't know anything about them), you need to discuss that with the therapist – eg. in terms of how you find people who are kind or cold attractive, or how you long for unattainable figures to love you, or how lonely you are, or what part sexuality plays in your life. If you find issues about authority emerge, for example, that the counsellor seems to be controlling you or stopping you from doing things, look with them at what this brings up from your past about your relationship with parents. You may need to be reassured that whatever secret or acknowledged feelings emerge, the therapist will respond in a mature and safe way – in other words, you may be testing the safety of the relationship and will only trust it if the therapist handles things in a way that is useful for you and non-exploitatively.

All good therapists will have supervision in place to where they can take their own difficulties in the therapy process including any feelings they have towards you that echo dynamics from their own lives - 'counter-transference'. Some therapists (particularly person-centred ones) will use their own feelings as a guide to feed back to you – *'when you do this, I feel.........'* *'when you say this, it makes me think what I have to say is of no value to you'* etc.

> *One therapist who clearly worked a lot with 'process' told me that she felt discounted when I started rambling and mumbling into myself – 'I have two hypotheses' she said 'it could be that you feel I am so much here for you that you have no need to articulate clearly to me – you think I already understand what you are thinking and feeling, or the converse – you believe that it is irrelevant whether I hear you or not, it won't make any difference'.*
> *We were able to discuss these ideas and I was able to look at how I might wander off in my communications with close others in my life and what it meant for me and them when I did that. In retrospect, in a more equal process, of course I could also have said 'I wonder why this bothers you as no-one else in my life has ever mentioned it.......'*

Trust The point is to avoid idealizing the therapist – we have a right to negotiate the definition of the therapy relationship with them whilst listening to what they have to say about the model they like to use and why they think it is helpful. We need to give them a chance but we need to keep our instincts alert too. This is a tricky business because it may be that the best therapy occurs when we develop trust in the therapist, and that we may want therapy because trust is a difficult issue for us. Having conflict with your therapist is not necessarily to be avoided – the difference is that with a good therapist, you can use the experience to explore your general approach to conflict and to consider new ways of handling it and learning from it. We have to take responsibility for ourselves and like with any other adviser or guide in life – our doctors, our car mechanics, our tutors, our bank managers, *we have to assess for ourselves the soundness of the service they are offering.* We have to listen to the longing in ourselves for a mother or God-like figure who forgives all and *work with* that energy, not give up our own power.

Therapy and real life One therapist with whom I worked for several years nevertheless failed to take into account at times the economic difficulties in my life, and encouraged me into explorations of the depths of my psyche which were difficult for me to cope with given the financial pressures on me. During a particularly painful period in my life, I regressed into states I must have been in as a baby, rolling around on a bed with my arms around myself and weeping copiously. Nevertheless I had to get up and get dressed up and go out teaching, and the split between the inner and the outer self became too much for me. The economic reality of my life – I had to earn money and sell my house – meant that I should have put limits on where I got to in the psychological journey and I didn't know how to do that.

The reality was that some of this therapist's clients could afford to be at home, doing creative and spiritual work, taking time to work through feelings. I could not. Perhaps I envied the fantasised other patients (some of whom I knew), who knows? Maybe I should have continued on into the womb of infant despair and in so doing, changed something forever, but my feeling was that I needed to save myself. There was no-one at home to hug me, and a job outside the home that had to be done to keep paying the mortgage. Going into the exposure of lecturing was difficult after I'd just spent the morning crying. It left me with a sense that the client should always look after him or herself in the process and decide when and how you can let go, and when because of the harsh realities of life, you can't. ***Make sure you're meeting your <u>own</u> agendas and not living out vicariously an agenda of the therapist*** (*or for that matter, the agenda of anyone else in your life*).

Final thoughts

Counselling and therapy have changed over the last 40 years. In the UK, it was far less common than in America, where in particular the Jewish émigrés from Europe established the psychoanalytic fraternity and made having a personal analyst fashionable. In the 1980s and 90s, I spent some years setting up training programmes in counselling and breaking down some of the prejudices about counselling in an area of Britain that had strong networks and family communities very much *in situ* - it was a place which was not immediately hospitable to the ideas and values of therapy. It was also a strong Labour and trade union context, and it is easy to see in retrospect that much as I succeeded

212

in bringing some small influence to the culture of the area with psychology, so I myself was changed forever by ideas about equality, discrimination, collective action and political activism. When I became a trade unionist, I realized how brutalized some of my fellow activists were by their experiences and how unexamined these were in psychological terms. I used my knowledge of psychology and therapy to develop a strong team, which I believe is essential to successful political action.

As Jack says, therapy can be used to pathologize and label the individual, supporting the idea that individuals have problems which need treatment, instead of recognizing that many of our troubles could be changed by changing the conditions of our lives. It's probably not just a joke that *'winning the lottery would sort out a lot of mental health problems'*. Living in intimidating housing situations, not being able to earn enough money to support your children, having few opportunities for leisure, having endless encounters with people, systems, employers etc. who reinforce poor self-esteem, etc. – I could go on citing the myriad ways in which people's material lives create the conditions for misery. Even if the problems don't stem from poor social conditions, the pressures on middle-class people to keep up with the Jones', to continually achieve, to be outgoing and publicly successful, and to conform to expectations regarding values, attitudes, roles and behaviour all create a level of stress that results very often in physical illness, emotional disturbance, debt, addiction and relationship breakdown.

Insist on discussing the social and economic realities with any therapist you decide to work with. Use any inequality you feel in relation to their situation (and some may seem in a cocooned bubble compared to you) to explore feelings about this (transference again!) – eg. envy, contempt, denial, discomfort, anger, safety etc. Get their take on their own life position and how they view social inequality. Finding meaning in our lives and determining how we position ourselves are things that therapy can help us with – I believe that we need political awareness, spiritual or moral depth *and* an understanding of our own psychology to be effective human beings.

213

Further reading

This list includes a number of texts and films which will inform you about the therapy world (not always in the best light) so that you can retain a critical mind-set when approaching therapy as a client or as a trainee.

There are a number of different fields of therapy including the psychoanalytic – with several branches including the 'Freudians' and the 'Kleinians', the British Independent object relations approach (eg. Donald Winnicott, John Bowlby, Masud Kahn), and the feminist approach initiated by Susie Orbach and Luise Eichenbaum; the analytical psychology path developed by the 'Jungians'; the person-centred approach initiated by Carl Rogers and later developed by Brian Thorne among others in the UK; the existential approach including the work of Irvin Yalom and Emmy van Deurzen; and other approaches to therapy by people like Alice Miller (who came to critique psychoanalysis), and Bert Hellinger who developed systemic family constellation work.

Some therapists have written stories of their work with clients and some examples by Susie Orbach and Irving Yalom are included below. This is always riveting and useful to people who are familiar or unfamiliar with psychotherapy but of course we should be mindful of the real people whose stories have been fictionalised to ensure confidentiality of their identities and details.

Eric Berne (1961) (2009 ed) *Transactional Analysis in Psychotherapy* Eigel Meirovich

John Bowlby (1951) *Maternal Care and Mental Health* report for the World Health Organisation New York: Schocken

Windy Dryden and Colin Feltham (1992) *Psychotherapy and its discontents* Open University Press

Barry L Duncan, Scott D Miller, Bruce Wampold and Marc A Hubble (2009)(2nd edition) *The Heart and Soul of Change* American Psychological Association

Luise Eichenbaum and Susie Orbach (1992) *Understanding Women* London: Penguin

Michel Foucault (1965) (2006 ed) *Madness and Civilization: A History of Insanity in the Age of Reason* Vintage

Sigmund Freud and Joseph Breuer plus Adam Phillips, Nicola Luckhurst, and Rachel Bowlby (2004) *Studies in Hysteria* London: Penguin Books

Paul Gilbert (2010) *The Compassionate Mind: Compassion-focused therapy* Constable

Erving Goffman (1968) *Asylums* Pelican

Phyllis Grosskurth (1991) *The Secret Ring: Freud's Inner Circle and the Politics of Psychoanalysis* London: Johnathan Cape/Westview Press

Paul Halmos (1965) *The Faith of the Counsellors* Constable

Linda Hopkins (2006) *False Self: The Life of Masud Khan* New York: Other Press

Gregorio Kohon (1986) *The British School of Psychoanalysis: the Independent tradition* London: Free Association Books

Rachel P Maines (2001 edition) *The Technology of Orgasm: 'Hysteria', the Vibrator and Women's Sexual Satisfaction* John Hopkins University Press

Joy Manne and Bert Hellinger (2012) *Family Constellations: A Practical Guide to Uncovering the Origins of Family Conflict* North Atlantic Books

Jeffrey Masson (1988) *Against Therapy* London: Collins including introduction by Dorothy Rowe

Alice Miller (2005) *The Body Never Lies: The Lingering Effects of Cruel Parenting* Norton

Norcross, J. C., & Goldfried, M. R. (Eds.). (2005). *Handbook of psychotherapy integration* (2nd ed.). New York: Oxford.

Susie Orbach (1999) *The Impossibility of Sex* Allen Lane

Adam Phillips (1997) *Winnicott* Fontana Modern Masters

Eric Rayner (1991) *The Independent Mind in British Psychoanalysis* London: Free Association Books

Carl Rogers (1961) *On Becoming a Person* Houghton Mifflin

Michael Rutter (1981) *Maternal Deprivation Reassessed* Harmondsworth: Penguin

Anthony Stevens (2001) *Jung: a very short introduction* Oxford Paperbacks

Anthony Storr (1988) *Solitude* Collins: Fontana Books/Flamingo

Thomas Szasz (1960) *The Myth of Mental Illness: Foundations of a Theory of Personal Conduct* Harper and Row

Brian Thorne (2012) *Counselling and Spiritual Accompaniment: Bridging Faith and Person-centred Therapy* Wiley-Blackwell

Paul Ware (1983) *Personality adaptations (doors to therapy)* Transactional Analysis Journal 13: 11-19.

Margaret Warner *Person-Centred Therapy at the Difficult Edge: a Developmentally based Model of Fragile and Dissociated Process* Chap 8 in Dave Mearns and Brian Thorne (2000) *Person-Centred Therapy Today, New Frontiers in Theory and Practice* Sage Publications

Bruce Wampold (2001) *The Great Psychotherapy Debate: Models, Methods and Findings* Routledge

Irvin Yalom (1989/2012) *Love's Executioner and Other Tales of Psychotherapy* Basic Books
http://www.mindfreedom.org/

Films:
David Cronenberg (2011) *A Dangerous Method*
Clint Eastwood *Changeling*
Tanya Wexler (2011) *Hysteria*
Documentary film:
John Bowlby and James Robertson (1952) *A Two Year Old Goes to Hospital*

6   emotional and mental health

See also our chapter on *Therapy* (including sections on *involuntary treatment* and on *diagnosis*)

This chapter is in two parts – the first part focuses on psychopathology and psycho-diagnosis, with the examples of narcissism and psychopathy given some consideration, and the second part looking particularly at the challenges for couples in handling mental health issues within close relationships, including the stress of not recognising what is going on, the fear of stigma, and questions around the idea of 'normality' which can prevent any of us from getting the help that we might need.

The first part is written by Jack and the second part by Julia

Part 1 - Jack

Putting people into psychological categories – is it of any use?

If you're interested in understanding problem personalities and their influence in society, it's hard to do this without looking into psychopathology in some detail, but psycho-diagnosis is not only complex but is a contested issue, involving a number of conflicting elements.

Psychopathology in psychiatry is based on the idea that people can be categorised into different groups and each group shares to some degree behaviours and beliefs.   People in different groups are regarded as *'pathological'* ie. their personalities have not developed normally, also that their problems are sufficiently serious that they cause problems to themselves and to other people.

With 'neurotic' problems, those with 'heavier' versions are labelled as having *'personality disorders'* of different types – eg. *'personality disorder paranoid type'*.   Other people with neurotic problems which are *less* classic or serious may be said to have traits eg. *'narcissistic traits'*.   There is also an issue about degree or depth of pathology, *'neurotic'* being less serious than a

217

'psychotic' level. Psychiatrists have largely claimed this territory of categorising personality types, calling them names like *'hysteric'* and *'schizoid'* and deciding how serious their issues are.

Psychotherapists (and remember that Freud and co. were doctors!) have also claimed some of this territory but in slightly different ways. Therapists claim that their use of psycho-diagnosis is more to do with *helping people understand and live with their issues.* So, for example, if someone has a problem and fits a particular personality type – say, *'paranoid personality disorder'*, therapists would attempt to individualise the diagnosis, see how it fits the classic paranoid picture, work out how deep and serious the issues are for that individual and importantly, construct a hypothetical developmental picture as to how the issues developed in babyhood or childhood. Remember here that babyhood and very early childhood issues are likely to be out of conscious awareness and stored as deep unconscious memories and as body memories (ie. memories linked to physical experiences and stored in memory as being linked to the body rather than in words or pictures). The idea then is to construct an individual's possible 'story' to enable understanding of issues and changes to be made in the present to behaviours which are largely caused by the past.

Thus in the case of someone with a *'paranoid personality',* the person may learn to be less secretive, feel less likely to be rejected, trust more etc. and understand their deep need for stability, as well as appreciating what their babyhood may have involved (a personalised 'likely story') and what the general problems are for people with paranoid issues. Contrary to information in the movies, paranoid issues are amongst the easiest to sort out.

The understanding of psycho-diagnosis to help 'therapise' or heal people is a quest for an ideal and sometimes for personality change ie. a radical re-structuring is thought about and aimed for but in reality, is unlikely to happen. What is more likely is that people build within the personalities they have, modify, understand and learn to live with them.

There is a huge dilemma for psychiatry, which until recently, has tended to hold onto its secrets and guard its territory of expertise.

Everyone wants to avoid populist labelling and the sensationalising of psychopathology (which is often done in horror movies), but this doesn't mean that we shouldn't have access to the keys to understanding different 'personality types'. Writers who are starting to publish books about psychopathology can sometimes pander to the populist mind-set but if we read between the lines there are often significant and useful pieces of information that can help.

It can be difficult for those of us with a liberal mentality to accept that some individuals may need boundaries. Because these are uncomfortable assessments to make doesn't mean that we should neglect the issue or let anarchy rule. It's important that we all recognise the prevalence and influence of pathology in society and if there are people at the helm of the 'world ship' who are not self-aware and are meeting their own needs rather than the needs of wider society, or imposing their psychologies on others, then we need to be able to intervene.

The issue often is *who* is qualified to judge? Are they neutral and fair and accurate and is it even possible to be neutral and fair and accurate? How 'mentally well' are those who make these assessments? How many psychiatrists, psychologists, psychotherapists, personnel officers are fully aware of their own pathological leanings? And what factors are influencing their judgements eg. looking after public safety, protecting their own careers, justifying their own theories, bowing to political pressure, following current trends in policy, fear of retribution from dangerous people and their associates, trying to meet employer demands for particular outcomes etc.?

At a deeper level, how much weight do we give to questions of love, wisdom, discernment in how we treat people with personality difficulties? We may recognise that there are difficulties in relating to them but do we have to ostracise them, ban them, fight them?

And if we have such problems ourselves, are we able to consider how we might stop hurting others around us, and reach out for help to stop passing on damage to others - including our children?

There are answers to this which are known by therapists. Yes you can be aware of your own developmental story and 'personality type' and its effect on others. Also working with personality types is an art-form (rather than an accurate science) and has to be done with sensitivity.

Problems with psycho-diagnosis

There are endless problems with psycho-diagnosis and most of them are pretty serious.

How it's used

1. at the extreme end of the spectrum, it can be used for labelling in order to exclude, isolate or even harm people

2. encouraging people to learn about and piece together an individual developmental *'likely story'* that fits for them and then working with them on as equal a basis as possible to enable them to strive for any achievable changes they want

3. somewhere in between these poles

Power issues:

*   legal concerns eg. defining *mental competence*

*   the use (or misuse) of *professional power* for example in psychiatry, forensic psychology etc.

*   power imbalances involved in *'helping'* and the therapeutic relationship in particular

*   the problem of *normalising* problem behaviours - if the culture and norms of society mirror those of narcissism as Alexander Lowen suggests, our idea of *'normality'* is now abnormal ie. a narcissistic culture prevails. If psychopathic individuals are setting up a new 'normality' of anti-social

behaviours, particularly in business (see the recent banking scandals), then we all need to be aware of this

- is psycho-diagnosis being used flexibly, creatively? diagnostic categories have possibilities for huge variation within each category

- is diagnosis being used in a human/humane way?

For many people, the idea that *a past which is hard to retrieve from memory, largely forming a personality type which has shared features with others of that type and can cause problems for individuals and society* just doesn't work, partly because even rough and ready 'typing' offends notions of individuality and personhood. In fact, if psycho-diagnosis is done sensitively and with respect for individuality, it can be helpful.

How people's problems affect us

There have always been people with problems who are destructive to others AND are in power - see for example, Ivan the Terrible, made *Tsar of all the Russias* in 1547, who among other things, managed in a rage to beat and kill his own son and heir. In more recent times, a man like Joseph Goebbels, who was Adolf Hitler's propaganda minister and close confidante almost certainly *was* narcissistic. Toby Thacker, who wrote a biography of Goebbels in 2009, indicates that Goebbels may have been the key instigator of the idea of exterminating the Jews in his discussions with Hitler. Certainly, Goebbels conducted the propaganda campaign associated with the 3rd Reich and encouraged people to fight to their deaths even when there was no chance of winning. According to another of his biographers, Peter Longerich, Goebbels had a number of affairs (including during his marriage), keeping records of them and being prepared to drop one important lover at Hitler's request because of her supposed racial 'inferiority'. In his epilogue, Toby Thacker paints Goebbels as an inveterate liar. Ultimately, Goebbels and his wife Magda killed their six children before committing suicide in Hitler's bunker. His psychopathology had massive effects on the lives of others.

In the time of Ivan the Terrible, who was totally dedicated to centralising autocracy, we needed only to be aware of the personalities of Ivan, the Church leaders and possibly our landlord. Under Adolf Hitler, there was a more complex structure of control and power.

Now, as modern citizens, we need to be aware of the influence upon us of a multiplicity of organisations with corresponding opportunities for people with problems to be in charge. Now, with more complex societies, there's even more scope for people in power to control us, harm us, lie to us, cheat us or take away our power.

Another structural issue that affects society is the loosening of agreed moral rules, happening much more with secularisation and a reduction in the influence of organised religion. For example, lying and manipulation regarded as 'anti-social' a hundred years ago is now part of life, as in for example, much advertising.

Based on the idea that leaders shape their organisations, if those leaders are unempathic, anti-social, controlling or have serious problems, then the feel and operation of their organisations will challenge our rights, wellbeing etc. as a consumer or customer as well as the rights and wellbeing of their employees.

Time and effort to understand the field

My experience of psycho-diagnosis comes both from being diagnosed as a therapy client (see *Therapy* chapter) *and* training in psycho-diagnosis as a therapist. Also I've used psycho-diagnosis in everyday life as a lot of psychiatrists and therapists do without admitting to it.

So why should anyone be interested in psycho-diagnosis?

- there's some truth in it
- it's extremely useful for avoiding obnoxious or downright destructive people

222

- we can use it to understand what drives public figures, including those in history and how history has been shaped

For example, possible diagnoses might be:

Alexander the Great – *narcissist* into world domination
Adolf Hitler – *manic* into world domination from a younger age
Joseph Stalin - *paranoid* mind-set
Marilyn Monroe - *hysteric*
Hermann Goering – some kind of babyhood issue

For those who want to follow this line of enquiry, there is an attempt at psycho-diagnosis from David Owen in his study of political figures, and there is a professional exploration of famous figures in the work of Alice Miller.

Used creatively, most diagnostic categories have their positive sides – eg. *manic depressives* can have a lot of energy, *narcissists* are often competent and focused, *paranoids* can offer healthy criticism etc.

It's important to turn your emotional health issues into something that can work for you – if you're *manic*, learn not to overdo the life and soul of the party and take yourself off to a quiet room before you drive everyone around you crazy; if you're *narcissistic*, volunteer for those jobs that require grandiose strategies and a belief that you can carry through project initiatives; if you're *schizoid*, use your concentration powers and your preference for solitude to develop ideas, invent things and produce detailed reports. Develop the ability to recognise how you're behaving and the effect it has on others.

Finding a balance

In dealing with other people who have personality disorders, it's important to bear in mind the following:

1) hold to a core belief that people in general are basically good

2) recognise that unless people are extreme types, most can change to some extent

3) recognise that with some 'order' in society, if it's functional for that society, most people don't want to be too 'anti-social'

4) psychopathology is never the whole sum of a person - people are individual and unique

5) classification is a 'rough guide' – it is used to benefit the individuals concerned so that they can develop self-awareness and change things if they want to, and to protect us from the worst aspects of someone else's problems where they might be destructive

6) people aren't still '2 year old infants', their life experience will have added to their understanding and their self-presentation, and in many cases, mellowed the rawness of their inner worlds

So how can I find out about it?

You can't do it easily/quickly but you can get familiar with the territory. A good starting point is to tell yourself that there is no area of knowledge that is taboo or which belongs to someone else or is exclusive to some professional club like psychiatry.

Then familiarise yourself with the main categories:

Do they have *psychotic* or *neurotic* versions or just *neurotic* versions? For example, *hebephrenia* has no *neurotic* version, *narcissism* has no *psychotic* version, *schizoid (neurotic)* is similar to *catatonic (psychotic)*.

You can do this with the help for example, of the American Psychiatric Association's *Diagnostic and Statistical Manual of*

Mental Disorders. The DSM is the main diagnostic reference worldwide but there are other diagnostic schemes (eg. for specific disorders) such as Hare's *Psychopathy Checklist* which is the internationally agreed scheme for psychopathic disorders.

The new version DSM-V is scheduled for publication in May 2013 (there hasn't been a new one since 2000). However, it's worth noting that decisions over what to include have been riven with controversy, including battles to get some members of the task-force evicted because of their particular views and experience. You can get a summary of the changes proposed from the web. One of the much-embattled categories is the one of *complicated grief* and at what point someone is considered to be pathological in their grieving and thus needing treatment – these days, there's often a sense that we take long to get over loss – life is too busy and anyway, 'there are plenty more fish in the sea'.

Interestingly, the UK British Psychological Society's response has been to question the over-medicalisation of ordinary unhappiness and psychological variation, claiming for example that definitions of personality disorders in the manual have not been 'normed' against the normal population. They also feel – as we do – that a number of diagnostic categories have been overly matched to current social trends and expectations rather than to a view of healthy normality that outlives eras of time when social ideas and values can get distorted.   Newer areas of diagnosis include *too much time (over a long period of time) spent on sexual activity such as masturbation, cybersex and looking at pornography,* and *'defiant oppositional behaviours'* from children under 5. The BPS would prefer to avoid diagnosis and labelling and work instead with symptoms and ideas about how people would benefit from particular treatment options.

More on diagnosis

I don't believe that this is an area for academics to just debate or an area to take black-and-white sides on; I think it's a complex area needing humanity and wisdom, and which, despite all its hazards, shouldn't be thrown out.

The current situation on diagnosis is roughly this:

'Psychotic problems'

There's a debate here about how many of these problems are due to *nature* and how much are due to *nurture*. Some people have had successful psychotherapy for psychotic problems called *re-parenting* based on regression to the stage of early development where problems began, developed by Jacqui Schiff in the 1960s and 70s, but it remains a controversial approach, particularly because of its intensive and powerful nature.

Practically, though, despite some changes in attitudes, having a *psychotic* level problem, you are likely to be treated in society as scary, problematic, a second-class citizen and as potentially dangerous.

'Neurotic problems'

Being in therapy can be seen as fashionable or as stigmatising depending on the context including where you live. A Hollywood star in therapy for *bulimia* is usually OK. Anyone with a serious *passive-aggression* problem will be seen as not-OK as most helpers find this problem difficult to work with.

Other issues

People with problems including violence or sexual issues are likely to be seen as not-OK and there is a lot of ignorance about these topics. For example, *'flashers'* are not likely to be violent but may be perceived as scary/potentially violent.

Gay people

One-tenth of people worldwide are gay, yet gay people have been discriminated against on and off – being gay in classical Greece was OK, in Nazi Germany it was OK until the SA Brownshirts had their power curtailed by Hitler. Psychiatry and psychology have played their roles in the world in attempts to eradicate homosexual tendencies and to 'convert' people back to heterosexuality.

Normality

There are huge problems deciding which (society) or who (individual) is normal. *'Normal'* ie. psychologically healthy people - seem to be quite rare in developed countries at present.

When people are in the psychological 'hinterland' of being *not extreme*, ie. not causing too many problems for self or others, they are classified as having *'problematic traits'* rather than being diagnosed as having a personality disorder.

See too the discussion about diagnosis in our chapter on *Therapy and counselling.*

The language of psychiatry and psychotherapy

It is truly awful. Here's a list of examples:

- disorder
- pathology
- psychopathy
- psycho-diagnosis
- schizophrenia
- personality disorder
  etc.

I would at least suggest using words like *'issue'* instead of *'disorder'*. The sterile, inhuman, cold approach to human issues in psychiatry, psychology and psychotherapy is dreadful.

The use of these words stems from the colonisation of the mind by the medical profession, and reinforces the idea of illness being behind symptoms. Yet there have been alternative formulations of emotional and personality difficulties – see for example the work of Thomas Szasz who wrote *The Myth of Mental Illness* and who argued that much of what is taken as *'disease'* should actually be defined as *'problems in living'*.

There are some attempts now to make things better – for example, a shift to a new *'trait-based'* more positive description of people versus the American DSM categories.

Positive approaches to diagnosis are backed for example by Martin Seligman, author of *Flourish* and a leader in the *'positive psychology'* movement.

So why not throw out diagnosis?

I think it's a 'baby and bathwater' issue and a practical one as well.

The 'baby' is the knowledge that *has* been gained about different personality issues, and how they may have arisen.

The 'bathwater' are all the problems with diagnosis being described in this section of the book.

On the practical side, if you have for example, *'post-traumatic stress syndrome'*, that's a diagnosis and it could be useful to know you have it so people can help you with it.

If you're damaging yourself and others in close relationships, it might be useful to find out where in your developmental history it may come from and you may be able to have more constructive relationships after some good therapy.

I think psychiatry should come with a health warning and you may be better going straight into psychotherapy for some issues, but remember that psychotherapy comes with a health warning as well.

Keeping or throwing out diagnosis depends on how you view the importance of babyhood and childhood experience and how these affect beliefs and behaviours later in life, assuming of course that you don't believe that personality is all a question of genetics.

See our chapter on *Therapy* for both a discussion of therapy and also for more on the issues in relation to diagnosis.

Some issues so far

1. Diagnosis is problematic – the best and 'ideal' use of it that I can think of is as a rough guide to developmental issues (ie. identifying when and how issues arose in infancy and childhood). This can lead to the creation of a developmental picture for someone which is then individualised to help people to sort out behaviours and beliefs which can cause problems. This can be done by therapists who are competent, warm and reduce the attendant problems of power, abuse, stigma etc. It may also be used to fix issues in the present without psycho-diagnosis but beware of the 'too-quick' fix.

2. The question of whether there's any genetic or biological basis for diagnosis is often not linked to social and cultural context factors in the person's life. R. D. Laing for example saw mental illness as a journey of discovery in which, given the right conditions to do so, a person might come to new understandings that could be healing. This was a central idea in the *anti-psychiatry movement* of the 1960s.

3. There's a major problems with diagnosis in terms of accuracy. Diagnosis within the DSM is in *categories*, not in *dimensional* or *continuum* terms, nor in *personality traits*, although there are now moves to change this. What this means is that to be diagnosed as having say, a *narcissistic personality disorder*, you would need to be very extreme, but the reality is that *people are on a continuum with any particular issue* and everybody in the helping business either knows this or they should read a book on it.

4. Power-abuse is an endless topic in psychotherapy, psychiatry and psychology – see for example, Jeffrey Masson's *Against Therapy* and *The Assault on Truth*. Clients/patients frequently come with problems arising from having their trust abused as children or vulnerabilities from the misuse of power by adults when they were young, so the relationship in therapy - which usually involves an inbuilt power imbalance - has to be handled very carefully, and people have to be very careful about the amount of power they cede to the psychiatrist or

therapist. It's impossible to know how many undocumented, unproven cases exist where patients have been manipulated or exploited, sometimes for the benefit of the therapist or doctor and sometimes through family members – eg. to stop people getting their inheritances or to silence them about intra-family abuse. Thomas Szasz's take on the writer Virginia Woolf is a shocking story.

5. Another problem is the political abuse of power within psychiatry, which is documented across the world, particularly in relation to regimes where human rights are not fully protected. China and the Soviet bloc have often been accused of being in this category, but see also Clint Eastwood's film *Changeling* which gives an example of how psychiatric diagnosis was used to protect the police force in America.

6. What about other avenues? For example, people may grow out of their problems with age (yet still be stigmatised). People may become spiritual to solve issues. An example of this is the notion of the spiritual used by *Alcoholics Anonymous* as a 'higher power'.

7. The awfulness of it all – stigma, exclusion, putting people in boxes, clinical language and treatments versus love and understanding.

8. Can really hard problems for society such as *paedophilia* and *serial killing* be included as needing a human response?

9. Psycho-diagnosis is a categorisation system taken from psychiatry, designed largely to categorise, allocate resources to (or not) and manage if possible. Psychotherapy has looked into causes of problems in childhood with a view to understand/cure, even if this is an ideal. In other words, *psychological issues are handled differently by different professions*.

My experience of being diagnosed

I've been diagnosed, misdiagnosed, partly diagnosed and then diagnosed as undiagnosable. My experience of being diagnosed has been both negative and positive.

So it was a mixed-bag.

At the age of 24, I had a massive 'neurotic-level' 'nervous breakdown' which left me in a state of paralysing anxiety and regression whenever I had to travel, go out, and be in certain social situations. I had no idea what was happening to me – it was physical and psychological - it took several months to come to terms with it. The regression I experienced initially was like feeling a very young child in an adult's body – a body which was experiencing all the signs of extreme fear. As a result of this I had to pay attention and I made a decision to 'sort myself out' and 'be normal', whatever that meant. My life was turned upside-down, the future looked awful, I couldn't travel, and it was a struggle to finish my degree course.

Apart from basic human support, I had no idea how to sort out the state I was in. What I intuitively understood though was to stay away from the medical profession and avoid psychiatry. In fact, my body was telling me that I had had a difficult babyhood and childhood which had not prepared me at all for life or survival, but I didn't know this at the time. There was no choice but to find help and I entered the world of private psychotherapy. I paid for help because psychotherapy wasn't – and mostly still isn't – publicly available in the health service.

The help I received had two aspects to it and either aspect on its own would not have worked. First, I was given support, on the phone and in person, for up to 10 years, but most importantly for the first 6 years. Second, I was introduced to a wealth of knowledge of psychology which helped me understand myself and other people, normal development and psychological growth etc. Also, I was introduced to a wealth of psychological techniques, some of which worked, some of which didn't and some of which were potentially dangerous.

The therapists I worked with had an interest in babyhood issues which I only had a 'body-memory' of, and they believed that diagnosis of personality types eg. schizoid, hysteric etc. gave clues to build the 'likely story' of what happened to me as a baby and as a child. I knew some facts, I was a heavy baby, my mother was still mourning the death of her first child and I was in hospital twice before and around the first year of life without my mother for neck operations.

Understanding the effects of my early life on me was helped ultimately by diagnosis in that I was able to construct a 'likely story' and see how any early experience may have affected me. For example, once in a therapy session involving regression, my body remembered having gas during the operation - which I re-lived. One problem was that I didn't quite fit a diagnostic neurotic category. Also, later childhood experience affected me in several ways, leaving me very unconfident and unprepared for life in important ways, BUT I also learned about the good messages, love, encouragement and freedom I received as a child.

What I learned from all of this was…..

– there's a chance of solving some very difficult *'neurotic-level'* problems; I even met people from the USA who had largely solved *'psychotic-type'* issues
– I had a mixed-bag of early experience
– diagnosis, if used in the context of trying to help, understand and resolve issues can be useful (the construction of a *'likely story'*)
– psychotherapy is an art; psychiatry largely claims to be a science but generally ignores psychology and psychotherapy
– diagnosis is often used inaccurately or badly or for the wrong reasons
– diagnosis is not an academic debate – it has practical, therapeutic uses and has been an important adjunct to my healing, at times
– there is no 'quick-fix'
– once you're on a growth path, it can go on and on and on

- I've been 'labelled' and by some, wrongly labelled, and this does hurt and exclude and puts a person in a 'box', but at the same time, in my case, it helped a bit.
- it certainly helped *me* to put together a 'likely story' of *my* past
- the biggest label and one that stays until you dump it is that you are a client, patient, somehow not normal (whatever that means) and not equal
- psychopathology (a horrible word) is actually very widespread – a lot of people have gaps in their parenting, they have personality issues and thcy have difficult character traits

'Narcissism' and 'psychopathy' as individual problems and as issues for society

Please also see the start of this chapter.

If you can accept diagnostic categories as having some value, there are several personality types that can cause problems eg. schizoid, paranoid types etc. if people have these as 'heavyweight' versions. *Narcissistic* issues have until recently not been viewed as a particular problem, yet in fact Western culture itself has a 'narcissistic' flavour (see Twenge, Campbell and Lowen).

Narcissism

Probably the best and most concise writing I've seen about narcissism is a chapter by J L Shapiro and S Bernadett Shapiro in *Mental Disorders of the New Millennium.* The reason that this chapter is so good is that it describes *cultural narcissism, narcissism as a trait and as a diagnostic category, how narcissism happens through poor parenting* and its *features.*

Since about 1980, when James Masterson was writing about this topic, there's been a steady development of knowledge about narcissism and cultural narcissism; now there's a big interest and a lot of writing about this subject.

We're now living in *'narcissistic times'* – an age of image, celebrity, control etc. which explains the need for this section of the book. This section is about one of the main biases in the developed world, which is the *normalisation and incorporation into the culture* of problem personalities and behaviours and those behaviours being a model for the majority - especially narcissism and psychopathy – and we'll look at each of these in turn.

Narcissism

Narcissism is both an individual problem and an issue for society and has led to distorted beliefs, behaviour and values. It's a serious topic. It's hard to 'sort out' but narcissism is causing a lot of problems so knowledge about it is becoming very important. Thankfully, there is now a large body of knowledge which has been growing since the 1970s. A recent example of this is the 2009 book *The Narcissism Epidemic* by Jean Twenge and Keith Campbell.

It's no longer necessary to sell the idea that narcissistic individuals can cause significant problems or that narcissism has adversely influenced society – it's now more a question of *'what to do about it?'* and *'how quickly can it be done?'*

In the chapters on *Therapy* and *Emotional health* where I've looked at diagnosis, I've described both advantages and significant problems in categorising individuals with psychological issues ('psycho-diagnosis'). In this chapter, I'm dealing with a psychological issue that is distorting society. It's not the only issue doing this but it's one that until recently was not widely accepted. *It is now.*

As a reminder to ourselves, a description of the Diagnostic Statistical Manual (DSM) (described in our chapter on *Emotional and mental health*) relevant to this topic is as follows:

1. The DSM was designed as a *categorical* approach, not to find the *quantitative distribution* of a problem. Having said that, in order to be diagnosed by psychiatry as having

a narcissistic personality disorder, you'd need to be quite extreme and to have got into the clutches of psychiatry.

2. The idea of a continuum of any category (*more or less* narcissistic, for example) is and was still possible with the current DSM which is soon to be updated (to DSM-V 2013).

3. The idea of having *'narcissistic traits'* is another way of expanding the issue.

4. As more narcissists who are nasty are being found, there are even suggestions to expand the category to include *'malignant narcissists'*.

As you can imagine, for people with narcissistic issues or traits, they may be less than keen to be 'outed', labelled, etc. This is not just because it's unpleasant and because there are rights issues, etc, it's also because, for example, celebrity culture is threatened by knowledge of narcissism. There is an emphasis on secrecy, manipulation and the presentation of 'more attractive' features of narcissists and the construction of their images.

Why is all this a problem now?

I think the main reasons are as follows:

- problems with parenting – Jean Twenge and Keith Campbell are good on this

- the rise of the media. There's a question here of whether the media *reflects* or *creates* a narcissistic society and I think the answer is – *both*. The media has enormous power to create a reality (see Jean Baudrillard on *'hyper-reality'*), to create 'mind-sets' and attitudes, and to exercise control over attitudes

- a values vacuum exists in society which is serious and is not just caused by secularisation – society is influenced by the distortion narcissism gives it and in turn it fosters more narcissism – see for example Jean Twenge and Keith Campbell

- narcissists can help the global capitalist economy to go round – they can be determined, focused, achieve things, build organisations, create images and reflect values such as competitiveness, status etc. This cultural reinforcement of narcissism fosters it.

- some negative narcissistic qualities are *lack of empathy, exploitation, ruthlessness and control of others* – they have obvious disadvantages

- narcissistic behaviours have been normalised

So where does narcissism come from and how do people develop it?

Most of the understanding of narcissism comes from psychoanalysis including the work of Heinz Kohut and there are many writers such as Jean Twenge and Keith Campbell and Jerrold Lee Shapiro and Susan Bernadett Shapiro who have done extremely good work on increasing our understanding of narcissism.

There seems to be a growing consensus about the roots of narcissism. Shapiro and Shapiro believe that it's caused in children by:

- a lack of empathy/love from parents

- a big disturbance of feedback (mirroring) of a child's normal achievements and competence, for example in walking etc. This can lead to the use of an earlier kind of self-love (grandiosity) which is a serious problem for self and others.

- a decision not to incorporate an ideal of a parent but instead to look for ideals in the external world to strive for, like status

- routine or pushy encouragement to achieve in conventional terms and be competitive by parents

- an over-indulgence, often not adequate limit-setting and spoiling children

- an encouragement by parents of an 'I+U-' position and a feeling of 'specialness'

- the encouragement of a kind of personality distortion where there is a constant need for adulation

In effect, narcissists are out of touch with their real selves and develop a false self. For a better understanding of the concept of 'false self' look at work by Donald Winnicott or Masud Kahn.

The diagnostic features for narcissism in DSM-IV (Diagnostic-Statistical Manual) are that people need *five or more* of the following:

- grandiose sense of self-importance
- preoccupation with fantasies of unlimited success, power etc.
- a belief that he or she is special and can only be understood by high-status people or institutions
- requires excessive admiration
- has an extreme sense of entitlement which is unreasonable
- is interpersonally exploitative, taking advantage of other people to achieve his or her own ends
- seriously lacks empathy
- has an issue around envy
- shows arrogant behaviours and attitudes

Don't underestimate the issues. Narcissism is one of the few personality problems where the level of aggression is often high and the damage to others can be high. Certainly the level of exploitation of others is often high. I would add to the DSM list that this is a personality problem where seeking control of others is common.

Most of the literature on narcissism describes people who look good and 'successful' on the outside, often having a cultivated image but who are damaged inside and feel very empty, finding it hard to relate to others. They are not in touch with their real selves, find it hard to be empathic and close and to form relationships that work. Also, they tend to be driven to achieve and perform.

What's so difficult about narcissism?

First, it's culturally accepted and reinforced; people with a narcissistic problem can be high-achievers and don't appear as though they have an issue that leads to psychological distortion.

Second, according to the DSM and most writers on narcissism, they have very difficult behaviours for themselves and others. This can be offset by the idea that there's a continuum of narcissism from tolerable to downright destructive people, or that some people with narcissistic issues have these as 'traits' – see Shapiro and Shapiro.

Third, people with a narcissistic problem are likely to be functional, successful, grandiose and have control issues. They are known as not wanting to seek change and hard to work with in a therapeutic setting.

[Please note that controlling others, aggression (including seeking revenge), manipulation, oversensitivity, and false self are features not included in DSM but are mentioned elsewhere].

Narcissism in a wider context

Shapiro and Shapiro state that there's a debate as to whether narcissistic behaviour is damaging to society but that narcissistic politicians are dangerous.

My view is that the use of power includes empathy, allowing freedom, rights, etc. and that narcissistic issues of manipulation, control and exploitation have no place in any power structure, whether it's in government or elsewhere.

There are times in history when different personality types have been in vogue. For example, in early Christian times, to populate the monasteries, *'withdrawn'* personality types were needed –for example, in DSM category terms *'paranoid'* or *'schizoid'* personality types. In a war, for example, World War II, society makes use of people who can kill without too much fuss – for example, the diagnostic category, *'psychopaths'*. It seems that we're in times where the DSM category *'narcissists'* is popular - until too much damage is done.

A need for control, lack of empathy, grandiosity and manipulation can help governments, companies and managers achieve goals and make 'tough decisions' – the problem is that this is often at a great cost to the people they control and manipulate, neither does it foster psychological, organisational health.

There's a move in TV programmes and popular magazines to start talking about DSM-style diagnostic categories and narcissism is being discussed in popular culture more and more and is being increasingly identified in criminal court cases and in news reports.

Relationship problems

Most of the psychological categories in DSM of personality types can cause problems in relationships and people with a narcissistic issue are no exception. There's now a growing field of writing on this subject.

A 2004 example is Joan Lachkar's *The Narcissistic/Borderline Couple* – this book though seems to over-extend diagnostic categories. People with narcissistic false selves are not operating from their real self – their core – and they lack emotional depth. There's a built-in problem with intimacy, trust and attachment, apart from all the other issues.

According to the psychoanalyst Heinz Kohut, one of the key problems with narcissism can be a *tendency to rage* in relation what are experienced as slights to the sense of self. Narcissists have a sense of self invested in being in control and in being perfect. They can feel the need for revenge often expressed through angry accusations and groundless attacks on the person who has dared to criticise them – or whom they *imagine* might be critical of them. To others the rage can seem unpredictable, unreasonable and without cause, but to the narcissist there is a need to destroy the person who has (often unwittingly) shaken the narcissist's sense of psychological safety, and thereby re-establish their own self-esteem. This process can be damaging to interpersonal and intimate relationships.

Good news

People with a narcissistic issue can learn to be more human but it takes time and effort. As narcissism is better understood and brought to a wider audience, it will be more recognised as psychologically distorted and the distortions in the wider culture have more chance of being fixed.

Joan Lachkar's book *How to Talk to a Narcissist,* which taps into Heinz Kohut's ideas on 'empathology', is an example of the stirrings of interest in how to deal with this challenge.

The person-centred therapist Margaret Warner describes her work with people in *'fragile process'*, often those with schizoid or narcissistic tendencies. Linking with work by Heinz Kohut, Margaret Warner believes that using intricately attentive listening, careful, accurate empathic responding and keeping the environment very stable can be helpful for people with difficulties like narcissistic tendencies, who feel at root that their very right to existence in the world is in question. She believes that saying the wrong thing and not understanding the fragility of the 'self' of the patient/client could result in them giving up therapy, whilst conversely the person may take time to benefit from and value the 'holding' that this kind of therapist could offer, perhaps in great contrast to most other people in their life (or in their infancy).

Psychopaths – do we love or hate them?

Robert Hare, whose diagnostic system for psychopathy is probably the most used has just co-authored a book with Paul Babias called *Snakes in Suits* where he describes the 'personality type' of 'psychopath' in a work setting. The psychologist Oliver James has also recently authored a book on similar territory: *Office Politics: How to Survive in a World of Lying, Backstabbing and Dirty Tricks.* Also I would recommend Martin Kantor's *The Psychopathy of Everyday Life: How Anti-social Personality Disorder Affects All of Us.* All of these authors have worked for a greater general understanding of 'psychopaths' and there is now a groundswell of interest and knowledge building which is similar to the interest in narcissism.

Robert Hare lists *features of psychopaths* including, for example, manipulativeness and lack of empathy, but as with narcissists, in order to be *diagnosed* as a psychopath, you would need to be pretty extreme. The less extreme 'white collar' psychopaths are described by Robert Hare and mentioned by Martin Kantor. These people are likely to be found in all middle-class professions, including the banking system.

At the start of this chapter we've tried to express some of the issues involved in psychopathology which we think it's important to be aware of. So with all the 'health warnings' and complexity, there is now a lot of interest in people whose behaviour can damage others or society. Highlighted in this chapter are the issues around 'psychopaths' and 'narcissists' but other problems can also cause damage too both at societal level and in personal relationships.

There are a number of categories that are only briefly covered in worldwide psychiatric diagnostic systems. It's possible for example to find classic examples of 'introverts' and 'extraverts' (see Carl Jung and Hans Eysenck) if you want to.

There's also the growing fields of forensic psychology and psychiatry which throw additional light on the issues. Hervey Cleckley based his 1941 book *The Mask of Sanity* on interviews

241

with incarcerated psychopaths. Cleckley tended to concentrate on men and the potential for violent behaviour, so reinforcing the idea (not necessarily correct) that psychopathy was more a disorder of masculinity. Cleckley's basic material is nevertheless still relevant today and became the foundation of our understanding about the problem. Robert D Hare has built on Cleckley's work in recent years and developed the internationally-renowned Hare Psychopath Checklist (PCL-R) and the version used for screening people for psychopathy and assessing the risk of recidivism in psychopathic criminals.

DSM is the main diagnostic system for psychopathology, and categorises psychopaths as having an *'anti-social personality disorder'*. There's been a big increase in forensic psychology in recent years, including greater knowledge about the brain, and this understanding of psychopathy is outside the psychiatric DSM system. This understanding of the so-called 'criminal mind' is growing parallel to the clinical/psychiatric classificatory system.

Psychopaths and society

Society is not as normal as we might think, and people with psychopathology are (without being paranoid!) 'everywhere'. Psychopathology is affecting our Western culture so that it is no longer clear exactly what *is* normal. As mentioned previously, the normalisation of pathology in society is I think partly caused by the abundance of opportunity for this to happen eg. in the media and celebrity world, but it's also caused by the break-up and questioning of an overtly more rigid moral structure since World War I.

Both extreme psychopaths and non-extreme ones go into fields like banking or become celebrities. Many of the people at the head of large and influential organisations have psychopathic aspects to their personalities, consistent with Paul Babiak and Robert Hare's suggestion that psychopathic characteristics can go well with leadership traits.

There are times where, however unpalatable, we've chosen to depend on psychopaths. For example, in extreme war situations and battles where we tend to recruit people for key roles who are not paralysed by empathy for the enemy or unduly concerned about ethics. In everyday life, some TV programmes revel in exposing people's flaws and frailties, demonstrating the grandiosity and insensitivity of the programme makers and presenters who are motivated by the desire to create excitement and are not averse to manipulating, tricking and humiliating the participants, strategies which have nevertheless been found to be entertaining and moneymaking.

Perhaps the most distressing thing about psychopathic people is that they often hide their lack of emotion, they pretend that they love, they charm and seduce us whilst shafting us behind the scenes. If this is the kind of personality we are promoting and encouraging, we're building a world in which there can be no trust.

What are psychopathic characteristics?

You can look these up, but some major features are:

- a lack of empathy
- preference for excitement
- manipulative behaviour, more so than with narcissists
- lying

Comparison with narcissism

Comparing narcissism with psychopathy, it's not easy to compare these as they overlap, but there are some differences.

The psychological damage for narcissists happens at around the age of 2 but much earlier for psychopaths.

Psychopaths are generally:

1. More manipulative than narcissists – usually they deal in webs of lies and it's very hard to keep up with them.

2. Narcissists are generally colder, appearing more serious, and are less superficially 'warm/human/charming'.

3. Narcissists often have a more fragile ego and self-esteem than psychopaths.

4. Psychopaths are often more 'edgy' and unpredictable and also often more impulsive.

5. Narcissists can seem more socially conformist than psychopaths who are OK with being 'original'.

6. Both narcissists and psychopaths are controlling but the feel of their control can differ – psychopaths' control can seem more basic and is around coercion and dominance.

Some plus sides to psychopaths

Since psychopaths often show no remorse and are exploitative, they can use people, exploit people, spend their money, waste people's money, etc. – thus can be efficient in our current world of 'value-free' capitalism (see our chapter *The Crisis We're In*). But could some of these qualities actually sometimes be *necessary*?

The research psychologist Kevin Dutton suggests that the qualities of psychopaths are ubiquitous – that *most of us share* some *elements of psychopathy to different degrees.* In particular, the ability to cut off from our emotions and deliver outcomes at the rational, cognitive level is one that he believes is key to the era we're living in. If we can add to our repertoire the ability to be charming and to not spend time ruminating on where we went wrong, getting straight on to the next job, we could probably make it to senior positions in our companies and institutions.

Because we're living in a scientific-rational era.

It's our contention that we need people to feel their emotions much more and to cultivate compassion and sensitivity to others, and to be in touch with the impact of their actions on others. However, there may well be times such as in warfare, in law courts and prison work, or in administering medical procedures and doing surgery, when too much awareness of the impact on others could be counter-productive and where a degree of psychopathy could be helpful.

Can we improve things for people with personality disorders who want to change?

Martin Kantor says that mild psychopaths are accessible and capable of some changes.

Summary

In summary then, it's important that we recognise that diagnosis is an incomplete way of assessing people – people are not pure 'types' – they are much more than that, and it's potentially dangerous and damaging to assume that they are just a 'type'. *It's an offence to human rights to treat people purely on the basis of assumed pathological personality characteristics.*

This is a complex domain but we can be alerted to the possibilities that people are not always what they seek to present, and that we need to be aware that people around us may not always have our best interests at heart, even if they say they do!

In close relationships, understanding psychopathology can help us to have compassion for the lack of insight that our partners or relatives may have into their own condition, whilst giving us the ability to protect and defend ourselves from emotional damage. At best, we can help people we care about to get support to change.

At the level of the workplace, consumer organisations, public and even religious institutions, we can be aware that people with damaging personalities may be seizing the initiative inappropriately and that others around them may be letting them out of fear, lack of awareness, their own needs, traditions, being hoodwinked, a need for particular outcomes, laziness or bewilderment.

We can decide that we at least will be 'on the ball'.

Part 2: Julia

In this section, I'm commenting on the effect of personality and emotional problems within close relationships. There are links to the rest of this chapter, to the chapter on *Close Relationships*, and to chapters on *Therapy, Effective Relating* and *The Self*.

The implications of biological and genetic breakthroughs in *psychosis*

The psychoanalyst, Darian Leader, has pointed out that we're in an era of significant breakthroughs in the field of biology and genetic science, with the result that more diagnosis – particularly of *psychosis* - can be based on a *disease* model. Contrary to the rhetoric that this makes it easier for people because they cannot have defended themselves against a physical disorder, Darian Leader believes that this carries the risk of *greater* stigmatisation and potential segregation (particularly of *psychotic* patients) as well as leading to treatment programmes that offer medication and require social compliance.

Darian Leader believes that psychological understanding and listening to patients' words offers a more hopeful, lasting and ultimately respectful outcome for people than programmes that discount what the patient is actually saying and attempt to replace patients' own thinking with ways of thinking developed by the therapists (or that actually *are* the transfer of therapist thinking to the patient's mind). In his book *What is madness?*, Darian Leader expresses concern about the way in which psychiatric systems often process people with psychosis without reference to their individuality and essentially do 'violence' to the 'culture and history' of the person by presenting a moral critique that makes the patient understand their own world as 'wrong'. His work, based on Jacques Lacan's ideas, helps us to understand the psychotic worldview and the struggle to know what *is* one's own world and what is *coming in from the outside* – because of these difficulties, we must be very careful about how we go about imposing treatment models which inevitably *are* outside the person.

Sometimes we want to relate to people at a level below surface consciousness – and indeed, doing so lets us into deep communication, and in such communication we can often ignore the words involved because something other than words matters. However, to consciously decide to ignore someone's words - someone's attempt to express their inner concerns – because we know better is to deny the value of that person's existence.

Personality and emotional problems in close relationships

Problems that affect relating can include *chronic or recurrent depression, bipolar* mood swings, flipping in and out of *psychotic states*, and personality disorders (such as *narcissism* and *paranoia*). Or there might be signs of disorders like *mild autism, Asperger's Syndrome*, or the early stages of *dementia* and *Alzheimer's disease*. Sometimes symptoms like *memory lapses, irritability* and *aggression, inertia* or *depression* and *anxiety* can accompany physical illness that has not yet been acknowledged or identified, or be related to taking particular medications. A number of medications and conditions can affect *sexual response. Over-use of alcohol, prescription medication, recreational drugs*, and *eating disorders* – which are all common in today's world, can all lead to problems, affecting for example how we feel about sex, the kinds of moods we are in on a day-to- day basis, and the potential for interpersonal conflict.

Many of our symptoms can be triggered or exacerbated by external factors such as *increasing debt, fears about economic survival, problems with housing, the challenges of parenting or looking after dependent relatives, accidents, chronic stress or overwork at work, bullying* etc. It can be difficult to face up to these and to take any action – simply recognising what is happening can be a first step towards change in the long-term.

At the beginning of relationships, things can seem good – the 'honeymoon period' during which companionship and sex can bring increased happiness. It can take time for problems deep within a person's psychology to become evident. It's helpful to see whether patterns in a person's behaviour are intractable or modifiable, mild or potentially damaging, rarely noticed or severely distressing, and if the person is aware or unaware of the impact they have on others - at some point, we make a choice about what we can live with. We also have to look squarely at our own psyche to discern if we too have a makeup that results in problems in relating. It's necessary for all of us to develop the capacity to imagine what another person might be feeling and to amend or shape our own behaviour and speech in relation to their needs and sensitivities – not too much and not too little - *being unable to do this may be the biggest stumbling block to successful relating that exists.*

Is it 'them' or is it 'us'?

There is a whole literature on *'co-dependency'* and whether we are participating in particular kinds of relationships because of problems of our own. This is not just about addictions such as alcoholism but may also relate to our ability to dovetail with particular disorders such as offering *'narcissistic supply'* to people who need admiration and reassurance, identified by psychoanalysts such as Otto Fenichel in 1938. Whilst this may be a useful way to look at our current relationship, and can help us to become aware of things we do that perpetuate problematic ways of relating, it's also important to look at ourselves in a more holistic way and not just in terms of how we 'match' or 'fit' the psyche of someone else, and to avoid blaming ourselves for someone else's problems.

This is a tricky area – it's important not to think of ourselves as OK and our partner or relative as the one who *'has something wrong with them'* – ie. not-OK. It's always best to look for OK-OK relating (see chapter on *Transactions*), and to look together if we can at where the problems lie. Looking back at previous relationships to see if we're repeating a pattern or if this is the first person with whom we've encountered difficulty can help us to see what is going on. However, it may also be a time in our life when with someone we love or trust, our own problems finally surface or we feel able to face up to them.

Sometimes when one person goes for help and starts to get 'better', their partner starts to crumble – their problems having been masked by the focus being on the one who 'officially' has 'problems'. It's important to be really honest with ourselves – have we been 'rescuing' our partner instead of tackling our own problems, or have we been unassertive in claiming space and time for ourselves, ignoring warning signs because we were looking after our partners. It can be too easy to scapegoat our partner, getting sympathy or other 'secondary gains' for enduring the challenges of life with a difficult or troubled person instead of admitting that we too have issues we should be tackling.

Working out what's 'normal'

Psychological difficulties in relationships that we thought were inevitable and intractable (and somehow 'normal') might be treatable through medication or psychotherapy or made manageable with regular support or access to a helpline. Sometimes the reason we don't realise this is that *similar patterns were present in our early years* and we think they *are* 'normal'. As we go through life and meet a variety of people, it may one day dawn on us that our 'normality' is different from other people's, and we might discover that we don't have to suffer as we thought we had to. On the other hand, it's worthwhile not measuring our relationship against idealised portrayals in drama or in magazines or even against the social presentation that our friends and associates give us. The reality of close relationships may be very different.

> *After several years of living near to an older neighbour who had a consistently cheerful, affectionate and vibrant personality, things suddenly erupted with the relative who lived with her and police vans were called to the house. It transpired that over the years, the relative had regularly shouted and physically attacked her and she'd often been in fear. We'd never known and she'd kept things hidden until she couldn't any longer. What had appeared as a calm and loving family relationship had been quite different under the surface.*

Sometimes we or our partner may be avoiding facing changes or not recognising what is happening. Sometimes florid emotional expression or a lack of response may have become normalised for us, but something – or someone - makes us start to realise that it isn't actually 'the norm'.

> *I remember when my friends starting having babies and watching them hug their infants, telling them they loved them and delighting in their company. I used to think 'how soppy' and be faintly embarrassed for them. When it happened again and again with different people, I suddenly had the realisation that* their behaviour might actually be 'the norm' *and that it was* me *who was unused to affectionate touch and expressions of love,* me *who in fact may not have had not had that kind of response as an infant myself. It was a shocking moment of insight.*

The times we're in

Our mental states often respond to the times we're in, not just because they do, but also because there are fashions in medicine, pressures from institutions like the pharmaceutical industry (which is good at 'inventing' new disorders), and cultural shifts during which people are 'minded' to view certain problems through particular lenses. Indeed there are different ways of seeing sadness and distress within different cultures – Cecil Helman, the medical anthropologist, for example pointed out that some cultures resist the split between emotions and cognitions that are often prevalent in the West, and medical practitioners view *physical* symptoms as indicators of *psychological* distress. In some cultures, the person who presents with disorder is seen as the catalyst for healing of a community, through ceremonies or shamanic practices which are designed to resolve conflicts, ease social tension, and release painful emotions within a social group, rather than being viewed as an individual in need of treatment, criticism or punishment which tends to be the Western response.

The writer Lisa Appignanesi (2008) suggests that illness often reflects the preoccupations of an era, eating disorders for example being common during times of abundance. Her work on women and psychiatry *Mad, Bad and Sad* is in the tradition of a number of writers who have observed the relationship between women's position within the culture and how their psychology has been 'constructed'. The feminist academic psychologist Phyllis Chesler

(1972) suggested that women who dared to step beyond the expectations for their gender and did not fit the ideal of mental health – essentially (at that time) a male construct – were frequently classified as mentally ill and in need of treatment to get them to adjust to their domestic and caring roles. This question of assessment and classification systems being culturally-biased is also touched upon in our chapter on *Creativity* in relation to intelligence-testing. The feminist psychoanalysts and founders of women's therapy centres in London and New York, Luise Eichenbaum and Susie Orbach, have made significant contributions to the literature on women's psychology as well as to the understanding of eating disorders in feminist terms.

In 2011, the UK voluntary organisation MIND released a new set of guidelines *Delivering Male* regarding men and mental health, recognising that men often avoid getting help for emotional problems and sometimes even have difficulty recognising that they have such difficulties. Making mental health services more men-friendly is a key objective. Keeping an eye on changing ideas about men and masculinity may be a good idea if you want to understand the context of men in your life or yourself as a man. The sociologist Jeff Hearn has been working in this field for decades including looking at men and sexuality and men and violence and has recently co-authored a book about masculinity across the globe.

Increasing our understanding of stressors

Most people's mental conditions, like their physical health, vary according to what is going in their life. Whilst we should not acquiesce to someone simply because they are aggressive or frightened (except perhaps to defuse a dangerous situation), *reducing stress* will usually help most people's behaviour to become calmer and can allow the space to start mutual exploration and problem-solving.

Sometimes *keeping a diary record* can help to identify patterns, cycles, triggers and things which help. Stress usually emerges from a build-up of pressures so it may take some time to truly reduce the effect of a variety of pressures. And it may also take time to discover *how* some things are stressing us (for example because they are echoes of similar things in childhood).

Researching problems ourselves and getting help

Putting our emotional struggles into perspective can be helpful. For example, estimates suggest that 1 in 4 of people in Britain has a *'mental health problem'*. According to the *UK Mental Health Foundation*, women are more likely to report *anxiety* and *depression* symptoms whilst men are much more likely to be dependent on *alcohol* or *drugs*, and 70% of people in prison have two or more *'mental disorders'*. It's often thought that women turn inwards and men turn outwards with their anger.

Data from the *Equality Trust* confirms that *'mental illness'* is more common in richer countries and in countries where there's greater inequality, so in the current economic crisis where disparities abound, it's likely to be on the increase. Richard Wilkinson and Kate Pickett's work underlines the damaging effect of *perceived inequity* on mental and physical health. There may be many reasons why mental illness might be more prevalent in different countries – for example, we know that where there is strong social support, most of us are able to look after our health better, and conversely, when we're isolated, atomised, lonely (as in much of the West) and under stress, we don't do so well. On the other hand, living with the fear of violence or abuse as people in many poor and war-conflicted areas of the world, do, won't do much for mental health either, but of course, distress in those circumstances may be seen as a rational response rather than as mental disorder.

We can help ourselves by reading up and finding out all we can, thus learning to understand ourselves and our partner's needs. There are a number of websites, organisations and groups where research on relevant material is available and support and guidance found. If a problem is beyond our own capacity to deal with, then contacting a relevant specialist voluntary organisation or a general one like MIND in the UK or our local doctor are possibilities, as well as considering discussion with a community psychiatric nurse or getting a referral to psychological or psychiatric services. Voluntary organisations often offer group meetings where over

252

time people can gain new understandings as well as meeting others with similar problems, thus reducing the feeling of isolation and uniqueness.

Leaving one person to battle it out alone in therapy etc. as one-half of a relationship is not the ideal – tackling things as a couple will often be the best course of action. Take an interest in how they are doing and find out what you can do to support them or change patterns. In the end, both parties have to engage with the decision to improve things – it's no good dragging someone into help if ultimately they're not ready to tackle things, but equally sometimes it's only when confronted by a new insight or idea or given a new form of support that someone may be prompted out of lethargy or hopelessness into new optimism. It's worth remembering the adage – *'the only thing we can change is our selves'*. Also *'the only thing we can change is our attitude to a problem'* can be a useful piece of advice – trying to change the behaviour and attitudes of someone close to us is not a legitimate goal – *'they have to want to change'*.

Stigma

Sometimes the fear of getting labelled and having our carefully-nurtured identities 'spoiled' can prevent us taking action. Yet worrying about this over-much can mean that we soldier on with painful and destructive situations for too long. The important thing is to think of diagnosis as something that can be a two-way process – things are not as clear-cut as the medical profession might like them to appear and we can have some say in when and what diagnosis is made.

Private psychotherapy and other 'alternative therapies' can often help us remain outside the official record-keeping system, especially as therapists have a strong commitment to confidentiality. This can reduce the possibility of feeling or being stigmatised by a label – this can be worth thinking about if this is a consideration in relation to employment status. It's worth looking at our chapter on *Therapy,* if private therapy is on the agenda. The film *The King's Speech* offers a moving account of the struggle for the monarch to find and accept therapy.

Doctors in the state system are often willing to 'negotiate' with patients about the nature of the diagnosis and the choice of treatment (and no doubt in the private system too). Some of our choices depend on the kind of relationship we already have with our regular doctor. Our chapter on *The Body* includes quite a lot of material about relating to doctors and also material about the mental state of doctors themselves!

I worked for more than 30 full-time years in higher education, teaching mainly social workers, nurses, and medical students, as well as people who worked in fields like banking, tourism, public administration, and engineering. Over those years, there were times where the circumstances of my life were tough – post-natal depression after the birth of my daughter, losing my home, relationship breakdown, bereavement, etc. and if I needed time off, I had to go and ask for a sick note.

I think that there was a negotiation each time with doctors – I often expected to be diagnosed as depressed even though it would often take something physical to get me into the surgery but doctors usually went on the presenting symptom such as 'exhaustion', 'abdominal pain', 'headaches' or 'post-viral'. My experience is that doctors tended not to dig too deep unless they had to and they like to deal with what's in front of them before rushing into things that could change our future forever. I don't think they're keen to label us unless we push for that. The point is that we often feel relieved when we get a diagnosis, sometimes whatever it is.

I found too that if I went with a report on what I was doing about things like 'going to Citizens Advice for financial help, getting some counselling re: my relationship problems or bereavement, taking some long walks, resting, cutting things out of my diet', doctors would be impressed with my taking control and be less inclined to insist on any formulaic treatments plans of their own as well as being more willing to give me time off work to sort things out. Unless a person is a danger to themselves or to others, there's usually room to share decision-making over any in-patient care or medication regimes, but you have to be clear about what you think is best for you and why.

It's also worth noting that research has at times offered us evidence that there are patterns in diagnosis that can tend to label people according to their social class, sexual identity, gender, age, and cultural background. We should not walk blindly into a situation where someone is likely to 'diagnose' us from a power position – we should do all our research beforehand and be ready to offer our own opinion. We should aim to get professionals on our side rather than accepting any social distancing from them. We can question any rush into 'labelling', and argue instead for help with *symptoms* rather than the identification of a *whole syndrome* for a while, until things are clearer.

Voluntary and campaigning organisations have often done a lot to dispel stigma and connecting up with these via websites and meetings can be very helpful. Ultimately, rather than fearing stigmatisation, we can decide to be open about our own condition and add to the growing number of people who are working to break down barriers and fear in the general population about psychopathology – and indeed, many health conditions too. Getting our doctors, nurses, social workers and therapists to play a role in defining 'our story' in a way that is not stigmatising can be an interesting and valuable challenge – the control of self-presentation should remain with us.

Sadly, sometimes it's people in our life who find it difficult to deal with how we are – perhaps not inviting us round or keeping us away from particular friends or relatives, being uneasy about admitting they are close to you to others, failing to stand up for us if we appear to behave outside the general 'norm' in social situations etc., or trying to minimise our difficulties rather than listening fully to what we're going through and trying to understand. Spending time to allay fears, provide information, and spell out what we need, can be worthwhile.

Sometimes we will have to accept the pain of letting people go from our life who can't share our journey - it may be unacceptable to us to have their prejudice and fear in our life or too painful to deal with their feelings of embarrassment and shame. We may have to take some time out from them until they find a way to change, if they can.

One of the best ways to reduce stigma is to remind people through our words and our behaviour that we have a range of roles in life and a variety of coping strategies – our mental health does not have to dominate our identity. Developing strategies which help to make our behaviour more predictable and manageable and informing people of possible triggers such as work overload and stress can also reduce other people's fears.

As always, there's both an individual response and a societal response to the question. In the UK, a number of organisations are working to reduce stigma and discrimination in relation to mental health issues. The *Time to Change* programme is the biggest new initiative launched by the charities *MIND* and *Rethink Mental Illness*, and is funded by the *Department of Health* and *Comic Relief*. The Royal College of Psychiatrists also has ongoing work in this field following their programme *Changing Minds*. One of the main aims of these kinds of intervention is to make people more aware that people can't just 'snap out' of mental health problems, to disseminate information and debunk myths.

To stay or to go?

Sadly, it may be the case that the mental makeup of someone close to us is so problematic that it's too hard for us to stay with them, and if that's the case, we should get support to separate. It's not a good idea to stay with someone if our own personality and/or life is being destroyed or if the other person is reluctant to take any steps to improve things. Nothing is clear-cut – sometimes we stay over-long, hoping for shifts that never happen, and afraid of regretting that we didn't stay if we leave without giving change a chance. Sometimes, if we're caught in an agonising dilemma, an interim break can help – going away for a short period, going on a retreat, getting a new base where we can stay away sometimes or agreeing to a trial separation. There are always risks with this strategy but usually it will give both parties a jolt and time to re-assess.

For some, talking to an 'outsider' will be the first step in breaking away from the symbiosis of madness that we can feel we're in. If we're afraid that the person we're close to may take their own life or fall apart or take action against us, we have to face up to these possibilities and in Susan Jeffers' terms, *'feel the fear'* anyway. Checking the statistics on the likelihood of this can be helpful, as can informing ourselves about suicide risks.

We may have to make the painful choice about effectively sacrificing our own lives to keep someone else going, or breaking free and finding out if they can make it without so much support from us. Sometimes we'll be surprised at the outcomes – sometimes people are able to replace us with someone else faster than we expected. *And we may have to face up to what we've been avoiding in our own lives.*

Psychological health and personal autonomy

As well as steadily increasing materialism, a cultural shift has taken place during the second half of the twentieth century, particularly in America but also across the globe, such that many of us in affluent societies have come to expect that *personal autonomy* is our right and that *self-actualisation* and *personal fulfilment* are entitlements. When this doesn't work out and we feel constrained by our roles as spouses, children, parents, employees, citizens etc. we've been encouraged to define our problems as *individual pathology* and as amenable to treatment or intervention, thus obscuring contextual factors such as economic pressure, repressive government policies, the all-pervasiveness of commerce, the propaganda nature of the media, and the decline of religious authority.

John Steadman Rice has written about the rise of *'liberation psychotherapy'* in the 1960s which persuaded us that *challenging conformity to social norms* is the pathway to psychological health – personal autonomy being the hallmark of a healthy person. Although this is the view that we take in this book, there are at least three provisos:

    a.   self-actualisation which ignores the impact on people close to us is not a mature or healthy position, and is not ultimately likely to bring us lasting joy or inner peace

b. individual growth without reference to the needs of society around us is unlikely to help the planet – we need to rebuild community and bonds between people if we are to survive as a human race.

c. the idea that antagonism between self and society is 'normal' is not a psychological issue – a scepticism about 'truth' and 'untruths' in society in our view *is* healthy and it's useful to remember that *'liberation psychotherapy'* emerged in a period of general freeing-up of society in the West the 1960s and 70s with much unrest (students, gays, black civil rights etc). This is not the same as developing *paranoia* where our distrust in 'reality' and our perception becomes overwhelming and where medication and psycho-therapy can help.

Emotional conformity

As we've said, one of the difficult things to get right is to determine how 'normal' emotional expression and experience actually is, and diagnosis will inevitably be made in the context of the times and the prevailing ideas about what is acceptable.

Frank Furedi, a British social commentator, has written about the *emotional conformity* that he believes is now rife in Western society, with the pressure to get our emotions sorted out by going into therapy or doing things like developing our *'emotional intelligence'* (Daniel Goleman) or *'emotional literacy'* (Claude Steiner). Approaches like these in Furedi's view are based on predetermined ideas about how we should feel and how we should express or contain feelings. Furedi suggests that we're encouraged to get in touch with our vulnerability and to see ourselves as sick, stressed, depressed etc. rather than getting authentically angry about external circumstances and feeling empowered to tackle the state of the world. He sees this state of general powerlessness linked to a widespread disengagement with the real political process – in this he alerts us to the need to question our attachment to therapy and to the medicalisation of economic, social and political problems.

It's of course true that every therapeutic model has an idea about what is 'healthy' and they won't all be the same, ideas sometimes reflecting the personalities of their founders. And organisations often have rules too about appropriate behaviour. We should feel free to resist styles of relating being imposed upon us (see Darian Leader's book) if they don't suit us. The era of narcissism that we seem to be in is increasingly being counterbalanced by writers on neglected personality characteristics like 'quietness' (Susan Cain) and 'timidity' (Polly Morland). We should however aim to use therapy and the development of our emotional repertoires to help us in our social activism rather than letting 'being distressed' become a normal or 'normalised' way of living. Instead of being afraid of our anger or our timidity, we should learn to channel these energies for good in the world.

Money and happiness

There's some evidence that 'winning the lottery' does result ultimately in greater 'happiness' for most winners over time (though initially there is some stress) according to research by Andrew Oswald at Warwick University. Yet, according to the psychologist Oliver James, in his work on *'affluenza'*, greater prosperity has not brought happiness to Britons. In fact, in recent years, the many factors involved in gaining more prosperity - such as increased work stress, seeing our children and partners less, and increased personal borrowing - have helped people to realise that money in itself can't compensate fundamentally for the losses in other areas of our lives – social, emotional, relationship, health, creativity and spiritual domains. The difference between 'lottery winners' and most of us is that we imagine that they can have unlimited time to cultivate the good things in life – from gardening to seeing their children frequently, and to make choices about how they live. Yet if we're prepared to let go of material goods, we too can allow more space for those things that are associated with the quality of life like engaging with nature, being creative, parenting properly, and being a loving partner – things which ultimately will strengthen our mental health.

Final thoughts

There is I think likely to be even more evidence for real satisfaction and optimism to emerge in our lives if we **take control of what's happening to us and work with others (if needed) to sustain our own wellbeing.** This I think will be as true at the *macro-level* of engaging with wider society for positive change as it will be at the *micro-level* of our personal relationships and inner psychological world.

Books and papers

Lisa Appignanesi (2008) *Mad, Bad or Sad: a history of women and the mind doctors from 1800 to the present* Virago
Paul Babias and Robert D Hare (2006) *Snakes in Suits: When Psychopaths Go to Work* Regan Books
Jean Baudrillard (1994) *The Illusion of the End* Polity Press
Tom Burns (2006) *Psychiatry: a very short introduction* Oxford
Susan Cain (2012) *Quiet: The Power of Introverts in a World that Can't Stop Talking* Viking
Phyllis Chesler (1972) *Women and Madness* Allen Lane
Hervey Cleckley (1941) (1988 5th ed) *The Mask of Sanity* William A Dolan
Kevin Dutton *The Wisdom of Psychopaths -- What Saints, Spies, and Serial Killers Can Teach Us About Success* Scientific America/FSG
Kevin Dutton: http://www.smithsonianmag.com/science-nature/The-Pros-to-Being-a-Psychopath-176019901.html#ixzz2Lw1mBYdv
Luise Eichenbaum and Susie Orbach (1983) (1994 ed) *What Do Women Want?* Harper Collins
Hans J Eysenck (1971) *Readings in Extraversion-Introversion* New York: Wiley
Otto Fenichel (1938) *The Drive to Amass Wealth* Psychoanalytic Quarterly **7**: 69–95
Frank Furedi (2003) *Therapy Culture: Cultivating Vulnerability in an Uncertain Age* Routledge
Erving Goffman (1963) *Stigma: Notes on the Management of a Spoiled Identity* Prentice-Hall/Penguin Books

Robert D Hare (1999) *Without Conscience* in: Thomas G Plante (2006) *Mental Disorders of the New Millennium* Vol 1 Behavioral Issues Westport: Praeger

Cecil G Helman (2007) *Culture, Health and Illness* Hodder Arnold

Linda Hopkins (2006) *False Self: A Life of Masud Khan* Karnac Books

Oliver James (2007) *Affluenza* Random House/Vermilion

Susan Jeffers (1987, 2007 edition) *Feel The Fear and Do It Anyway* Vermilion/Random House

Martin Kantor (2006) *The Psychopathy of Everyday Life: How Antisocial Personality Disorder Affects All of Us* Praegor

Masud Khan (1974) *The Privacy of the Self* Karnac Books

Heinz Kohut (1971). *The analysis of the self: A systematic approach to the psychoanalytic treatment of narcissistic personality disorders*. Perspectives.

Joan Lachkar (2004) *The Narcissistic/Borderline Couple* New York: Brummer/Routledge

Joan Lachkar (2008) *How to Talk to a Narcissist* Routledge

Laing, R.D. (1960) *The Divided Self: An Existential Study in Sanity and Madness*. Harmondsworth: Penguin.

Christopher Lasch (1979) *The Culture of Narcissism* New York: W W Norton & Co.

Darian Leader (2011) *What is madness?* Penguin: Hamish Hamilton

Peter Longerich (2012) *Joseph Goebbels: Biographie* Pantheon Verlag (German version)

Alexander Lowen (1984) (2004) *Narcissism: Denial of the True Self* Simon and Schuster

Jeffrey Masson (1989) *Against Therapy* London: Collins

Jeffrey Masson (1984) (1992 edition) *The Assault on Truth: Freud and Child Sexual Abuse* London: Harper Collins/Fontana

James E Masterson (1988) *The Search for the Real Self: Unmasking the Personality Disorders of Our Age* Free Press/Simon and Schuster

Alice Miller (1990) *The Untouched Key: Tracing Childhood Trauma in Creativity and Destructiveness* Virago

Alice Miller (2005) *The Body Never Lies: The Lingering Effects of Cruel Parenting* Norton

Polly Morland (2013) *The Society of Timid Souls* Profile

David Owen (1987) *In Sickness and in Power: Illness in the Heads of Government during the last 100 years* Methuen

John Steadman Rice (1998) *A Disease of One's Own: Psychotherapy, Addiction and the Emergence of Co-dependency* Transaction Publishers

Elisabetta Ruspini, Jeff Hearn, Bob Pease and Keith Pringle (eds.) (2011) *Men and Masculinities around the World: Transforming Men's Practices* Palgrave Macmillan

Jacqui Lee Schiff and Beth Day (1970) (1974 ed) *All My Children* Pyramid Books

Jerrold Lee Shapiro and Susan Bernadett Shapiro *Narcissism: Greek Tragedy, Psychological Syndrome and Cultural Norm* in Thomas G Plante (2006) *Mental Disorders of the New Millennium* Vol 1 Behavioral Issues Westport: Praeger

Martha Stout (2007) *The Sociopath Next Door* Bantam/Doubleday/Dell

Thomas Szasz (1961, 1977) *The Myth of Mental Illness: Foundations of a Theory of Personal Conduct.* Harper & Row

Thomas Stephen Szasz (2006) *"My Madness Saved Me": The Madness and Marriage of Virginia Woolf* Transaction Publishers

Toby Thacker (2009) *Joseph Goebbels: Life and Death* Palgrave Macmillan

Jean M Twenge and W Keith Campbell (2009) *The Narcissism Epidemic: Living in the Age of Entitlement* Free Press/Simon and Schuster.

Margaret S Warner (1991) *Fragile process* in L. Fusek (ed) *New directions in client-centered therapy: practice with difficult client populations* (Monograph Series 1). Chicago: Chicago Counseling and Psychotherapy Center, 41-58.
http://www.focusingresources.com/articles/fragileprocess.html

Richard Wilkinson and Kate Pickett (2009,2010) *The Spirit Level: Why Equality is Better for Everyone* Penguin Books

Donald W Winnicott (1960) *Ego Distortion in Terms of True and False Self* in *The Maturational Process and the Facilitating Environment: Studies in the Theory of Emotional Development.* New York: International UP Inc. 1965, pp. 140-152.

Film
Tom Hooper (2010) *The King's Speech*

7   the body, health and illness

In this chapter, drawing on my work over a decade of teaching medical students and working with doctors, I cover a number of themes which centre on the question of who has responsibility for and how we experience our physical selves. Science and technology, philosophy, cultural beliefs and rituals, including those of health practitioners, all play a role in shaping what we expect of the body and how we view ourselves as physical beings or as beings separated from our physical selves.

Touch is an important issue for most of us in experiencing our physicality, and I give some thought as to how we can engage with our needs for touch and how touch is a conduit in power relations.

Health professionals play a major role in shaping our perceptions including the question of who or what is to blame for ill-health and whether indeed we are to be considered sick, but there are risks in putting our trust entirely in the health service for treatment or even for permission to be ill, not just because of all the pressures and influences on health practitioners, but also because they may not be addressing their own emotional and health needs, and because the organisations in which they work may not be 'healthy' cultures.

I also give some pointers towards ways in which we can resist the pressures to conform in presenting our physical selves to the world, in defining ourselves as ill or well, and in constructing or deconstructing the reasons why we experience ourselves as 'ill'.

This chapter is written primarily by Julia.

Do we 'have' bodies or *are* we our bodies?

One of the things that has been long debated is the question of how much we *are* our bodies/our bodies *are us,* or if 'we' exist as distinct from our bodies, which we temporarily inhabit (ie. during our earthly life) or even 'own' – and which, like a casing, we shed at death.

It can be very important for a number of reasons that we have the ability to transcend our physical reality – for example if we are:

- suffering serious pain or injury
- being tortured
- being subjected to unwanted sexual attention such as in rape or prostitution
- having unpleasant medical procedures
- doing difficult or dangerous physical jobs

At such times, we may be capable of dissociating from our physical body, of 'depersonalising' in order to cope, *"this isn't really happening to me"*, or *"this is happening to my body but it is not 'me'"* or *'I can ignore the physical feelings and think about something else or about when it's all over'.*

In war, it's long been recognised that humiliating people physically and sexually through the exertion of power over their bodies, such as happened scandalously to prisoners at Abu-Ghraib in Baghdad (and as happens in most 'domestic' rape and abuse) - can cause damage to self-esteem and social standing that eats away from within, affecting a person's future intimate relationships and sense of wellbeing. In war, the systematic rape by soldiers of their opponents' wives and daughters is designed to deliberately destroy the morale of the enemy rather than having much to do with the need for sexual release. In their shocking report for United Nations Population Fund 2006, Jeanne Ward and Mendy Marsh collate data on women raped in war-zones such as Sudan, Rwanda, Bosnia, Sierra Leone, and the Republic of Congo etc. and indeed note that the United Nations accept that women and children nowadays constitute the *majority of victims of war* (although at the moment more men actually die). Ward and Marsh comment on the often public nature of physical/sexual abuse – ie. carried out in front of families or other soldiers and in her chapter in a collection of essays on war and health edited by Ilkka Tapale, Ruth Seifert discusses the power of rape in warfare to establish male hierarchies as well as to attack the culture of the 'other' group. In addition, authors like Helen Benedict and researchers like Jessica Wolfe explore the reasons behind significant numbers of military personnel (mostly but not always, female) reporting sexual harassment and assault from their male colleagues and raise the possibility that the psychology of military recruits has often been coloured by the experience of emotional, sexual or violent abuse before joining-up. And whilst we're still struggling to take on the facts of women's suffering in warfare, we tend to take it as the norm that injury to the body – loss of limbs, wounds and infections, etc. will happen, particularly to men, as the currency of battle.

Even if we think of our bodies as something we can distance ourselves from, it can be difficult to eradicate memories of how we or our partner of offspring have been 'despoiled' or damaged, if this is what has happened. Therapy to help people recover or move on from trauma and abuse has to address this issue of people's mental strategies to cope with horrifying experiences, in which both the physical experiences (often with long-term consequences such as genital damage, pregnancy, miscarriage, becoming HIV), and emotional experiences encoded in memory are difficult if not impossible to separate.

In some Eastern disciplines, people choose through the practice of meditation to deliberately cultivate the skills of transcending suffering resulting from desire and attachment to others (as in betrayal, or abandonment or bereavement), thus realising mental equilibrium and harmony, and in some cases, a 'higher' spiritual awareness. Such paths may vary on the extent to which the body is thought of as separate from the mind or the idea that awareness and the *object of* awareness are identical.

'Dualism'

However, it may be that the 'normal' state is for mind and body to be integrated as 'one'.

There's been much philosophical debate about this. The philosopher Rene Descartes clarified the case for *'dualism'* – in which it's clear that there's much human experience that's not 'physical', particularly thinking, mental desiring, remembering, and dreaming. This leads us relatively easily into the case for both the intellect and the 'soul', for something that's above the base physical/animalistic nature of human beings, and which justifies us thinking ourselves different from animals who can't escape their physical nature – an idea that's been important within some belief systems.

The question of *'sentience'* – the ability to experience pleasure and pain, and therefore being able to suffer – has often been applied to the way in which we relate to animals and invertebrates with for example, some laws offering protection to lobsters, squids, crabs and octopuses. Recent campaigns such as that by the *Born Free Foundation* have sought to rescue dolphins from captivity for tourism purposes arguing that they're suffering immense stress from containment and noise, resulting in health problems for the dolphins. We make distinctions between species we're happy to hunt or slaughter, eat or otherwise exploit, domesticate or worship and these distinctions vary across cultures.

Accepting the idea of dualism also means that we can 'defer gratification' because we can understand higher issues such as morality, principles, religious rules etc. and can control our physical urges with the power of our minds.

'Cartesian dualism' has been the foundation of our modern Western preoccupation with medicine as primarily about the body, and illness as primarily amenable to physical, pharmacological and technological interventions. However, conversely, Ayurveda and Chinese medicine are based on the contrasting philosophy – that *mind and body are one* and that it is the *person* who needs to be treated, not the disease.

Alternatives

If we appreciate that psychological events affect physical ones and that the body can affect our emotions and thoughts, the evidence for a dualistic approach tends to evaporate. The West still offers its support to this approach grudgingly, with space given to 'alternative' or 'complementary' practitioners, and some acknowledgement of psychological symptoms being linked to physical ones. However, Western medical training generally still prioritises and privileges physical approaches, and there are huge financial investments in treatments that are delivered to the body

266

as if it is a machine and as if psychology and social context have little to do with the health of the person.

This debate matters because *it affects the way we treat ourselves* and the health problems that we can stack up if we don't look after ourselves. For example, evidence is accruing that positive emotions, love and support can reduce our stress levels and increase our resistance to disease, and conversely, being lonely, anxious and depressed may damage our survival chances.

A few months before writing this, I had a severe car accident in which a lorry skidded into the back of my car on a damp road at traffic lights, crushing the back of the car and shunting my vehicle forward some distance. At the time, I thought that I had escaped lightly, initially being shocked, and then over the next three or four weeks, suffering a bit of neck soreness and feeling a bit nervous about driving for a while. However, four months on, my back started to hurt and my neck occasionally caught me with a burning sensation. I was referred to a cranial-sacral therapist who initially lay me down and put her hands under my head. After a few minutes, tears ran down my face, I remembered that every time I now drive, my back tenses in anticipation of a replay of the accident with vehicles slowing down at the back of my car at every junction and roundabout, and I realised that my sense of competence as a driver and as a person who was the main family driver, had been seriously dented. I found that the physical therapy was releasing deep distress about having nearly died and my failure as a parent to insulate my daughter (who had been in the vehicle with me) from trauma. It was a good example of mind and body affecting each other.

Becoming separated from our physical selves

We live in a perverse age. Health practitioners rely increasingly on technology and we're encouraged by them to rely on the outcomes of technological testing – blood tests, CT scans, blood pressure measurements, angiograms, endoscopies etc. which tell us about our own bodies, often habituating us to ignore the signs and symptoms of our own experience. Thus we've long been encouraged to lose touch with a holistic sense of ourselves, yet we're often criticised for not recognising symptoms at an early stage and examining ourselves for signs of disease, or for failing to exercise and eat our 'five-a-day' fruit ration. We're both put into a position where we become *split off* from our physical selves AND expected to be *aware of* our physical selves.

We know that touch can be important for healing; we use technology to standardise patient diagnosis and treatment and to make these more precise, yet in the process we distance patients' bodies from that of the health practitioner and make it less likely that we will experience any hands-on connection. Health staff may feel released from the need to engage with a variety of bodies, imagining that this is safer from a health and safety point of view and feeling the benefits of distance from the physical reality of patients, which has always been seen as the mark of higher status. Yet nursing can become more arduous if we become sicker as a result of lack of physical and emotional care and support. As physical care recedes from us, being done at a minimal and least-skilled level within the health system and supplanted by machinery, so also we're finding that 'emotional labour' is becoming more expensive and less easy to access.

Inexorably, healthcare becomes mechanised and impersonal, even whilst we discover from research that we need the opposite.

Bodies that are like machines and can be repaired

It's important too that we consider the context of capitalism in which we can all too easily expect that medicine can always repair or replace body parts as if we simply 'have' an old or damaged vehicle, rather than taking responsibility for the care and maintenance of ourselves as a whole, recognising that our life stories are 'writ' on our bodies. Our posture, for example, can convey how beaten down or energetic we feel, what kind of occupation we have, and how we've treated ourselves over the years. Not for nothing do we have the adage that an employer can decide in 30 seconds of seeing us whether to give us the job or not.

This aspect of ourselves as repairable machines is fed by the new technology that we have that can transplant major organs, alter DNA, clone organisms, and develop bionic prosthetics. Equally, human beings in desperate plights can be kidnapped or offered money so that their bodies can be plundered for organs to meet the health needs of the rich, just as if they were simply the sources of 'parts' (with no feelings, lives, relationships or psychologies). Nancy Scheper-Hughes, who at one time described herself as a 'militant anthropologist', has done much to highlight the plight of people treated in this way, particularly in countries like Brazil, including setting up the *Organ Watch* website.

Donna Haraway documents what she sees as the 'metaphor of immunology' whereby we're encouraged to imagine *'terrorism inside the body'* and to see the immune system as a *'battlefield'*, whereby medical treatments such as chemotherapy and drugs like interferon 'attack' the evil within. This is why *visualisation* can be a powerful technique – whilst it may be used to support this kind of metaphor it can also be used to enable us to address our bodies in less militaristic terms and in fact to see ourselves as mind and body in one.

Seeing our bodies like machines also implies that we see doctors as mechanics – we go to them as we take our cars to the 'body shop' garage. But if we expect doctors to offer us something *more* than technology, to see us as people with feelings, lives, relationships and values that matter to us, then we're suggesting that our bodies are *more than* simply casings for the mind and soul – we're relating as entities that have physical, psychological, spiritual elements and social contexts.

'Bodily integrity' and self-definition

Opponents of circumcision – male and female – talk of the way in which 'bodily integrity' is breached as if our bodies are ours to do with what we want (see for example readings in the book by George Denniston and colleagues, and more on this topic in our chapter on *Sexuality*). The right to a 'self-defined sexuality' was a watchword of the feminist movement in the 1970s. There have been struggles about peoples' rights to define their sexual identity as heterosexual, transgender, gay etc., for women to establish that rape can exist as a crime within marriage, for spouses to choose sterilisation or vasectomy, for women to choose abortion without needing their partner's permission etc. As I write, there's a story in the news claiming that the practice of sterilisation, sometimes without women's consent or even awareness (done at the same time as Caesarean sections) is being used in a country as a method of population control as well as a strategy to reduce infant mortality statistics, and we now know that the one-child policy in China is partly achieved through a massive programme of abortions.

So the extent to which we have power over own bodies varies at different times and in different situations – to what extent can the state intervene? to what extent do we consent to our religious authorities requiring control of our sexuality? to what extent are our bodies to be used in warfare - being sacrificed sexually and physically? what freedom do we have to refuse work in employing our bodies in hazardous industrial and construction projects?

Perfecting the body

Looks have often been seen as the source of power, sexuality being a strong force for influencing others and getting what we want. *If I have a perfect body I will find love.* Whilst much of the justification for circumcision of males and infibulation of females (notwithstanding the primacy of the religious and cultural rationales) in Asian and African cultures (particularly), has been to ensure acceptability of people to future partners, many people in the West choose to access modern medical technology to modify their bodies. Round the world, piercings and tattoos have been popular ways of enhancing the body, whilst facelifts, breast implants, liposuction and lipo-sculpture, 'nose jobs', Botox treatments, vaginal 'upgrades', clitoral and penile modifications are widespread in the West as ways of expressing dissatisfaction with what is given and exerting our power to determine self-presentation.

Another arena in the politics of the body has to do with symbolic presentation for example, in relation to hair - restoring hair in baldness, alopecia, post-chemotherapy etc. as well as electrolysis of hair in sex change, in-growing eyelashes, hirsutism etc. not to mention the enormous investment there is in hairdressing – colouring, perming, cutting, grafting extensions etc. All this is because we attribute meanings to things like hair, particularly in relation to gender, age, status and cultural identity.

One of the problems with the role of medicine in the case of children born with ambiguous genitalia labelled 'intersex' is the pressure to define an infant as male or female and medical practitioners usually advise parents on the most amenable gender to which to align the patient, usually no doubt forcing this foreclosure on gender identity motivated by the wish to save children from bullying and abuse.

Perhaps the key issue is how much real self-determination there is in all this, and how much people feel pressured to conform to the cultural context in which they find themselves.

The way we see ourselves - the body's size and shape and how we feel about it

How we feel about our bodies has a lot to do with the context we are in. Most of us in the West are embedded in a culture which exalts the sexual and material beauty of the perfectly coiffured and contoured body, slim and gym-fit. But in Nigeria there are fattening rooms where potential brides to be go to be fattened up before the wedding, and in parts of Asia, where weight is associated with eating well and affluence, the plump and heavy woman can be seen as more erotically attractive than the slim. In some parts of the world what looks in the West like anorexia nervosa is very similar in presentation to the emaciated body of the malnourished.

The psychoanalyst Jacques Lacan wrote about different levels of experiencing ourselves, and the challenges of dealing with *imaginary, symbolic* and *reality-based* ideas of the self, in particular the idea of mediating our deep-felt sense of things through (but not exclusively) language, so that as we learn to experience the world through words and symbols, we can become split off from our deep self (an idea not so different from Carl Rogers' idea of the split between the socially constructed *self-concept* and the more 'real' *organismic self*). It's helpful to recognise that we don't have an automatically accurate perception of ourselves; indeed, from the moment that we first see ourselves

271

reflected in a mirror or a shop window, we're dealing with both our internal sense of self and the one we are given from outside. In *anorexia nervosa*, people typically have a distorted sense of their physical selves – seeing themselves as fat, whilst others see them as dangerously thin. *Weightwatchers* include in their teaching the idea of distortions in the way people see food and portion control, suggesting for example that food served on smaller plates will look like more.

Throughout life, our experiences in relating to others and the events in our life provide us with feedback about ourselves. The trick is to bounce back some of these messages and make a sense out of them that works for us. We don't have to accept someone else's definition of us. The feminist writer Mary Daly was good on this idea, of redefining the meanings of words ascribed to us by others. And we have to take care in receiving messages even from the world of healthcare where prejudices and criticism and revulsion can still prevail. We need to listen to the language in which things are couched and evaluate it for ourselves, *finding our own words and giving new meanings to the words that are used about us.*

The way others see us, or we imagine that they do

I've worked in a medical school where students took a dim view of my overweight and indicated their disapproval, seeing in it a rebuke to their chosen vocation, believing that with an act of will I could do something about it, and become (like them) *svelte* and supple. They didn't see the beauty and trauma of my life written into the curvature of my spine and my painful knees, the now-permanent split on my lip from a fall at a party, the pelvic scar from the caesarean at the birth of my daughter, the curved stomach from years of drinking and eating in order to stave off the pain of a difficult relationship. Their youth requires that the world responds in a logical and efficient way but in mid-life we start to see that things accumulate, things problematize, things resist, things are complex. But to my lover, older than me, older than them, with a body of his own racked by injury, surgery, misuse, iatrogenesis, my body is a source of beauty and delight and comfort and companionship. It's a question of context.

272

How we present our bodies to the world

What are we saying to the world through our bodies and how much control do we exert over our self-presentation? Rightly or wrongly, our size and shape expresses to others something about our relationship to the most primeval material, eating and drinking and sleeping and sex. To some, the anorexic body is the final site where a child or lover can say 'no' to the overwhelming nature of parental control or the requirement to be sexual. For some, fat is the expression of helplessness and giving up while for others, fatness reflects a defence and a rejection of sexual competition. Obesity exposes the greed of the West so the West demonises the obese, desperately trying to hide it. Anorexia is horrifying culturally because it represents the choice to starve whereas for many in the world there is no choice. There is a long tradition of hunger-strike as a form of political protest. Women won the vote. Concessions – eventually – were wrung out of the British government in Northern Ireland – see Steve McQueen's *Hunger*.

Fat activists in America claim that overweight people (even when in other terms they're healthy) are discriminated against on *aesthetic* grounds – there is something more than simple health concern afoot. In San Francisco, legislation outlawing discrimination on height and weight made things easier for people of all shapes and sizes to get around.

The problems associated with disability are often less of impairment itself than of societal barriers and challenges impeding those with disabilities from engaging fully with life. See work by Michael Oliver and Colin Barnes on disability politics. Sometimes, our physical state is one that removes us from notice, edits us out of the fray – we can often be discounted because we're older, fatter, blander, or obviously disabled. Robert E Murphy, an anthropologist, reflects on how he became invisible to colleagues and an object of affection rather than the subject of respect from students when he was struck down by illness that rendered him quadriplegic. For some, association with someone who is in cultural terms physically unattractive or low status renders them too as carers and partners subject to rejection, stigmatisation, neglect and discounting.

273

The effect of 'norms' on our feelings about ourselves

A visiting colleague to the medical school said to me of our first meeting *'as soon as I walked into the room, I knew you were the sociologist'*, meaning that something about my presentation distinguished me from the 'norm' of how people in a medical school usually look. Taken aback initially, I decided I was OK with that piece of feedback.

Susie Orbach, psychoanalyst, writer and social activist, established the *AnyBody* website and has long challenged ideals of beauty and the organisations that profit from them for their effect on people, particularly contributing to problem eating among women. She suggests that women are constantly judged on how well they come up to cultural aesthetic ideals. The Western ideal of beauty is being marketed across the globe in fashion, advertising, film, and pornography, and women in other countries strive to meet it, unless there is a strong counter-pressure to celebrate their own aesthetic. Susie Orbach believes that dieting can't work to keep weight off in the long-term as the body eventually cries out for a binge to replace the foods it's not previously been allowed to have, and in any case, the focus is on conforming to an ideal rather than valuing who we are. This kind of idealisation also applies to the way we think about sex, believing that we can have ideal sex only with a partner with the right kind of looks – we need to loosen up about all our ideals and get real. In any context, it's important that we find ways of presenting ourselves confidently to the world without being dominated by 'norms' that make us feel we don't match up. In doing so, we are relating to ourselves in a loving way.

According to Susie Orbach's *Anybody* website, women are subjected to bombardment of images that are of women who are not the norm, and the average size 16s and women with disabilities are in general excluded from the media. In 2007, Vivienne Westwood complained that fashion magazines rarely included black models on their covers and discovered that this is because revenue goes down massively when they do. Women have to bear the sense of inadequacy engendered by media imagery throughout their lives within the culture. Looking at TV, film and magazines, it is clear that the average person in an ordinary life is not what we are seeing. Photography plays a key part in presenting to us people in beautiful kitchens, smart cars, top fashion clothing accompanied by articles and programmes that depict challenging conditions and disfigurements as peculiar and ordinary life and existence as pathological – in need of upgrading, improving, healing. Advertisers not only identify but create need so that we buy products to repair and replenish ourselves for supposed deficits. What we need to do is get attuned to our real hungers – both for food and for love, and then do something about them.

How do health practitioners figure in this?

Health practitioners must be careful not to reinforce people's inner hatred. The most 'beautiful' in any given context is not necessarily the happiest, the wisest, or the most spiritual. Inner beauty is where it's at, and ultimately an external presentation that emerges from inner beauty will find its own expressiveness. 'Ugliness' may come from the internalisation of negative messages – we flourish in conditions of love and support.

We often go to health practitioners to find out if we're 'normal' and expect that medical staff will refer to statistical data and their experience to tell us the answer. Children are measured against norms of development and are corrected when they fall behind the progress of their peer group. The bereaved are given but a short period of time before being diagnosed as stuck in 'abnormal grieving'. Surgery is often performed because something in our body is outside the norm of what is deemed healthy or normal. It can be very hard to fight against the groupthink adopted by the health service and our community if we want to do something against the norm – for example, let our child take his/her own time to learn to read or talk or swim, or for us, to go out and about without hiding the loss of a breast after mastectomy or attempting to cover up a facial disfigurement.

The charity *Changing Faces* commissioned a study which indicated that bad teeth, scars and burns were viewed as the most common indicators in film of evil or villainous characters, thus reinforcing fears and prejudices towards people with faces and bodies outside the 'norm'. They also found that children with disfigurements are perceived less positively on social skills, happiness and achievement and campaign on their behalf to change attitudes, not least those of the children themselves.

Internalising messages from others is a powerful mechanism and we need to really challenge any that are negative – *getting a sense of OK-ness is a vital tool for wellbeing.*

Psychological pain in the body

We know that many of us have conscious or unconscious memories of 'adverse childhoods' or abuse (in childhood or later on) stored in the archives of our bodies. There is now evidence that suggests this may be a key factor for some of us struggling with obesity. See for example papers by T B Gustafson and D B Sarwer, and by Jennie Noll and colleagues which indicate that it's worth doing more research on this.

Unhappiness and grief is often accompanied by illness and death – a significant number of us die within weeks or months of our partners.

Reichian therapy (though not a method to use lightly) works to reach us through the body armour we've created, layer by layer over the years, using breathing, massage, screaming, re-enactment – anything that will unpack the embedded trauma. The way we hold ourselves, the way our faces crinkle or don't – every aspect of our relationship to others and to the world is encoded in our physique.

Cranio-sacral therapy works more gently to reconnect us with our bodies, and regular therapeutic massage can also have powerful effects.

When we want to change our life, we have to start changing our relationship to our body; *to change our relationship to our body is to start changing our life.*

276

Being ill

Increasingly, the boundaries between the two categories 'ill' and 'well' are less clear - in the UK, NHS doctors are now required to complete *'fit to work'* notes rather than *'sick notes'*, and can identify those areas of a person's work that they are capable of continuing even when *'sick'*.

The sociologist, Talcott Parsons, (1951), described the *'sick role'* as a special identity to which we are given access by doctors, through which the normal requirements of daily life are suspended. Though there are many exceptions to the way in which Parsons defined the sick role, nonetheless it is useful to think of *'sickness'* as a state in which we are allowed to be - and expect to be - *protected from harm because we are more vulnerable than usual.* However, in today's world, it is not sensible to assume that we will be treated specially as *'vulnerable'* or *'delicate'* – paradoxically, we may have to use all our strength – or that of our friends or family - to get what we need.

> *After a short spell in hospital, J, aged 59, came home but a couple of nights later started coughing up blood. We rushed him across the night city streets and through the dark countryside to the local A & E department, where in a large shabby room flanked by policemen and burly security officers, sat a variety of people in various states of alcohol-fuelled aggression, a mix of people with impromptu bandages and slings, pushchairs with crying babies, couples in conflict etc. It was a frightening and miserable place and the energy level was high. We learned that the night before a patient had bitten a nurse. J was feeling very vulnerable, especially as he feared a bleed from the lungs. We were asked to sit and take our place. The sign above our heads said the average waiting time was 5 hours. It was difficult for me to argue that we were more urgent than others because of my belief in equality and fairness, but it was impossible for us to sit in that room without the stress creating a dangerous situation for J's health and for my state of mind. I felt sure that after a few minutes I would be the one being restrained by the police. In practice, what we achieved was removal to a quieter trolley-zone where we waited in a curtained cubicle away from the waiting-area for another two and a half hours before seeing a doctor, but the reduction in stress allowed us all to become calm and less frightened. Asserting our needs on this occasion had been the right thing to do.*

We may find ourselves angry and stressed throughout the 'patient journey' if we're not treated with care and loving attention. It's important to be prepared for this not to be the case, to look at our own expectations and experiences both within the family and outside it, and to recognise that a state medical system is not necessarily equipped to offer the kind of sensitivity and support that we need. Staff are often overwhelmed with personnel shortages, over-detailed bureaucracy (note how many times you're asked the same questions), low pay for long shifts and a lack of support and supervision. Add to this mix the dominance of science, technology and pharmacology in healthcare and the scene is set for psychology to play a very small role in our care programme. Evidence-based healthcare which has been in vogue for some years now tends to favour those treatments which have outcomes that are easily measurable and demonstrable – subtle, complex human skills don't easily fall into that category.

Entering into the sick role – sometimes a difficult decision

The medical sociologists Annette Scambler and Graham Scambler and their colleague Donald Craig, researching in the 1980s, found that women tended to consult with a variety of others (husbands, friends, female relatives) before consulting with a doctor. Consulting with family tended to encourage women towards a consultation with their GP, whilst talking to friends tended to put them off.

Perhaps friends collude with us sometimes in our desire to disregard the significance of symptoms or with our tendency (particularly as women) to let other things take precedence before going to the doctor about ourselves. We know that once we do, something might change.

Perhaps these days, most of us consult with others about whether it's a good idea to step over the boundary from *'being well'* to *'being ill'*. There is not always a clear-cut difference between the two states in terms of what it 'feels' like – it is often about *the permission to act differently*.

For example, in accepting a definition of being 'sick', we can:

- stay off work
- rest more and slow down
- take proper action on our health
- avoid social encounters
- make life-changes
- spend time with whom we love
- be there for our children (even if not fully-functioning)
- tackle problematic ergonomics and psychodynamics at work and at home
- take time to make the most of counselling and complementary therapies
- have the opportunity to reflect on the meaning of our symptoms

But it also might mean putting ourselves in situations where we face:

- waiting-lists
- waiting-rooms
- brusque care
- standardised routines which take no account of our patterns and processes
- intrusive questioning
- unwelcome judgements on our health behaviour
- invasive and sometimes risky procedures to find out what's wrong with us
- trying out medication that may or may not agree with us
- a struggle to get information about our condition and to understand its implications
- a battle to get the medicine or treatment we believe we need
- a struggle to get the time and rest we need to heal from 'family' and home demands, work demands, economic pressures, and doctors' permission-granting
- being under the control of hospital systems with reduced access to people close to us
- a need to be vigilant about what is proposed for us by others
- fear and anxiety waiting for the results of investigations or treatments or trying to find the courage to have them

It may be worth reminding ourselves that the World Health Organisation defines 'health' as:

> a state of complete physical, mental and social well-being and not merely the absence of disease or infirmity.
>
> *Preamble to the Constitution of the World Health Organization as adopted by the International Health Conference, New York, 19 June - 22 July 1946; signed on 22 July 1946 by the representatives of 61 States (Official Records of the World Health Organization, no. 2, p. 100) and entered into force on 7 April 1948. The definition has not been amended since 1948.*

and bearing in mind that for anyone relying on a state health system such as that in the UK, true 'health' is not the goal. Minimisation and management of symptoms may be all we can hope for under this system. Many treatments carry problems in their wake such as side-effects of drugs, risks of damage to our bodies, and negative long-term implications which have to be balanced against the benefits, since we may come to feel unwell but in a different way. It can feel like swapping one bad thing for another, the main difference being that we might have been promised longer-term survival or the hope of symptom remission.

'Health' in the true sense of the word may be up to us. If we want 'health' we will have to take responsibility ourselves and recognise that it is quite a luxury product. We will have to look after ourselves carefully and invest in our health as we do any other part of our lives. Looking after ourselves involves money, time, energy, thought and ingenuity. We may need to talk to new people, find out about things, undertake a positive action programme, be ruthlessly honest with ourselves, confront situations and relationship dynamics, assert ourselves, engage in new activities and accept new vulnerabilities. Very often the path to deep wellbeing involves engaging in creative, spiritual and psychological healing as well as a new approach to the way we see our bodies and treat them.

Defining ourselves as 'ill' or 'well'

We will often go on working or functioning with a variety of underlying disorders, aches and pains, and worries, but are - technically speaking - 'well'. The moment when we finally decide to go to see a nurse or doctor is the time when we have decided that that protected status or labelled identity is of more use to us than struggling on as if we were well. Some are still stuck in the dichotomy between being fully well and fully sick. For the conscientious, being 'off sick' can mean that anything other than being prone and taking lots of medicines would look like malingering. Being out on a bracing cliff-top walk with a friend, sitting in a beachside café downing fishcakes and beer and watching the waves, looking round an art gallery or having one's hair cut and coloured all look like things we should not be doing on an employer's sick pay. Yet all these things might be good for the spirit and morale, reminding us that there is more to life than work, that it's important that we get the work-life balance healed, and that being well is about a lot more than the lowest common denominator of having a body that appears not to be distorted or in pain.

As patients, we write our own narrative story about our illness, telling and retelling the story of how we came to be ill and finding the significance of events and context in the genesis of 'unwellness'. Traditional history-taking by health professionals encourages us in this process, but it becomes particularly necessary when our symptoms remain with us and we are required through the new acceptance of disability, chronic fatigue, pain, disfigurement, immobility, embarrassment and other restrictions on our lives, to *explain to ourselves* how this came about and how we incorporate these factors into our identity.

Talking to people in our lives and exploring the significance of events in our lives for our states of wellbeing and unwellness may be a helpful process in coming to that understanding and resolving a path for future management of our conditions.

In serious illness, we may need to decide what our approach will be – will it be to accept the inevitable as in Elisabeth Kübler-Ross' well-known model of facing up to death, or will it be as in Dylan Thomas' poem *'Do not go gentle into that good night'*? But in fact in every case of physical or mental disorder, we need to find our own path through it, whether we will get ourselves the rest and replenishment we need, whether we will battle through it and live with chronic niggling inconvenience, take whatever the doctor or occupational nurse hands out or seek out treatments and help from people who really understand our condition.

What's our illness about?

We may also need to ask ourselves the question: do we actually want to get better or does the 'illness' serve a purpose in our life? Are we simply 'going through the motions' of getting help because we actually prize our symptoms as ways of getting attention or avoiding other challenges?

Illness can be a way of masking deeper feelings, and in particular it could be a form of passive resistance, of refusing to go along with what is expected of one – eg. to be a dutiful employee/colleague/pupil/partner/parent/child/soldier/etc. where the channels for open refusal are blocked or dangerous. Illness can be about brokering transition that we find it hard to ask for or give ourselves permission for in the cold light of practical realities. Depression is often categorised as a mask for buried anger, anger which is turned in on oneself. Illness sometimes allows a person to resist expectations and to escape from unpalatable situations or situations where there is a 'double-bind'.

Illness can also be based on a series of learned behaviours from childhood. We learn to react to injury from the way parents and others react to us. When we fell over and cut our knee, did our parents hug us and reassure us, did they rush for the antiseptic and plasters, did they ignore us, did they tell us to stop being a 'cry-baby' and concentrate on the job in hand? Thus doctors see patients with serious illnesses who take matters in their stride and people with minimally worrying symptoms who think the world is at an end.

Our response to what's happening to us is individual and linked to our cultural background. Indeed, the very notion of illness 'happening to us' - like the notion of germs or viruses visiting us from outside ourselves - may have much to do with our own belief system. In contrast to this idea of ourselves as the passive victims of unpredictable, mobile disease, some of us imagine that illness is

282

the result of stress (to which we have often contributed by accepting heavy workloads, ignoring physical symptoms, eating and drinking heavily etc) on our body and mind, creating weakness in immune responses and making cells atrophy, mutate, adhere, misfire, multiply, synthesise in ways that they shouldn't etc. Some of us believe 'old wives' tales', that walking on cold floors in bare feet or getting caught in a rain-shower causes colds, that not expressing our anger causes cancer, etc.

In some Asian cultures the notion of 'depression' doesn't exist, in France, the liver is revered, in the UK, the heart. In some countries surgery is more common; in others management of conditions is preferred. See Cecil Helman's work on the cultural expression of illness. Our social class and local culture will have attitudes towards different illnesses – if keeping working is central, then we will be expected to overlook symptoms and to tough out discomfort. It's not just a family or occupational culture thing. We have to choose between a *passive response* - being incapacitated by our symptoms, and *being proactive* - taking steps to get control of what is happening, informing ourselves and finding out the choices we have, preventing distress and seeking out the best support, as well as learning to understand the deeper reasons for our sickness. We may have to step out of our family or cultural context and seek answers and perspectives that are new to us.

Timing

Darian Leader and David Corfield in their book *Why do people get ill?* discuss the timing of illness and how it is common for people to present themselves at doctors' surgeries with symptoms on significant anniversaries that are out of conscious awareness. And people *do* die of 'broken hearts', with coronary problems and other illnesses often following the loss of significant others. Leader and Corfield are able to trace back in case histories the possibility that illness sometimes emerges at times that were significant in the family system eg. to a parent or a previous loss not yet grieved for, rather than having an obvious correlate in the here and now. It may be enlightening to look at *when* things happen in our lives and the meaning of why they happen then, to illuminate our understanding of the causes and what we can do. Feeling unwell may happen in harmony with the timing of trauma within the family system. The pull to follow a key person to the grave can sometimes be hard to resist.

> Years ago, a man I knew was interested in a woman friend of mine for a relationship but she wasn't sure she wanted to get involved. At the time, she was packing up her life in one city and had got a job elsewhere and a new flat. She also ended her existing relationship. On the weekend of her move, she went to stay with her parents. Whilst taking a photograph of her parents, she fell backwards off the garden steps, fracturing her leg in several places. She was suddenly hospitalised for several weeks. This had the effect of giving her time to process the big changes in her life that were taking place and to receive visits from the man I knew (which did eventually lead to a relationship between them).

Letting illness speak to and for us

There are lexicons available whereby we can look up 'the meaning' of our symptoms – eg. is a sore throat to do with not wanting to speak out, or leg pains to do with not being ready to move forward in your life. Louise Hay's work is seminal in this respect. But a standardised approach is unlikely to be of much use except in terms of stimulating our own thoughts. What is likely to be of use is to spend time thinking about what is troubling *us* in our body, understanding how the illness or condition is affecting our life, what meaning the body parts involved have for *us*, and what can be drawn from the illness for our life.

The following tables give examples of this kind of analysis.

What's troubling me?	*Headaches*
Effect on my life	*Can't concentrate on my work at work, need to lie down on occasions several days in a row, intake of painkillers increasing*
Meaning of head to me	*I imagine my head as full of all my knowledge, but also full up with data and administration which is at times overwhelming. My head is the place where battles are fought out about where I should be and who I should be spending time with.*

What can be drawn from this	Is too much of my life lived in my head? Should I look to giving attention to the rest of my body and getting more balance between head and heart? Are there conflicts in my life I need to resolve? Do I have a need to institute some time-scheduling to give myself more of a rest from my work and organise things differently, bring in more help or delegate? Do I have a need to question the pressure I am under and ask if I am in quite the right role? Is this a warning sign that eventually I will need to make some life changes? Would some counselling help me? Do I need to do some de-cluttering?

What's troubling me?	Irritable bowel syndrome – pain, bloating, fluctuating bowel movements etc., fatigue.
Effect on my life	Affects my sexual relationship because I don't feel attractive or physically comfortable. I get to withdraw from looking after my children because I have to sit down and nurse myself. I can put off supper gatherings with friends because I am unwell without feeling I am rejecting them or them feeling that.
Meaning of bowels to me	Central feature of my functioning. Makes me feel vulnerable in a deep way and aware of my mortality. Bowel movements and eating not entirely under my control when I was a child, retreated to the loo to get away from family arguments and gatherings. Bowels are to do with the evacuation of waste – do I need to look at anything in my life I can't afford time for – eg. cut back on entertaining both friends and my children? What do I need to explore about my sexual relationship – am I avoiding it, feeling guilty about it, not giving it enough time, feeling ambivalent about it etc? Bowels affected by my diet – is there something I need to be doing to control what comes into my body?
What can be drawn from this?	A need to review things in my life in terms of the allocation of my time and energy. A need to get control of what comes in and what goes out of my body. A need to get serious about my life.

Although this kind of analysis may be useful, the important thing is to recognise that bodily symptoms are *the manifestation of unconscious processing*. Things in our life which aren't getting attention, particularly buried trauma, will find ways of reaching our conscious mind. Dreams will be one avenue, but particularly if we don't listen to them, our mind and body will eventually acquiesce to the pressure on them and resort to things like pain, discomfort, self-destruction, or depression and anxiety. Very often illness is helpful to us, making us slow down, pause, review and if we are sensible, making us instigate changes in our lives. Depression is often about the need to have a cocoon for a period. Sometimes we need more than one communication, and we suffer several bouts of illness before we are prepared to hear 'the message'. Sometimes if we continue on without listening, and treat the symptoms with heavyweight pharmacology to suppress them, the unconscious material will bubble up in a new format, with a 'new illness'. The important thing is to see ourselves in a holistic way - as a whole system - and symptoms as communications about the state of ourselves.

The energy to live

Taking our lives seriously is perhaps the single most important step we can take to look after our health. We need to ask ourselves: what *will* do I have to live my life as happily and as long as I can?

Life energy is central to being able to do something about our health. If we don't want to go on living, then tackling health problems will only be cosmetic.

There are many ways in which the will to go on is sapped and we have to allow healing and facilitate the cultivation of our life energy:

- we may need to take time to allow our depression to speak to us rather than busying onwards.

- we may need to allow the pain of our past to break through into conscious awareness and to weep and to be held.

286

- we may need to address guilt at surviving the loss of someone important in our life and the doubt we have about our right to have a fulfilled life of our own.

- we may need to acknowledge that we were not wanted wholeheartedly by our parents, and learn how to live our life for ourselves and give ourselves the parenting we need.

- there may be a legacy of murder, manslaughter, or suicide in our family background that we have to overcome to find a way of both honouring its shadow and coming into the light.

- we may be treated as malingerers and depended on very heavily by employers, business partners and family members and we might have to struggle to get the seriousness of our bodily woes accepted and investigated, rather than letting ourselves die psychologically or physically.

- we may be going through the menopause, having a hysterectomy, or finding out that (male or female) we cannot produce children because of infertility – finding our lives worthwhile in the absence of reproductive power may take strength.

- we may be getting old and suffering changes to virility, feelings of attractiveness, physical energy and physical changes and feel that there is no longer any hope of an intimate relationship – we may need to find a way of finding ourselves worthwhile regardless of the messages coming towards us from the external world.

Getting what we need from health services

The sociologist Erving Goffman showed us that interpersonal relations can be seen as a drama in which we play our parts – doctors, nurses, cleaners, patients, each being covered by role expectations. The sociologist Talcott Parsons cast the doctor in the role as 'gatekeeper' – as do many governments - and one way of looking at our interaction with health services is just this – *how to get our share of the resources to meet our needs*. Even if we agree to the notion of a fair and equal allocation to all, we recognise that our needs may be different from that of other patients – *equal* does not mean *the same*.

Thus our relationship to healthcare professionals may be one of participating in a negotiation for examinations, for drugs, for information, for other treatments, and most difficult of all, for the time to talk things over. We shouldn't accept any agenda where we're rushed through, made to feel we're a cog in a big machine, are given minimal explanations, or otherwise treated badly. It's OUR health, perhaps the first and only time we've had a particular illness (even if they've seen thousands of cases) and we have a right to good treatment and care.

The General Medical Council's *Good Medical Practice* guidelines in the UK stress that *making the care of patients should be the first concern* for doctors, and the second is *working in partnership with patients*. These kinds of concerns are echoed in similar documents in the USA and Australia and no doubt in many countries across the world. There's also usually a *duty* on doctors to report misconduct and bad practice, legitimating 'protected disclosures' whereby they are supported to raise difficult concerns with management.

We can claim the doctor's attention and concern in the light of their *code of ethics*. Codes of ethics or conduct are somewhat abstract and it's possible that doctors and others drift away from them over time, only remembering them when a crisis occurs and they're about to be sued by a patient. It's important to clarify who is responsible for ensuring that people stick to them.

Healthcare is driven by things like pharmaceutical business, investment in technology, the pressure to cut costs from government, the pressure to get research findings from researchers, etc. Patient pressure groups come low on the overall agenda.

Is illness *our* fault?

One of the problems with medicine is that practitioners can focus too much on us as individuals and 'pathologize' our problems – we are to blame: we didn't exercise, we didn't notice the symptoms, we didn't get prompt treatment, we didn't eat or avoid eating the right things, we kept doing things that were bad for our health, we didn't follow the health regime properly, we kept working and failed to reduce stress etc. when in fact, there are often wider forces that contribute to ill-health.

Epidemiology provides us with data on causal patterns and correlations for disease. In 2009, the World Health Organisation listed factors responsible for 25% of all deaths in the world as: *'childhood underweight, unsafe sex, alcohol use, unsafe water and sanitation, and high blood pressure'*. Our environment can make a major contribution to problems with health – factors such as poverty, famine, limited availability of condoms and sex education and lack of investment in irrigation and sanitation. Dramatic climate change such as flooding, contaminated injections (in healthcare settings), occupational carcinogens, asbestos, lead poisoning, urban pollution, and availability of illicit drugs are all factors that contribute to morbidity and mortality across the world. Even how difficult it is to take a walk near our homes can be taken into account, or how far away access to exercise is and what it costs. This is not a blueprint for saying that it is the government's fault or the employer's fault that we are ill and that we have no responsibility, though watching films like *Erin Brockinovich, Insider* or *Silkwood* may make us feel like that. The point is to be vigilant and to counter negative effects eg. by making sure that we get in lots of fruit and vegetables, not living near pylons, insisting on proper health and safety procedures in the workplace, etc.

Psychotherapy and counselling have this problem built-in. The very fact of going for therapy suggests that we accept that *we* are responsible for our mental/emotional condition. Or our parents are. Or our siblings. Or our colleagues. No matter – the problem is an *individual* one, requiring support, understanding, insight, or treatment.

But isn't the individual at the mercy of the context......?

Advanced capitalist societies are bound to lose a few souls for whom it is all too much. The endless work pressures, the stresses, the personality culture, the financial cut and thrust, the impersonality, the regulatory frameworks, the transitory nature of things, the commodification of relationships, the constant monitoring and surveillance etc. - it can be predicted that a certain percentage will get depressed, anxious, burned out – that's the cost of a fast-paced, profit-driven, competitive society – the 'collateral damage'. But it's worse if – when exhausted or troubled by things - we also take on the ascription of being at fault, deviant, weak or wrong in some way rather than there being an acceptance that this kind of society isn't particularly good for anyone and that it's inevitable that some – usually those of us with a particular mix of unfortunate pressures and circumstances – a boss who bullies us, a difficult childhood, redundancy, a friend who dies etc – will go under at some point.

Research backs up this kind of point. For example, we know that alcohol-related illness, injury and death can be affected by things like drink-driving policies, age-restrictions, opening hours for licensed premises and sales of alcohol, education about safe drinking limits and the dangers of alcohol, advertising, legal enforcement, taxation and pricing limits, and alcohol labelling. We also know that people's drinking habits will be affected according to the drinking culture in which they live – their own families, whether or not there's any attempt at moderation or abstention around them, the kind of alcohol available – beer, wines, spirits; whether alcohol is drunk daily, with meals, at festivals, etc. and what the tolerance levels are for drunkenness. Thus when someone comes into surgery with serious alcohol-related illness, to treat them as if they are solely culpable is unjustifiable.

We know that the state of the economy affects people's mental health - for example, researchers are looking into the extent of correlation between debt and mental disorder; the stress of inequality (felt differently by both the poorer and the better-off); the increase in suicides during recession and downturn etc.

However, recognising that factors around us contribute to our state of health doesn't mean that we can let go and give up working on our own response.

Taking responsibility

The point is to look critically at the question of causation and responsibility, and to take responsibility for what we *can* change. Often in life, it's not the outward things we can change; it's *our response to them* that we can alter. For example, we can:

- decide to take care of our bodies and improve our fitness or flexibility
- find out everything we can about our health conditions, look at alternatives to allopathic medicine, discuss approaches with health practitioners and health advocates, and make sure that our healthcare is what we need it to be
- get together with others with the same condition and fight for improvements to services; meet with local health representatives to discuss shortfalls in provision and what can be done
- find out about others with whom we can join to seek redress for any harm or injury – this need not be individual redress but could mean negotiating investment back into the community from companies and organisations that have been negligent etc.
- reduce personal stress - if necessary, by dramatic action such as leaving work, giving up our home, sharing childcare with relatives etc. or by cutting back on complexity, detail, perfectionism, over-involvement, mollycoddling, attachment to things which distress us etc.
- down-shift, budget and monitor expenditure, reshape our finances, consider including exchange and barter as an adjunct to money
- press for better health and safety regulation at work
- switch off the TV and ignore advertising and the messages of celebrity culture that make us feel low
- phase out people in our lives who don't help us to feel good or worse; get help to get out of situations where we feel bullied or intimidated

- boost our morale with mental exercises such as affirmations, visualisation, collages of our dream future etc.
- invest in things that will help – from walking boots and tents to a new hobby
- improve our social skills, whether it's getting feedback from friends and ex-partners on our approach to dating, or going on an assertiveness or negotiation course
- give up or reduce alcohol and caffeine intake (read up on it, prepare, find alternatives, get allies, change drinking situations etc)
- write our memoirs or our first novel
- talk to new people and get some fresh perspectives
- notice our neighbours and build a sense of community
- find meaningful things to do – help with a social or political campaign, record books for visually-impaired people, offer conversation or listening skills to literacy and language learners, help set up a credit union/community newspaper/befriending service/youth club etc.
- enhance our relationships by building in quality time; invest time in talking to our children, partners, parents, siblings
- set up a new group at work such as meditation or prayer, environmental sustainability, developing an artistic eye, peer support – anything that attends to wellbeing
- find out about drugs – legal and illegal – learn about the dangers for people who experiment with recreational drugs and how to offset them; stop being naïve about drug companies and the safety of prescription drugs etc.; find out about balancing medication with things that ameliorate the damage (eg. like replacing intestinal flora after taking antibiotics)
- explore our family history through therapy, memories, photos, talking, writing, art, return visits to family haunts, archives - to put perspective on our current situation (like repeating patterns of behaviour or attitudes)
- find out about the economic situation, study facts and figures, inform ourselves and take decisions based on the best projections

- get to know our local political representatives, start to have an influence on local decision-making – be a contributor

Perhaps an important point here is that *the body can't be separated out* – our physical wellbeing is intricately tied up with our social self, our emotional health, our financial situation, etc. and our health depends on feeling in charge as much as possible.

The second point is equally important and is a key message of this book – *don't be passive, don't let external circumstances dominate, be active and powerful.*

The body can often overwhelm us so that we feel unable to exert any power over things, but unless we are in intensive care, there is probably always *something* we can do to improve things, to assert our will on events, to break down ignorance in ourselves and our caregivers, and in so doing, come to feel better.

Health activism

When health resources and support aren't available or are inadequate, we can feel very stressed and angry and hopeless, and it is painful to find that we are forced to fight for proper treatment. There are many movements and groups that have been started up by people who've suffered illness or disability either directly themselves or through caring about someone who has – for example, Alzheimers', breast cancer, and HIV-AIDS. They have had various degrees of success and like all social movements experience schisms and divisions about strategy, goals and outcomes – sometimes depending on the extent to which they have threatened pharmacological providers, healthcare providers, and the nature of medical science. The range of approaches by both the medical establishment and the health industry and the health activists who've challenged the status quo, goes from 'defiance' to 'co-option' – however, one of the important points for those of us who are suffering is that engagement in fighting for improvements and changes might in itself be good for us compared to remaining in a passive, victim position.

293

Countering stigma and discrimination – fighting for equality

Sometimes we're not fighting for resources but for changes in attitudes – countering stigmatisation and discrimination. One of the key elements in the disability rights movement has been the focus on justice rather than charity. The approach must reflect the aim – it's no good insisting on equality but asking for help.

> The specific goals and demands of the movement are:
>
> - accessibility and safety in transportation, architecture, and the physical environment
> - equal opportunities in independent living, employment, education, and housing
> - freedom from abuse, neglect, and violations of patients' rights
>
> http://en.wikipedia.org/wiki/Disability_rights_movement

One of the arenas where developments have occurred since the Second World War, following the leadership of injured war veterans, is in the idea of the Paralympics, where people with a variety of disabilities including cerebral palsy, intellectual disability, wheelchair-bound, visual impairment, and multiple sclerosis compete in parallel with the Olympics. Both the International Olympic Committee and the International Paralympic Committee are committed to equality and events are now always held at the same time and in the same venues.

However, the battle for equal rights and the right to be consulted over policy developments is not an easy one. In Bolivia, in January 2012, there were reports that police may have used excessive force against protestors (who had in many cases, travelled long distances to demonstrate about being included in decisions about disability provision) allegedly using pepper sprays and electric shocks against people, many of whom were in wheelchairs. Increasingly, people with disabilities are claiming their space as equal members of society: for more on this, read work by Michael Oliver and Colin Barnes.

Touch

It's important to give thought to the of role touch in our lives, and in particular, its role in power relations.

- health practitioners are allowed to touch us; *we're* not allowed to touch *them*

- health practitioners can instruct us to undress, to cough, to breathe in and out; *we* can't do the same to *them*

Some touch is *'instrumental'* – ie. it's to find something out like palpating our chest or putting on a blood pressure cuff or to get us to move in a particular way for say, a physical examination, or to get us out of the way of danger.

Perhaps surprisingly, nurses and doctors rarely use touch as a *therapeutic tool*, though some may hold our hand or touch our arm to steady us, or to calm us down before breaking difficult news or administering an uncomfortable procedure. It tends to be 'alternative' practitioners who provide *healing through touch*, such as chiropractic practitioners, masseurs, acupuncturists, and osteopaths, though in some contexts, nurses have explored the use of 'therapeutic touch'. Sometimes with people we're looking after, as laypeople, we use strokes, massage, compresses, ice cubes, lancing etc. to bring about change in the body. And of course the way we undertake any procedure such as bathing a baby or helping an ill or disabled person with toileting will reflect our feelings about the person and about physical things in general. Our own ease or unease with physicality will be relevant.

As a tutor in a medical school, I remember an argument about the question of whether doctors should touch their patients when patients were distressed. There is some guidance in the code of ethics for doctors but some things can't be completely predictable or legislated for. Students tended to be horrified at the idea, fearing misinterpretation by patients of what the doctor might mean, whilst some experienced doctors thought that a human response of touch to a patient who was crying would be quite appropriate and would reflect their spontaneous compassion. I think the general consensus was that touch would be used according to the style and approach of an individual doctor and their reading of a particular patient – trust has to be there on both sides. There was for example some debate about gender and whether a male doctor was more restricted in this and that perhaps touch from a female doctor was less contentious, etc. The point here is that touch is simultaneously symbolic of concern – (though whether the concern was real or 'professional' was also debated), deeply reflective of the power relationship and embedded in cultural systems and expectations. In the end, deciding on boundaries may be something that is negotiated across the space between professionalism and patient perspective.

If we find touch difficult, we can learn to reconnect with our bodies through physical therapies – in cranio-sacral therapy for example, the practitioner puts their hands under relevant parts of the body and holds them there for a while, helping the person to become aware of how their body feels and what the symptoms are expressing, and listening to the rhythms inside the body. Therapeutic massage from a skilled and sensitive practitioner can also help restore trust. Both therapies can bring up powerful feelings from the past and we should ensure that we are able to work through issues safely with the therapist and that we have support in our lives in between sessions for anything that comes up.

Touch between people is a powerful mechanism for bonding and for manipulation. Witness any salesperson and their use of the handshake. There have been various studies showing things like the idea that people are more likely to return to a shop where the cashier touched their skin as they gave back cash – even when this is unconsciously done or felt (unless of course they didn't like the cashier) or where healing touch before surgery or other health procedures results in better survival chances etc.

Look into the role of touch in your life and explore what happens when you resist it. Most of us will find that people get very upset when we try to change the dynamics of touch.

> I was brought up in a family where no-one touched each other except the occasional hugs my parents gave each other, or the wrestling fights my siblings had with each other. Years later, on a visit 'home', my mother came towards me expecting a kiss goodbye as I prepared for departure.
> I found it very difficult to give her such a kiss after years of never receiving affection in that way but I had to accept that people don't stay the same as they go through life.

Resisting sex can result in violent reactions from some partners, partly because a sexual relationship brings up not only feelings of bonding, but also of vulnerability shared – choosing not to have sex with someone can evoke powerful feelings of abandonment, or in cases where a partner feels that we 'belong' to them, of anger. We may need to make good preparations and build in support if this is an area of our life where we want to make changes. Good communication is needed if we want to assure someone that we still love them but need to change the dynamics – eg. a new approach to sex itself, or refraining from sex when one or other is drunk or feeling unwell, or if we're actually feeling a difference in our own sexual reactions etc.

Exercise: consider touch in your life and identify examples:

Who touches me?	When?	Do I touch them?	When?	How do I feel about this relationship – is the level and balance of touch where I want it to be?
Person A				
Person B				

Consider where in your life you would like more touch and where in your life you would like less. Getting in contact with our own needs for touch is important. If there is no touch in our life and this is something we'd like to address, we can make an action plan for what to do about it.

It could include items like:

- get feedback from others on what they think about our touchability (questions like: *do I have funny social skills that put people off/does my physical appearance and manner need attention?*)
- try out some touch with a few sessions of massage
- consider some counselling or a group-work weekend to explore patterns from the past that may be encoded in the body and in our approach to touch and sexuality
- look at problems in particular relationships that may be blocking the natural expression of love through touch
- consider venturing into internet dating if a new partner is wanted but of course following appropriate safeguards and taking time to get to know someone – it is obviously no good simply pursuing someone for touch
- test out being more physically affectionate to people in our life and discussing the effect of this if it goes wrong – genuinely explore what the dynamics are
- consider if we are too dominant or powerful and if this getting in the way so that people feel manipulated or coerced, not free to refuse or able to express themselves
- work on issues of grief, previous hurt or loss that may be blocking us on moving forward into something new, consider if we are truly ready for this yet

Mind and body

Like others who have followed her, Louise Hay, a founding mother of 'self-help', believes that anger and resentment often lie behind physical and emotional symptoms and runs workshops on forgiveness to help people move beyond these feelings and heal.

The idea that developing forgiveness might allow for healing of physical and mental ailments resonates with the kind of work done by shamans – anthropologists have long understood that shamanic processes often involve addressing conflict and tension between individuals and within communities. 35 million copies of Hay's pioneering work *'You can heal your life'* have been sold, suggesting that people feel an instinctive rightness about the ability to link meaning to physical disorder, whether or not they accept Hay's particular suggestions. Reading our symptoms may need as much skill as interpreting our dreams, and in this sense, we should welcome our symptoms as the language of the body.

One of Louise Hay's most powerful ideas is that our thinking affects what happens to us and that thinking negative thoughts make it difficult for us to open to the possibility of good things flowing into our lives. Thus affirmations and visualisations and strategies to wish good things into our lives make it far more possible that they will.

Jeremy Hazell, whose work as an object-relations psychotherapist included heading up a university student counselling service, suggested that events like exam failure and being caught out plagiarising someone else's work are often connected to a struggle to go beyond the success of someone key in our lives – a fear of becoming a 'survivor'. In a paper he wrote in 1982, he emphasises our need to attend to the 'unconscious significance of motivational blockages'. To tread into territory where our parents or mentors or beloved friends didn't venture – because they died or because they were afraid, can seem like disloyalty. Our bodies or minds react and tell us that they are not ready to go forward. Healing will have to address the nature of the rift that is imagined if we outstrip someone who was once close to us. The capacity to stake our claim to living even though others' journeys have faltered or ended is a difficult one, and might be a reason why we fall into illness, feeling trepidatious about being well and healthy or ambivalent about being the lucky one. It can be easier sometimes to stay in the sadness and badness. Feeling fantastic and joyful and happy and well would be a position in which others might feel envious of us. We might be called upon to face up to new challenges, of love, of fulfilling or creative activity, of social or political or spiritual engagement, that we might have been avoiding.

When I started to get powerful abdominal pains linked to the diverticulitis that had been lurking for several years, I reluctantly acceded to tests for coeliac disease and irritable bowel syndrome. My brother had died at a younger age from bowel cancer, and coming out of the barium scan, I sat down on the hospital toilet and wept, acutely aware that I was alive and he was not. I recalled that he had died in the middle of his career as a jazz musician and just after getting married for the first time.

Although the doctor wrote down 'abdominal pain' on the documentation for work, I knew that I had a lot of work to do on recovering my mental energy. My sick leave was in the end filled with walks in beautiful places, reading, time with my new partner and my daughter, tackling piles of unsorted books and papers and ultimately getting in touch with my spirituality. I also learned to read my body and started making links between unexpressed feelings and the occasions of intestinal attacks, when I would lie on the bed burping painfully for hours.

Medication helped but **the primary healing came from accepting that I needed to slow down and to build quality into my daily life, and that I had the right to carry on living even though key people in my life had died.** When I went back to work, I wasn't fully 'well'. I still had abdominal attacks but I now had a very different framework from which to view and tackle them.

Illness as the path towards change

Illness thus can sometimes be the way in which transition to another stage or phase of our lives is brokered. Unable to express that we can't go on as we have been, our health cracks and we find that we have good reasons to argue for change that are less equivocal: we find that arguing on health grounds for change is more 'legitimate'.

Thinking about the motivations and drivers of other stakeholders in our health is a helpful way to look after ourselves. Doctors for example have a strong stake in protecting their own knowledge, power and rewards, whilst family members and friends often want us to carry on fulfilling the same roles as spouse, friend, parent, child, colleague, employee etc. we have been doing in their lives. Each has a stake in our continuity and it can be hard to go against this in our drive to change. Recognising the importance of our own needs and desires and how they may be getting lost in a lifestyle may be an essential task of healing. Standing up for what we need rather than acceding to what others think, identifying and naming our own state or deciding for ourselves on the meaning of diagnoses rather than taking on labels and definitions as stigmatising or disempowering may be the path to mental and physical health.

It's important not to abdicate our responsibility to ourselves to health professionals, and to consider the idea of *shared* responsibility.

Critics of the medical system such as Ivan Illich and Bryan Turner suggest that in the drive to maintain and expand medical power and implement social control for the furtherance of capitalism, doctors – and the manufacturers of technology (from pharmaceuticals to Magnetic Resonance Imaging scanners) - have succeeded in many cases in *separating us from our own knowledge about ourselves and what we need*. Rebuilding our trust in ourselves can address this. Informing ourselves about our condition (or about differential diagnoses) and the possible treatments is a first step; arming ourselves with ideas about what we need to make us well (which may not fall neatly into existing government guidelines or contemporary medical paradigms) is the second.

This is not a blueprint for ignoring contemporary research or for deciding never to consult doctors again or for insisting on what we want to the cost of others – it's about recognising who's in charge of our health and healthcare, and being able to discuss our healthcare on an OK-OK basis with healthcare practitioners. It's about making our own assessments based on good research and advice as to the value and use of science and technology in our healthcare programme and not being naïve about the varied motivations in their being made available to us.

301

Responsibility for our health

Throughout this book, we've put forward our belief that looking after ourselves is an important life skill. This can mean a variety of things, including listening to inner 'scripts' and 'voices', divining the wisdom of the body, telling others where our boundaries lie, and expressing our feelings and wishes. Getting ill is not only often seen by ourselves and/or others as a *failure* to look after ourselves, but it's a time when our self-protection and self-care skills really need to come into play.

Questioning the systems and procedures to which we're expected to conform – from the way in which we have to telephone a surgery at a specific time to get an appointment or a prescription, to signing our agreement that a hospital will not protect our property during our stay there can make us start to realise that we have had very little input into the way things work, and that now might be the time to start influencing things.

At a recent visit to a state-run urban hospital, I noticed that all the glass doors along a vast corridor to flowered courtyards were locked. None of the patients or their relatives could access the fresh air or sit on the park benches provided. On enquiry, the main reason given was that patients had tended to smoke there. So all participants in the drama of the hospital were forever sealed in, and smokers congregated at the front of the A & E department. I was referred to an administrative office that was 'not open today'.

Once upon a time we knew that beautiful spaces and oases of tranquillity were healing, and people with diseases often went to rural sanatoria to recuperate, and people created healing gardens. Psychiatric hospitals in particular used to be situated in acres of gardens, not just so that people could be housed away from the community, but so that nature could play a role in healthcare.

The hazards and limits of medicine

The basic thesis of much medical sociology is that doctors are so keen to maintain and enhance their own prestige as a profession, they are prepared to deny patients' innate (and cultivated) self-knowledge and to offer powerful tools of technology, pharmacology and surgery that at times cause us to be worse than we felt originally. And that it is quite wrong to assume that we will find doctors to be altruistic and caring. According to much medical sociology, that is just simply not what they are about; the evidence is that they have systematically developed and expanded their 'power-base' and their personal rewards through 'medicalising' much of modern life.

However, there's hope that today's rhetoric of 'patient-centred medicine' and the idea that people should look after their own health because the health service can't cope with demand, may work back in our favour. GP surgeries tell us that our GP's time is precious and expensive, list the number of 'did not attends' at reception, and exhort us not to waste doctors' time and to limit our 'story' to ten minutes. Hospitals limit our visits to relatives and lovers severely, lest our presence upsets the regular routines of the ward or perhaps allows us to garner too much information about the quality of care. Receptionists tell us that no doctor is available unless what we have constitutes an emergency. A nurse can tell us off if we're not on our bed ready for when the consultant arrives on the ward. Even porters are afraid to chat in case they say something that can be used against the hospital. Everything conspires to get us to conform to our place in the hierarchy of the health system, with doctors (and sometimes managers) at the top and patients somewhere near the bottom. Increasingly, the health service is afraid of an interactive relationship with us, so much so that it's difficult to see any encounter as anything but 'litigation-defensive'.

There's no need for us to become afraid of that relationship ourselves. We can claim an OK-OK relationship with doctors and approach medical consultations as *negotiations*. We can make the assumption that our bodies and minds belong to us and consult with doctors and other health professionals for their advice. We don't have to give over to them that power, nor do we have to imbue them with any magical qualities, despite the evidence of their status and prestige confronting us at every stage. We can recognise that *our* time is important too. We can recognise that *our* knowledge and experience has relevance. We can face the responsibility of taking decisions about our health ourselves and seeking the best possible information, much of which doctors - if so minded - can tell us.

The National Institute for Health and Clinical Excellence (NICE), the UK government's advisory body in relation to evidence-based medicine and ultimately the allocation of health resources, plays a key role in the kind of advice and recommendations that doctors give. UK NHS doctors have only a limited palette of what they can offer in terms of drugs and treatments and are increasingly under pressure to make cutbacks. These are spelled out in national framework guidelines; many patients, if they have the means, are forced to buy treatments they need outside the system. Increasingly the NHS offers the basic minimum of healthcare and **it's important to keep vigilant about what we're prescribed and what is dispensed and administered.** We can familiarise ourselves with reports from organisations like the National Patient Safety Agency – for example, appreciating that errors in administration and prescribing medication make up a significant proportion of serious incidents reported, and that incidents involving injectable medicines are the most commonly to be associated with death or severe harm.

We learn too that the UK led a new initiative from the World Health Organisation through introducing a *surgery safety checklist* similar to that used by pilots in aviation, an idea promoted by the surgeon Atul Gawande – but also note that in the UK, reported errors in surgery, not all of which have resulted in harm to patients, are annually above 100,000.

'Iatrogenesis' – doing harm to the patient

There are numerous cases of what the philosopher Ivan Illich called *'iatrogenesis'* – including the VIOXX scandal, the infecting of haemophiliacs by blood transfusion, thalidomide babies, and injuries in drug trials, quite apart from a wide range of annual failures to treat or to diagnose correctly. In Britain, organisations like the GMC, NICE and the Cochrane Reviews work to combat medical risk – it is our job to be 'on the ball' about their findings and recommendations. Druin Burch in his 2009 book *Taking the Medicine* tells us something of the history of medical

304

experimentation, the attachment of doctors to their methods and beliefs and the lives that have sometimes been damaged or lost as a result. Ben Goldacre in his recent book *'Bad Pharma'* asserts that pharmaceutical research and development can be distorted and results hidden from view – the more we can be educated about this the safer we may be.

However, Ivan Illich also thought that by medicalizing ordinary problems (from baldness to the management of death), medical institutions were extending their reach into areas of life that should be social rather than medical, issues that people ought to be able to manage for themselves, and that this in itself is harmful to people. It's ironic that today helping professionals often blame patients for not looking after their own health properly in areas that medicine itself has appropriated as its own, thereby putting patients into a kind of 'double-bind'.

Doctors' roles in collusion or whistleblowing

It's essential not to be naïve in our thinking - altruism and objectivity cannot always be assumed on the part of the health professions despite their rhetoric. Institutions seek to survive. Professions seek to survive. The medical profession's role could be construed as identifying individuals as troubled or diseased, and in some cases, as irresponsible or deviant, and sometimes neglecting to mention or even concealing from us and from wider debate the role that pathogens (eg. viruses, bacteria, fungi) and other phenomena around us (eg. pollution, toxins, drug effects, medical error, poor quality food, poor housing, location of pylons, social policy and business decisions, psychopathology and distress/fatigue among professionals etc.) have played in the aetiology and outcomes of our illness. Doctors may not always do this consciously or intentionally – it may be that they too have accepted unquestioningly precepts and systems that they should have looked into more deeply. Taking a stand and rocking the boat are things that we should expect doctors to be willing to do when necessary, yet recently, following the scandal of the unusually high death rates at Staffordshire Hospital in the UK, senior doctors have spoken of a culture of fear and coercion within the NHS and the paralysing fear of damage to careers that can inhibit whistleblowing among medics. New helplines and guidance are now being introduced to address the problem and the British Medical Association is working to 'normalise' the 'raising of concerns' as part of medical culture rather than emphasising the dramatic nature of 'whistle-blowing'. The surgeon and author Atul Gawande in his book *Better* suggests that *finding the energy to fight for patients* is an essential task for doctors.

The social commentator Vicente Navarro, writing since the 1970s, describes medicine as a mechanism for depoliticizing the harm that is done to the population by capitalistic interests such as disregard for ethics, health and safety; pollution and toxins; harmful products, goods and foods; work and travel stress etc. As well as normalizing for us these unwelcome negative outcomes, medical practitioners also attempt to provide the repair to the damage done by prescribing tests and treatments, thus, whether willingly or unintentionally, inevitably fulfilling the business interests of pharmaceutical companies, laboratory testing organisations, researchers, and equipment manufacturers.

South America has long been known for its pioneering work in 'social medicine' kick-started by activists and political leaders such as Salvatore Allende in Chile and Ernesto/Che Guevara in Argentina, who promoted the ideas that poor health resulted from social conditions, inequality, poverty etc. Some who have followed in these traditions have paid the price for their work in suffering persecution. For more on this see the article by Howard Waitzkin and others listed in the references.

Thus one way of looking at healthcare professionals is to see them as conduits between the damage done by industry and commerce and the provision of further services and solutions tendered as therapeutic - which nevertheless may also do damage. Blaming patients for their inability to stop eating, drinking, smoking or manifesting couch-potato habits is arguably an abrogation of doctors' moral duty to challenge tobacco companies, breweries and distilleries, licensing authorities, slimming product companies, diet regimes, the producers of food with high (and sometimes hidden) levels of salt, fat, sugar etc., and the inaccessibility of gyms, lack of walkways and safe areas for leisure and exercise.

It's through *people-power* that improvements can be made and challenges to malpractice and corruption made. We may decide – particularly when ill and feeling vulnerable – to argue purely for what we need at an individual level. At other times, or after we have gotten improvements to our health situation, to consider if there are lessons to be learned or communicated to the health organisations and practitioners with whom we've been dealing, to complaints bodies, to patient organisations, or to the public through the press. ***Becoming a health activist is one life position we can choose.*** Ann Marie Rodgers from Swindon was an example of someone who fought an individual court case which had wider ramifications: she challenged the decision of her health authority to refuse her a prescription for Herceptin for early-stage breast cancer: *"I did this for all women battling this dreadful disease"*. Her friend, Barbara Clark, said *"When she won her case it had a domino effect across England and that is her legacy"*.

Putting our trust in health practitioners

Our own experience of being cared for as infants will shape the way we feel when we're vulnerable and what we anticipate from health professionals, so that if for example, they don't match up to how our parents were, or if they appear to reinforce punitive or uncaring attitudes, this triggers frustration and anger in us.

However, recognising that doctors and other healthcare practitioners are rooted in their own social positioning with its particular prejudices and values, that they make mistakes and are subject to their own psychology, sharpens the mind when subjecting ourselves to their gaze and power. Fatigue, inexperience, stress can all affect healthcare personnel.

Problems in medical care can result from a multiplicity of factors which can affect direct care, such as:

- administration systems that aren't properly linked up resulting in a lack of relevant information at the right time
- errors in diagnosing and prescribing, including failure to spot potential drug interactions (eg. through lack of information)

- difficulties in communication – cross-cultural misunderstandings, poor handwriting, confusion of similar terms and names of drugs etc.
- diffusion of responsibility – eg. lack of clarity about who's supposed to have done what
- cutbacks resulting in work being done under too much time pressure, without proper safety checks or using out-dated equipment

Health warnings on health practitioners

Nevertheless, it's worth noting that doctors and nurses come with their own 'health warnings' – often suffering from psychopathology of their own. David Malan coined the term *'helping profession syndrome'* – whereby a practitioner feels compelled to give others the care they would like to have for themselves, for example, because in childhood they were expected to look after their parents rather than being cared for, or because they want to repair damage done to them when they were ill and weak as children - such patterns of *'giving out of well of unmet need'* have also been identified by Susie Orbach, the feminist psychoanalyst commenting on women's psychology.

In rare cases, there have been examples of the contentious *'Munchausen by Proxy'* syndrome, probably suffered by the nurse Beverley Allitt, who was given a life sentence for killing a number of young children in her care or narcissism and psychopathy, as may have been the case in Harold Shipman, a GP who was jailed (and later killed himself) for bringing about the deaths of patients (most of them elderly women) with morphine injections (possibly ultimately totalling 250). Both practitioners were highly valued by patients and relatives who thought they were wonderful. Where health practitioners – or more commonly, parents - fabricate or induce illness the person exaggerates or induces the health problems in others and then reaps a secondary gain by being solicitous and helping towards them and those who care about them, thus gaining the attention they desperately seek. Sometimes they have themselves been the victim of parents who gave them attention if they adopted the sick role – something which, in moderation, many of us can identify with. In Harold Shipman's case, there's a suggestion that he needed to replay the death of his own mother, where she was given morphine to help her cope with the symptoms of cancer when he was a boy, and in those 'replays', it would be he who had the power of saving or ending life and not something arbitrary beyond his control, which was how he might have felt as a child.

Above-average levels of emotional detachment and the denial of personal vulnerability, identified by W. Johnson, apparently characterise significant numbers of health professionals, and this is reinforced within medical culture. This makes it difficult not only for health practitioners to admit to problems and ill-health themselves because of anxiety about stepping into the patient role, but also means that they cannot empathise with patients' needs. The position of a patient becomes 'one-down'/not-OK and the healthcare practitioner finds it impossible to accept being in that place themselves. Perhaps too they know all the small humiliations and indignities that patients are frequently subjected to, and can't bear the thought of suffering that way themselves.

In a moving paper on the retained organs controversy at Bristol and Alder Hey Hospitals in the UK, Alistair V Campbell and Michaela Willis make a plea for medical practitioners to pay more attention to their *own* physical experiencing, indicating that it was doctors' tendency to treat the body as *object* through the lens of scientific-rational thinking that led to the tragedies for relatives who saw the body as belonging to people they *loved,* and could also lead to doctors submerging their own personal health needs.

None of this is written to frighten us into thinking that going to the surgery or hospital will be a nightmare, but is intended to help us all to be on the alert for the way we're treated and to insist on psychologically healthy, OK-OK communication and shared decision-making. In a climate of shortages and cutbacks, it's all the more important to double-check everything and make sure that our care and treatment is accurate, safe, appropriate, and the best that can be given in the circumstances. We need to stay in charge – informing ourselves before and during treatment – and remain ready for discussion with our carers and physicians. Taking our share of the responsibility makes the chances of good outcomes a lot more likely.

Being sensitive to the needs of health practitioners

It might also be a good idea to check out how our doctor or nurse is feeling themselves – there's no need for us to treat *them* impersonally even if they're treating us that way. As we said in our *Effective relating* chapter, it's good sometimes to *do the opposite*. Humanity should be shown both ways. The challenge in healthcare is for practitioners to balance pacing themselves through a variety of emotionally gut-wrenching cases so that they can keep on dispensing care, yet not 'go under'. And in today's high pressure and under-resourced environments, many choose to pull back on the *'emotional labour'* that creating social relations and talking sympathetically to patients and relatives involves – it can seem simpler to do the minimum, to deal with the technicalities of physical care, to use the technology available, and to avoid complex human encounters that will take more energy and more time.

Unfortunately, this is a misapprehension – litigation against the medical profession is apparently much more likely when there's been poor communication, and human connection is much more likely to yield the critical clues to what the patient needs than simply going through the motions in a medical protocol as well as likely to reduce symptoms like pain and anxiety. Indeed, some studies show that good communication can reduce the time each patient takes – just as with parents and children and between partners, giving a small amount of quality time when needed reduces time-wasting calls for attention and complaints later on. So as health consumers, we need to insist that our health practitioners properly attend to us, for everyone's benefit.

The surgeon, academic and author Atul Gawande reminds us of the mystery and unpredictability in medicine, and how doctors have to come to terms with the limitations of their expertise, often with much anguish. Leading the introduction of checklists into surgical practice, he shows how ideas from other fields in life can sometimes cross-translate. Trying to be error-proof is an art that takes much from science. Equally, as consumers we have to recognise that medicine can never offer the answer to all ills.

Some final reminders from Jack about taking charge of our own health

See also our chapter on *Effective relating*.

- be very assertive and active regarding your own health
- get knowledgeable; get the gist information about treatment offered – 'does this stuff work?' 'how many people do you give it to?' – be informed and read everything going.
- treat people (whether doctors, nurses or patients) as equal
- make it personal - relate to others as human beings
- let others know you won't accept nonsense and that you expect a 'top-rate' service
- get what you want, don't follow others' agendas - act like a citizen and not like a sausage in a sausage machine.
- watch out for any bad treatment, bad goods, incompetence etc.
- watch out for any agendas to save money etc.
- don't treat health practitioners like experts - treat them as *advisers to you* – **you** make the decisions about your health and treatment
- be proactive, not passive
- aim if necessary to fit into 'educated, sincere and serious' category of patient/relative rather than getting into the 'troublesome/nuisance' category
- offer nurturance to the health professionals (who are usually overworked and stressed themselves) and don't expect it from them
- insist on a partnership and talk
- make health a priority in your life and where necessary change lifestyle to suit
- learn to recognise stress and adjust to reduce it
- keep informed about diet for our body and mind
- find a way of using the body through exercise and activity which is helpful, and ensure you do keep active tap into

beauty, plants, water, rocks, air quality, connection with animals, accept the mystery of nature
- bring more water into life – drink it, swim in it, look at it, ride on it, touch it
- look at 'compliance', find sources of energy that we do have, look at resistance etc.
- tap into the unconscious, use positive thinking, visualisation, dream-work, creative mind
- live holistically – integrate body, mind, emotions and spirit
- tackle addictions
- develop passions
- get emotional and social support
- avoid over-using the body, pushing it around, listen to pain and discomfort
- rest – let body and mind have time and space to heal
- get in touch with anger and despair and grief and fear
- be realistic
- get in touch with others with same disorder
- publicise or look at public fora, campaign for resources, help, anti-discrimination etc.
- build a balance of structure, routine and freedom in our life

Books and papers

Peter Anderson and Ben Baumberg *Alcohol in Europe: a public health perspective: a report for the European Commission* Institute of Alcohol Studies, UK June 2006
Helen Benedict (2009) *The Lonely Soldier: The Private War of Women Serving in Iraq* Beacon Press
Phil Brown and Stephen Zavestoski (2005) *Social Movements in Health* Oxford: Blackwell
Druin Burch (2009) *Taking the Medicine* London: Chatto and Windus
Alistair V Campbell and Michaela Willis (2006) *Narratives of embodiment and loss* in Frances Rapport and Paul Wainwright (2006) *The Self in Health and Illness* Oxford: Radcliffe
Mary Daly (1984) *Pure Lust* The Women's Press
George C. Denniston, Frederick M. Hodges and Marilyn Fayre Milos, (eds) (2009) *Human Rights and Circumcision* Springer

Deborah Franklin (2012) *How Hospital Gardens Help Patients Heal* Scientific American 19 March 2012
http://www.scientificamerican.com/article.cfm?id=nature-that-nurtures
Atul Gawande (2008) *Better: A Surgeon's Notes on Performance* Profile Books
Atul Gawande (2008 2nd ed) *Complications: A Surgeon's Notes on an Imperfect Science* Profile Books
Atul Gawande (2011) *The Checklist Manifesto: How to Get Things Right* Profile Books
Ben Goldacre (2012) *Bad Pharma: How the Drug Companies Mislead Doctors and Harm Patients* Fourth Estate
T B Gustafson and D B Sarwer (2004) *Childhood sexual abuse and obesity* The International Association for the Study of Obesity Obesity Reviews **5**, 129–135
Donna J Haraway (1991) *Simians, Cyborgs, and Women* London: Free Association Books
Jeremy Hazell (1982) *The unconscious significance of some motivational blockages in students at university* British Journal of Guidance & Counselling Volume 10 Issue 1
Louise Hay (1984, 2004 edition) *You Can Heal Your Life* Hay House www.hayhouse.com
Cecil G Helman (2007) *Culture, Health and Illness* Hodder Arnold
Ivan Illich (1976) *Limits to Medicine: Medical Nemesis: The Expropriation of Health* London: Marion Boyars
W.D.K. Johnson *Predisposition to emotional distress and psychiatric illness amongst doctors: the role of unconscious and experiential factors* British Journal of Medical Psychology, 1991 Wiley Online Library
Elisabeth Kübler-Ross (1973) *On Death and Dying* Routledge
Darian Leader and David Corfield (2007) *Why do people get ill?* London: Penguin Books
Robert F. Murphy (1990) *The Body Silent: The Different World of the Disabled* New York: W W Norton
Vicente Navarro (1986) *Crisis, health and medicine: a social critique* Routledge
Jennie G. Noll, Meg H. Zeller, Penelope K. Trickett and Frank W. Putnam (2007) *Obesity Risk for Female Victims of Childhood Sexual Abuse: A Prospective Study* Pediatrics Vol. 120 No. 1 July

1, 2007 http://pediatrics.aappublications.org/content/ 120/1/ e61. short

Michael Oliver and Colin Barnes (2012) *The New Politics of Disablement* Palgrave/Macmillan

Susie Orbach (2002) *Susie Orbach on Eating* London: Penguin

Annette Scambler, Graham Scambler, and Donald Craig (1981) *Kinship and friendship networks and women's demand for primary care* J R Coll Gen Pract 1981 December: 31(233) 746–750.

Nancy Scheper-Hughes (2000) *The Global Traffic in Human Organs* Current Anthropology 41:2 April 2000

Ruth Seifert *Rape: the female body as symbol and sign* in Ilkka Taipale (2002) *War or health?* Cambridge, Mass: International Physicians for the Prevention of Nuclear War (IPPNW) and Zed Books

Richard Tillett *The patient within – psychopathology in the helping professions* Adv.Psychiatr.Treat 2003, 9:272-279

Bryan Turner (1995 2nd ed) *Medical Power and Social Knowledge (A Handbook of Experimental Pharmacology)* Sage

Howard Waitzkin, Celia Iriart, Alfredo Estrada, and Silvia Lamadrid *Social Medicine Then and Now: Lessons From Latin America* Am J Public Health. 2001 October; 91(10): 1592–1601

Jeanne Ward and Mendy Marsh (2006) *Sexual Violence Against Women and Girls in War and Its Aftermath: Realities, Responses, and Required Resources: A Briefing Paper* Prepared for: Symposium on Sexual Violence in Conflict and Beyond 21-23 June 2006 Brussels (Belgium) UNPFA

Jessica Wolfe, Kiban Turner, et al. *Gender and Trauma as Predictors of Military Attrition: A Study of Marine Corps Recruits* Military Medicine 170(2005): 12, 1037.

David Wootton (2006) *Bad Medicine: Doctors Doing Harm Since Hippocrates* Oxford University Press

Safety in Doses: improving the uses of medicines in the NHS Learning from National Reporting in 2007 National Patient Safety Agency

Films
Michael Mann (1999) *Insider*
Steve McQueen *Hunger*
Mike Nichols (1983) *Silkwood*
Steven Soderbergh (2000) *Erin Brockovich*

8 sexuality

This chapter is divided largely into two sections.

The first section incorporates practical proposals for improving our sex lives on the basis that many of us don't have a good sex-life and that most of us could learn to enjoy it more. We also look at the importance of touch for our wellbeing and how we can develop it.

A key message in the second part of the chapter is the fluid nature of our ideas about sexuality across cultures and stages of life, bringing into question long-established views on sexual identity and gender.

We've both contributed to this chapter, with Jack mostly having written the first part and Julia the later part.

Jack

My position

The simple version of my position is that I see sexuality as linked to our 'sensual self' and our 'touch self' and our 'emotional self'. I think the problems around sex centre on splitting off sexuality from other parts of the self and then trying to regulate sex with distorted attitudes or through being judgemental (designating things or people as 'not OK').

The way out of this situation as far as I can tell is to:

1. accept our sexual selves
2. understand all the conditioning from self and others
3. get real instead of following myths, ideals etc. and realise that sexuality is an important part of ourselves
4. integrate our sexuality into our everyday lives and give it priority
5. communicate with partners from an OK position
6. learn to develop sexually, find out what pleases us and our partners, ask and give; make sex creative and playful

7. create a situation in which we're able to feel safe and are safe
8. try and understand the breadth of sexual behaviour and learn something about the more disturbed or damaging behaviours and how these develop

The world of sexuality is full of unhelpful myths around performance, 'attractiveness' etc. Maybe the main myth is that in the developed countries, we've 'sorted out generations of not-OK programming in recent times and are all now having fantastic sex lives'.

I think the truth is that in a climate with mythology, wonky attitudes, misinformation, sexploitation etc. around, people are not fully enjoying or being their sexual selves. I think too that there's a lot of backwardness, prejudice and not-OKness about sex when people could be growing/developing their sexual selves and having fun.

Give your sexual/sensual self priority – nobody else will until you do

Carl Jung's idea that accepting our sexual selves as part of the process of developing as a person (individuation) seems important. This means acceptance without censorship or conforming. If our sensual/sexual self doesn't have priority, then we can put it back into our lives as a priority, by devoting time, care and attention and thought to it, otherwise we'll end up reading endless magazine articles about how to get our sex lives going and getting nowhere. By giving our sexual selves a high priority we're doing the opposite of what many people do, which is to fit everything else in, then wonder why they're unhappy.

Love or lust............. does it matter which?

For a lot of people, the distinction does matter and sex is better the closer you are to the person (or people) you're having sex with. This doesn't apply to everyone and I think there shouldn't be any judgement beyond 'doing no harm' - see below.

Sex and harm to ourselves or others

It's important to get things right as ultimately we must decide for ourselves and be responsible, particularly if our sexual lifestyle causes real harm to us or others in the culture we're in or with the relationships we have – ultimately we have to live with the consequences. Here I'm not talking about vaguely upsetting some people or raised eyebrows but actual or potential harm.

In the 'real harm' category, I would include for example unsafe sex, sex addictions, forcing people to do things without consent, having sex with inappropriate people and destroying trust in existing relationships by having new ones.

It's not true for most people that sex takes people over and stops people thinking, looking after themselves, or considering others. We're always capable of taking responsibility for our actions.

The risks of sex since HIV

I think that unconsciously people are more scared of having penetrative sex outside their longstanding partnerships than they used to be, since HIV became an issue and it's worth being informed about sexually-transmitted diseases but not to be put off sex and not to discriminate against people with problems they could transmit to us. There's a lot of moralising about sexual behaviour and this can confuse the picture with people who have sexually-related diseases. Stigmatising people is enormously hurtful and also means that we can exclude people who otherwise are or would be interesting and attractive to us.

What's 'normal' and who's 'normal'?

It's hard to arrive at normality (even if we all knew what it was!), especially as we're all conditioned by our culture, and perhaps particularly through films.

A lot of us still get very little information about sex from our parents and families, schools or professionals that's useful - in other words there's usually an information gap that we have to

317

make up for, and this can make us uneasy about the range of possibilities available to us in our sex lives.

We should make room for the expression of sex which 'pushes boundaries' – whatever we call it - 'exciting', 'kinky', 'risqué', etc – we needn't dismiss it out of hand. We should get consent from each other, have fun, learn about each other. We can be experimental and keep our sex lives alive, evolving and creative.

Being creative and imaginative

Being creative and imaginative in sex is important, including allowing and sharing fantasies with partners, experimenting with ideas gleaned from reading, the media, our own desires etc. Being relaxed and open to what emerges can be the best approach rather than operating according to a regular formula. Getting used to the uncertainty of what might happen (as in our chapter on *Creativity*) may be an essential skill – we don't have to control or predict everything, we can afford to be adventurous and to follow where our partner leads, to listen to our inner selves more acutely than before, and to find out what happens when both partners create something new together.

Enjoying sex and making it fun

Thinking of sex as something to enjoy and making it fun, tackling anything that's worrying us and getting things to work in a way that suits us. For example, creating the right setting and making ourselves ready for sex.

Sex is something that is 'free' and available to us as a happy, enjoyable part of living and it's mad not to value it and make the most of it.

Many of us choose partners with whom we can share humour during sex – it's a good idea not to take things too seriously or too intensely. It's helpful to look at the longer-term and recognise that sex doesn't have to be perfect every time – sharing a good and happy time together is what's important.

318

Talking about sex

Sex can be the great un-talked about subject in our lives. If on the other hand we find that others around us 'over-talk' about it, trivialising sex or joking about, it may be time to start clarifying that sex has a value for us and to spend time with people who do actually want to talk about sex meaningfully.

Talking about sex with our partner can include a variety of aspects: developing our allusions to sex around the home and when we're out so that we relate as 'live' sexual partners, using sexy talk during sex, sharing fantasies and desires, exploring memories of sex, discussing how we'd like things to develop or what's in the way of having good sex (including previous bad experiences or the memory of good times with other partners). Non-verbally, we can build more touch into our life *as a language* rather than saving it just for when we have sex. This can enhance our sensual awareness and shouldn't just be instrumental, though sometimes it will of course be a prelude to sexual activity.

What's most important is to create a climate in which we can ask for what we want in relation to sex without being judged by each other. Sexuality is about *intimacy* – we explore a variety of issues in this chapter which can be discussed in more detail at our workshops on this theme.

Caring about our physical selves

We have important aspects of ourselves that need caring about, including our sensual, touch, emotional and bodily selves. See also our chapter on *The Body*. It's not just about eating right and doing exercise as part of some kind of self-mortification that matters – as many in the West seem to think – what's important is to care about our physical selves and to nurture our sensory side, our experience of touch, the emotions that affect our physical state, and our experience of our bodies. This might mean having an aroma-massage or a languid bath, choosing music that suits our mood, giving in to the need to cry or laugh, doing some physiotherapy on aches and pains or getting into some dance, rejecting invasions of our bodies such as medical interventions we're not happy about or a sexual relationship with someone we no longer respect. When we enter into a sexual encounter with a partner, we should feel happy about the way we live in our body and feel in charge of ourselves – only then are we ready to relinquish self-control without fear.

It's good to get fit and avoid slipping into lazy habits about self-care, but it's also important to distance ourselves from the stereotyped images of young, 'beautiful' people in magazines, films, advertising etc. Real sex doesn't depend on matching up to these images. We can develop our own aesthetic style and enjoy the encounter with ourselves and our partner's physicality even through illness, ageing etc. with a sense of joy and exploration – the history of our lives is written on our bodies.

Making sex a priority and building it into our lifestyle

To prioritise sex means scheduling it in formally or informally, not being afraid to say to others, *'oh, I'm having some time with my partner then'* and refusing to let that time be overridden by other demands. It's important to make that time and hold to it. Our difficulties with this are sometimes linked to a lack of self-valuing, being afraid to say to others that our relationship with our partner matters and that we want to give it the space it deserves. (See our chapter on *Close Relationships* for more on this issue). Sometimes it can be a sense of 'shame' built in from childhood, (when for example we might have been punished for masturbating), or because sex has been treated as a taboo subject, or we might work in a field of work where sex is a loaded subject (eg. social work).

It may be easy to prioritise sex at the beginning of a relationship when we feel 'in love' but that feeling needs to be re-evoked over the long-term by the excitement of scheduling dates with one another, and ensuring that time together is protected from the intrusions of others (actual or mental).

Building sex into our lifestyle includes making it a priority – not putting it at the bottom of the list of things to do. Sex should not be something we only do when everything else is done and we're exhausted (though if it happens then that can be cool, too). It's worth finding out what sex feels like when we have it in the middle of the day, or unexpectedly in the middle of a busy time of work or stress etc. Sex can be about increasing our sense of being bonded to our partner and can help dissolve tensions and worries that are blocking us in our work or daily activities.

OK-OK feelings and power within the sexual relationship

Learn how to recognise what OK-OK feels like and withdraw from interactions which don't feel like that. Confusion is exploited by magazines and media – making us feel NOT-OK, that we must be lonely if we are alone on a Saturday night and in need of telephone sex, that we need after-shave or perfume or a super-sports-car to feel OK, etc. Reject any messages that sex is not OK for our status such as being an older person or being divorced etc.

Recognise different styles of interacting sexually (and socially) - dovetail/negotiate/jettison behaviours – we can lead, follow, and share at different times.

Look where things are matched/mismatched in your life – eg. being socially powerful at work and being mastered/mothered at home; flirting in the external world and committed at home - check out if you need to change any of your behaviours or interactions with people and how compartmentalised or integrated they are. In some families and groups, although men seem the powerful ones externally, it might be that women wield a lot of power within the privacy of the family. Consider the patterns you experienced in your own background and how much you've been able to make your own choices of how to be as a sexual person. Allow what suits you and change what doesn't.

Sexual culture or aesthetic styles

Conflict of styles can be a problem – recognise that each person has their own family, cultural and historical background shaping their sexual aesthetic. In a new relationship, it may take some time to merge or share or come to terms with each other's preferences and habitual ways of doing things such as being passive/submissive or active/initiating/dominant, being edgy,

321

enjoying cross-dressing, enacting fantasy roles, being romantic, joking around, liking sex in the open air, enjoying fetishes like high heels or soft fabrics.

Being close to our partner

Being close to our partner can emerge from making sex an important and valued element in our relationship with them. Clearing out things that bother us about our relationship can help create space for good sex – expressing our concerns and seeing what possibilities there are for change can enliven us with new hope that things can be happier; likewise we should offer ourselves up for feedback and listen carefully to what our partner says. Relationships can be great resources for personal growth.

The idea of sex is that it enhances bonding between partners – if it doesn't and if through sex we come to feel more distant, unsatisfied, lonely, hurt, etc. then things need to change in our relationship or in our life. If we have an idea in our mind of how sex should be and actual sex is falling very short of this, then talking this over with our partner or if not possible, with a counsellor or therapist, is the next step. It can be very painful to broach issues in relation to sex because they are so intimate and so deep, people can quickly imagine that they are being criticised or found wanting when in reality, there may be issues from buried history that are getting in the way or beliefs and understandings that are outdated. Sex is about sharing our vulnerabilities as we build trust with each other – if one or other in a relationship is finding this difficult, patience will be needed and a commitment to being reliable and trustworthy and caring. It's important too to remain OK-OK and to see that problems often reflect a particular dynamic in the relationship rather than identifying one person as 'the one with the problem'. Our response to 'the problem' will have a huge effect on how that problem resolves itself.

Dating through the internet

We should recognise that the internet dating industry is just that, and that those who run dating sites are looking primarily for profits. Thus they may want us to conform to standard ways of

322

presenting ourselves to get lots of 'hits' rather than helping us to present ourselves as the unique and unusual individuals we may be. We shouldn't be afraid to be authentic and to wait for the right connections, whilst being open to a variety of people who might fit the bill. It can often take one to two years to find someone depending on our criteria and our luck.

Our guidance (from experience) would include:

- looking around at dating sites – some have good records on people getting together for the long-term and there are also plenty of 'niche' sites based on mutual interests or values or social groupings – checking out too their policies and guidance to find sites we feel comfortable with
- being OK with ourselves <u>before</u> dating
- not judging others
- being honest <u>from the start</u> about ourselves and what we're hoping for – being ultra-clear
- dropping ideals and avoiding looking for an idealised, fantasy person – being open to a range of possibilities
- dropping *persona* and *ego* as much as possible (see chapter on *the Self*)
- avoiding game-players and destructive people and avoiding playing games ourselves – it's not to get attention or to disturb others, it's to find a partner
- watching out for characteristics and patterns that we would find it difficult to relate to (see our chapter on *Emotional health*)
- realising that people may still be 'interviewing' candidates until they make a decision and being prepared to handle our upset when they don't choose us; keeping open the right to choose for ourselves too
- tackling loneliness and our needs for touch before we go dating if we can – nurturing our friendships, developing our interests, getting a regular massage etc. – going out dating when we feel lonely or needy puts us in a vulnerable position
- being creative around rituals and clarifying expectations about arrangements, who pays for what etc. – there's no need to do things based on outdated notions of 'dates' –

we can relate in creative ways and organise social meetings using our own flair

- checking out our own internal permissions and not agreeing to anything we don't feel ready for
- watching safety, taking sensible precautions (like letting someone know where we are and not putting ourselves in vulnerable positions) but not being paranoid

The use of pornography in our sex-lives

Pornography is an industry – a very lucrative one. The original intention was to provide an addition to people's sex lives, and it's now particularly targeted at men as an aid to 'wanking'. It also transpires that a lot of its use is in the workplace. It's often not talked about and there can be a lot of 'moralistic' judgement about it. Its use is now so widespread that it's becoming normalised as part of a lot of people's lives – witness for example the astronomical sales of E L James' *50 Shades of Grey*, which is sold in supermarkets along with food and household goods, fast becoming one of the biggest selling books ever.

There can be good and bad elements to pornography – it can inspire experimentation within a sexual relationship and also provide some relief for us when there's no-one to have sex with, but it can also become addictive, with the risk of undermining a relationship because it's 'easier' than bothering to engage with a real partner and the risk of distracting from getting on with fulfilling work or parenting roles.

Researchers Ogi Ogas and Sai Gaddam indicate their awareness that women are (perhaps not unexpectedly as they are most of the 'gazed-upon') more attuned to the social messages in pornography than men who tend to focus on the sexual material itself. Exploitation may be mutual – of the people providing the pornography and of the consumers of it, while for some, the production of it may have been as enjoyable as the use of it. For some of us, making our own videos or writing our own material may be a way of enjoying pornography as 'producers' rather than feeling that people are being exploited as 'performers' or as 'users'.

324

Julia:

Sex will feel different and require different approaches at different times in our lives:

- *experimentation when sex is new*
- *early passion*
- *routine sex*
- *sex for procreation*
- *sex after miscarriage, abortion, stillbirth*
- *when one partner is involved in a second relationship*
- *repairing after conflict*
- *when a relationship is breaking down*
- *occasional sex after formal separation*
- *stranger sex and one-night stands*
- *sex in a group context*
- *sex which is paid for*
- *friendship sex*
- *sex in a relationship across distance (eg. transcontinental)*
- *e-sex – by telephone or computer*
- *forbidden sex (eg. when a partner or both are committed elsewhere or when it contravenes institutional role boundaries etc).*
- *mature love in a long-term relationship*
- *when a partner is dying (eg. cancer)*
- *sex as we get older*
- *when one or both partners are ill or disabled*

Recognise that what's true right now may not go on being the same in the future. All situations ultimately change, life is transient, and relationships can take new forms. Sexuality can help us to change our feelings about something and can give us memories for ever.

Our sexual needs change throughout life

Sometimes our life situation dictates our sexual practices – a partner becomes disabled or ill or dies and we start to masturbate as a regular practice; we're confined to an environment where sex isn't possible and we become celibate; we fall in love with someone much older or very different from ourselves or someone who is not fully free to be with us etc. and we work hard to relate to them as well as coping with others' censure; a relationship that was happy ends and we find it hard to find a new partner who understands us as well; we soldier through a long-term abusive relationship and find that even when we break out to find someone kinder we are haunted by memories of the past. Our sexual life is not static and it's good for us to recognise that we can continue to change.

Touch and non-verbal behaviour

We're primarily non-verbal creatures, but modern life has taken us into the realm of thinking and language, almost as if nothing else exists. Perhaps the visual culture of our modern life – endlessly presented through digital media – is the nearest we get to recognising this, tapping as it does into our 'right-brain'. To accept our non-verbal selves may require an acceptance of our animal nature (which is antithetical to the teachings of some religions) – it's sometimes much easier to imagine that we are rather like machines, but that doesn't do much for our love-life. A great deal of our communication is non-verbal – when going on a date with someone we haven't met before, much of the necessary information will be conveyed as we walk towards each other. We spend a lot of time and money trying to influence the presentation of our non-verbal selves, designing our outfit, shaving, showering, putting on scents, styling our hair, and in more drastic cases, training our voices, posture and behaviour, and using smiles and eye contact strategically.

Touch is one of the most powerful elements of our non-verbal cache, communicating coercion, tenderness, reassurance, inducing relaxation and reducing pain. Ina May Gaskin has presented *childbirth* as **a phase in an ongoing psychosexual and spiritual**

relationship and sees loving touch as vital to that process, reducing anxiety, limiting pain and fostering closeness. Childbirth within this framework is a sensual, even sexual process.

James W Prescott's work links **deprivation of touch to violent behaviour**, and indeed suggests that people and countries which have the least physically affectionate styles of family life could be the most violent and war-mongering. If this interests you, have a look at his writing.

Some thoughts on how to use touch in your life

- stay in touch with your partner at gatherings through eye contact and casual touch as you pass
- evoke memories with smells and scents and create moods with them
- use touch for reassurance and connection
- value touch in your life when you or partner has to face pain or anxiety-provoking treatment
- consider how to build touch into your life without feeling it has to be sexual – eg. increase hugs with people, having a massage, stroking a pet, having sensual experiences – eg. swimming, mud-baths, going to the hairdresser

Touch is an important barometer of how things are – if we're not comfortable with someone's touch, find out why (*is it you? is it them?*), negotiate changes or get out of the relationship. See also section on *Touch* in chapter on *The body, health and illness*.

Sex and spirituality

Incorporating sex as part of our spiritual selves can sometimes go against ingrained attitudes to the way we've been brought up or indoctrinated within our culture or religion, particularly if in our early background, sex was isolated as something done for procreation or done 'behind closed doors'. Being truthful about ourselves and accepting our sexuality – even if our sexual identity is not what family or those close to us would wish – is important in being an authentic, fully alive human being. Sexual energy is about being fully alive and about loving ourselves and others.

Being blocked about our sexuality could result in us being resistant to change, remaining narrow, being judgemental of others, denying life-energy and remaining distant from others. Even if we can't enjoy an actual sexual relationship, cultivating our awareness of ourselves as sexual beings is an important human right and is something which connects us to all others and to the stream of life.

Sexuality and spiritual institutionalisation

It's important of course to look carefully at attitudes towards sex within any spiritual organisations we join – there can be hazards with an over-control of what we should and shouldn't do as much as there can be the danger of being required to accept sex with someone we don't want, because they're charismatic or 'suitable'. The point – as always – in our book, is to listen to what *we* want and don't want.

Some religions have powerful prohibitions about sexuality – if you are affected by fears about breaking teachings that have been around in your life since childhood, give time to look at why these ideas are there and whether you are relating to the spirit of your religion or to narrow teachings or interpretations. If you want to stay within such teachings, work hard to make your life congruent. If you're beginning on your own creative approach to spirituality, then *make sure you find your own base of ethical behaviour and seek the true heart of how and why sex might be important in your life.* Don't accept positions that make you or others feel bad or not-OK.

It's not always overt religious teaching that restricts people's sex lives – it can simply be the general moral culture. Many people find the idea of imaginative sex-play repellent and in parts of modern America, there are still legal sanctions against non-marital sex, oral sex, anal sex, and the use of sex-toys (even if few cases are brought). The important thing is to listen to yourself and your partner and find an aesthetic for sex that suits you both. We don't have to accept the kind of sex culture that is marketed by big organisations – we can create a world that incorporates the beauty, fun, spirituality, humour, sacredness etc. that appeals to *us*.

328

I was brought up with the instruction to 'save' myself for marriage, a message somehow transmitted as a mix of secular and Christian teaching. When, against my parents' wishes, I lived with my first boyfriend outside marriage, I found that their disapproval persisted during the five years of the relationship. When we finally separated, my parents disapproved of that since the situation could only actually be redeemed by marriage. I spent years feeling that I was a bad person because of my sexuality and sometimes tried to run away from it, living as if God was (like my parents) forever disapproving.

Eventually, I realised I had to live my own life. I moved to faraway cities so that I wouldn't cause my parents embarrassment through my lifestyle choices. I lived my life with lots of loneliness and in later years, I was established in places far away from my family so that sadly, I wasn't able to be near themas they aged and died. This was the price of my determination to have my own sexual autonomy and of their original rigidity, something which in the end mellowed over the years through the challenges brought by parenting not one but four children as well as the changing *zeitgeist*, perhaps epitomised by divorces in the House of Windsor, which undoubtedly helped a lot of families to appreciate the strength of social change around them.

Ideas about sex within spiritual practice

Many philosophers and religious writers have written about the power of orgasm as a way of reaching beyond to something transcendent. And indeed we can feel that we've 'lost ourselves' in the moment of coming. Sex can allow us to merge with another for a brief time, or in controlled spiritual practice, to connect with something deeper even than the humans involved in that limited place and time.

If this is an area that interests you, read up about it. Tantric Buddhist and Taoist texts explore these issues – eg. Tsultrim Allione's work. Linda Hurcombe's (1987) book *Sex and God* contains a number of interesting pieces of writing on the themes of religious experience and sexuality. Some may find the combination of magic, sex and politics in Starhawk's work inspiring. Find your way to the books that speak to you. Recognise that some religions are more concerned to regulate sexual activity and even to separate it from the spiritual domain whilst others (or other branches) have found ways to integrate sexuality and spirituality.

History and context

It's helpful to understand our sexuality in the context of history and cultural difference. In doing so, it soon becomes clear that our attitudes and experiences are not only genetically and biologically determined, but are also powerfully shaped by the context in which we live.

Furthermore, in Western society (and in countries that are 'Westernising'), films, TV, advertising and the internet suggest that sex is available everywhere, 'happening' and endlessly varied. Yet the reality for most people may be nothing like this, and this cultural 'mask' conceals a mass of unfulfilled lives, sexual frustration, boredom and absence of sexual joy for many people. The cultural 'front' distorts our ideas about what we should or could be having and makes us feel even worse about ourselves since we're obviously not enjoying the party. The Sex Census 2012 undertaken jointly by the UK *Relate* relationship counselling organisation and the Ann Summers retail chain questioned over 25,000 people in the UK, concluding that people in their thirties were much more likely to be at risk of unhappy sex lives with the pressures of money and parenting weighing heavily on them, and that enjoyment and confidence in sex seems to be greatest the older we get, with people in their fifties, sixties and seventies getting more satisfaction and being prepared to go and find what they need. This picture is not necessarily what's portrayed in the media.

Our intention in exploring the variety of cultural and historical fashions regarding sexual practice is to encourage an openness to sexuality by making it clearer that attitudes and values emerge from families, groups, institutions and cultures, and that we are limited in our own approach to the extent that we're 'embedded' in these. As with so many things in life, we usually have to fight for our autonomy and the right to make our own choices, and to keep those rights. It's important that we feel able to challenge narrow views of sex and that we cut through our own ignorance about sexual matters and inform the next generation. In modern capitalist society, much of sexuality is experienced through the 'virtual' world – actually having fulfilling sex with another person may be much rarer than we are led to think.

Reading about the history of sexuality, we can see the changes in attitudes that there have been over decades and indeed, centuries e.g. to masturbation, homosexuality, female pleasure, masculinity, pregnancy outside marriage, intersexuality, monogamy, contraception etc. We're not in favour of ideas of 'tolerance' which sounds patronising; rather, an OK-OK position requires us to be open to diversity within the population instead of assuming that there's a single orthodoxy to which other ideas are subordinate.

We know that at times in our history, medical authorities have tried to change homosexuals into heterosexuals and advised us that masturbation will result in blindness, impotence, madness, mental exhaustion etc. We know that governments round the world have different policies on same-sex sex – countries like Saudi Arabia, Iran, Egypt for example having at times implemented strict punishments, whilst the Soviet Union has varied in its apparent tolerance for a Gay Pride march and subsequent crackdown. Some countries have severely punished women for adultery, whilst in the West, some consider adultery to be so common that the model of long-term monogamous marriage barely stands up. We know that HIV has taken root in some parts of the world such as sub-Saharan Africa more than in other places. The point really is that sexuality is something that is shaped by governments, public attitudes, environmental factors, religious movements and cultural mores. We come to understand our sexual selves in the terms transmitted to us by our culture – by the media, by art, by stories and life-stories, by rules and regulations, by threats and fears, by taxation policies, by rewards and punishments, by social attitudes, and by families who use a variety of strategies to influence us.

Gay rights

There's a wide range of sexual behaviour, and what at one time is labelled abnormal or deviant may become normalised, particularly

331

if it transpires that a particular practice is very common (whether or not everyone agrees that it's 'right'). Being gay in the 1950s would have been understood by many in the West as having a physical or mental disorder, and life would have felt very sad and conflictive, lived in fear of the law and perhaps suicide would have beckoned. There was a climate of fear for men with 'homosexual tendencies', with dismissal from jobs and arrest for soliciting being real possibilities. Men were often forced into medical treatment including electric shock or pharmacological intervention to avoid imprisonment – (it looks as if Alan Turing, the gifted mathematician and Bletchley Park wartime code-breaker may have committed suicide when offered this option). Many would have married women resulting in inauthentic relationships for themselves and their families. Kinsey's 1948 survey of male sexuality revealed that 37% of men admitted to having had sex with other men - this helped challenge the notion of 'homosexuality' as a disorder.

Although there were developments in law and in social attitudes, being gay in the 1980s could still be felt as a stigmatized position – in the UK, the Thatcher government brought in Clause 28, forbidding the subject to be taught in schools, and there was the additional burden of homosexuality being associated with the initial growth of AIDS and the experience of friends and lovers dying in a horrible way. Alan Hollinghurst's novel (later filmed) *The Line of Beauty* evokes the pain of this position when it was still a shock that AIDS was taking hold in the West.

Being gay in the 2010s is different again - in the UK there are new legal protections, the recognition of civil partnerships, the possibility of adopting children and the future of gay marriage under consideration, and in contrast to earlier times, positive anti-homophobia policies in schools and places of employment.

Yet across the globe, *Stonewall*, the gay rights organisation reports that being gay is still illegal in 80 countries and in some countries, the penalty for homosexuality is death. *'For more than 200 million gay people worldwide each day is filled with the fear of being beaten, imprisoned or murdered at any moment'*. And however far we have got in America and Western Europe, let's be clear that the experience in daily life in these countries does not match up exactly to the rhetoric and the law.

Being heterosexual

Being heterosexual in 1950s Britain meant that pre-marital and extra-marital sex was severely frowned upon, women usually had to relinquish employment if they got married (whether from expectations by husbands and family, pressure from employers, or the restrictions of having children), and the guidelines on 'how' to be married were relatively clear – it was a lifetime commitment and sexual fulfilment was a bit hit-and- miss (especially as many started married life with little sexual knowledge). In some parts of the world, marriage can take place at the age of 13, in other places not until 20 or 21; marriage is generally thought of as monogamous but there are some groups in the world who have practised some form of polygamy.

Today, there are many more choices of lifestyle and relationship, there is much more access to relationship help and to sex information, and more freedom and choice about who to relate to and for how long. People may no longer think that being in a long-term heterosexual relationship is the only 'norm' – it is a choice or a lucky (or unlucky) break. We need to guard against the idea of taking heterosexuality as the barometer of normality even within Western society from which other kinds of existence are marginalised and measured. *Accepting diversity means starting from an equal base, not privileging one group over another.*

The idea of love and romance

Neither should we take the idea of love and romance, so prevalent in Western society, for granted. Arranged marriages are popular in south and south-east Asia, Africa and the Middle East and love may not always be the main consideration. Some writers (eg.D Liu and colleagues) consider that in order to build countries like China and India into the vibrant economic forces they are today, it's been necessary to push love and romance into the background and collective action and bring hard work to the forefront of

333

personal lives, partners sometime having to go away to work projects for months on end. The meaning of 'love' for many people has become associated with sadness rather than joy. With increasing urbanisation have come new expectations for more sexual fulfilment and greater relationship quality for those who can make their lives in modern cities, but such expectations may remain a luxury for the privileged.

In the West, people on low incomes who work hard often have to suffer long shifts or long times away from the family, putting personal and family relationships under stress, just as those on high-power career paths only 'visit' their families and are often preoccupied with the life of headquarters or 'Westminster village' or the 'Washington Bubble'. In a programme about 'Tory wives', one participant suggested that the avenues open to them to ameliorate their loneliness were religion, alcohol or an 'affair'.

How ideas about sexuality are transmitted through the body

In Britain, the new princess – the Duchess of Cambridge - publicized that she was going on a diet because it's so much the norm that women in this society should be slim before their wedding; yet in Nigeria, wealthy women go to 'fattening rooms' in order to prepare for theirs. There is diversity across the globe in relation to the way in which we see the body as attractive.

Round the world, *male and female circumcision prac*tices are fiercely defended on a number of grounds by religious and cultural groups whilst secular international organisations try to restrict them.

This is a complex issue and there are a number of strands to it.

- there are a variety of types of circumcision ranging from minor to major surgery and there are risks to life as well as to physical and psychological health in the procedures – the World Health Organisation estimates that some 140 million girls and women are currently living with the results

- the secular view on female *circumcision* (which has a variety of forms, some more dramatic than others) voiced by the World Health Organisation who call it FGM - *female genital mutilation* - is that it's a travesty of *bodily integrity*

- although a number of the immediate health problems (such as excessive bleeding, infection, trauma etc) could be ameliorated by moving the practice into sanitary medical contexts (and out of cultural and religious contexts), international organisations are reluctant to push for this because it might seem to condone and legitimate a practice which many people find unacceptable in today's world and thus could make it harder to eradicate. Indeed, the World Health Organisation specifically discourages health professionals from taking part in the procedures.

- there can be longer-term damaging effects of FGM such as difficulty in childbirth, urination problems, cysts causing infertility, the necessity of cutting open and re-sewing the vaginal orifice (in cases of full infibulation) for sex and childbirth, post-traumatic stress related to sexual activity and problems with sexual desire, sensitivity and orgasmic capacity. In male circumcision, there is some evidence that penile sensitivity can be reduced and some men choose to have their foreskins restored in adulthood

- the *rights of the child* are relevant in many instances since circumcision (male and female) commonly takes place in childhood or adolescence (– in the case of Jewish boys for example, it happens within 7 days of birth) – and some of the trauma experienced in adulthood is about coming to terms with the imposition of something so drastic on the body before the age of consent – in some cases affecting the relationship between child and parent

- for many people, finding a marriage partner depends on this external sign of conformity to orthodox religious practice, and demonstrating one's commitment to religious society is important eg. in cases of religious conversion

335

- respecting religious and cultural diversity is important and a universal rule that seeks to eradicate a cultural and religious procedure is inevitably in conflict with this principle

- circumcision has preceded most religious organisations, dating back for example to 5000 years ago – we accept so much else that modernises our lives, yet some countries and groups are reluctant to let go of practices which others consider barbaric (such as circumcision and *suttee* – the burning of widows) and also oppose a range of practices such as abortion, contraception, homosexuality, masturbation and wearing immodest attire, all of which have a place within contemporary states.

- religious organisations are often fearful of modernising, opting instead to hold onto traditional power and ritual (eg. arguments over the ordination of women) and in the process, causing much pain and division in their ranks

- the emphasis on sexual freedoms in the West is not automatically portable to all corners of the globe. The belief in the rights to self-defined sexuality and gender equality is not shared by everyone. It represents Western liberalism and attempts to impose this on societies that think differently can be seen as a form of colonialism. This is a problem because it's not clear that international organisations are without bias.

- circumcision of males or females is primarily symbolic of conformity to a cultural rule-system (usually religious) – refusing it is an act of 'rebellion' that many families and individuals do not have the stomach for, even if they disagree with it. Institutionalised support for change from outside the family – eg. bringing in legislation and educating attitudes, can help override the pressures on individuals.

- valuing the *symbolism* of religious and cultural practices and stopping the actual physical procedures could be a way forward - some groups are *already* substituting milder procedures and techniques as a concession to modern values. Some religious groups and cultures would still believe in the importance of women's subjugation to men or that men's sexual desires should be contained, which would disappoint those who imagine that taking away the procedures would strike a blow for sexual equality.

Setting boundaries on sexual behaviour

In Western society, we've been steadily facing up to the range of abuse – sexual, physical, social and emotional – that has been meted out to children in the care system, within the churches, and within families, as well as attempting to challenge the edifice of human trafficking and the forcing of vulnerable and poor people into physical labour and prostitution. In recent times, abuse of power in relation to young people within the media industry through sexuality has come to light in the UK and received public censure. We rout out and punish people who collect or download or produce child pornography. We have laws about zoophilia – making it illegal to have sexual relations with animals whether opportunistic or regular and exclusive. We require formal monogamy in legally sanctioned relationships while some groups and cultures still allow forms of polygamy.

We draw boundaries on what's acceptable and what's not – at *this* point in time and within *our* society (whichever one it is), but historical and cultural research may reveal that some of what liberal people consider obscene and damaging has at different times and in different places been taken as the norm.

Lone sexual activity

Masturbation is a practice that's had a chequered history. Whereas in the late nineteenth and early twentieth century, there was considerable investment in stopping people from masturbating with much terrifying propaganda, now medical and social authorities are encouraging people to do it. At one time, it was thought that people would exhaust themselves and not have the energy to relate to the other sex for procreation and the

337

cementing of marriages. Considering that the main purpose of internet pornography is to facilitate 'wanking', it's perhaps not just our outrage against the imagery (if we have any) or the development of the industry that bothers us but the same concern that people won't bother with real relationships. On the other hand there are those who believe that getting plenty of sexual satisfaction from masturbation will reduce the likelihood of rape, or that it will help us to heal anything from headaches to cancer. There's a whole debate about the urgency and demand of male sexuality, perhaps much exalted, and different cultures and particularly religions have attempted to control it. One view of the Islamic *hijab* and *burka* is that they reduce women's visibility to people outside the immediate family, particularly other men. Christianity has perhaps attempted to control men by promulgating rules about sexual conduct such as forbidding 'self-abuse' and the Ten Commandments.

Whilst we may think of masturbation as something particularly common for young people whose sexual energy is high, it's also possible that significant numbers of older people, especially once widowed or disabled, find satisfaction in masturbation.

As an example of how far attitudes towards self-pleasure have changed in the UK, hundreds of people raised money for the Terrence Higgins Trust and the Marie Stopes International Agency by staging a *"wank-a-thon"* in 2006, which also had the aim of reducing shame about an activity that most people do. Since people had to get signatures for sponsorship they *had* to engage people in discussion about it.

The compulsory nature of the (heterosexual) female orgasm

One of the reasons that masturbation is important is that we have discovered that the vast majority of women can orgasm through self-stimulation, as evidenced by the late twentieth-century *Hite Report*. The emphasis on male penetration of the vagina promulgated in contemporary Western culture and through the development and promotion of drugs like *Viagra,* not only puts pressure on men to perform in a traditional manner and to worry about erectile dysfunction, but also renders women as inadequate

338

or frigid if they cannot 'come' during heterosexual penetrative sex. In fact, a vast number of women have difficulties in coming in this way, and many choose not to bother to penetrate the vagina during masturbation.

The social emphasis on penetrative sex serves to reinforce the myth of male domination and to ensure that men and women continue to work at coitus. But for mutual pleasure, stimulation of the woman's vulva and clitoris by hand or mouth or with sex toys is much more likely to produce orgasm and create the right conditions for male satisfaction through intercourse or through stimulation of the penis outside the vagina.

This is an essential piece of information for anyone involved in sexual activity with women, but it's worth noting that these findings have been very controversial. Critics (including religious groups) have feared that women might abandon their husbands once they discovered that they have their own sexual autonomy. The edifice of contemporary sexuality, which includes attempts to reduce sexual sensitivity through infibulation of women in a number of African and middle eastern countries, and the pressures in most societies to keep women within heterosexual marriage (eg. through the lack of effective policing of rape and the social censure on women who abandon their families), is built upon the idea – the myth - that men – and men's penises – are necessary to women's sexual satisfaction. Once we accept that this is not the case, we weaken the social structure of the family because men and women have more choice.

The fact that we should choose to love one another and to stay together because we love each other is perceived as too much of a risky basis on which to build society because of the uncertain nature of free love. This was one of the main reasons why the *Equal Rights Amendment* was opposed in many American states in the 1970s – because it was felt that only the law could compel men to stay with women and children; love alone would not suffice as sufficiently reliable 'glue'. If you're interested in the history of the anti-feminist movement in America, see *The Flipside of Feminism* by Suzanne Venker (niece) and Phyllis

Schafly (aunt). We discuss some issues related to love in our chapters on *Close relationships* and *Values.*

The fact is that most societies build in censure and punishments – from stoning and execution to social disapproval and ostracism – for women who do not conform to the social norm of being a good wife. Heterosexual penetrative sex has many lovely and satisfying qualities and it's of course possible for many people to have mutual or separate orgasms during it – the point is that it's not the *only* method, and this knowledge is liberating and facilitates a more creative approach to sexual pleasure.

Celebrating difference

We need to recognise that we're all different culturally - whether it's due to religious prohibitions and rituals – eg. Jewish prohibitions on sex and menstruation, or different ideas about releasing ejaculate (eg. Tantric sex), or simply the lessons we've learned within our own families and in our schooling about touch, openness, privacy, meeting emotional needs, shame, body confidence, discipline, aesthetics, courtship etc.

Culture isn't just about people from different places or races – every family has its own culture. Some of us pick people who come from very different backgrounds because we wanted to get away from our own family culture, or because we learned to be open and curious about people who are different from ourselves. Others will always want to find people who seem to share the same patterns and experiences and cultural background to themselves. Families will vary in their attitudes to singlehood, promiscuity, infidelity/open relationships, sexual orientations, single parenting, etc. People's attitudes often evolve from things that have happened within their family. It's important to remember that the way things happen in one family is not necessarily the way they're experienced in a different place or time by other people.

> *I remember doing jury service in a city at one time and coming up the stairs as the last one to join the group one morning where we were all waiting outside the court to go in. As I got to the top of the stairs and looked round for where to sit, I saw that all the women were on one set of benches and all the men on another. It was clear to me that I would be made to feel very uncomfortable if I chose to sit with the men.*
>
> *To me this reflected attitudes in the city which I saw as generally conservative and traditional and gender-based – different from those I was used to in academic life where I believe people would have sat with whomever they found interesting, regardless of gender. To me, it was an example of a powerful social mechanism through which we were all expected to conform to unwritten rules.*

Maybe 'gender' is something we *do* ………

We may change our sexual identity through our lives, and people differ in terms of the balance of male and female energy and perhaps genetic makeup. Sexual identity includes our physical and genetic makeup, the way in which we 'learn' to play our role as male or female, and our sexual preferences or orientation. The idea that gender is a fixed two-category thing is slowly being dissolved. Judith Butler is a key theorist who suggested that the feminist focus on the politics of women's lives was not helpful – a more fluid approach to gender was needed if we are to understand the way in which society tries to fix us into roles. We *perform* our roles as people according to the lessons of our childhood and the pressures upon us through life to be masculine or feminine.

Sex is embedded in a lot of social presentation including the use of sexuality in the workplace (eg. to signify status and compliance and dominance – porters and cleaners are often expected to be the butt of sexual joking; office staff, junior research staff, receptionists etc. are expected to be sexily dressed; television presenters have significant clothes allowances to ensure they look attractive to us etc.). See for example Nigel Rapport's participant observations on hospital porters.

People who don't present as clearly male or female (or any other uncertain category eg. social class) can unwittingly challenge others to feel uneasy about their supposedly 'fixed' characteristics and people want to avoid that anxiety. On the other hand, presenting in drag or playing with the presentation of gender has sometimes been very successful for performers such as Paul O'Grady/Lily Savage and Barry Humphries/Dame Edna Everage although these kinds of performances may reinforce stereotypes. And films like *Yentl* and *Mrs Doubtfire* have depended on disguised gender.

Once we grasp the idea of gender as performance, we can see that sex itself can be fluid and that we can be creative in how we relate to one another. There don't have to be fixed ways of having sex or of relating to one another, or even about whom we relate to.

> *After my husband died, many people in my life were wonderful – they came to help, they invited me and my daughter round for meals, they gave me things, they offered time to talk, they suggested walks, they folded and put away my washing etc. but after a while I realized that women were ringing me up and saying 'oh, my husband's away that night, why don't you come round then?' It felt as if I was no longer to be invited to social gatherings with couples – the 'main' currency of socializing; I was to be kept in the backroom, having private girl-chats.*
>
> *It was the beginning of recognising that my social status as a widow was different from that of a wife, and learning that other people might have a hand in defining that, even if they did so unconsciously and kindly.*

Audre Lorde was a black lesbian poet and activist in the USA, active during the middle and late twentieth century. She was concerned not only with the differences between groups of women (eg. white feminists and black lesbians) but between conflicting differences within the individual. Her refusal to be placed in a particular category, whether social or literary, was characteristic of her determination to come across as an individual rather than as a stereotype. We can take inspiration from people like her – to define our own sexual identity in relation to current ideas about sexuality and societal sanctions.

And maybe biological gender is not as definite as we thought..........

Studies of intersex and trans-sexual people help us to understand that, as a population, we're not made up of people who are all definitely and fully male or female – there's a spectrum, and indeed it can take years for us to recognize what we come to feel is our true sexual self. People born with ambiguous genitalia have to negotiate their gender status in conjunction with medical possibilities and parental wishes to find what they feel they can live with. Assignment to the category of male or female is done by doctors and family, sometimes involving surgery and the way in which the child is trained to present him/herself to others. There are a number of cases where in the past decisions have ultimately proved to be difficult to cope with and in some cases, the choice of gender has been reversed in adulthood.

Anne Fausto-Sterling, biologist and historian, reminds us that masculinity and femininity can vary in terms of *genetic material*, *hormones* and *anatomy* – there are many variations on these themes and the spectrum of gender is much more complex and nuanced than the simple dichotomy of *male* and *female* we are used to, would have us think. Anne Fausto-Sterling has written about the biological basis of sex at length, and suggests (even if somewhat lightly) that because of the varied distribution of genetic material across the genders, we may do rather better to consider five genders; as well as **male** and **female**, there could also be at least three other categories – *'herms'*, *'merms'* and *'ferms'* depending on how much ovary and testes material and how much of our genitalia are 'female' or 'male' in structure.

Some people marry and pass as heterosexual for a decade or two before realizing that they have feelings for someone of their own gender, some individuals struggle with a discord with the body they have and their perceived sense of gender identity and choose to change sex, some people have been homophobic for years but through a son or daughter coming out, or the impact of social attitudes and employment policies, start to change their views.

It may be time for all of us to view gender as a far less fixed 'given' in our lives than we used to – this is an aspect of our existence in which both science and social science have given us the opportunity to question a fundamental 'truth' and crack it open, recognising that some groups may have vested interests in sustaining or even exaggerating the division between the sexes.

The 'economics' of sex

Sex is rarely 'free' of cost. Even if we're not technically paying for sex, there's usually some material investment needed to gain access to sex – whatever our sexual identity and gender status.

- *to meet people (joining dating sites, going to meetings and gatherings etc, telephone calls)*
- *to fund encounters (travel, meals and drinks – whether out or at home, tickets, etc)*
- *looking after appearances (perfume/aftershave, gym membership, new or cleaned clothes, hair care), cleaning/tidying, decorating or improving home, updating or re-organising music or DVD collections, having car or bike valeted or repaired etc.*
- *to access most porn requires magazine purchase, online subscriptions, etc.*
- *setting the scene - buying sexy underwear, sex toys, bedding, bath or massage oils, candles etc.*
- *to arrange childcare, work cover, a hotel room or weekend cottage etc. to create the space and privacy for sex*
- *the time involved – going to nightclub or party, chatting to people online, on the phone, in person; going for walks or meals, building trust, spending time having sex itself and relaxing afterwards*

The costs of internet sex

However, on a wider scale, the global sex industry is enormous, with the US being one of the major producers of sex videos and pornographic web pages and China supplying most of the world's sex toys – presumably much of them through online purchases. It's important to recognise that commentators on usage have their own agendas for the statistics they quote. Julie Ruvolo in *Forbes* quotes Ogi Ogas and Sai Gaddam, authors of *A Billion Wicked Thoughts* who from their extensive internet research on sexuality give a conservative estimate of about 4% of all internet sites and 13% of internet traffic, whilst others say there is much more. These authors suggest that although the number of sites has grown, the actual usage may have dropped in recent years. Dismissal from employment happens increasingly in relation to internet use, and of these incidences, evidence such as that posted in *Personnel Today,* indicates that the majority are related to pornography. Disturbingly, Ogas and Gaddam are able to highlight the racial divide that is represented in porn usage, with most people featured in porn material being women from black, Asian and Latino communities.

The cost is not just financial. A significant percentage of adults admit to an internet sexual addiction. Reasons for this could include ease of availability, the privacy (we don't have to go into a shop or premise and can be away from our main partner and the home), the impersonality and the ability to hide aspects of the self (eg. by giving false information or just by being an 'anonymous' user), the freedom from being rejected, the wish to enter a virtual world which is easier to handle than the real world of people, the freedom from sexually transmitted diseases, and believing it's harm-free.

However, becoming addicted to internet porn can seriously interfere with or replace real relating and is now a significant causal factor in relationship breakdown. Perhaps the key factor is that we can hide ourselves in the process – little is required of us and the pain of self-disclosure, a necessary element in relating to others, is avoided. This is not to say that people who can avoid dependence can't find it a useful source of stimulation.

The sex business

A massive organized crime industry across the world brings women and young people continuously from poorer countries into richer countries to work as prostitutes. A recent study of men in London who went to prostitutes by Melissa Farley and colleagues indicated that it was often to assuage immediate sexual need, and frequently followed on from using pornography, giving them ideas about what they wanted that they didn't feel able to enact with the partners in their lives. It's often not that the partner they pay for can or will do more or better than their 'regular' partner – it's perhaps that the men feel less exposed by sharing their real needs in an impersonal way, or that they can convince themselves that the money they pay is a fair exchange for services they can demand. The men mostly chose to ignore evidence of abuse and oppression of the women they turned to, sometimes distorting their own perceptions in order to carry on. We commented on the way in which can be distanced from our physical experience in our chapter on *Health and the body*. Research suggests that men who buy sex are more likely to be involved in violence in other areas of life than men who don't, and the extent of violence and cruelty experienced by prostitutes is truly horrific.

Janice Raymond, a passionate advocate for action against prostitution has documented the 'health consequences' to women of being involved in prostitution including broken bones, concussions, other injuries, sexually-transmitted diseases, the risk of HIV, chronic pelvic pain, depression, post-traumatic stress and trauma, as well as the likelihood for many that they seek amelioration of their suffering through alcohol and drug addiction. Many lose their children and contact with their families, and some have involuntary pregnancies and miscarriages, as well as disengaging from their own enjoyment of sexuality.

There are also women at the top end of the market who may escape these fates by being in a position to market their services autonomously, choose their clients and how often they work – but a significant part of the business involves women (and sometimes men) who have little choice because of their impoverished circumstances or because of having been tricked into the network of crime.

An important aspect of the sex industry is that *it can benefit from the shame and stigma we feel about our sexual needs* – whilst on the other hand it can also create a sense that we should be having orgasms regularly and having sex round the clock with beautiful people. Any sense of dissatisfaction we have can be exploited by the industry.

Thus it's important that we face up to ourselves as sexual beings and accept our desires as a positive part of ourselves. For example, for those who like pornography, the trick is to resist dependence and to use it for ideas about making sex more imaginative and creative.

'Sex for pleasure' and 'sex for procreation'

One of the arguments against homosexuality comes from the idea that that sex is designed for procreation only. The existence of gay sex makes explicit the idea that people have sex for pleasure. Many societies through the ages and across the world have sought to insist upon conception as the sole function of sex (including the Catholic ban on contraception). If procreation is seen as the only function, sex is denied to many: people in prisons, hospitals, single people, young people, gay people, people with fertility problems, people who no longer want to have children, post-menopausal women and ageing people.

The idea that God works through us and brings us children or not as He/She sees fit – eg. through 'barrenness' or miscarriages and stillbirths, and whether able-bodied or with disabilities, can be difficult for some of us to dismiss, so that intervening to affect sexual outcomes through amniocentesis, contraception, abortion, and surgery (vasectomies and sterilisation) represents a challenge to deep teachings and raises questions about bodily integrity. In contrast, of course, some religious practices involve acting *on* the body to prepare people for marriage or childbirth.

However, some Christian authorities nowadays accept that within committed and sanctified relationships, as well as procreation, sex also has a bonding function. This is important because it allows for the possibility of sex to heal hurt and to build closeness in an ongoing way throughout life.

Nevertheless, there's strong pressure from the media and the culture to commodify sexuality – to find partners through the marketplace of the internet, to dial up instant sex, to look at people as sexual objects, and a wide variety of opportunities to step across new sexual frontiers and break taboos. In a society that's confused about values, we can find ourselves without rudders when confronted with endless choice and the excitement of risk-taking.

Perhaps what's important is to decide a position for ourselves – finding a balance between the polarities of valuing sex as a sacred and precious gift, shared between true lovers and retained as a natural activity without enhancement and subjecting our sex-life to Western commodification and commercialisation not just in its process but also in our choice of partners and types of relationships. We can be creative in deciding for ourselves what we think is important and how we wish to live our emotional and sexual lives in relation to spiritual guidance or secular freedom. Our view is that retaining a sense of the value of ourselves and of the other person is essential – activities that reduce self-esteem or make us feel bad about ourselves are never going to be a good idea. We believe that honesty, trusting our instincts and good communication remain central to a good sexual relationship.

Exercise

This is designed to help us explore 'messages' about our sexual selves that we've internalised and think about what's useful in each 'message' and what we want to change or challenge.

Message or behaviours modelled	From whom?	What's useful in the message/ model?	What's not helpful for me in the message/ model?	How do I/could I challenge it?
Example: *People who have sex outside marriage are somehow bad*	*Parents*	*Made me think carefully about the seriousness of sex and the value of commitment - conveyed my parents' concern about emotional (and practical) safety*	*I felt bad about myself for many years, and separated from any sense of a God - it didn't seem an open and loving attitude to have, nor very playful; overly influenced by 'religious' precepts without looking at the real value issues*	*Through my life choices and therapy to feel good about myself and others; clarifying that what's important is to save sex for people I really care about and that it doesn't have to be linked to marriage; revisiting concept of spirituality to include stewardship of planet, equality and less focus on sexual rules*
Message/ model:				

Message/ model:				

Books and papers
Eve Esler (2001) *The Vagina Monologues* Villard/Random House
Anne Fausto-Sterling (2000) *Sexing the Body* Basic Books/Perseus
Melissa Farley, Julie Bindel and Jacqueline M. Golding *Men who buy sex: who they buy and what they know* December 2009 Eaves, London
Ina May Gaskin (2002)(4th ed) *Spiritual Midwifery* Book Publishing Co.
Elaine Hatfield and Richard L Rapson (2005) *Passionate Love, Sexual Desire, and Mate Selection: Cross-Cultural and Historical Perspectives* Page 227 www.elainehatfield.com/ch80.pdf
Darian Leader and David Corfield (2007) *Why do people get ill?* London: Penguin Books
D Liu, M L Ng, L P Zhou, and E J Haeberle *Sexual Behavior in Modern China: Report on the Nation-wide Survey of 20 000 Men and Women* New York: Continuum 1997, pp. 586 (Chinese edition: Joint Publishers, Shanghai 1992, pp. 866)
Audre Lorde (1984) *Sister Outsider* Crossing Press
Veronique Mottier (2008) *Sexuality: a very short introduction* Oxford University Press
Ogi Ogas and Sai Gaddam (2012) *A Billion Wicked Thoughts: What the Internet tells us about Sexual Relationships* Plume Books
James W Prescott (1975) *Body Pleasure and The Origins of Violence* The Futurist Bethesda, MD. reprinted in: *The Bulletin of Atomic Scientists*, November 1975, pp.10- 20
Nigel Rapport (2008) *Of Orderlies and Men: Hospital Porters Achieving Wellness at Work* Carolina Academic
Janice Raymond (1995) *Report to the United Nations Special Rapporteur on Violence Against Women: Prostitution and Trafficking* Coalition Against Trafficking in Women.

Julie Ruvolo *How Much of the Internet Is Actually For Porn?* Forbes http://www.forbes.com/sites/julieruvolo/2011/09/07/ how-much-of-the-internet-is-actually-for-porn/
Starhawk (1982) *Dreaming the Dark: magic, sex and politics* Boston: Beacon Press
Suzanne Vender and Phyllis Schafly (2011) *The Flipside of Feminism: What Conservative Women Know – and Men Can't Say* WND Books
Bernie Zilbergeld (2004) *Better than ever: time for love and sex* Crown House Publishing
Medline Plus – Intersex http://www.nlm.nih.gov/medlineplus/ ency/article/001669.htm
http://www2.hu-berlin.de/sexology/GESUND/ARCHIV/ MAY_97.HTM
http://www.personneltoday.com/articles/2002/07/09/13721/web-porn-at-work-leads-to-high-number-of-dismissals.html

Films

Chris Columbus (1993) *Mrs Doubtfire*
Barbra Streisand (1983) *Yentl*

Sexuality in fiction and films

The following brief selection explores aspects of gay relating, heterosexual relationships, ageing, social class and disability. All have the potential to generate discussion.

Books

Rita Mae Brown (1973/1994) *Rubyfruit Jungle* Penguin Books
Alan Hollinghurst (2004) *The Line of Beauty* Picador
Philip Roth (2007) *Everyman* Vintage Books

Films:
Pascale Ferran (2006) *Lady Chatterley*
Beeban Kidron (1989) *Oranges are Not the Only Fruit*
Damien O'Donnell (2005) *Inside I'm Dancing*
Steve McQueen (2011) *Shame*

9   dependencies

This section of the book (like some other chapters) is a tour of the territory of addiction/dependency, designed to present a fresh view and start people thinking and discussing the issues.

This chapter has been written entirely by Jack

In this section, I'm looking at different kinds of 'dependency' as a broad category which includes a lot of different kinds of behaviours from addiction to drugs to compulsive TV-watching. I've worked as a therapist/counsellor for more than 20 years, and for 7 of which I specialised in drug/alcohol addiction.

My position is that we're in a messy difficult world with an uncertain future and that we are *'fiddling while Rome burns'* and that the dependencies of entertainment and consumerism particularly are ways of not solving 'bigger problems' as well as avoiding the resolution of individual problems or issues.

I think dependency is a way of not moving on in your development as a person. Jung had a view that people can feel empty if their personalities are not fully integrated or whole and dependencies, pastimes or even relationships are ways of filling that void.

I would include *workaholism* as a socially acceptable dependency.

With the 'trans-theoretical' model of dependency they published in 1983, James O Prochaska and Carlo DiClemente constructed the stages of change for addictive behaviours. The model has been adapted worldwide for a range of addictive behaviours.

Strengths of the model are that it allows for relapse and shows how people move through different stages. However, it is not a linear process – you can shift from any stage to any other stage.

The main stages of their model are:

pre-contemplative	*- not considering change*
contemplation	*- thinking of changing*
preparation	*- ready to change*
action	*- making changes*
maintenance	*- staying on track*
relapse	*- coming out of maintenance stage*

Main points about dependency:

Some are self-evident, some just positions in the absence of 'proof'.

1. dependency-type behaviours whether it's a compulsive shopping or heroin addiction are a problem in themselves but they also are a frequent 'cover-up' for other problems and block 'personal growth' or social growth

2. dependency behaviours often mean that there is a lack of balance in us and they interfere with the balance between mind, body, spirit, emotion

3. anything more deep and complex than problem behaviours are often NOT addressed or resolved by a focus on JUST the problem dependency behaviours

4. help is available for dependency behaviours but we need to put effort in as well and be ready for change

5. losing control is a feature of dependency becoming a problem and can be used to define dependency

6. often 'deeper issues' for example a stressful job, having an empty life, being psychologically stuck etc. are masked by dependency behaviours

7. dependencies are growing and they are becoming socially accepted and encouraged, as in the following examples:

via consumerism, which is by my definition a dependency for many people, it may be mild, but can be entrenched and compulsive and may also be integrated into self-concepts – *'I'm the type of person who buys x product, has x lifestyle'* etc.

people have become dependent on the kind of instant payoff they get from technology, including TV, cell-phones, cars, etc. etc. in one sense convenience, speed, pseudo-choice, have become dependencies.

8. dependencies can also induce or cover *passivity* (if this interests you, see work by Aaron Schiff and Jacqui Schiff on this); be compensatory (a treat); can be an escape; can anaesthetise feelings or substitute psychological needs eg. for security.

9. people use dependency to alleviate stress or to escape from painful situations

Dependency is on a continuum from 'big problem' to 'manageable issue' - here I'm defining dependency as a behaviour which is causing significant problems to people or others and/or when people have lost control over the behaviours and they have a compulsive feel to them. To illustrate this with a consumer example from the world of shopping, someone who HAS TO shop daily and cannot control their spending and is running up a huge debt etc. has a dependency on shopping. Someone who enjoys shopping, hasn't run up huge debts and isn't compelled to shop is in control of their shopping behaviour and is in my schema not dependent.

Dependency and/or addictions DO have positive payoffs, they give people pleasure etc. as well as having negative consequences. Stopping dependencies is easier when the negatives outweigh the positives. (See James O Prochaska and Carlo DiClemente's *'contemplative phase'*).

An older psychoanalytic idea that has lost favour is the idea of the 'addictive personality' – the quest for an addictive personality is now over.

There has been a growth in the scope of what has been called addictive/compulsive/dependent behaviours to many areas of life eg. eating and compulsive TV-watching.

There has also been a trend to use cognitive-behavioural approaches to 'solve' these 'problem behaviours'. In the past, it has been a maxim in the dependency and addiction world to solve the addictive behaviour and then examine the problems behaviours underneath.

Now the focus has shifted to solve the addictive behaviour but not necessarily to solve what may be underneath.

Often this is driven by a political and resource agenda.

Cognitive-behavioural methods seem logical, can be understood by government and law enforcement agencies, and can be time-limited. They don't involve feelings or noise or the 'troublesome unconscious' like some other therapy methods. They are a 'one-size fits all' method offer when you are ready (contemplative) or not (pre-contemplative).

There are not necessarily big personal/social issues lurking beneath a dependency behaviour; however, most dependencies take over and have their own momentum and lifestyle.

Common features of dependencies are that they depend on availability, are reinforced eg. socially, and are compounded by an accompanying mind-set eg, denial.

Chemical dependencies

These have unique features which include tolerance of the drug – including alcohol – often a non-mainstream lifestyle including eg. crime (and sometimes sex-work) and sometimes physical as well as psychological issues in withdrawal from the drug. Some drugs

355

are dangerous or difficult to physically withdraw from. Harm reduction used broadly means a range of ways of reducing harm – for example, by prescribed drug maintenance, issuing sterile injecting equipment to prevent spread of disease that would ensue from sharing equipment etc.

The 'model of change' (James Prochaska and others).

A descriptive model of addictive behaviour came into being and has been used and studied endlessly in the addiction/dependency world. Here I am referring to the James O Prochaska and Carlo di Clemente paper cited in the bibliography. This is a model designed to explain the behaviour of smokers who stopped smoking or didn't stop, perhaps relapsed etc. It's well worth a look at the model to understand the basics of it. What the model did from the outset is:

1. reduce the idea of a judgemental approach in addictions
2. try to match interventions to the stage of addiction someone is in
3. accept relapse as part of addiction

Stage of change and depth (level) of problem in the model

However, the model changed over time. In the article cited, there was a notion of 5 **levels** of psychological problems in addiction from (1) being *symptom/situational* to (5) being *intrapersonal*. (p.17) and that 'the deeper the level that needs to be changed, the longer and more complex the therapy is likely to be and the greater the resistance of the client' (ibid p.18).

The idea of 'levels of problem' in the everyday use of the model has been dropped and therapy of addictions is now mostly cognitive-behavioural and mostly at the symptom/situational level. This is a 'one-size fits all' narrow approach which simply doesn't work for a lot of people.

Here's an example:

> *A person is addicted to alcohol after growing up in a family that used drink to suppress feelings and helped them to cope with a car crash in which two family members died during her childhood. Cognitive-behavioural focus probably isn't going to solve her experience of family grief - perhaps nothing can, although it may give some pointers to controlling her use of alcohol on a day to day basis, but when emotional pain surfaces, something deeper is needed to help her release emotion and move on.*

Here's another example:

> *Disappointment with solving eating disorder leading to 'overweight' problems because this may come from babyhood and eating is associated in a person's 'baby thinking' with love or survival.*

To say as some eminent doctors and others do that dependency/addiction is just about dopamine is narrow and merely describes a chemical process which may be attached to a larger psychology. Worse still, the psychology may be from early childhood or babyhood and may not be easily accessible.

Life scripts

Another useful way of looking at addiction/dependency is in the Transactional Analysis idea of *scripts*, which is the person's 'programmed' life-course (see Ian Stewart and Vann Joines).

The problem *scripts* associated with self-destructive chemical addictions would be *third-degree* or *hamartic scripts* where there is significant bad experience from caretakers or the environment – in fact, many of the people who follow these extreme scripts may have been unwanted from babyhood.

If dependencies are causing significant but not total harm, they may fit a *non-winning* or *loser* script in TA terms.

357

Moving away from dependency

A lot of moving away from dependencies is a desire to get organised and to be in charge of your life and to have moderation (the *'middle way'* in Buddhism) and balance (*mind-body-feelings-spirit*) in your life.

Getting out of the stuckness and passivity of dependency does need:

- a feeling that you *can* 'do it' (self-efficacy)

- a position that it's worth it to get out of distorted self-centredness and problematic 'pleasure' with its 'quick fix', short-termism and denial.

If you're 'in it' for the excitement and pleasure, ie. experiencing dependency as a kind of entertainment, with problem dependency, this experience tends to get less enjoyable over time.

Ultimately people may need to create their own excitement and pleasure in less easy or less harmful ways. Sometimes this is known in the addiction world as building into our lives 'positive addictions'. Creative activity, good relationships and spiritual development could come into this activity.

People need to develop self-awareness to end dependencies and need to want to 'grow' psychologically and develop their inner life and sense of self-esteem and OKness and be active and responsible.

Also, a difficult part of solving dependencies is to be prepared for difficulty versus a 'quick fix' and also, (with many people), to unravel and solve blocks/problems/causes including issues from their past which may be hampering their development.

Drug and alcohol dependency

If you need support and/or help overcoming dependency on chemicals, there is (theoretically) a wide range of services available including:

- medical help with withdrawal from drugs or alcohol

- information about drugs (– this should include the information that cannabis is now much stronger in the UK than it was and is now hallucinogenic and much more dangerous than in the past)

- support for coming off drugs or alcohol and staying off eg, drugs or alcohol counselling

- possible 'rehabilitation' ie. live-in or community (Christian or spiritually based or independent)

- support groups

- different kinds of help eg. drug use and pregnancy

- counselling (often private)

In practice, state support and free support are often in very short supply. It's worth working hard on the internet to find groups and organisations which can help, starting with state health service links. There are organisations like *Talk to Frank* and *Drinkline* which offer telephone contact, and there are also organisations which offer support to parents, partners, friends and children of people struggling with dependency problems. Going private will give faster access to support and ensures confidentiality.

Remember that there is a bias towards cognitive-behavioural methods in the addiction world; if you want something else you will probably have to hunt for it.

Other dependencies

Examples include *workaholism, shopaholism, eating problems* –
help for these issues is probably seemingly less comprehensive
than for chemical dependencies but would include counselling and
therapy (private or not).

References

James O Prochaska and Carlo DiClemente (1986) paper. *Toward
a Comprehensive Model of Change in Treating Addictive
Behaviours* in W R Miller and N Heather (eds) *Treating Addictive
Behaviors* New York: Plenum Press pp.3-27
Jacqui Schiff and Aaron Schiff (1971) *Passivity* Transactional
Analysis Journal 1: 1 (Jan 1971) 71-78
Ian Stewart and Vann Joines (1987) *TA Today: A New
Introduction to Transactional Analysis* Life Space Publishing

10   the unconscious

In this short chapter, we argue for the importance of tuning into our unconscious processing and introduce subsequent chapters on the techniques of dream analysis, visualisation, using memory and reminiscence, and creative activity.

Jack

As a focus of academic study through the ages, the 'unconscious' has moved from being fashionable (eg. through psychoanalysis) to being unfashionable with some exceptions such as looking at creativity. The founding 'father' of psychoanalysis, Sigmund Freud, was one of the first to highlight the role of unconscious material – which in his view, was often the more difficult material such as fear, anger or jealousy – feelings and thoughts that we find it hard to accept in ourselves or to express to others, but which nevertheless influence our reactions and choices even though we are not aware of them. His sense of the unconscious mind was that it determined most of our behaviour and his therapeutic/analytical work with patients was usually designed to elicit unconscious material, such as through dream-analysis and the 'free association' of ideas.

Study of 'the unconscious' has sometimes been neglected or relegated to 'cinderella' areas of research with little funding. Does this mean it is not significant? No, it means it's hard to quantify and to evidence in a 'scientific' way, and in this scientific age, it's been easy to dismiss it. But if we evaluate what a scientific approach means, we can see that a lot of wisdom has been lost. Paradoxically, recent developments in brain research are bringing the unconscious back into the spotlight, getting us to examine questions about its role in important aspects of life such as choosing sexual partners or recovering features of our functioning when there is damage to linguistic and cognitive processing.

The unconscious mind is HUGE. It's important not to underestimate that – the unconscious mind offers us VAST resources for understanding ourselves and for creative problem-solving, and thus is an essential part of our survival kit. It's like an iceberg, with only a small part of what is in our mind being in conscious (surface) awareness.

Dreams, visualisation, reminiscence and creative activities are the direct routes into the unconscious mind; they are holistic and involve mental, emotional, visual and sensory experiencing, but are primarily non-verbal. In this way, they are often equated with the powers of the right brain as distinct from the cognitive, rational left-brain. The 'unconscious' can feel mysterious, unfathomable and scary but learning to define it, tap into it, and use it empowers us with an amazing and rich resource for living life.

The simple definition we're using is *'every part of the psyche that's not obviously conscious'* though there's always overlap with unconscious activity going on within the conscious mind.

Key features of the unconscious mind are:

- it's big
- it pushes to be heard
- it speaks to us in its own language (eg. through dreams, through the body, through symbols)
- it slips at times into consciousness (eg. through unexpected things we find ourselves saying, forgetting things etc)
- it has enormous power – both through its contents (like the contents of dreams) and its abilities (like the power to visualise)

Unconscious activity includes a long list:

- instinctual behaviours
- the fight-flight response in 'survival' situations
- feelings
- the spiritual
- the creative so-called right brain
- dreaming
- old memories (including physical and sensory memories)
- memory of pre-verbal events such as birth

- attraction
- non-verbal events eg touch
- the parapsychological
- the ability to heal your body
- survival shutdown of the body
- intuition, memories and decisions from childhood

It's perhaps odd to describe the unconscious as a 'thing' – to 'reify' it as an active entity, as the *subject* of sentences - but *owning for ourselves* the concept of material being processed within us at unconscious levels helps us get round this etymological problem. If we accept that much of our mental, emotional and spiritual processing takes place in non-verbal, non-conscious ways, then it may be helpful to use a shorthand feature of *'the unconscious'* to quickly refer to all this activity.

The unconscious mind in this way often seems like a being that steers our life for us. We can feel in touch with organic (perhaps both biological and spiritual) processes in which our mind tells us what to do or how to respond to something.

The 'unconscious' pushes to get heard – we know, for example, from studies of post-traumatic stress that people may experience repetitive nightmares calling for their attention – listening to the dream messages can help bring about healing. But we can also exert our own control – we do not have to have a passive relationship with our unconscious mind.

The main useful techniques for accessing the unconscious mind are:

1. dream interpretation
2. visualisation
3. using memory and reminiscence
4. facilitating creativity

and these are explored in the following sections.

Books and readings

Walter Evans-Wentz (1935) *Tibetan Yoga and Secret Doctrines* London: Oxford University Press

Paul Ricoeur (1970) *Freud and Philosophy: An Essay on interpretation* New Haven: Yale University Press

David Stewart (1989) *The Hermeneutics of Suspicion* Journal of Literature and Theology 3:296-307

Carl Zimmer (2010) *Meet your secret master* The Brain Fall 2010 pp.47-49

Man, Myth and Magic – original journal contains many articles of interest.

11 visualisation

The point of this chapter is to give clear information on visualisation, to put visualisation in perspective and to help get you into a position where you can start to use it in your life.

This chapter is written by Jack

I've found the best book on visualisation is *Visualisation* by Adelaide Bry. Do beware though of people making grandiose claims about visualisation and be prepared to read about it and put in some practice.

Adelaide Bry is one of the early proponents of the power of visualisation. Essentially, things are more likely to happen in our life is we visualize them happening, and less likely if we don't. Keep your mind on misery and pessimism and you'll get more of the same. Focus on great outcomes and watch them emerge.

Serious interest in visualisation started about fifty years ago and the technique is now used in many areas; sport, cancer treatment, business, therapy and counselling, and for healing physical conditions.

Visualisation is a powerful psychological technique and it is used widely, for instance in sport to enhance performance and in treatment for cancer. It is taken extremely seriously in sport and is highly developed and often included in 'packages' with other psychological techniques. The fact that it's been used for many years as part of cancer treatment including with people with 'terminal' cancer may give some idea of its usefulness. The Simontons are pioneering doctors in the USA who introduced visualisation into their programme of conventional treatment.

Due to resistance and narrowness in the medical profession and a resistance in the public, who tend to listen to the 'experts', not to mention the vested interest of medical suppliers (for example drug companies), a lot of useful psychology and psychological techniques have been largely ignored by the medical establishment but interestingly, not by the world of sport. The main objections lie in the difficulty of 'proving' its effectiveness and demonstrating 'how' it works – it's clearly a challenge to demonstrate how it works in a field where mind and body are more often kept separate than integrated (see the chapter on The Body) – the technique strikes at the heart of this dichotomy because it assumes at least a bridge between mind and body and at best, a unity of mind and body.

Frequently grandiose claims are made for psychological techniques and visualisation is credited with getting you anything you want, overlapping with parapsychology, and being a near substitute for religious experience. These claims are not true but visualisation *is* powerful, particularly if it's included in a 'bigger' package of change which could include support, changing attitudes, learning, and counselling/therapy.

What is visualisation?

Visualisation is not owned by a host of indispensable 'experts' whom I think don't want to admit that it's fairly straightforward as a technique and that we do it in our everyday life anyway. As I've already mentioned, it can be incorporated into a bigger 'package' and I think this package is what is being mystified by some. Critics of visualisation often do not understand how the unconscious works, downgrade the effectiveness of the unconscious and/or find visualisation too simple.

Visualisation imaginatively and naturally serves the unconscious mind, which is geared to survival and alerts us to and focusses on future events. It can be used for rehearsal of events about to happen and can focus energy in the present. It also has an inbuilt problem-solving capacity.

> For example, if you're driving on a difficult, busy or perhaps a dangerous road you can stop in a safe place and picture yourself being relaxed (both in the present and in the rest of the journey), being competent and safe and arriving at your destination with ease.

366

In this case it would be enhancing performance by directing the body, monitoring your state of arousal, improving alertness and perception and possibly changing attitude and endurance.

Visualisation has been around since humans evolved, so it is not a new technique that anyone can claim as their own. People visualise naturally - it is the process of *imagining something in the present or the future* by *creating visual images or creating a fantasy*.

> For example, if you are going to give a speech, you may picture yourself 'naturally' as being nervous and create a negative fantasy in which you perform badly. In this case, you can substitute a positive fantasy of yourself being confident and delivering the speech well, instead of the negative fantasy.

Visualisation and the unconscious mind

Visualisation is a way of focussing the unconscious mind, training our perceptions and ultimately shaping our behaviour.

For example, we can visualise having a successful job interview or finding a parking space – visualising positive outcomes relaxes us and makes us far more alert to possibilities around us and what to do about them. We need to develop our skills so that negative fantasies are naturally converted into positive images – if we do, we create the best conditions for heavy-duty healing and successful results in a variety of life situations. Try visualising a good outcome before meeting with people with whom you are in conflict – reaching out for those positive images is ultimately engaging with your deeper spiritual self. *Persist and practise.*

Visualisation and illness

The Simonton Cancer Center Patient Programs launched from Fort Worth, Texas, and now available in Europe, Australia, and South Africa, are based on the concept that *'beliefs, feelings, attitudes and lifestyle are important factors affecting health'*. The programme focuses on the influence of beliefs and belief systems and participants are taught mental imagery and creative thinking along with relaxation, counselling and gentleness, and challenges to the role of illness in their lives, such as the secondary gains from being ill. The programme's success owes much to its advocacy of personal power to influence one's own health, and a belief that harmony and balance between the different domains of one's self actively facilitate health improvements.

The Simontons have had remarkable success in turning back incurable cancers – critics of their approach have probably been worried that it looks too basic, too simple, too obvious and unscientific – their approach threatens the current drug/technology/expert monopoly. This kind of approach is helpful in all areas of healing (and in sport) – our mind can have a huge effect on our body. It can be tempting to underrate the power of our thinking on our health and wellbeing, but the Simontons provide us with examples of how with practice and effort, benefits and transformation can come.

If you're interested in the Simontons' approach, they're contactable via the internet. Alternatively, you may be able to find a doctor who could be in touch with the Center and work out a programmed visualisation for you.

How it works best

To start with, it helps *to learn and read about visualisation*. I found Adelaide Bry's book OK, but I have read others that exaggerate, are crass, silly etc. Like most things, it's not instant and you have to stick at it as you are training or retraining parts of your psyche.

When you are visualising, *the more you can do it the better*. When rehearsing future events it's useful to *put in as much detail as possible*.

Create time and space for it.

Visualisation is not just a relaxation technique but it helps to *be relaxed when you do it*. It focusses unconscious energy and can do complex tasks with tremendous efficiency and elegance, tasks that are done far less well by the rational or verbal parts of the mind. Also it has the capacity to replace negative 'alarm' fantasies with positive ones.

Putting it into practice

Adelaide Bry uses three main visualisation categories: these are: *open* (unstructured), *guided* and *programmed* (a fantasy closely linked and standing for a process, for example a process in the body).

Open visualisation

This kind of visualisation is often used for responding to reality or directing yourself to influence real events in the present or future, it is self-directed and the closest to the kind of visualisation that we do naturally.

You can picture yourself and or others in a certain way, for example calm, effective, listened to in different situations - if you do not know what the situation looks like then imagine a generalised one.

If the fantasy involves complex physical activities like sports, put in all the physical and movement detail you want.

There is no limit to your fantasy, you can make it as simple or complex as you like.

> For example, if you are going to visit people you
> find difficult at the weekend imagine yourself as in
> charge and unflappable whatever others are doing.

If you want to take the fantasy into a symbolic realm you can do this:

> For example, imagine yourself as a hero/heroine
> figure from the film world with whom you can

identify, coping with everything, or having a companion advisor with you etc etc.

You can use visualisation to handle emotional situations:

For example, if someone has annoyed you, visualise not losing your temper in the next few minutes.

You can use it to reward yourself when you are doing a tedious job:

For example, imagine the weekend and having time off. I have known people relax in aggressive meetings by picturing their aggressors dressed in silly outfits or comic underwear.

Guided visualisation

This type of visualisation can also be called 'guided fantasy'. Guided fantasy is a term often used in the therapy world.

Usually the guide is another person but there is nothing to stop you designing your own structure.

An example would be having your idea of the perfect future family gathering - go through the morning, the afternoon and the evening and put in all the details of what you would like to happen and what you are doing - for example, being in charge or just relaxing or both.

Here some of the structure has come and continues to come from another person, for example in asking you for more detail about how you are relating to the people at the gathering etc.

Or you can be guided/guide yourself to a fantasy realm to find things out, for example what you would *ideally* like to happen.

A simple example would be to imagine you are on a desert island in paradise - what would you like to happen?

A different example from the world of work could be: you enter a new office and decide what you would like the décor, colleagues, restaurant etc. to be like, then move on to working on a mix/balance of ideally enjoyable and fulfilling tasks and describe them.

With this fantasy, you could include lots of detail - for example, how colleagues respond to you (support you, praise you), whether you have peace, how much autonomy /trust you have, trips away and travel, and you could be guided or guide yourself into many areas of 'work'.

The learning from this could be to pinpoint what you would like and to discover how your current job falls short and in what ways.

Programmed visualisation

This kind of visualisation is when you substitute a fantasy for reality but the point of the fantasy is to *match the reality*. This is the type of visualisation that is used to focus unconscious healing power in the body and is used by the Simontons to directly address physical conditions - whilst it seems simple, it works.

Here are the principles to make it work:

1. Get a doctor to explain the physical condition with some visual input, for example, a diagram.

2. Develop a fantasy to match the condition - for example, if it's an infection and involves immune system cells overpowering the infection, the fantasy could be of piranhas nibbling away at other fish etc.

This may sound too simple, but the point is to understand the condition and then to develop a fantasy that is easy to use repetitively and which closely mirrors the condition.

Then it's a question of persisting with using the fantasy.

It's important not to use visualisation as a substitute for conventional treatment but alongside it. It's also important to find a doctor who is not ignorant of the unconscious and is not narrowly 'scientific', but this can be done, even in the UK.

My experience of the use of this technique is with someone who had multiple sclerosis, lived in the UK, and had a sympathetic GP, is that it helped arrest the condition.

Books

Adelaide Bry (1979) *Visualization: directing the movies of your mind* Harper Collins

12 dreams

The idea behind this chapter is that you will be more confident about deciphering your own dreams, have a rough guide to what is useful to read and can start in a practical way to use dreams in your life.

This chapter is primarily written by Jack with some material from Julia at the end

Understanding your dreams without 'experts' is possible: in today's world, you can be your own expert.

If you are understanding your dreams, you should be more in touch with deep parts of yourself, will be finding out what you want, making decisions that are right for you and saving the huge amount of time wasted by the conscious mind which often goes round in circles trying to find answers because it is not connected to your deep intuitive self.

If you're not used to deciphering them, coming to understand dreams is a bit like learning a new language - dreams are a picture language and have some 'rules' of their own and you will have to practise and 'stick with it'.

Please, though, forget about all those books which tell you the 'meaning' of a particular symbol, animal, or person in a dream. As each person develops their own individual dream language, the language of a dream alters depending on how the dreams are being deciphered – this is because your unconscious wants to get through and make life easier for you.

Some background and history to dreaming: Sigmund Freud, Carl Jung, Calvin S Hall, and Ann Faraday

Being able to understand dreams to guide your life or understand yourself has actually been made more difficult by 'experts'.

Sigmund Freud emphasised how big and powerful the unconscious mind is compared to the conscious mind – this, I think, has been very useful and it is a position that has a lot of supporters. He also thought of dreams as the 'royal road' to the unconscious mind – in other words, your dreams are a direct 'plug-in' to your unconscious mind, if they are deciphered properly.

The problem is that people like Sigmund Freud have spoilt useful dream processing to some degree. Ann Faraday in her helpful book *Dream Power* thinks that interpreting dreams rigidly, as often happens in psychoanalysis (Freudian or non-Freudian), is 'tyranny'. Why is this?

In Sigmund Freud's case, he tries to fit dreams into his theories, so that his theory would explain why the dream is produced, why the unconscious mind disguises a dream's content and why experts are needed to decipher the dream. A simpler explanation is that the unconscious minds of the dreamers that Freud studied did not want to cooperate with him as a therapist and didn't think much of his theories. So they may have masked the dream's content. Looking at Freud's original work, for example, *Studies in Hysteria* and *The Interpretation of Dreams*, I certainly wouldn't want to be one of his clients. These 'works' give an idea of his expert mind-set, his personality, and what is useful or outrageous about him theoretically. His biography and lifestyle are also very revealing. What's interesting about Freud is that despite huge problems with his theories, that he's had so much influence and there is extensive literature about Freud which could be time-wasting or interesting, depending how keen you are. My view of Sigmund Freud is that he has value as a pioneer but barked up a lot of the wrong trees.

Your unconscious mind is concerned with survival and health and doesn't care about the debates and disagreements of experts and academics – it is simply there to work for you in an incredibly effective way whether we realise this or not.

Carl Jung (initially a follower of Sigmund Freud) thought that the dreamer is the best person to decipher their dreams in any way they liked. Also, he thought that dreams were best interpreted as part of a sequence of dreams and that dreams were concerned with understanding and resolving current issues in people's lives. He also thought that the unconscious has a forward-looking bias and that people push towards psychological health.

In the early 1950s, rapid eye movement (R.E.M.) sleep was linked to dreaming in research by Nathaniel Kleitman and Eugene Aserinsky, whom Ann Faraday calls 'the Chicago pioneers'. Their ideas were that sleep is for brain growth and it's divided into R.E.M. and non-R.E.M. They observed that there is more R.E.M. sleep towards waking and that non-R.E.M. sleep produces different dreams from R.E.M. Faraday compares R.E.M. and non-R.E.M. dreams.

In her book on dreams, Ann Faraday says that R.E.M. dreams are:

- *more visual*
- *long*
- *detailed*
- *episodic – the 'scene' in the dream changes*
- *richer*
- *more emotional*
- *less vague*

and that non-R.E.M. dreams are:

- *shorter*
- *less vivid*
- *less visual*
- *less dramatic*
- *less elaborated*
- *less emotional*
- *less active*
- *more 'plausible'*
- *more concerned with current life problems*
- *more conversational*
- *more thought-like*
- *usually do not involve a change of scene*

Ann Faraday proposes three levels of depth for dreams:

Level 1
Insight about events in the outside world not emphasised enough by the conscious mind
Level 2
Dreams as a distorted mirror reflecting inner beliefs of the dreamer
Level 3
Insight into the deepest inner self

and she suggests looking at your dreams starting with level 1 – *is the dream explicable in terms of telling you a simple message about your everyday life?* - should be the first thing to look at.

As the level of your dream deepens, there's likely to be more symbolic content, multi-meaning and meaning which needs to be deciphered.

In Level 1, Ann Faraday classifies dreams like *reminder dreams* and *warning dreams.*

She also mentions Calvin Hall, a psychologist who studied thousands of 'normal' (not 'neurotic') dreams in the early 1950s, who found that everyone can decipher their own dreams on their own without expert help. He also found that:

- dreams show a lot of processing of everyday events
- dreams are like a letter to yourself – they are personal and rarely describe public events
- he agrees with Carl Jung that they reveal the present state of the dreamer
- dreams are to do with making sense of your inner life
- dreams involve a conversion to picture language, which can be symbolic
- dreams express the true versus the constructed or social self
- the dreamer is responsible for their own dream creation

- he agrees with Carl Jung that dreams are better read in a series
- he suggests that multiple views of the inner life are possible within a dream
- he agrees with Carl Jung that they're a very elegant, condensed, highly efficient way of communicating, if they're understood and there's no attempt by the unconscious to distort a dream so that it's hard to decipher

There's a wide variety within dreaming and it's a very individual process but it must be mentioned that some people do repress their dreams, presumably because they don't want to know what's really bothering them etc. It's also true that there's a wide interpretation possible to a dream which is why it's best that the dreamer interprets their own and sometimes they have multi-levels of meaning. A lot of doubtful literature on dreams says that there are universal symbols within them – this is a possibility but don't be too rigid about it. Also Carl Jung developed this idea extensively in his work on 'archetypes' - universal unconscious symbols. Calvin Hall found from analysing towards 50,000 dream diaries that there were remarkable consistencies across them as well as of course individual variation.

My experience of dreams as a dreamer

I've worked as a therapist for many years and have my own ideas about the unconscious mind and dreaming. I also have an unshakable faith in my unconscious and the importance and accuracy of what it tells me through my dreams, and I've been using my dreams to guide or direct my life for many years. What I've found out from this is that I can be in touch with the 'real me', solve problems, and know where to go next in my life in my life. My dreams have helped me through various times of crisis, in the making of big decisions, and keeping me on track in many ways - for example, in my creative work and in relationships.

Travel in my dreams

How I'm travelling in my dreams often suggests the speed or nature of change and how I'm developing in my life. If I'm driving a car in a dream, that usually means freedom and high speed in my life. If I'm walking, I'm taking time to reflect and consider. Journeys on trains usually suggest that I'm relying at the time on the already organised world of routine, working with authorities or organisation and being less responsible personally.

During one period when things were happening fast in my life, unknown to me I was becoming diabetic and having less energy. During this time I dreamt that I was in a car coming to a crossroads and whichever gear I chose or route I wanted to take, I lost power and control of the car.

Recently I was involved in a social/political issue and deciding how to be involved. I dreamt I was flying in the cargo hold of a plane. Julia was there but unseen in the body of the plane.

Buildings or landscapes in my dreams

A house or building in my dreams usually means my personality or creative potential. If I'm in a large empty house in dreams, there is room in my life or personality to start a new creative project.

If I'm in a flat or small, cramped house that usually means I'm hemmed in, in my life or in terms of personal development.

If I'm going through a learning period, usually this is reflected in dreams of being at college etc.

The sea/water in dreams

To me being near the sea is usually being near my creativity and/or unconscious mind. Sometimes there's another layer (see *Buildings* above) and I'm in a building representing my personality or creative self. The kind of issue my unconscious mind is engaged on is reflected in what's happening in the building or the nature of the building. How I enter or exit water and/or the building may also be relevant as is the relationship of the water to the building eg. surrounded by water, a small stream beside the walls, crashing waves outside the windows.

Some things I've noticed about the unconscious and dreams……………..

I agree with Calvin Hall that dreams are best translated into conscious thought as a series of dreams

This does not mean that you can't translate a single dream, it just allows you time to learn the language the dream is 'talking in'- remember that dreams talk in pictures, they're a bit like watching a movie and contain their own rules, distortions and symbols. It also allows the unconscious mind to adjust to how it's being deciphered, and if it's not getting through to you in the way it's being deciphered it will adjust until it gets through.

Here's an example of a dream that has been part of a series to do with my art work where I've long ago established the meanings of 'movement', in this case walking, and an 'art- college-like' studio or building, which means learning or development or solving problems in my painting work. If I'm walking in a dream it means usually I'm taking time to explore something closely and slowly.

> *Recently I dreamt I was walking in an art college type studio- far bigger than my normal one. I was doing a bigger canvas than usual, and was thinking about developing my 'realistic' work – then the dream shifted (a sign of R.E.M. sleep) and I was walking into an office building, with an unknown companion, and going past a woman in a business suit whom we ignored. The feeling accompanying this dream was of being happy, confident and creative.*

This dream was also in the context of thinking about doing some realistic work as I'd been doing some drawing and design work with my daughter (my usual work is abstract) and I'd been thinking too about doing book illustrations. The dream told me that yes, I was thinking about doing realistic work **and it did not say** *'don't do that'*. It told me I was into a time of learning and expansion and that this was also true for my normal work which is abstract.

I took the companion (an unknown benign figure) to be some kind of trusted advisor who wasn't a real person but was part of me and was maybe a bit unknown at present.

I took walking past the well-presented woman in a business suit to mean that I didn't need help or someone else to promote my work.

As since I had this dream and figured it out, I've not heard from my unconscious, I'm assuming the interpretation is on track.

What you do *not* dream about is important.

In the art-college-like dream above, I was **not** told *'don't do realistic work'* and before going to sleep, I asked myself to tell me in a dream about any current significant issues - I dreamt about work *not my relationships,* so I assumed that there were no problems to sort out in close relationships.

There's a dialogue with the unconscious in dreams, dreams adjust to the way they're being deciphered - you get better at speaking their language.

You can ask your unconscious a specific question and get an answer in a dream -for example: *'tell me how to solve an issue with a particular person'.*

Or you can ask a general question and get the answer in a dream - for example: *'what is really important right now in my life?'*

Usually, as people become less known and recognisable to you in a dream they are more likely to be symbolic or parts of *yourself,* so commonly, if you dream about a friend it's likely that the dream IS about that person.........

For me, this isn't always true....when I dream of my brother whom I never see, I'm usually dreaming about a 'business-like' part of me'- I've always seen my brother as efficient and good at business.

If you ask a question before sleep and the dream answer is unclear you can ask your unconscious mind for clarification or simplicity.

Dreams can be multi-layered and have multi-meanings

Dreams can be very humorous

Sometimes a dream will give you a message which is obviously not relating to a current reality – it tells you what your reality ISN'T. For example, sometimes I *dream I am late for work* – but I'm freelance so often this type of dream is saying *'come off it, you're worrying about life in the past, it's no longer relevant'*. In this case, the dream is pointing me back to a new difference in reality.

More on how we can tap into our dream-life:

- 'the unconscious' can be asked specific questions – identify what you want to know before falling asleep and the answers will often emerge during sleep

- if the answer is unclear, 'the unconscious' can be asked to clarify

- the language 'the unconscious' is deciphered in is the language it will get used to communicating with

- dreams can be multi-layered and multi-meaning – take time to decipher them in relation to the context of your current concerns, your emotions, your questions

- accept how funny imagery and activities can sometimes be within our dreams

- recognize that dreams can be an elegant way of communicating, with beauty, concision, creativity

- understand that the 'unconscious' will 'talk to the dreamer' in the language it is being deciphered in, so the most reliable language is *your own personal language* – be aware that models such as Freud's counter this approach

- deciphering dreams saves the time-waste of endless conscious processing

- dreams are not rational – they will come from all parts of you eg. from feeling, intuitive and spiritual parts. They may tell you things you were not aware of at a conscious level.

Jack says: *my approach has developed from:*

- taking years to decipher my dreams
- my own experience of therapy
- working with dreamers as a therapist
- extensively using my dreams to guide my life
- particular features of my dreams
- exploring my dreams in periods of illness, introspection and uncertainty
- being interested in how my dreams get through to me/my dream language
- using imaginative interpretation

Practical notes for working with dreams

- have a notebook beside the bed to note dreams down – this is essential
- ensure no interruptions when you're remembering them
- make an intentional effort to remember them - replay them several times, making an active effort to remember them
- persist with your dreams and if necessary, find someone to help who has an open, flexible (not 'school of therapy') approach
- avoid silly dream interpretation books

- when deciphering, consider: *what are the associated feelings? what's in the detail? is the dream saying what the reality is NOT? think about the <u>context</u>*
- ask for answers or clarification before you go to sleep
- if there's no answer from the 'unconscious' then it's probably not important.. is a very good guide
- beware of distortion through drugs and alcohol, food etc.
- practise – develop your skill over time and learn your personal dream language to help you decipher meanings

This section includes contributions from Julia

I've not concentrated on my dreams as much as Jack but occasionally a dream has stood out and I've spent time exploring it or being moved by its power. Soon after my father died, it seemed as if he revisited me in a dream, taking me out on a boat on a big peaceful lake and then steering me safely through rapids. It felt like a gift from him and I felt much more secure in the world.

Freud suggests that dreams are about wish-fulfilment and others believe that they are the re-working of the events of our day or week, whilst some, like Jung, believe that dreams might have a more proactive, forward-looking motive, illuminating the possibilities that might lie ahead. This is consistent with the Apollonian view of the prophetic power of dreams. For Freud, if we remember dreams, it suggests repressed material bursting through into the conscious mind.

The main people to look at dreams are Sigmund Freud and Carl Jung, but the field of psychoanalysis of which they were both pioneers has been criticised by among others, Karl Popper, on the general issue of being non-scientific and unfalsifiable, and as being dependent on case study analysis which it is difficult to evidence - and is thus unreliable - depending as it does on the honesty and integrity of the therapist/author. But to be too critical and logical can mean that we lose access to the main source of knowledge about our unconscious mind, and to attempt to subject dream-work to rational, deductive evaluation is like trying to explore an underwater treasure trove full of organic life with a pair of scissors and a tweezer – the tools don't necessarily fit the job. It's better to look at what material emerges and let it speak to you in your own terms: there are no absolute answers as to what dreams mean and no-one else can ultimately explain them to you. In the end, you have to be your *own* dream 'therapist'.

Paul Ricoeur and David Stewart have identified thinkers like Sigmund Freud and Frederic Nietzsche as masters of the *'hermeneutics of suspicion'* – thinkers like these have shown us how to look beyond the face value of things, and given us tools with which to deconstruct and interpret text. In this book, we constantly urge you to view with suspicion the prevailing story – whether it's in the media, politics, economics, medicine, organisations or culture. With dreams, there is an immediate chance to develop our skills in exploring the symbolism of surface imagery and digging deeper to 'read' the real story underneath and appreciate what is going on in our unconscious. Dreams are a part of the general exploration and attentiveness that we need to pay to our unconscious for our mental, physical and spiritual health.

Sigmund Freud's ideas

Sigmund Freud thought that dreams were always about desires and wishes – *about 'repressed impulses'* sometimes called material from the *'id'*, often deep, early wishes from babyhood that are not always explicable in words but which can emerge in the graphic and pictorial images in our dreams. The most common desires are grandiosity and ambition and sexuality. These wishes are contained in our daily life by the control of the conscience, our internalised parental/authority-figure messages or *'super-ego'*. In sleep, this control is somewhat relaxed and we can do things that normally we would not allow in thought or behaviour. Freud believed that these wishes were nevertheless often disguised and thus we can only discover their meaning and our feelings about them through interpretation. An example of this is when dream material is sometimes the apparent *opposite* of what we really feel or mean. Repressed wishes and desires are hidden even in dreaming because they seem to us so unacceptable – through the *'defense mechanisms'* that psychoanalysis works to unravel - but

384

their repression can hamper the free flow of our energy and our capacity to love people and our work. In dreams, the struggle between the *'super-ego'* – a censoring force - and the *'id'* – the instinctual desiring force - goes on with psychological mechanisms functioning to keep important material contained, hidden, fictionalized, or socially acceptable.

Other people's ideas

However, more recent analysts of dreams suggest that there might be other issues going on in our dreams that are not always about such deep desires – they may for example be ways of working through problems that are worrying us and sometimes offer us creative solutions. Ann Faraday in her 1970s work on dreams suggested that dreams are often about the processing of material experienced in the conscious mind over the previous two or three days.

Antti Revonsuo in Finland has suggested that animals and human beings dream in similar ways, primarily *rehearsing threats to our survival*. Dreaming about our fears and external threats, and keeping our self-defence instincts sharpened may be a significant motive in our unconscious world.

Some writers believe that particular images have particular meanings and there are numerous dictionaries or lexicons that purport to identify these. Sigmund Freud himself offered a few such as seeing the self represented by a house or death by a journey. Carl Jung believed that this kind of symbolic analysis could be widened to a 'collective unconscious' – that there are universal 'archetypes' that recur in different people and in different cultures. Carl Jung saw *individuation,* a process of integrating opposites within us such as male and female energy and the conscious with the unconscious as key elements in our maturation. See our chapter on *The Self* for more detail on this. He identified a number of common *archetypal figures* such as the *hero*, the *wise old man,* the *earth mother,* and the *trickster* who appear in most people's dreams across the globe at one time or another.

Thus, in dreaming, although there may be clear images eg. a *mother*, the real meaning is that of the feminine or emotional side of one's nature or the longing to 'go home' rather than a literal reading of the image as one's own mother. Or there may be common images - *house* is *structure, travelling* is *movement.* Carl Jung did not agree with the idea of dream material always being about material repressed from consciousness; rather, he thought dreams were themselves a new language for us that connects us to the *collective* unconscious, which he saw as at a level below our *personal* (individual) consciousness. One of the mechanisms we might use is that of *'compensation'* whereby we attempt to balance out aspects of our psychological material, such as dreaming of sexual desire, but repressing this strongly during our work in a professional role. Jung believed that as well as dealing with material from the external *'objective'* daily life, dreams may be tapping into the deeper *'subjective'* world of the person's own psyche.

Of course, from a scientific perspective, it's possible to contend that dream material is purely random activity within the nervous system; yet these days, the unconscious is no longer left unmapped. Researchers into brain functioning are increasingly finding evidence of unconscious processing – what Carl Zimmer, writing in *The Brain*, calls the *'inner zombies'*. People appear to 'know' things which are not expressible in the conscious mind – for example, amnesiacs and people with damage to their normal brain functioning being able to process phenomena which in their conscious mind they could not recognize. We know a lot about the brain's structure and where things happen: for example, we will recall the details of an accident from the *hippocampus* and react emotionally and physically (eg. in anxiety) in the weeks afterwards from the *amygdala.* Undoubtedly we may be able to make links between different types of sleep like slow wave and rapid eye movement sleep and our experience of dreaming, but the new development is that scientists are now becoming interested in the potential of the huge amount of important mental processing that goes on without verbal language and without a formal logical order.

But even if we're inclined to dismiss the psychoanalytic approaches (and we may not be), it's important not to throw everything out and miss things that could be useful. Perhaps what's important about the unconscious is the chance to honour the spiritual, mysterious and creative within us – something less tangible and explicable than the conscious mind, which seems to guide us, unravel conundrums, and release emotions underlying issues and events, often unexpectedly, with surprising outcomes and without conscious effort.

In the end, *it's a matter of opinion* how important the unconscious mind is and what it does.

Ann Faraday pioneered much modern dream work, which Jack has discussed in the previous section. In her work at the reflective level of dreaming, she believed we could understand more about ourselves through exploration of the characters, animals, houses, places and methods of transport in the dreams. Carl Jung emphasized the distinction between the *objective* characters within a dream which represent literally themselves – ie. a house is a house, and the *subjective* and symbolic elements whereby a house might represent for example, stability and safety. There are of course many general guidebooks to imagery in dreams of varying value, but as Jung believed, it is important to relate any symbolic analysis to the individual's life situation and personal psychology. Meanings have to be related to the context of the person's life.

Like the Gestalt therapists, Ann Faraday recommended **initiating dialogues with dream characters** to facilitate understanding of the messages in the dreams, work which can be done upon waking or in a subsequent therapy or personal meditative session. *Lucid dreaming*, linked to the work of *'dream yoga'* mastered by Dzögchen practitioners within Tibetan Buddhism, involves **talking to dream characters** *whilst dreaming* – this is an advanced meditative technique and may take some practice.

Whether or not we are practising Buddhists, there is potential here to learn from our dream-life, to puncture the fears we may have (particularly within nightmares), and to move within the unconscious world, developing our awareness. Becoming skilled in *knowing that we are dreaming whilst we are dreaming* enhances our awareness that our everyday experience is more transitory and illusory than we tend to think - this is a powerful tool that can help us live our lives, bear the pain of events and changes, and ultimately face death.

References and books

Ann Faraday (1972, 1997 edition) *Dream Power* Berkley Trade

Ann Faraday (1975, 1990 edition) *The Dream Game* Harper Collins

Sigmund Freud 1899 *The Interpretation of Dreams* (1980 version) Avon Books

Calvin S Hall (1953) (2012 ed) *The Meaning of Dreams: their symbolism and their sexual implications* Iconoclassic

Nathaniel Kleitman and Eugene Aserinsky (1953) *Regularly Occurring Eye Periods of Motility and Other Phenomena, During Sleep* Science New series 18:3062 September 4, 1953 273-274

Antti Revonsuo *The reinterpretation of dreams: an evolutionary hypothesis of the function of dreaming* Behavioral and Brain Sciences (2000) 23: pp 877-901 Cambridge University Press

Paul Ricoeur (1970) *Freud and Philosophy: An Essay on Interpretation* New Haven: Yale University Press

http://www.psychologytoday.com/articles/200710/dreams-night-school

http://www.freud.org.uk/education/topic/10576/subtopic/40030/

http://www.carl-jung.net/dreams.html

http://en.wikipedia.org/wiki/Carl_Jung

http://www.dreamresearch.ca/pdf/jung.pdf

http://en.wikipedia.org/wiki/Dream_yoga

13   reminiscence

In this short chapter we give some pointers as to how we can use our memories to benefit our lives and some exercises to get you started.

This chapter is contributed by Julia.

Mining our memories is a tremendous technique that we all do naturally.

- consider one of those moments when you're suddenly asked to wait somewhere, eg. because of an unexpected delay at an appointment or on a journey or while a treatment takes effect and you don't have a book or computer or companion with you. What often comes into your mind are memories.

- when we meet a new partner the first thing that builds a bond between us and them is often the sharing of memories – how and where we grew up, a previous relationship and what went wrong or right, places we've been

- walking into a room, someone's perfume evokes a memory of someone else we once knew or the smell of baking reminds us of an earlier time when our mother or an early caregiver cooked something similar

- deciding to go for therapy – unless it's someone who's determinedly only working with current process, you'll find that recalling events from earlier times in your life is helpful in deciphering strands of your own psychology, providing explanations of how patterns have developed in how you behave or feel

- driving down the road to the shops, work, school gate etc., perhaps talking to a companion in the car, turning the wheel competently round corners on a familiar route, listening to the radio, and thinking about the stops you have to make on the journey, you may not be conscious of the skill you have developed at a deep level in driving itself – the skill has become 'automated' – it's engaged but not conscious unless something interrupts it like a collision or the car stalling

- you try to teach someone piano-playing, or to make a plumbing repair, or to do a maths sum or how to meditate or to make a white sauce and find yourself making a mistake – you thought you knew how to do it, but as you try to bring your unconscious processing into consciousness, things don't go quite right

- away from a loved one, staying in a guest room, and find yourself feeling a bit lonely, recalling what it's like to go to bed with the other person, or a happy time together, but can't quite bring to mind their face or their voice – you make a call and as you hear their voice, you're connected up to a template deep in your memory system where their voice is already stored, and you feel comforted

- nervously getting ready for a performance or an exam or a talk, you wonder how you will cope…..as you walk on stage or start to write the answers to exam questions, your voice flows calmly, your pen moves along the page swiftly, your fingers play beautifully – words come and things stored in your memory are retrieved, apparently effortlessly

- in the middle of the supermarket, as we reach for a product high on a shelf, we turn round and there's someone we know in front of us – for a moment, we can't 'place' them – they're out of context and wearing 'mufti' – then our unconscious mind offers an answer and we 'know' who they are and we decide to smile or perhaps, to beat a hasty retreat

Long-term memory

In all sorts of ways, we depend on our memories and we tap into them all day long. If anything, our task ought often to *stem* the flow of material from memory in order to live in the present, as in meditative states or when we are trying to be fully 'alive'. However, the point here is to *utilise* the memory for a number of purposes.

Most of what's stored in our memory is out of conscious awareness at any one time. We couldn't possibly hold it all at a conscious level. From the moment we're born we're encoding material for 'storage', and in old age, we can more readily access material from this long-term storage facility than we can remember things recently put into our short-term working memory like a person's name or whether or not we've just taken our prescribed tablets.

Memory is not just a mental process

Memory is not just a mental, thought-based process. Our memories are also stored through the body. We can evoke a memory of when we hurt ourselves in a fall or a bash against a wall or in a car collision every time an old bodily ache disturbs us. But intriguingly, it seems that much might be stored at an even deeper level.

Darian Leader and David Corfield in their book about illness document the numerous cases of patients turning up at doctors' surgeries with ailments on particular anniversaries (eg. the same day 5 years ago when a spouse died or a particular time within the family system). Many symptoms can appear to reflect memories which are not conscious. They suggest that the body is particularly prone to these effects when events are difficult for us to process or make sense of, suggesting that illness is often about unresolved emotional business, or about events that are so traumatic – as in the case of people who have been tortured or raped or deliberately abused – that ways of dealing with them through language are not enough.

Perhaps if we can't deal with something through the conscious mind – and there might be much in life that comes into this category, the only route for the material to take is through the body. And removing the symptoms of physical distress can sometimes trigger mental breakdown because the mind is unable to deal with all of the psychological material.

Michael Balint, who ran groups for GPs to discuss the role of doctors' own beliefs in relating to patients' illnesses, cautioned against violation of *'the patient's right to fall ill'* and Leader and Corfield write convincingly about the way in which people might *need* their symptoms, their *somatization* of psychological material, or indeed the reverse, the symptoms of mental illness than when relieved, might be followed by physical illness. In other words, it is possible that much is held in the unconscious in non-verbal ways that we simply do not have the means to process and deal with in our conscious mind. Emotional material and knowledge of traumatic events may be ultimately expressed through illness in mind or body to protect us from complete collapse.

Using memory for healing

'Reminiscence therapy' is used with older people who may be struggling with increasing dementia or disorientation as they move into care home contexts, or needing to alleviate depression or apathy. 'Therapy' involves gathering together artefacts from earlier times including photographs and ornaments, and playing music from eras and situations that they might recognise. Relatives, friends and associates can play a role in helping bring memories alive, particularly if they too lived through the same periods of history.

Survivors suffering from post-traumatic syndrome can sometimes be helped to overcome physical and mental disorders (things like headaches, depression and bowel disorders which they may not connect with their original trauma) through the use of therapies (such as hypnotherapy) which are designed to re-evoke memories and thus help them to release the fears, anxieties and anger which have long been buried. Others find that creative expression helps without fully articulating or unearthing memories in detail.

Is our memory fixed?

The storehouse of long-term memory is not a fixed place. Not only are we constantly adding to it, and perhaps sometimes letting some things go, but if we are dedicated to our personal growth, we will find that we are able to change the meaning of material already stored. It doesn't have to stay the same. It can be revisited and re-filed in a new place or in a new way. Irvin Yalom wrote eloquently about his work in existential therapy with older people, and about the benefits of therapy in later years, where there is the possibility of new insights changing the way in which we view the past. But ordinary life can also change the way we think about the past. A new partner can make us review an earlier partner – perhaps more harshly or more kindly, for example, accepting that what we experienced in the former relationship may have had more to do with our own contribution than we liked to believe at the time, or gobsmacking us with the idea that someone new loves us properly and that what was purported to be love by someone else was in fact, not. We have an argument with our parents and discover a new truth about our relationship with them, or we trace an aspect of family history that makes us review something we thought was true about our identity or background.

Although there's a debate these days about the benefits of 'grief therapy' and whether talking about loss is helpful to people who are bereaved, many of us can identify with the idea of taking some time to indulge in a 'sob session' where we gather memorabilia associated with the lost person and wallow for a contained period of time in our memories, perhaps weeping, perhaps feeling angry, whatever the exercise evokes. For some people this can be helpful, and the more particularly so, because it comes to an end at an agreed time and allows us to feel able to get on with other things in our lives more freely, less burdened.

Recent changes to the American diagnostic code means that people are allowed less and less time to grieve before they're considered in need of treatment, a guidance that that many doctors disagree with. Suppressing grief with anti-depressant medication may have its place for those of us who have other pressures on us to carry on or because something is too painful to bear at the time, but grief should not be hurried into as a matter of course.

The point is that our memory can be a powerful fount of material for healing.

Accessing the past is a basic tool of therapy and counselling, but you don't necessarily need a therapist to help you do it. Whether you want someone there with you may depend on how painful the memories are. The idea that we must choose how much pain we can handle is put forward in Irvin Yalom's novel, *When Nietzsche Wept,* and it seems relevant here. Our memories can be wonderfully uplifting and keep us going through adversity as in many novels about soldiers who keep going with images of the men and women they love. But they can also be agonising – if we were abused or violated, we may need a lot of support before we can go back to times we've chosen to forget, and we may need convincing as to whether or not doing so is good for us. Memories can also be agonising just because they're beautiful – remembering times of happiness and joy and knowing that they're irretrievable can be exquisitely painful. So we need to take on board the concept of reminiscence with a lot of care, perhaps letting in painful memories step by step, and turning each one into something positive for the future – *I will never let that happen again, I am grateful that I was loved by that person, I understand now that I am strong because of what happened* etc.

Activities to try using reminiscence

Select a photograph or artefact from the past and find a piece of music that was around at the time. Sit down in a quiet corner, close the curtains, play the music, look at what you've chosen and spend some time letting your memory of that time be evoked. After a few minutes write down everything you can remember about that time. Write down an affirmation for the future that emerges from letting in the memory. Choose someone with whom to share the experience and its outcome and talk about how you made your choice of photo and music and anything that's different about the way you view that time now from when you were actually there.

Enrich your long-term memory store by looking at the history of the time when you were growing up. Read about what was happening in the world when you were, say, aged 6. Look at food, prices, transport, housing, sexual attitudes, religious institutions, the political scene, wars, economics. What effect does understanding the pressures on those bringing you up and educating you have on the way you now view them? Does a deeper awareness of the world you were living in affect your sense of yourself now – are you able to modify long-held memories in the light of new knowledge?

Books

Michael Balint (1986 ed) *Doctor, his patient and his illness* Churchill Livingstone
Darius Leader and David Corfield (2007) *Why do people get ill?* London: Penguin Books
Irvin Yalom (1992, 2005 ed) *When Nietzsche Wept* Harper Perennial
Irvin Yalom (2012) (2nd ed) *Love's Executioner* Basic Books

14   creativity

> Our main focus in this chapter is on how to foster creativity,
> navigating the resistances around us, getting organised,
> finding support and the right conditions, understanding the
> balance of rationality and unconscious processing, and
> recognising the political and social nature of creativity within
> the wider culture.

Most of this chapter has been written by Julia, with comments from Jack towards the end of the chapter.

The importance of creativity

Creativity is important. It's what life is about.

Creative people are the ones who will help us survive when marooned on a desert island.

Creative people are the ones who will help governments and organisations solve problems and lead people out of difficulty.

Yet it can be hard to think of our own creativity as mattering. It is often derided, neglected, devalued, and left till last on the list.

In rebuilding iconic buildings bombed in war, or restoring collections of art or literature destroyed in warfare, food and housing can easily be seen as more pressing – *'culture can wait'*.

Yet *life itself* is the biggest creative project we have. Every religion knows that, even as religions strive to tame and contain our lives. Governments tend to forget that, even as they find rationales to control and watch us.

We hope in this chapter that there's enough to make you think about the role of creativity in your life and what you can do to foster it. Much of what we say applies to the person who wants to really get down to some creative work *per se,* but many of the suggestions can equally apply to someone who wants to become more creative in their approach to existing problems in their life.

First on the list is the need to think of creative activity and creative production as *important.*

Art and political dissent

Governments and businesses have always been aware of the importance of art and culture, both because of the opportunity to use it for furthering their own ends and because dissent and rebellion are most often expressed and fuelled by artists and intellectuals.

It's important to look carefully at the balance between governments' legitimate roles in managing the protection to minorities and individual rights that they agree to provide and the legitimate rights of artists and intellectuals to free expression of dissent and challenge. Russia has recently been in the spotlight because of President Putin's avowed intent to support religious expression (after decades of suppression of religion) and those who challenge this including the case of *Pussy Riot,* musicians who claimed to be protesting against government legislation against women and to be linked to the global anti-capitalist movement, and *Yuri Samodurov* and *Andrei Erofeyev,* curators of a *Forbidden Art* exhibition in Moscow, in which banned and irreverent pieces of art were to be displayed. We have to decide whether the issue is one of freedom of expression, one of genuine dissent in relation to human rights, or one where individuals are intending to build their career reputations through being associated with shock value, regardless of their effect on fellow citizens' feelings, dignity and values. The issues can be complex.

The novelist and human rights campaigner, Arundhati Roy, no stranger to controversy, a spokesperson for many issues in Indian politics, has often crossed swords with the government on issues such as the independence of Kashmir and the Narmada Dam Project. The artist Ai Weiwei, ranked highly in *Art Review*'s guide to the 100 most powerful figures in contemporary art, helped design the *Bird's Nest* for the Beijing Olympic stadium and exhibited *Sunflower Seeds* at the Tate Modern in London, has long been a thorn in the Chinese government's side, gaining international standing as a dissident for human rights in China. He's been imprisoned, claimed injury by the police and that charges of tax evasion against him are politically motivated. Their stories are worth exploration because they're people who risk much - ranging from social disapproval to prosecution and personal danger – to bring issues to the attention of an international audience. Understanding what motivates creative people to step beyond traditional comfort zones and live in the spotlight of controversy can be instructive –for example, particular kinds of personality, personal history, having resources such as personal contacts and money, and having supportive partners may all be factors which make it more possible for some to do this kind of work than others.

The political leader Adolf Hitler designated modernist art as 'degenerate' and mounted an exhibition in 1937 of what he meant by 'degenerate art' - each work displayed was commented on in terms of its failings, including *mockery of religion, insulting to women, glorifying racial stereotypes, mental illness and disability, distorting of faces and bodies* etc. Adolf Hitler viewed modern movements in art such as cubism, Dadaism, fauvism, surrealism and Bauhaus as degenerate. Work by artists like Otto Dix, Paul Klee, Max Ernst, Wassily Kandinsky and Marc Chagall were included in the exhibition, and many such artists had to lie low, run the risk of being banned from teaching positions or from selling their work, or escape to exile for many years. It was a reaction to the developments in art and music in the inter-war years under the Weimar republic, which some viewed as having been unnecessarily influenced by American styles and values, such as jazz music, and which had been viewed negatively by conservative groups. In the 3rd Reich, Hitler also wanted to gain control of 'high art' with a view to propagating the Nazi ideology and eradicating critique, whilst he apparently initially refrained from challenging ordinary culture for the masses.

The era of McCarthyism in the USA in the 1950s was about emphasising the distance that needed to be put between the capitalist world and the threat of Communism, which it was felt was prevalent in left and liberal culture, and particularly among creative and intellectual people. Abstract Expressionists evaded much of the American McCarthyism censure because they chose to express their feelings and views in abstract ways which could not be pinned down and identified. Many others who put their feelings and perceptions into figurative art, film, and the written word lost their jobs or means of making an income or gaining recognition.

We should not be naïve about the way in which governments and big business want to use the cultural world to influence the public mind and can intervene directly or indirectly in the 'natural' marketplace to do so. For example, the airing and publicising of issues of public policy often takes place through the vehicle of soap drama, and funding policy for the film industry can shape what is produced.

The current developments in 'entertainment' and celebrity culture which catapult people of often questionable talent into mega-stardom and unimaginable wealth do little for the development of true creative work, and serve to undermine ordinary people's self-esteem, whilst offering false hope to many (particularly young people) that they too might 'make it' if they try hard enough. This culture also distracts us from the sometimes difficult conditions of our actual lives, filling our minds with the ins and outs of the personal lives of the famous which can take precedence over our own worries, and serving as an indirect advertisement for the trappings of upward social mobility, thus fuelling our hunger for goods and our motivation to work hard to afford them.

Art and culture can be the place where we find the best launching pad to challenge things in our society. For Howard Zinn, historian and social activist, the arts are the locale for a kind of 'guerilla warfare' in the sense that guerrillas look for the gaps in the culture where they can make an impact. Artists, musicians, writers, dancers have a privileged opportunity to inspire others to critique and challenge things. In our view, the opportunity should not be wasted.

We don't have to have the label 'artist' to do something creative as a way of opening up debate.

'Protest art', comedy, conceptual art, and resistance art are all forms of expression which are utilised to question assumptions and expectations and to critique existing ideologies. As the American Abstract Expressionists realised, dissent doesn't always have to be expressed through open confrontation.

War - destruction and reconciliation

Enemy nations have often targeted iconic buildings and collections of art, or burned books in public to symbolise the obliteration of a cultural tradition, to define the end of a previous era, to demoralise people and demonstrate their power, and to make it clear that the power structures that have previously prevailed are no more.

And the loss of domestic artefacts as people flee their homes renders people disorientated and homeless in a cultural sense as well as a practical sense. Perhaps 'reminiscence centres' are not just there to help people recover their personal memories but to rebuild their sense of continuity and connection with a culture after fragmentation and loss. After war, museums don't have to demonise the enemy – there are opportunities to convey messages for peace, but sometimes – particularly when justice has not been seen to be done and reparation has not happened - people are not ready for this.

Nevertheless, projects to make good the physical damage to cities and valued symbols of a culture are not always developed through a sense of hatred or anger. Damage has usually been inflicted on both sides. Sometimes such work holds out possibilities for reconciliation such as through pairing and twinning arrangements of cities and villages. In Dresden *Frauenkirche,* destroyed by Allied bombing in the second world war, when 25,000 people were recorded as being killed in a single campaign, the Coventry Cross of Nails now stands on the altar in the rebuilt church as *'a symbol of reconciliation and new beginnings',* and the new cross was financed by British donations amounting to £600,000. It was designed by Alan Smith, the son of an RAF man who had been in the sky bombing Dresden during the war. His father had later become a pacifist. And in 1940, the day after Coventry Cathedral was devastated by the Luftwaffe, Provost Dick Howard promised to build what has become a base for reconciliation ministry throughout the world: *'the Community of the Cross of Nails',* at Coventry.

The creative process

One of the most important messages we want to give is that creativity should be a joy. If it can be fun, that is good. If your approach is more sombre, so be it, but *enjoyment* through engagement should be key. This is because art – in its widest sense – only really speaks to people when it emerges from that love of the work. You may have other motives – reconciliation or protest, expiation or reparation, self-expression or reworking etc. but the primary reason for doing something creative probably has to be pleasure. *It should flow from you.* Consider yourself a vehicle for creative energy, let it emerge and flow out from you.

Graham Wallas, in his work *Art of Thought*, published in 1926, presented one of the first models of the creative process. In the Wallas stage model, creative insights and illuminations may be explained by a process consisting of 5 stages:

preparation	preparatory work on a problem that focuses the individual's mind on the problem and explores the problem's dimensions
incubation	where the problem is internalized into the unconscious mind and nothing appears externally to be happening
intimation	the creative person gets a "feeling" that a solution is on its way
illumination	where the creative idea bursts forth from its preconscious processing into conscious awareness
verification	where the idea is consciously verified, elaborated, and then applied

It's clear here that logical thinking is employed in the process as well as inductive and intuitive processes, and indeed, it may be important to note that both conscious and unconscious processing, both cognitive and non-verbal processes may all come into play in creative work. There's a long tradition in the idea that creative production depends on *preparatory work*, setting the scene. Gathering the materials, making the design, getting to know the field, reading around the subject, *engaging*, and then time when *incubation and reflection* may take place, and insight, problem resolution, synthesis or the ultimate selection of outcomes takes form in the 'mind's eye', often when away from the site of the work, when relaxing or allowing free play of the mind, before a *final stage* of putting the work together, refining it, preparing for marketing or performance. Many people talk about moments of insight which come to them when in the bath, walking on a hilltop, in the middle of having a drink with friends etc. This is not a charter to down tools, but a recognition that not all creative solutions come through a direct whittling away at the problem – sometimes there has to be a stage of free play to allow unconscious and conscious processing to meld.

Some people may be more 'logical' or focused and plan their work meticulously before they take brush to surface, chisel to stone, pen to paper, with results coming quickly once they actually 'engage'. Others may go straight into working with materials, waiting to see what emerges after immersion in colour, light, sound, words, images etc. Others still might come across a creative idea 'by accident'. There's no one way to 'do' creative work.

> I used to have long late-night conversations with a dear friend, which persisted over the course of some months. Each phone-call lasted nearly two hours. I discovered after a while that I had a growing collection of doodles on paper, reflecting the waxes and wanes of the discussions and my unconscious processing whilst our voices dealt with the words. If I'd wanted to, these doodles could have been collected and turned into a creative project.

However, it's worth making the point that we don't have to be talking only about people who 'do' creative work. Everything in this chapter can be relevant to someone who wants to be more creative in their work or daily life, even if that work is not normally seen as specifically creative or within a creative industry. Developing a new system of timetabling, or setting up a space for colleagues to meet and have coffee, taking a new approach to problem-solving, working out how to save time on a task, taking an alternative route, finding a different way of remembering data can all be examples of creativity at work. Creativity is not the exclusive province of those who work in marketing, design and development departments or in music and drama colleges.

Don't skimp on investment

Be prepared to put the effort in on preparing the ground and doing the actual thinking, feeling, and doing. Shell out some money without begrudging it: tools, studio space, clay, wood, metal, a new laptop, filing system, some new books, a better musical instrument, some lessons or advice, a new printer etc.

Being in touch with your creativity

People who are in touch with their creative capacities are likely to be *willing to take a degree of risk* – starting on a blank page or canvas involves taking a step into unknown territory and seeing what comes out, going into a group of people and outlining a novel approach to working practices takes courage.

Creative work usually requires *concentration*, and in the solitude of that concentration, our *inner life* develops, our unconscious material is tapped, our memories and our imaginations are engaged. This enriches us, and also gives us *a measure of independence* because we can live within our inner world without particular need for the stimulation of other people.

For many, there is often *a willingness to open to material and stimuli around us and perhaps too to different ideas and values* which challenge us. On the other hand, for some, creative play with ideas that we've long-held may serve to *reinforce and articulate long-held ideas and values* more clearly and forcefully. This difference in permeability can mean that some creative people seem obstinate, bullish, and definite about what they do

403

and believe, whilst others may need to protect themselves from the outside world at times because they can get overwhelmed by external stimuli which they soak up as source material or buffeted by a range of ideas from outside themselves so that they find it a challenge to develop a single or unified response.

Creativity for many is automatically linked to the capacity to *critique the status quo* because it's the opposite of accepting what's given and being passive – it's about being productive and energetic.

All of this adds up to the possibility that we will be more challenging and critical of organisations with which we are associated, and perhaps more threatening to others, not conforming to what's expected, offering new ways of seeing things, generating alternative approaches. We may not always be popular for this, and may leave others feeling criticised for being staid, uneasy about the risks of change and concerned about any lack of anchors and safeguards.

Schools, colleges and workplaces whilst paying lip service to the idea of creative abilities being welcome if not actively encouraged, may nevertheless suppress innovation and novelty, quieting people who try to be different and failing to reward or even recognise the creative contribution. The international author and adviser Sir Ken Robinson argues that organisations need people who *'think outside the box'* but that institutions are deeply ambivalent about the reality of dealing with creative people and bringing them into the mainstream of decision-making. Schools, struggling to manage large numbers of children or teenagers, may prefer those who fit in and cause no trouble or extra work. The link between creativity and the rebellious spirit is one that society needs but about which it's deeply wary.

I worked with a practising artist on representations of the body with medical students and found that we met a lot of resistance to the project with both colleagues and students – people did not automatically think it was as great an idea as we did, and in fact, did not want to be shaken out of their comfort zones and regular ways of teaching and learning. Sir Ken Robinson argues that the current education system is *"educating people out of their creativity"*, and this example seemed to me to epitomize this idea.

So don't expect it to be an easy road – if you're doing good creative work, you can expect to meet with reactions ranging from a lack of interest (may be defensive) to unease or outright persecution. Part of the job will be *working with these responses.*

Adversity

Although we can frequently feel that it's not possible to do any real creative work because of the pressures on us in our lives, there are numerous examples of people who have felt able to overcome adversity, if not even found that adversity is the spur to their creative work.

> *Novelist **Fyodor Dostoevsky** suffered the death of his mother whilst he was a boy, the murder of his father by his father's own serfs, the death of his first wife, and the death of a child. He had a lifelong struggle with debt and the regular need to pawn domestic goods and flee from creditors, an addiction to gambling and the experience of lifelong epilepsy.*
>
> *Composer **Wolfgang Amadeus Mozart** had difficulty getting any sufficient and secure income and was often frustrated by the work that was on offer to him through the royal courts. He and his wife lost four of their six children in infancy. He frequently had to borrow money and to struggle to make ends meet.*
>
> *The artist **Frida Kahlo** grew up in revolutionary times in Mexico with gunfire in the streets. As a child, she contracted polio and as a teenager, she was involved in a traffic accident that left her with serious injuries for which she had a series of operations throughout her life and suffered recurrent severe pain. A long-term effect was her ultimate inability to have children, and the sadness of a necessary abortion and a miscarriage.*
>
> *Journalist **Jean Dominique-Bauby** wrote 'The Butterfly and the Diving Bell' whilst suffering 'locked-in syndrome' before his death by dictating his words to an assistant through eye-blinks.*

In the current climate of recession, austerity and international conflict, there are opportunities for creative responses to flourish. Indeed, we would argue that survival through these times *depends* on a creative response for/from each person.

Creativity, the brain and intelligence

Some thinkers have developed tools to help us learn and deal with information, two of the most well-known are *concept mapping* - Joseph Novak - and *mind-mapping* - Tony Buzan - with the idea that these may be more congruent with the way the mind acquires, stores and retrieves data than found in the *linear* way most of us write notes and read books. Such tools have been used in the organisation of material for learning, for memory recall and exam revision, and for creative brainstorming eg. in business. They are also quick ways of mapping out the content of a whole field of knowledge. *Concept mapping* may be more helpful for representing material which has a variety of interconnections and concept relationships and in some cases, hierarchical sub-structures, whilst *mind maps* tend to relate everything to a central concept with discrete clusters branching out centrifugally.

We can use these kinds of systems to get a sense of an area of knowledge and to plot how concepts and ideas might fit together when we're trying to kick-start our creative thinking.

'Left' and 'right' brain ideas

Such ideas have been related to the idea of the brain's bi-laterality based on the original work by Roger W Sperry that indicated that the left and right hemispheres might be specialised to different functions. We now know that it's a bit more complicated than that, and that left and right-handedness don't always correlate to the relevant hemisphere dominance, because there is a lot of variety in human beings and how they are formed. Maybe the details of how our brain functions don't really matter to most of us, until we (or people we know) have a stroke or a brain tumour or a traffic accident and we struggle to regain particular kinds of functioning, or if we suffer from disorders like *dyslexia, dyscalculia*, or *dyspraxia*. However, the idea that precise, 'scientific', rational thinking and language can be separated from intuitive, emotional, pictorial, musical and non-verbal functions has been a powerful element in human experience.

Indeed, our education systems and our investment as societies have often reflected this divide. In recent eras, government and business money in modern nations has gone into scientific and technological research, and artistic people and projects like local theatres and art centres have had to struggle for funds. It has been easy to prioritise things like developments in pharmaceuticals, computing, genetics and weaponry over cultural innovation and social support although it would be disingenuous to suggest that the former didn't sometimes tap into 'right-brain' skills as well as logic and rationality.

The point is that 'left-brain' activity tends to get revered above right-brain activity, and particularly so since the Enlightenment, when for a number of reasons, key figures privileged empiricism, scientific rigour, and the challenging of religious authority. Superstition and the supernatural became objects of suspicion, and along with them went much of organised religion.

As well as the 'right-brain' idea being associated with creativity and artistic ability, it's also been credited with the more subtle decoding of emotions in visual and sonic material giving a basis for intuitive thought, whilst the more detailed 'cognitive' material involved in mathematical problem-solving, the structure of language and critical thinking tends to be associated with the idea of the 'left brain'.

Today, there's a small but steady increase in acceptance of the value of 'right-brain' material, including brain research that acknowledges the power of unconscious processing, previously highlighted by figures such as Sigmund Freud and Carl Gustav Jung, who worked in clinical contexts rather than laboratories, using their intuition to handle the emotional material of their patients.

Intelligence is more complex than we thought

Intelligence testing through the twentieth century has focused on verbal reasoning and mental calculations. Early critics questioned the bias in the original tests, demonstrating that people of 'low intelligence' according to test results were nevertheless able to handle complex life tasks in familiar settings, and Margaret Donaldson, querying Jean Piaget's model of child development, showed that making tests culturally meaningful to children made a significant difference to their test results. Nevertheless, even if controlled for social class and cultural difference, intelligence testing for many years continued to focus on 'left-brain' skills. Even now, thinking efficiency including speed of processing and memory retention are considered key elements of 'intelligence'.

Then Howard Gardner introduced us to the idea that intelligence wasn't a single entity - he believed we have *'multiple' intelligences* including for example an ability to be sensitive to processes in our own internal world and in other people *(intrapersonal and interpersonal intelligence)* and the ability to pick up on and respond to cues with our bodies – skills that are well-honed in dancers and sportspeople *(bodily-kinaesthetic intelligence)* and suggested that *cognitive intelligence* is over-valued. He also suggested that our development might be at different stages for different intelligences – thus for example, one person may be well developed linguistically but weak on interpersonal sensitivity.

Even within the cognitive framework, more than one type of thinking was identified. The military psychologist, J.P. Guilford produced a framework that identified a large number of cognitive skills including the ability to generate multiple solutions to a problem, the ability to judge whether or not information is accurate, consistent, or valid and the ability to make predictions, inferences and imagine consequences.

Not everyone accepts Howard Gardner's ideas – some consider not only that they are 'unscientific' but that they are simply variations from a *general* intelligence level that *can* be assessed by psychologists. Gardner also felt that the emphasis on single IQ scores as they are traditionally measured helped to match children and students to traditional learning opportunities which focus on cognitive left-brain skills - but maybe what we actually need is a more holistic form of education where people with different potentialities are supported to develop.

We should perhaps consider whether these academic debates have implications that matter in today's climate, and ask ourselves whether we need to think 'outside the box' on intelligence, such that high intelligence purely in its own right may not be attractive if it's not accompanied by good mental health and altruistic or ecological values. And we can note that parents of children with low scores on intelligence tests – children who are considered to have 'learning difficulties' - quite often report valuable emotional and spiritual experiences that have transformed their inner worlds and their lives for the better.

Who is best at 'imaginative and rebellious ideas'?

Liam Hudson was a Cambridge educationalist who found that convergent thinkers were capable of imaginative and rebellious ideas when invited to write freely or to imagine the part of 'mad artists' and that divergent thinkers were no more original than convergent thinkers. He concluded that many factors were involved in creative thinking including cultural background and expectations and self-image.

The point is that the quest to measure or detail creativity has met with a variety of outcomes and no absolute definition.

People with high intelligence quotients on primarily 'left-brain' cognitive tasks may or may not be more creative than others. Research suggests that intelligence and creativity appear to be independent of one another, but of course it's important to recognise that creativity cannot be defined simply through the number of ideas generated but also the quality and originality of ideas, factors which are more difficult to assess in laboratory studies. Guilford's (1067) *Alternative Uses Task* asking people how many uses they can think of for a brick can be scored on a variety of factors such as originality and fluency as well as how many. Contemporary brain research indicates that creative expression emerges from the interaction of parts of the brain and is not limited to any concept of the 'right-brain'. See for example Alice Flaherty's work.

What's become of more interest is the task of *mapping* the different ways in which people use their minds - as discussed earlier.

We have different preferred learning styles

David Kolb identified different styles of learning preferences among learners, which included those who liked practical *experimentation,* those who like immersion in *experience,* people who tend to *reflective observation* and people who are comfortable with *abstract conceptualisation.* People with different combinations and strengths in these areas can be identified and learning designed appropriately – a system which has potential for application in a variety of educational contexts.

A key issue has often been the distinction between didactic instruction – perhaps at its most extreme where a teacher simply reads from notes for students to take down in their books and at the other end of the spectrum, explains and outlines how to do something in a lively and interesting way – and 'discovery' learning, where students are given experiences such as ingredients for cooking or building or the opportunity to go exploring on a field-trip, and the teacher builds on what the students discover for themselves. The latter is of course seen as likely to engender creative and problem-solving thinking, but where students are given no help at all can sometimes result in boring experiences and little discovery. Sometimes we have to be helped to 'see' as for example, to recognise plants and birds, or to recognise smells and flavours, and ideas – perhaps drawn from the history of the subject – about what can be done and has been discovered before.

It may well be that there are also different styles of readers for books and different styles of approaching works of art – not all art and literary fans are the same. In producing art, people differ as to how much they're interested in empathising with the recipients of

410

it – some artists feeling that their work should not be compromised by any consideration of the public, others being acutely aware of particular sensitivities, especially if they're exploring painful themes like child abuse, rape, the holocaust, racism etc.

It's perhaps best to enjoy the rich range of skills that individuals can bring to any creative task, be it logical, deductive thinking and planning or a wide-open approach to seeing what emerges.

What are the best circumstances for helping us to do our creative work?

The paediatrician and psychoanalyst, Donald Winnicott, observed that children whose mothers did not *'impinge'* on the psychological space of the infant, were able to get lost in their reveries of play and imagination, and that this cocoon was good for the psychological development of the child. We suggest that this is space that is necessary for everyone – the ability to allow us to *'be alone in the presence of the other'* - a *'facilitating environment'* in which the people close to us leave us alone to get on with our work without interrupting us or making demands or disturbing our psychological mood with their own feelings of resentment, envy, depression, anger, boredom etc. - is the best gift anyone can give us. It doesn't mean that people disappear on us or threaten us with abandonment; it means that they are around in the background doing their thing and happy that we are doing our thing.

Having a secure sense of connection that does not need constant reassurance helps us to enjoy the necessary solitude to get on with our creative work. And helping our children and our partners to feel that sense of confidence is good for them too. Let them know you love them, thank them for their love of you, and encourage them to get on with their own creative activities and to respect that you have yours to get on with. It can be very important to have the opportunity to go into a 'creative dream-world' where you are fairly sure no-one will interrupt you with phone-calls, conversation, requests or demands. Whilst few of us can get this for hours on end, making sure that you have some time to yourself regularly is probably an essential for most people to protect their sanity and to have any chance of productive activity.

Getting that creative space for ourselves

Don't expect that others will automatically give you this space, particularly if they've been used to you being available on demand. It may be necessary to be harsh on your friends and family for a while, making it clear that this is a new phase in your life, and setting clear boundaries. *'On Friday and Saturday nights I won't answer the phone at all'; 'I've bought this new garden hut and when I go into it I don't expect to be interrupted'; 'I want to have two hours to myself every Sunday morning after which I will do everything that is expected of me'.* The transition to this can be painful and you may need some trial runs. Put up notices reminding people where you are and when you will come out. You may need to explain very carefully and assertively what you're doing and what you need and why it's important to you. Discovering how hard it is for others to give this to you can release emotions as the underlying dynamics of relationships and transactions emerge, but see it through. You owe it to the child inside yourself to give it room to play, room to heal, room to explore, and to the adult you are to produce something that expresses some of your inner world.

This is similar to the idea of spiritual discernment and involves pruning distractions from your life. Decide if you really need to iron sheets or tea-towels or t-shorts. Consider sending Christmas cards out every other year. Do you really need to go down the pub with friends or spend time with your brother on the phone? Could you live with the idea of your teenager getting themselves to and from town on their own? Where can you cut out extraneous social and practical commitments to free up your own time?

Play and creativity

Nurture this concept of 'free child' and don't be afraid to make a mess, to create areas of chaos and to leave them, to experiment. Have fun, let go of rules. If you have been academically trained, stop looking everything up and checking every reference. If you've been an engineer, work with a palette of colours and a range of textures and patterns to break away from your usual visual and sensual stimuli. If you're a nurse or social worker, write a story in fantasy where there are no regulations or safety considerations. Tap into your unconscious world and mine memories and dreams and imagined worlds.

On the other hand, bear in mind that some people like to be very disciplined about their work. They may ensure they have every colour in the spectrum available and organise their pastels, pens, paints, brushes and papers in specially labelled trays, or track and record every note and reference on index cards and computer files. Don't confuse getting organised for your work – the preparation – which can be very important as a starting point, with the nature of the creative work itself, which may need to be playful. If you didn't have much play as a child and were over-controlled, think about ways in which you could learn to loosen up and extend your own boundaries. Doing a spot of dancing – even going wild to music in your own living-room or running along a beach or woodland path may help you to start freeing up.

Think about whether you have *permission* to paint, write, dance, toboggan, make things, think creatively, to innovate. What would your friends think if you sent them a home-made card rather than a printed one? Could you drive a home-made vehicle down the road or float a home-made boat on a pond without feeling embarrassed? How strictly are you adhering to unwritten dress codes at work – what would happen if you ventured out without a tie or tights or had your hair striped with pink highlights? Think about giving yourself that permission, start thinking of yourself as a free individual and fighting off all the inner demons that hold you back. This will be a necessary process for when you want to allow in quirky or challenging new ideas – you will need to silence those inner voices that denigrate your efforts and make you doubt yourself. Start being your own best parent. Be your own 'creativity facilitator'.

413

Support and sabotage

In contrast, consider how much praise and 'positive stroking' you need. Free yourself from the need for external encouragement. *Encourage yourself.* Keep going with any projects until you have a finished product. Cultivate your own energy and directedness. Believe in yourself and accept that just doing the activity is its own reward.

Don't be thrown off-course by showing your ideas to other people too soon and having them damned with faint praise or petty critical points. Avoid any tendency in yourself to self-sabotage by offering yourself up for discouragement by others. Don't be naïve about this – remember people have a number of motives and feelings in relation to someone else's work – some conscious and some unconscious - distance yourself from these, you don't have to solve their problems for them.

Build the framework for your work – go into that hut or cocoon every week even if you don't have anything specific to do and *see what emerges.* Allow pessimism and depression and disappointment and scepticism to float around if they want to, but *don't stop doing what you're doing.* Change direction if you want to, have fresh starts if you need to, but don't abandon the essential project of doing something creative. Put all the material you have to hand – documents, reports, books, tools, fabrics, cottons, clay, paints, musical instruments etc. ready for you. Immerse yourself in them and see what comes.

Watch the film *A Beautiful Mind* if you want to see how a scientist like John Nash struggled with his own hallucinations – visual and auditory, his mental illness and the attitudes of some of his colleagues – and ultimately became a Nobel prize-winner.

Look rigorously at the people in your life and decide who is truly supportive and facilitative (if anyone), who wants more of you (your time, your affection, your help, your attention etc) in competition with the energy you have for your creative work, and who is nervous or threatened by your new activity and why (makes them feel jealous because they're not doing what they need to, worried that you'll be more creative than them, afraid you may move on in life and not want/need them anymore, feel as if they might be pushed into changing themselves, upset that they didn't do more in their own past etc).

This is part of your *preparation* phase – if you have to let go of people who hold you back or put them on hold whilst you move forward and cope with the emotions in them and in yourself that this involves, face up to this as the price of personal growth and recognise that this may be the best thing that happened to *them* – they will have to look at their own demons instead of hanging onto *you*. (In therapy, often when treating one half of a couple–relationship or parent-child bond, as one person starts to improve, the other starts to fall apart, leading ultimately to recognition that the other party has at least as many difficulties to contend with as the official 'patient'). There is no need to be brutal, but there may be a need to recognise that it is time to have more healthy relationships.

Make your life creative

Look at the pie-charts in the chapter on *Change* and determine which areas of your life need creative/novel solutions. Balance rational, focused, direct concentration on things with the *use of your unconscious mind*.

Aim to break routine, act on fresh ideas about how to do things. Make something different for dinner, or better still pack up a picnic and drive out to watch the moonlight. Pause the car on the way home from work and turn down a road you've never gone down before. Answer your partner in a different way from usual – ask a different kind of question that explores something new in your relationship. Think about what irritates you at work and push your mind to think how things could be done differently, then arrange to discuss the idea with a colleague to test out support. Don't be put off. Persist. You may not get things right first go. Develop an attitude of mind that is spontaneous and forgiving of mistakes. Try out ideas in different media – if writing is your thing, play something on the piano; if wood-carving is what you do, try some dancing. The unconscious mind will be processing ideas that can transfer across media to the field you are really concentrating on. (But don't dissipate too much).

Look at your own 'ancient' problems, stuckness or lack of fun. Challenge messages from family, teachers, previous partners, friends or colleagues that stick in your mind and keep you from feeling confident. Produce responses that affirm your ability to move forward, to develop and express yourself, to honour the creative energy within you and stick them up on your walls. Consider going for a short course of counselling if your history troubles you. If relationships are troubled, try to settle things before attempting to concentrate on creative activity as a sense of calm may be helpful. If there is unhappiness in your life, allow creative activity to be cathartic or therapeutic – allowing you to process and work on issues and to articulate things that are in your unconscious mind. Consider your creative activity to *be* your healing path. Take responsibility for your own growth as a creative person and start rejecting any messages from the past or now that hold you back.

In the end, being a creative person is a very individual thing – how you organise things for creative activity, how you use it in your life will depend on what you want and what you can live with, but of you have struggled up to now to have the time or space to do anything creative or to reflect on the way you are living, recognise that the process of getting them requires dedication and sometimes, pain. You will find out who understands and supports you and who doesn't.

Organising yourself

Decide if you need to set up your own special environment – a hut in the garden, an evening out a week, a retreat weekend, a table for your own work that isn't used for meals etc., a studio, practice room, workshop, study, corner, flower-bed or allotment etc.

Decide if you need to have rituals and patterns for working or not – reserving a special pen; re-shelving of your books; organising of all your tools, mending and replacing as necessary; organising some music or sound to help you concentrate; getting a comfortable chair or stool; making sure your computing needs are met; having a croissant and coffee before you begin; finding a time when you want to work on things (will it be regular or opportunistic or when you feel inspired?) etc. (*Some people can't work until everyone else is asleep, others prefer the dawn, others need the afternoon light, some like to have an hour before or after dinner or to work when everyone else is out doing things*).

Practise *retrieving* material from your unconscious store - don't put all the effort into further *inputting* of material or training, observation, research etc. Make sure that SOME of your time is spent DOING the activity, pulling things out of yourself, *expressing* things, and *practising/getting used to* doing this.

If stimulation or inspiration is needed, plan exciting or helpful activities to refresh your approach – eg. a journey away to look at something relevant, going to talk to someone who is of interest, getting some new materials, looking at something which contrasts with what you know about to gain perspective – take responsibility for interesting yourself in your own field and don't feel that the work has to be tedious. Infuse your creative journey with enthusiasm and passion.

Take a break if necessary, especially if you feel blocked or tired. Direct whittling away at something has its advantages but there may be a moment when, having laid the groundwork, you would benefit from walking away, taking time to reflect and letting the unconscious processing happen. You may find a connection with what you're doing in something completely unrelated. Don't fill your mind with trivia if you can help it, but do something which gives your mind a different space for a while. Going for a walk or a swim is a good idea, particularly if it helps you to move out of head-work and integrate with your physical and emotional and sensory self. Check out the compartmentalising of these aspects of you and put them back together – smell a flower, run round the block, taste some yogurt, do some bending and stretching, look at some photos or play some music.

Locate yourself within any context or framework of work that you think is relevant, if you want to – eg. look at similar books to your own, learn about new developments in design that your ideas might supersede etc. but DON'T let anyone else's work depress you, intimidate you, stop you. Find ways to provide self-talk that work, or decide to shut out all external stimuli for a while (ie. don't look at others' work). Protect your own mental processes, remember that you can find your own voice, make your own unique contribution, express things in *your own particular way*.

Tap into a variety of sources for inspiration, particularly your unconscious mind, both memory stores and real-time dreaming and dream-world activity. Remember that it works differently from the rational mind eg. it pushes and repeats, it's multi-layered, it's visual and sensual, it can be surprising, it can provide symbolic material etc.

Our emotions and creativity

There are many links between mental health and creativity that can be explored including those who were very successful but whose lives were ended through suicide or punctuated by attempts at suicide - Sylvia Plath, Virginia Woolf, Robert Schumann, Ernest Hemingway etc. It's worth asking the question *'to what extent did their creativity help them to stay alive or make sense of their troubles?'* rather than making any quick assumptions of causal links with the stresses of creative activity. Kay Redfield Jamison's book *Touched with Fire* explores links between manic-depressive illness and the artistic temperament.

Going public

We can be paralysed by the fear of letting others see our work – there are many cases of people who've stockpiled paintings or novels over many years which no-one else has ever seen –and if this is satisfying, so be it. But what does matter is if we have something we want to say but are afraid to say it. Going to people who do support us for some feedback can help, as can practising our own definitions and responses, perhaps imagining comments and views and working out how to counter them. Disseminating what we create is part of the job and facing up to our anxieties about this is an important part of the creative process. Ensuring that we're doing what we're doing because it matters, or because we have a mission can also help to overcome our fears. Finding an ally to talk things over with or accompany us to the public unravelling of our work can be a good idea.

Jack

Julia's section on creativity is so good, I haven't got a lot to add.

The idea of *'thinking outside the box'* ie. *being creative at times* needs to be separated from *living your life creatively, being in a 'creative' profession,* and *acting creatively in an emergency.*

Being creative in emergencies/survival situations

This involves speed in finding what will work or may work. Do generate options if possible. In survival situations, choosing fast what to do, trying a new tack if it's possible and the first actions haven't worked. I think extraordinary focus, processing and action is needed in these kinds of situations. It does help to practise and 'overlearn' your responses to crises where fast action is needed - the military for example are good at this. You can figure out 'Plan A, B and C' creatively in advance for difficult situations and rehearse in practice if appropriate use visualisation for example, to aid the process.

Thinking outside the box – looking for novel solutions

I call this being creative 'at times'. Here the idea is option generation in relation to a problem but do remember that you need to identify the problem and its importance first. This sounds obvious but often this isn't done. The idea of 'outside the box' is to plug into your right brain/creative unconscious, drop 'the rules', and come up with new ideas. Generate as many as you can even so-called ridiculous impossible unusual ones, keeping the idea of evaluation and critique quite separate. This approach is now widely used in business and other fields.

Being creative as a lifestyle

This is a bigger project and may involve change, an adventure, risks and re-evaluation of your life, home, relationships etc.

It's not for the fainthearted and you may want to partly do it, delay it until you have the money, retire etc.

It's not *just* a change in your life - it means *re-examining* what you want and the first step is to ask questions and sometimes, to plug into fantasy to imagine new possibilities:

-    do I want a change?
-    what do I want to change?
-    what are the pros and cons?
-    how big a change is needed?
-    what are the likely consequences etc?
-    what's wrong in my life or missing?

It can mean thinking more freely and seeing life as a series of problems to be solved. It can be described as being 'outside the box' most of the time. It also involves flexibility.

'Creative' work

What I've found useful in my art and design work that may be helpful for you is:

- realise that when you get 'stuck' in your creative process, it's important to take a rest and let your 'right brain' work on solutions using little intentional effort – solutions pop up later
- have all the means there in terms of materials, equipment etc. of the best quality
- see creative work as important AND everyday – even if you do just a bit, it's all practice and rehearsal
- make up your own rules to suit you – these are rules governing the work and how you operate best
- if the work needs you to be open, childlike, emotional, try to explain this to close others in your life and/or whilst

you're in a creative/vulnerable/open mode, protect
yourself
- know when to stop, you can ruin work by over-perfecting
it
- keep fresh and alive
- do work which FLOWS – if work is tedious, there's
something wrong and it may be a good idea to re-think it
- be your own best critic, but guard against being grandiose
and thinking you're wonderful
- find your own 'voice' then listen to it – it will tell you
where to go and experiment, then shape it more – it's a bit
like watching a garden grow – at some point it develop a
life of its own
- see creative work as a *process* in contrast to fixed points

Becoming a professional

It's OK to be messy in creative production but NOT in business
setup mode!

Give careful thought to the presentation of your work, to people in
your life and to the outside world. Consult books and people to
get good advice, but don't be afraid to do it your way. Here are a
few brief pointers.

- have a developed body of work before you bother

- be confident and realistic but not grandiose re quality of
your work

- don't go for normal rules ie. being part of culture norms,
entertainment system norms for culture, locate yourself
where you think you should be, find niches that are unique
if necessary

- define your own work – don't accept any attempts to
pigeonhole you in traditions, schools of thought, styles,
unless you agree with them

- be clear about your goals and stick to them – don't be swayed to be more ambitious or less ambitious than you want to be

- sort money out at all stages

- look efficient and professional

- ask for specificity in feedback and recognise that any comments on your work may be different at different stages

- if you feel put-down, go immediately to I+U- position (see chapter on *Effective relating*) and look after your self-esteem

Egograms

It's worth looking at ego states from T.A. in the book by Ian Stewart and Vann Joines *TA Today*. Essentially, we're best served by being in a *Free Child* state with a *Nurturing Parent*, and worst served by being in an *Adapted Child* state and a *Critical Parent*. It could also be helpful to try some ego-grams.

Exercises to try:

You win 10 million in the lottery - how would you spend it?

Think of new ways to save £s in the recession – 'adversity is the mother of invention'.

How do you already use your creative mind? What examples can you find of novel solutions, answers to problems you have found?

When were you last at your most creative – what was the context? What helped?

> How important is creative activity to you?
> What's in the way? eg. *money, time, interruptions*
>
> What 'blocks' are there – what *internal permissions* do you
> need and how can you get them?

Links within the book

This chapter links particularly to the chapters on the *Unconscious*
mind and creative techniques for accessing the unconscious mind
such as *visualisation, dream-work* and *memory* work.

Books, papers and websites

John S Allen *Creativity: Adaptation or a by-product of increased
intelligence?* April 29, 2010
http://www.psychologytoday.com/blog/lives-the-
brain/201004/creativity-the-brain-and-evolution
Jean Dominique-Bauby (2008 ed) *The Butterfly and the Diving-
Bell* Harper Perennial
Claudia Bauer (2007) *Frida Kahlo* Prestel Publishing
Tony Buzan (2009) *The Mind-mapping Book: Unlock your
Creativity, Boost Your Memory, Change Your Life* BBC Active
Julia Cameron (1993) *The Artist's Way: A Course in Discovering
and Recovering Your Creative Self* Pan Books
Margaret Donaldson (1978) *Children's Minds* Fontana/Croom
Helm
Fyodor Dostoevsky (1866) *Crime and Punishment* SMK Books
Alice Flaherty (2005) *Fronto-temporal and dopaminergic control
of idea generation and creative drive* Journal of Comparative
Neurology 493:147-153
Alice Flaherty (2005) *The Midnight Disease: The Drive to Write,
Writer's Block and the Creative Brain* Houghton Mifflin Harcourt
Howard Gardner (2006) *Multiple Intelligences: New Horizons*
Basic Books
M Gonzalez (2005) *Kahlo – A Life.* Socialist Review: June 2005.
Liam Hudson (1967) *Contrary Imaginations: Psychological Study
of the English Schoolboy* Pelican

Kay Redfield Jamison (1993) *Touched with Fire: Manic-Depressive Illness and the Artistic Temperament* New York: The Free Press.
A Y Kolb and D A Kolb (2011) *Kolb Learning Style Inventory 4.0* Boston MA: Hay Group
Robert F Murphy (1990) *The Body Silent: The Different World of the Disabled* W W Norton
Josef Novak and D B Gowin (1984) *Learning How to Learn* Cambridge University Press
Sylvia Plath (1963) (2005 ed) *The Bell Jar* Faber and Faber
Sylvia Plath (1966) *Ariel* Harper and Row
Ken Robinson (2009) *The Element: How Finding Your Passion Changes Everything* Penguin/Viking
Ken Robinson (2001) *Out of our Minds: Learning to be Creative* Capstone
Arundhati Roy (2002) *The Algebra of Infinite Justice* Flamingo
Arundhati Roy (1997) *The God of Small Things* Flamingo
Roger W Sperry (1980) *Mind-brain interaction: 'Mentalism, yes; dualism, no'* Neuroscience **5** (2): 195–206
Thomas Szasz (2006) *My Madness Saved Me: The Madness and Marriage of Virginia Woolf* New Jersey: Transaction Publishers
Ian Stewart and Vann Joines (1987) *TA Today: A New Introduction to Transactional Analysis* Life Space Publishing
Anthony Storr (1988) *Solitude* Flamingo
Graham Wallas (1926) *The Art of Thought* Johnathan Cape
Donald W Winnicott (1965) *The maturational processes and the facilitating environment: Studies in the theory of emotional development* The Hogarth Press and the International Universities Press psycnet.apa.org
Howard Zinn (1994) *You Can't Be Neutral On A Moving Train: A Personal History Of Our Times* The Beacon Press
http://www.telegraph.co.uk/news/obituaries/1486082/Professor-Liam-Hudson.html
http://larussophobe.wordpress.com/2009/06/08/putin-escalates-the-persecution-of-artists/
http://www.guardian.co.uk/news/2001/mar/20/guardianobituaries.highereducation Anthony Storr

Film
Ron Howard (2001) *A Beautiful Mind*

15   spirituality

- *territory to explore not ignore*

In this chapter, we've shared a lot of personal material as we believe that spirituality is not something that can be explored a great deal through rational thought but is something that is a *felt* experience, evolved through a changing lifelong journey. We make the distinction throughout between organised religion and spirituality and discuss secular approaches to living which some consider still to be 'spiritual' whilst others would vehemently deny this label. There is also information in the chapter which we intend to be useful for clarifying issues, such as ideas about God, our relationship with animals, spiritual discernment, marking events in life with ritual, handling complexity and ambivalence, appreciating things and taking responsibility.

Whilst religion and humanism can offer important anchorage in a bewildering world, we feel that people are free to detach from religious institutions if they choose and can create a spiritual life that has meaning for them without intermediaries, rules or things being defined for them by others.

The first half of this chapter is written by Jack and the second half by Julia.

Jack

I find debates about organised religion irrelevant to my spiritual being. This includes a lot of topics, for example, *the afterlife, the creation, original sin,* etc. etc. Some religious ideas about spiritual development I do find useful, for example, *the middle way* and the *reduction of ego* in Buddhism. To me, it's not questions about single or multiple deities that matter; it's whether or not we're engaged in *spiritual growth*. It's not about being a spiritual consumer and having battles about 'brand loyalty'. It's about something from the *inside*-out, not something from the *outside*-in. The process of spiritual development is bigger than something like psychological development – it's holistic and all-encompassing.

There's a huge confusion about religion, God and the spiritual, to the point where the *New Atheism* doesn't acknowledge the existence of *'the spiritual'* and confuses it with organised religions.

Alistair McGrath in *Why God Won't Go Away* in 2011 explains the position of the philosopher Isaiah Berlin (1909-1997) who groups human convictions into three categories:

i.   those that can be established by empirical observation
ii.   those that can be established by logical deduction
iii.   those that cannot be proved in either of these ways.

It's hard to prove or dis-prove the existence of God (through observation or deduction) – my position is that *the spiritual is not primarily mediated through thought* but is built on *felt* experience.

It's widely accepted that words are not able to express the spiritual world adequately and that's also my position. My advice is to be discerning and questioning from a *felt* spiritual position rather than trying to work it all out intellectually. A lot of my comments about spirituality are about *worldly* problems that people bring to spiritual development.

It's a good idea to go into a childlike space – to get in touch with a sense of innocence and freshness and accepting mystery – that we can't reduce everything to something understandable, rather than engaging with the cynicism and misery of worldly critique. One of the problems with the scientific-rational mind-set is that everything that can't be observed, measured, identified is ignored, neglected, denied, devalued. This leaves out a lot of human experience.

Something about my spiritual journey

I've been on a spiritual (not a religious) path for some time in my life and this is not something I can put to one side or do in my spare time as my spiritual self and spiritual development are central to my life. My experience of the spiritual is that I am aware of another level of being that is beyond the worldly, that is in *me* and *others* and in *the world;* this level has a life of its own and rules of its own. This is not static - I'm developing this part of me. My spirituality can direct my life and my decisions and it helps me deal with larger issues and everyday life. My spiritual side has intuitive, inbuilt values - for example around equality, tolerance, compassion and self-expression.

The scientist Albert Einstein, who 'discovered' relativity, quoted in Ann Edwards' *How to Nurture Spiritual Development*, was able to write in 1931 about the sense of 'religiousness' that can accompany scientific discovery.

Throwing the positives of 'spirituality' out along with religion needs real thought (see Frederic Nietzsche's work) and involves taking significant responsibility (both as a philosopher and as an ordinary person). With all its faults - including its role in social control - religion in developed countries nevertheless did provide a moral framework, an awareness of spiritual development, encouragement to strive to be a 'better' person, humanity, love and forgiveness, all of which we still need.

I think it's hard to feel complete or at peace without developing your spiritual self. Most of my experience is from the Christian religion in the UK, with some from Buddhism and most importantly, there is my own inner spiritual experience to draw from.

New Atheism

Organised religion is open to a lot of criticisms, but the *New Atheists,* critiqued well by Alistair McGrath, have missed some very important points.

1. they're attacking religion, not the spiritual and are unaware of the difference between these.

2. they're supporting the mind-set of scientific/rational fundamentalism which has been at war with religion for a few hundred years.

3. they're likely to encourage entrenchment of religious views by being over-aggressive and egotistical.

Attacks on religious institutions and the subsequent widespread abandonment of faith has left society without much of a spiritual core, and this has created the space for ruthless capitalism and unbridled consumerism. Being in touch with our spirituality is potentially a significant challenge to materialistic capitalism, which is maybe why so many people, wedded to the free market project, aren't keen on the idea. Whereas some of the early wealth creators like Andrew Carnegie in the USA, did make the link between capitalism and the moral/spiritual duty to give back to society, this idea (though sometimes there as a rhetorical idea in corporate mission statements) isn't being implemented much these days.

Bureaucratic and legalistic approaches to reject sexism, racism, religious prejudice etc. have not quite captured the ground since people are made to adhere to external behaviours out of fear of sanctions but are not tied into caring and ethical value-systems or supported to develop their own inner value-base.

It's interesting that the *Giving Report*, carried out by the Charity Aid Foundation in each of the last five years, has counted not only financial giving, but also volunteering behaviour and 'helping a stranger' across the globe. In some countries, it's possible that the economic pressures on people to work hard and earn are so strong that the giving of time to others (without asking for pay) is just too much. In some countries, and Ireland is one of the top-hitters on this, it may be that a strong spiritual/religious ethos drives good behaviour towards others and results in a more generous-minded culture. (More on philanthropy is in our final chapter on *'The crisis we're in'*).

What are we talking about?

There's a lot of confusion when we talk about *spiritual life* or a *spiritual dimension*. By definition, *'the spiritual'*, *'god'* and the *'soul'* cannot be man-made. Religions and churches are man-made and institutionalised - they are also subject to political and economic influence and have power issues attached and are often hierarchical. By talking about spiritual life, I'm talking about something which is vast, is unseen but often felt, something which most people agree is not explicable, and is beyond words. It's a mystery which people in different cultures have debated, wondered about, and disagreed about. The *'spiritual'* is both complex and there's a simple version, and it's often hard to develop your own spiritual life and to get clear information. Despite all the problems I've come across, and all the distractions, I'm glad I've listened to my spiritual side.

I think those wedded to science and rationality have tried to throw out the worst aspects of man-made *religion* but have unwisely at times *also* thrown out the *spiritual,* often giving licence to organisations (including governmental ones) to do so. What this can mean is a less ethical, more egocentric/selfish, materialistic, loveless and self-destructive world which is confused, not pleasant to live in, and on a road to nowhere. The corruption and bad practice witnessed in public life in recent times is testament to this.

Something about religions that is not easily dismissed and which has been noticed for example by the analytical psychologist Carl Jung is that they can have a lot in common despite developing quite separately. And sometimes there are big misunderstandings - for example, the idea that Buddhism has no deity or god figure which is strictly true, but it is worth looking at the idea of a parallel spiritual dimension to a worldly dimension described by Soyen Shaku in *Zen for Americans.* And some Buddhists would say that Buddhism was not a religion but rather a 'psychology'.

According to the author Karen Armstrong, the main worthwhile thing the major religions have in common is *compassion.* Armstrong believes that *transcending selfishness* is the key to changing our world for the better. In the worldwide *Charter for Compassion* that she launched in 2008, she calls for a commitment to alleviate the suffering of others and to honour human rights as the path not only to 'enlightenment' but also for a 'just economy and a peaceful global community' – she believes that people from any religious faith can sign up to this.

Some of us get stuck or confused about spirituality, and there's not even a general consensus on the meaning of the word – for example, it can be synonymous with the concept of religion, or at the other end of the spectrum it can be identified with a code of ethics that has nothing to do with any ethereal or supernatural entity.

Descriptions of spiritual awareness

Spiritual awareness and spiritual development are not new ideas and often religions describe these processes or create ways to encourage them. Sometimes these methods are rigid or ineffective - for example, Karen Armstrong describes the enforced and exacting spiritual journey in her training to be a nun (in her book *Through the Narrow Gate*) as a process which was intended to eradicate the personal 'will'.

Carl Jung has described a model of personality with an organising core which is largely unconscious - he calls this the *'self'*. Jung suggests that *the self* is returned to throughout life to integrate different parts of the personality, including a spiritual part. Jung's mystical archetypes (like the 'wise old man', the 'hero' or the 'earth mother') are perhaps not so compelling nowadays but a *'collective unconscious'* is still worth thinking about. Jung sees his integration process - called *individuation* - as being a main task of the second part of a person's life – something which can lead to a feeling of wholeness. (See our chapter on *The Self*).

If Jung is right, a main problem in life for many people would be *a felt lack of wholeness* that they may experience without integrating the various parts of their personalities, particularly a spiritual part.

People may also try and fill this incomplete state with, for example, consumerism, relationships etc. in order to try to feel whole.

Another writer who describes stages of spiritual development is James Fowler; M. Scott Peck produced a simplified version of Fowler's model.

Scott Peck's stages are roughly:

stage 1	chaotic and egocentric
stage 2	'blind' faith /faith in authority
stage 3	scepticism
stage 4	enjoying the mystery (but with more self-direction)

As people move through the stages there is more *inner* versus *outer* direction, so for example, at stage 3 or 4, people may not feel the need to be a part of a church; at stage 2, people want more outer direction.

In Fowler's model, it is suggested that people grow towards containing more paradox and complexity as they go through life, and that if they reach the final stages of spiritual development, they will be operating from general principles like love and justice that transcend particular religious paths or specific dogmas.

When we look at the model it can appear hierarchical and user-unfriendly but may have some truth. I do think people develop spiritually over time, some more than others whilst at the same time they have equal rights.

Discernment

In many religions, there is a notion of *spiritual discernment* - that is, deciding for oneself who or what is good for spiritual development, who or what holds you back. Buddhism for example offers the advice of *'avoiding obnoxious people'*.

This can seem harsh, and I'm still not sure whether this is a way of being OK yourself and seeing others as not-OK, but I think it could be used like that. Nevertheless, most of us can find people around us who hold us back or activities in our life which are not good for us, and it's important to do something about this.

More importantly, if you're growing in any area of life it's best done with awareness.

Suffering

In the West, we've tried to alleviate every form of pain and discomfort from human experience, whether it's through pain relief medicine and surgery, tranquillisers and anti-depressants, or central heating, air conditioning and electrically operated windows, so much so that we not only find it difficult to tolerate anything that isn't perfectly comfortable and OK, but we'll quite readily take legal proceedings against anyone who hasn't made it like that for us. This of course is what has led to a 'nanny-state' mentality because everyone is afraid of being sued for not having anticipated something that could go wrong.

Yet life *is* full of pain and difficulty (– if your life isn't like this, you've been lucky so far!) and many people have gone to religious organisations for support at times of particular trouble.

We can't be compensated for all that happens to us, and even when we do get some financial recompense, it can rarely make up for the rest of what we have experienced like physical suffering, emotional pain, changes to our lifestyle or relationships etc.

The point is that in the West we've tried to distance ourselves from suffering whilst in Eastern traditions, suffering is accepted as the basis for spiritual growth. We can use our suffering as a basis for development, for understanding things, for changing our relationship to life, to people, and to ourselves.

For example, there are many stories of people who have transformed their lives after terrible things have happened to them like Simon Weston, the soldier who was seriously burned in the Falklands War, who has given his energy to charity campaign work, and Lesley Payne, mother of Sarah Payne, the daughter who disappeared and was found murdered in 2001 who has campaigned ever since to make the world a safer place for children. Many people who emerged from the Second World War have contributed to the world through their writing and therapeutic work like Victor Frankl and Primo Levi.

432

Although many do find solace and renewal by working in the external world in this way, this isn't compulsory.

The key point is that we can find compassion for ourselves and others around us through the softening of our personalities that ultimately follows trauma and sadness if we let it. If we don't attend to the spiritual dimension (whether or not we recognise it as 'spiritual'), there is a risk of becoming bitter and frozen in our responses.

Everyone's spiritual and life journey is unique. It is not what happens to us that is key, but *what we make of* what happens to us.

How I started

I was brought up as an 'atheist' and I was taken out of religious studies at school. As I mentioned in the chapter on *Therapy*, when I'd finished doing tons of therapy - a huge and necessary job - I realised that something was missing and that development as a person doesn't stop when the most obvious problems are fixed.

At this time, I had a lot of contact with my mother with whom I'd not been in touch for ten years and learned that she had looked quite deeply into her spiritual side and had also studied Eastern approaches to spiritual life. I talked a lot about spiritual life with her, went to several Quaker meetings/conferences/retreats, read a lot and visited several nonconformist churches; I talked to people of all faiths. I also went to Christian study groups and did the Alpha course. I was baptised by the then Bishop of York on an impromptu basis at what was my then my local Anglican church.

I think spiritual life has a territory of its own.

My view of the spiritual world is that it is a mystery and not subject to logic and scientific enquiry and cannot be defined by any one society within that society's worldly terms. I believe that the spiritual territory is not for any one religion to colonise.

433

What put me off my spiritual journey, and what I liked

The usual history

History is full of religious intolerance - between religions, between churches, and within the same religion - for example, between Protestants and Catholics. There is often conflict between believers and non-believers. The history alone is so bad it is enough to put anyone off as it involves cruelty, persecution, abuse and judgement, all of which are still happening, and all of which seem deeply unspiritual. Some examples of books on the history of religion are given at the end of this chapter, including the savage critique of religion by Christopher Hitchens (who was of course a New Atheist).

The non-standard history I became interested in

In terms of Christianity - there is a non-standard Christian history for example of the Christian churches' incorporation into states including the Roman empire, the history of the creation of orthodoxy in the Bible, the missionary movement, the crusades, and the history of taking the spiritual out of life - *'secularisation'*.

There are a variety of histories of Christianity available – two of the most thorough are by Paul Johnson (1976) and Diarmaid MacCulloch (2010) who have both written versions published by Penguin Books, as well as the 'people's history' of Christianity by Diana Butler Bass, who reminds us of the good things that have been achieved and retained and of the importance of the links with fighting for social justice.

Pointless debate, debate

I think *the spiritual resides in the intuitive unconscious mind* not in the logical conscious mind and that a lot of debate is pointless as it depends on rationality, which has its limits - as has been described in texts on western philosophy. *As far as I can tell from what they say, many critics of belief do not experience a spiritual part of themselves and think belief is about debate and logic. This is a huge stumbling block to understanding religion.*

434

There are plenty of quite good', often waffly, sometimes ranting, thinkers over the last few hundred years who have questioned and explained religion from all shades of opinion, but in the main they have been critical of all the worst aspects of *organised religion* rather than of *a spiritual life* itself. There is an argument also that science/rationality is itself a blinkered, narrow approach to life, which has its own dogma and its own priesthood who think they have all the answers. A scientific logical approach with over-dependence on language does not suit everyone, can be grandiose and egocentric, human-centred and may be pretty useless explaining life's mysteries. Fortunately, mysteries such as the spiritual, the unconscious, love and goodness persist despite being distorted or explained away.

People who are against the spiritual world usually choose one religion to criticise, often choosing rigid views held by one religion and attacking dogma, interpretations, theology, history, politics, rituals or structures, and early beliefs etc. These can usually be criticised quite easily as they are man-made.

What people cannot criticise is any one individual's spiritual world, which I think depends on an individual's *felt* experience. Also, anyone should be able to experience their spiritual world in a way that suits them, talk about their experience how they want to, and belong or not belong to any group or religion without any judgement. This is the kind of freedom that is intended in the United Nations Human Rights Charter which gets forgotten about when it is not convenient.

False self

My experience of 'churches' is of the Quakers and the Anglicans in the UK and I've noticed particularly in the Church of England, the common development of a social self or *'persona'* or *'false self'*. This 'self' is not radically different from the usual middle-class social self of good character, status, etc. except that it has a Christian flavour. In any event, a false social self is non-genuine - we are all flawed and there is competition involved. Social selves are by definition worldly and impede spiritual growth.

435

Hierarchies

A lot of religions seem to have an organisation like that of the army (except the Quakers who have a flattened hierarchy). I suppose this makes the Archbishop of Canterbury a type of supreme commander. You can argue that hierarchies come from history, or reflect social structure, or that those further up are more spiritually 'sorted out', but hierarchies seem to have nothing to do with the spiritual world.

Conformity

Most religions expect conformity to some degree because they are rooted in orthodoxy and history. Most religions expect the 'givens' of their beliefs not to be questioned too much or even made relevant to today – as for example, in the Church of England, over the issue of women clergy. On the other hand, a lot of churchgoers adopt a pic'n'mix approach so there's an inbuilt conflict between the clergy and an individual choosing what they want to believe in. When this tension is too much, there are breakaway churches formed, for example, the Non-conformists and the Gnostics and the Protestants. Individuals got together to form those movements but the first tension is between individual belief and orthodoxy. Historically, conformity has also been part of social control – many religions were incorporated into, or ran parallel, to the state and it's very convenient for governments to have obedient citizens.

Rules

There's a thread in Christianity which can be described as anti-fun/play/in service to others/judging others and self, etc. which has the feel of a rigid, controlling Victorian parent. The Catholics seem to accept that they are imperfect and can sin and be forgiven, the Protestants don't seem to get round to doing any sinning or living life with enjoyment in the best sense.

Most religions are fostering spiritual growth by having moral codes/rules but these cannot be too rigid and I think ideally an individual 'built-in' ethical course is best, one which is based on

436

humanistic/spiritual values. Rules are outside people, and can be dropped, or used against people. If you have to keep looking outside for what's right in life you may go round in circles.

Lack of really useful writings that are not partisan

Religions sometimes feel a bit like football teams and you have to be the biased supporter, but developing your own spiritual football skill is a process that doesn't have to belong to one team. Any religious rituals and writings can serve to make spiritual knowledge hard to find and they may seem dated, rigid or compromised in a worldly way. Critics of religion tend to focus on the parts that are easy to attack and use rationality to attack a *mysterious and largely unconscious, felt experience.* (For more about this see what I've said about Carl Jung in *The Self* chapter and about a wide, accepting view of the unconscious part of the psyche in the section on *The Unconscious.*)

Choices when thinking of belonging to a religious group

People may join or not join religious groups for many reasons, including one or many more of these positions - some of which are spiritual, some not so spiritual, and some worldly:

1. not joining, developing spiritually on your own
2. joining with a pic'n'mix approach to all the things you do not like
3. trying to fit in and keeping your doubts
4. accepting everything
5. accepting everything to avoid persecution or death
6. joining several different churches
7. joining in a half-hearted way
8. joining for reasons other than spiritual ones like social reasons
9. joining and ignoring what you don't like
10. starting your own church or religion
11. joining and trying to change what you don't like
12. finding a different church or religion that suits you better
13. joining to enhance your career and to network with people
14. joining to improve your social standing

15 joining to get support and encouragement in your spiritual journey
16 having a pic'n'mix approach to religions as well as to the church
17 finding a more liberal or conservative branch of a church or a religion
18 joining to deepen your sense of spirituality
19 joining to learn
20 thinking of history, dogma, rituals as quirky and then joining anyway
21 joining with a view to developing a religious career
22 joining to improve your chances of getting your child into a faith school
23 joining to find a partner/relationship or to make friends
24 hoping to become 'more spiritual' by becoming immersed in religion
25 hoping to meet like-minded people with whom you can discuss things
26 joining to find love and support especially at difficult times in your life
27 joining to get help with healing - psychological and/or physical
28 joining to feel less alone in the world
29 joining because it is expected by others
30 joining to alleviate fear

I've joined several churches and explored others, mostly in the past when I was learning about my spiritual life. I noticed that initially there were both spiritual and social reasons behind my decision   - and others' - to join these religious groups but in retrospect, I think some of the outcomes were different from what I had expected.

Just as an example:

Joining an Anglican church introduced me to prayer (see below), which I then used in my work very productively and later developed into a very flexible and powerful practice. And hymns helped me to develop my singing ability.

These are some of the real positives I found from joining various religious groups:

- I found that joining aided my spiritual journey **at the time** and that there was in a general sense an acknowledgement and interest in my spiritual awareness from others, which I think was sincere. The fact that in order to move on spiritually, I may have had to leave religious groups to find other ones until I left them completely does not matter, as I saw this as a process of finding out and reacting against things that did not suit my development, which helped me define my beliefs.

- A sense of belonging and inclusion in a positive sincere group (and sometimes also a global community). This I found very useful as I find there is an overall tendency for society to be competitive, materialistic and excluding, and being excluded has affected me quite seriously, I have been a good candidate for exclusion, having had a breakdown, having health problems, and being an original thinker and artistic.

- I felt a sense of love and welcome and importantly later understood and felt what is often described as the *Holy Spirit*, which I felt as a strong exchange of loving energy amongst people - this is notoriously hard to define. I would not bother with a church where this was lacking. In a Christian church with the Christian emphasis on love and forgiveness, I have experienced this. Nowadays, I would beware of any unspiritual processes – this includes judgement, which I have also come across.

- Generally also I have found spiritual groups to be more aware of a value-base than secular society and there is always an opportunity to become involved in social action.

What happens if people develop their spiritual life, whether they join a religious group or not

There is a lot written about developing your spiritual life and there is a lot written about how to do it in the best way and what obstacles you might find on the way.

These are some things that many people have described in terms of what you can expect as you develop spiritually, but remember that at best, *words* do not describe spirituality. They do not fully describe *love*, for example, so it is useful if you can accept something that is on a different plane, is mysterious and is at a deeper level than an 'ego-bound' life. For more about the *'ego'* see our chapter on *The Self*.

- experiencing a sense of deep belonging and connectedness to other people and the world
- being less in your ego/ material self and less individualistic
- having more of a focus on the good and not the negative possibilities in the world
- being connected to spiritual world with its own ways - very different and not understood by worldly approaches
- making the world make sense - it's not just about the selfish individual operating in a world where eg. goodness is at a premium - you can be a part of something much bigger, more loving, more positive
- as spiritual self gains/regains importance in the personality, integrating personality becomes easier – you are more whole, for example (see Carl Jung on this)
- finding other psychological positives, including feeling OK
- becoming become part of a mystery which is on another plane and saves you the trouble of figuring everything out
- discovering that there is a natural goodness and morality directing life without effort
- realising that you can accept your own faults as well as feeling OK and confident

- finding that a lot of things make sense that did not before (because you were looking at them or trying to find solutions on a worldly level)
- discovering there is a different feel to a lot of experience and revaluing it - for example, the idea that time has an endless aspect in spiritual terms
- becoming less bound up with worldly attachments - this alone makes a huge difference in people's lives
- experiencing a tremendous feeling of direction and peace etc, which enables people to withstand a lot of worldly difficulties
- for some, being in the present and being fully aware
- making a transition from being small-minded to being broad and generous with people

This list is a selection of what people who are sincere about developing spiritually have described and the literature is huge, cutting across cultures and religions and going far back in time - all that experience cannot be dismissed easily.

If you can make your spiritual life the centre of your life, everything in life will be different and very fulfilling in many ways. Don't expect quick results though, spiritual development is a *process;* it can be a long one and can have ups and downs. The idea that it's quick or instant is not true for most people.

In his poem, *The Dark Night,* St John of the Cross indicates that when we feel most lost in our spiritual quest, we are often at our closest to a spiritual answer or resolution. It's quite common to feel a sense of *'spiritual homesickness'* as J G Bennett describes it, without having named exactly what or who it is that we are missing.

Another aspect of spiritual development that I've noticed is that, although you may be able to put it on hold or become worldlier at times, there is actually *a growing momentum* as you develop your spiritual self.

Ideas that *'God is on my side'* – the spiritual in service of personal gain or ego - usually come out of misunderstanding the spiritual dimension or having a spiritual life that is fairly superficial.

The idea that you develop a kind of false 'good person' *persona*, denying your needs and being dour and miserable is I think, misconceived.

Remember as well I am not talking here about one religion, or the dated ideas and texts and social structures that any one religion may offer, nor about convoluted debates which are largely *'rational'* and completely ignore *felt* spiritual experience.

Retreat

There are some ideas that *are* worth thinking about - for example, *having a break from the world to develop your spiritual life*. Material on Buddha and Jesus who were both very conscious and aware of their spiritual process is worth exploring in this regard.

There are many retreat centres, some near your home and some across the world, where you can go to have a true break from your usual routines. These can range in style from silent retreats and retreats with strict discipline to others which can be very active where you join with other people, talk, share food, undertake activities together like yoga and meditation etc.

But remember it's also possible to find a place in everyday life where you can go to develop your spirituality – it doesn't have to be an expensive trek to the Himalayas.

Updating religious practice

In our chapter on *Sexuality*, we discuss conformity to religious and cultural systems in relation to our bodies e.g male and female circumcision. Religious institutions often fear modernising yet by not doing so they frequently alienate and fail people and cause much suffering and division. Harmonising with ideas of human rights and equality *can* strengthen religious groups, particularly if they prioritise their values rather than the survival of traditions.

Julia writes:

What's happening today in spiritual terms?

I'm not going to attempt a comprehensive review of what is happening in religion across the globe or even just in Britain, but I will give a few comments on the subject. There are plenty of writers to consult if this is what interests you. One of the liveliest is the religious commentator, Cole Moreton, who suggests in his recent book about faith in the UK that Britons are increasingly stepping away from rule-based religion. Having been alienated from the orthodox churches by sexual and financial scandals and bigotry, he sees resurgence in forms of paganism and rural folk religion. He believes this revival is fuelled by a renewed desire to value and protect the planet and to be in touch with nature, a belief in some kind of higher power or powers that is shared by large numbers despite a lack of agreed definition or label, and a new inclination to express emotions more powerfully and collectively than ever before.

The Church of England struggles to hold onto congregations, nevertheless quoting average weekly attendance of around a million people in the UK and that 4 in 10 people in the UK consider themselves as adherents, the biggest religious 'group' in the UK. Cole Moreton finds from 'polls' that some 26 million people in the UK believe in some kind of God or gods – however, they're not aligned to any particular religious institution. Cole Moreton makes the point that many of us prefer a spiritual path that allows us to drop in and out (eg. by attending a festival or an event) rather than to be committed to an organisation long-term or bound by a constricting dogma. *We're starting to realise that we're free.*

Neo-paganism is on the up across the globe. With its provision for a *female Goddess* as well as the *male God* of the Abrahamic religions, and its fusion with contemporary liberal values, it offers a way forward that offers a spiritual home for many who are disillusioned with or marginalised by traditional religion. *Radical Faeries* is an example of a group that explicitly opens its doors to gay men, allowing them to be both politically and spiritually active.

There are *'red letter Christians'* like Diana Butler Bass who has written *'A People's History of Christianity'*, challenging what she sees as the Christian right's takeover of the spiritual agenda in America, refusing to be squeezed out of her rights as a Christian to say it like she sees it and arguing for more attention to be given to matters of social justice.

There are *'Jews for Jesus'*, *'Jews against Circumcision'*, *'Jews for Justice in Palestine'*, and *Keshet UK* (who lobby on behalf of Jews with different sexual identities) etc. – across the world people have taken up challenging positions even within their own religious institutions and no doubt often against much criticism.

What is amazingly refreshing is the idea that spirituality can be ours without the confines of a stultifying institution, that the big institutions don't actually *own* the concept of spirituality, don't have the patent on being spiritual, and that we can step away from them and find our own path or stand up for our own concept of what is right even within their structures. We can also be joyful – the centuries of institutional stranglehold are finally giving way. Indeed, some believe like Karen Armstrong, linking to the work of Karl Jaspers on the original 'axial age', that we are in the throes of a third 'axial' – pivotal - era of spiritual awakening. Philip Sheldrake, scholar and writer, suggests that spiritual traditions have their day, evolving into something new and exciting at the beginning and ultimately facing the choice about stagnation or change as they 'age', when maintaining the institutional structures can seem more important than refreshing and evolving the wisdom-base.

So we have at one and the same time new spiritual awakening, a decline in support for traditional religious orthodoxies and strong advocacy for secularism.

What kind of spiritual path do we want to tread?

Some religions or paths within religions (such as monasticism) emphasise *ascetism, renunciation, abstinence* – abstaining from sexuality and avoiding physical comforts (perhaps even *mortification*), and sometimes also forgoing the pleasures of the mind – reducing reading and thinking to a narrow preoccupation with specific texts, as well as limiting social contact – living in silence or denying any closeness with other human beings so as to focus all one's energy on the deity and to develop a deep level of spiritual awareness. This holds some allure for people outside it so that some choose retreat experiences to tap into this way of life, even if it is just for a weekend. For the ordinary member of a church, the priestly advice has sometimes been for the individual to practise self-denial and self-discipline in accord with theological rules even where this has meant unhappiness for the person and others around them.

In contrast, some religions may encourage money-making in order to do benevolent acts within society, or to build beautiful places of worship to emphasise the power and strength of the religious path and to provide a safe place for worshippers to congregate and bond with each other. Others, keen to evangelise and expand the reach of the 'church', encourage large families and community engagement. In contrast to *renunciation, transmutation* involves acting spiritually *through* one's engagement *IN* life. In this way, everything we do holds the possibility of spiritual learning and practice, but one of the problems here is that we can get too caught up in the challenges of daily living and 'tempted' by pleasures and material rewards so that holding firm to ethical living and spiritual discernment can become very difficult. There are many who convince themselves and others that their choices are spiritually-driven, when in fact they reflect inner psychological confusions and misguided justifications for following what feels easy or pleasurable.

What kind of 'God' or spirit do we relate to, if any?

I have no specialist knowledge or experience in the spiritual domain (but see below for a bit about my journey) but it seems to me that it's a good idea to tackle this domain of our experience and become more confident and more 'sorted' about it - this is something I'm beginning to face up to myself. There can be a lot of confusion and we may spend years, even decades of our life, neglecting this side of things and failing to benefit from the help it can give us.

In my case, I've often drawn towards me strong humanists, existentialists and atheists and have been happy with that position, leaving it unexamined and 'on the shelf' for later review. Having got together with Jack, I've been challenged to attend to the question of spirituality afresh.

For those for whom Christian thinking seems outmoded, John Selby Spong, who retired from being Bishop in the Episcopal Diocese of Newark in New Jersey, offers some refreshing – and contentious - new insights.

What's our idea of 'God' and do we have need of a concept of 'God'?

For example, is our God a personal one who should give us things, protect us from harm, and make things right when things go wrong? Is our 'God' omnipresent? Are our 'gods' benevolent or wrathful, male or female, or all of this?

How much is our concept of God a projection of learning from childhood - perhaps we longed for a perfect parent figure who didn't punish us for burgeoning sexuality or 'bad behaviour' as our real parents may have? Do we avoid the spiritual just because it hovers around us like a Freudian 'super-ego' conscience tapping into feelings of guilt or shame that we'd prefer to let go of?

Do we tap into our spirituality to gain energy for fighting wrong or for accepting what cannot be fought, to set things that are personally painful into a wider perspective?

It seems to me that it might be helpful to get some clarity in our thinking about spirituality and secularism and I've identified five main approaches:

446

transcendent

This is the idea of an externalised or 'higher' power or God, or a *personal* deity, angel or ancestor - someone or something that is omniscient and far removed from everyday life, perhaps something perfect. This is the God who has created the world, who is distinct from the world. This is often associated with dualism, separating the spiritual from the material world. We might have direct access to the spiritual Being, or we may accept someone who mediates the communication process like a priest or elder. This approach will often involve us in the process of worship, engaging in religious rituals, making a shrine or icons, prayer.

immanent

This is the idea of an omnipresent God or spiritual energy, someone or something that is present everywhere and within us. We can experience this in nature, in the stars, at a concert, in the kitchen, in the bedroom, or in a group. It's available to each of us, emanating from inside ourselves so that handling the challenges of life rests within our own spiritual nature and has nothing to do with any figure on a white charger who can rescue us, or anyone who can be blamed when things go wrong. We may want to meditate or practise listening to the inner voice inside ourselves.

There may be traditions which fuse both transcendance and immanence but generally speaking, these are logically inconsistent with each other.

mystical

This is when we yearn for spiritual *experiences* – blissful ecstasy, 'nirvana', something perhaps akin to orgasm where the boundaries of self and other, the world and the other-world seem to dissolve for an endless moment, and we feel closely *connected* (dualistic) to our God or deity or *at one with* (non-dualistic) our spiritual self. In some spiritual communities, shamans or medicine men and women ingest substances like strong herbs which enhance trance or spirit possession. Fasting, playing music, drumming, chanting, burning incense, waiting for darkness, etc. can help us to move beyond the everyday reality.

Letting go of regular clothing may help – sharing nakedness or wearing robes (done for example in some pagan ceremonies), putting on special makeup, ornaments, flowers and headwear (as in Balinese Hinduism) etc. - can make people in a group feel that everyday roles and insignia are gone, and that one has temporarily stepped into a different world where worldly and social differences can be forgotten.

The 'vision quest' in American Indian and some Inuit traditions in which people find guidance on their path or direction in life, is often embarked on over a few days, and can involve sleep and sensory deprivation, fasting, and spending time in the forest or wilderness. We're told that Jesus spent 40 days and nights in the wilderness – this is a time-honoured tradition.

secular

For those of us who tend to the secular, we may nevertheless want to spend some time regularly catching up with an account of our week and chewing over the ethics of situations in which we are involved. We may make that time special and even build in rituals, whether that's having some regular time alone or going fishing every Wednesday night with mates. Or we might go to Quaker meetings, which it is possible to attend without adhering to faith, where we can listen to ourselves and others in a silent group.

We may work with a sense of something bigger than conscious individual life or even a self-aware society, the sum and synergy of things that are beyond human control and which cannot be fully predicted. For example, we might call it having a sense of 'fate'.

Even if events which happen in our lives are random and accidental, we may feel that a sense of the 'sacred' is appropriate in dealing with them even though we don't call it that – respecting a person's need for space, offering support when someone is in trouble, celebrating achievements, honouring courage and fortitude, commemorating a person's life when they die etc.

We may feel that our daily life is very much dominated by conscious and left-brain material and want to become more aware of our right-brain – the non-linguistic processing and the creative within us, and to cultivate our ability to tap into unconscious material.

ethical

It may be that we're primarily concerned with the ethics of living – a need to develop or relate to a set of moral principles (such as that espoused by the Humanist Associations as well as by most religious organisations), or to develop skill in assessing situations and determining the wisest course of action perhaps by finding the widest possible consensus – for example as in Richard Rorty's *'contingent morality'* approach. In such a view of the world, we may find ourselves hesitating before swatting a tiny fly in our wine-glass, looking for every alternative avenue to letting an employee go because we've run out of funds to keep them on, and feeling ambivalent about visiting parts of the world where people can't afford the simplest things in order to give ourselves a holiday, not to mention totting up the air-miles that contribute to pollution. We may have decisions to make about joining campaigners for change or speaking out about injustice.

If up to now we haven't articulated our principles very clearly, this might be the time to examine how we make such decisions and whether we are operating consistently across different situations or whether we have some areas that merit more attention than others.

Religions and spiritual paths face us with a variety of complex issues to resolve or live with, particularly the question of how many gods, whether there is a 'god' or 'higher power', whether that god is singular or for example, *Trinitarian* (Father, Son and Holy Spirit), or pluralistic (eg. Sun, Moon and Stars). *Pantheism*, the idea that everything is sacred, that everything is part of a universal cosmos rather than there being a material world with a separate, overarching or transcendant God, has been returning to popular consciousness. Buddhists mostly dispense with any notion of a god, yet utilise the energy of many 'sky-dancers' and deities (including wrathful ones) in their meditative practices.

Philip Sheldrake's introductory text on *Spirituality* offers some good categorisations of different kinds of spirituality, including the (contentious) idea that much of what is described as secular can nevertheless be considered as secular *spirituality,* whether that's Mahatma Gandhi's doctrine of non-violence, the transcendent feeling an explorer or climber might get from the top of a mountain, or a scientist who recognises that the more we know, the more mysterious it all seems. Some 'seculars' will be annoyed at this colonisation of their experience by the 'spirituals', but it is perhaps worth wondering if we're talking about qualitatively similar things even though we may argue about the nomenclature or about whether there is anything mystical 'out there' or 'in here' or not.

Fear and religion

It can be frightening for us to stand up and be counted for our religious or spiritual identity, which may be one reason why we hesitate to come out about our beliefs and practices, or even to allow ourselves to wonder about them. In anthropology, we can read studies of witchcraft within different cultural contexts and in history, including stories of those who have been afraid of being accused of being witches because of the punishments or social exclusion that might follow. Many religious adherents have been persecuted at different periods in history, the persecution of Jews in the Second World War being perhaps the most horrific example, and the crucifixion of Jesus being one of the most iconic images of persecution in the western world. There have been many famous examples of martyrs who have stood up for their faith. Yet even today, we may fear telling an employer or our customers about our spiritual affiliation lest we encounter prejudice. Recent cases of countries outlawing the wearing of religious markers such as crosses, beards, turbans, and veils damage our confidence about religious tolerance, openness and equality.

In an era where we believe we've got religious freedom in many countries, **it can be disconcerting to find that prejudice and intolerance of religious expression is in fact the reality**. Once again we have to look beyond the rhetoric and think what is *actually happening* around us.

It's also been difficult for people to abandon a religious or spiritual path. We've heard for example stories of how painful it is for teenagers and others to be liberated from groups labelled cults which appear to wield such a powerful hold on them that kidnapping them back and subjecting them to intensive 'debriefing' has been necessary. Perhaps it's been difficult for many people to walk away from the Abrahamic religions such as Christianity, even in the face of corruption, cruelty and abuse because of the key concepts that God is *all-knowing, all-powerful* and *eternal.*

Deists have been able to separate their respect for God as creator of the world from dogma, seeing this as the manipulations of human beings who set up religious institutions, shoring up their power with superstitions, mystical beliefs and threats of punishment and damnation. Even though we know with our rational minds that there is no 'hell', it can be hard to set ourselves free from unconscious attachment to the security of punishment for 'going it alone'. Even though we no longer believe in 'sin', it can be hard to dismiss programming that has been there in our own families which criticises us for attempting to live sexual lifestyles outside community 'norms'. The fusion between ideas of God and our own childhood indoctrination, however subtle, can be difficult to unravel.

When I read Cole Moreton's optimistic and joyful last chapters, I found it hard to imagine that spirituality could be like that – free, energetic, happy, empowered, creative, fun. It would be good to think that the revolution we are experiencing in rejecting political dictators round the world, is also happening within the spiritual domain, as we start to move away from religious authoritarianism, take control ourselves and dare to choose how we want to experience life – and spirituality.

'Religious' diversity

Around 400,000 people in the UK and significant numbers in Australia, New Zealand and Canada have started identifying themselves as *'Jedi'* in answer to government census questions about religious affiliation, of whom a proportion (albeit perhaps a small proportion) actually do subscribe to beliefs linked to the Jedi Knights, who originated as fictional figures in the cult programme, *Star Trek*. Even in their refusal to be pigeonholed into religious identity and in their mockery of the system, a number of people who feel that way prefer to be labelled *Jedi* – with its association with spirituality – rather than *atheist* or 'coming out' about their true spiritual beliefs. Among the people who see themselves as part of a new *Jedi* movement, there are some astonishing stories of prejudice against them by those who find the idea that Jedis *could actually be* spiritual too upsetting, or conversely, feel so strongly about their own religious status that they find *the possibility of mockery* deeply challenging.

Even the term religious 'tolerance' can be deeply offensive rather than religious *freedom* and an acceptance of religious *diversity*. At the top of James Fowler's list of states of religious awareness, there is the idea that spiritual maturity would mean that we can allow and enjoy the challenge of different spiritual ideas rather than being threatened, including being open to the possibility of modifying our own beliefs and practices, just as would be the case with intellectual maturity. We don't have to hold on to dogma like 'grim death' or defend a particular position fiercely – not only because perhaps it's all one spiritual world, but because what one person believes or does doesn't have to hurt us. The difficulty we have in cultivating this kind of openness is at the heart of problems we have around the world with living alongside or being integrated with people of different cultures.

Reactive philosophy

Many of those who advocate the 'death of God' had themselves strong upbringings within traditional faiths. The philosopher Frederic Nietzsche comes to mind. Alice Miller tells us that he grew up in a dysfunctional family in which he was often arbitrarily punished and disciplined in the name of Christianity. Sometimes when people are strongly arguing for atheism and a purely scientific view of the world it is interesting to discover that they may be reacting against the very religious tenets that appeared unfair or controlling of them in childhood. A friend of mine who has an unbreakable existential and humanist commitment and is

452

deeply critical of the supernatural nevertheless uses a variety of Christian references in his speech eg. *'Christ, that's terrible!'* etc. thus conveying unconsciously the link with his own early experience of going to church, being in a choir etc. which he has since rejected.

There are approaches which have sought to reconcile science and religion, including Christian Science developed by Mary Baker Eddy, which has health and healing as central to its work. Charles Darwin, though offering us the theory of evolution that would sweep away much of religion's hold on us, struggled to reconcile his own faith with his scientific work. There are organisations such as *Christians in Science*, who work to integrate evangelical Christian teaching with their scientific research and stewardship of the planet.

Rationalists like Baruch Spinoza held that God is at the very most a *philosophical* concept whilst Immanuel Kant allowed that there were some things that could not be known simply through *reason* – we need *experience*. It's important not to approach spirituality purely through our *thinking* processes (if even through thinking at all) ; much of our experience of spirituality comes through other channels – instincts, senses, bodily experiences, unconscious processes like dreams, emotions, and channels of knowing that we may not even have labelled. Getting a sense of something beyond our *individual consciousness*, and even beyond our *collective consciousness* – our connectedness to others, may have to do with things much bigger than the overwhelmingly *cognitive* discipline of philosophy.

Reclaiming a path

Sometimes, when we feel stultified spiritually we may be stuck in a structure or set of beliefs or rules that we can't get our head round. We are just 'in' it. This is when digging into the literature about our religion or spiritual 'field', talking to people elsewhere and listening to critiques and alternatives can come in useful.

Diana Butler Bass, a teacher of church history and a Christian writer, exemplifies the way in which people can find their way even through their own traditions to come up with different and perhaps surprising conclusions from what has become the dominant take on it, mining the history for different examples and interpretations. In this way, for example, she has provided a text for new 'generative Christians' to chart a path within American Christianity which reconnects with social justice and opens up belief to a more fluid approach (for example, changing denomination or having simultaneous membership of more than one tradition), and the practice of a true ecumenism across conventional religious and social boundaries. Indeed, after reading her book, it's possible to consider that rather than mourning the decline of 'structured' Christianity, this is a time for celebrating the possibility of exciting new spiritual avenues.

This approach does not have to belong purely to Christians. It is a strategy that increasing numbers of academics and writers are developing with their 'people's histories' in a number of fields.

Being definite about things like good and evil

In the later part of the twentieth century, post-structuralist thought helped us to move away from the starkness of dualistic thinking, of *good* and *evil*, of *right* and *wrong*, of *rational* and *emotional*, and *mind* and *matter*, *body* and *soul*. We are now able to think in much more nuanced ways, understanding that any concept is appreciated in relation to its context and to other concepts with which it is compared, contrasted, juxtaposed.

This of course is part of the approach that says that there is no absolute truth, which is problematic for many in fundamentalist religions, and those who rely on religious texts to define 'right' ways of living. Many of our concepts have been changed forever as a result of this philosophical shift, coupled with more subtle insights derived from science, such as the challenge to the idea of 'male' and 'female' or 'black' and 'white' as fixed categories. Some of our ideas have been defined purely through their capacity to be measurable, such as 'intelligence', yet we have discovered for example that people with low outcomes on cognitive intelligence tests can have high scores on interpersonal sensitivity or commonsense functioning in the world. We have discovered that little is as certain and definite as we would want it to be, and science has often had to understand its task as one of engaging with uncertainty and offering interpretations of the complexities rather than of seeking signposts to clear answers.

There are various ways in which religious movements have perceived existence, with some understanding the *material* world to be inferior to the *spiritual* domain, while others portray spiritual life to be a battle between *good* and *evil* forces. *Gnosticism* for example is generally based on a dualistic struggle between the forces of *light* and *darkness* (though there are of course a number of variant strands, some of which see this struggle as that between equal forces and some between unequal forces).

Are we 'above' animals' or 'one' with animals?

One of the critical elements of Judeo-Christian and Muslim thinking is the idea that human beings are seen as on a different plane from that of animals, distinguished by things like our language, the fact that we stand up and can carry things and that we have a capacity to regulate our own behaviour (sometimes!), whilst in some other traditions like that of the American Indians, in Shinto, Buddhism and Neopaganism we are *animistic,* believing that objects – animals, insects, rocks and mountains for example - are animate and have souls just like we do. In *naturalistic pantheism,* there is a reverence and respect for all nature, a respect for the sacredness of the universe, and the idea that we are recycled organically when we die.

The results of *non-animistic* religious thinking can be various. Seeing ourselves as different from animals and the natural world, we can come to believe that we can control our environment, exploit it for our needs, use animals and plants for food and adornment. Nevertheless, there are expectations on us to look after animals. In the Catholic Catechism, for example, there is a consciousness of our duty of kindness to animals in the context of a 'religious respect for the integrity of creation' alongside the recognition that we may use them for food, clothing and medical research. Similar ideas are expressed within Islam.

In Christianity, there has been a softening of attitudes towards animals and the environment towards a sense of stewardship rather than exploitation, as there has been in the general population.

In Islam, the practice of *halal* slaughter of animals for meat has included the requirement for good treatment of the animals and measures to reduce their fear and there is now increasing acceptance of the measure of pre-stunning animals, which is practised in secular abbatoirs.

A key element in categorising animals as distinct from humans is that it allows us to deny or repress our physicality and feel ashamed of our (animal) sexuality and we have seen how this has played out in many religious situations, for example where celibacy has been enforced on clergy, where there has been child abuse within the church, where dogma and prejudice has fuelled the pronouncement of judgements on people for sexual 'transgression', and where there has been harsh treatment of unmarried mothers and their babies.

Perhaps one reason why Westerners have turned at times to Eastern religions and paganism is that these have a more positive attitude to sexuality. The attempt to keep sex strictly within heterosexual, marital, monogamous and lifelong partnership limits has brought unhappiness to many and eroded their spiritual joy. Of course, protection of children and preventing the pain of emotional abandonment and separation are important considerations but there are many ways to achieve these aims without creating additional suffering.

External and internal resources

Another way to look at things is to consider the *external* and the *internal*.

For example, if we're feeling trapped within a life-role, and out of touch with our spiritual self, we should consider what we can do to gain more freedom – either *outwardly* through making structural or practical changes – going for a walk at lunchtime somewhere beautiful or making a significant life-change eg. in relation to employment, or *inwardly*, like Brother Lawrence, who found something of God in anything that he was doing – experiencing an inner freedom and personal growth through meditating, praying, or reflecting on our connectedness to people across the globe.

If we're caught in work that feels dry or meaningless, we have to go into ourselves to develop our inner world, for example thinking about people everywhere who are in similar situations, attending to what we can do to make things go well for ourselves and people right next to us, remembering times that were better and finding something positive about the present, such as the wider meaning of our work, and dreaming up ways of making the overall working systems better. If relationships around us are not good, we can work on ways of doing something about that. Sometimes we just have to stick things until the situation changes, waiting for things to shift imperceptibly, drip by drip. The time will come when we either have to become proactive and change things dramatically, or when we realise that the situation has already changed whilst we were waiting. It is no longer what it used to be like, and some of the reason for that is *how we have been.* This is not a 'left-brain' process – such shifts come about by allowing unconscious processes to work.

Can we handle an individual approach to spirituality?

Jack has made a strong case for distinguishing between the *institutionalised* religious path (which whilst being helpful for many, has also resulted in others turning away from spirituality altogether), and taking an *individual approach* to spirituality.

Mid-life might be the best time for a more individual approach because we can tolerate more uncertainty and diversity and be less self-centred, perhaps having had some of our needs met in adult relationships, parenting, caring, working, creating and playing.

Klaus Riegel's work on *dialectical thinking* suggests that maturity brings a greater possibility of handling ambivalence and dissonance – we don't have to foreclose so sharply on opinions and ideas and feelings, we can hold conflicting thoughts and feelings without having to deny one or the other. We can handle emotional discomfort better. This is consistent with James Fowler's ideas about the later and more advanced states of spiritual development in which we're more open to being challenged by other forms of thought, are less spiritually fragile, and have less need to defend our ideas and beliefs by keeping others out.

In the model of human development put forward by the psychologist, Erik Erikson, the later stages of life can bring an increasing ability to focus on the next generation's needs and on the wider community through *'generativity'* and *'integrity'*. We shouldn't forget the downside of these – *stagnation* if we fail to be energetic and creative, and *despair* if we fail to pull together the strands of our life and experience.

We don't have to be a member of a religious community to pray or work for the good of others and to focus less exclusively on the needs of ourselves and our personal family. It is perfectly possible to see ourselves as connected to international brother-and-sisterhood and to be concerned about the world we are leaving behind to future generations *inside* or *outside* a religious organisation. However, ultimately, we will usually need to link to others to get things done – even if this is through social or political groups rather than through religious groups. What the institutions and groups are that we connect to may matter less than the question of *being clear about our own motivations and commitments*. If these are OK, we will be able to avoid involvement with groups that are psychologically or structurally unhealthy.

It's very sad that religious organisations are often more concerned with buildings than with the lives of their communities, or that certain cliques have gained control of the culture and values within them to the exclusion of others. If we can get over these kinds of hurdles, then we may find that we can find fulfilment in the company of others that is more readily available to us than doing the hard work of building a spiritual life on our own. The important thing is that we have a choice.

Living spiritually

Living spiritually usually means building *quality* into our lives – doing everything with care and love and attention, not living at breakneck speed and skimping over everything important whether that's tidying up or paying attention to what our child is saying. Living with quality in our lives is likely to mean that things take longer and that we cannot do the same number of things we used to.

It's likely to involve things like:

- developing awareness of the spiritual world and the spiritual self
- setting boundaries around our time and energy – telling people when we're tired, cutting back on entertaining, being selective about whom we spend time with, protecting our peace, reducing the amount of chatter in our life and starting to talk about things that matter.
- learning to live with less materiality around us, resisting consumerism
- repairing things, doing some sewing, enhancing old items, sanding old table tops, conserving things etc.
- spring-cleaning rooms, clearing out drawers and boxes, thinning out our wardrobe
- simplifying, getting rid of clutter, developing storage systems, thinning out
- bringing a sense of order into our life with good administration, filing our papers, ordering our books, photographs and music, systematising our housekeeping with routines and lists etc.
- living within a 'budget' – whether financial or practical eg. how much we decide to eat and drink or how much sleep to have
- reducing dependence on entertainment provided by others (eg. TV) and putting energy into production eg. making things, being part of community activity
- relating to nature, valuing and appreciating simple things like the sky and plant-life

- relating to animals, respecting their dignity and showing them kindness
- safeguarding our inner life – setting boundaries on who and when we allow other people into our world
- finding people who are inspiring to us in spiritual ways; pasting up on our walls and doors aphorisms and sayings that we find encouraging.
- stopping the search for satisfactions in relationships beyond good spiritual connection – recognising and challenging patterns of instrumentality, need gratification, or a wish to control – seeking for peaceful connection and letting people be as they need to be.
- spending time in reflection

Ritual and the sacred – 'marking' events in our lives

We're often propelled to find our way to spirituality or to recognition of our spiritual nature when disaster strikes.

That song sung by Edith Piaf – *Les Trois Cloches/The Three Bells*, about 'Little Jimmy Brown', whilst rooted in a clichéd model of life, nevertheless reminds us that life tends to be bounded by ceremonies around our birth or naming, around making a partnership, and at the time of our death.

But there may be many other occasions too when we want ceremony:

graduating or achieving the outcome of studies
gaining a promotion or success at work
experiencing a separation or divorce
moving into a new home
completing a project
reaching a particular age
starting out on a journey or other departure
returning or reuniting with people
becoming pregnant and having a child
losing a child at any stage through death or departure
trauma that needs recognition
receiving a windfall

having to downshift and move on
recovering from illness or surgery
taking on a new identity or role
etc.

Sometimes the ways in which these events have been commemorated may seem hackneyed or commercial – it's important to consider how we can bring freshness and meaning to them in our own terms. We don't have to go to a conventional funeral director and have a coffin brought along in a black hearse to a crematorium with piped muzac. Consider for example a basket carried into a bluebell wood with a woodland/forest burial among the squirrels and robins and having friends play our favourite music on a saxophone.

There *are* radical alternatives to what's served up as 'the norm' in every avenue of life if we look hard enough, and ways to ensure that the key events in our life are marked with personal significance rather than bureaucratised and commercialised.

We can be creative about *every* aspect of our lives. Like growing our own organic vegetables or choosing handmade jewellery or making our own clothes, we can move beyond the easy offerings of high street or TV and imbue the important moments of our lives with a sacredness of our own design. There's a different energy – a vibrancy - that comes when we take control of our life.

The point of ritualising passages, transitions, and events is often to assist us all to cope with their emotional impact. Thus for example, we need a retirement party to say goodbye to colleagues and to launch us into a new way of life, but our colleagues too need something that underlines our departure from the team and reminds them that they too are on a journey towards endings; it helps everyone to recognise that change is inevitable, that life moves forward and doesn't stay still, that we're all getting older, and that everything ought to be done in the awareness of the preciousness of this time now.

Funerals have a multiplicity of meanings – planning for our own can help us to keep the idea of our demise in mind whenever we are tempted to waste time in our life and keep us focusing on the people who matter to us before we go. On the day, it can seem as if the event is 'for' the person who has died, but it's also very significantly for the people who've been left behind (even though of course they may not all agree about it). I was reminded of this when a dear friend died, someone who'd shared with me on many occasions his clear commitment to atheism and indeed rejected relationships with people who 'had religion'. When I turned up at the funeral, his relatives had organised a Christian event. I felt it was a significant betrayal of the man I'd known and the principles by which he'd lived his life, yet I recognised that his family needed to feel *for themselves* that they had laid his soul to rest. Once I got over my outrage I decided that he might well have laughed at it all, reflecting affectionately how little his family had understood him. The question is - *whose* funeral is it???

Changes and losses in our lives that go unmarked or unacknowledged can remain problematic. There's always time to go back and do it later, if we missed it at the time. 'Renewal of vows' and memorial services can technically be done whenever we need them, not just at official junctures (eg. ten years). Just having a gathering or creating a special event to commemorate something may be what is needed. Exorcisms in new (or old) houses are usually about recognising that there are unquiet spirits who need acknowledgement and sometimes people who need 'closure' on traumatic events.

Purpose and taking responsibility

Another significant area that comes into the spiritual domain is the issue of 'purpose' and assessing our life for its meaning and whether there's more we need to do to develop a sense of adding something to the earth.

Relating to people around us in more meaningful ways than previously, might be enough. We can for example consider that we might need to be inspiring to the young people in our life. We need to create time for partners, older relatives, children, and animals, but we also need to relate to them from a place of spiritual engagement and demonstrate how to engage with the world by making our own contribution to life.

We need to consider how we might contribute to the future of the planet, whether it's through prayer, through posting online messages, blogs and tweets to inspire others, making a renewed attempt to recycle and conserve, giving money to environmental campaigns, developing gardens or allotments or getting involved in bigger, more sociable or more practical ways to change things on the earth, working with decision-makers or researchers, or initiating new developments in our work to take account of ecological concerns.

Two writers who've given thought to this aspect of our existence are:

Don Cupitt, author of the *Sea of Faith*, who believes we should find the *joy in life* and make *an active attempt to add value to the human lifeworld.*

William James, psychologist and philosopher, who said: *The greatest use of life is to spend it for something that will outlast it.*

Appreciating things

Finally, we can remember that happiness is an active thing. If we let in too many of the negative messages from the news, the media, other people, it may be difficult to keep up our own morale. We can choose to think positively. We can tackle any depression we may be suffering from. We can do things that are joyful – visit beautiful places, find the tiny flower emerging in a concrete wall, notice the grass trying to grow up around a drain, praise what is good in a child's behaviour rather than criticising all that is bad, give positive strokes to our partner and value that they're choosing to be with us, be grateful for all that life gives us, honour the good that there is, cultivate contentment at every opportunity. A spiritual approach to living means moving on from complaining to finding love in life and experiencing gratitude for all that there is.

Perhaps a useful concept is that of returning to innocence and simplicity, taking up a childlike freshness to our experiencing of life and taking steps to protect ourselves in that state of vulnerability. This has to be done alongside an ongoing awareness of the many hazards in life – they are parallel processes – remaining open to experience *and* taking steps to survive the pressures of life.

We can remember that all is transient and that people who are here today may not be tomorrow, and that our own health and wellbeing requires energy to maintain it, and that anything can be taken away suddenly, or slowly. We can make the most of every day.

Above all, the idea is that spirituality is an energy that's already within us – the task is to tap into that resource for enriching our lives, and to find a way that works for us.

Building our own path

As you will see from reading the next section (if you do), my own path in life has been very fragmented in spiritual terms, and the history of my religious identity is unclear. It seems to me that each of us has to chart our path and make sense of it as we can. Perhaps it doesn't matter where our influences and resources come from, perhaps it's OK to make our own tapestry in an eclectic way.

Yet there will be *some who have always known who they are in spiritual or religious terms*, perhaps coming from a family whose provenance like social class and ancestry is known to them – eg. generations of Catholics or Protestants etc. However, even within each religious institution, there is variety – an example of which is made clear in Mary Loudon's interesting set of interviews with Anglicans.

I believe that our spiritual path can be as creative and variegated as it needs to be – and can be *our own* – but I would wouldn't I, coming from a fragmented background. If you have the benefit of a clear religious affiliation, you may be able to see a clear track ahead of you to deepen your spirituality, or you may be wondering if there are things you can do and ideas you can learn from by exploring more widely, learning about other religions and unravelling long-held beliefs about people outside your usual community.

The history of religion is one of schisms and wars and changes of directions. Sadly, within the Church of England these days, (where I was christened but never 'confirmed'), these kinds of splits over matters such as gay marriage, gay clergy and women bishops - are proving hard to resolve. Over the decades, differences between Catholics and Protestants, established and non-conformist, Shia and Sunni Muslims, Christians and Muslims, Arabs and Jews etc. have raged. Within countries, whichever group is in the minority or in the less dominant position has often suffered discrimination and exclusion from political office. These days there are often moves to broker peaceful co-existence as an alternative to the exacerbation of difference which can be fuelled by.external parties whom it suits to have conflict rather than positive action - we need always to look at motives both in action and in the presentation and interpretation of action. Being open to people of all different faiths and of none is a sign of confidence in our own path.

What follows is my own journey through spirituality and religion – which illustrates the variegated approach to all these matters.

My relationship to spirituality

I was christened in the Church of England and for most of my childhood believed that this was my basic affiliation, although rarely went to church. I went sometimes to Sunday-school. Going to church for a wedding or ritual event, my father used to giggle and make faces – I learned not to take things in the church service too seriously. Years later, as I neared my fifties, it began to emerge that the history of the family was not as simple as this kind of tenuous Anglicanism. It appeared that my maternal grandparents were non-conformist chapel-goers, lived simply, and were committed to pacifism, plain speaking, temperance and trade unionism. My father's parents were in business and ran a pub, and it transpired later, may have had some links with Judaism.

465

With such contrasting backgrounds, my parents' marriage was more or less bound to be turbulent and my life likely to be involved with questions of diverse views and the mediation of conflict.

When I was around 30, I met my first husband on a counselling training programme. During the four years we were together, he introduced me to his work and practice in Tibetan Buddhism and many people congregated at our house for teachings and meditations. I met Buddhist teachers and went on some retreats, but I remained a guest/observer rather than an adherent, not convinced that I wanted to fully participate, particularly as I couldn't connect culturally with it. I learned quite a bit from my husband (and others) about the nature of mind – for example, the idea that there may be fewer distinctions between our waking, sleeping and after-death states than we tend to think – they may be part of a single continuum of consciousness, and this can help us with detaching from things and people in our life since everything in one sense can be experienced as an ongoing dream-state rather than as a solid reality that we can cling onto. Certainly through meditation and the observation of thoughts arising and dissolving in my mind, I came to appreciate the transitory nature of everything – an insight that was of course prescient of all the changes that were to follow in my life.

There were many I met during that time who were very sincere in their spiritual journeys but it was a good lesson in not being too idealistic about spirituality. I saw people – as there are in any spiritual community - who sought to gain power, money, influence and identity in that world – I hasten to add that I don't think these motives are specific to Buddhism, although the tendency to 'guru-worship' can be strong there because spiritual practice depends on getting teachings from specific Teachers. It was just that that was when I first stopped having illusions about spirituality - it's too easy to think that because something is labelled 'spiritual' or even 'psychological' that it's somehow going to be free from the usual problems that beset other kinds of organisations and groups. Around that time (late 1980s), I also went on some American Indian retreats with friends, including sweat lodge ceremonies we ran in the countryside. I liked the way we spent the day building the lodge and the sacred fire, heating the stones for the sauna, and then sat in a circle inside the lodge watching the glowing stones, telling stories and experiencing the true closeness of a group.

Becoming anxious to define where I did stand spiritually, I chose to attend local Quaker meetings and went to the Quaker UK retreat centre in Oxfordshire, Charney Manor, and to Woodbrooke College in Birmingham. This was the first decision I had ever made myself to follow a spiritual path, and I liked the non-hierarchical approach and felt the power of regular silence in my life. In particular I valued the regular accounting to myself for how I was living, a kind of review of my spiritual life every Sunday (something of course that people across the globe do, but in Quakerism, this was not defined by a priest or intermediary). However, when my life went into crisis, I withdrew from Quakers – which in retrospect seems a pity – I should have felt it to be an opportunity to reach out for support.

With my second husband, I had a daughter and as she got older, agreed for her to start attending a local Catholic primary school, as it seemed to have a strong pastoral element and it was my husband's preferred choice. Although uncertain that I wanted anything to do with the church, I was warmed by the welcome I got from the then pastor, who created services that encouraged and recognised the role of mothers in their children's lives, including celebrating Mother's day with candles and flowers. This touched me because at that time, I had to work away from home a tremendous amount and found it quite painful to relate to my role as a mother. I was surprised by the lack of emphasis on theology and the belief in the power of love that that pastor talked about.

In the last year of my husband's life, it became clear that spiritualism was important to him, and I also recognised that he had experienced a broken line to a Jewish heritage in his family background. I was very lucky in the hospital chaplain I found who was willing to conduct a funeral service that was both broadly Christian and acknowledged this Jewish element.

In my 50s, I discovered that both my paternal and maternal grandfathers may well have been Jewish; probably coming to

Britain in the late 19th century pogroms, but any Jewish heritage was suppressed and never mentioned. In recent times, I have started looking at how Judaism in my distant family history might be influencing my personal psychology, how I am processing the events of the last century, and what it means to have a significant part of my family history destroyed or hidden.

As I got more involved in academic work, and coped with the loss of several key people in my life and the disorientation and worry of losing my home too, I guess it became easy to think that there was no God looking after me. Indeed, at times, as the darkness of my life deepened, I sometimes felt that conversely, (and superstitiously), I might be being punished by a God for the life choices I had made (living an unconventional life, failing to adhere to a spiritual path etc). During some of the most painful times, I remember thinking consciously that suffering had its own value and that there was an enriching and deepening of myself through *what I was experiencing. I did not rush out looking for distraction – I went deep into the experiences and learned what I could learn from them. Conscious that my daughter had lost her father, I took her to Aberfan, South Wales and showed her the graves of children and teachers (144 people died in the coal-tip disaster in October 1966) and said, look there,* you are not the only person to lose someone! *Brutal perhaps – and of course, I was also speaking to myself. It seemed to me that only in our connection to the wider perspective on death can we get a handle on our own sense of being bereft.*

During this time I went to a large inter-faith event, at which representatives of different religions each had time on the stage. Although it was a joyful meeting with dancing, drumming, singing etc., it struck me that the meaning of spirituality had got lost in what had been turned into a series of cultural displays. Furthermore, the meeting was addressed by local dignitaries including the local chief of police and it seemed to me that the idea of inter-faith had been hi-jacked as a vehicle for the management of inter-racial relations in the city, perhaps a laudable aim but not what the inter-faith initiative was in my mind, really meant to be for.

Slowly, people came into my life including some I already knew who showed me much kindness, and some who were new to me, but accepted me even though my life was in free-fall. I learned that for a while, I was finding it difficult to run my life by myself – I needed the support of others to get me through. As part of the process of receiving help from others, I lost a sense of privacy – people folded laundry for me, looked after my daughter whilst I went to work, cooked meals for us, helped to pack and unpack my possessions each time I moved home, sat with me whilst I faced up to debts and the need for budgeting, mended my broken toilet and bed, categorised all my books, listened to my sorrows, gave me health advice and encouraged me to start internet dating. It was a huge shock to find that my lifelong sense of independence and capability was in question and that I was now in need of others' ministrations. I was touched by others' compassion – a kind of unconscious spirituality in action by each of them. But it also meant that I received much advice about how I should live. I had a sense of somehow having gone wrong on 'the path', as if the life journey should always be about onwards and upwards, about measured change and predictable success, and that somehow the unfortunate events in my life were obscurely the result of my living unwisely.

When I met Jack, he remarked upon a sense of my spirituality, which involved openness to others that I hadn't perhaps given myself credit for. Whilst accepting that I do respond to people in a loving way, I am also now learning that it is perfectly OK to draw boundaries again around my life and to claim back my space for me. This is a complex spiritual task – to decide when and where to be receptive to people, to be both grateful for the help I have received and to try to be reciprocal, and yet to protect my own time for development, looking after myself and family, engaging in creative and spiritual work. Sometimes, people who have 'rescued' me don't feel comfortable with me doing anything to change the balance of the direction of giving, and that has been a painful lesson to learn, sometimes resulting in relationships that cannot continue, and sometimes meaning that I need new people in my life who don't remember me during the time when I was in trouble. Others have weathered the storm of change and remain in my life. These are tricky issues that I think any church or community has to manage, particularly as people often turn to them when they are vulnerable.

I have a strong sense of having been 'in the wilderness' and having returned from it, aware that there are further difficult times ahead - some I can anticipate and some I can't and I have to build my inner resources for those times. I am changed by the experiences of my life, and by my awareness of the relentless cruelty of life. I need too to be thankful for the good things in life.

Over the years, I've met a variety of people who are (neo-) pagans and shamans – I like the way in which for some, spiritual practice is integrated with political consciousness and activism – particularly on ecological matters and our stewardship of the earth - as, for example, in the work of Starhawk. *I like the way that psychology can permeate spirituality, and that understanding how a community works might be important in resolving* individual *conflicts. I believe that we should always remain in touch with political realities and where we can, work through political channels to help the world.*

I realise that long-held truths in any field of endeavour that I look at – medicine, psychology, finance, cooking, for example – can all be questioned. Most of my life I've been told that there is only one God. It's refreshing to look again at even that idea and ask myself if I believe that, if I think there is any externalised God, if it might be that there are many spirits - in trees, flowers, mountains, the sun and the moon, and also to reflect on the spirits of those I have known who've died yet who continue on within me, with their voices and beliefs and habits and achievements – and who can still divide or bring people together long after their earthly life is over.

If religious institutions are standing up for people rather than servicing the structures of the political élites, then I think their existence is important for us all. They have an opportunity to be part of the great changes that are happening across the globe and to help us all find our way in the challenges that face us. The Church of England had to cross this kind of rubicon when members of the Occupy movement camped outside St Paul's Cathedral – individuals in the church were divided about where they stood, and the lack of cohesion among senior members of the church was testament to the fragility of its spiritual mission. Although monuments like great cathedrals and even tiny 'listed' chapels are wondrous and awesome, my feeling is that we are entering a time when if necessary we should ditch the investments in property and develop a religion that can be shared on hill-tops and in the street and in our homes.

With Jack, I've had to address again the question of spirituality in a more rigorous way. Even when I've felt sure rationally that there was no God I've nevertheless often wanted to call upon a fantasy God when in trouble and have often felt that my life was about a kind of retribution from a wrathful God. I was always postponing any idea of reconciling with God, not sure I could make any kind of commitment and totally against any kind of dogma or human control system. Often I haven't liked the aesthetic culture of religious ritual – fonts and altars, robes and incense, bells and drums, daggers and trumpets. Fire and water have always seemed the purest so I light candles for the dead and happily go to a fire ceremony by the sea to celebrate a friend's PhD.

I find that I no longer support a clear division between the secular and the spiritual – if we take 'spiritual' to imply many of the good qualities discussed in this and the next chapter in this book, I'm not sure if it matters whether or not someone 'believes' in a spirit world. To me, the spirits are often symbols for material in our minds and hearts – whether they 'exist' or not is not the crucial issue, and whether we believe 'power' is outside us or inside us doesn't necessarily make a big difference to the result.

I find myself unhappy with oppressive or aggressive presentations of religion or secularism despite often useful critiques in their messages, and feel reinforced in a belief about the importance of something kind, something that speaks to all creatures, something that reaches out across the religious and political and cultural dogma across the globe and connects us in resistance to authoritarianism, connects us in the joint project of environmental stewardship, connects us in the project of fighting suffering, oppression, egotism and cruelty wherever we find it, connects us in building a world of connection.

As an exercise, write a page or more about your own spiritual path.

Checklist

Do I need to make a choice between engagement within a religious institution and finding my own spiritual path or are they compatible?
Have I looked at philosophy and how it can help eg. in recognising the difference between my own and others' ideas, or notions of the self and of phenomena?
Am I in touch with my spirituality as a *felt* thing, not as something cognitive?
Have I started avoiding conversations that are trivialising or attacking because logic may not be an appropriate tool for understanding spirituality?
Do I need to split off from the pressures of daily life (perhaps by going on retreat), or can I integrate my spirituality with my daily life, do I need to make changes in the way I live?
Am I safeguarding my spiritual life, practising spiritual discernment eg. being selective about activities and people?
Can I build quality into my life, take time, establish order, reflect, talk deeply?
What sort of spiritual *persona* do I want to have and am I ensuring this does not take over the real issues? Can I be authentic and real, and not false and 'perfect'?
Are there any Inspiring figures I want to learn from?
Can I practise equality, not morality?
Can I set suffering in a wider perspective than simply that of my own life?
What is my idea of God –how much (if anything) is separate from the self/how much emanates from within; do I want to select a personal god from a pantheon, etc?
Can I 'add' something to the earth during my lifetime?
Can I be happy/content, find the joy in life; or do I need to tackle my own depression or reduce negative inputs from the external world?

Books for interest and inspiration:

Tsultrim Allione (2000) (2nd ed) *Women of Wisdom* Snow Lion Publications

Karen Armstrong (1981, 1995) *Through the Narrow Gate* Harper Collins/Flamingo

Karen Armstrong (1986) *The Gospel According to Woman* Harper Collins/Fount

Karen Armstrong (1993) *A History of God* London: Vintage Books (also later book in 2006)

Martine Batchelor (2007) *Let go – a Buddhist Guide to Breaking Free of Habits* Wisdom Publications

J G Bennett (1992) *The Way To Be Free* Maine: Samuel Weiser

Diana Butler Bass (2001) *A People's History of Christianity: The Other Side of the Story* HarperOne

Julia Cameron (1993) *The Artist's Way: a course in discovering and recovering your creative self* Pan Books

Church of England   http://www.churchofengland.org/about-us/facts-stats.aspx

Don Cupitt (2003) (3rd revised edition) *The Sea of Faith* SCM Press

Mary Daly (1973) *Beyond God the Father* The Women's Press

Ann Edwards (2010) *How to Nurture Spiritual Development* Blue Ocean Publishing

Albert Einstein (1931) *Living Philosophies* New York: Simon and Schuster

Erik Erikson (1998 ed) *The Life Cycle Completed: A Review* W W Norton

Christopher Hitchens (2007) *God is Not Great* London: Atlantic Books

Stephen A Hoeller (2002) *Gnosticism: New Light on the Ancient Tradition of Inner Knowing* Quest Books

Immanuel Kant (1781, 2007 translation) *Critique of Pure Reason* Penguin Classics

Karl Jaspers and Michael Bullock (tr.) (1953) *The Origin and Goal of History* London: Routledge and Keegan Paul

Paul Johnson (2001) *A History of the Jews* Orion/Phoenix

Paul Johnson (1980 ed) *A History of Christianity* Pelican

Brother Lawrence (1981) *The Practice of the Presence of God* Hodder and Stoughton

Mary Loudon (1994) *Revelations: the Clergy Questioned* Penguin Books

Diarmaid MacCulloch (2010) *A History of Christianity: The First Three Thousand Years* London: Penguin

Alistair McGrath (2011) *Why God Won't Go Away: Engaging with the New Atheism* SPCK Publishing

Alistair McGrath (2007) *The Dawkins Delusion: Atheist Fundamentalism and the Denial of the Divine* SPCK Publishing

Kristin Madden (2005) *Exploring the Pagan Path: Wisdom from the Elders* new Page Books/Career Press

Alice Miller (1990) *The Untouched Key: Tracing Childhood Trauma in Creativity and Destructiveness* Virago Press

Bel Mooney (2003) *Devout Sceptics: Conversations on Faith and Doubt* Hodder and Stoughton

Cole Moreton (2010) *Is God Still An Englishman?* Abacus

Klaus F Riegel *The dialectics of human development* American Psychologist, Vol 31(10), Oct 1976, 689-700.

Soyen Shaku (tr. by Suzuki) *Zen for Americans: Sermons of a Buddhist Abbot* www. forgottenbooks.org

Philip Sheldrake (2012) *Spirituality: A Very Short Introduction* Oxford

John Shelby Spong (2011) *Re-Claiming the Bible for Non-Religious World* HarperOne

Baruch Spinoza (tr. Edwin Curley) (1996) *Ethics* Penguin Books

Starhawk (1982) *Dreaming the Dark: magic, sex and politics* Boston: Beacon Press

St. John of the Cross (1972 ed) *The Poems of St John of the Cross* New Directions Publishing

Richard Tarnas (1991) *The Passion of the Western Mind* Random House/Pimlico Books

Andrew Wheatcroft (2004) *Infidels: A History of the Conflict between Christianity and Islam* London: Penguin Books
http://jewishchristianlit.com/Texts/dss.html

16 values

In this chapter, we consider the place of religious and secular approaches to life, including how political institutions in the past have been glad of religion to absorb and mute people's frustrations and potential rebellion and how conversely the attack on spirituality in today's world feeds into justifications for a value-less culture in which science, technology and bureaucracy rule and people are treated without empathy, kindness or respect. We consider the question of values that are external to us or internally-generated and maintained, asking questions about our cultural and political leaders, and about the value (if any) attached to 'suffering'. We look too at how we might treat each other in social relations, including the way we might look at questions of truth, lying, loyalty, kindness, fairness and love in our personal relationships and reverence for life itself and whether we can find any anchors in a world which has been dominated in the last few decades by the fluidity and contingencies of post-structuralist thinking.

This chapter is written by Julia with a response from Jack towards the end.

Why bother to be a 'morally conscious' human being?

In the terms put forward by the philosopher Immanuel Kant, exercising our moral duty (eg. by working for the good of society or of specific others, making ethical choices etc), is the main indicator of our dignity as human beings. Being a morally conscious and ethical human being is possible when we have *autonomy*; being *'unfree'*, we can't give full consent or make proper choices, which is why for example, we don't see children as capable of acting fully in their own right and adult advocates or guardians are often needed in legal cases.

As we shall see elsewhere in this book, the question we think of is one of *how* we engage with a level of experience that we call 'spirituality' but which for some is simply living by humanist or secular values - and whether we're able to discern human power-mongering and pressure to conform to accepted 'truths' in any religious teaching or institutional rule-making, and whether we find support and strength in our spiritual life, or the guidelines on living that we follow and through connection with others for positioning ourselves within society.

There have always been plenty of people who criticise religion from an external value position, such as the left-wing and anarchist critics of the past: Emma Goldman, international anarchist and political activist, writing in her *Mother Earth* journal of 1913, claimed that rulers use religion to protect against 'rebellion and discontent' – she believed that religion is a mechanism far more potent than military or policing measures.

There are plenty of writers who follow the idea (most often credited to Marx) that religion is the *'opium of the people'* – Lenin, writing in 1905 also believed that workers were encouraged by religion to be *'submissive and patient'* whilst pinning their hopes on a *'heavenly reward'*.

Towards the end of the twentieth century, in contrast, Starhawk writes lucidly about how she's engaged in political activism from a base within her spiritual path - the Wicca tradition, which through the lens of stewardship of the planet has included opposing nuclear power.

Dietrich Bonhoeffer, a Christian pastor put to death by Hitler, believed that Christians had a duty to oppose evil through 'direct action'. Bonhoeffer didn't follow German Christian fellows into collaboration with the Nazi regime; he stood out against the regime and worked subversively to overthrow and kill Hitler.

Humanist social activists have played a key part in fighting for human rights and ensuring that global affairs are guided by organisations like the United Nations. Quakers have played a part in conflict resolution and mediation in the world.

The point is that we have choices about how we position ourselves even within the institutions we find ourselves part of or choose to join.

Raising consciousness, 'grand narratives' and the significance of knowledge

One of the difficulties in engaging with a sense of who we are and how we position ourselves in the world is related to *epistemology* – the study of knowledge. Jean-François Lyotard, a philosopher writing in the 1970s and 80s, suggests that (aided by new technology) knowledge has become a commodity which is bought and sold. Knowledge is no longer about truth, but about marketability. Who owns knowledge or controls access to it has become a major issue in modern life, and it's becoming something that will be fought about in the way that land and physical resources like oil and money used to be.

Lyotard writes about the *'grand narrative of emancipation'* the idea that has been very prevalent in shaping our Western world, that *knowledge liberates people* – i.e. that people will be free if they understand the mechanisms of how they are oppressed. Political activists such as those inspired by Marxism, feminism and post-colonialism have usually believed that *'raising consciousness'* among people is the necessary requisite for protest, change and revolution. This particular 'grand' or 'meta'- narrative' has been the justification for education, for science, and for writing books like this one.

Meta-narratives
knowledge liberates people
the progress of history
the knowability of everything by science
the possibility of absolute freedom

Jean-François Lyotard argues that we've lost our belief in the idea that one theoretical position can possibly *account for* or *fuel change in* or *define* huge numbers of diverse human beings. Overarching ideologies and definitions are usually created and promoted by those in power seeking to enforce a regime and cannot be simply mapped onto the chaos that is human life on the planet without a struggle – clearly we won't all accept the same model or answer, so inevitably there's conflict as a particular group tries to impose the prevailing 'narrative' on the population.

Moreover, we find our ethical stance in each particular situation, not in abstract conceptual notions of principles such as *justice*.

For Jean-François Lyotard, the method of resistance is to *develop more and more micro-narratives. 'Disruptive critique', 'avant-garde art'* and *'small, local narratives'* are effective challenges to the great overarching project of capitalism. In the 'post-structuralist world' that he believed in, diverse and multiple perspectives are the norm, there's no one definite answer or agreed perception of anything. Of course, this could also be a new 'grand narrative'!

However, not everyone is disillusioned with capitalism. Whilst it may be difficult to defend recent malpractice and greed in the financial systems, this doesn't necessarily mean that capitalism isn't the best system for the world, with its harshest outcomes softened through benevolent welfare policies for the most vulnerable; its messages of hope, freedom, democracy, equality; its support for individual endeavour and enterprise; and its challenge to the cruelties that can prevail in some non-capitalist dictatorships.

Are we making progress?

Martin Seligman, author of *Flourish* and proponent of positive psychology, tots up the positives that we've achieved in the twentieth century which he believes includes improvements to healthcare and survival rates and stronger challenges to injustice.

However, reviewing the *United Nations Millennium Development Goals* for 2015, the fight against poverty and hunger in the world is not a story of unremitting success. Whilst the world *is* building towards sustainable outcomes for the environment and for its people, a number of challenges to progress continue to hamper development such as increasing population (with the resultant increase in absolute numbers of the poor) and the world financial and economic crisis. Food prices are not being controlled, the

478

spread of HIV is not under control, climate-related disasters affect agricultural production, and increasing urbanisation of some populations brings new social challenges.

Whatever our views, the point is to look clearly and deeply into how things are presented to us and to seek to understand how things work and what contribution we wish to make, remaining sceptical and cautious about overarching abstract ideas.

Are there any truths?

In any case, perhaps inspired by Frederic Nietzsche's statement that *'there are no facts, only interpretations'*, during the twentieth century, a number of philosophers have attacked the idea that there is any immutable or fundamental truth.

Richard Rorty, for example, suggests that we do not need any kind of absolute moral law for us to live ethically – in conversation and community with others, we can formulate good ways of living with each other and contributing to the world within each specific situation that presents itself, and based on wide consultation with others.

Whether we agree with this, or prefer the idea that we should have an agreed and shared code of ethics that anchors us and guides our actions and decisions, isn't necessarily the issue. Perhaps what matters is *our intent* to live life ethically, and to challenge whenever orthodoxies and the interpretation of policy and guidelines threaten to stifle life energy, propagate injustice and suppress dissent.

One of the criticisms of following a religious path from secular critics is that religion exhorts us to look to the 'next life' rather the one here on earth and that this is *'life-denying'* rather than *'life-affirming'*. Religion can get us seeking something that transcends the sufferings of this life, which can at times seem attractive, particularly if we are trapped in situations – in a *gulag* or prisoner-of-war camp or suffering from an intractable disease.

There may be times when to immerse ourselves in spiritual experience as a way of disengaging from seemingly intractable troubles or reaching out for bigger energy beyond that which is available to us as individuals (perhaps when suffering from fatigue, responsibilities, burdens, incapacities or a sense of powerlessness) is a sensible investment to make.

However, on the down side, religion can provide the justification for accepting our circumstances such as lower social and economic class positions (such as within the caste system in India or within the British class system) and hold us back from protest or opposition or from making positive life changes.

It's important that we don't avoid facing up to the realities of life, because to do so reflects a more healthy state of mind and because there might be things we *can* do about situations that could bring us more happiness and more of a sense of human potency than we are getting from closing our eyes, and because the more of us that do so, the better the world could become. Being too positive in our thinking can blind us from looking at painful things squarely in the face.

But it is *not* an *'either-or'* choice – spirituality can fuel our political energy, and political activity can be a spiritual path, if it is infused with a love for our fellow humans and a commitment to looking after the planet for the next generation.

Although our connection to spiritual energy may wax and wane as we go through life, spirituality isn't something that we should necessarily pick up and put down whenever it suits us – the idea is to engage with an energy that remains with us through whatever is happening in our life. Spirituality doesn't have to be a rescuer or a 'fair-weather friend' – it can be present at all times.

What about a secular approach?

The National Secular Society emphasises that people have the right not only to be free to choose their religion but also to be free *of* religion. Secular life, whilst its advocates may sometimes seem to be abrasive, offers the possibility of seeing life from an entirely different perspective, without any reference to spirituality. Orthodox religion of any kind provides readymade guidelines for living – once we ditch it, we can find ourselves in a sea of uncertainty and have to decide what values will guide us. There are organisations which can fill the void if we are uncertain about deciding for ourselves.

Roughly speaking, the word humanist has come to mean someone who:

- trusts to the scientific method when it comes to understanding how the universe works and rejects the idea of the supernatural (and is therefore an atheist or agnostic)

- makes their ethical decisions based on reason, empathy, and a concern for human beings and other sentient animals

- believes that, in the absence of an afterlife and any discernible purpose to the universe, human beings can act to give their own lives meaning by seeking happiness in this life and helping others to do the same.

British Humanist Association

Advocates of secularism claim that it offers neutrality and that that is the proper basis for government but some, like the academic Tariq Modood, have questioned the promotion of secularism at the expense of people's spiritual beliefs.

For some peoples, however, the idea of government without spiritual values is unthinkable – Tibetan Buddhists for example. Theodor Adorno is one who reminds us that making judgements (for example in a court of law) without reference to both intellect and emotion is likely to be flawed – we need to balance both reason and feeling in order to live ethically. In Britain, the link between government and the 'established' Church of England is currently being challenged – for example, the practice of having Christian prayers before council meetings has been questioned, the *Occupy London* movement has challenged the Church authorities to put compassion and fairness before its concerns with tourism and church income in the City of London, and as we write, both the Catholic Church and the Church of England are at odds with the government in respect of gay marriage proposals.

It is of course theoretically possible for secular governments to include a balance between intellect and emotion and ethical values without invoking the idea of spirituality, but the history of governments that have outlawed religion does not give us confidence in this regard.

Christopher Hitchens who became a leading spokesperson for *New Atheism*, contended that organized religion is a key source of hatred in the world, being linked to violence, bigotry and coercive attitudes towards women and children. Organised religion may not be able to effectively defend itself against many of these charges but this is not the same as 'spirituality'.

One of the freedoms that secularists particularly value is the freedom to a *self-defined sexuality* without the rulebook that is present in most religious institutions. The point that we make is that *spirituality* too can be self-defined – and is (perhaps troublingly) quite separate from the religious institutions that claim to house it.

The joy of defining *ourselves*, of being *free*

Jean-Paul Sartre, a leading existential thinker, gave the green light for the student protests of 1968 and the hippy movement by proposing that human beings uniquely (eg. as distinct from animals or material objects) have the power and freedom to define themselves. Throw out religion and you have to define yourself. You no longer have a preordained purpose or obligation. You are *free*. But being free is still a challenge, if not a burden in its own right.

In the aftermath of the 1960s, we found nevertheless that everything was not perfect in the hippy paradise. Women felt abused by the concept of 'free love', which, supported by newly available contraception, meant there were few reasons to say no to sex and left them often hurt and bewildered as men were no longer bound by the obligations of commitment and respectability. There were many demonstrations of protest on the streets as well as some breakdown in social order and the beginnings of large-scale use of recreational drugs. Nevertheless, it was very much an era in which authority and tradition were challenged and it broke new ground in sexual freedoms and gender equality.

The joy of suffering

During the 20th century, the development of science and medicine has affected people profoundly. The suffering associated with disease, pain, unwanted pregnancies, sexual dysfunction and shortened lives has been significantly ameliorated through the development and distribution of antibiotics, targeted painkillers, Viagra, HIV medication, synthetic insulin and contraception - to some extent, these have also given us freedom from the consequences of our actions.

It's possible to argue that this era of proliferation of both illegal and prescribed drugs – whilst giving us much greater ease, also gave us higher expectations that life should be free from pain and trouble, and made us less willing and able to bear difficulty and discomfort. This is problematic in spiritual terms because we learn much more from struggle and suffering, and in a life of ease it can become very tempting to distance ourselves from others who are not so fortunate.

As a people, we will always work towards the eradication of things which frighten and hurt us and which affect us negatively against our will like illness – the point is rather how we *interpret* these experiences. The medication which helps us can also mask the deeper elements of our malaise - for example anti-depressants which can dull the reality of difficult life circumstances or painkillers that allow us to ignore worrying physical symptoms - and can result in a failure to address the real causes of our problems.

The developments that have emerged from scientific enquiry have been truly awesome but they should be kept in perspective and scientific thinking should not be allowed to become the dominant discourse; scientists cannot and should not dictate the 'new ethics'.

Self-actualisation

Within the therapy world, the *Human Potential Movement*, led by people like Carl Rogers, Abraham Maslow and latterly, Denise Hay, emanated from the West Coast of America, and offered the belief that we would all naturally evolve towards goodness (organic biological development, just as blossom inevitably becomes fruit), and advocated 'self-actualisation' as the goal, focusing on the further development of the healthy parts of the self rather than looking at pathology.

Available to people across the globe who either work as healing professionals and want to refuel, or to those who can afford to go to California for self-development and healing, there's a wide a range of growth and therapy experiences to be had including: *primal scream, rolfing, tai chi, massage, yoga, rebirthing, bodywork, eco-literacy, self-awareness, couples work, holistic sexuality, encounter groups, constellation work, hypnosis and sound healing*, much of which has now transmuted into (often) more dilute forms in cities across the Western world. However, because of the costs involved and perhaps the culture, many people accessing these therapies are members of a privileged élite and it's taken a long time for humanistic practitioners to shake off the image that their work encourages self-indulgence and self-obsession, despite the fact that much of it has a 'spiritual feel' to it.

The UK philosopher and therapist Emmy van Deurzen, who put the idea of therapy derived from existentialism on the map in Britain, believes that facing up to difficulty and pain at times of challenge gives us an opportunity to engage with deeper questions and 'ultimate concerns', and is in that sense, to be welcomed. The answer does not lie in seeking escape, relief, solace or even self-fulfilment. We need to find a solution that deals with things like meaning and purpose, dilemmas and paradoxes, questions of death and continuity (such as leaving something behind in the world). Van Deurzen believes that facing up to the truth of ourselves and accepting the limitations of the human condition are vital ingredients in authentic living.

The point is that – in our opinion - spirituality is *what we choose it – or find it - to be.* Spirituality is not in itself about attending rituals and wearing funny clothes (though both can be part of it), it's not about easy answers and rapid change. It might come from slow patient waiting or the long hard work of sustained change or 'spiritual discipline'. It might be about developing an inner life, a base of tranquillity that is a resource for the times when things get choppy around us, it might be becoming a discerning person and reducing time spent on things or people that waste our time, it might be finding the courage to speak out and take action to change things, it might be listening to others and helping them to move forward, it might be tapping into something bigger than ourselves and recognising that life is precious and transient, and that death happens to everyone.

So how do we live an ethical life?

Sometimes we can feel that it's impossible to have an effect on the world, or even on people around us.

Sometimes we can feel afraid to stand up for values.

If we have a sense of our self as an ethical person, it becomes easier to assume that everyone else will also behave ethically, and the world can appear less threatening, more logical, predictable. But if we begin to see ourselves differently, if we take steps into unethical behaviour, we will come to believe that others are also capable of same and the world will seem more dangerous. Behaving ethically can reduce a sense of anxiety about the world and make us more confident about tackling problems.

If we fill up our life with material goods as compensation for spiritual and emotional emptiness, if we absorb entertainment and celebrity culture instead of enriching our own inner world, we may ultimately feel uncomfortable with ourselves (if we let ourselves really feel that). If we live in a context of inequality, we will feel a lack of ease about relating to others. If we rarely give out to others, the imbalance will eventually inculcate a sense of guilt (unless we lack any empathy). If we acquiesce or adjust too much to the remit of others, we will feel a sense of disappointment and unhappiness about our lack of authenticity. Eventually we will die unfulfilled unless at some earlier stage, we seek to change the balance.

When we first take those steps to get our life into a better balance, we will be likely to be starting to live more ethically.

Resistance

Conscious awareness of external factors – like the effect of the dominance of big business or of an over-controlling government – can ultimately push us to our limits, and we decide that resistance of one form or another will follow. Such resistance may have taken the form of falling ill, refusing to work, avoiding responsibilities, evading or subverting rules, escapism into porn or violent films, alcohol or drug dependence or being demotivated but we can choose to make proactive choices like joining with others in a trade union, pressure group or political party, in non-violent protest, in developing creative expression, in starting up projects to offer alternatives, or in simply appreciating the small things in life and concentrating on the positives. The pattern of our life, our own ageing processes and perhaps even our male and female qualities will all have their own rhythms which we will have to heed. *Our unconscious self will find the right time for our energy to be released.*

Ethical relating

As well as defining the parameters of our belief or experience such as which gods or higher powers are involved, how exclusively we should worship or honour them, and/or practices such as fasting, prayer, observance of festivals, rituals, charitable donations and acts, vision quests, pilgrimage etc, most religious codes have sought to regulate or guide our relations with other human beings.

The areas that frequently come under the 'remit' of many faiths and spiritual pathways in respect of our relating to people include:

- honesty
- emotional and sexual fidelity
- admonitions not to envy or steal
- attitudes to family and parents
- avoidance of damage to others

Some apply what is called the 'Golden Rule' of reciprocity – that we should *'do as we wish to be done by'*, treat those we come into contact with as we would like to be treated.

In addition to how we relate to human beings, sometimes there is guidance on how we relate to animals, care of ourselves – including our bodies and our health, and how we relate to the planet, and even in some cases to the extra-terrestrial.

However, we're also naturally influenced by a drive towards *'self-interest'*, which can militate against altruism. Much of religious thinking is about how to conquer that drive, how to reduce 'ego' (see relevant section in chapter on *The Self*), and how to work for the good of others as well as taking care of ourselves.

How our values depend on our situation

Social scientists across the world have been mapping values and how they vary across cultures in something called the *World Values Survey*, started in 1981. Their work shows that we tend to develop values in accord with the situation we find ourselves in – they compare the transition to 'industrialised' societies with the transition to 'knowledge' societies. Thus, if we're struggling for basic survival, we are less likely to be able to find the energy for ideals like equality and fairness in our efforts to get essential resources. And in the process of industrialisation, there has been a tendency to move from traditional values of religion, family ties, marriage, national pride etc. to 'secular-rational' values which accept events like relationship breakdown, abortion, euthanasia and suicide without judgement. As a nation becomes more 'knowledge-based', a choice it tends to make when it's more confident about being able to survive, so its members come to value self-expression, including democratic rights, an openness to diversity, care for the environment, and teaching imagination and tolerance to children over and above the 'protestant work ethic'.

However, although in 'knowledge societies' who do have the confidence about survival, sometimes even in a time of plenty, there's been a lack of empathy and philanthropy - the psychological climate having allowed the greedy and the selfish to rise to positions of power and influence and resistance and self-discipline having been softened by material comfort.

It's also possible that following severe wartime conditions or times of deprivation and shortage such as rationing or famine, people go on operating as if survival were at issue, even when life is relatively very comfortable. Martin Seligman's research on *'learned helplessness'* (although controversial in its methods) helped us to understand that even when a punishment is no longer likely, we can go on behaving as if it were (- this opened up a lot of understanding for the treatment of depression).

It also depends on what or who is at stake – for most people, saving our children, partners and close family members will take precedence over anything else. However, there have been cases where men who've invested everything in material gain, when threatened by bankruptcy and insolvency, have killed their wives and children (and themselves), believing perhaps that survival without material resources makes life not worth living, and that their role as a provider (and therefore as a man in their terms) has completely failed.

Values vary across cultures – and the *World Values Survey* has been able to map clusters of values across the globe. The UK and Ireland, Australia, Canada and the US – the English-speaking countries - score high on self-expression and medium on secular-rational values, whilst 'protestant Europe' including Scandinavia, Germany and Switzerland is very high on secular-rational values. North Africa and parts of south Asia are both traditional in value and very survival-oriented.

In contrast to the idea of *'moral relativism'*, we have to accept that there is also *'moral universalism'* – that there are key moral ideas that are universal across all cultures. This kind of idea has underpinned attempts by the United Nations to lay down global policies for example in relation to female circumcision and infibulation (called by its opponents 'genital mutilation'), challenging the idea that the meanings of such rituals in different cultures should make any difference – if something is wrong or in this case, invasive of human rights, then that is so everywhere. However, for many, female circumcision (and male circumcision for that matter) is an important indicator of suitability as a marriage partner and of one's submission to a shared religious orthodoxy, and to legislate against it is to impose a universality that is disturbing for people within that culture.

It can be enormously difficult to legislate on a worldwide basis without steadily eroding the nature of different cultural contexts – for example, the spread of capitalism usually challenges long-term established dictatorships and brings about a push for democratic freedoms.

When we transgress the cultural rules of the context in which we live (eg. neighbourhood, religious group, nation) we're often judged and ostracised. Trying to understand why we may be feeling isolated or rejected by others, we may be able to recognise that somehow we're not playing by the rules of the group of which we've been an apparent member, and this may be the basis of our *'intuitive morality'*. It may lead to us deciding to move away from that context and searching for like-minded people with whom to associate.

Ethics under pressure

When organisations find themselves under economic pressure, fighting for their survival, things such as equality policy, anti-discriminatory practice, human rights, employment protection legislation, trade union rights etc. can go by the board, as if they were 'luxuries' that can be jettisoned at the first sign of difficulty.

But there are always exceptions. The Marriott hotel chain for example remains committed to values in employment strategy, food, and entertainment in their hotels and markets this. The

Ethisphere Institute, a New York-based organisation, compiles a list of the world's most ethical companies to work for. However, being on the list doesn't mean that companies like these are necessarily always immune to challenges over things like hazardous waste, animal testing, and tax avoidance: being large companies makes it both possible and impossible to get it right all the time.

Buying goods always involves us in ethical dilemmas whether we know it or not. Goods which are priced at a level at which is intended to pass on a significant proportion of funds to 'majority world' producers (under 'fair trade' agreements) do not always meet that aim, sometimes resulting in much smaller percentages being given to recipients than consumers imagine. Companies long famous for their ethical stance in bringing cosmetic and toiletry items to the public have nevertheless found that maintaining that ethical hallmark has been difficult at times – for example, the supply of palm oil for beauty products from Colombia was for a time associated with deforestation, affecting natural habitats of wildlife, carbon emissions, and displacement of local farmers.

In recent years, controversy has followed the supply of cut flowers to the West, not least because of the number of air miles involved in transporting them. Following the realisation of abuse of a variety of labour rights for women workers in parts of the flower industry, a number of developments have happened – welfare and gender committees established; stricter pesticide controls; better conditions of work, pay and housing, and organisations like the *Horticulture Ethical Business Initiative* have been established. Other claims are that the flower industry, with its use of fertilisers and pesticides, may be polluting natural resources like lakes which have been habitats for wildlife and tourism attractions, and that the amount of water needed to produce items like flowers for the West is detrimental to countries which are prone to drought and famine.

As Western consumers, we're faced with a bewildering array of ethical dilemmas when we go shopping – and making ethical choices often costs more than products that are brought to us cheaply, for example, clothing made in factories that employ child labour.

The consumer marketplace is the crucible of inequality across the globe – paying more for products that meet ethical standards is a sign of our wish and intention to start equalising things and to stop benefiting from exploitation.

Discrepancy and consistency in our values – why we do particular things

Some recent studies such as that by researchers for Ogilvy and Mather, Graceann Bennett and Freya Williams, have shown discrepancies between people's *overt* ethical behaviours such as buying green products or recycling and other behaviours in their lives, for example letting the water tap run and run when washing-up or cleaning our teeth. Hypotheses for why this may be the case include the idea that if we work hard to demonstrate our 'goodness' credentials, we let slip elsewhere where we're not being observed, or that we do ethical things and buy ethical products to indicate higher social status but are not actually really invested in it. So next time we're tempted to buy a bottle of 'green' washing-up liquid or a pack of recycled toilet rolls, which cost more than the usual products, we need to ask ourselves if we really believe in the moral rightness of doing so or if we're just doing it to show off to the book-club members when they come round.

In their study *Moving Sustainability from Niche to Normal*, Bennett and Williams argue that we need to move away from the 'specialness' of green products to making them feel 'normal' and mainstream. Describing one group as those who feel most guilt about the world in comparison to those who reject green products, they show that our emphasis on 'buying green' is actually putting people off doing the right thing for the planet. Apparently, many people don't actually want to feel different from the norm – for example, because they might associate green products with hippies or with élites that they don't want to join, and in general, they're less persuaded by altruism than by concepts such as fun or hedonism.

So – the call to moral or ethical behaviour doesn't always work because aiming to be the best we can be isn't necessarily everyone's automatic goal.

Is morality to do with reasoning or intuition?

The most famous model of moral reasoning was that developed by Lawrence Kohlberg, suggesting that our *rationality* is the key element in moral action, in other words, that our *thinking about things* is what guides us to be ethical in our behaviour. However, if this were all, we could find that we all could act like people with personality disorders such as narcissism and psychopathy – there would be no feeling for others, no care and concern underpinning our choices – and clearly in healthy individuals, there *is – there is more than simple rationality.*

One of the key points in Lawrence Kohlberg's model of moral development is the progress through stages towards a greater awareness of the impact on others of our actions – allowing us to be guided by a sense of what would be good for everyone. In order to be ethical beings, we need to be aware of how we affect others, and how others might be feeling. This capacity for empathy allows us to be sensitive to other people around us and ultimately to take the bigger decisions such as looking after the planet *for our grandchildren's generation.* One of the ways of training social workers, healthcare professionals and business executives, is to practise role-play, allowing people to imagine how someone else might feel.

In the *social intuition model* of moral thinking, developed by the social psychologist Johnathan Haidt, our moral judgements are reached *intuitively* – rapidly, effortlessly and without any conscious awareness of how we derived them – they're gut feelings and instinctive taboos, similar to aesthetic judgements as when we respond to a painting or a piece of music, we know when something seems to us morally repugnant or disgusting, but we can't usually explain *why*. It might be for example that the analytical psychologist Carl Jung is right about there being a deep universal order to life, experienced through what he calls the 'collective unconscious'. Such judgements stand in contrast to

492

slowly reasoned arguments (usually post-hoc) about the rationality behind our actions, which we might call *cognition.*

The implications of this are that we're not particularly amenable to reasoned persuasion to change our minds. Only a shift in something *social or emotional* could change our view – for example, if someone we love likes something that we don't - such as a particular sexual practice that up to now we've considered abhorrent, or a beloved family member experiences degrading or disgusting symptoms of illness that we would normally wish to avoid, or in a very different situation our son or daughter falls in love with someone from an ethnic group that until now we've rejected or been fearful about – we're faced with the dissonance between our hearts and minds which we have to resolve.

Our moral judgements are also affected by the powerful forces that make us conform to the perceptions and views of others, particularly the wish to avoid conflict and to maintain harmony in social relations. Some of us are simply more attuned to saying right out: *'but momma, he's wearing no clothes!!'*

As we say in the chapter on the unconscious mind, the evidence is accruing for the role of unconscious processing being a very significant part of what guides our actions and feelings. We may be learning to 'read' and understand more of what has hitherto been unconscious, just as we may be becoming a bit more sceptical about logical reasoning.

First, do no harm

In medical ethics, there's a dilemma between acting through *beneficence* – the wish to do good to your patient, and *non-maleficence* – 'do no harm to your patient'. One of the reasons for this has been the enthusiasm in medicine to try things out with good intentions that have nonetheless caused harm to patients. For some enlightening examples of medicine's painful journey through experimentation, see Druin Burch's *Taking the Medicine.*
In life, it might be a good idea to decide to avoid doing damage to anyone in our lives before we give ourselves the role of rescuer or saviour, or requiring ourselves to do good in the world. Are we

sure that we've looked fully at ourselves and have all the prerequisite skills and self-awareness we should have before wading into situations that involve helping people in our lives?

Respect for others

The principle of 'right speech' from Buddhism would seem helpful to us in guiding us not to speak badly of others, to keep confidences and to keep our privileged access to information about people confidential, and to honour people in our life with respect for their privacy and their standing as people. Slagging people off in public does no good to other people's sense of *us* as someone to trust with *their* confidences. I believe we need to keep our counsel on things we know about other people – not just in or out of professional contexts, but in general social life as well. If we do decide to share something about someone to a third party, it should be done with a sense of respect and care for that person and a sensitivity to how that person would feel if they knew they were being described or discussed, and there should be a good reason for doing so, such as our concern and a need to get ideas, guidance, further information or support from others about the situation.

Loyalty

Becoming someone's friend or lover is a significant commitment – it means that at some level, we decide to be loyal to them, even if others criticise them. We decide that because on balance we've already assessed them as being worthy of our loyalty through our knowledge of them over time. It doesn't mean a blind faith in that person – we might recognise that sometimes they're wrong or behave other than we would wish, and we might – in private – decide to take things up with them about this. But our public face is one which supports them and does not side with others against them, let alone mock or joke about them with others. Some people will find this difficult – they may think for example that you stick up for the truth of a situation even if your partner or friend has to be sacrificed. But sacrificing someone who matters to you usually means that someone else in the room matters more to you than the person who's your friend or lover, either because you love them, or because you're connected to them for matters of business, status, group membership etc. which at the time seems to matter more to you than the relationship you think you're part of.

If the 'truth' of an issue really does seem to you to transcend or contradict a value that your friend or partner is espousing, you need to find a way of interposing doubt or an alternative way of looking at things which does not smash through what they have said. Damaging the standing of someone you are with (whether they are present or not) - in a social situation – is a risky enterprise and usually signals that something is not true or right in that relationship.

Much has been written and dramatized about 'fidelity' within sexual relationships. Perhaps the main reason is that 'pillow talk' often can involve being disloyal to the other partner, breaking their confidence, sharing information about them, even laughing about them, and certainly lying to them or hiding something from them. If we can avoid all these elements, then relating sexually or emotionally to someone else doesn't have to be the painful betrayal it often is. If we decide to be with someone else regularly or temporarily etc., we need to make it as respectful of all parties as we possibly can.

Living positively

Surely the measure of us as persons is not *what* happens to us but *how we have responded*. We can choose how we respond; if not at the time, retrospectively. We can steadily make something of what we've gone through, weaving and re-working our life narrative to make sense of things, and finding new things to be glad about and to value.

There are many examples of people who've been able to make contributions to the wider world after going through enormous trauma. Some examples include:

- *Victor Frankl*, psychiatrist and Holocaust survivor, wrote about the importance of 'responsibleness' to counterbalance 'freedom' and the importance of love for human beings

- *Aleksandr Solzhenitsyn* wrote novels exposing across the world Stalin's *Gulag* forced labour-camps where he had been incarcerated

- *Diana, the mother of Suzi Lamplugh* (a British estate agent who disappeared whilst visiting a client) established a trust to educate people about personal safety

- *Maggie Keswick Jencks* who ultimately died of cancer herself, set up Maggie's cancer centres in the UK where design of beautiful and inspiring buildings is seen as a therapeutic tool

- *Jimmy Boyle*, whose violent youth resulted in a life sentence at Glasgow's Barlinnie Prison, later became a writer, speaker, sculptor, husband and father

Albert Schweitzer, who, armed with qualifications in both theology and medicine, chose to run a hospital in the interior of the French African colony, Gabon, came to the conclusion that a vital ingredient for living is the positive 'affirmation of life' - what he later termed **'reverence for life'**. In 1952 he was awarded the Nobel Peace Prize for this philosophy, and gave perhaps his most famous speech relating to this *The Problem of Peace* in 1954. Once we recognise our own will to live, we're able to be respectful of others' will to live, including non-human creatures, and this principle he saw as a vital element in anyone's ethical code for living. It's more than just our own will to live, it's the will to live amongst others who have the will to live. Thus we need to be able to foster the wellbeing of others around us in order for ourselves to feel that life is worthwhile – it's not OK to selfishly pursue our own fulfilment regardless of the situation of others around us.

Schweitzer saw the ability to *refrain* from killing and damage to others or to the earth – an idea developed from Indian Jainism – as a key spiritual element. We should struggle less to *do* something in the world and a bit more *not* to do certain things. Schweitzer campaigned until his death for the abolition of nuclear weapons. The key is to live life with a sense of awareness about everything we do.

Life gives us chances every day to respond differently from yesterday, to make good what we got wrong before, to start living anew each day. We can live *as if* we can find life worthwhile, *as if* we can make a positive contribution to the world or even just to someone in our life with whom we have contact, even if that has narrowed down to our child or our carer.

Investing in ourselves, daring to believe in a future and in our capacity as human beings to continue to make the world a better place, are things we can do that are transformative and inspiring.

Appreciation

Writers on 'happiness' such as the philosopher Sissela Bok and the psychologist Martin Seligman, emphasise the value of concentrating fully on what we're doing in the present, fully *'engaging'* as a route to personal satisfaction and vibrancy. We can teach ourselves to appreciate what's around us, to take care with everything that we do, making every action worthwhile and every production or transaction of high quality. We can train ourselves to *notice* what others do in the world and *express gratitude and recognition to others* for the things that they do in our lives or in the world. This isn't just about feeling good ourselves – it's about living more deeply, giving attention to people and things around us, and ultimately putting good into the world.

Truth

We've come into a time when post-structuralist thinking, expressed by authors such as Michel Foucault, Jacques Lacan and Judith Butler, developed during the mid-20th century, has cracked open much of our thinking. In a post-structuralist world, there are no absolutes, there is no truth. Things mean what they mean through their juxtaposition to other things. Thus 'happiness' means something when it is contrasted with 'great misery' – for example in someone who has just been released from imprisonment or slavery – and something different when compared with 'security', 'boredom', 'pleasure'. Things become *'relative'*.

Thus someone who asks us if we love them gets an answer that is 'relative' – *do I love you more than anyone else I've ever known? do I love you more than my child, my parents, my God? do I love you differently from my closest friend(s)? do I love you more than the money I can earn by taking a high-level job? do I love you more than the alcohol or porn sites I am addicted to? do I love you now but might someone else next year? do I love you now but would stop loving you if you were 'unfaithful'?*

Outside this way of thinking, we might be able to answer absolutely, *'yes I love you'* without qualification.

In post-structuralist terms, it's not just our answer that matters but also what the other person hears or *thinks* they hear from us – *yes you love me absolutely,* or *you love me conditionally, you love me for my money or my ability to look after you etc.* Any communication is made up of a number of reference points that are not all clear or articulated, and some which will only become clear retrospectively. *I now realise that you thought you loved me but actually you weren't really free to love me; I now realise when you said you loved me, you didn't have the faintest idea how that would be tested or what would be demanded of you, you thought it would be easy...etc.*

We have to decide what the best way to proceed is and where our truth resides.

Lying

Sissela Bok, the philosopher, who wrote a ground-breaking book on 'lying', suggests that lying is for 'free-riders' who rely on everyone else telling the truth and *believing* that everyone is telling the truth. If everyone told lies, nothing would have any meaning. She also considers that we need to think about how we would feel if *we* were lied to, the idea being that lying is part of a system of communication that on the surface – officially - is about truthful statements.

In modern society, we no longer trust the media or politicians with any confidence, and increasingly we're unsure whether we can trust professionals – *is that doctor under pressure from the pharmaceutical company to prescribe this drug? did that nurse really get it wrong in my care or should I believe them that what happened was a random or unlucky event? is this lawyer hurrying my case along because they're eager to get their money or do they genuinely think that's the best thing to do? is this priest or teacher really pleased with my singing or are they interested in me sexually? has this plumber really mended the pipework or did they just do a cover-up job?* It's become very difficult to rely on statements from anyone in such a climate, and we have to be very careful about how much we're prepared to trade integrity in personal relationships as well as how much we're prepared to go along with institutional falsities, propping up regimes that have traded away their moral basis (if they ever had one).

At what stage in a relationship do we start undermining the truth – is it in the way we present ourselves when we first meet? At what stage do we start to *'come out'* about the truth of what or who we are? It can be difficult to come back from a lie, and the pain of that position may be something that we're so keen to avoid that we commit ourselves to always telling the truth. If we have particular conditions or truths about ourselves such as sexual identity, a hidden disability like epilepsy and diabetes, or a history that includes a 'spent' criminal conviction etc. we're confronted frequently with situations where we have to decide whether to 'pass' or to tell. Sociologists have long been interested in how we make these kinds of choices including Erving Goffman and more recently, Graham Scambler, who's looked at the issue of 'stigma' in health conditions.

Or we may decide that we have to set an example to our children, yet find ourselves unwilling to tell them the truth about their other parent fearing it might damage them or the relationship between parent and child. We're unsure whether to tell the school our child is ill when they need a day off for fear of letting our child think that 'white lies' are OK, because we don't want them to lie to *us*. There are no simple answers in the realm of ethical relating.

We need to give careful thought to what we consider to be lying – the construction of our *persona* (see section in chapter on *The Self*) may be designed to deceive or convince others that we are something more than we are or than we feel. Sometimes pushing ourselves forward, trying to be confident, showing off about what we have or have done may be false, hiding our real inner feelings of insecurity, uncertainty and diffidence. We may be successful in this presentation, hoodwinking others that we are this charming, confident and successful person, but we won't gain the intimacy and trust with others that could bring deeper satisfaction.

On the other hand, we may feel that we have to try to 'fit in' in a society that relies on and demands these kinds of presentation. We may think that we need to project this *persona* to attract people to us but that our real self can come out over the longer-term.

We make our choices.

Being truthful to ourselves

There's also the question of being truthful to ourselves as well as to others. It might be a good idea to push ourselves to find our own inner truth – deconstructing our dreams, catching our 'Freudian' slips, noticing any self-sabotage, feeling our feelings in our bodies, monitoring our physical reactions, watching what we actually *do* rather than what we *say* etc.

If we can become independent from others, reliant only on ourselves for our self-perceptions and our own 'strokes' – giving ourselves praise and recognition for our efforts, we're more likely to arrive at accurate perceptions and viewpoints because they will not dependent on conforming to those of others. This brings us towards a sense of integrity.

In today's society, it's important to understand the world we live in and the lies about it that confront us every day. At the moment, critical abilities are not particularly valued; there is a backlash against intelligentsia, whereas there *is* an emphasis on doing well and gaining status, particularly through the spending of money. In order to keep up with others, many of us are having to work extra hard and take on debt. We're replacing the love we need from others with material objects, accepting material rewards in exchange for rarely sitting down for a meal together, or being there when our children come home from school. We believe – and want to believe – that our parents – and along with them, alternative parent figures (such as people in government) are effective authorities, wise and mature, even when the evidence contravenes that. When this obscures that we ourselves have our own wisdom, we've lost our own power.

Love

How do we give love? Is it in being a truthful and forthright companion or is it in flattering someone's ego and letting them think they're marvellous? Do we tell our children that they're great even when we personally doubt their choices or the standard of what they're producing? Do we insist on loving ourselves so that we can be inspirational to others, or do we meet someone's else's every need, convinced this will bind them to us, or because we believe in fostering their talent more than cultivating our own? What exactly does love mean? Over time, most would agree that there should there be a balance of reciprocity.

Most observers of close relationships also comment on power and the need to neutralise it eg. by finding a way of equalising things. Love flourishes when given freely – coercion and fear tend to destroy it, although we may comply with delivering loving behaviour, or in some cases, feel bonded through emotional pain (and even as some of us do, through physical violence). We're all familiar with the tendency to right balances by inviting back people who have entertained us or giving gifts – and if a partner looks after us for a long period of time or provides childcare or housework etc. we may often seek to repay that in later months or years by doing something similar for them. Even if we're not balanced in terms of wealth or strength or education, we should find ways of supporting our partners proportionately – it's not good to make a habit of taking without communicating clear appreciation of what the other person offers. The 'stroke' economy is relevant here – letting someone we love know that we value what they are doing – even if that's the most obvious things like taking out the rubbish or earning a living – not taking them for granted is very important.

Perhaps one of the most important aspects of love is acceptance of another person, 'warts 'n all'. No human being can ever be the fantasy lover or companion of our imagination (if we still do this) – we need to learn to love and value the person who is *in front of us*.

If we can't, we'll need to decide what to do – such as accept and communicate that the relationship is not based on love, or leave the relationship behind. Love is a process, not a once-and-forever moment – although we may in a single moment realise that we love someone, we have to go on making that realisation a reality over time.

Kindness

One of the most significant values we can have is an intention to treat others kindly – go the extra mile, respond sensitively to their distress, help when they need support, give praise and encouragement and recognition, accept apologies, show interest in their projects, listen when they need to talk, act thoughtfully in relation to what they need (eg. by giving them a gift that is carefully chosen for them) , introduce them to people who might be good links for them, invite them into our home, share childcare etc. Clearly we can't be kind in these ways to everyone we meet, because we'd run out of time and energy for our own lives, but the general intention to speak warmly and thoughtfully to people may be appropriate.

How do we balance such kindness with the need to ensure our self-esteem isn't dented by bad behaviour on the part of others (eg. from narcissistic or angry people)? Being kind doesn't mean being a walkover for people with exploitative personality traits or taking a victim position in relation to others who are aggressive or competitive or elitist etc. Perhaps kindness is best expressed through seeing people clearly for what they are and being honest with ourselves (and sometimes to them) about our ability to reach them and to have any impact.

We need to be kind to ourselves as well, and not use the value of general kindness as a way of avoiding being assertive in our own right and standing up for ourselves. We can be discerning about whom we offer our kindness to and on what occasions. It doesn't mean rescuing others from their fate.

We can remind ourselves of the moments in our life when others have been kind to us, and how such unexpected moments leave us with a feeling of belief in human nature and hope for the future. Armed with such memories (and if we don't have any, we may be taking things a bit too much for granted), we can ourselves join the human race and make our own contributions.

Damage and reparation

Recognising that we've damaged others through our behaviour, we can decide to do something about it. There's usually something that can be done – an apology, a gift, an explanation, a phone-call, a letter, a meeting – even if we don't know what we might say. Just being there, however diffidently, might be enough. We can tap into our unconscious and wait intuitively for the right things to emerge in any renewed contact. If we can't find a practical method (if for example, someone doesn't want to see us any more), we can send our wishes for healing into the ether – as in prayer or affirmations – believing that our longing for repair can somehow reach the other person and create change.

Changing *ourselves* is always the first step – understanding why we hurt someone, what motivated us and why we weren't connected or loving enough to avoid doing whatever we did to them. This doesn't mean that we blame the other person – sometimes as for example in a sexual or emotional relationship, love wasn't really there in the first place or it dwindled or faded or was neglected and died. If we had our own difficulties in being ready for a relationship, or believed there was something or someone better out there, or we wanted something else in our life (like a career opportunity or a change of sexual identity), or we responded to someone else in our life whom we (also) loved, or our own 'demons' from our past were triggered etc. we need to face up to these 'truths' and use the process of doing so to prepare us for living more authentically and with greater self-awareness in the future. We can admit to mistakes. We can say sorry. We can attempt a balanced discussion with the person who is feeling hurt, recognising that their hurt is our hurt too.

Sometimes we have to wait a very long time indeed for healing to happen. Sometimes by our own behaviour, working towards genuine growth in ourselves, we create change around us. Sometimes we hear: *'The best thing you can do for me is to get yourself together and get off my back!'*

As in so many examples in therapeutic work, we can't always work the thing out with the person concerned – we can only do it with the internalised person we carry in our hearts and memory. Exercises like writing a letter we're never going to actually send, talking to a pillow, doing something creative to express what we feel about things, going to 'confession' to a priest or therapist or friend - can all help to bring about inner transformation.

The wish to repair damage isn't an easy path but aiming to find reconciliation in our self for what we have done to others is a powerful way of going forward – it's another part of taking responsibility for who we are, and ensuring that we're doing our best to live life as a worthwhile human being.

Fairness and justice

Having a concern for fairness and justice will involve us in many dilemmas, and is about reaching out to people in many walks of life and across the globe. How we think about others will inform every transaction. Once we recognise that there should be a general equality between human beings, we can no longer walk about 'blind'.

I find it hard to look at the beautiful buildings in cities like Bristol without thinking of the money that was made from slavery that must have been used to build a number of them – that awareness changes my whole approach – I might still enjoy them but there is a deeper reality that I have to deal with beyond enjoyment, one that has to take into account what has built or created the pleasures that are available to us.

I can't hear someone make a sexist or sexual joke without thinking about the pain of people with mixed gender identity issues and of the people who have struggled for gender and sexual equality often at great cost – life takes on a deeper and richer hue and I realise that the task of making this a better world is endless.

This doesn't make me want to give up or to join those who never started – it makes me feel privileged to already be on a path where I can see what is wrong and where I have an opportunity to make a difference. It's not always clear how we can engage but the answers will come to us eventually.

The value of fairness and justice commits us to a path upon which there are many painful things to observe and where sometimes it is very challenging to stand up for justice, and even to decide where we stand. The struggle for a Palestinian state, for the ending of apartheid in South Africa, for compensation for Jews and others after the Second World War, for recognition for Tibet, rights for Aborigines, equality between Catholics and Protestants in Northern Ireland, the needs of human beings for pharmaceuticals and the rights of animals not to be experimented on etc. etc. are examples where people on both sides are or have been on collision courses – and conflict has been the result.

At the micro level, we can look inside our own families and communities and check out if choices made and resources allocated have always been fair and if we have spoken up sufficiently for equality within situations close to us.

It can be difficult to take sides sometimes – not just because we might be afraid of the consequences – but because we can understand the motivations and pain of both or all parties. We

505

may have to decide if our choice is a 'spiritual' one where we offer reflections, hopes, and skills for mediation and reconciliation and recognise claims (and usually a history of loss and investment in the struggle) on both sides or whether we are willing to be 'political' and throw in our lot with one side or the other. It may depend on which particular situation presents itself to us – we don't have to get equally involved in every argument – some may seem more worthwhile or more conflictive to us than others.

Deciding what's fair and just tends to be informed by our political beliefs as well as being underpinned by unconscious processes, and is not always rational or clearly explicable. Putting such principles into action often requires the facing up to conflict. For those of us with a pacifist leaning, this may be more difficult to reconcile than for those of us who are willing to enter into a battle. Most of us are prepared to fight about some things and to recognise in other situations that the time is not yet right, or that we have no allies or resources, or that the price of a battle is too high, or that we simply don't care enough. We need to have the ability to look accurately at the claims of each side and decide for ourselves what we think of each person's or group's 'story'. For each of us this is ultimately uncharted territory – even if we are a member of a group, ultimately at some point, we may disagree with groupthink and have to branch out on our own, recognising that our sense of fairness may be different from someone else's, or that the 'group' is no longer what we thought it was. Some conflicts are too difficult and we don't know what is right – we may have to pray or wait or take an interim decision or even withdraw. We can't get it right every time.

'Equality' is not the simple concept some people would like us to believe. The upheavals required to bring about a complete equality among people and peoples might be too costly in terms of conflict or human life. It may be that we have to think – in the circumstances – what would be fair and just? Whatever we decide – whatever 'horse' we decide to back – is always going to be challenged. We may decide to go for more than we think we can get – a tried and tested negotiating strategy – so that something better than the present situation can be achieved but we recognise that it may not be as much as asked for at the beginning.

It may not be up to us (– for example, women in the developing/majority world have often told Western women to attend to their own) – the issues are sometimes best understood and battled for by the people involved themselves. Every politician – and ultimately every voter – has to make painful decisions about whether to intervene or to leave people to fight it out themselves. The concept of 'forgiveness' is not something that can be easily put into practice, particularly when there's a long history of pain and damage on one or both sides.

Holding to what we believe is fair and just in all situations takes courage and a sense of individual integrity that we have to 'grow' in ourselves.

Some of us will feel moved to give back to society through charitable acts – giving money or time to others, and we're increasingly able to map how this kind of activity is distributed across the globe and within countries. It's interesting that people who have the most aren't always the most generous and conversely that people with less sometimes give more proportionately from their income than those who are better-off. More about philanthropy is in our chapter on 'The crisis we're in'.

Not going for quick and easy answers

The psychologist Klaus F Riegel suggested that we can reach a stage of thinking that is *dialectical* – where there is an interplay between ideas such that we can tolerate paradoxes and ambivalence without trying to settle the conflicts involved easily and quickly by denying the force of one side rather than the other – rather we hold the contradictory possibilities in our mind together and sometimes find new syntheses or creative resolutions. Rare before mid-life, James Fowler's idea of *'conjunctive faith'* suggests that (if we're lucky) we become able to work with apparent contradictions and paradoxes in our lives, struggling to reconcile opposites and to bring together our own pasts with our present reality, our inner self and the experiences and views of others, the awareness of our own lives and of others' and the pain of all that. Mid-life and 'conjunctive faith' thus offers us the chance to move forward in our development without settling on easy answers or denying truths.

Living a meaningful life

Deciding to live a meaningful life means living life to the full – not rushing off round the world on holidays or spending money on entertainment – but attending to each moment, appreciating everything around us – and having a position on everything that happens (even if that position is having 'no position'). It means understanding that we're in charge of our reactions to other human beings and all in the universe, and we alone can decide how to behave, how to respond, how to feel, and what to do. It means we're prepared to be *accountable*. It means we have to face our own fears and uncertainties and make the effort – when we can or when we deem it right - to speak up.

It means that we're continually learning to see more accurately, deeply, vividly; to question what we experience and see; and to hold ambiguities and ambivalences and conflicts in our hearts, knowing that there are often no easy answers, but prepared to take a step forward, risking criticism, risking being wrong, risking being human. It means that we know that any joy is tinged with the knowledge of pain – in our own histories and in the lives of others simultaneously, but that it's important to experience our joy anyway because not to do so is to deny the point of life and what people everywhere are struggling for. We negate one another's struggles if we resist accepting life with its joy and its pain.

Jack's response

I like Julia's section on values and I'm adding a few thoughts here. The gist of this section is that whilst looking at values can be complex, there is a simpler way of describing them. Also, I'm talking about the process of *using* values and how they can be identified and updated.

The big picture

I think the big picture that runs throughout the book is a global clash between two positions:

materialism,	vs	less ego, caring
negative ego *(see 'ego' in Self chapter)*		co-operation, love
individualism	vs	humanisation, the spiritual
dehumanisation, greed exploitation	vs	taking care of self/others and nature/the planet
concern with status and inequality	vs	nurturing the social

Or an even simpler big picture -

> ### Individualism and materialism/greed
> versus
> ### the humane and the social

The humane, which includes not destroying the planet, is presently losing the contest.

Values are crucial in moving away from materialism, but a lot of people are concerned with how to put values back when the moral bar has been lowered (or stolen?) and the norm in society has been to be value-free or to dilute values in many areas. Values are everywhere but there is pretence that they are not - but what are these values? *The unregulated free market and unsustainable growth depends on the values of individualism, competition, that it is good to possess more and more and OK to have inequality.*

Government is increasingly adopting a 'value-free' approach and politicians seem like economic managers with no idea of the shape they want a functional society to take - for example does society nurture young people or leave them unemployed, does it dump old people or care for them? More on this in the final chapter of this book, *The crisis we're in*. The separation of religion and politics – clearly desirable in some respects, has nevertheless resulted in a secular bureaucracy in most Western countries that celebrates impersonality as a positive virtue.

How did we get into the crisis we're in

I think there's a simple version of this and it's caused by fear of the future, greed, and conformity.

This could be called *'let's party now, and get what we can, as the party will soon be over'* and the last things wanted in this party are responsible behaviour, regulation, concern for society, morals, honesty etc.

The Club of Rome published *The Limits to Growth* 1972 and spelt out the dangers of exponential economic growth and its depletion of world resources and ensuing environmental problems. This report was largely ignored by 'experts' and the public. *The Limits to Growth 30-year Update* published in 2005 has been widely accepted and its main gist is that we need environmentally sustainable growth.

Unfortunately either consciously or unconsciously, people have kept on with unsustainable, irresponsible growth - even though there's been plenty of evidence about the environmental and social damage it was/is still causing.

Both of the philosophers Frederic Nietzsche and Jane-Paul Sartre sought freedom from rigid, externally imposed values coming from organised religion or bourgeois norms but recognised that *then* the individual *had to take responsibility for their behaviour.* This hasn't happened.

Most organised religions including Christianity, however flawed they may be, have in-built moral codes. These actually became moral straightjackets for many but part of their function was to provide a rough and ready moral guide, which aided spiritual growth and put some love and consideration for others into the world. If values are dropped or eroded, society suffers and individual greed, lack of caring etc. come to dominate. With secularisation, spiritual and moral values have been thrown out along with the dropping of rigid, external organised religion, and materialism and a negative individualism has taken over.

Two world wars and a lack of psychological knowledge haven't helped, nor has the proliferation of a cold inhuman scientific approach to life both through scientific endeavour and bureaucratisation. The positive sides of Christianity were love, forgiveness, and striving to 'be a better person'. Dumping religion (because of its many faults) risks dumping these features of it.

What many critics feel now is that there's a crisis in parenting, resulting in parenting gaps, lack of time and love for children, and distortions – around competitiveness for example (see *The Narcissism Epidemic* referred to in the chapter on *Narcissism*) which has consequences for developing morality. All around us are questionable cultural influences including those in the media - the 'heroes' of our culture may not be the best models in terms of values, and there has been a ruthless exploitation of the naïve 'teenage market' resulting in a fixation in many young people on electronic gadgetry, appearance and fashion and trivia.

As people are operating less and less from an internal moral frame of reference (because one hasn't been built up or emphasised), there is more felt need in society for external regulation and rules. Also in the developed world, governments and society have become more controlling.

What I'm saying here is that in an historical process of questioning values, the significance of values - and the building of internal values - has been neglected, and the results of this are dangerous.

How serious is the lack of values a problem for society?

I think most people who've thought deeply about this are worried and realise that values are not a luxury. Without values, society is in deep trouble.

First of all, are we talking about *individual* value systems or values *in the culture*?

We're talking about moral values which are both individual *and* cultural - they may overlap, and external values can be internalised.

At present values which we might regard as universally social and humane and obvious - for example, fairness, honesty, respect, and caring – can no longer be assumed.

A lack of values, compromised values or deviant values (eg *'bankers are gamblers with other people's money in the speculative financial casino'*) leads to huge problems everywhere. This includes personal relationships within families, in the professions, in society, in government, in the world of 'knowledge' as well as the compromising of truth and wisdom in politics and finance, with for example, the clash of egos and turf wars.

External rules to guide us such as those in relation to political correctness are less useful than acting from our own internal value systems. At present, many people seem to be conforming to the crooked/valueless distorted 'values of the day', ignoring their own inner values (if they have them) - this constitutes a sort of moral panic in reverse. It may be that *fear of the future* makes us reckless and we think none of it matters any more.

What about cultural and political leaders?

Another key problem in the field of values - resulting in distorted values - has come from people with psychopathic and narcissistic personalities achieving huge influence in society. I recently asked a neighbour what she thought of the banking crisis and she said *'they're all conmen!'*

For good reading on personality problems try Martin Kantor on *psychopathy* in everyday life and the chapter on *narcissism* by J L Shapiro. The suggestion here is that problem personality behaviours like lack of empathy, lying and manipulation are now

512

more tolerated in society and copied by people conforming to the belief that this is the way to 'succeed', particularly if outwardly, people with such behaviours appear to be successful. However, these behaviours create damage for others, don't actually repair psychological damage for the individuals concerned, and bring about a distorted and unhappy society.

The experts who've been wheeled in to analyse the economic crisis, good or bad as they may be, tend to be limited by their intellectual narrowness, but there are some signs of change and people are thinking more broadly for example about 'pathology', spirituality, sociology, psychology, politics, power etc and making links between these areas.

In relation to psychopathology (which need be no longer the private, mysterious knowledge of psychiatry), people are beginning to learn about the distorted personalities of members of élite professional, economic and political worlds and celebrity culture. Those 'successful' people, the rich and powerful may indeed often have personality problems which affect others in negative ways. For more on this, see our chapters on *Emotional health* and *Therapy*.

What are *internal* and *external* values in psychology?

In the work of Sigmund Freud, the conscience has been described as residing in the *'superego'* – ideas internalised from our parents and teachers about how we should curb our natural inclinations arising from the instinctive *'id'* (which is full of desires) in order to live in a social world. In this model, it is our 'ego' that mediates between these two forces, but we vary on how well we're in touch with our *'id'* and how much we're ruled by our *'super-ego'*.

In Transactional Analysis (TA), *moral and religious 'codes'* are internalised in the *'parent-ego state'* and *norms of behaviour* are internalised in our *'script'* and *'cultural script'*.

There are now also models - psychological and spiritual - of how we develop our *moral* selves. James Fowler describes the way in which we might grow through levels of *spiritual development* and Jean Piaget and Lawrence Kohlberg describe stages of *moral development,* dependent on increasing levels of sophistication in our thinking. (See our chapters on *Spirituality* and *Creativity*). And in describing *individuation,* (which we look at in the chapter on *The Self*), Carl Jung is putting forward ideas of spiritual and value development.

There are different ideas in the psychological models about the relationship between the self and the outside world, with some viewing human beings as more passive recipients of social influence and others seeing us active in our engagement with the world and thus playing a part in the way in which we construct our own development.

The development of internal values

Psychological theories of moral development such as the one proposed by Lawrence Kohlberg are useful in that they cut through the morass and confusion about values and they offer hope, and they leave value development to the individual and are not imposed from the outside. Also such theories tend to conceptualise moral development as non-static.

On the minus side:

1. they don't describe the process of value systems in action (which I do later on)
2. they could be seen as hierarchical or élitist

Whilst these are valid criticisms, they go against everyday observation as some people are very developed in moral/values terms, some are not, and some are stuck.

Also criticisms of élitism are only relevant if those in a hierarchy who are 'highly developed' morally or spiritually (as described by James Fowler and Lawrence Kohlberg) are about to discriminate against those who are less developed, which is unlikely as they should be mature enough to refrain from judging others or discriminating against them.

514

Basically, Lawrence Kohlberg describes development in moral reasoning from childhood to adulthood in six stages. His work was inspired by the child psychologist, Jean Piaget, whose model he extended. For Kohlberg, Stage 1 is *'external'* where the child learns to obey rules, then there is a possible progression to an increasingly *internal and self-chosen morality* based on ethical principles where individual conscience is involved more than external influence.

The Kohlberg progression is similar to Fowler's *'stages of faith'* in that people can develop their morality and as they progress, come to operate more 'internally' rather than following 'external' rules and influences.

External values

These are many and various and include laws, moral codes eg. religious ones, social mores, institutional rules, unwritten codes eg. of 'polite formal behaviour', rules for roles (professional codes), ideas and lists of human rights etc. External rules can be internalised.

The problem that we have now in the West is that we have a well-developed and articulated code of ethics, a bureaucratised set of rules, an anaesthetised administrative system that offers us a framework for behaviour and sanctions for not conforming to it, that is 'secular' and 'neutral'. But without love, compassion, and an understanding of paradox and complexity, we're going to get it wrong quite often when we try to sort out problems that arise. Without the wisdom of spirituality and its ethos of love, we're stuck in a morass of rules and regulations that are supposed to apply to situations we've already anticipated, and that fit all cases.

It's clear that this can't and doesn't work. It's a charter for officialdom, pomposity, and insensitive implementation of rules. We have little guidance for 'discretion', and what discretion is exercised is usually outside the rules and not based on a shared value-base.

It's painful to think that a society where values were internalised by the majority of people would not need the raft of legislation on equality and anti-discrimination that many of us have had to fight so hard for – now that we have such legislation, it's difficult to make sure that it's implemented because ultimately good practice requires people to have internalised true wisdom, and that cannot be taken for granted in today's world.

The idea behind this section was to find a straightforward way of looking at values.

So why bother with values? Are they a luxury?

No, they're not a luxury; without them we have big problems. Any society not acting enough on values - as is the case now - has endless problems, conflict etc and prioritises goals that can in the worst, destroy our environment. So the whole question of values is very serious.

Values though, are ideals – we don't always come up to our own values and we compromise them at times.

I think that in the individualistic culture we have - where cheating, competing, greed and selfishness are not only tolerated but held up, with whatever subtlety, as 'normal' - there has been a compromise which has resulted in the 'moral bar' being lowered or thrown away.

It has probably always been the case that people reduce or compromise their ideal values in survival situations – the difference is that now *daily life is thought of as a survival situation*.

As our value system becomes more developed and individual, external rules and systems are there to follow, ignore or contest – they are far less important than following our own value path.

Spirituality relates to values and if we reach a spiritual point where our internal spiritual development is strong, there will be more clarity without external rules.

516

Values and value-driven behaviour may seem a bit 'unprocessed' by the logical 'left' conscious mind - we shouldn't worry about that, so much of life is elegantly and powerfully 'right' brain/unconscious if we but listen to it.

Updating values

We're constantly updating and developing our values throughout our lives; these systems develop according to our life experience, our development as people, the experience of having or looking after children and parent/childcare/mentoring roles etc. The point here is that for most (but not all) people, there is an evolving process happening.

Some people, sadly, do not have much in the way of internalised values from parental figures, so have to process all value decisions from scratch logically, or be confused or operate without values.

Another group of people have 'crooked' values, this fits for some criminal families etc.

Some people's cultural values do not mesh with the culture of the country or area in which they are living.

Another process that happens constantly is that of values being tested and challenged by circumstance and I think it's worthwhile to understand our own individual values and see how we use our values in our everyday lives.

We all have a 'values package'

We all have a values package which comes from parents, grandparents, society, the culture, religion etc. and we do an estimation of how to employ the package, assessing each situation. We use values for our own behaviour as well as for handling situations and dealing with other people.

This can create an endless headache - processing guilt, dealing with feelings of not-OKness etc. - but it is nevertheless a process that people do and they do it not just according to the situation or

517

in relation to survival, but in relation to their 'egos', the cultural norms they are affected by, and if you agree with developmental models, their level of moral development.

My own values package is devised from several sources:

1. input from family - includes grandparents, parents, some Victorian values
2. input from others, teachers, colleagues, therapists etc.
3. an intuitive feeling of 'rightness' based on empathy, the spiritual, reflective, empathic self
4. the culture
5. internalised rules
6. therapeutic professional self includes 'do no harm', 'keep confidentiality' etc.

The gist version of my values package includes:

equality   freedom   rights   do your best

Julia: Once I got this idea of a 'values package' from Jack I couldn't wait to put it together:

My values package includes various messages gleaned from life – I don't necessarily agree with all of them but they've all been there influencing me for good or bad

However, it's important to question the motivations and feelings behind these pieces of 'wisdom'. For example, my parents would have been concerned that none of us children got into trouble with the law, but was this an actual ethical belief? I used to dispute the stress put on manners but in modern life I sometimes wonder if we should bring it back when I see how a lot of people behave to others in the street, in shops, on the roads etc. Are some of these actually *values* or are they guidance for staying out of trouble? Maybe it's important to sift the list and refine out what are the real values.

- Work from within the organisation to change things (mother)
- Always look presentable, put on a good front for the world, and have immaculate manners (mother)
- Women have 'got it made'; don't 'rock the boat' with feminism (mother)
- Kindness and gentleness are important (father)
- Humour can break down barriers and intensity (father)
- Finding a long-term permanent partner is an important life goal (parents)
- Doing something interesting with your life is important (parents)
- Career and marriage are not compatible, especially for a woman (mother)
- Stealing is absolutely wrong (parents)
- It's important to keep within the law (parents)
- Borrowing and getting credit is not good (father)
- Free speech is important and worth fighting for (mother)
- It's important to be an individual and not just follow the crowd (parents)
- Courtesy is utterly important in every avenue of life (parents and relatives)
- Choose your friends carefully (parents)
- Creativity is more important than having things (brother)
- Having good friends around you is valuable (brother)
- Be creative with money, be confident about negotiating settlements and agreements (friend)
- You can't manipulate love – it's either there or it isn't (therapist)
- Love and support is important and needs to come from a whole person, not just gleaned in little packages (therapist)
- What is important is being a person, not achieving (therapist)
- No job is unimportant, or too humble for me to do (intuitive belief)
- Everyone in a community has an equal right to recognition (intuitive belief)
- Collective action is better than individual effort (co-activists)
- The vulnerable need to be looked after and fought for (professional and political culture and intuitive belief)
- People with intelligence and ability have a duty to contribute to society (writers I've read)

My 'gist' these days would include:

- have compassion for others
- trust love, don't manipulate it
- give time to the people who matter to you and love them well
- stand up for what matters, find the courage
- never be supercilious or bragging, be happy to pitch in and help
- always be sensitive to what the most 'lowly' person is doing and needs, don't be dazzled by the extraverts and narcissists in a room
- be inclusive
- respond to each person individually, don't generalise or operate on stereotypes
- the best is best for everyone not just for grown-ups
- individual difference (gender, sexuality, ethnicity, disability, age etc) is what makes life rich
- always strive to give to the world and make it a better place

---

Consciously update your values package.

1. Look at any values package you have and where it comes from

2. Think of a time when you made a mistake of not living up to your own value-base

3. Think of a time when you have stuck up for a value for its own sake irrespective of personal advantage

4. Identify where something in your past values package needs to change or has changed

5. Identify something that needs to be added or modified in your values package

Books and web material

Theodor W Adorno, Else Frenkel-Brunswik, Daniel Levinson, and Nevitt Sanford (1950) *The Authoritarian Personality* Harper and Row

Graceann Bennett and Freya Williams (2011) *Moving Sustainability from Niche to Normal* Mainstream Green: The Red Papers : Issue 4 Ogilvy and Mather

Sissela Bok (1999) *Lying: Moral Choice in Public and Private Life* Vintage

Sissela Bok (2010) *Exploring Happiness: From Aristotle to Brain Science* Yale University Press

Dietrich Bonhoeffer (2001 ed) *The Cost of Discipleship* SCM Classics

Druin Burch (2009) *Taking the Medicine* London: Chatto and Windus

Judith Butler (2006) *Gender Trouble: Feminism and the Subversion of Identity* Routledge

Emmy van Deurzen (2012) *Existential Counselling and Psychotherapy* London: Sage

Michel Foucault and Paul Rabinow (1991) *The Foucault Reader: An Introduction to Foucault's Thought* Penguin Books

Victor Frankl (1946) (new ed 2004) *Man's Search for Meaning* Rider

Erving Goffman (1963) *Stigma: Notes on the Management of a Spoiled Identity* Prentice-Hall/Penguin Books

Emma Goldman (1972 ed) *Red Emma Speaks: Selected Writings and Speeches* New York: Random House

Johnathan Haidt (2001) *The Emotional Dog and its Rational Tail: A Social Intuitionist Approach to Moral Judgment* Psychological Review 2001. Vol. 108. No. 4, 814-834 http://www.nd.edu/~wcarbona/Haidt%202001.pdf

Johnathan Haidt (2012) *The Righteous Mind: Why Good People Are Divided by Politics and Religion* Allen Lane

Louise Hay (1984, 2004 edition) *You Can Heal Your Life* Hay House

Christopher Hitchens (2007) *God is Not Great* Atlantic Books

M H Van Ijzendoorn, F A Goossens and R Van Dee Veer *Klaus F Riegel and Dialectical Psycology [sic] in Search for the Changing Individual in a Changing Society* University of Leiden https://openaccess.leidenuniv.nl/bitstream/handle/.../7-703-175.pdf

Martin Kantor (2006) *The Psychopathy of Everyday Life: How Antisocial Personality Disorder Affects All of Us* Praeger

Lawrence Kohlberg (1981) *Essays on Moral Development* Vol I: *The Philosophy of Moral Development* San Francisco: Harper & Row.

Simon Malpas (2003) *Jean-François Lyotard* London: Routledge

Abraham Maslow (1962) (2010 ed) *Toward a Psychology of Being* Martino Publishing

Donella Meadows, Jorgen Randers and Dennis Meadows (2004) *Limits to Growth: the 30 year Update* London: Earthscan

Tariq Modood (2013) *Multiculturalism* Polity Press

Frederic Nietzsche (2004 ed) *A Nietzsche Reader* Longman

Jean Piaget and B Inhelder (1962) *The Psychology of the Child* New York: Basic Books

Carl Rogers (1961) (2004 ed) *On becoming a person* London: Constable and Robinson Ltd.

Richard Rorty (1989) *Contingency, Irony and Solidarity* Cambridge University Press

Richard Rorty (1999) *Philosophy and Social Hope* Penguin Books

Graham Scambler (2004) *Re-framing Stigma: Felt and Enacted Stigma and Challenges to the Sociology of Chronic and Disabling Conditions* Social Theory and Health (2) 29 - 46.

Anthony Storr (2000) *Freud: A Very Short Introduction* Oxford Paperbacks

Albert Schweitzer (1954) *The Problem of Peace* – speech delivered for the 1952 Nobel Peace Prize
http://www.nobelprize.org/nobel_prizes/peace/laureates/1952/schweitzer-lecture.html

J L Shapiro (2006) *Narcissism: Greek tragedy, psychological syndrome and cultural norm* in Thomas

G Plante (ed) (2006) *Mental disorders of the new millennium* Greenwood

Peter Singer (2001) *Marx: A Very Short Introduction* Oxford

Alexandr Solzhenitsyn (orig. 1973) (2007 abridged ed) *The Gulag Archipelago* Harper Perennial
http://www.ethicaltrade.org/in-action/projects/kenya-flower-project
http://www.treehugger.com/natural-sciences/are-cut-flowers-killing-the-wildlife-in-kenyas-lake-naivasha.html
http://www.guardian.co.uk/environment/2010/apr/19/uk-virtual-water

17   stress
managing ourselves in a stressful world

In this chapter, we consider the idea of becoming more aware of and more informed about the worldwide crisis we're in because understanding what's going on will help us to live in the world more effectively. Recognising the choices we have about the way we respond to information about the world and how much of it we let into our psyches, and the extent to which we search for truth rather than buying into 'hyper-reality' and untruths makes a difference to our experience of stress.

Taking responsibility for our own lives, paying attention to signs of stress and the risk of burnout, simplifying things, maintaining a respect for human life and human beings, and finding meaning in our lives are all strategies that all contribute to our survival and growth.

The first section of this chapter is by Jack and the second by Julia

Jack

Apocalyptic thinking

Changes in the 'shape' or 'flavour' of society and processes which influence people's lives, directly or indirectly, have always been there, but they happened **more slowly** than today. In twelfth century Europe, people had a real dread that the world would soon end in the 'apocalypse'. Now it's more certain that the apocalypse is coming unless we organise thoughtful intervention. So we're in a nightmare which is getting more dreadful all the time.

And *not only is the apocalypse nearly here, but we've helped cause it.*

Julia thinks that this movement towards taking responsibility is an indication of *our becoming more mature as a society*, facing up increasingly to our shadow side, although it's also inevitable as we gain so much more information about *how* we are causing damage in the world.

It's up to each of us how we interpret what's happening and whether we think what's happening is a temporary blip in our onwards and upwards path to growth and success, or whether we think the end is nigh, or whether we are able to make a more nuanced and sophisticated analysis somewhere between these two positions. And our personal, individual will to live and to make something of our lives will be related to our view of the overall picture. Our vibrancy as individuals will emerge or die according to whether we choose to insulate ourselves, link with others, find meaning, invest in something creative or spiritual, fight for change, retreat into illness, give up bothering etc.

As spelled out throughout the book, the processes which are having an impact today – some more subtle than others (and you'll probably like to add more) are explored in most detail in our final chapter – *The crisis we're in.*

For me, these can be summarised as follows (– some are more subtle than others) and you'll probably like to add more. I've divided them up into rough groups for convenience

Impending DOOM
- loss of the environment and animal species
- scarcity of resources
- pollution
- natural disasters – to include tsunamis, volcanoes, meteorites, viruses and superbugs etc.
- over-population – with psychological effects, problems of resources etc.

Social decline - mostly a decline in:
- values
- morality
- relating
- parenting
- personality
- decline in standards in public/professional life (see phone-hacking in UK)
- erosion of 'culture' – effects of entertainment, celebrity

Social control/less freedom and trust

- controlling societies with most developed nations becoming more controlling, and a shift to intolerant uncaring right-wing politics
- surveillance
- manipulation – eg. through distorting or withholding information, which applies to multi-nationals, advertising, government

Other

- secularisation or lack of spirituality
- materialism
- effects of technology
- encouragement of greed, selfishness (negative traits)
- increase in shallowness vs depth
- rise of status vs notions of equality
- increase in 'terrorism'
- increase in addictions
- increase in 'anti-social behaviour' – we're all doing it
- rise in power of the big companies
- DELUGE of over-detailed information
- dehumanisation and commodification of people (eg. older people as past their 'shelf-life')
- globalisation

As I've indicated before, I think one main way of describing the 'crisis we're in' is a clash between:

materialism, ego **and** *individualism*

versus

values, 'being human' **and** *spirituality*

(We have explorations of these terms in other chapters – materialism in *The crisis we're in*; ego in *The Self*; values in *Values*; Spirituality in *Spirituality*).

Clearly, these things have different effects depending on the nature of our individuality, where we live on the globe, the culture we're part of, and our membership of social groups. Some of the processes affecting us are universal such as globalisation and environmental issues – but nevertheless can affect different sets of people and places more acutely. See for example Anthony Giddens' work on this. Epidemiology is also relevant here as such research can plot factors which make particular groups and populations more vulnerable to disease or disaster than others, and our ability to do this is one of the things that science and technology has enabled us to get better at.

Please add to my list of processes or make up your own list and if you like, make a note of how you usually cope with any particular process and whether it works or not. For example, with *'intrusive technology'* on a daily level, I do the following:

intrusive technology		
what affects me	**what doesn't work**	**what does work**
spam unsolicited phone-calls bad TV programmes conversation interrupted by cell-phone/mobile	*flick through it answer the phone read whilst TV is on interrupt talk and wait to restart it*	*get another email address leave the phone select programmes carefully tell people I won't have phone interruptions*

Guidelines for surviving the crisis we're in

- think of ourselves as important

- trust in our perception

- drop notions of the 'ideal' lifestyle – no-one has them, do they?

- slow down, create more time, develop more simplicity/drop complexity

- check 'process' in relating to others – make observations on what you think is happening or what you're feeling - and be *in the present*

- develop self-awareness: *how compromised or conforming am I? what am I frightened of? what or who is 'driving' me? am I competing and if so, is that helpful or necessary?*

- do something about stress in our lives – *am I overworking and if so, why? is it compulsive or necessary? do I have too many running conflicts – can I resolve them or drop them?*

- become aware of the world – *seriously question sources of info from politicians, the government, media, any institutions, economic world, knowledge, power, hegemony including academia, seek alternative sources and a range of opinion*

- drop myths and fairy-stories, stop the denial of reality and be prepared for the pain of this

- drop status and ensure we relate to others on an OK-OK basis – enjoy the surprises this brings

- clarify our values and our belief in them

- be aware of our rights, fight our corner wherever necessary

- be willing to change and be flexible

- reduce ego – see our section on this in the chapter on *The Self*

- think social, then go social (including via the internet) – network and make helpful links

- think kindness and cooperation – nip in the bud any tendencies to exclude or discredit others and consider that in the future, we will need a much greater amount of sharing

- invest in creative activity or be creative around problem-solving

- work to improve relationships in our lives; if necessary, cut out ones that aren't working and enhance the ones that have potential for mutual support and inspiration

- develop our communication skills, challenge putdowns, insist on clarity, ask for information, negotiate 'deals' – don't just accept what people suggest etc.

Seriously question	Look at ourselves
Science	Update values
Academia	Be critical
Government	Examine our compromises and biases
Media	
Any institution	
Economics	
Knowledge/power hegemony	

Stress is a booming industry and a big field

Stress management, particularly to make workplaces more efficient and to reduce absenteeism has become a big industry in recent years.

There are lots of books, courses, loads of training and generally **too much** information about stress – in fact, there's so much it's becoming stressful!! This overload of stressful information is about stress at work, in general, stress in relationships, the stress of life, etc etc. The books tell us that a certain amount of stress is important for performing well and that positive stress (called *'eustress'* by initial researchers like Richard Lazarus and Hans Selye) is something that people like.

528

In this section, I'm going to provide a rough overview of stress and include things that are often left out. I'm doing this because I find having missing information very stressful!

Stress management is usually divided into:

work stress
general stress

A typical book on general stress is Mike Clayton's (2011) *Brilliant Stress Management* and there's a lot of information here about stress at work, including how to deal with obnoxious colleagues. Remember as well that *work stress* is subject to health and safety legislation in the UK and elsewhere.

Stress in Turbulent Times by Ashley Weinberg and Cary Cooper is a useful text about stress in today's climate, offering support for how to cope with and survive in times of uncertainty. Their interests have always been in organisational psychology and recently some of their interest has been in the field of stress experienced by politicians, which is relevant when we're assessing the mental state of those carrying responsibility for big decisions.

A quick history of stress and the body

Older studies of stress focused on the *amount* of stress. Holmes and Rahe scored the life events of patients in their last year as a predictor of illness. They scored different life events -for example retirement 45, imprisonment 63 personal injury or illness 53. A score of 300 in the last year was a good predictor of illness.

What they didn't differentiate between was positively and negatively perceived stress. If a stressor is perceived as positive, it can become excitement and not stress. The body's response to anything an animal or human perceives as threatening wellbeing is called a 'fight or flight' response – a term coined by Walter Cannon in 1915. *Many body changes happen in a fight or flight response, preparing people or animals for action.*

Ideas about stress gradually progressed into *looking at how people could perceive and respond differently to stress* particularly by changing thinking about it and how stress could be successfully managed. Some features of stress have become clear. One is that it's easier to manage if it's more under a person's control and secondly, that it's easier to tolerate if you can predict it. It's important though to realise that the perception of what *is* stress is very individual; stress management is individual; and recovery from too much stress is individual.

A definition of stress is not as simple as it looks, as one person's stress is another person's excitement. Generally, stress is *a response to a perception of a psychological or physical danger.*

Hans Selye and stress – a key idea

Hans Selye thought about adaptation to stress with his General Adaptation Syndrome (GAS for short) and his ideas have been in fashion, then out of fashion, and now in fashion again. I have used his ideas to help people who are on the verge of burning out or who have burned out. *Burnout* is the state people get into when they have been adapting for too long to stress without a break. Selye's idea was that the body responded to the total amount of stress by adapting to it, after a short alarm phase - **these body changes are complex but involve all systems in the body working harder.** Then there was an exhaustion or resting phase where body functioning dropped below a normal baseline of function – this is in diagram 1.

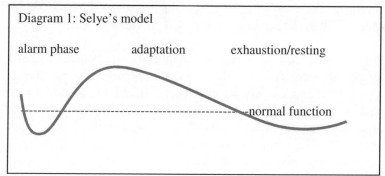

Diagram 1: Selye's model

alarm phase   adaptation   exhaustion/resting

normal function

Diagram 2

Selye's model and Burnout

over time with continued alarm and adaptation but no exhaustion or resting phase, leading to eventual deep physical and mental exhaustion/resting.

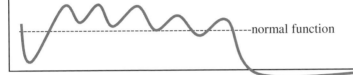

----normal function

It doesn't matter what the stressors are in Hans Selye's model – it could be a virus, noise, psychological stress, experience in a war zone, an obnoxious colleague or partner or debt.

In diagram 1, the adaptation phase is followed by an exhaustion/resting phase which is necessary for recovery. During this resting phase, the body's functioning is not up to normal. You can see this in everyday life. Teachers get ill in the first days of their holiday when their immune systems are run down and they're not up to normal functioning in their resting phase. When people don't rest after adaptation and when this happens repeatedly, then a long and deep rest is necessary in order for the body and mind to recover and this is called 'burnout' – see diagram 2.

Burnout

Burnout has several features, including Selye's exhaustion/rest phase. If someone is seriously burnt out, they may need to be off work for some months, sometimes six months or longer. This is an individual matter and likely to be fiercely resisted by people and their employers. All the messages and pressure on a person – internal and external – are to be back at work, so people need to understand that they're exhausted, not in a normal state, physically or mentally. They may be anxious/depressed or very unmotivated, but still feeling the pressure to be back in the fray that caused the burnout in the first place. Features of people at risk of burnout are *paranoia* and *denial of the problem*.

531

When people are recovering from it, the first job for them, apart from resting, is to slowly build up their bodies, their physical strength, and their closeness to other people. *It's common in people who've burnt out that they've focused too much on goals and not enough on being close to other people.* John Bowlby in his attachment theory suggests that we need to be attached to other people as well as goals.

What usually isn't in stress books because it's inconvenient, politically or economically

Selye's theory and 'burnout' tend not to be written about enough. Problems with people, particularly work colleagues, tend to be written about very well - the focus is often on mediation, relating to people and what makes a good manager. What most stress books do is to create a *one-size fits all* approach where for example, sensitive people don't get a look-in and individual differences are not fully recognised. Susan Cain's new book *Quiet: The Power of Introverts in a World That Can't Stop Talking* is one that questions the discounting of people with more gentle personalities and the terrible waste that this can be for society and for organisations.

Also there's a strange 'ignorance' of the process of burnout. Quite a lot of knowledge about stress is taken from military experience, from the First World War onwards. Early in World War I, troops with mental breakdowns were shot for cowardice and battle fatigue was only slowly accepted. Even today people can be discriminated against for letting the side down through feeling stressed or getting ill. There **is** a tendency in real life by organisations and governments to blame the victims of stress.

There are several stress responses which are usually not mentioned in general stress books - for example, extreme or sudden panics, traumatic stress, post-traumatic stress syndrome, learned helplessness etc.

A character in the 1944 Jean-Paul Sartre play *Huis Clos/No Exit* states that *'hell is other people'* – this kind of feeling can relate to individuals, people organised into groups or workplaces, the wider society or the state of the world at the time. See for example the burgeoning literature about psychopathy and narcissism in the workplace (see our chapter on *Emotional and mental health*).

Psychological survival in an age of change

Like most people, I'm worried about the future, dissatisfied with the present and am tired of being rendered powerless, voiceless etc. BUT I do think that humans are endlessly adaptable and can survive, especially if they have some hope, so here's a quick recipe for survival:

1. stop what we're doing and think
2. be prepared for the worst
3. be flexible
4. stop being greedy, selfish, individualistic etc. and come up with something more caring and social
5. change what we can
6. generate hope, however we do that
7. generate some happiness for ourselves that's real
8. stop conforming and do something more mature, for example, go spiritual or alternative or caring
9. be brave and put something into action NOW in our life

What *I'm* doing on my checklist is following point 2: *being prepared for the worst,* and: *being happy* – point 7; *promoting thought* – point 1; and *changing what I can – writing a book –* point 9.

I do think by going *'spiritual'* or *'value-based'*, people can achieve a lot:

- short-term – we could find that as more damage happens (personal or global) there's a possibility that it leads to more change of a positive kind

- long-term – we could find ourselves having to leave the earth to the animals (ie. the ones that haven't yet become

533

extinct including lions, tigers, elephants, crocodiles, reptiles, birds etc) who will have a different approach to the earth

It's important *both* to FACE THE REALITY as we interpret it *and* to THINK POSITIVE. Looking back to our chapter on *Values*, you will be able to read about *dialectical thinking* (usually attributed to Klaus Riegel) – our capacity as humans to live with paradoxes and conflicting feelings or points of view – however hard that is, and to see what creative resolution can emerge.

Things that can stress us, including other people's decisions and work organisations

Money issues can stress us, as can war, illness, badly organised organisations, inefficiency, people's mistakes, badly made clothes and cars. Other people's energy can be stressful, so can a lack of trust and lack of motivation. Working to deadlines and targets can be stressful and so can boredom and the *muzak* designed to alleviate it. Putting important and boring things off, for example, tax, accounts, papers etc. can create stress. In the world of work, sometimes the values of an organisation, not just the organisation of the organisation creates stress. Organisational and governmental policies can stress us. Some life events like retirement (which is supposedly a positive step) nevertheless create stress for some.

Good news about stress

People are individual in the type or quantity of stress that they can handle. Some people, though, are 'hardy' or resilient during stress. I think what's helped me with stress has been *being persistent selectively, being creative, getting enough rest, and getting good information.*

Early on, I mentioned controllability and predictability of stress as having been found to be useful. I would add to these:

- *getting support and connecting to people*
- *awareness and analysis of stresses*
- *looking after our physical self*

- *getting information in stressful situations*
- *listening to our bodies for signals – for example, increase heart-rate, headaches*
- *keeping positive and hopeful*
- *doing things we're putting off instead of being passive*
- *slowing things down and putting non-essential things off*

Organising techniques, such as creating efficient admin systems, time management, not overloading ourselves, can help. Also *management skills or 'healthy' organisation skills* can help. *Learning how to understand 'difficult' people or interactions is also very useful –* we could do worse than study psychopathology (see our chapter on *Emotional health*), acquire conflict resolution strategies and read Dale Carnegie's *'How to win friends and influence people'.*

Julia

Symptoms

Stress can involve a huge variety of symptoms that in early stages can involve difficulties with sleep, feeling irritable, fatigue, over-eating, anxiety, depression, loneliness in the midst of family life, dread of the future, finding it difficult to make decisions, having more conflict than usual and conversely, a desire to avoid conflictive situations. If we continue onwards without making any changes to our lifestyle and the pressures on us, without pausing or changing the pace, and **without understanding what's important in our life**, worse may follow.

Existential therapy is a great approach for getting us to think about what matters in our life and our relationship to life and death - see Emmy van Deurzen's work on this.

Stress in relation to pessimism and optimism, hardiness and resilience

There's increasing interest in the question of *pessimism* and *optimism* as elements of personality, with some evidence that an optimistic outlook is more likely to bring about positive outcomes.

Certainly this approach underlies *visualisation techniques* – *imagining* good things is more likely to make them happen. See also our chapter on *Positive thinking*.

Western culture has tended to take us down the road of 'glass half-empty' rather than 'glass half-full' thinking. Although financial disaster is often 'talked-up' on TV programmes, much of the news is negative and we're given little to hope for; steps taken by government and institutions to tackle things are frequently described as 'too little, too late'. In this context, if we've been brought up to be superstitious or overly-cautious, we may become pessimistic and wonder if it's worth doing anything.

Cultivating a confident approach, whilst also building in sensible safeguards or fall-back positions, may be the best way to proceed. That confidence is best built on the basis of one's own abilities and determination, rather than on a vague sense of benign fate. Of course, this will depend on our spiritual outlook – for those who believe in a God, perhaps the most helpful phrase that comes to mind is *'God helps those who help themselves'*. This also resonates with what we know about the creative process where *incubation of ideas works when there's been good preparatory work.* Looking after ourselves and hoping for the best is most successful when we've taken clear steps to *lay the groundwork and set up strategies for handling difficulties should they occur.* Such behaviour doesn't mean that we expect negative outcomes – it means we're sensible about trying to ensure good outcomes.

Psychologists such as Suzanne Kobasa are investigating ideas of *hardiness* and *resilience* in the face of stress. Whilst most of us eventually break down at least health-wise under chronic high stress, nevertheless it appears that there *are* some recognisable features of those who keep going the longest and are considered 'hardy'. One of the mental processes that's helpful is *finding a context in which to set the stressful event(s)* so that it's seen as less daunting.

When my husband died of cancer one February, my nine-year old daughter and I drove to Aberfan, where 144 people had died, most of them children, after a Coal Board slag-tip slid down on top of the primary school after heavy rain in October 1966. I felt that it was important for us both to set our loss in the context of other losses and to realise that loss happens ultimately to all of us. We wandered among the graves, and read all the messages left by parents to their children, and visited the beautiful memorial garden.

For a few minutes, my daughter played in the playground (which was empty) and then two children came and threw stones at her. I imagined that the fact of people visiting – and there are many who come there from all over the world to assuage their own pain - might also be seen as intrusive, even if this is at an unconscious level for children of a later generation.

We drove on and into the starkness of Snowdonia in February where we spent a few days in the mountains, addressing our own sadness. When we came back, loving friends invited us for meals, and we began the long fight-back to functioning again in daily life.

Meaning

In the end, it's the *meaning we attribute to life events* that makes them particularly stressful. We've long known from anthropology that people can tolerate higher levels of pain and discomfort in initiation rites and cultural rituals than if were they to be administered as torture or even as Western medical procedures when they would be experienced as intolerable.

It can be very helpful to use the technique of 'reframing' – find a different way to perceive what is happening, and in particular, even if we've had little choice, to take charge of what's happening and make its process your own. We shouldn't hand over to others the role of defining what's happening and management of our path through it. Even in intense grief, it should be us who decides what it's about and how we want to handle it. Feedback from others on how they perceive the situation should be evaluated in terms of what we know about the person speaking and whether we trust their motives and observational ability. Doctors for example are currently under pressure to get people moving through and out of grieving very quickly when in fact we may need a long time to process loss.

Pressure points

Space, pressure and surveillance

New homes built today are often too small for family life, furniture, books, play and eating together. Cost-saving 'hot-desking' in modern organisations can make people feel marginalized or anchor-less within the organization. Call centres have proliferated as workplaces where high work volume, target-driven approaches, close monitoring of work and lack of privacy become the norm.

There's often a feeling that there's no room to escape from other people or from surveillance. Motorways, streets, squares, shopping malls and even the interior of shops and fitting-rooms are on camera, emails and telephone calls can be watched and listened to, and the number and content of our bin-bags is monitored. As we know, the UK has the highest level of surveillance in Europe but there is no clear relationship between reduction in crime and the proliferation of cameras, nor is there a clear justification for it in terms of guarding against terrorism when the government doesn't ensure tight security at airports as became clear during 2011, when people were allowed to walk into Britain without proper checks.

In a few areas (like Middlesbrough), pilot 'talking cameras' apparently issue reprimands and warnings to the populace, whilst *Keep Britain Tidy* has pioneered *'talking litter bins'* in Liverpool and a number of police forces are using Smart CCTV cars to catch speeding motorists. The *Police.com* site has continued to expand the data it can offer the public about crime in their area, and *Googlemaps* users can now travel in the virtual space of the road in which someone lives on *Streetview,* looking at the property and quite often, the resident's car outside. Even the insides of our bodies are regularly invaded with tests of our blood and urine, biopsies, endoscopic photography and ultrasound scans. Little can be hidden from the eye of the state and in many cases, from private operators in their own right or on behalf of the state.

The point is that whether it's the demands of work, the number of people around us or the intrusion of monitoring systems, we have a problem in carving out the space we need for ourselves and our needs. Reaching out for another drink, tablet or piece of food is not an effective answer to this problem.

The decline in personal space and privacy can have detrimental effects on us such as greater conflict because of overcrowding, disturbed attention and concentration and consequent mistakes, feeling stressed, losing our ability to multi-task, emotional fatigue and irritability, and the possibility that we will cease to care about protecting personal dignity and privacy for others with whom we work such as patients or customers. There's a sense of regular intrusion with the consequent need to seal the doors and hatches, and often this can seem uncaring towards others and can result in relationship difficulties when we don't feel like talking, or answering the phone, text or email.

The mixed-blessings of technology

With the growth in state-of-the-art technology, originally developed to save us time or increase what we can achieve, there have been resultant problems. For computer users, there has been an exponential growth in information load and more demanding expectations of what IT can offer. Yet often our growing dependency on these advanced systems results in extra time being devoted to waiting all day for an engineer to come to mend something or a carrier to deliver something (– we don't yet have the capacity to schedule things to suit), having to maintain paper backup systems in case the computer crashes (thus losing the benefits of the 'paper-free' office), and being hooked into paying for highly-priced printer ink cartridges or annual anti-virus and anti-malware products. Business telephone lines designed to help our businesses nevertheless are open to channelling a high rate of spam phone-calls selling us things we don't want and taking up our precious time to filter them. We ring an organisation to sort something out and have to spend hours on moving around audio menu systems, listening to inane 'muzac', and being required to give personal data repeatedly to people who have no accountability and no personal link with us. Not only is there often a negative counter-balance to most benefits, there is also a sense that systems have been developed for the benefit of providers rather than that of the consumers, leaving us feeling that we are powerless, that our time and feelings and explanations and individual situations don't matter.

We need to believe that we *do* matter and find a way to take control.

Respecting human beings

On the TV, a variety of people - some of them with vulnerabilities - having been chosen for their entertainment value, are paraded in front of us as losers ("you *are* the weakest link!", 'I'm sorry, it's three *'no's'*) or as people in need of medical intervention, stricter parenting, professional singing tuition, fashion makeovers, presentation skills, harder work, or dietary advice. This constant lack of respect and valuing of human beings, their efforts and aspects of their lives and selves that should be private, permeates our consciousness gradually so that we can forget the efforts people *have* made and how special each person is, including ourselves. We learn that intimate space and personal material can be regularly trashed and it slowly becomes easier to let slip on personal ethics in our own lives.

On-line dating and friendship sites, whilst offering us opportunities to meet new interesting people and potential partners, nevertheless also carry the hazards of devaluing our humanity. They invite us to describe ourselves on questionnaires with limited menu choices about our food preferences, activity preferences, values etc. which can encourage us to think there are only a few choices about what matters (eg. *do you like 'piercings, tattoos, erotica'?*). The huge numbers of people listed on such sites can make us feel that there is so much choice and availability it doesn't matter how we treat someone, there are plenty of others in the pool – the same kind of commodification of people, with which governments, employers and armed forces have long been familiar. These are all pressures we have to resist.

'Headless chicken' syndrome

We can find ourselves living like a 'headless chicken' – decentred, stressed, with unmet needs, over-complexity, shifting 'goalposts', lacking a proper focus, dealing with trivial detail and missing the bigger things that really matter. In contemporary western life, it has come to seem that we have to chase everyone to do their job properly. Unless we keep an eye on everyone, it seems as if mistakes will be made all over the place – the garage will 'forget' to tell us that the new model of car has had asbestos removed from the clutch thus making it necessary to drive more on the accelerator, the company sending us goods will use the old address we had instead of the new one even though they have it on record, the surgeon might omit to spell out the post-operative challenges, we get home to open up our takeaway and find that they've sprinkled masses of salt all over our chips without asking whether or not we wanted it or not – and we don't. The recent debacle over the descriptions of horsemeat and in some cases, pork, as *beef* has eroded public trust in something absolutely fundamental – the supply of food to a mass market.

We need to slow down, reduce the number of things we tackle at any one time, become proactive - ask questions, check things, insist on proper treatment, alert people to our needs, watch how they do things, double-check administration.

We need to stop worrying about being 'nice' or chatting and concentrate instead on making sure things are done as they should be. Otherwise we will find our time taken up with complaining and moaning and regretting – taking time that could be used more profitably.

We need to stop walking round in a daze, responding to people as they want us to, fitting into systems that don't suit us - we need to start waking up!

The challenge of awareness

One of the reasons that we may not have realised the necessity for being 'awake' is that is that we are frequently unaware of how much we are lied to and hidden from. It is so easy to believe in the 'truths' that are put before us.

We know for example from the therapy world that people have great difficulty in coming to terms with the idea that their parents might not have been the loving people they have always thought they were. We know that some women who flee violent men have difficulty letting go of the myth that their relationships are about 'love', even when the evidence of abuse is substantial and long-term.

We can also find it very difficult to believe that the employers upon whom we project the idea of institutional parents are not actually benign. They may be covered by humane legislation, but we may not realise that the legislation actually functions to protect the employer and not us, or we may find that the employer's interpretation of the law is different from our own. When we're sick, after the initial disbelief or chaos, there are at first messages of concern and exhortation to take it easy; later we may find ourselves sitting in an interview to warn us that our long-term employment may be in jeopardy. The employer is not after all, a benevolent 'parent' – it is an organisation trying to make a profit or fighting for its survival.

The example of St.Paul's Cathedral initially being unable to respond effectively to the *Occupy London* protestors in the autumn of 2011 revealed that our beliefs about the Church as an advocate of the people might have been mistaken, or at the very least, that the Church itself is riven with dissent and ambivalence in its ranks rather than offering the clear moral leadership we might have expected.

We may imagine that the government's benefit system or our pension scheme is there to provide for us when we are in trouble or old and weak but discover, when the chips are down, that if there is a way that payments to us can be minimised, they will take

542

it. They are not compassionate bodies – *they are administrative systems.*

We cannot afford to be naïve in our way of living. We need to grow up and understand that we have to take responsibility for our own survival. This doesn't mean becoming aggressive and selfish; it means concentrating on what matters and becoming aware of where truth really lies. It means thinking strategically, creatively and sensibly about our relationship to organisations, to sources of our funding – customers, employers, funding bodies, government etc., to people in our lives, to the professionals upon whom we depend for maintaining the health of our bodies, our cars, our computers etc., to the suppliers of goods, to the teachers and tutors who teach ourselves and our children. Anyone who's lived through the crisis of money management in the West cannot afford to ignore this message: it's no longer (if it ever was) a good idea to rely on others to do their jobs honestly and with integrity without paying them any attention. We need to live proactively, and reduce our anxiety and powerlessness in the process. *We need to stop trying to please, communicate directly and authentically, reflect on social interactions and work out what's going on.*

The difficulty of recognising what's real

We need to recognise the *'hyper-reality'* in television, films, games, internet porn - address the *reality* in our lives. It's useful to realize that use of porn takes up an enormous percentage of internet traffic – Sebastian Anthony of Extreme Tech suggests the figure could be around 30% of all data transferred across the internet. It's a multi-billion dollar industry (with key providers including America, China and South Korea). We can look beneath the surface and ask questions about how the news is presented to us – every TV presenter is carefully coutured to fit norms of attractiveness and to make it seem as if all is 'well' or 'in hand'. *The government is in control. The bankers are sorting it out. The United Nations Security Council will decide what to do.* There's no suggestion that it is up to *us* to advise the government. We're told of the most appalling tragedies and human rights abuses by people who look as if their most difficult life challenge has been choosing their clothes for the show. The people invited to give

543

views may not be a fair cross-section, and people with varying levels of 'credibility' don't necessarily get treated evenly by journalists.

We need to seek wider information and not rely exclusively on any one source, particularly not television. Finding the 'truth' about any situation needs research, discussion, questions, and a variety of sources of information. *We can ask provocative questions of our friends and local community and beyond – get different viewpoints and surprise ourselves.* We'll be much better equipped to assess the 'reality'. We can travel. *We can speak to people in different organisations or different places.* Chat to the gasfitter who comes to mend our boiler. Ask the person who serves us a meal in the canteen or café what they think of the political or environmental situation. Read newspapers – different ones. Press journalists are sometimes a lot braver than TV ones in expressing alternative viewpoints. Inform ourselves. Go outside our comfort zone. Stop following the crowd. Disturb our social scene. Listen to our instincts and attend to unease. As Quakers say, *'live adventurously'*.

Environmental and political factors

There are big issues bothering us about the wider world.

- *Yellowstone Caldera* hovers with its potential to erupt 'overdue', nuclear plants get damaged, earthquakes and tsunamis overwhelm us, superbugs proliferate, oil leaks damage birdlife and sea-life, blue whales, giant pandas and snow leopards are some of many species threatened with extinction. We struggle to comprehend the extent to which we are responsible for the problems and are uncertain about the likelihood that we will find the will to tackle the problems that we can, before they overwhelm us.

- states organise extraordinary rendition of people for torture, protesters against state regimes are fired upon or imprisoned at the decision of government officials, women are raped and their husbands and children killed or beaten up; whole peoples are forced to transfer their family lives, humiliated at checkpoints and left to find their way to refugee centres where often they perish from disease, starvation, further attack or grief.

- banks exploit their customers and damage state economies, the media industry turn murderers and (other) violent criminals into characters in dramas, journalists hack into people's phones and paparazzi invade people's privacy at times of stress

- governments whom we may have long thought of as there to organise things on our behalf start to look less trustworthy and less benign, presiding over an unfair world and deepening the divisions between people, squeezing the poor and nearly poor and making the better-off insecure and frightened

The history of the twentieth and twenty-first centuries provides clear evidence of the bullying and intimidation by governments to implement policies and to intimidate protestors. Josef Stalin's tactics in eastern bloc countries after the end of the Second World War, the Rwandan and Bosnian conflicts, Saddam Hussein's government in Iraq, and recent battles in countries like Libya, Bahrain and Syria between rebels/demonstrators and their ruling élites are examples of situations where enforcing the hold on power on populations by those in power has been catastrophic.

Sometimes we may feel that the human desire for territorial imperative or political control is taking precedence over 'green issues' to our detriment – *'fiddling while Rome burns'* – arguing and battling whilst icebergs melt, animals disappear, the globe warms up, congestion and pollution choke people and the population continues to increase. We may be able to appreciate that human rights and land and autonomy are things that across the globe people feel so passionately about they are prepared to fight and die for them rather than worry about the survival of the planet.

But not only are peoples arguing and battling – behind the scenes, key players in the way the world works economically and politically are making their moves and implementing their strategies – foreign aid policies are increasingly linked to desired political outcomes, multinationals and international banks have more influence than some national governments – shifts in power structures are gradually re-shaping our world. Whilst we may feel that there is not enough of a brake on greed – developments seem to be in the interests of those who would be rich, in control or wedded to the continuation of the *status quo,* there may also be a sense of progress as international organisations increasingly regulate and monitor situations around the world, and technology allows us to build data banks that provide instant information about any subject under the sun.

There is always a balance to be struck, and not everyone makes the same choice about priorities or makes the same interpretation of facts.

The way our culture is being distorted

The way in which celebrity culture and the entertainment industry fills our heads with distraction and motivates us – or our children – to be *wannabes* needs to be examined. The flaunting of wealth and the creation of iconic status for people who have questionable talent can overshadow the poverty and difficulty in much of our own society and elsewhere. It is laudable that some celebrities front up charity programmes for disaster relief, set up funds for disadvantaged groups, fly out to war zones to visit armed forces-bases, or swan round the globe highlighting suffering, and maybe this does go some way towards helping some of us to look beyond our own concerns, but the overriding message of celebrity culture and the commercial entertainment industry is that success, fame and fortune is for the few, and that those few are the chosen ones, whether or not they are the most able. We can see from contemporary TV talent-spotting programmes that thousands of people long for fame and success and are prepared to have a go at reaching their dream, but we need to consider carefully if living our lives trying to fit alongside many competitors and going through a 'narrow gate' is the right way to go.

The school system also echoes this approach – our young people are forced to prepare hard for qualifications in order to enter the employment market competitively rather than to develop their characters or to question ideas and beliefs about the world. It's inevitable that the education system will have been distorted to serve the capitalist machine and it's important that we remember our rights to have our needs as human beings in the equation. Not just because our rights matter (which they do). But because the world needs (and deserves) more than clones turned out to feed the great project (and fantasy) of perpetual economic growth.

The deliberate and sometimes inadvertent glorification of criminal activity or violence through the endless array of detective and horror dramas and the sensational way in which serious crimes are sometimes reported has resulted in the risk that criminality can seem a route to fame and notoriety for those who are desperate to be noticed and suffering from pathological disturbance. War itself is a major field of entertainment – in films, reporting, novels and games, and again can fill our minds with the idea that jingoistic aggression is praiseworthy. Avoiding the negative and destructive messages within our culture – sometimes conveyed simply by the sheer *volume* of its content *(look at the balance of programmes in any evening's TV listings)* – may help us to find a healthy direction for our energies and that of those in our charge or care.

It may be a good idea to stimulate effort and personal development to enter competitions and aim for prizes but not at the expense of deep human values. *We need to live our lives feeling good about ourselves and the way we live,* not hoping for a better tomorrow, not mortgaging our current lives for a fantasy of what may never actually come to us, and riding on the highs and lows of winning and losing. Of course we all hope to create good things in the years ahead – that is not the issue – the issue is that we should not deny the importance of our time now, with the opportunity to value our relationships, our interests, and our emotional and physical health.

The effect of history

70 years after the Second World War, the generation that lived through it and those who fought many of its battles is dying off. There is a special gratitude among many of us for the sufferings they had and the sacrifices they made, as well as a painful ambivalence about the way we have allowed the world to develop since, including sadness about the erosion of human rights after so much had been achieved in post-war commitments to human freedom.

It may be that as this generation leaves the picture, the rest of us are more able to look squarely at what happened then and discuss it dispassionately. Certainly, there is almost an obsession with documentaries and dramas linked to that war, going over again and again the strategies, the battles, the atrocities, the resistances, the collaborations, the privations, the weaponry, the delusions, the romances and the separations, and the losses and the grief. We need to understand and to piece together how human beings came to participate in such mass horrors – including Okinawa and Iwo Jima, Stalingrad, and the Shoah/Holocaust. It's possible that this history – the biggest conflict in human existence, with estimates of 50-70 million dead and mammoth numbers of families bereaved and destroyed – has left the human race in a peculiar state. Losses came primarily from *military action and collateral damage, crimes against humanity, prisoner of war deaths and starvation from famine and migration.* Among some of the most horrifying statistics is the loss of 25% of the population of Belarus, c. 23 million Chinese people and c. 24 million people from the Soviet Union and c. 6 million Jews and the deaths of perhaps 1 million Roma people. Getting definite statistics and agreements on statistics is of course impossible since what is being measured and what people admit to will be difficult to specify.

The point here is that it's hard to see how we can come to terms with this. Can we imagine the numbers of families that must grieve the loss of family members (many of whom they never had a chance to meet), the number of people who were injured mentally as well as physically, the families that were destroyed even though huge numbers survived.

For a personal and meticulously researched exploration of the post-war experience in Europe, Tony Judt's book *Postwar* is recommended. There are of course many valuable histories of the twentieth century, each with their own flavour. For example, Eric Hobsbawm in his *The Age of Extremes* is considerably more sympathetic to the Soviet Union than Tony Judt, Hobsbawm being a lifelong Marxist and Communist.

It's hard to see how we can have rebuilt lives and nations, brought children into the world and brought them up – and we *have* – the world population having more than trebled since 1940. It becomes easier to appreciate the psychology of the decades since then, to recognise that there were times when personal liberty felt terribly important and more important than our current obsession with health and safety, for example; to imagine that after starvation and rationing, people began to eat and eat until obesity has become a major problem in the Western world.

The stress we feel today must have some relationship to the psychology we have inherited from our forebears and from the unresolved material that we are still processing. There is the destruction of family lines so that many people are dispossessed of their place of origin and of knowledge about their identities. There is the denial of grief, with so many plunging into 'newbuild' and the project of post-war economic growth, a project that has been so all-engrossing across much of the world that it is a wonder anyone had time to parent anyone at all or to look fully at how to love our partners. There are also the post-war stress disorders that we now know affect the soldiers who come home. There are the long-term effects of trauma on those whose countries are ravaged, their cultural heritage bombed, their land and their bodies left with lifelong scars.

It's worth looking into the history of our own families and our long-term origins, as well as considering fully the aftermath of huge conflict on our psychological being. We are not simply floating in a vacuum – our psychology is made from the decades of history that precede us, and our capacity to take in, resist, and survive stress will have some relationship to the context in which we were constructed.

Being blamed and whose responsibility is it?

In my 40s, I was travelling on average 16-20 hours a week to and from work, I had a young baby, and a husband who didn't drive or use the computer. My work was demanding and difficult, with a series of short-term contracts always making continued employment uncertain. I was heavily over-borrowed with a large mortgage, a large personal loan and credit-card debt, all of which had been necessary to sustain our lifestyle in a three-storey house overlooking the sea in a rural environment, which my husband continually improved and upgraded. My health began a slow process of decline, I became alienated from my husband and started to invest in relationships at work instead of at home; conflict at home became the norm.

Sometimes I even imagined turning the wheel and driving off the edge of a major bridge on the way home. The years went by – the eventual outcome was that my husband developed cancer and died, and I faced up to the debt situation with the support of friends, and ultimately gave up my job in order to save my health. I lost my home but saved my life, and started to prioritise the love and care I needed to give my daughter and myself.

The problem is that we can be blamed for stress as an individual problem, and come to believe ourselves as weak or in the wrong. This can only exacerbate the situation.

In my own story (above), there are a number of factors from the outside world that affected my situation. This included:

- declining work opportunities in the rural areas so that travel to work in the cities became necessary

- years of fixed-term contracts which kept me endlessly trying to prove myself worth 'keeping on', attaining short-term goals, never being able to invest in long-term career development, in an employment setting which relied on keeping large numbers of people on flexible employment contracts and grateful for work

- financial borrowing made easier but ultimately mortgage and borrowing rates increasing, insurance policies etc.

front-loaded onto cost of loans etc. (a financial context which found more and more ways of making money out of people's struggles)

- changing culture in the workplace which made things increasingly tougher (eg. new systems for monitoring sick leave, introduction of targets, more complex requirements within the job, increase in workload, decrease in the rewarding areas of work, more legal accountability for getting things wrong etc)

- more traffic congestion with new shopping centres bringing in more traffic and more people travelling to work, and more road-works as repairs increasingly needed to sustain roads no longer fit for higher volumes of traffic

- accessibility of food and drink made easier (eg. late night shops even in rural area, more and more delicious things sold, wider choice of products, ease of preparation, cost of alcohol kept manageable with special offers and cut-prices etc)

- a culture in which it became increasingly acceptable to have a stay-at-home father and a working mother, regardless of whether that was what I wanted – the idea of 'work-life balance' hadn't really permeated my consciousness and the ideology of feminism which I'd always promoted meant that I supported challenges to traditional roles

I mention these things not to reduce the 'blame' that might be appropriately accorded to me by many, but to show that we exist within a culture and systems that have built-in problems and are also intentional. We are at the mercy of grander and wider systems than we like to think.

When I was first employed at one college on a short contract, I was told by the person appointing me that they wanted people who were 'lean and hungry'. Some years later, still on short-term contracts in the same institution, when I was clearly (and perhaps inevitably) suffering from stress, instead of the care and concern that I longed for, my boss was critical and distancing.

In retrospect, I understand that I should have parented myself – I was wrong to expect the institution to do anything other than look to its own profits and ambition, yet I carried on like a child looking for love from abusing parents, hoping that the organisation would somehow help me. It was an example of my not 'taking charge'.

An example of how we can manage a stressful event – 'moving home'

For many people, moving home is a stressful event, even though it's not high on the Holmes and Rahe's Stress Scale (they obviously never moved house!!), but of course, it is the *meaning* that will make this more or less stressful. Losing your home because the bailiffs are in is quite different from selling your house because you have decided to go travelling round the world for a year in a camper van.

The key ingredients are usually:

the sense of control we have over events
and
the *amount of emotion encoded in them.*

If having a home has always come easy to us, we will have an optimistic outlook on being able to get one again and we may be unaware of the deep emotions that can be unearthed for some people through losing a stable base. It will depend too on the sense of safety we got when we were infants and how confident we feel about being able to look after ourselves or to get help.

If we've spent years working to service a mortgage and are very proud of owning our own home, or paying high rent to live in an attractive place, then losing it because of financial pressure may feel like an attack on our competence as a human being.

Re-framing what's happening

If we've been unable to keep up mortgage payments because of over-mortgaging ourselves in the past and rising interest rates, or other borrowings, or other financial commitments that have increased and put pressure on our overall outgoings, or because we've lost our job or business been unable to keep up our income etc. it can be easy to blame ourselves. Understanding that millions of people in the Western world have been manipulated financially into just this position may help us to feel less personally culpable. Of course if we don't feel at all responsible, maybe we should consider that we *could* have taken action sooner to cut back or looked for alternatives etc – it's always good to try to get an accurate view of our situation!

> When I lost my home after my husband died I felt very unhappy and blamed myself for the financial situation. In order to settle debt, I had to hand over the entire inheritance from my parents' house when my mother died – I was very upset at having to do this, but after a while, I came to see things in a completely different light. I saw that as my parents had been unable to help in any way with the upbringing of my daughter this inheritance was really a retrospective 'grand-parenting' contribution to those years when I had needed help and had had to borrow from the bank and they hadn't had any liquid assets to share with me. This re-framing of the situation helped a lot.

Getting information about the context and our options

It's important to get information about our situation – not simply about our own options, but about the wider scene. It may help us to learn how many people have been forced into foreclosure on loans and mortgages and whether we are in the main target group. This kind of data could help us to accept the wider social and economic shifts and to stop blaming ourselves. Accept that life stages are transitory, that things are always moving on and that having a home might be something that will fit one phase of life and isn't going to fit in another. Adopt a Pollyanna approach and look for the things we can be *glad* about such as:

- new freedom
- getting to understand a different way of life
- meeting others whose lives have become more difficult
- less pressure to 'keep up with the Jones'
- a sense of relief
- a chance to start again
- no need to do any major repairs
- no surprises re: maintenance costs on a property

We can research our new options as widely and fully as possible:

- *backpacking and hostel stays*
- *buying a campervan and travelling about*
- *joining a travelling community*
- *travelling by car, train or bus and staying in new places whilst we do 'reccies'*
- *advertising for what we need*
- *renting a property – watch out for discrimination and hunt for a landlord we like and a property that has something good about it for us*
- *downshifting to a cheaper area or property*
- *moving to where there is more work in our line or more social openness*
- *joining a communal housing project*
- *getting a live-in job or tied-housing post*
- *going into social housing such as deals with housing associations and council housing help*
- *staying in bed and breakfasts or finding a permanent/semi-permanent hotel base*
- *buying or renting a mobile home or chalet*
- *setting up temporary residential arrangements (eg. going on a course or retreat, staying with a friend)*
- *joining a religious or social community that provides residential accommodation*
- *investigating the availability of grants, charitable help and financial support etc.*

Then put a decision-making process into action – this will almost certainly require going to see or talk to people. Remember that some steps may lead to further ones. They are not all permanent choices. Things change over time as we pick yourselves up and move through change.

Overall, we can consider the way we relate to *ourselves* – challenge any tendencies to recriminate or chastise ourselves, fight any pessimism, keep up our morale, look for the good around us, and get stuck into the new challenges. (See also our chapter on *The Self*)

Develop control over our situation:

- gather information and ideas
- find some meaning in the situation that makes sense of it for us
- enlist support
- connect with others
- create positives around us
- create our own individual space, however small.
- make our own rituals – *walk to the same place every day, have a regular hour when we reflect on things, always have a coffee-break, sit down with our children once a week in the fish and chip shop and talk with them.*
- take decisions
- take control of money, however problematic it is
- look after our health – eating, rest, play, sleep, medicine, health monitoring
- *tell* others what we need, *don't* ask *them* what they think we need or can have

Exercise

Try working on something happening in your life that you don't currently feel in charge of.

Event	How I can re-frame it	What I can do to take charge of it.

Looking after ourselves and 'being in charge'

We need to look after ourselves – this means treating ourselves with care and attention and with a loving approach. Exercise, good food and regular rest are all part of maintaining our health for the long-term. Recognising and reducing the kinds of events that can stress us is important. The most important thing that stresses us is *not being in charge*.

There has long been evidence that we can bear painful, uncomfortable or scary medical procedures better if we have some control over their delivery – for example, being able to interrupt proceedings and say 'can we pause now', or 'that's too painful' or 'can we go a little more slowly' etc. Being able to exercise *some* control allows us to handle more. We can handle heavier workloads if we can exercise *'worker-paced control'* – if we are able to slow things down sometimes or take a break – when work comes at us without us being able to influence its pace at all, we feel stressed. It is interesting that 'working from home' often produces better results than 'working at work'– one of the reasons may be that we feel we can take breaks and vary the pace more freely than when under the watchful eye of an employer.

Letting go of having to get it right

The pressure to get it right – to find the right partner, to bring up our children right, to have the right occupation can be a major stressor. The pressure to maintain our status – often a key feature of middle-class existence - can literally finish us off – particularly at times of economic downturn when being able to keep up with financial commitments comes under pressure.

The trick is to find our identity beyond crude external measures of success such as having our children go to university or living in the right area, and to ensure that we and our children find meaning in existence beyond material markers.

Books, papers and websites

Sebastian Anthony *Just how big are porn sites?* Extreme Tech April 4, 2012 http://www.extremetech.com/computing/123929-just-how-big-are-porn-sites

BBC India *The rapes that India forgot* 5th January 2013 http://www.bbc.co.uk/news/world-asia-india-20907755

BBC News Europe:
L'Aquila: Italy Scientists Guilty of Manslaughter 22nd October 2012 *http://www.bbc.co.uk/news/world-europe-20025626*
http://www.bbc.co.uk/news/uk-politics-19167590

Johnathan Bloom (2010) *American Wasteland: How America Throws Away Nearly Half Its Food and What We Can Do About It.* Da Capo Lifelong Books

John Bowlby (1951) *Maternal Care and Mental Health - report for the World Health Organisation* New York: Schocken

Susan Cain (2012) *Quiet: The Power of Introverts in a World that Can't Stop Talking* Viking

Walter Bradford Cannon (1915) *Bodily Changes in Pain, Hunger, Fear and Rage: An Account of Recent Researches into the Function of Emotional Excitement* Appleton

Dale Carnegie (1936) *How to Win Friends and Influence People* Simon and Schuster

Mike Clayton (2011) *Brilliant Stress Management* Harlow: Pearson Education

Emmy van Deurzen (2012) *Existential Counselling and Psychotherapy* London: Sage

Margaret Donaldson (1986) *Children's Minds* Harper Collins

Jack Dusay (1972) *Egograms and the constancy hypothesis* Transactional Analysis Journal 2(3)37-41.

EurActiv.com *Parliament pushes to slash food waste in Europe* 19th January 2012, updated 9th March 2012 http://www.euractiv.com/cap/parliament-pushes-slash-food-was-news-510225

Anthony Giddens (2011) *The Politics of Climate Change* Polity Press

Stéphane Hessel (2010) *Time for Outrage!* London: Charles Glass Books

Eric Hobsbawm (1995 ed) *The Age of Extremes: The Short Twentieth Century 1914-1991* Abacus

Thomas H Holmes and Richard H Rahe (1967) *The Social Readjustment Rating Scale* J Psychosom Res **11** (2): 213–8

Tony Judt (2006) *Post-war: A history of Europe since 1945* Penguin Books

Suzanne C Kobasa (1979) *Stressful life events, Personality, and Health – Inquiry into Hardiness* Journal of Personality and Social Psychology **37** (1): 1–11.

Richard S Lazarus (1966) *Psychological Stress and the Coping Process* New York: McGraw-Hill Book Co.

Paul Mason (2010) *Meltdown: The End of the Age of Greed* Verso

Robert Peston (2012) *How Do We Fix This Mess? The Economic Price of Having it All, and the Route to Lasting Prosperity* Hodder and Stoughton

Eleanor H Porter (1913) *Pollyanna* L C Page

Klaus F Riegel (1976) *The dialectics of human development* American Psychologist, Vol 31(10), Oct 1976, 689-700

Jean-Paul Sartre (1944) *Huis Clos/No Exit* Vintage

Hans Selye (1974) *Stress Without Distress* Philadelphia: J B Lippincott

Ashley Weinberg and Cary Cooper (2012) *Stress in Turbulent Times* Palgrave Macmillan

Irvin Yalom (2008) *Staring at the Sun: overcoming the dread of death* Piatkus

TV

Wonderland Series 5: *Young, Bright and On the Right* (2012) BBC

18 change

> Throughout the book, there is an underlying assumption that you might want to make changes in your life. Factors like identifying how big a change is needed, deciding how much we want change, recognising how natural a change seems or how sudden or unexpected it is, letting go, facing up to our fears, being willing to risk things, dealing with resistance in people around us, networking and building support, and being willing to make and rectify mistakes are all part of changing things in our lives. Maximising the feeling of choice in relation to the elements of change and the process of change is important.

The first part of this chapter is by Jack and the second by Julia

Jack

Change is happening all the time - the world is changing and we are changing. We need to decide about and take charge of changes within ourselves, for example, our attitudes or making changes in our lives or in the world.

The pace of change in the world is fast – I'm not sure people can keep up. In ageing we usually get less flexible when we need to become more flexible as there is more to handle eg. health issues, insecurity etc.

Why is the world moving so quickly? Answers to this question are discussed in our chapter on *The crisis we're in* as well as the one on *Stress* but an important shorthand version would include the pressure for different nations and companies to compete with each other in order to survive economically, and the anxieties associated with the state of the physical world and its dangers.

A possible model is:

1. what's the problem?

2. nature of the problem

internal	external
big	small
easy	difficult

3. is change wanted?

yes
no
later

This model works in relation to many problems. It's a deceptively simple model but it's tried and tested.

Examples:

- loss of internal values
- too much society intrusion
- difficult work situations
- feeling unworthy because of psychological 'put downs'

Identifying the nature of the problem or issue is an important step – often, changing something at the individual level is easier than making an impact on the wider world, but sometimes we live our lives trying to change something big and external to ourselves because issues at home seem so intractable.

In all situations requiring change, there will be levels of resistance.

General point: we're never *entirely* responsible but we need to act as though we are.

Internal	*lack of confidence needs to be turned into confidence*	external	*material inequality needs to be addressed so that things are fairer and more equitable*
Big	*financial debt needs to be turned into solvency*	small	*forgotten birthday needs to be salvaged with apology and gift*
Easy	*not spending time with family needs to be changed into finding quality time*	difficult	*alcohol dependence needs to be healed and replaced by mild social drinking*

What to be careful of with change:

- resistance from others, organisations etc.
- trying 'more of the same' – see Brief Therapy

'How' as well as 'what'

We need to look at *the way we go through the process of change* as well as focusing on *where we're aiming to get to.*

It's important to look after our own survival but important too, to consider how we treat others and the whole question of our 'social fabric'. We need to be socially conscious and sensitive to the kind of society we want to have. We need to *be* the change we want to see.

Julia's comments

Events don't have the same meaning for each of us

We don't experience 'marker events' in the same way as each other – thus it's not clear that we all experience for example, pregnancy or retirement in the same, pre-programmed ways. We can't necessarily anticipate how something will 'take' us. Getting married or confirming a relationship is often expected to be a happy event but it can bring up grief at what has gone or memories of a previous relationship or new responsibilities that are more onerous than we anticipated etc. And the ritual ceremonies for key moments in life can sometimes be worrying in themselves, involving complex negotiations among people (eg. who to invite to a funeral) or expectations regarding how much to spend on the event.

Pie-chart analysis

It can be a good idea to assess the amount of effort and time we invest in aspects of our life, and how much reward and satisfaction we get back from that investment, as a prelude to deciding how to go forward. For example, some things may be 'bothering' us yet we may not invest much time or energy in trying to tackle them, or we may be surprised that something which brings us lots of satisfactions doesn't in fact match up with the time and energy we're currently investing in something else that doesn't seem fulfilling. We may be over-worried about things that don't ultimately bring us much satisfaction or in which we're not currently investing much time or energy – perhaps if we gave that area of our life more attention, our worries would reduce.

Try working out for yourself where your energy goes and what comes back.

The pie-charts that follow are fictional examples. Developing charts for ourselves can lead to all sorts of questions about how we're using our energy and how to amend our investments of time and resources to bring about more rewarding outcomes. This could mean switching some of our energy and attention to something else, or it could mean that we notice a mismatch and decide to see if we can use our energy in a more skilful way.

time spent

Possible key to colour shades:

Pets
Friends
Close relationships
Sexuality
Parenting
Caring roles
Working
Non-close relationships
Money
Spiritual life
Creativity
Social activism
Listening to the unconscious

concern/worry

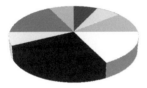

resources invested

For example, if we said *medium grey* was 'sexuality' we might find that we invest little time or resources on it, and thus that concern/worry is there and we have low levels of satisfaction. If *white* was 'parenting' and *black* was 'working' we might find that we're investing time, worry and resources in these roles but not getting much satisfaction and we might need to look at whether we're doing the right things in our parenting or working roles. Conversely if *deep grey* was 'pets' we might find we don't worry much about them, but that they give us loads of happiness.

satisfactions

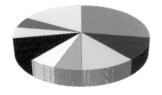

Do we want the change?

The degree to which something is wanted and anticipated is a key element in how we handle things.

Unwanted/unexpected	Wanted/unexpected
Closure of factory/office/ department	*New relationship possibility arises*
Rape	*New opportunity arises in work or housing*
Accident	*Winning a prize*
Sudden relationship breakdown/ betrayal	*A stressful neighbour moves away*
Unwanted/expected	**Wanted/expected**
Redundancy or redeployment	*Pregnancy or birth of a child*
Financial failure	*Marriage or civil ceremony*
Academic failure	*Retirement*
Bereavement	*Academic/professional/sporting success*

The closure of a workplace, which might be unwanted and unanticipated, could nevertheless result in a surprising new horizon appearing, for example new and deeper bonds with people in the same boat, the development of a hitherto neglected hobby, or a richer engagement with spiritual questions and the transitory nature of institutional structures.

> When I found out I was expecting my daughter (at the age of 44), I went to see the doctor who was older than me and she sat back for a moment, pen perched on her earlobe, and slowly said *'well, I think that's wonderful!'* It was a caring response but though ultimately she was very caring, at that moment she wasn't actually dealing with the mixed feelings I had about it and my fears for the future.
>
> cont'd

When I went to the 6 week ante-natal course, the midwives talked about fortifying my home against toddler damage and installing locks and guards around the home to protect the toddler. They talked about spending seven hours a day feeding the baby, sterilising bottles and making up feeds etc. To me, who up until then had been a busy 'career woman' with hardly the space in a day for a coffee break, it was a huge shock. Tears just quietly rolled down my face. No-one addressed how I *felt*, and no-one talked about the psychology of the infant. And little did I know then that those feelings might have echoed my own mother's feelings when she was expecting me and had to give up her exciting career at the age of 23.

This 'one size fits all' approach can miss many essential aspects of a situation.

And if something is expected we can plan for it whereas if it's sudden, we may find ourselves unprepared for the feelings as well as the practical implications.

Try using the following table to identify different aspects of a change and to think about how you might respond to them.

Dealing with change

Wanted elements	Unwanted elements	Anticipated elements	Unanticipated elements
How do I value these?	How can I incorporate these or act on them?	How do I deal with these?	How can I incorporate these or act on them?

Whose change is it?

In his novel *Everyman*, the writer Philip Roth describes the pull of desire as his central character faces up to the changes in himself and around him in relation to women he has known. In particular he describes a time when he found happiness with a younger, peaceful woman but knew that within a year his desire for her would evaporate against his rational will. He knew too that he had destroyed his former marriage through following his sexual desire into a powerful but ultimately unfulfilling affair. Sometimes we can feel moved to external changes by compulsions and forces within ourselves that we don't understand or that we struggle to control.

We might want to 'go into' therapy or search our personal memory archives to appreciate our own processes and understand how we seek and find love and satisfaction (sexual, spiritual, creative, professional etc) in our lives (and how sometimes these quests become distorted into addictions and problematic foci). Religious teachers and preachers have often provided a strict moral framework for getting on top of natural desires and compulsions, and legal and regulatory frameworks often enshrine moral principles of the society within them.

The work of creating change in ourselves may need *both* deep understanding of how we tick and for us to implement management strategies (eg. practical steps, new ways of thinking etc). The example of looking after our health – physical and emotional and behavioural, comes to mind. For some of us, attending courses or groups may be helpful even if we have to do some research to find them - *anger management, assertiveness skills, parenting skills, handling headaches, living with depression, carer support, diabetes management, alcohol, drug and smoking cessation groups, etc.*

Accepting things is part of changing

What's important is that *we* **get in control of change to the extent that we can**.

The *Serenity Prayer*, which exists in a variety of forms, and has disputed provenance but is generally attributed to the theologian Reinhold Niebuhr, is used by *Alcoholics Anonymous* in their meetings. What is helpful here is the idea that *we may have to accept some things about life* as part of our change process, and to distinguish between things we can change and those we can't.

For example, we may have been projecting an ideal fantasy onto someone we know rather than relating to them with a realistic appraisal of them – thinking of our child or partner as essentially good when they're really a thug and a bully, believing that a colleague's grandiose plans really are going to work out this time when time and again they've led us into financial trouble etc. Or we may have been denying the changes going on in our own body, believing that we can carry on doing high-stress work or driving long distances when our heart or brain is giving warning signs that it can't cope.

Accepting limits may be the change we need to make.

Linked to this kind of idea is the issue of **updating our perceptions and beliefs.** Struggling to keep up with a sense of who we're supposed to be – *the perfect health professional who never makes mistakes, the son who doesn't get divorced and doesn't bring shame on the family, the wife who's always well groomed and stylishly dressed, the friend who is always there for troubled souls, the mate who can always afford the drinks* – **we can wear ourselves into the ground by not setting boundaries between self and other, between expectations of others and our own deep self** – what the psychologist and therapist Carl Rogers called the 'organismic' self. (See our chapter on *The Self* and the one on *Therapy*). We have the absolute right to say what we need and what we can no longer do – we can't maintain façades that aren't true, we can't be all-giving, we can't keep up unrealistic standards any more, we can't do all the driving anymore. We can be surprised at what a relief it is to be more authentic.

> My father had always been the main family driver. In his seventies, he agreed to be the driver for my mother and relatives on a long car trip around Britain, staying with various friends and in hotels. They were all enthusiastic but it all went wrong when my mother had a heart attack *en route*. Eventually he had to drive the few hundred miles home on his own without a navigator. Within the year, he had two strokes and died. Although of course not possible to make a definite link, the question remains that perhaps he should have said 'no' to doing all the driving and should have looked after his own stress levels.
>
> But a lifetime of a pleasing 'script' and of being the stalwart figure in the family meant he had no experience of changing his behaviour and that didn't help him as he got older – he couldn't change when he needed to.

Fear

Change is frequently and sometimes inevitably linked to fear – we can counter fear by analysing it or by shaping it – unshaped fear is much more anxiety-prone.

Businesses are often asked to produce plans for optimistic, expected and pessimistic outcomes and this kind of strategy can be helpful at a personal level and at a campaign level.

Actions	Optimistic outcome	Expected outcome	Pessimistic outcome
Leaving home	*Find new flat at perfect rent, meet the love of my life, still feel happy one year later*	*Find a flat which isn't quite where I want it to be and the rent's a bit high, make some new friends, sometimes miss the family but feel proud of my newfound independence*	*End up living in a horrible bedsit, abused by a sadistic landlord, so lonely I end up crawling home and begging to be let back into the fold*

Initiating a new direction for a social/political campaign	Team members think it's a great idea and start to implement the new strategy with enthusiasm. New policy has an effect and social/ political situation starts to shift. Morale goes up and more people are able to benefit from the service or initiative.	A small cohort agrees with new strategy, it gets adopted but we lose a few people who don't go with the new direction. I have some uncertainties about the plan and it has some effect – probably have to review it and rehash it a bit in a few months' time.	Quite a few people in the team walk out, my credibility as leader is damaged, people see me as betraying our original objectives, and people aren't willing to move with change. New policy is dropped. Former strategy reinstated but is ineffective. I have to resign or move out of campaign.

It may be an idea to explore our fantasies about the worst possible scenario. Often our fantasies are linked to childhood experience and the reality may have moved on from what we experienced or believed then. The housing estate we were frightened of may now have tenant support services, and active government investment in aesthetic and security measures and community initiatives, the dental work we always dreaded having may be pain-free and delivered by a team who are kind and sensitive to our anxieties, the friends who used to put pressure on us to 'keep up with the Jones' may be replaced by people who are more relaxing to be with and more imaginative about life, the search for cheap nourishing food on a low-budget may turn out to be fun and involve us in thinking about nutrition properly for the first time. Not giving anyone any Christmas presents may help us to balance our own bank account and bring us enormous relief from stress as well as kick-starting real discussions with people in our life about economic pressures. Going bankrupt may free us from stress that may have been slowly killing us.

The spectre of stigma and danger can be challenged and linked up to horror stories we absorbed when we were young. We're unlikely to have kept up with all developments in modern life –

it's good to check things out to see what new systems and steps have been put in place – notwithstanding our critiques of contemporary life, there ARE also many improvements.

Choosing how to respond

There are lots of ways in which we might respond to pressures that are mounting around us and some of these are listed in the box below:

Areas to consider in problem-solving change

Ritualising	Protesting	Going with the flow	Linking
organising a ceremony, memorial, plaque, feast, saying a prayer or poem, visiting a grave or special place	organising a campaign, taking legal action, amassing arguments, getting in touch with powerful allies	crying, letting feelings come up, going into a cocoon, grieving, incubating energy	networking, bonding, sharing, exploring, setting up or joining groups
De-stressing	**De-cluttering and making space for the new**	**Being practical**	**Being creative**
taking a holiday or break, listening to music, going to look at the sea, doing some exercise	clearing up mess, getting rid of old things, repairing broken things, giving away what we can	organising funds, borrowing, finding new ways to raise money, talking to financial advisers	writing a narrative, evolving a new look, moving home, accepting a change in identity or status

What helps?

Things that have been helpful for me at times of change include:

- discussing with friends and allies the options – the more I talk about the possibilities the more real they become

- writing out lists of advantages and disadvantages of different options and giving them weightings

- doing as much as I can to find out about the future possibility eg. visiting the new place, asking people about their experiences of the new situation

- carrying out ritual closure on the past eg. with a goodbye party, proper speeches, thank-yous to those who've been part of the past etc.

- establishing things to help in new situation eg. contacting any contacts I have in new situation, looking up relevant organisations that could be of help, getting or producing my own maps and guidebooks – including maps of how to get around buildings, lists of useful contact details, reading up on information and tips about how to handle things (eg. a health condition, a new social status such as 'widow', new stepmother, being a newcomer etc); tapping into 'local' knowledge, finding a counsellor to talk to while we settle into new ways of living and to help us challenge old patterns.

- handling my feelings and keeping calm, recognising that things will be uncomfortable and unfamiliar and scary for a while, giving myself positive messages for the courage and initiative I'm demonstrating, reminding myself of why I'm doing what I'm doing

- being clear about the external factors that have contributed to my situation such as the world economic context, the changes in policy affecting my work, health crises among people in my life etc. and ensuring that I don't take the blame for difficulties entirely on myself

John-Paul Flintoff, in his useful and wise book *How to change the world*, suggests that turning our vague ideas about what we want to change into operational, clearly defined goals will help us to take action and move forward on things, and that linking our specific ideas (eg. close to home) to wider concerns may help us to value the small steps for change we make every day.

Undervaluing what we are doing and the effect it is having on others is an easy but perhaps costly mistake to make. It can be all too easy to walk away from a person, job, project or campaign because we feel unappreciated only to realise later that there was a problem with communication – they didn't think they needed to tell us, we didn't think to check the matter out – too many assumptions were made. Going back to Jack's ideas about OKness in the chapter on *Effective Relating* may be helpful in these circumstances – we should act with a belief in our own value and communicate clearly to others that we need to know how they find us.

'Willingness to risk'

More than any other writer on change, I've always found Gail Sheehy's work on adult life development inspiring. In her original book *Passages,* she outlined a stage approach to adult life development and really put the idea of lifelong growth and change on the map with a model that suggested we shed a psychological 'skin' roughly every seven years and steadily grow a new carapace, often feeling vulnerable during the phase of shedding and new growth. She gave us a plan of what to expect at each stage of adult life whilst giving enough room for each of us to negotiate such passages in our own unique ways.

In her later work on *Pathfinders,* Gail Sheehy elaborated on her original themes and studied the responses of sixty thousand people to her life history questionnaire. Her section *'what to take into the woods'* is very useful, including the idea of *'willingness to risk'* and a sense of the *'right timing'*.

In fact, Gail Sheehy makes an explicit link between the phases of the **creative process** (see our chapter on *Creativity*) and the process of negotiating a life 'passage', with *preparation* and *incubation* phases being followed by the risk of dipping our toes into the water of change and actually starting the change (or creative activity) before getting to the place where we *incorporate, edit* and *consolidate.*

We all differ on how much we're prepared to handle risk. Gail Sheehy found that people had a higher sense of wellbeing if they went with change in their lives rather than holding onto stability and continuity against the stirrings of their inner selves or the pressures of shifting life circumstances. The question of timing includes the issue of making changes before disaster strikes, taking preventative action to avoid catastrophe, taking steps to protect oneself, organising things to best advantage rather than letting someone else dictate the timing.

Most of us cling tightly to 'comfort zones', unless we happen to be someone who likes taking risks – extreme sports or daring business ventures, and even there, we may have stability zones in our lives, a mother we come home to or a mentor we talk things over with. Perhaps most of us aren't big risk-takers but living with a spirit of adventure will help us.

Letting go

Waiting for an organisation to make us redundant may be a good thing to do in order to get the redundancy pay, but is it the best in terms of opportunities for new training or taking up an offer to work on a new project with someone? Letting our relationship slide into self-destruct because we're afraid to let go could be damaging for our self-esteem and confidence and bad for the wellbeing of our children. *We don't always save things by holding onto them.* Sometimes letting a person go is the best way to find out if they really love us. Sometimes taking a risk with our career is the best way to demonstrate that we have entrepreneurial qualities.

Making changes may mean that we lose our fantasy of being a perfect organisation person or a married-for-life person. But many people have found out to their cost that fitting in and conforming and behaving perfectly doesn't actually bring all the career success or relationship happiness that they wanted. We can find 'betrayal' – emotionally or professionally – hits us very hard. It's as if the (silent) 'deal' we've made – often without making it explicit – with our employer or spouse has been reneged on, and it can be very hard to accept that the betrayal is actually something belonging to us – **that *we* have been afraid to grow** and partners and employers have sensed that and chosen someone else who *is* willing to grow.

We need to delve into our bank of personal resources to help ourselves especially if the change is unwanted. Buddhists would describe what is needed as 'letting go of attachment', freeing ourselves from wanting the things we used to have. Often the things we're attached to most are those things that give us our sense of ourselves. But we can go with a new notion of ourselves and recognise the continuity that exists in our inner life as we develop.

If we're 'downshifting', whether from a conscious choice or because we have to, we have to come to terms with the sense of loss we have from the materialistic life we've led previously and embrace the new freedoms we have as we unshackle ourselves from the treadmill of keeping up with others and struggling to pay high bills. We can enjoy the simplicity and the new challenges rather than seeing ourselves as victims.

> *During a particularly fraught phase in a dying relationship, I and my then partner started arguing and shouting both at home and outside. A row could flare up anywhere. I used to get embarrassed when it happened in a café or shop or at the library. One day we had a huge row in the supermarket, witnessed by lots of people. I sank to the floor and sat there holding my head in my hands. I think at that moment I knew that I was never again going to be the person that I had been. I would no longer always try to hold onto a formal* persona, *in control of emotions and interpersonal interactions. My sense of self underwent a change. It wasn't how I wanted it to be, but it was what was happening. I had to get used to this more vibrant but perhaps less 'pretty' sense of self.*

Deciding when……..

Deciding on timing may require a careful assessment of the right moment to make our move or it might be acting quite suddenly on a new insight or intuition.

There are no rules about when or how to make changes, and sometimes an exit has to be *right now*, even if the necessary preparation hasn't been done.

One of the important things that helps with change – and with so many things in life – is the support of people who like or love us or believe in our worth, talent or potential. Finding out what kind of support is available to us may affect our choice of timing, as will our decisions about the effect of our changes on others in our life. We might for example wait for children to take exams or leave school or parents to die etc. before separating. We often wait for a key support person to be around before making a change such as establishing things with a new partner or making sure a previously absent friend, family member, colleague or teacher is going to be available. However, there's no rule about this – for example, there can be a risk of emotional damage to children by parents who need to separate but are afraid to make the break – or similarly risk to ourselves through staying in a manipulative or violent relationship. Sometimes we can't wait any longer – we have to make a move for our own sanity regardless of other consequences.

We shouldn't forget the value of listening to the views of all players – our children or parents or colleagues might have a perception or opinion that surprises us. We may find that they've seen our unhappiness or frustration and have been aware that we've tried to deny it (even to ourselves).

Comparisons to people in our lives

It can be good to review who constitute our reference points.

We may for example compare our life progress with people we went to school with or served in the forces with, and re-union events bring this kind of comparison to the fore. Our thoughts may not be that attractive: *how come she did so well? how come an idiot like him became so rich? how come she managed to inspire people when she has so many glaring personal problems?* etc. and we can find ourselves berating ourselves instead of valuing what we *have* achieved. Quite often differences come down to people's self-presentation skills rather than the true nature of what they appear to have done.

Or we may compare ourselves to people with whom we're forced to spend many of our days at work, in hospital, in prison, in school or college, in sports teams etc. Subtle (and direct) comments from others can ensure we continue to conform to group norms. Within social class networks and institutional groups like churches or clubs or political organisations, there may be clear messages about expectations and groupthink, affecting anything from how much makeup we wear to whether we feel brave enough to criticise government or church policy.

The effect on others

In order to change we often have to face the fact that we can no longer sustain the relationships around us in the same way. There will be changes and losses as people seek to keep us where we've always been – perhaps useful to them if not practically, then psychologically – and as they struggle to accept choices we are making that feel like disapproval of their choices.

Negotiating a parting of the ways without rancour is a difficult challenge – leaving the door open to future contact can feel reassuring but in a little while, you may find that the differences between you have increased as you move forward.

And we need to remember that without us, people don't always collapse or even stay the same – they sometimes move forward in new ways themselves and we may find ourselves wondering why they felt so stuck when we were around. It can be a salutary experience to realise sometimes that in fact others needed *us* to change and move before they could make moves themselves. We go back to the office we left and find a whole raft of new systems in place that we hadn't even thought of. We visit our ex-partner and find that since our separation the house has been completely revamped to reflect their personality in a way that we wouldn't have anticipated. We walk out on a project group and find that they go on to greater success than we achieved when we were there. ***What's important is that we had the courage to go, and that our path (however uncertain it feels) is the right one for us for now.***

Making mistakes

Our fear is often of doing the wrong thing or of regretting a step we make.

Sometimes making a decision, right or wrong, is better than living in long-term indecision.

Sometimes if we do regret a step taken, we can negotiate a way back. Sometimes we can't but we can go on to build something similar with other players.

Sometimes we have to live with consequences of a 'wrong' decision *but we have to make our decision 'right'* through what we do in the months and years ahead. It's up to us.

We have to accept that we can't live life perfectly. Life is a creative process, and not every brush stroke can be exactly what's needed in the overall picture. Life has many twists and turns and if we got it right once, we can do so again.

Alternatives to big changes

If we're finding a decision difficult to make, one of the things that can be useful is to make *interim* changes......trial separations, a period of time away from a situation, going on a course or retreat, taking a room in town, organising a secondment to a different team or project.

If we feel trapped or unable to leave a problematic situation, one of the things that can be useful is to do steps that are *preparing for the future* when we will be more ready to make a move, such as acquiring new skills, getting fitter, tackling finances, organising more independence for ourselves etc.

A sense of safety

If we're frightened of being unprotected in a new situation, after years of feeling 'safe', we could consider whether that former safety would have been guaranteed to continue. And if it really was as safe as we thought. For example, we may have protected ourselves from violence or the sack by overly pleasing behaviour or overwork, either of which could have systematically eaten away at our mental or physical health. Our job may have seemed safe but who is to say that new developments might not have changed the goalposts later on?

We can set about *building new safety* around us. We can equip ourselves to cope, balancing the new anxieties with a feeling of exhilaration about new-found freedoms, learning how to cope with for example less money and being creative around that, learning self-defence or reinforcing the safety of our home, and shutting off the negative messages from people we know who think we're crazy. We can start thinking about safety coming from the exercise of our *own* abilities rather than safety provided by *others*.

We can free ourselves from old patterns of self-comforting like smoking, eating, watching TV and drinking. We can recognise old fears from infancy and childhood and recognise that *we're grown-up now*.

Books

John-Paul Flintoff (2012) *How to Change the World* Basingstoke: Pan Macmillan
Gail Sheehy (1976) *Passages: predictable crises of adult life* New York: Dutton
Gail Sheehy (1981) *Pathfinders: how to achieve happiness by conquering life's crises* London: Sidgwick and Jackson
Philip Roth (2007) *Everyman* Vintage

19   positive thinking

> The way that we think can have a significant effect on the outcomes of our lives and of any projects in which we get involved. The relationship between positive thinking and good outcomes is however not as clear-cut as used to be thought. There are some strategies in this chapter that can be used to foster positive thinking, but there is also some attention given here to the dilemmas associated with concentrating too much on grandiose or over-optimistic thinking instead of building in things like reality-checks and contingency plans.

The first part is written by Jack and the second by Julia.

Jack

Positive thinking has been around since people have been around. POSITIVE THINKING IS NOT NEW.

Positive thinking does not belong to anyone – there are usually some people trying to claim this territory as their own and build careers and empires on it. Various people have added bits to it or formulated slightly new angles despite all the grandiose claims that are made.

A lot of the 'positive-thinking industry' is American. People can think positively without the help of this industry.

There is a difference between positive thinking and the positive-thinking *industry* – nobody is actually saying how positive thinking works.

In this section, I will talk about two simple approaches allied to positive thinking, the positive thinking mind-set and the positive thinking industry. Being focused and mentally strong and disciplined is a very powerful way to approach the world and can make huge differences. Mental strength can involve the unconscious and conscious minds working simultaneously. Positive thinking is an aspect of people's ability to increase their mental focus and direction and motivation.

The positive thinking world

Positive thinking overlaps with 'success' and 'self-help' and with the 'growth movement'. An early example of fixing on getting rich is Napoleon Hills' (1937) *Think and Grow Rich* which is still worth a read to get an idea of his methods and value base. Then of course there was Dale Carnegie, whose landmark book *How to Win Friends and Influence People* (first published in 1936) is a commonsense book on treating people in a creative way to get a positive result. Both of these books though are probably over-optimistic and over-focused on influence and success as defined by money/power definitions, which were nevertheless important within the zeitgeist of their times. It's interesting though that Hill's 17-volume series of books was called *'Mental Dynamite'*!

Next to come along was the growth industry fuelled by some good ideas for example, Abraham Maslow and Carl Rogers to do with treating people as OK and capable of realising their potential. Important in this phase was the idea that we should focus on people's healthy aspects and potential for change and growth rather than on their neurotic and psychopathological distortions, which had been the main focus within psychoanalysis.

Next came the 'self-help' industry, usually with the idea that people could use simple, quick techniques to solve their problems, get rich and become successful.

Recently there's been a new interest in positive thinking. Martin Seligman is interesting in this context, building on these ideas for people in organisations like the US military and adding a research and evaluation underpinning to the ideas.

I think there's much that it's useful to learn from all these developments and they all offer some good things.

Some interesting problems in them though are that they are:

- conservative
- focus on individual 'success'
- often make too big claims and sometimes false claims

- tend towards claiming territories and empires for themselves out of ideas which are neither new or very original
- are over-concerned with acquisition of wealth, status, power etc.

How does 'positive thinking' work?

- it's active
- it's a way of being in control
- it creates focus
- it gives hope
- it gives meaning eg. to boring or difficult parts of a job or task
- it creates positivity and meaning in negative or difficult situations
- it keeps up morale and motivation

Usually positive thinking is part of a package which is geared to changing attitude and getting on and making changes. This is important as **there needs to be positive *doing* as well as positive *thinking***. It's a very useful approach for individuals; governments and big corporations have realised that it works to motivate people and make them more efficient.

Affirmations and retraining

Bearing in mind it is usually part of a bigger package, here are two positive thinking approaches:

Affirmations

Louise Hay is perhaps the person who's done the most to promote the value of positive affirmations in recent decades. Julia has written about the relationship of mind and body in the chapter on *The body, health and illness*, highlighting the power of our thoughts on our wellbeing, and Louise Hay is well worth reading in this respect.

Ultimately, affirmations are a very simple technique which involves you telling yourself something positive. For example, if you're doing your tax papers, which is often experienced as boring and difficult, you can say to yourself all day, at intervals, *'I'm doing good work here and it's helping me reach my business or career goals'*.

The idea with affirmations is that they're simple, positive, in the present, and involve motivating or praising yourself.

The part that's trickier is that affirmations need to be frequent and relentlessly repetitive.

Exercise:

Think of something (a task) you don't like doing. How can you use affirmations to help motivate yourself?

Reframing

Cognitive restructuring originally associated with Milton Erickson's work and later linked to ideas in cognitive therapy such as Aaron Beck's work on depression, involves challenging and disputing negative or 'dysfunctional' thoughts, a practice which can sometimes result in people suppressing or avoiding certain thoughts.

What we're talking about here as *'reframing'* is a method of *changing the psychological or emotional meaning or value of an event* and it's a way of seeing often negative or difficult events in a more positive way. For example, losing a business in an economic downturn may be seen as a catastrophe or as giving you an opportunity to spend more time at home with people you care about or starting a new business which has fewer of the problems than those you had with the old one.

Reframing is usually very helpful in the process of seeing what are experienced as quite bad events as an opportunity for growth and learning. Theoretically, you can reframe any event, even very traumatic ones, like terminal illness.

I think people have to come up with their own meanings in the end though you may be able to suggest new meanings to other people or get ideas from others. Not all situations are easy to reframe, especially where there's great loss and trauma.

Exercise

Think back on past events (big or small ones) that looked very negative or reflect on current ones that look negative and identify how you can reframe them positively.

Mental strength

Perhaps the important thing is *mental strength* and the determination to see things through. Having a positive view of life itself can help with this, having something or someone to live for. There are many stories (and films) of people who've gone through combat situations, buoyed up by the memory of their loved one(s) and the hope of being reunited with them. Many people have found courage to cope with frightening or difficult situations through their religious or spiritual beliefs. Having a belief in our own resilience helps; we can look back over situations in the past that we've successfully negotiated to remind ourselves about this.

Identify your own sources of mental strength.

I draw my strength from:

People in my life ....

....

Beliefs ....

....

Other
sources...

Julia's comments

Some extra points about affirmations

Affirmations are usually phrased in the present tense such as:

I am making healthy choices
I am a loving person and good partner/parent/child
I am letting go of my past

They can be spoken like mantras, although some have provided variation, for example, by giving them rhythms and melodies. For some people, they can be like prayers.

Some people use *visual* affirmations which can vary from putting the words up around the house to collecting and displaying imagery – for example, if you want to have a holiday but don't initially see how you can manage it financially or practically or both, pin up a noticeboard and collect everything you can in relation to the holiday – ideas, pictures, handy hints, testimonials from others who've been there, alternatives that are similar but cheaper etc. This could be done in conjunction with an affirmation *'every day I am getting closer to having that holiday'* or *'I am worthy of this holiday'*. This kind of idea was taught to me by the 'soul coach' Denise Linn at a workshop to 'manifest' desires.

Although dieting may not be the right route for many people (see chapter on the Body and also Susie Orbach's *Anybody* site), weight-loss gurus often suggest that we put up pictures of our former slimmer self, or identify clothes that we will be able to fit into or things we will be able to do when we have lost weight, and there is little doubt that this kind of activity will have positive effects towards reaching your goal, not least because if you find the energy to do them, you are already motivated. The important thing is not so much a future focus as an acceptance of ourselves in a positive way – a good affirmation might therefore be: *'I am living in harmony with my body'*. If we repeat this like a mantra regularly, we will find increasingly find it hard to put ourselves into 'cognitive dissonance' by doing anything which is bad for our body.

Not only does this kind of activity focus the mind in a positive way, it publicises to others what we're aiming for, it cultivates a belief in us that we can get something we want, it opens our soul to our needs which may have lain buried, it can work on the unconscious mind to release blocks and start us unpicking things in the way – people who object to us going somewhere, limiting financial problems, resistances around us and within us.

One of the most important messages to take home about affirmations is *the need for perseverance*. Just keep that affirmation going through thick and thin, whatever life throws at us, and we open ourselves to the positive energy that affirmations create. Creative artists (writers, painters, musicians etc) have always had to accept that they may have to make many efforts before finding the acceptance, recognition and opportunities they seek.

The social, cultural and political context of positive thinking

One of the important things that Jack is pointing out, but I think could be emphasised more, is the *social, cultural and political context* of this material. Just as we say in chapters like *The Body* and *Therapy*, it's important to avoid putting everything onto the individual. Things are as they are very often because of external circumstances, the historical moment, the times we are in, the geography of where we are, the kind of people who are in power – in our family, community, employment, and country. Thus people like Dale Carnegie and Napoleon Hill were responding to a time when people were struggling out of the Great Depression, when the ideals of their country were under serious review; people had lost out economically and individuals had to rebuild their lives. For many, fantasy and entertainment were a way of escaping from the grim realities of their lives and the Hollywood film industry provided this. People who'd lost their farms and businesses often had to migrate across America – many to California and start again with nothing.

There was a questioning of the rationale and processes of capitalism (and even democracy) which now seemed to have had brutal human consequences. Social 'programs', state regulation (eg. of the banks) and unionisation started to emerge – it became evident that collective and government help was needed to organise things and ameliorate and avoid the worst extremes of unfettered capitalism. Positive thinking was offered to help people find the energy to fight their way through these tough times.

The human potential movement in contrast came at a different time, in the aftermath of the second world war, when men returned to America from their tours of duty as soldiers with new insight and ideas about human rights and equality, and women who'd been able to taste new work opportunities and family decision-making on their own were no longer willing to go back to traditional roles. Abraham Maslow was a second-generation Russian Jew, born in New York, who battled with a lot of anti-Semitism in his growing up. There were lots of questions to be asked and answered about human rights, civil rights and black power, feminism, and the anti-war movement. It was important to emphasise that all people were equally worthy, equally capable of positive growth, equally meriting of resources and support. It was important to overcome the downgrading of Jews, blacks, women etc. that had marred history so acutely in previous decades and centuries, and to rehabilitate their human status alongside the white middle class male.

The late flowering of the billion-dollar 'positive thinking industry' needs also to be put into context. The expansion of technology and the open flaunting of wealth are hallmarks of the 1980s as more and more people borrowed to live up to the images and ideals that were projected. In America, under Ronald Regan, there was a return to conservative values, cutting welfare payments to the poor and reducing taxes for the rich, increases in defence spending and national deficit. The influence of the religious right and those in the Californian *'Sun Belt'* grew strong, and it's from that root that many of the lifestyle gurus emerged. The answer to the plight of the poor in mid and north-east parts of America - the *'Rust Belt'* - lay in their taking more responsibility for their lives, not in generous social policies. At its most extreme, the philosophy could be taken to suggest that being wealthy meant that God was on your side, and being poor was a sign of your moral laxity. Positive thinking gurus offered a way of moving forward and upwards by believing in yourself and opening yourself to 'abundance'.

In the 1990s, during the Bill Clinton era, it seemed as if the economy was recovering – yet America's position in the world went from being a fantastically rich nation to being one of the world's biggest borrowers. The struggle to be 'OK' for many people came to mean borrowing heavily to keep up and to seem affluent, a feeling that is in much of the West today. But being too positive can fuel an inappropriate grandiosity and sense of entitlement.

There's no doubt that positive thinking motivates people and comforts people and that people can gain from using the techniques. Many institutions have invested in positive thinking programmes for their staff, including currently the US military, and many businesses. Positive thinking teachers have thousands of testimonials to the effect that their methods have helped people.

In my 20s and 30s, I was enthused by work by Susan Jeffers and Louise Hay which helped me to overcome anxieties about my self-worth and my ability to survive, and at a time when I was struggling to throw off the habit of self-criticism, they created a new discourse for me that was loving and kind towards myself and others.

Think about the goals for which the techniques are to be used. As Jack has said, positive thinking has often been employed in the service of making money, perhaps especially in sales contexts. Medicine has found it to be helpful for people to overcome uncomfortable treatments and to be motivated to stay well as well as to handle tragic prognoses. Sport has found it to be essential for the development of mental attitude, critical to high performance. But it could equally well be used for people involved in social action – it doesn't have to be about individual self-aggrandisement – for example, reframing what happened at a demonstration in terms which help you to return again to the struggle rather than being dispirited or developing affirmations which inspire you to lead or join with others in campaigns that last a long time. *If positive thinking is harnessed to social objectives, it can be released from its origins in conservative, capitalist and at times, religious, thinking.*

Cautions

The point that Jack and I both feel is that we need to question *whom* the positive thinking ideology serves. Take charge of your own engagement with it – if it benefits YOU, that's good; if you can use it to further your own goals, that's good. But be wary if it is being used by your employer or other institutional powers to put all responsibility on you and evade their role in properly looking after you and supporting you or creating the conditions in which you can flourish.

Barbara Ehrenreich, an American commentator, has critiqued the positive thinking industry, reminding us that contemporary 'gurus' are moving on from the *quasi-religious status* that previous ones have achieved to presenting as *evidence-based practitioners* who use academic research and evaluation studies to back up their work – she particularly focuses on Martin Seligman in this context. Other examples include Paul McKenna who uses techniques honed from hypnosis to help people, and neurolinguistic (NLP) practitioners who tie their work to research on how the brain processes information and communication theory. There is less need to present positive thinking methods as part of a holistic, spiritual package as positive thinking gains academic and therapeutic credibility, yet Ehrenreich's feeling is that they still require a kind of magical thinking, a leap of faith that positive thinking will result in good outcomes in our lives or in the world.

It's noteworthy that the most well-known positive thinking pathways have also benefited from the persuasive power of charismatic individuals who've been supremely successful in promoting themselves and their work, for example through pointing to success stories, being clear and definite about what works, or through promoting a loving and spiritual ambience that helps people to feel good about themselves and people around them.

The problems with positive thinking

One of the problems with positive thinking is that if you don't succeed in society's terms, *you can blame yourself - or find that others blame you - for not putting enough energy into motivating yourself.* This can happen for example in healthcare, where practitioners may warm best to those who have a positive attitude and castigate those who don't 'try'. Paradoxically, I remember hearing a medical sociology paper about a group of medical students being uncomfortable with cancer patients who were 'in denial' about their condition – the example given was of a woman who went out dancing in a pretty dress even though she had terminal breast cancer – it was felt that she should be 'accepting' her illness and getting ready for death. Oh she *was*, she *was!*
Sometimes we just don't feel positive, and indeed, have reason not to be. See the chapter on *The Self* for work that has been done on optimism and pessimism.

The point here - as made often in this book - is that we can benefit from using the technique(s) to help ourselves so long as *we remain in charge*, but we shouldn't allow ourselves to internalise shame and failure for feeling low or miserable about circumstances beyond our control. If we're facing a context of high unemployment or a run on the bank that means we've lost our savings or a raising of college fees that puts university education out of reach, we don't need to start castigating ourselves for not being positive enough.

Barbara Ehrenreich feels that an over-emphasis on positive thinking in the business world over many years has contributed to the ridiculously unrealistic worldview that led bankers and financiers to take the West into financial meltdown, and that an over-emphasis on positive thinking for cancer patients (and Ehrenreich became one) can result in a sense of desperation when people *can't* beat the cancer, not to mention the struggle to deny and repress the expression of natural anger and misery.

Oliver Burkeman in his book *Antidote* also questions the idea that positive thinking is positive and offers a variety of other approaches to getting us through. According to him, we're likely to make more thorough preparations, plan alternative contingencies and make more effort to avoid hazards if we anticipate the worst. And in fact, as he says in *Psychologies* magazine January 2013, we may be better advised to concentrate on developing our coping strategies for what we may have to face in the future than practising our positive thinking.

Oliver Burkeman's exhortations to focus on *'negative capability'* remind us that accepting the value of experiences of failure and uncertainty and the reality of our mortality can be very important for living our lives in the present. Indeed, his book offers us a rationale for living in a *process-oriented way* rather than focusing on goals in the future, which can cause us to miss important things in the here and now and ultimately to regret the way we've lived when we get to the end of our lives. This is consistent with teachings in most religions.

Allowing ourselves to release negativity can be as essential as finding something to be glad about. 'Welcoming' illness into our lives can be a way of integrating mind and body and learning to understand the processes in oneself that have led to our condition - perhaps ways of processing emotions and early dynamics that have never previously been explored or tackled, and for some of us, give rise to transformation in our personal relationships.

It's important then to do a reality-check and not imagine that positive thinking *in itself* will necessarily or automatically solve our life challenges. Good 'market research' – finding out about the odds stacked against us and the real standing of our talents and abilities and resources is always important. However, *it really depends on us*. We may be one of those people who *want* to put their faith in positive thinking as a belief system, and can find real personal transformation by its practice. We may be someone who tends to depression and passivity for whom positive thinking is an effective antidote, helping to get us moving and being creative and active about our situation rather than giving in or giving up. Or we may find that exploring catastrophic scenarios is what propels us into action.

The point is that that what makes the difference between the person who gets the job, makes the million, survives the recession, leads the revolution – whatever we want – and the person who doesn't, may really lie in our capacity to energise ourselves – and others.

Books

Oliver Burkeman (2012) *The Antidote* Canongate
Oliver Burkeman (2013) 7 Ways to Success *Psychologies magazine* Kelsey Publishing January 2013
Barbara Ehrenreich (2009) *Bright-sided: how positive thinking is undermining America* Metropolitan Books
Barbara Ehrenreich (2010) *Smile Or Die: How Positive Thinking Fooled America And The World* Granta
Grinder, John and Richard Bandler (1983) *Reframing: Neurolinguistic programming and the transformation of meaning* Moab, UT: Real People Press.
Jay Haley (1993) *Uncommon Therapy: Psychiatric Techniques of Milton Erickson M.D.* W W Norton
Susan Jeffers (1987, 2007 edition) *Feel The Fear and Do It Anyway* Vermilion/Random House

Louise Hay (1984, 2004 edition) *You Can Heal Your Life* Hay House

Denise Linn http://www.deniselinn.com/index.htm

Martin Seligman (2011) *Flourish* London: Nicholas Brealey Publishing

Marjorie E Weishaar (1993) *Aaron T. Beck (Key Figures in Counselling and Psychotherapy)* Sage Publications Ltd

20   going freelance

> Going freelance is an important step to consider taking if you want to have some autonomy and make your own choices about survival and growth rather than being hitched to someone else's star or to an institutional framework. There are some new responsibilities attached to going freelance that need consideration: it's not an easy path but there are significant potential rewards if you get it right.

The chapter is written by Jack with a personal contribution from Julia.

We had to make choices about what we cover in this book, and we decided not to write a specific chapter on 'work' itself (ie. particularly working for employers) but chapters like *Stress* and *Effective relating* are very relevant to those in employment.

Jack

In this section on 'work', I'm looking at *working for ourselves* and picking out what I think are important elements.

Key messages include:

look after your health
manage stress
organise money
find best ways to optimise your productivity
stop all timewaste (bear in mind that *rest* is not timewaste – the unconscious mind is working away in the background)

Working for ourselves is different from 'being an employee'.

It has a lot going for it in terms of freedom and flexibility, but with the freedom comes responsibility.

Most of my family have worked for other people and then successfully been self-employed.

I've been self-employed for several years and have also worked as 'employed'.

There's a lot of information on working for ourselves available and there are quite a lot of 'dos' and 'don't' wisdoms; paradoxically, there's also a lack of information and I will try and fill some of the gaps from my experience both as a self-employed person or through knowing people in that world.

Why self-employment is important is not only because of the *freedom* involved but because of the *choice of work* we have. And moving into self-employment (even temporarily) can help with developing a different work direction when we're changing and wanting to do work that is more in line with us as people.

What are the demands of self-employment?

Put bluntly, these are:

- the risks
- the responsibility
- the skills needed
- the energy and activity needed

Most of the books I've read about self-employment focus on acquiring business skills, like marketing or general skills relevant to most businesses, and they miss out important information that most self-employed people realise make all the difference.

What is self-employment?

It's everything from making things which we sell to providing services and running an organisation that's our own. It can involve the kind of work that isn't usually found in employment for example, being a writer – and it may or may not involve working alone. It may or may not overlap with employed people's work to varying degrees - for example, specialists/advisers who may visit or be 'employed' as advisers by organisations. The main features of being 'self-employed' are that we're in charge more than 'being employed' – we are our own boss.

Goals versus process

We need a balance between goals and process - most freelance activity is too *goals driven* and you need to take care of yourself as well, whilst most employed work is too *process driven* and there may not be enough reward for achievement.

The 'work-smart' programmes for efficiency miss the point that most non-high-flyers don't love their jobs and efficiency in capitalism is a cover for more inhumanity.

Going freelance, it's important to build in time for yourself, time to keep up your morale, time to remember the joy of living and the joy of freedom. Being self-employed can mean putting in a lot of hours but at least you can choose when those hours are!

In fact, the point about working for ourselves is that the effort we put in is or should be highly linked to our own life journey, rather than giving our life energy to someone else or to an organisation for a relatively small compensation. Of course there are people who find employment doing something that they love, but for others, this is only really possible when they go freelance, because only then can they do 'their own thing' and do it their way.

How free is the 'freedom' of self-employment?

This depends on our market/customers and how much we want to adjust to other systems, organisations and cultures. I've met people for example who 'advise' organisations having much of their work and behaviour dictated by these organisations and it neither looks or feels like freedom.

Also, working in certain conservative areas of endeavour, we may have to compromise our own way of being. I think it's best to control as much as possible of our ways of working, our freedom, our time etc.

Some people combine working as self-employed and being employed part-time.

Myths of self-employment

Total freedom

Unless making money is not an issue (which is unlikely for most), we're still connected to the economy, other organisations, the fashions of the day, and our market base etc. The amount of freedom and type of freedom will depend on us and our situation.

I can do exactly what I want

Yes we can, but we may not 'make a living'.

The sky's the limit

Theoretically, in terms of income, there's some truth but not absolute truth in this – there are often constraints. Also, just doing something for income may not work.

A study of millionaires has shown that what mattered successwise was that they chose to make money *doing something they loved.*

It's easy

No, it's not, it's harder in some ways than employment and about two-thirds of small businesses 'go under'. Also, looking at millionaires again, most of them are 'risk takers' (a human type in psychology) and some go bankrupt at least twice before they 'make it'.

Anyone can do it

Yes, usually they can, but they may need to learn new skills, increase existing skills, use helpful personality traits and look after themselves, do research, get organised etc.

Everyone will like me and my work

This myth is a version of the 'it's easy' myth. We need to decide if we want to market a likeable product, and if so, check out its 'likeability'.

In any event, we need to have a belief in what we're offering, ideally not an inflated belief. Also we need to not undervalue what we offer.

What a lot of self-employed people do not do, which they need to do

If I had to pick out what works and isn't done enough by the self-employed, it would be:

a.   looking after their health (physical and psychological)

To me, this is the number one priority and includes a huge range of things, from finding a good dentist, learning about health, not being pushed around by experts but being equal, resting, taking exercise, eating well, etc. It's a big list, but it's more of an attitude of *'being important'*. So yes, we are worth it. We're worth the investment and focus on health. Health is vital, it needs organising and isn't entirely predictable, so we need to take charge of it as much as possible.

b.   managing stress

(see also the chapter on *Stress*)

As well as the general stresses on most working people, self-employment can create particular stresses: for example, overworking, not creating efficient paperwork systems, or if we work at home, not getting out enough.

It's worth examining our situation on a regular basis and looking for solutions to anything we're experiencing as stressful - even trivial things.

597

c.   choosing what they really love doing and are good at

If we go freelance doing something we really love doing, it's more likely to 'flow' and make us happy.   If we're *good at* doing something that can help, but that won't be a substitute for *loving* the activity.

Whatever we decide to focus on, develop confidence in doing it as *self-belief* is important in the freelance world.

d.   being active/taking responsibility

This is not as self-explanatory as it looks – things rarely just happen.   And yes, we *are* responsible for everything as a freelance.

e.   focusing on quality

This is allied to what we love doing/are good at and the quality of our products/services but it also applies to how we're organised and how we relate to customers/clients.   I would always be reaching for high standards as an ideal.

Julia: **Some reflections**

After a lifetime of working for large institutions – national newspapers, universities, and hospitals – I've taken the plunge into a freelance life and it IS scary. An important element I would suggest is funding yourself to have some time to get on top of things – there's always likely to be a backlog of things not done from an employed working life because few of us get enough time to both live and work whilst conforming to an organisation's pace. I spent months clearing up, de-cluttering, organising filing systems, restocking my library, actually reading, and designing systems like housework rotas and financial budgets. It was like having a large 'overdraft' of time that needed to be paid off.

I found too that I had a backlog of things I wanted to do and went out and about, amazed at my new freedom, visiting landmarks and places I'd never had time to do before and actually sitting in cafés in the daytime. So it's a good idea to build in a bit of de-briefing time if you can, getting used to the new freedoms whilst at the same time, developing all your new skills and systems. That time can be very useful in its own right, letting go of tiredness and allowing for reflections and observations which can feed into your new life.

The process of going freelance is underpinned by anxieties about money – few of us can get round that one, but for me, it was important to recognise that this was also true in the large organisation I used to work for. The work we had to do was endlessly about helping the organisation extend and survive into the future, and jobs (though traditionally protected within the public sector) were in reality always on the line in recent years. And if it wasn't my job itself that was threatened, it was certainly my 'career' – with others vying to have more power or a bigger share of the cake that would edge me out of mainstream. In the end, I decided that emphasising the 'different' perspectives that I can bring would be better done from an independent base.

I found that leaving 'work' changed many of my social relationships – some people I hadn't expected to offered new connection and encouragement, whilst others whom I'd known for years found it hard to relate to me on a more equal basis, preferring the old 'in-role' me. Becoming freelance has meant that I've had to work much harder at being OK-OK with others and realising my human rights – I've been astonished at what I 'allowed' within the institutional system because of expectations about hierarchy and role-playing.

I've had to get used to more isolation, because time is at a premium in a new way, and interestingly, contrary to expectations, to having more authentic relationships and less instrumental ones – relating to people for what they can do for you seems to be endemic in institutional life. As a freelance, the answer to what others can do for me, is very often, nothing. Being freelance puts you on your mettle – you have to find out how to do absolutely everything yourself and if people are to help you, you have to offer something in exchange (like a later discount for your product) or pay for their time as you would expect them to pay for yours.

599

Seeking out people who are encouraging is also helpful and making friends with others in the freelance world can be rewarding and inspiring.

Although I've spent my life talking to groups of people in working groups, lecture halls and committee rooms, I've realised that I'm rather more naturally at home in my own room, getting on with thinking and writing and I can now see how hard it's been for me to push myself to fit the extrovert ideal of our culture. So I've been glad to find Susan Cain's spirited new book on the value of introversion which she believes has been treated as 'a second-class personality trait' (p.4). She discusses examples like Rosa Parks and Eleanor Roosevelt and Steve Wozniak (of Apple Computer fame), and demonstrates that great things have been achieved by people who haven't been loud, assertive or sociable types – but were instead able to concentrate hard and to tolerate periods of solitude - developing things and ideas that we need as a human race, whether it's a new invention or standing up for human rights.

Nevertheless, being self-employed has required a shift in attitude and in confidence for me. For example, I've had to develop confidence on the telephone again – it was years since I'd rung a tax office or a supplier and I had to work on honing assertiveness and negotiation skills to fit new situations and to argue for myself rather than for others. Suddenly, there's no human resources or finance department to do it for me. I've had to tackle my self-doubts and keep going – not overly inflating my sense of self, but quietly, determinedly, happily, overcoming the scepticism and lack of interest of others (including my own internalised messages from the past), relishing my enjoyment in what I do and cultivating the knowledge that I am free to do it. In fact, in a capitalist economy and a democratic society, going freelance is – or should be – one of the best entitlements we have.

Susan Cain (2012) *Quiet: The Power of Introverts in a World that Can't Stop Talking* Viking

21 finding our own direction in today's world

This chapter is for those of us who need to review our direction in life and the kinds of contribution we want to make to the world, depending on our assessment of our personal resources (eg. health, energy, money, relationships, skills etc) and our view of the situation that faces us at any particular time. We need to be able to find an ethical position but also resist those who would pressure us to contribute in ways that don't suit us. Understanding the relationship between individuals and the state is important, as is understanding ourselves and where we're at, at different points during our lives. People around us have different stakes in society and different reasons for doing what they're doing. We may feel that the promises made us have not been fulfilled but we may also want to examine the expectations we had in terms of our own psychology as well as in socio-political terms. We need to retain critical awareness and a creative sensitivity to what's needed and be truthful to ourselves about our motives for choosing particular paths. In this way, we can be at our most effective and make our most meaningful contributions to the future of the world.

This chapter is written by Julia

I wanted to write this material because in my own life I've often exceeded my energy and damaged my health by being driven to 'do good' in the world as well as just working, running a home and trying to have a personal life. I've also sometimes got caught up in social activism through my relationships with people and know from experience how tricky it can be to separate out our own beliefs and aims from our connections to others who may have a different take on things and have different resources from us. So this is about being our real selves AND thinking about how we can contribute to the world in accord with our own selves and situations.

The idea of the 'social contract'

In all societies, there is some kind of contract between the individual and the wider society, whether spelled out or not. In the

West, in all countries, the contract has been embedded in a variant of the great capitalist project, with the promise (implicit or explicit) that if we work hard, things will get better. Our conformity to rules, expectations and pressures is manipulated by dangling in front of us the idea that something good is to be achieved – that if we study hard we will pass exams and get a job; if we work hard and avoid controversy, we will get promoted; that if we wed ourselves to institutional goals and outcomes, we will have a better lifestyle than others with holidays, sick pay, nice clothes, a comfortable home and a good district to live in; if we put in the years, there will be rewards once we retire; if we pay our mortgages we will own our own homes, and if we pay into a national or private insurance system, we will be looked after when we are vulnerable. Sometimes we are given presents or hints that we are going in the right direction, as we go along, like pay rises, bonuses, new opportunities and initiatives, tax cuts, and the supposedly reassuring propaganda that others who 'milk the system' will be closely scrutinised, if not fully routed.

However, *sometimes it doesn't work out like that.*

We discover that people less talented than ourselves are favoured for opportunities on the basis of their schooling, their connections, their money, or their personalities. We find we are not eligible for social welfare benefits. We lose our home with negative equity. We cannot live on our pension, and the date for receiving state pension benefits recedes ever farther away.

In recent times, the relationship between expectations and results has become more strained, as the troubled global economic situation translates into troubled individual country economies, and the nature of the contract becomes clearer. Populations start to consider how they want to relate to their governments and how far they want to protest about the shortfall in what is delivered in relation to their efforts.

Political philosophers such as John Locke and Jean-Jacques Rousseau have discussed the question of a 'social contract' including issues about the relationship of people to each other within a community (eg. agreements not to hurt one another or the responsibility of one generation to another), or between individuals and the state.

One of the difficult issues is how any consent to a political system is gained – Philip Pettit (1997) has argued that a *failure to rebel* confers legitimacy on any ruling élite, because *if we did not agree, we would protest.* Perhaps this is why, even when there is little hope of changing our government's mind about something like welfare, pensions or health reform, it's important to make our resistance to and unhappiness with proposals explicit (eg. as people have done through staging public demonstrations) – to *make it clear that our consent is not to be assumed.* In medicine, much is made of the concept of *'informed consent'* – things cannot be done to us if we do not consent and if we were not fully aware of what we were consenting to (except in exceptional circumstances like a life-threatening emergency). How often do we feel fully informed about what is being done to us in social and political terms? How often do we *make sure* that we *are* fully informed?

Is it that the responsibility to make sure rests with us, the people, or should there be a duty upon government to keep us informed? The economic historian Niall Ferguson emphasises that governments should make us aware of all the assets and liabilities they incur – that they ought to have a duty to have transparent accounting – but he laments that at present they don't have to do this.

How our consent is taken for granted

The point is that we are all generally pressurised to *conform* to a social system. We are signed up from birth with an implicit agreement to behave properly, to work for the good of the nation, in times of war to supply ourselves and/or our young to fight, to help (directly, or indirectly as in the public sector) to produce the nation's wealth etc., and to act appropriately towards other members of our society (eg. without violence or malice). It might be that most people consider these to be naturally good aims on which there would always be a consensus, but the point is that our consent is *assumed* –rights and responsibilities being enshrined in our constitution and our agreement reaffirmed through our votes at elections. But how many of us have ever consulted the Bill of Rights for our country, looking clearly at the law on matters such as:

Often what is expected of us is made explicit in a variety of specific 'sub'-contracts such as home-school agreements and employment contracts, all subsumed from wider national sets of duties and responsibilities, and often transmitted through county council or state policies, copies of which (in today's world) can usually be found on the internet –- they are rarely given to us - we often have to be proactive to find them.

Not conforming to expectations usually results in challenging consequences – for example, witness the 'Arab Spring' and the tragic outcomes of protests, sometimes erupting into full-blown civil war, or take any case of individual whistleblowing such as those illustrated in films like *'Silkwood'* starring Meryl Streep about Karen Silkwood and the nuclear industry or *'Insider'*, starring Russell Crowe, about Jeffrey Wigand and the tobacco industry.

History is rich with stories of human resistance to oppression and injustice. Studs Terkel's (2003) book of oral histories of activists says it all in the title: *'Hope Dies Last'*. Historical record-making is often controlled by the victors or the dominant parties so we have to take care in our research to ensure that we hear different voices, and that we recognise the contested nature of storytelling. For example, among numerous films that appear to document the passive victim status of Jews in the holocaust, there is the (inevitably controversial) film *'Defiance'* which documents Jewish partisans and refugees fighting the Nazis and establishing a community in the forest which enabled more than a thousand people to survive the second world war.

Chris Harman's (2008) *'A People's History of the World'*, John Newsinger's (2000) *The Blood Never Dried: A People's History of the British Empire*, and Howard Zinn's (2005) *A People's History of the United States* are examples of history told from a non-traditional perspective.

When to review our direction

When we don't agree with either the substance of these expectations or the way they are interpreted, or feel that we have lost a connection with our representatives and no longer have a say in matters pertaining to our lives, we might need to review our position and consider if and how we want to engage in the political process, taking into account our resources and constraints. If we are already socially or politically active, we may need to take a fresh look at whether we are being effective and for how long we can sustain our energy.

Sometimes, even when we lose hope of making a difference, it's important to register our disquiet, to put it on record that we disagreed at the time. The anti-war movement has used the phrase *'Not in my name'* to indicate that withholding our approval in relation to any given issue, *itself has a point to it*, even when we have lost hope that we can stop an action or change a direction. Whatever we do, sometimes it's important just to not join in with the 'shit'. And sometimes not doing so signals our belief that we think there will one day come a reckoning or a better time.

Sometimes in order to survive or protect others, we pretend to join in – going through the motions, but our unconscious mind resists. It will bide its time. Material stored at unconscious levels threatens to break through even though we try to suppress it.

We can't always make a difference on the outside – we might decide that instead of spending our energy fighting external opposition, we will invest elsewhere, carving out a niche where things happen as we think they should.

There are many wonderful examples where people have set up alternative communities and organisations to further aims that governments or orthodox institutions would not at the time, follow or support. *Findhorn. The Child Growth Foundation. Greenpeace. Amnesty International. Women's Aid. Terence Higgins Trust. etc.*

Remember that it's important to survive ourselves. It's no good trying to do superhuman things if we eventually burn out and are no use to anyone. Our efforts will bear better fruit if we're healthy and peaceful in ourselves, rather than strained and stressed.

Sometimes we have to wait to see if there is enough of a groundswell of opinion around us to bring about change; we cannot do it all alone and survive. And in the end, change that does not have a constituency of support may not last. We always benefit from a network of core people who have the same aim, so let's not give up on building consensus.

We should think carefully about worrying about people far away whilst people near us go hungry for our attention. It's a good idea to know how we're prioritising – to be able to tell people near us why we haven't got time for them and why we think it necessary to give time we would have shared with them to the work of helping people in worse conditions.

Is there truly a need to act on the world at all? Look at what 'scripts' we're acting out from childhood. See Claude Steiner's work referred to in our chapter on *The Self*, and general work on Transactional Analysis. Were we brought up to feel we *should* always be philanthropic? And to whom? Are we reacting to an upbringing in which we were spoiled or allowed to be selfish? We need to identify our inner messages and own them or cut them out.

Passion

An important driver for investing our energy is feeling passionately about something. We might for example find ourselves cheated or experiencing injustice. We might feel very distressed on learning about the plight of others – during the writing of this book, I've found myself very disturbed by many narratives - for example, the experience of women in prostitution and warfare - knowledge that can push us to want to help to bring about change. It's important to listen to our hearts as a guide.

The question of 'expertise' and our trust in it

In recent times, our attitude to professionals in all fields has changed. On the one hand, our fear of taking responsibility for our own lives has kept us in thrall to the concept of 'expertise' and with increasing complexity and an exponential growth in data availability, we turn to 'experts' rather than trusting ourselves to make decisions. We want professionals to advise, recommend and even better, take decisions for us. *'What would you do if it were you?'*

But on the other hand, there is a welter of information through the media about the mistakes and mess-ups made in a whole range of areas and the travesty of trust in others. The wider context is one of politicians, bankers and businesses which have been carried away by greed and corruption, or in the kindest view of things, simply failed to monitor, regulate and sanction properly. But in many other fields we learn about failings. Across the Western world, we hear of abuses, errors, negligence, neglect and wrongdoing. Medics have removed the wrong organs or limbs, left instruments inside the body, failed to give correct anaesthetic, diagnosed people dead when not, given the wrong sperm to a fertility patient, and overdosed patients on the wrong drugs. Priests have abused children under their spiritual direction. Teachers have had affairs with their teenage pupils. Lawyers have embezzled clients' money. Politicians and police officers have taken backhanders and acted criminally. National leaders are potentially indictable for war crimes.

The people whom we ought to be able to trust need watching carefully, whilst most of them spend their time working out ways to watch *us*. Susan George wrote years ago about world hunger and exhorted us to spend less time studying the poor and hungry and turn our spotlight onto what the rich and powerful are doing.

This does not mean being blitzed by the glamour of media presentation and propaganda – it means being wary of pronouncements, never taking things at face value, asking yourself why things are being done as they are, and taking all necessary safeguards to protect yourself and your close associates and family members. We can never afford to be taken in by someone's position or status. We can never assume that a professional mantle means that the person will act appropriately or correctly. Contemporary life means that there is no excuse for naïveté.

The ownership of expertise

The effect that this collapse of belief in social structures has had has been manifold.

In the public sector, driven partly by technology and the profit motive, but also by the desire to no longer depend on individual expertise and particular individuals, we have developed systems that are mechanised, computerised, modularised, formula-bound, systematised, standardised, guided by the perhaps laudable aim of 'quality control' intended to ensure that every customer or patient has the right to the same standard of care.

Where possible expertise has been taken from individuals and put onto databases. Doctors and nurses can diagnose and treat with the aid of computer programmes. Social work and healthcare practitioners use standardised assessment programmes, online counselling programmes, controlled resource allocation systems, centralised information systems and every function they have to do is spelled out in job descriptions and protocols so that their practice is litigation-defensive. Lecturers in many cases no longer hold the copyright to their material – their expertise is mined by the institution so that their material is held on electronic databases, students can access it whenever they want and the institution can ensure that what is taught meets particular standards and is targeted at addressing specific learning objectives. Television engineers who used to have a great deal of knowledge about electronics and radio systems have been replaced by factory-level design and technology and semi-skilled workers who replace whole modular units or disposed of the machines if repair is too complex.

This is a massive shift in the ownership of knowledge – 'knowledge is power' and we now have to pay for it on a scale hitherto unprecedented. We can't go far on a web-based search engine before we have to pay for access to reports, articles, news, and advice. Even academics themselves are upset about this kind of gatekeeping and profiteering. We have to have the resources to have access to expertise. Expertise is standardised and quality-stamped but unfortunately in this process, something is missing.

609

Jean-Francois Lyotard's work on commodification is relevant here (– see Simon Malpas).

The individual diversity has gone. There is a kind of 'one size fits all' dumbing-down quality to everything, in which nothing is too disturbing, everything has a pleasant, anodyne feel to it, everything is set at the middle-range of the market and the choice is the same for everyone. There is a cosy sameness and a confidence that everything has been checked and tested for safety and quality.

But if this were all, we might even be able to tolerate it.

However, at the beginning of the twentieth century, behaviourism came into fashion – the science of psychology based on the idea that the only things that are valid are those that we can see, touch, taste – in other words, things that are *observable* and *measurable*. Since then we have had difficulty with anything that can't be entered onto a computer database, that isn't easily *validated* or *measured*. Thus emotions, intuition and instinct, individual needs and perceptions, and uncertainty – these things are generally edited out. We find ourselves in a Kafkaesque world with human beings we don't believe or trust, and a mechanised, inflexible, computerised and formulaic world to which we are expected to conform.

How do we decide how to position ourselves in relation to the world?

Modern life is characterised by a lack of money, time and space. Many of us feel overloaded with work and pressure, by too many demands and choices, and with an endless permeability such that we can't defend ourselves very well against it all.

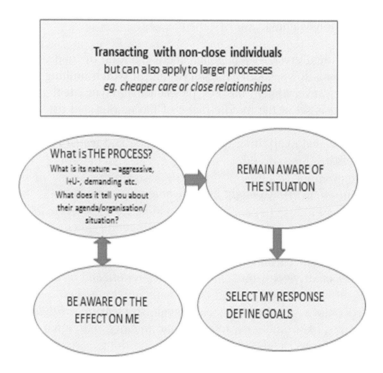

In the diagram above (discussed in more depth in the *Effective relating* chapter), we aim to show that our experience of what things feel like *at the time* is a good barometer to what is going on. Look at 'the process' – do you feel ignored, discounted, devalued? Use the awareness of your feelings to analyse what might be going on in the other party's mind – does the government fear people's reactions? Does the employer have an unethical aim it doesn't wish to disclose? Does the supply company covertly want to get away with supplying shoddy goods for cheaper prices instead of maintaining quality? Select your response – fight, flight, modify, work out, discuss, negotiate etc. – and determine the goals of your interaction with the world.

The important point is to decide what our base is, the 'ground' on which we stand. We recommend that *health and wellbeing* should be the fundamental ground, because without these, we are less able to make and sustain contributions to the world, and without these, we are more likely to cause damage around us eg. by neglecting people, by being unaware of others' needs because our own are too urgent, by requiring too much of others. Being in touch with our own needs, and getting those needs met in healthy and appropriate ways means that when we do try to help others we are doing so from a healthy place, and are able to assess effectively what is needed, what is true, and what is most possible and sensible to do. We will not be trying to meet our needs in distorted ways, overly rescuing others, seizing control to make us feel good, trying to do things our way rather than in terms of what the situation needs, plunging into workaholism, becoming distant from those around us and avoiding sorting relationships out, getting overly close to people as a substitute for tackling problems etc.

What's important in our view is that we keep ourselves well and remain mentally/emotionally healthy as a first priority.

You may have a different priority at this stage of your life – you may believe that tackling a wider social injustice or ill is vital and urgent, whatever the personal price.

> Cary Cooper, a psychologist specialising in stress, indicates that lack of emotional support and long hours in political work frequently correlates with psychological problems in politicians, particularly those in government roles, and most of us could probably identify someone in public life who does not appear to have everything 'sorted'.

> *For many years, I told my therapists that work was my priority and that my personal life was secondary to tackling the problems of the world. I pretty well thought about little else, and expected relationships with partners to fall into a subsidiary category. No wonder they hit problems – I didn't spend time 'shopping' for them, I didn't spend time maintaining them. I was convinced that helping large numbers of disadvantaged people was more important than spending time with family, friends and partners.*
>
> *I didn't realise that I felt a lack of entitlement to a loving relationship and that my obsession with work filled the gap where love should have been.*

Going activist

There can be strong pressures on us to fight for causes – we need to think carefully about our involvement, where we put our energy and how we can best be effective.

The slogan *'not in my name'* gives us permission to express our dissent in many situations even when we feel powerless to do much but withhold our agreement.

The recent report by Darra Singh *5 Days in August,* makes it clear that *having a stake in the world* is a significant protective element for people – people who did not loot or riot in UK in the summer of 2011 indicated that they had something in their lives that they did not wish to jeopardise by involving themselves in lawless activity. Every individual needs to know that he/she is significant in the world and to find a way to live meaningfully and distinctively. Investing in communities so that people feel they care about the world they live in is one response that governments can make, but are not always inclined to.

John Bird, who established *Big Issue,* indicates that protest movements, while dramatic, haven't always had the impact hoped for, whilst Howard Zinn, historian, civil rights activist and author (now deceased) would no doubt argue for the value of political protest. We have to decide (a) whether protesting is appropriately targeted and likely to have a desired result (b) what our energy is like for the efforts required (c) how well organised it is, what support there is for protest and how much support we can galvanise (d) whether we're doing it to feel better about ourselves or whether there is a better, more strategic alternative (eg. like consumer boycott, making a legal challenge etc).

Graham Scambler and Annette Scambler, writing as sociologists, highlight the desperation and lack of concern about the outcome even to themselves that looters may have felt in the summer of 2011, in a world that has been designed by the 'capitalist executive' as allowing freedom (and a lack of punishment) for those at the top and 'exemplary retribution' for those at the bottom who dare to protest and cause 'damage' (even if it is to their own locations and communities). This kind of world in which it seems as if the dice are loaded to fall in one particular direction and those who dissent are discredited and heavily punished makes it a painful choice for people to step out of comfort zones, however miserable or dispiriting these are.

Winning a campaign or securing concessions can bring about a great personal 'high' as well as bringing about changes or a refusal of changes that matters to lots of people. Often there is a lot of human bonding between people involved in the process over time (often forged through insider battles!). It will usually also be tinged with the pain of what has gone on during a campaign – sometimes the cost of 'winning' is high. It's important to listen to our instincts about right and wrong in how we do our fighting.

Some people believe that 'win-win' outcomes are best, where we aim to avoid the other side losing face, and all sides get something from the battle. There is less likelihood then that the battle will resurface to be fought all over again, as some believe was the case with the idea that the Second World War emerged from unresolved conflict left over from the First World War. The idea of 'winning the battle but not the war' is relevant here, it may be very important to be in for the long haul, or to recognise (and make it clear to others) that we're just lending our help for a one-off effort.

How do we want to live?

The question is *how do we want to live ourselves* – how do we position ourselves in the face of all these challenges to life and way of life?

It's easy to be judgmental but the fact is that any direction we take in relation to life can be transformed into something positive. Thus, developing our skills in making money for our own life can be useful at a later stage for resourcing social action. Escaping into drugs, alcohol, and/or sex could ultimately be turned into experience which underpins a compassionate concern for others or creative, self-expressive work. People who work politically at the local level can contribute actively to problems in front of them whilst others may fly right across the world to help out in a distant war or famine zone. Illness can give us time to reflect and absorb the messages from the media and perhaps to undertake internet research, whilst denial of a problem by someone close to us can make us realise how many others are struggling to address a particular reality. Research skills can be geared towards positive change and ethical outcomes, and indeed those of us who are engaged in work of any kind can consider how it could be extended to produce more human-friendly, planet-sustainable and ethical outcomes. Obsessive tendencies can be turned into determination to see things through and fanaticism into attention to detail. Humour can be turned from general cynicism to politically acute satire which alerts people to what's going on. A tendency to procrastination can become a skill in assessment of situations. See the diagram on the following page for some of the possibilities.

Deciding on our direction

Work such as that by Jack Dusay suggests that we meet *resistance* at every level of our endeavours, and it's going to be sensible to anticipate this before we step outside our own space to introduce new ideas or start new projects.

It's helpful to look at where we're trying to make a difference and to assess our inner capacity for change first. Perhaps it's the idea that unless we ourselves can accept or make changes, how can we expect anyone else to? Not much good promoting a green recycling policy for society if we don't ourselves take every step possible to recycle things in our own home and avoid buying everything new. But if we don't manage to be perfect, should that necessarily stop us encouraging others to be better?

depression /anxiety

focusing on bringing up a family

choosing a cause close to home

escape into sex, drugs, sport, music, travel

looking after relatives

developing a creative voice – art, music, dance, writing

prayer and meditation

more materialism – new car, new kitchen, clothes, iPods etc.

investment in work or study

developing or helping with projects in the community

physical illness

denial/ remaining blinkered

researching a problem, collecting data

analysis and theorizing

treading water/ procrastination

fund-raising or philanthropy

obsession/ fanaticism

making money for self and family

developing and offering skills

tackling health, getting fit, managing stress

performing and speaking

developing humour

choosing a cause far away

campaigning, representing people

The kinds of choices and assessments we may be faced with include:

- we might need to prepare to make a contribution to life by going through the pain of therapy and personal change, or sorting out our personal financial debt or health issues, and coming to an understanding of the difficulties of our own and others' lives.

- we might need to look after our own health and deepen our understanding of ourselves as a route to not being a burden and not damaging others.

- we might need to check out what 'life scripts' we're feeling compelled to live out (see Claude Steiner's work and our chapters on *The Self* and *Therapy*) and work out for ourselves what we *really* want to do with our energy and time.

- we can find ways of coping with carer responsibilities that are inspirational to others - this can mean that we understand the value of love or duty and that we enrich our own inner world and emotional strength.

- we can endure dry committee work if it means that we're influencing wider policies or we can decide that the daily satisfaction of delivering interventions to meet immediate needs is what we need to do to feel real and able to go on.

- we can find that social activism calls us, with the right allies and networks and the necessary health or freedom from work or family responsibilities.

- we might find that this is a time when reflection, prayer, meditation, and going on retreat seems to be the best thing to do for the planet.

- we might feel that we're best at making money for family, the community or the wider world – fundraising through work or projects, developing confidence in our ability to survive and build for the future.

- we can use our practical skills to provide materials, equipment, storage, accommodation, administration, cooking, care for the environment, plumbing, cleaning, furniture, writing, 'business'- planning, book-keeping, growing things, conservation, transport etc. for our family or for people in the wider world

We have to find what suits us at a particular time in history and in our own life stories. There is room to change at another point, another time in our life. There is room to accept ourselves and what we can manage. There is no right way to be. Engage with others without criticising the position they've taken, recognising that there are many reasons why someone is where they are and how they are dealing with things. Find your position, recognise that it might evolve, enjoy the clarity of knowing where you're at, defend it with the confidence that you understand why you're where you're at, and start investing in it fully.

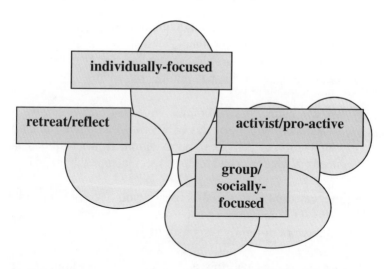

In the diagram above, there is recognition that we might choose different life positions at different times in our lives. There may be a time when we decide to concentrate on our individual needs, but at other times, we work within groups to achieve social outcomes. We may accept that our personality or life situation doesn't suit social activism and choose instead to pray or write letters, to research or to reflect and generate thoughts on situations. Life is a 'broad church' and there is room for all.

What follows is an audit table that suggests a number of questions that we can ask ourselves about our readiness and capacity for engagement in life.

QUESTIONS	AUDIT OF RESOURCES	ACTION IDEAS
SELF		
what energy do I have?		
what is my state of health?		
what are my skills? do I need to develop them?		
what do I know about? do I need to know more?		
what are my motivations? in what way am I justifying this new investment of my time and energy?		
what's the state of my finances?		
what time can I give to this?		
FAMILY/CLOSE CONTACTS		
what emotional and practical support do I have in my life and how can I enhance it?		
am I free to do anything other than look after my family, go to work, etc, or are these for the time being, all-encompassing?		

are there things I can change to get people around me to think about things differently?		
can I help to release time and energy for others so that they can get involved with me?		
what patterns and 'scripts' are there within my family unit that block change?		
can I help people to express their anxieties and fears about changing things? can I recognise that some reactions eg. anger, disinterest – may be masking fear?		
COMMUNITY AND WORKPLACE		
what contacts/networks do I have?		
am I individually-focused or do I work well within groups and teams? what difference will this make to the way I go about things?		
if I'm doing creative work, sport, research, or business development, have I asked myself questions about the purposes my work serves or could serve?		
WIDER SOCIETY		
how do I respond to messages in the media (especially negative or depressing ones) – am I able		

to think creatively or energetically to tackle problems or do I collapse in a heap of despair? if latter, how do I pick myself up again?		
do I need to approach a group or an organisation, or do I already have access to what I need eg. a prayer group, the internet, etc?		
where is 'society' *at,* at the moment? are people ready to accept what I think they need? is my timing right?		
where is the most resistance likely to come from – can I focus my efforts where they might have most initial impact and thus gain early small successes on which to build?		

Books and papers

John Bird (2012) *The Necessity of Poverty* London: Quartet Books

Julia Cameron (2011) (7th ed) *The Artist's Way: a course in discovering and recovering your creative self* Pan Books

Jack Dusay (1972) *Egograms and the constancy hypothesis* Transactional Analysis Journal 2(3), 37-41.

John-Paul Flintoff (2012) *How to Change the World* Basingstoke: Pan Macmillan

Erich Fromm (1969) *To Have or To Be?* Abacus Books

Susan George (1976) *How the Other Half Dies: The Real Reasons for World Hunger* Penguin

Stéphane Hessel (2010) *Time for Outrage!* London: Charles Glass Books/Quartet

Roger Housden (2001) *Ten Poems to Change Your life* Harmony

Susan Jeffers (2012 25th anniversary edition) *Feel the Fear and Do It Anyway* Random House/Vermilion

Simon Malpas (2003) *Jean-François Lyotard* London: Routledge

Paul Mason (2013) *Why it's STILL Kicking Off Everywhere* Verso Books

John Newsinger (2000) *The Blood Never Dried: A People's History of the British Empire* London: Bookmarks

Virginia Nicholson (2007) *Singled Out: How Two Million Women Survived Without Men after the First World War* London: Penguin Books

Philip Pettit (1997) *Republicanism: a theory of freedom and government* Oxford University Press

Philip Pettit (2001) *Deliberative democracy and the discursive dilemma* Philosophical Issues Volume 11: 1 268–299, October 2001

Graham Scambler and Annette Scambler (2011) *Underlying the Riots: The Invisible Politics of Class* Sociological Research Online, 16 (4) 25<http://www.socresonline.org.uk/16/4/25.html> 10.5153/sro.2556 30 Nov 2011

Darra Singh *Policing large scale disorder: lessons from the disturbances of August 2011* Parliament: House of Commons Home Affairs Committee

Starhawk (1982) *Dreaming the Dark: magic, sex and politics* Boston: Beacon Press

Claude Steiner (1990) (2000 edition) *Scripts People Live* Grove Press

Anthony Storr (1988) *Solitude* Collins: Fontana Books/Flamingo

Studs Terkel (2003) *Hope Dies Last: Making a Difference in an Indifferent World* Granta Books

Ashley Weinberg and Cary Cooper (2012) *Stress in Turbulent Times* Palgrave Macmillan

Howard Zinn (2002) *You Can't Be Neutral on a Moving Train* Beacon Press

Film:
Edward Zwick (2008) *Defiance*

22 the crisis we're in

In this chapter, we include a number of issues about modern life including the state of the financial and resource base of the world, ecological challenges, the risks of new scientific developments, wrongdoing and corruption, the pressure to be materialistic, the shifting world order, inequality and the players in the world system from financial predators to philanthropists (including those who discredit the poor) and political dynamics from short-termism and varied models of democracy to social revolutions underpinned by technology and fuelled by the unequal way in which the effects of free-market capitalism are distributed.

There's a lot of material here and we don't have one simple answer - we offer our opinions and suggestions as to how to survive and grow individually as well as daring to consider what the world itself should be doing.

In the main, we echo increasingly widely held reservations about going for economic growth that depends on further exploitation of the world's diminishing resources and reinforces the divide between rich and poor, and argue for an approach that is dedicated to fostering a world community where creativity, fairness, honesty, emotions, spirituality, sustainability and shared values are at the top of the list and free-market capitalism is tempered by concerns of a social and ethical nature.

It's easy to live in denial about the state of the world; it's important that we face up to what's happening and choose our place and role in the world, taking on our responsibility as world citizens.

Jack did most of the initial thinking about this chapter and devised its main structure whilst Julia did substantial amounts of the research and expanded things. It's important to bear in mind that we're social commentators rather than economists, scientists or climate change experts and that our coverage of these areas isn't intended to be exhaustive or comprehensive – what we have here is our 'take' on what we've discovered.

Introduction

This section really needs a whole book. It was a chapter we didn't plan originally, but we're including it because our work on the book led inevitably to an appreciation of the general situation which we're calling 'the crisis we're in'. As we wrote the book, it became clear that we had to understand the conditions that are shaping the world in order to understand our individual relationship to the world.

We're concerned about the way current times are being described and handled generally by commentators, ways which are usually not holistic and seem to depend on 'experts' following single disciplines like economics. In addition, a lot of the people involved seem to be compromised and unwilling to be truthful. Well, sorry to say that but it's too serious for people to dilute the seriousness of the situation or for them to not describe the *whole* crisis. Indeed, our belief is that some aspects of the crisis – eg. financial wrongdoing or ecological irresponsibility - are being covered up or modified by the media so as not to panic the public. Clearly the 'crisis we're in' problem is big and complex but there's a gist version which hasn't been made clear.

We're not interested in joining in a debate with *'more of the same'* which can be stated as *'here's the problems - now be rational and find solutions quick and work together'* as we find this position unrealistic and leading to slow change at best and much denial. Instead, in this book, we're providing a 'rough guide' to the *'change the crisis'* business, and then presenting our view.

As citizens, we're entitled to take our own 'helicopter view' of the world – sometimes during the writing of this chapter, we've asked ourselves if it's grandiose to do so. Then we realise how easy it is to be duped into thinking that such big issues are the sole province of those at the top of the UN or of individual governments and realise that if we don't take responsibility, we're abdicating from our roles as citizens to analyse what has gone wrong and advise on what to do.

Every one of us can do this and this chapter is designed to help you – the reader – to play your part in the democratic process before it's too late – too late for democracy and too late for the earth.

It's a painful process – facing up to the state of the world is in our experience deeply saddening and worrying – but it has to be done. There's no chance of saving the earth and building a future for the next generation(s) without doing this. Just because it's frightening and upsetting doesn't mean that we should avoid it. Our psychological, spiritual and creative talents can take us through and help us to fathom a way that we want to take to survive personally and to help the world to survive. Furthermore, tackling our own individual situations – psychological, physical, practical, economic, ethical – all come into focus when we set our problems into the wider context and understand the driving forces and challenges around us. We need no longer go through life puzzled about how we're feeling or unsure why things are happening. Being informed and empowered will help us to survive.

A quick progress report

We've written this book between 2011 and 2013 and during that time we've seen evidence through a series of high-profile cases that the 'clean-up' of wrongdoing and corruption in public life, the financial sector etc. in developed countries is beginning to happen, so much so that it's possible to believe that we're on the crest of a new wave. However, most of the changes to financial regulation are internally-driven and are unlikely to work because they're not independent or don't have enough 'teeth'. And most financial commentators still want growth *per se* (at any cost?) rather than sustainable growth.

There's an alarming increase in state regulation especially in the USA where foreign policy has remained imperialist and interventionist.

Round the world there's unrest, with pictures transmitted worldwide on a daily basis following the Arab spring and the imposition of austerity measures in Europe. There's hope that change will come as people seek more true democracy but the process of bringing about change is painful.

We've written about the necessity to now operate from values but as evidenced by the continued existence of Guantanamo Bay

625

detention camp etc. the developed world still accepts oppression and torture despite the United Nations *Universal Declaration of Human Rights* prohibiting such activities – so where's the progress on human rights and equality?

Structure of our analysis

To make 'the crisis' more manageable, we've divided it into sections. We're not intending to 'fix' the problems but mainly to demonstrate that the situation *is* complex, to emphasise that problems need to be identified properly and that the solutions need to be much more informed than they are in the present context.

Sometimes the solutions are clear – *'less of the same'* or *'do the opposite from what we're doing'*. Sometimes they're in a particular section, suggesting *alternatives*. There are ideas about how to deal with *individual* change in our chapters on *Managing Stress* and *Change* (as well as several others); in this chapter, we focus on *social* change.

'The crisis we're in' usually refers to the global financial and environmental situation, which is a favourite topic for people in the economic and eco-economic change industries and the usual presentation of this is as an *economic, environmental* and *equality* nightmare. We see this as a limiting presentation and so we're extending our analysis from these three main aspects to several elements, including *what's in the way of solving things*.

Our list includes:

- being clear about who's in charge
- historical factors
- the scope of the financial 'crisis'
- the hidden economy
- the myth of 'recovery'
- myths of capitalism
- from 'myths' to 'truth' – what are the downsides of capitalism?
- what's in the way of developing 'eco-friendly' capitalism?
- how we view climate change and climate 'justice'

- but it's not just climate change : nanotechnology and biological dangers
- the issue of different agendas and aims for change
- wrongdoing and fraud in the financial world
- power
- sham democracy and the people's voice
- inequality: what it is, how we handle it, what we do about it
- financial predators and financial givers
- short-termism
- how we experience materialism/consumerism
- the scientific/rational versus the holistic mind-set
- psychological/behavioural issues

Some books on 'the crisis we're in'

There are many books on the crisis we're in - two recent ones we've found of some use are those by Tim Jackson and by Richard Heinberg. Both of these books are emphasising that *economic growth of the type we have known recently is over, due to depletion of world resources* including the reduction in oil. We're running out of the basics eg. oil, copper, silver etc. needed to support growth. At the same time, we're facing more pollution and clean-up costs, for example, as in the recent BP accident in the Gulf of Mexico, and an increasing number of natural disasters, such as *Hurricane 'Katrina'* and *Superstorm 'Sandy'*.

At the same time, the population has grown from c. 3 billion in 1960 to above 7 billion in 2012. And in addition, we're still in a financial crisis.

Kalle Lasn, whose ideas have been credited with inspiring the *Occupy Wall Street* movement, and co-founded *Adbusters* magazine and media corporation, has proposed a new approach to what used to be called 'economics', including coming up with concepts of *"psychonomics"* – economics that takes into account human behaviour – and *"bionomics"*, economics which bears in mind the cost of environment damage. His book *Meme Wars: The Creative Destruction of Neoclassical Economics* is intended to challenge traditional economics teaching and get the economics

627

community to think again. It also challenges the traditional way of presenting information through its creative format.

It appears to a number of writers that the world is in the grip of old-fashioned ideas about economics that are no longer fit-for-purpose. John Quiggan's *Zombie Economics: How Dead Ideas Still Walk Among Us* is very much about this view and how an unthinking faith in a market-led economy is destroying us. Steve Keen's *Debunking Economics* is also a useful critique of 'mainstream economic orthodoxy'.

The first *Limits to Growth* in 1972 by the Club of Rome predicted a crisis in global growth due to resource depletion. It's now 40 years later and the crisis has become chronic, so an important question is:

> *– what's stopping the world dealing with the crisis?*

Mike Hulme's book *Why we disagree about climate change* presents us with a measured and analytical view of the different players and forces that shape our perceptions and fears, including spirituality, the media, psychology, scientists and politicians, and this is a very useful categorisation of the variety of factors that make it somewhat impossible to put a coherent synthesis together for collective action.

Economic commentators tend to be narrow and conservative and stick to their single discipline of economics – they're also engaged in a turf war between free marketeers and the others.

Important questions to ask about economic commentators are:

- how 'detached' are they?
- how 'holistic' are they?
- how 'compromised' are they?
- how 'expert' are they, and what are the problems with these experts?
- how do their 'scientific' models work – are they growth-dependent?
- do they include 'externalities'?

There's a crisis of trust in general at present and a crisis of trust in the economic world. We're not told the truth because various élites are 'covering their tracks'. We *have* however, made *some* progress on resolving the 'crisis' but it's been slow. The political commentator Susan George has described economics as fundamentally being about *politics* – sometimes it's not necessary to go into the detail of the economics but instead, it's important to work out the key political agenda going on.

Being clear about who's in charge

It's always a good idea to explore the backgrounds of those who are charged with responsibility for running – and changing – things. This can help us establish their credibility, including how well-prepared they are for their roles, and see how much social distance there is between them and the vast majority of people they will be affecting through their decisions.

It's perhaps easiest though not simple to get data on politicians (because they've often had to be fairly transparent), but exploring the backgrounds and interests of those in other fields like banking, the armed forces, the Church, big business, protest movements etc. will tell us something about motivations and values in a variety of cases.

According to the US website of *'Defeat the Debt'*, significant numbers of US Congress members lack an academic background in business or economics. In Britain, according to the Smith Institute, the majority of MPs at present are university educated with c.25% having gone to Oxbridge. A very small percentage of of Labour MPs have apparently worked in finance whilst more than a third of Conservatives have done so. Labour MPs tend to have worked in the public and voluntary sector and in blue collar occupations. More Labour and LibDems have been in academic and teaching roles than the Conservatives.

In the US, apparently more than a third of Congress members and more than half of Senate members are millionaires, and in Britain, *Wealth X* rates the UK Cabinet as a whole as worth about £70 million. In Russia, the opposition party have highlighted the luxury lifestyle of their leader Vladimir Putin, who has access to more than 20 'palatial residences' and a massive fleet of cars and aeroplanes. Increasingly, in order to get into power, politicians need both personal wealth and the clout to attract wealthy donors and investors.

One of the problems is that it becomes difficult for people who aren't 'in the club' of privilege to enter politics and thus varied perspectives and voices are lost from the democratic process. The BBC documentary *Young, Bright and On the Right* attempted to highlight the challenge it is for boys from comprehensive school backgrounds to break into the Oxbridge political 'training ground' (in this case for the Tory party).

However, there are alternative examples if we look, and the president of Uruguay appears to be one of them - José Mujica, former guerrilla leader - who lives on an 'austere' farm owned by his wife where they cultivate flowers for a living, and runs an old Volkswagen Beetle, giving 90% of his income to poor people and entrepreneurs in his country.

Politicians are not of course necessarily *in charge*, they're often just the 'front-men' (and 'women' in rare cases). And even within parties, there are different groups with different agendas who may exert pressure on officially elected leaders. In the UK Conservative party for example there are *One Nation* Conservatives (who seek civic harmony), free-market 'Thatcherites', and traditionalists. In the American Republican party there are a number of 'factions' which include traditionalists, fiscal conservatives, social conservatives (including the religious right), and moderates (some of whom are fiscally conservative and socially liberal) etc. It can be in our interest to get wised up on who represents what so that we can assess what is being advocated and what might lie behind the rhetoric.

These days, more often than not, it's big financial players who are influencing the government. Working out who IS in charge in any society is always going to be a challenge. And it's not always going to be the government. For example, there's no shortage of estimates on the internet regarding the small number of people who might actually be 'running' the US.

Of course, the real truth may be that we – the people – are in charge, but we're not using our power sufficiently – part of the reason for this is that we fail to recognise our own power, which is one reason why we've written this book.

Historical factors

Here's a short list of main factors leading to the 'crisis'. The list isn't exhaustive but you can see that we're talking about large events and powerful attitudes.

- for 200 years or so, industrialisation was based on fossil fuels

- there was an explosion of growth and surplus

- in the last 100 years there have been:
    - two world wars
    - Cold War and nuclear arms proliferation
    - two major financial crises: the Depression and the current crisis
    - more information emerging about the state of the planet

- the ideal of consumer society pioneered in USA in late 1940s has served as a model for the rest of the world and powerful consumer mind-sets have taken root

- the world's population has increased from around 2.3 billion people to 7 billion people since 1940 – that's a fantastic, exponential increase in only 70+ years.

- there's been a 'deconstruction' of society, things have been thrown out (such as many religious values) and this has left a vacuum

- since the 'fall of communism', unbridled *free market capitalism* worldwide has led to 'corporatism'

In recent years, the economic system has involved a major turf war between the *free market camp* and other economists including those interested in *sustainable capitalism* – which includes both the *eco-economists* and the *socially-conscious* styles of capitalists.

This turf war (see later) is partly responsible for the slowness of change in the economic system, which must be changed for both environmental reasons and to avoid economic turbulence.

Essentially, the *free market* school of economics has dismantled regulation, including regulation designed after the great Depression to prevent financial collapse. Professor Yaneer Bar-Yam of New England Complex Systems Institute (NECSI), interviewed by Max Keiser for RT states that deregulation was like *'taking away supports and beams from a house which then needed external support from governments as it had become dangerously unstable'*.

The scope of the financial 'crisis'

The 'crisis' is huge. The problems are worldwide. It depends how things are calculated but the size of the 'crisis' is absolutely unimaginable. Even on the meanest calculation and the best estimates, the world debt – apparently well into tens of trillions of dollars - is appallingly gigantic and utterly impossible to pay back. Check out *The Economist's* online Global Public Debt Clock for the latest figure – and remember that this is just the *public* debt. And if we divide it into the 7 billion people on earth, we start to get a sense of the weight of debt on every one of us. The intention here is to give a sense of *scale* and to encourage you to do your own research and to make your own comparisons.

The hidden and irregular economy

The world economy is difficult to gauge, not least because official figures tend to present the straightforward (though complex) data of the regular market – they do not include huge amounts for the irregular economy including the illegal drugs trade, arms trafficking and prostitution. On a website called *Havocscope*, the global 'black market' economy is estimated in billions and possibly trillions of dollars, and covers a wide range of activities from counterfeit, illegal and prescription drugs, prostitution, human trafficking and human smuggling, to illegal gambling, fishing, waste dumping, video and music piracy, organ trafficking, arms trafficking, and counterfeit items from passports and diplomas to toys and batteries.

Because the details are hidden and difficult to ascertain, there are widely varying estimates of how many people are forced into prostitution, domestic work, dangerous and unpleasant manual work and farming (such as the cocoa trade). The UN believes there are 2.5 million people in forced labour (mostly sexual exploitation of women) at any one time in the world whilst *Free the Slaves* estimates from the International Labour Organisation that there are *at least* 12.3 million people enslaved in the modern world.

Whatever the correct figures, *forced labour is the third largest hidden economy after drugs and arms* and as an industry, the human slave trade is on the up. Trafficked people - including a significant proportion of children - are forced not only into prostitution and domestic servitude but also into organised street begging, shoplifting, leaflet delivery and factory, salon, restaurant and unskilled building jobs in the West. There's also a ghastly trade in human organs – especially kidneys, hearts, lungs and livers, with human beings being trafficked for the specific purpose of 'harvesting', which includes those who have in some form or another, 'agreed'.

However, one of the problems with this way of looking at the irregular economy is that it focuses on the worst excesses, and can miss the widescale economic activity that falls outside the mainstream, regulated systems but which represents business activity by millions of people who can't get into the regulated economy. This might include for example medicines which may be OK but which aren't subjected to the research, development and testing undertaken by the global pharmaceutical companies, or companies which make mobile phones and computing equipment which are a lot cheaper than ones made by the giants of the industry. The fact is that many people choose to enter the economy despite or because of cartel activity, price-fixing and restrictive regulation that would make it impossible for them to join in formally. This doesn't *necessarily* mean that their products and services are inferior – but they don't carry the quality stamp (including usually guarantees of ethical practice) – or designer label - that international operators can both claim and impose, and they're often designated as 'illegal' or discredited as poor quality or dangerous. Nevertheless, there's a significant market in those who can't afford the more trusted and well-established brands. Since items can vary from fake design products to perfectly well-tested drugs without the brand-name price-tags, there are judgements to be made about whether exclusion is justified or is about protecting the big fish in control of the market-pool by keeping new entrepreneurial players out. As we demand ethical and ecological accountability in the supply of goods and services, it may be that alternatives that fall short on these elements may burgeon.

Selecting indicators

Of course there may be other indicators of the scope of the crisis than the ones we've selected – but whatever examples we choose to listen to, we need to take care not to accept presentations that try to boost the facts artificially and play down the awful reality of the situation.

The myth of 'recovery'

The financial mess is bigger than anyone previously thought. Based on the slowness of economic recovery in the 1920s and 30s, recovery in the early 21st century will be slower than governments tell us and want it to be.

Here's a list of issues involved:

- the financial amounts involved are huge

- it's worldwide

- it's affecting most people negatively

- recovery is slow

- recovery is complicated and consists of a conflict between free market economists and the 'others'

- resource depletion is unquestionable

- recovery has been paid for by the public - both in terms of bailouts to banks and other economic institutions and by austerity measures.

- democracy has been eroded in recent decades with 'corporate capitalism'.

- amongst the causes, deregulation wasn't a good idea but financialisation and toxicity have caused incredible damage

- generally the financial world is rigid and conservative.

- the 'shadow' banking system (including under-reported profit) is worth a huge amount and a significant proportion of the total financial system, is not regulated and is used as a conduit for getting round the rules

The extent of corruption in the economic world is being relentlessly played down by most of the media except RT.

Economic recovery is still being thought of as back to the free market bubble *'boom and bust'* mind-set and doesn't take into account resource depletion.

The recent history can be caricatured as taking away the controls in the financial world (de-regulation) for investors and bankers to gamble in the 'last chance saloon' knowing that the ecological end is nigh (whether this was done unconsciously or not) then they got into fraud or a mess, then asked the public and government to bail them out and imposed austerity.

To change capitalism is a big issue but most sensible people think that capitalism needs to be more humane, less corrupt and have its powers limited.

Social mythology and some myths of capitalism

By myth, we're talking about at least two kinds: 'cover up fairy stories' and manipulations.

For example, history abounds with mythology. The myth of 'our brave pioneers going West' and American Indians being 'dangerous' covers up the reality of genocide and broken treaties in the quest to establish communities and businesses in America; land seizure, slave labour and cruel practices to bring about social compliance all feature. (See for example Howard Zinn's book on American history).

In an article entitled *'Masters of cover-up: How the Establishment closes ranks to protect its own and deny the people the truth'*, Stephen Glover outlines the range of key institutions that no longer live up to the expectations that the public used to have in them.

The myth of *'British fair-play and justice'* covers the reality of justice often being expensive and largely reserved for the rich. Recently in the Independent Report on the Hillsborough disaster in Liverpool where 96 football fans died due to crowd mismanagement, we've seen the role of delays and police corruption exposed. It took more than two decades for the families led by parents like Trevor Hicks and Margaret Aspinall to get at the truth and have it recognised, whilst the police appear to have hesitated in cases like that of (Sir) Jimmy Savile, brought to their attention on different occasions by allegations of sexual abuse of young people again and again without any action being brought. In the North Wales Waterhouse Inquiry into sexual abuse in the

636

Bryn Estyn and other care homes, we learn nearly 20 years later that the inquiry was restricted to the care system and that claims that others from public life were involved were denied expression, and demonstrating once again how difficult it is for the abused and vulnerable to have a voice and to be believed. See Alice Miller's work on abuse to discover how important it is for *someone* to believe us.

One of the things at stake here is the *use of language* which can serve to define and shape our impressions, when in fact the reality may be different. For example, the notion of *'peacekeeping'* suggests something good when in reality, it's impossible to have unambiguous decisions about military interventions across the world – officially these should always be *impartial, consensual, and defensive* – yet problems range from *failure to intervene* to *'mission creep'* and the challenge of how much to 'enforce' peace. In the avowed aim of preventing persecution of some groups, the UN inevitably at times takes action which results in support for one side rather than the other, with Rwanda being one of the key examples of this. Andrzej Sitkowski's 2006 book discusses these issues.

It's difficult to see the wood for the trees sometimes in any institution or set of circumstances, especially when we want to imagine that good work is going on. When Kathy Bolkovac, a former American police officer who specialised in tackling sex crime, alleged sex trafficking by people involved in the UN peace mission in Bosnia (illustrated in the film (and book) *The Whistleblower*), it became clear that it was a huge and courageous effort on her part to fight obstacles to bring this to light. This was true too of Karen Silkwood who was a union activist at the Kerr-McGee nuclear facility in America, who raised questions about conditions of work and plant safety - a story that was illustrated in the film, *Silkwood*. People who bring things to light often pay a high price to do so – since the majority of people often keep quiet, the few individuals who raise their heads above the parapet may in fact be highlighting simply the tip of an iceberg. It's good to learn as we go to press that in Britain new protections for whistle-blowers are planned.

There are many other myths in our society such as *'banks are respectable'* which falsely lead us to believe in organisations and products which no longer merit our hopes and expectations. A browse through advertising slogans – some of them now ditched – will give the flavour of the way in which we can no longer trust even household names in product development - new myths are created daily. Not only do many products not do what they claim to do any longer, but updates (promoted as improvements) are often worse than their previous formulations (often due to the pressure to cut costs and maximise profits), and there's an increasing number of 'product recalls' as manufacturers discover that they've failed to anticipate risks associated with their products or perhaps hoped no-one would notice. Recent exposure of horsemeat purveyed as beef has shaken consumer confidence in trade descriptions and regulatory controls.

Our childlike trust in leaders and belief in myths are a problem.

The recent history of political corruption and increasing access to information on leaders who demonstrate very distorted personalities (see *Psychopathology* chapter) should alert us to the facts that

(a) leaders are human/fallible and have distorted personalities (everything from grandiose to self-aggrandizing)

(b) leaders are often young, good-looking, and rich and hope that these qualities will hide their basic lack of competence

When we look at leaders and leading teams (in for example politics, financial institutions and academia), we need also to remember that *policymaking is not rational* – it is the product of a variety of dynamics between personalities, each with their own pathologies, idealisms, values and strengths – the policies that emerge will be a synthesis of different interests and the result of who wins out in the struggle to achieve an outcome. Usually this battle is backed up by the threat of force/action – military, political or financial.

We also need to look closely at the results of policymaking and recognise that what seems easy to us may in fact be built on hidden facts. The ethics of keeping prices down in the West are often highly questionable, resting as they do on the exploitation of people round the globe including the use of children in the coffee, cocoa and cotton industries, women being given very short contracts and few rights in clothes and cut flower production, and indigenous farmers being ruined to allow for expansion of Western food and drink production. Many of the products we buy in the West are directly produced in contexts of poverty where bonded labour, lack of rights, and damage to health are commonplace, but little of this background knowledge is made clear on the packaging.

Nevertheless, for both the 'free market' and the 'others' to some degree: capitalism is basically preferable to other systems and accepted as OK – particularly in terms of the freedom for private enterprise and initiative that exists, but the ideas of creativity/innovation and endless progress have been part of a 'grand narrative' (see Jean-François-Lyotard's work), which is no longer sustainable, and the fallout of brute capitalism – the abuses, corruption and lack of social responsibility - has seriously damaged its standing.

From myths to truth - what are the actual downsides of 'capitalism'?

- it depends on exploitation of others (often 'big eats small') – often those who are most poor and vulnerable

- it perpetuates and normalises inequality

- it's open to corporate power and greed, – Richard Heinberg describes many financial organisations as *'psychopathic corporations'*- their methods promote inhumanity, lack of values and anti-social perspectives, and furthermore, often compromise democracy

- it allows for corruption and abuse

- it tends to generate competition instead of cooperation, creating winners and losers and celebrating this

- it tends to focus on novelty rather than value and quality – unnecessary novelty is now structural

- it reduces everything down to efficiency and profit motive, in the process ditching humanity for hardness and ruthlessness, and exchanging love for sexualisation and romance – eroding values and making society rudderless

- corporations are now so powerful that they're eroding democracy and distorting values

– in short, it's *anti-social, inhumane and unspiritual.*

Whether capitalism can be humanised, made fair or socially responsible or be regulated is a matter for debate – in the meantime, we should question its nature (eg. competiveness, negative exploitation of human and environmental resources) and its form. This not only holds out the promise of the world being a happier place to inhabit but is vital if we are to feel motivated. Being cared about and valued are not simply cosmetic exercises – these are necessary for us to go on. Having a world that is not full of envy and hatred is essential for effective functioning if we are to avoid sabotage, aggression, inefficiency, and conflict which deflect energy and resources from the main task of survival.

What's in the way of developing *eco-friendly* capitalism?

Answer: the whole competitive world system - a military and industrial complex with different sectors and groups vying for financial and power advantage. Progress in terms of changing mind-sets eg. academic economics, changing power structures etc. is likely to be slow and piecemeal and chaotic. It's possible that things may need to get tangibly worse before change can come about within existing power structures simply because people continue to think that they can keep going without fundamental change. Also it may be good to remember the adage that *'adversity is the mother of invention'.*

There are two main environmental issues – resource depletion and pollution.

We've chosen to focus on *depletion of resources* vs. *pollution* as the case for *depletion* is clearer – see both Tim Jackson's and Richard Heinberg's work.

With emissions, there's finally an agreement that global warming above 2°C will lead to serious problems – there are various dates on offer as to when the trouble starts between 8 and 37 years away. The problem here is that with emissions, science cannot yet either fathom the effect on the planet, nor separate global warming as due to Man's activities from a natural *new ice age*-type event. One of the main sticking points with regard to global control of emissions has been the refusal of USA to be a party to the Kyoto protocols. The lobby of 'climate-change-deniers' and 'skeptics' – some of whom may have financial interests in opposing new regulation - include both scientists and politicians who question the Inter-governmental consensus (IPCC) on global warming on factors such as whether the causes are natural or man-made and just how dangerous the risks are. The book by Nancy Oreskes and Eric Conway, *Merchants of Doubt: how a handful of scientists obscured the truth on issues from tobacco smoke to global warming,* is relevant here.

Another problem is that emissions targets are not defined clearly or regulated well, which parallels what we've also seen in the financial sector.

Yes, it's sloppy and political – global political cooperation has been traded for national self-interest.

Problems include:

- 'peak oil' – whereby the production of oil is deemed to have peaked and to have gone into terminal decline – whether we've passed this point or it's fairly imminent is really a quibble about when and how soon oil-dependent countries can develop alternatives (and how difficult will be the relations between oil-producing and oil-dependent nations)

641

- emissions from the 'greenhouse gases' – methane, carbon dioxide, fluorinated gases and nitrous oxide – which are emitted through activities such as fossil fuel use, changes in land use (forests etc), waste management and fertilizer use – all of which affect global climate change.

- it's also worth mentioning population growth (– China is notable in its efforts to control this but the human cost of enforced family restriction through the one-child policy has been deeply disturbing) which threatens to exceed our capacity to feed everyone effectively and to put unsustainable demand on our resources. However, there's some debate as to whether waste and over-consumption in affluent parts of the world are more of a problem than rising birth rates.

How we view climate change

One of the issues is the variation in the ways in which people perceive the world. Mike Hulme, in his book *'Why we disagree about climate change'*, tackles this. Based on Mary Douglas' and Aaron Wildavsky's (1982) model of the four 'ways of life', he outlines different perceptions of risk linked to our ideas about the significance of social contact and social regulation, and (interestingly) how we view nature - as *unpredictable* or *controllable, benign* or *precariously balanced*. All these factors affect the extent to which we feel afraid.

According to Mike Hulme, our views are likely to be shaped by many factors including the cultural and practical world we live in (such as the kind of media messages we get, the distance we have from actual physical dangers or the particular emphasis on comparative dangers we get – such as the risk of terrorism or contagious disease) and our religious/spiritual beliefs. If, for example, we've grown up with a sense of responsibility to the planet, we may identify with a sense of guilt about what we've done and not done in relation to the natural world and expect 'retribution' eg. in the form of volcanic eruptions, floods, tsunamis, earthquakes etc. for the damage we've 'caused'. Some of this of course may also relate to the primitive feelings we have from our childhoods – see Lawrence Kohlberg's model of moral development and Sigmund Freud's concepts of the *super-ego* and *id* (expanded upon in our chapter on *the Self*).

But Mike Hulme suggests that an appeal to apocalyptic visions of the future is unnecessary and can backfire – such that the sense of urgency and concern promulgated under the banner of wanting to stimulate energy for change, could backfire and generate such despair and hopelessness that in fact we stop trying to do anything and even increase our decadent behaviour convinced it's not long before we all experience the ultimate destruction of our lives and the earth. Social psychology has long demonstrated that fear is not the most effective mechanism for bringing about attitude change.

Climate justice

Another factor Mike Hulme identifies is the question of *'climate justice'* in which different players in the world have to address the fact that they are not equally responsible for the problems nor equally able to put things right, and that the question of who bears the greatest responsibility – and obligation – *individuals, governments, corporations, previous generations etc.* - is not easy to resolve since we all have different ideas about this. Equally, we are not all at similar levels of risk for ecological damage.

Anthony Giddens, the British sociologist, for example, reminds us that poor countries where the geography renders them particular vulnerable to events like flooding or drought, may also lack the quality of housing, warning systems and emergency infrastructures to withstand ecological trauma that richer countries may have. Greenhouse gas emissions created in 'majority world' countries for their survival are not the same as emissions generated in richer countries for non-essential (luxury) living standards. Wealthy people are more able to operate in ecologically friendly ways than poor people – for example, by installing solar panels and modern waste disposal systems in their homes and buying low-emission vehicles, whilst poor people often have to fight against the dumping of waste and pollution close to where they live.

Trends in consumption have not been evenly balanced across the world. Industrialised countries make up only a fifth of the world's population yet have the greatest responsibility for their massive pollution of the planet. Anthony Giddens says that consumption increases every year for industrialised and developing countries, whilst it has substantially reduced in parts of Africa. The wealthy, he explains, are in the best position to consume and also to be far away from the negative results of consumption – for example where the waste goes, the pollution happens, the forests are chopped down, and the people are exploited to produce the goods etc. It may be this distance that accounts for the cavalier attitude of many of us in the West – we simply don't have any connection with the problematic effects of our consumption and can go on ignoring the facts.

Thus it's very difficult to get global agreements on emissions targets and the Kyoto Protocol has not been entirely successful. The future of environmental justice will depend on our ability to go forward with social, political, economic and spiritual commitments to collaboration and good practice.

The many meanings of 'climate change'

What's uplifting about Mike Hulme's work is his dissecting of the climate change debates to show us that the issues are not purely or wholly *scientific* – there are deep and symbolic meanings for us in understanding the concepts of 'climate' and the 'earth', and concentrating on what we need to do to 'save' the planet can mobilise us to give of our better selves – to link with others and dig deep into our spiritual, psychological, and social resources to produce a more hopeful future.

But it's not just climate change.......

What about nanotechnologies?

Nanotechnologies are about a whole new way of doing science, now that we have the power to work with and intervene at the level of atoms and molecules. Although at an early stage, this technology has already transformed the world of digital computing 'toys' and machines (including miniaturisation), made our cycles and batteries more lightweight, helped us develop new fabrics, cosmetics and cookware and given us hope for reducing the side-effects of chemotherapy and creating artificial tissues to replace livers and kidneys. There's also the potential to develop the nutrition in our food and to create safe water in places where it's hard to supply this at present - aspirations to which the world desperately needs to give serious attention. Nanotechnology has the potential to revolutionise our world, but it does not come cost-free. Because the materials, substances, and processes operate with (or on) such infinitesimal matter, it's possible that air, food and water could become contaminated or modified, including the pollution of soil and groundwater and creating damage deep inside our bodies through respiration of material that we cannot see or even detect.

There's a strong need for regulatory agreements to control these developments, which threaten our survival just as much as the earth's natural processes may do, and some believe that there is a chance as never before for human beings to work together - scientists, governments, businesses, and the public - to develop voluntary controls and regulatory frameworks to ensure safety. *The Project on Emerging Nanotechnologies* and the *Center for Nanotechnology in Society* are both accessible on websites which offer an insight into the debates that are taking place.

And it's not just nanotechnologies...what about biological dangers?

As disaffection grows across the globe, so does the risk of bioterrorism – with risks particularly for people living in cities in huge numbers, and of course for people who are less able to fight disease and infection, whilst ecological disasters, the 'side-effects' and aftermaths of warfare, food-borne viruses and pandemics all hover as potential, frightening dangers.

The counter-industry of bio-surveillance, which aims to collect data from a variety of sources including electronic health records, school attendance records, emergency call-outs, hospital data-capture, and laboratories is designed to protect us from risk (eg.

with vaccines), alert us at an early stage to the detection of any threats (which may not always be immediately apparent), and to equip us for responding rapidly to events.

Unfortunately, this may have the effect of making us more than ever suspicious of people with dissident views or who seem to be 'loners' as we all join in with the mass paranoia that this must generate. Trying to work out exactly when and where a dangerous incident might occur is an impossible task, although no doubt some predictive capability is possible with modern 'intelligence' systems, and a culture of vigilance, distrust and inform-on-your-neighbour is cultivated, destroying our relationships with one another and our potential for building community.

And of course, the spectre of disease generated from other 'natural' causes haunts us. Our way of living involves trillions of road and air-miles of travel and massive movements of people across the globe (including within their own countries as people migrate to cities and in the future, away from areas at risk of environmental disaster). Global warming may bring diseases into countries that had previously been free of them, such as malaria. At present, TB, HIV, and resistance to antibiotics are some of our most potent threats.

There's much to be worried about, and climate change may not be our only concern. However, how we respond to our fears will be a major factor in determining the kind of social world we want to live in. Already, we find it hard to manage health and safety agendas to make us comfortable and safe and being so intrusive that we are frightened to play conkers or light a campfire. Our longings to live in a pain-free and worry-free world may drive us to create such a controlled environment that life might no longer be worth living.

The issue of different agendas and aims for change

The difficulties about what to do

A 'more of the same' approach of slow, add-on eco-friendly behaviours and ad hoc projects isn't going to solve the eco-crisis.

It's valuable but without other changes of mind-set, values, political cooperation and the creation of responsible capitalism, it's not going to solve things. Neither is simply persuasive communications and 'educating the masses' though it all helps.

Change is coming about because of other factors – for example, the great capitalism project is manifestly full of holes - corruption, exploitation, over-extension and debt, toxic products, fatigue and disillusionment, and ecological fallout such as the BP oil spillage in *Deepwater Horizon*, Gulf of Mexico and the Japanese tsunami affecting a nuclear installation, both of which have links to current business practices. As Daryl Hannah points out, there's disquiet over new procedures such as *'mountain top removal'* and *underground 'fracking'* as we try to find cleaner and 'more natural' ways of accessing fossil fuels, and as people experience the downsides in their daily lives of environmental damage, they are steadily organising themselves to protest.

However, as the *Big Issue* entrepreneur John Bird emphasises, protest in itself is often not the answer. He advocates shifting our allegiances as consumers and refusing to support the 1% rich through our purchasing patterns. If we stop buying things and services from the key players they will soon need to rethink.

There's clearly a dilemma for public and private sector initiatives to provide ongoing fuel supplies without creating further damage to the planet – the pressures to do so will come from a variety of sources including a questioning of the whole idea of 'growth'.

Agendas for change

Different regions/countries/groups have different agendas for change which include the following:

- working on an eco (sustainable) economic approach

- implementing a free-market economist approach

- wanting western-style consumerism/growth/ technology/infrastructure

- developed countries wanting to 'develop' emerging nations (and to profit from doing so)

- those who want to develop *as* emerging nations – there are problems here (see Heinberg); being in the process of trying to develop their own standing in the world economic system

- wanting basic needs met – clean water, food, infrastructure etc.

- wanting 'democracy' (where even the somewhat sham democracy in the developed world is better than what they have)

- looking for equality where there is unfairness with other cultural, tribal, ethnic groups within the same culture/country/region

- being positioned within a fundamental disagreement – for example, the Muslim world is faced with an obtuse Western secular approach which is user-unfriendly to a society guided by a spiritual/religious dimension

- having a radical anti-capitalist or capitalist critical/ radical approach eg. the *Occupy* movement

- campaigning on interests around employment, rights, pay etc.

- having a unique cultural historical bias

- having particular power and rights issues (including gender equality)

- dealing with old historical clashes between regions/countries where distrust/difference and unfinished business has been 'handed down' generationally through time

- resolving ethnic and religious conflicts

There are points of difference here but also some major clashes.

For example:

1. wanting Western consumerism vs an eco-friendly economy which wants to rein back consumerism (growth/non-growth)

2. having a culturally important emphasis on the religious/spiritual dimension vs countries which have pared back their idea of capitalism to completely value-less systems (– the spiritual vs. the ultra-secular)

3. wanting Western consumerism without an increase in democratic rights or gender equality

The short version is that there are very varied and often competing agendas for change between countries/regions and also within countries/regions.

Wrongdoing and fraud in the financial world

Wrongdoing and fraud is *structural* in the financial world and not mentioned enough by economists.

There's a long list of corporate scandals since the Second World War. For example, take the case of *Enron*, which rose to be America's seventh biggest company within 15 years and was then revealed to be riddled with hidden debt, hidden profits and potentially scandalous money-dealing, finally going bankrupt in 2002.

Recently, since the 2008 financial crisis, the dazzling scale of fraud and wrongdoing in the financial industry has come to light. For example, Greece – a country now in serious economic trouble – apparently didn't meet the stringent financial regulations for its original entry into the European Union but presented as though it did.

At best, the wrongdoing can be described as completely misleading people – for example, the process of financialisation has involved *'selling something as a cherry cake with only half a cherry in the whole cake'* – this is the view of Max Keiser, the current main critic of the financial world on *Russia Today* TV channel (RT). Here what is being described is the wrapping up of financial toxicity into an exotic financial product that very few people can understand.

Also perhaps 'at best', it's failure to declare what's going on. The economic historian Niall Ferguson, who gave the 2012 BBC Reith lectures, believes that governments fail to present the true picture of the relationship of their assets and liabilities to their populaces. Huge amounts of liabilities are simply not declared. Furthermore he believes that not only should they be required to account in ways similar to businesses, but that they should also be required to show forward thinking and the burden of debt they are saving up for future generations.

The LIBOR (inter-bank lending) rate 'fix' exemplifies the scale and seriousness of fraud. Follow Max Keiser on RT.com or RT TV channel for details of actions brought, fines, personalities etc. The fraud is huge and legal action is pending, so we're keeping fairly quiet! The point here is not names but 'business as usual' within the regular and the shadow banking system, the markets are generally unregulated, can be fraudulent in a legal sense and look structurally corrupt. The idea of banks as 'pillars of society' vetting individual customers has become ridiculous; the credibility of banks has been destroyed. Whilst Barclays and UBS have already been fined millions, other banks are also implicated. The scale of the creation of toxic financial products is huge. Many organisations rely on the LIBOR rate as a reference point for financial transactions so the damage is enormous. It's a violation of law and has apparently already cost billions for the international business community.

Some of the major financial institutions have been accused of greed and recklessness and even money-laundering. Fraud destroys trust and adds to the problem of an unstable financial system.

Academics and others compromised

Charles Ferguson in his recent book on the *'financial heist'* has spelled out examples of academics who have received large fees for providing the academic credibility for economic and banking policies, and he also criticises academics for *not* speaking out, for their huge silences when they were in a position to comment.

In his book *How do we fix this mess?* the BBC *News* Business Editor Robert Peston asks questions about whose job it was to pick up on the growing financial crisis in the years prior to 2008 - bankers, investors, regulators, politicians and us as consumers. Perhaps we should look too at academics and whether they should have more or less of a role in advising key players.

As the bank scandals and swindles and frauds are numerous and currently may be under investigation, we suggest you follow the news from a good source to keep ahead. What is important about the crookedness and distortion in the system is that it is huge, structural and probably not just caused by a lack of regulation and professionalism, but also by the *personal psychological makeup of individuals* in the financial world who set the standards of what to get away with.

Inquiries, truth and reconciliation

And sorting out problems with corruption and pathology costs money too.

It's not easy to find out the precise costs of inquiries and tribunals – the following are approximations from the data we were able to find: the Waterhouse Inquiry in the 1990s into child abuse in care homes in north Wales - possibly £13 million; the Leveson Inquiry may have cost around £6 million to run whilst News Corporation may have spent more than $167 million on legal fees; the Saville Inquiry into the *Bloody Sunday* shootings in Derry may have cost £195 million; the Hutton Inquiry into the death of UK weapons expert Dr David Kelly may have cost £2.5 million.

And it's not just the cost of inquiries and trials themselves. After the collapse of *Enron* in America, there were dozens of legal suits with compensation pay-outs to staff (in the millions) and investors (in the billions). Settlements from News Corporation after the Leveson Inquiry may run into millions of pounds. And of course there's the cost of new regulatory systems and the arguments over what these should be.

It's good that we appear to be facing up to our problems but important to remember that this isn't a cost-free exercise in itself.

Power and democracy in the world order

Power is a big issue but in essence, we're looking at big shifts in power across the globe on economic, political and cultural grounds.

The dominance of the USA in the world is under threat, particularly as new power blocs and alliances are being formed, and America (like many others) struggles with its economy (not to mention its political situation). Geopolitical analyst Ian Bremmer describes his concept of a *G-Zero world* where he sees a breakdown in global leadership as Western influence declines and other players are not strong enough or unified enough to lead a global agenda.

There are various ideas about emerging economies in the new world order, and indeed financial commentators are falling over themselves trying to predict which players are worth watching.

As well as the BRICS – *Brazil, Russia, India and China*, there are other groups. Jim O'Neill of Goldman Sachs has identified the *'Next Eleven'* based on factors such as economic stability and political maturity, the so-called N-11 countries. Investment in education systems is also important when assessing growth potential. There are *Asian Tiger* countries and *Tiger Cub* countries – where selling to the West is important, and there are the CIVETS identified by Robert Ward of the Economist Intelligence Unit and Michael Geoghegan, previously of HSBC, countries with business potential including young populations, sophisticated financial systems and often a diversity of industries. Then there's the MAVINS – picked out by Joe Wiesenthal on the basis of commodity advantages (like oil and metal reserves) and under-utilised population and land. If groups of countries pulled together, they could form powerful economic and political units to rival the West but co-operation is not a simple matter.

New players including the BRIC countries look like they will have more economic say in the future, but it's difficult to say how much. The political scientist Ian Bremmer reminds us that the BRIC countries have little in common with each other, and may even come into greater conflict with each other in the future, for example over resources like water. The hope that emerging economies like the BRICs will save the world situation is short-lived claims Ha-Joon Chang, since in his view, their economies will never proportionately match those of the richer countries, nor are they free from being affected by difficulties in the bigger economies because of their interconnectedness through trade, and in some cases have much internal conflict to deal with, making it unclear exactly how things will go for them.

There are big questions over the nature and reality of democracy in a variety of contexts – Samuel P Huntington's concept of *'waves' of democracy* is helpful here, with a number of current democracies remaining fragile (sometimes including enforcement by military might), and a new 'wave' beginning with the Arab 'spring' revolutions.

The Economist Intelligence Unit (linked to *The Economist* newspaper) produces *The Democracy Index* each year which categorises nations across the globe on a scale from full democracy through to authoritarian regimes based on the results of a number of assessments such as transparency and efficiency and how free and secure the elections are. Bodies which attempt to define democratic progress run into lots of difficulties about how they interpret data and make their assessments and whose interest(s) they serve or if they can be truly independent. Despite the questions over objectivity, many researchers (and no doubt financial political operators) find them useful as a guide.

Samuel Huntington also raises questions about whose ideals and values will prevail – suggesting that people in the West need to take on board more the fact that the values and practices of the West - using the *rule of law* to ensure a reasonable degree of civil liberty and to protect both religious and secular diversity - are not universally accepted across the globe. And in any case, recent examples of corruption, greed, bad practice and unexposed abuse all make it less likely that the West will win over other countries to our ways of doing business. Samuel Huntington foresees an increasingly conflictive world.

Although many of us will equate the concept of democracy with the idea of freedom, John T Wenders argues that 'democracy' stifles 'freedom' and that to preserve freedoms, we need to protect ourselves from democratic processes. He defines *democracy* as dealing with *public* matters and *freedom* as dealing with *private* matters (including financial transactions and property deals), and believes that the natural tendency of democratic processes (the rule of a majority) will be to *restrict individual freedoms* so that a constitution is necessary to protect them.

However, this critique of democracy can miss the point that democratic governments are supposed to operate on the will of the majority rather than making it easy for the few to get what they want out of the system – and we could equally well argue that the democratic process in too many countries has been perverted in its course by powerful lobbies and wealthy factions, undermining the moderation that might have been expected from a properly representative body.

On the other hand, we can't always expect that 'majority' governments will be moderate or even-handed, or even that the 'majority' really *is* the majority – in the UK for example, the electoral system frequently ensures that the majority of people do not have the government that they want – the group in power is simply the one that managed to get the biggest vote together whilst a host of other groups remain out of luck. And in many states round the world, powerful and wealthy lobbies and blocs exert influence on larger groups of others to guarantee votes.

Whilst we may be in a phase of facing up to the endemic corruption within Western culture (such confessional times are to be praised), if we don't repair things fully, we run the risk of remaining compromised in any legitimacy we claim for intervening in regimes where we believe wrongdoing is occurring.

Sham democracy and the people's voice

We've lost real democracy and representation in much of the West. One problem is the big increase in the size and power of big corporations and the way in which governments appear to have become managers of money, lacking in real power themselves and administering the populace (such as imposing austerity strategies or social control measures) so as to maximise economic outcomes desired by the real power-brokers. Neither do we have confidence that our representatives have the autonomy they need to speak up for us; very often they're compromised by their own career aspirations, by being members of factions and by groupthink within governmental systems.

People can be left feeling voiceless as the mainstream media fails to reflect their opinions, is not open to public involvement, and appears as the mouthpiece of government. There's not only commercialisation with the race for ratings, but a convergence around supporting the careers of the élites who have control of the media that is tedious and undemocratic. People whose faces we've seen for years on the television are given lucrative contracts to travel across the globe and 'show us' other countries, whilst the general population is prevented from access to the media. Anchor-men and women and news presenters deliver ever more polished presentations – yet who wants news of disasters, exploitation and human misery delivered by people in perfectly coiffured hair and smart ties that match the background graphics? We could be satisfied with natural communication, informal presentation, something authentic, but instead ordinary people have their stories organised and packaged into sound-bites by professional journalists.

At present, though to outside eyes it may seem that people in the West live in democratic states, to many of us who live in the West it feels as if what we've got is 'sham' democracy. For example, Jack Campbell from the University of Buffalo reckoned that the pool of 'persuadable' people in the American 2012 election was as little as 2-3%. *Super-PACs* - independent political committees - were allowed to raise funds and run advertising campaigns for their favoured candidates and against their non-favoured ones, with no limits to the amount of donations they could raise, and in America in 2012, these ran into millions if not billions of dollars. We're excluding people from the democratic process. The American *Declaration of independence* put together in 1776 by Thomas Jefferson and fellow associates, emphasised the rights and equality of human beings and questioned the legitimacy of any government which failed to support these. Yet, in the 2012 American election, parties like the Green Party and the Justice Party got hardly any look-in on airtime.

What all this actually does is to protect the 'system' within these fields such that people who don't fit in or come from a particular 'world' end up excluded or disheartened, and the 'system' replicates itself, losing vibrancy and diversity whilst society itself becomes more and more divided.

We don't need leaders to look like film stars and speak like actors. What we need is for them to be emotionally mature, wise and well-informed, and above all, able to challenge and fight for those they represent on ethical grounds. We're not convinced that current processes maximise the chances of these kinds of qualities coming to the fore.

Good news about life in a democracy

People in power in a democracy can't ultimately get away with bullying or manipulating people or not listening to them.

Although media is controlled – we're fed only what 'they' want us to hear – ultimately, in a democracy, the people *will* be heard, especially if they get together on the internet or gather on the streets – in fact, ultimately, the people can't *not* be heard. John Bird reminds us that the total 'wealth' of the consumer population is far greater than the 1% of multi-millionaires/billionaires, and believes that if people use their consumer power effectively they *can* create change.

The political scientist John Keane describes our current age as characterised by *monitory democracy* in which there's a multiplicity of forms of pressure and scrutiny on governments, beyond simply the old forms of representation – modern democracies include cross-border and international organisations, global corporations, media scrutiny, human rights organisations, non-governmental organisations, as well as digital systems like *Twitter* and blogging.

On the one hand we have increasing variegation of organisations and bodies to deliver public outcomes and thus the opportunity for less governmental accountability and on the other, a huge range of organisations and bodies whose role includes scrutinising, monitoring and critiquing the functioning of the state. Furthermore, it's not at all clear where the boundary between the 'state' and the 'people' lies, with increasing fusion between public and private and overarching non-elected bodies and global corporations exercising power over and above individual governments. It's easy to find examples of these confusions such as the UK's struggle with the US over extradition of its citizens; the struggle for governments to levy taxation on international companies which are not necessarily 'domiciled' in the country where sales take place; the movement of investment in countries from one to another in order to profit from lower labour costs or more lax environmental regulation; business sponsorship of and investment in educational establishments and hospitals.

Human rights are an important issue within human societies. Ronald Dworkin, a philosopher of law, argues that the rights of the individual against the state exist *'outside of the written law and precede the interest of the majority'*, while Ayn Rand (often taken up by the right-wing) thought that protecting rights was important to counter the *'tyranny of the majority'*. This is an important issue within the concept of democracy which prioritizes the will of the majority. According to Kenneth Arrow's *'impossibility theorem'* (he applied 'game theory' to political science) there is no such thing as the *'general will'* and in any case, people vote strategically in elections so that the results do not actually reflect what people want or feel. Thus, whatever the results of an election, there's always a sense of dissatisfaction among a significant number. Human rights therefore often applies to those in *minority groups within democracies* – where these are not respected, a democracy feels oppressive.

Inequality

Alarmingly, whilst millions/billions struggle to make life work, a few people get more and more. *Occupy Wall Street* and other movements in America and round the globe have exposed the divisions in what they call *'99%/1%'* - the 99% who don't have and the 1% who do have. According to E N Wolff (2007), of the financial wealth created within the US between 1983 and 2004, the top 1% got 42% of it, and the bottom 80% of society got only 6% of it. For a detailed rundown on the structural inequality of American society, see G. William Domhoff's website material *Who rules America*. Among many interesting statistics, he shows how the relative wealth of chief executives has increased astronomically over recent years compared to the very small increases in income of the average worker, reinforcing disparity.

We already have the situation whereby the net worth of political leaders demonstrates the social distance there must be between not only leaders and 'the poor', but between political leaders and the 'average working person'. The scale of disparity between ordinary people and celebrities is phenomenal, whilst millions on low incomes watch, *admire* and *emulate* celebrities whose personal wealth is sometimes many hundreds of times greater. And to add salt to the wound, often the money generated for that wealth is *from the poor people themselves* through phone-in voting systems, quizzes, licence fees and their responses to advertising (including simply watching the programmes in the first place, thus boosting rating figures and attracting the advertisers). All round the world, wealth is generated by the harsh lives of the poor.

In Britain, the *Trussell Trust* is opening a record number of food banks to distribute food to the poor, in both 'deprived' and wealthy areas of Britain, feeding people through churches and community centres. They report feeding a third of a million people during the period 2012-2013, and suggest that 13 million people live below the poverty line. *Fare Share* redistributes food from supermarkets and other sources to the poor, and in 2013 reports serving the needs of more than 36,000 people a day.

There are a number of questions that inequality of employment income raises:

- in addition to the numbers of people in the *Sunday Times Rich List* or the *Forbes Billionaires* list (including people who've made their fortunes in business), we seem to accept that TV chefs, footballers and commercial musicians should gross colossal amounts of money and that jobs like heading up prestige universities should command huge remuneration packages; why should salaries for people who *manage large amounts of money* necessarily have to be set at what represents a significant proportion of that money, rather than being set as a reasonable rate for the skills of the job?

- why should doing *what we love or have chosen to do* be rewarded with funds tens or even hundreds of times greater than those whom we serve? why should people doing *dead-end or boring or dirty jobs* be paid any less? perhaps they need compensation?

- who decided that if we *spend years as a student* – rewarding years in which we're investing in our own skills and knowledge for our lives ahead – that we should necessarily get more money than those who haven't had that opportunity? perhaps we should get *less*?

- how do different jobs get rated? should people who *deal in life and death* – whether that's cleaners, health professionals, food preparation staff, health and safety operatives or emergency services get the most money? should people who *do the most complex work* be paid the most? should *talent* be rewarded with anything other than the satisfaction of seeing others enjoy the fruits of our efforts? should people (and their families) who do *difficult or dangerous work* be compensated for taking the risks involved? what about people who *produce lasting things for humankind* – building bridges, making scientific discoveries, composing songs?

- at the moment, what we often have is that *those who have been able to lobby for the most resources get them* (whatever the methods they've used – old school tie, collective bargaining, etc); maybe we should all get the same?

- perhaps we need differential wages according to our age and stage of life, rather than according to the job we do? the idea that older people can manage on meagre pensions is partly dependent on the idea that older people have already got their housing, furniture, clothing etc. sorted out but this isn't true for everyone.

- in his book *The Necessity of Poverty*, John Bird argues that many jobs (particularly middle-class ones) are only created and sustained by the existence of the poor; what would happen if we started to see the populations who 'feed' those in jobs like social work, prison and probation service, healthcare, teaching, benefits administration, employment services in a different light, as those who make it possible for all those people to *have* jobs?

We don't know the answers but we do believe that it's time we reviewed these kinds of issues and asked ourselves questions about what appears to be immutable *status quo*.

Who bears the brunt of capitalist enterprise?

It's not just that rich and poor are *divided*, it's that *the stakes are unfair*. The economics commentator Ha-Joon Chang emphasises this unfairness by spelling out that it's the poor who are thrown into survival mode, with fewer and fewer protections, cuts in public spending, austerity measures, and at the mercy of damaging environmental conditions etc. - in other words, **the poor bear the**

brunt of the free market outcomes whilst the rich are looked after with bailouts, big payoffs, and are allowed to escape justice measures for their mismanagement of funds - in other words, **the rich are protected from the vicissitudes of the free market.**

Careers

The writer Christopher Lasch in his book *The Revolt of the Elites*, bemoaned the loss of 'third places' where élites and working people used to have opportunities for discourse, and saw the widening gap between rich and poor reinforced by the retreat of the élites into gated communities, big cars, insulated environments and closed cartels wherein only those who went to the 'right' schools or have the 'right' credentials are let in.

The emphasis on 'careers' and looking after one's c.v. reinforces this kind of idea – to the poor, there is no real notion of 'career'. The idea of *career* means that we make decisions that protect our personal long-term interests rather than what's in the interests of the people in front of us – of course, sometimes we can marry these up, but where we can't, the career usually wins unless we have a strong personal sense of values and ethics. The difficulty comes when we consider ourselves in relation to our peer group, believing that if we drop out, we'll never get back in or that others who've 'kept their noses clean' will be preferred for opportunities. We have to take our chances and make our choices – are we for moral action and for what we believe in for the world, or are we going for (what may ultimately prove to be short-term) personal advantage?

The question of career structures, whilst good for people who get into élite jobs, nevertheless denies opportunities for those outside the big organisations who offer them. Students within fields like law, medicine and politics are trained to protect their career and their reputation like gold-dust, carving their path carefully, looking good, cultivating the right contacts, getting the right kinds of experience and ensuring that all their opportunities are high-quality and of good status. The increasing emphasis on *internships* that require considerable self-funding is further excluding those without the means to do them. The emphasis on 'career' means that we have a homogeneous 'club' across all main fields of work wherein particular kinds of well-off people collude in maintaining a network and system that administers to others lower down in the hierarchy, expects services from them, and ultimately exploits them, making their money one way or another out of them.

Furthermore, the idea of protecting a career can seriously affect people's ability to highlight malpractice, to whistle-blow on ethical issues, and to challenge people whose personalities and emotions are negatively affecting their work and the way they handle significant responsibility.

Doing something about inequality

The *Global Call to Action Against Poverty* (GCAP) unites numerous anti-poverty coalitions round the globe, (including the *Make Poverty History* campaigns), and works to put pressure on national governments to meet the UN *Millennium Goals*, eradicate poverty and reduce inequality. It produces an annual report called *The World We Want* 2011 and reports on a massive range of work round the globe. They are committed to eradicating *extreme poverty* 'within a generation'. This makes for sobering, interesting reading.

The UN Millennium Goals

- eradication of extreme hunger and poverty
- universal primary education
- gender equality
- reduction of child mortality rates
- improvements to maternal health
- reduction of HIV, malaria and other diseases
- ensuring environmental sustainability
- global partnership for development

Yet poverty isn't always just about the material. The GCAP sees *human rights* as likely to be the leading edge of the post-2015 goals for the world.

The UN Human Rights Council is working on the development of *Guiding Principles* which make it clear that *human rights* are intricately linked to questions of inequality because those without the means to have a voice are denied their human rights. The UN has long stated that poverty includes the inability to engage in 'civic life' rather than being solely about mere subsistence or below-subsistence existence.

Inequality isn't just about the material level of existence

'Happiness' doesn't have to mean money or goods – we discover that in some parts of the world even without many material resources, people are happier with simplicity, time to be with people, and a sense of identity, history and community – much of the Western world has destroyed individuals' sense of history identity and belonging and it's not easy to put it back (though there's a lot of interest in family history searches, archaeology, museum exhibitions, TV history programmes etc). Karma Tshiteem, who is the secretary of the *Gross National Happiness Index* in Bhutan, says that it's well-known that happiness is a *'state of mind'*.

However, feelings of life satisfaction and a sense of 'having' may also come from essential freedoms and democratic rights.

The economist Amartya Sen and the philosopher Martha Nussbaum have led the way in thinking about the way in which we measure development across the globe. Together with economist Mahbub-ul-Haq, Amartya Sen drew up the *Human Development Index* for the United Nations, to measure improvements in wellbeing as well as objective economic advances.

Their thinking is that *capabilities* are economic assets, not just material things, money or access to services. These might include the ability *to live to old age, engage in economic transactions, or participate in political activities*. People value essential freedoms and rights and these should be taken into account when we compare the development stages of different nations. This makes a big difference to the way in which we view poverty, because if we have a sense of strong human rights we may feel less poor and frustrated than people with a lot more money who are deprived in terms of life expectation (eg. through stress or ill-health) or the right to express themselves (through political activity or artistic pursuits).

There are many improvements in the rights of groups in society in some countries – including for gays, women, and children – but in some countries there are decreases in rights. Martha Nussbaum has defined a number of capabilities that she thinks we should value including *bodily integrity* (see our chapter on *The Body, Health and Illness*) - which includes freedom of movement, choice over reproduction and sexuality, freedom from fear of sexual assault etc; *being able to make plans for one's life; being able to have a range of feelings and their expression; being able to hold property and apply for jobs on an equal basis with others.*

However, it's important that we don't think that we can get away with depriving people financially just because we've allowed them a bit of political freedom. Surely the idea is that (as we outlined in our chapter on *Effective relating*), seeing relationships between politicians/power-brokers and people as OK-OK is likely to generate a more equitable distribution of resources.

Areas where attention needs to be given include:

- workers' rights - like the trend towards more flexible work contracts and reserve labour forces which make us less able to plan or feel economically secure

- the general increase in social control – including the control of information sent out by the media and public and employment surveillance methods and how this interfaces with human rights

- economic development round the world causing difficulties for sub-sections of populations (eg. suffering in rural environments whilst urban élites flourish)

- huge distances between élites and 'the rest' – more social distance between those who are making and delivering policy and those who live with the results

- inequality across nations (eg. Kyoto climate change targets resulted in some key players producing dangerous emissions that cancelled out the efforts of many other nations to cut their own)

- the feeling that bankers have 'ripped off' society and then required bailouts paid for by austerity – people in developed countries are feeling that things are unfair let alone those in developing countries. There's resentment caused by a banker getting millions in payouts and someone not even being able to earn enough to feed their family after a month's hard graft.

- the increase in size of the media industry versus the lack of a voice for the public - though thankfully the internet provides some opportunity for people to express themselves. Even with the internet, the 'official' media shape and control the news, public opinion and recently, intrude into the lives of citizens eg. by phone hacking, the subject of the recent Leveson Inquiry in the UK.

- the growth in corporatism ie. the influence of large corporations and their (non-) values which appear to be diluting democracy and the values by which governments have traditionally operated.

How we handle inequality

There are different ways of calculating inequality which include:

- income
- rights
- development/technological progress
- basic needs eg. food and water

Richard Wilkinson and Kate Pickett have long pointed out the negative effects of *perceived inequity* within societies, particularly on mental and physical health. Now there's more *obvious* disparity *within* countries including in Western nations, so that it's visible rather than hidden, and through the internet and media, disparities across the world are now evident to most people. People can no longer pretend that they don't know about inequality in the world and this awareness is leading to social unrest in many places, as people without start asking questions about *why.*

There's a fear for the future eg. possible conflicts over food and water availability and social dissatisfaction and disruption. Since the protests of 1968, developed countries have developed a great deal of social control mechanisms from camera surveillance to the building of huge databanks (including bio-surveillance) and more repressive legislation (often under the guise of state security and anti-terrorism).

In addition, social mobility is now much less possible as the élites tighten their grip on their power bases and cultural worlds.

Discrediting the poor

A significant clue to the decline in values is the creation of a *not-OK* 'underclass'. After the Second World War in Europe, governments were concerned with providing employment, free healthcare, education etc. and democracy and human rights were taken seriously. The 'working-class' were idealised as honest, hardworking etc. Owen Jones in his book *Chavs* skilfully demonstrates how a group such as the British working-class has been demonised and badly treated through a number of strategies over time. It's immoral and unspiritual to create and treat people as 'second-class' citizens and it has got to stop. And in defining those who live off 'benefits', there are echoes of course in current discourses from the Victorian 'deserving' and 'undeserving' poor. We need to catch ourselves every time we're tempted to write off another person or a group and remember how sinister this kind of habit can become, witness the persecution of minorities and cultural groups, the most significant of which were the Jews, in the Second World War.

In India, the recent protests about the unacceptable rapes of women within the culture has also served to highlight the discrediting and discounting of the Dalit community – formerly the *'untouchables'* a word that now translates as *'the broken ones'* - who do most of the unattractive jobs within the community. According to reports (eg. BBC India), many Dalit women are subject to rape and abuse by higher-caste men and have little recourse to law; in some cases where fathers have tried to get justice there've been serious reprisals against the families for complaining. Young women from the Dalit community are *blamed* for things like not being married yet, for going out unaccompanied, being with a boyfriend etc. – in other words, they are turned into *the problem* rather than being recognised as *victims,* **painted as responsible for the crimes of the powerful and influential**, and their efforts to better themselves through work or study or marrying well are destroyed.

What's at stake in these examples is the social structure of societies – those who are situated in weaker positions are not only abused and forgotten, stolen from and cheated, raped, beaten up and in some cases killed, and excluded from the majority of opportunities *but are also presented as 'bad', lazy, lascivious etc.* The effect of this process of labelling and discrediting is several fold - concealing the evil in the oppressors who can deny their own guilt (even to themselves) by blaming the other; deterring those who have aspirations out of their ascribed 'class' or caste membership; frightening those who might want to protest or complain or seek justice into backing off; keeping society operating along well-travelled lines of gender, race and social class divisions rather than facing the challenges of equality and a fairer distribution of opportunities and resources.

We need to inform ourselves fully about the situation of those in vulnerable groups and recognise how they can be discredited by those who are more comfortable and who have greater power and greater ability to present themselves in a good light within mainstream culture.

Financial predators

As if issues of global inequality were not bad enough on their own, some people are making the situation worse with gobsmacking levels of greedy, exploitative behaviour, demonstrating a complete disdain for their fellow human beings.

'Vulture Funds are international predators. Their victims are the poorest people in the world'. Sally Keeble, UK MP, said after bringing in *The Debt Relief (Developing Countries) Bill* to stop Vulture Funds profiteering from third world debt by suing poor countries for the full repayment of debts that they have bought up cheaply.

Now it appears that some companies are profiteering from Greece's suffering, although as yet (2013), UK legislation on Vulture Funds (where some are located) doesn't cover European countries. In February 2012 the Greek Debt Audit Campaign wrote that a *'social Armageddon'* brought about by austerity measures was being forced on the people of Greece to *'pay the state's creditors'*.

In February 2012, social movements across Europe took to the streets in a campaign called *'We are all Greek'*. The Jubilee Debt Campaign argues that much debt in the world has arisen from irresponsible lending by rich lenders in the 1970s, and the *Drop the Debt* Campaign has as its first demand a 100% cancellation of *'unpayable'* debts – ones where countries (including Greece) cannot afford to pay while meeting its people's basic needs, and *'unjust'* debts which include those made on unfair terms.

The political scientist, Susan George, does not view the debt crisis in much of the world as simply about 'irresponsibility' but rather links it to *political intentions*. She has criticised the policies of northern hemisphere countries in shoring up despotic regimes with so-called *'odious' debts* - loans that are made not for the benefit of the country but in order to maintain dictators in positions of power - and for maintaining poor countries in the southern hemisphere in debt - a position which ensures their political compliance and their willingness to let in foreign capital and accept the 'free market'.

> The *Drop the Debt* campaign is critical of the World Bank/IMF's Debt Sustainability Framework because '*the Framework does not promote a human-needs approach to sustainable debt levels, does not share responsibility for lending decisions equally between creditors and debtors, and it does not provide an answer to the call for much broader responsible lending standards*'.

Anyone who's had to repay individual debt to creditors knows that there's always an amount you're allowed to keep to meet your basic needs like food, childcare, travel to work, housing and medical care. It seems that this isn't always done at the global level, and vulture funds are making the situation worse.

As Ronald Dworkin tells us, **rights have to be paid attention to and constantly reasserted and fought for – *otherwise they tend to be taken away or eroded.***

Inequality across the globe is affecting agreements on climate change targets; it's also there in attempting to get agreements on fiscal policy and economic direction. The crisis in Europe is very much about this with attitudes from the richer countries affecting the treatment of countries in trouble and a host of feelings and prejudices that probably underlie decisions taken – eg. those countries that benefited from the post-war Marshall Plan, those countries where they have failed to save or which have lived beyond their means etc. There is a great deal of moralising in the field of debt, as we can see from our experiences of personal debt – *people without the immediate means to pay back are stigmatised and discredited as irresponsible*, and this is as true for countries and companies as for individuals.

Financial givers

The moral basis for giving

In his 1889 article *The Gospel of Wealth*, Andrew Carnegie suggested that the rich (especially the self-made new rich in America) should recirculate the bulk of their fortunes into society, seeing them as 'trustee[s] of the poor', more capable of administering funds for the general good than the poor would be themselves. These days, we may have to question whether or not those who make money are any more wise about how to use funds for the public good than the potential recipients of such money might be, but it's interesting that similar to the idea of ourselves as stewards of the earth, Carnegie saw the rich as *stewards* of money, rather than *owners* of money.

Within a capitalist framework, Carnegie also believed that in donating to charitable causes, money should primarily be used to help people create yet more wealth (rather than for example, reinforcing a 'benefit culture'). Nevertheless, he believed that there was a spiritual good to be achieved by giving away one's wealth rather than spending it on oneself and one's family and accumulating private goods. Today, there is no shortage of testimonies from people who 'give' that they experience positive feelings of reward from doing so.

The social and cultural critic Christopher Lasch felt that those who've gained status and wealth through education and career in America, colonising and trading in fields of knowledge, lack the sense of 'reciprocal obligation' that previous generations of aristocrats who inherited wealth have had, feeling glad to have escaped from the working class, protecting themselves by insulating their lifestyles, living in gated estates, staying within tight frames of reference and social circles, and keeping mobile and cosmopolitan. Not all aristocrats have felt benevolent but there is clearly a feeling that many used to see philanthropy as a part of their civic duty, an approach that seems chillingly absent from many of the young people in programmes like *Young, Posh and Loaded* and *Made in Chelsea*. Ian Hislop's programme *When Bankers Were Good* highlights the work of Victorian reformers like George Peabody, Angela Burdett-Coutts and Samuel Gurney, and gives more than a hint that modern-day financiers have lost the plot on this one.

Who gives?

There are differences between nations on the activity of 'philanthropy'. According to reports from the Center for

670

Philanthropy at the University of Indiana, America is the highest giving nation in the world, (followed by the UK), with high-earners giving away c.£90 per £1000 of their wealth compared to their peers in the UK who give £2 per £1,000. Nearly 100% of top tax-payers give to charity in America whilst just above a quarter of top-taxpayers do in Britain. Wealth in America is often defined by how much people *give* as well as how much they *own (*or *earn)*.

However, in Australia, it's possible that people may be much quieter about their giving activity. Some see transparency about *giving* activity as 'bragging' whilst others believe that publicly 'modelling' *giving* encourages others. Research at the Australian Centre for Philanthropy and Nonprofit Studies at the Queensland College of Technology indicates that corporate giving is lower in Australia than in comparable 'big hitter' countries, and Miriam Steffans of the Sydney Morning Herald supports this view in her 2011 article on the topic. However, it's important to locate comparisons about philanthropy with countries' industrial and business record (such as Australia's booming four decades of mining compared to perhaps more sustained income generation in some other countries) and their taxation and social welfare policies (such as high taxes and generous welfare). On the other hand, the *World Giving Index* 2012 lists Australia unequivocally as the *most generous country in the world* – certainly in attitudes - with over two-thirds of the population giving money to charity and helping a stranger and significant numbers doing voluntary work.

It is hugely difficult to make cross-cultural comparisons. On the measures used by the *World Giving Index* (financial donations, volunteering and helping strangers) Thailand has the 'highest engagement' in donating money whilst Liberia has a strong ethos of 'helping a stranger'. India comes low on the index for giving behaviour in total, yet the 165 million people in India who give to charity in a typical month exceeds the 143 million people who do so in America. In the report *India Giving*, 84% of people in India have given to an individual or organisation in the past year – in the UK, this measure is around 72%; Ireland, close to Australia at the top of world-rankings for giving, achieves 79%. Measures for percentages and proportions have to be disaggregated from actual amounts; it's not the place here to go into this in detail – suffice it to say that assessing ideas like 'generosity' is immensely complex.

What's striking is that highest rates of giving behaviour aren't always consistent with affluence even at national levels, so that *some rich countries are less generous and some poorer countries give a lot to others.*

Inequity about *who* gives is reflected in many ways. Quite often the evidence is that poorer people give a greater *percentage* of their incomes to others than rich people do. And Stuart Etherington (knighted in 1994 and chair of the National Council for Voluntary Organisations), in his Attlee Lecture on the theme of philanthropy, indicated that around *a third of adults in the UK do most of the volunteer work and charitable giving.* Much of the money for charities in Britain comes from *London and the south-east* and in the nation as a whole (and probably across the world) *older women* are the most generous with money and time.

Where should the money go?

And there's naturally disagreement about *where money is best spent.* Much charitable giving by the rich is personally motivated, for example, giving to people whose work attracts them or to a medical cause because of a relative's illness or an arts development because they like that kind of music etc. Conservatively, most money in Britain from rich donors goes to higher education institutions, on the lines of the Carnegie idea that money should help people to create more wealth, being spent on funding research institutes, building projects on campuses and bursaries for studies etc. Medical research and international projects are popular, as are arts and culture (most often in the capital city). One of the difficulties for big donors – those who give over £1 million - is to find organisations big enough to handle and use such large donations, so there appears to be a tendency among the rich to give lots of money to big existing organisations rather than funding small projects and innovation (although of course some of the foundations and large organisations distribute money to these). The Coutts report written by Beth Breeze gives further details on million-pound donations.

672

One of the advantages of being able to give is the opportunity to shape the world according to your wishes. Susan George (2007), commentator on global development issues, suggests that the American right-wing have been advancing their ideological 'social-Darwinian' agenda over the last 30 years through funding think-tanks, research centres and individual academic posts which then feed into some of the biggest financial institutions.

According to data from the National Council for Voluntary Organisations, more 'ordinary' donors to charity – *equating to more than half of the UK population* - tend to like medical research, hospitals, children and animals. Worryingly, only a tiny fraction of charitable donations go to 'the elderly', despite poverty and isolation being growing problems for the older generation.

Author and playwright Bonnie Greer, commenting on the future of charity for the independent grant-making body the *Esmée Fairbairn Foundation*, believes that giving to cultural projects can *foster social bonding* as a counterbalance to the social forces that drive us apart from one another. Gerard Lemos, social policy writer and researcher, who's been involved with a number of social action projects such as chairing the *Money Advice Centre* in the UK, believes that charitable work in the future should include making links between people and nature, creativity and spirituality, because these have important non-material benefits such as *grounding ourselves, exploring our identities* and *developing a sense of belonging.*

As the state becomes less able to meet the needs of the poor, private and charitable resources will increasingly be called upon to make up the deficit and to enter into joint arrangements with matched-funding for example.

Getting people to give more

Although the number of people giving may be becoming more diverse, the actual amount of money raised through philanthropy has reduced in recent times across the globe and effort has to be made if this is to be turned around. For example, moves are already afoot to entice the average worker into giving through their employment pay and for people to give at hole-in-the-wall cashpoints, and many supermarkets give regular spaces at their entrance doors to charity collectors. In addition, rich donors who receive tax benefits on their donations will be increasingly required to demonstrate that they have done all they could to ensure their charitable donations are used effectively (rather than for example languishing in foundation 'funds' or simply supporting prestigious administration centres).

Signs that the tide may be changing include the 2012 Forbes 400 philanthropy summit in which 161 'billionaires and near-billionaires' got together to discuss the moral and emotional imperatives of philanthropic and boost their *Giving Pledge*. Nearly 100 have committed themselves to giving half their fortunes to charity.

However, *the whole issue of 'charity', 'giving', and 'aid' not only raises questions about the strings attached, but also of course highlights structural inequality which shouldn't be there in the first place.*

Short-termism

Some societies in the past had a 'seven generation rule' - see Richard Heinberg's work - which was designed to protect future generations. This wise approach suggested that with any change, thought needed to be given to its effect for seven generations, which actually needs imagination. *Now we're not even planning for the* next *generation.*

In an article entitled *Fiscal Child Abuse American Style*, the US economist Laurence Kotlikoff and co-author Scott Burns reckon that funding the older generation in America is leaving a *massive* debt for their children and grandchildren, whom they suggest are not defending themselves – for example, they're much less likely to vote than the older generation, and have fewer resources to employ in influencing social policy than older people.

Not only is this kind of borrowing – on the backs of younger, less informed members of our society and without their true consent, immoral – it's not designed to create social cohesion in the long-term.

One reason amongst many for this position is the belief in the myth/fairy story of technology and science which runs: *'whatever mess we make, science has the power to put it right'*. Unfortunately, this is a myth – the prolific use of antibiotics to fight infection for example is resulting in the development of drug-resistant strains of bugs/viruses, the systems for breast screening in the UK may be damaging more women than it is saving (although of course it does save some). And the idea that we can put right our financial woes is now running out of steam, as many of the solutions we thought of have produced new problems such as virtual financial portfolios - money that doesn't really exist.

For those who want to follow up on *iatrogenesis* – when medicine does more harm than good, see our chapter on *The Body, Health and Illness*. David Wootton outlines his belief that the obstacles to progress in medicine lay in the way doctors saw themselves and thought about established medical knowledge and methods – they were lost in their own world with little ability to critique themselves – this may well be true too for those involved in the financial world and is a dangerous situation to get into. This chapter is particularly about economics and politics – fields which could be described in similar terms to Wootton's doctors – whereby we are holding onto old ideas and impeding progress in order to support cultural institutions and patterns that are past their sell-by date.

Another factor in 'short-termism' is the nature of government in democracies, governing teams being wedded to the need to stay in power and to ensure that they win elections. Thus it's very difficult to govern for the long-term unless politicians are convinced that their place in history will be assured through investment in long-term projects regardless of whether they're in power at the time. In this sense, stable dictatorships have more of a chance of pushing through reforms for the good of the country or the world than political parties in power for 3-4 years. The instability of democratic systems is arguably a problem for capitalism, as are the difficulties of governments elected on promises and enticements rather than on educated wisdom or values which give direction on things like the nature of a healthy society.

Democratic processes themselves take time – elections take time, committees and inquiries take time, consultations and referendums take time, and for those who believe themselves to know what needs to be done – just as for those whose aims are to make rapid profits - democratic processes can feel excruciatingly time-consuming and not fit-for-purpose.

The scientific-rational mind-set versus the holistic mind-set

Throughout the book and particularly in chapters like *The Unconscious* and *Spirituality,* we've emphasised the MYSTERY in life. Not everything can be known, we're often not in touch with our inner selves, there are surprising events that couldn't have been predicted, we can't always know what is ahead, there is much that we still don't understand etc.

The main problems with the *scientific/rational* approach to life as the 'new religion' are:

- it's like a *single-discipline approach* with strict rules whereas *holism* includes wide-ranging wisdom and knowledge

- it's full of turf wars based on divergent values/egos etc. and protection of empires

- it's subject to the effects of academic career values and competitiveness of individuals and institutions

- it makes the assumption of a rational and organised world + rational policymaking when policymaking is self-evidently affected by circumstances and personalities – if these personalities are distorted (see our *Psychopathology* chapter), the policy will suffer

- it's often compulsive and relentless – developing ever more into new fields and applications, sometimes regardless of the implications for humanity, and sometimes defying calls for regulation or giving them only 'lip-service'

- at the same time, change can sometimes be conservative and slow (partly because of the necessity for debate, red tape and research to establish the 'evidence')

- the work of academics has often been appropriated by governments and companies looking for support for their policies and products under the guise of 'independent' study which they have nevertheless funded (Ben Goldacre's work on pharmaceutical research is relevant here)

- the knowledge world has been significantly colonised by business interests such as journal publishers restricting access to material to those who can pay, book publishers and stockists determining whose work gets distributed and promoted, colleges who want to run courses that have high 'yield'

- the models that have emerged are problematic or faulty or too limited – eg. it's essentially silly to measure GDP; *externality* is frequently not included in the calculations ie. factors that are often 'hidden costs' and don't come to light until well into the future; models of the world are developed *assuming growth*. Particularly important here is the treating of ecological damage as *'externality'* not to be calculated into economic models. Environmental issues that need attention include *resource depletion, the gap between population and resources, and pollution.*

- there's conformity and group-think and a discrediting or neglect of ideas that don't conform to prevailing paradigms (see Thomas Kuhn's work)

- there's a lack of explicit recognition that economics are embedded in and help run industrial military complexes *(eg. that economic situations are frequently reinforced through the threat or application of military might)* – in fact, this is quite often hidden from view and left out of presentations

- the scientific-rational mind-set emphasises *'objectivity'* at the expense of *subjectivity*, often resulting in perceptions governed by a lifetime of looking at the world with a particular set of values including unexamined gender, class and race presuppositions as well as economic 'truths' and pretending that these are 'givens' and 'absolutes' and are somehow neutral

- there can be an emphasis on *'evidence-based'* approaches to knowledge – things which are *'observable'* and *demonstrable* which can drive agendas to focus on surface issues and things which will be easily testable and 'provable' – thus undermining and discounting initiatives and experiences which are more subtle, more profound, longer-lasting, and more complex

- there's been too much emphasis on *cognition* in academia and in the laboratory and a failure to look enough at 'the passions' of life including emotions and motivations and the physical and spiritual aspects of human experience

- there's been an emphasis on the idea that human beings are selfish and untrustworthy *rather than a view of human beings as likely to grow towards healthy outcomes* (as for example believed by the humanistic psychologists of the 1950s and 60s), thus negatively influencing public policy in the direction of surveillance and control rather than support and encouragement

This is probably not a fully comprehensive list, but it does cover a number of the main objections to the domination of much of the world by a scientific-logical mind-set in the quest for 'intellectual freedom' that's been underway since that period of history known as 'the Enlightenment'. (For a chatty guide to the Enlightenment, see Kieron O'Hara's *'Beginners Guide'*).

Getting the balance right between science and art is also a challenge. An example of people who've used a scientific mind-set in a creative way to express a political statement are the New York based Adam Harvey and Johanna Bloomfield, who've designed 'stealth-wear' fashion for 'counter-surveillance' including anti-drone burqas, hijabs, hoodies, scarves and 'off-pocket' technology to conceal phone signals from thermal-imagery surveillance technology, as an explicit statement of challenge to modern surveillance – what they call the *aesthetics of privacy*.

Of course good science depends on creative thinking, but it's quite evident that we've become too dependent on scientists to sort out the world's problems when the world's problems are not all scientific. It's clear in our chapters on *The body, health and illness* and *Emotional health* that medicine may have gone too far in medicalising ordinary human states (eg. of baldness, grief, etc), whilst we for our part look to medicine for too many answers and solutions. The relationship between science and the public is not just a problem of dissemination of 'results' – it needs to be a much more transparent discussion of aims, responsibilities, and parameters. There needs to be far more involvement across disciplines so that science is put to work in combination with other fields such as spirituality, art, sociology and anthropology, history, insights from the unconscious mind, emotions and intuitions, politics and economics. Alternative approaches need to be examined (eg. including different ways of doing medicine across the world). There needs to be an acceptance that there are many ways of knowing and that empirical research has considerable limits.

How we experience materialism/consumerism

Commentators on this don't really seem to tackle it. What we think is that materialism 'makes up' for psychological needs like our longing for love and acceptance that are often not being met - instead, we accept the myth that actual or symbolic *things* can make us happy, can fill the void, and can give us a sense of *importance in the external world.* Carl Jung tackles the idea of emptiness in his work, as does Erich Fromm. Recently we met a man who drove a great Jaguar car and had a powerful business and technical role, but who had the sadness of two adult daughters each with serious mental health difficulties. His life choices had not answered or made up for the challenges of his family life, which perhaps might have benefited from more of his attention in earlier years.

Furthermore, we're encouraged to *buy* rather than to *make,* although it's interesting that despite economic worries, hobby shops are doing rather well in the current climate. Generally we spend too much energy on being *consumers* rather than *producers,* going shopping rather than staying at home and producing things which not only give us functional objects for our lives but also give us a sense of accomplishment and joy (as well as keeping alive traditional and new skills).

Materialism ignores the spiritual dimension of life which has the contrasting mind-set ie. *less is more, less attachment is more, social responsibility and caring for others* is more important than *individual consumption, less ego is better than more -* greed hinders our development as people and also of society – greed is there in our work where we go on extending our reach, updating, expanding and exploring new developments, creating more markets when this is no longer necessary and straining people beyond healthy limits. This kind of activity can become addictive and compulsive, ignoring natural boundaries.

Our chapters on *Values, Spirituality* and *Finding our own direction in today's world* also tackle these issues.

'Modernism'

What stands out for us is the sheer number of processes, the speed of change, the seriousness of the situation, the lack of control we seem to have over processes and the sheer destructiveness of the situation. This negative/destructive aspect of the 'electronic age' or the 'postmodern world' is counter to expectations as we've been conditioned into believing in the high ideals of 'modernism' such as progress and justice.

'Modernism' rejected traditionalism and realism and encouraged the use of any kind of science, technology or art form to explore new ways of going forward. Modernist art and music has used strange and dissonant features and abstract forms to break with the past. The decline of modernism and people's disillusion with its goals and myths ('metanarratives') has been described by Jean-François Lyotard, in his holistic overview of the times we're in. He also describes the negative aspects of global capitalism and the commodification of knowledge, ideas which are helpful although they lack any explicit link with the concept of spirituality.

Post-structuralism

We've benefited from the breakdown of traditional ways of thinking – such that we've been able to take on ideas from 'post-structuralism' which, to put it simply, attack traditional structures and easy ways of knowing and allow us to juxtapose a whole variety of things to one another and be much more creative in our thinking and able to 'deconstruct' the power relations in all areas of life. However, whilst this has had a tremendously freeing energy, it's also enabled us to ditch all our anchors, something which has left the world feeling rudderless and chaotic, and this has been profoundly disturbing for the Western world. Throughout the book, we've both offered ways of freeing up our thinking and experiencing, and suggested that we need to find 'bottom lines' and values which can guide us. It's important that we find a way of synthesising both the best of the old and the new. For an introduction to post-structuralism, see the short guide written by Catherine Kelsey and Gary Gutting's introduction to the work of Michel Foucault.

How we're coping

We think the processes we've listed are very difficult to cope with psychologically and that people are responding with:

- being stressed
- fear
- confusion
- a sense of impending catastrophe
- a feeling of powerlessness
- over-adaptation and conformity
- denial
- conservatism
- conformity
- escape into entertainment
- escape into addiction
- magical, naïve thinking [*'surely the people in power will fix everything, surely they will have the same commonsense priorities as me'* - assuming that countries cooperate, are at the same stage of what's termed 'development', have similar histories and agendas, and that their policies are constructed rationally instead of for convenience, political expedience or prey to the personalities and whims of those with power.

Conformity as a response to the 'crisis we're in'

We've mentioned conformity in a number of chapters including *Therapy* whereby clients mostly need to conform to middle-class values and expectations in order to be seen as 'well', processes that can be similar to those within institutionalised religion and within medicine and education and careers where to be seen as successful, people need to be able to manage health, pass assessments, and be suitable candidates for promotion. The problem here is that our culture is distorted ie. competitive, materialistic, etc so that 'normality' is in fact abnormal; furthermore, the ideal doesn't exist – people pretend socially to have an ideal lifestyle, but in reality it's aspirational rather than fact.

Social conformity brings with it a standardisation of behaviour, lifestyles etc. which can be rather boring as well as dangerous for the world because it limits awareness and problem-solving and brings in its wake other difficult issues such as intolerance and exclusion. We would call social conformity actually *anti-social*.

Standardisation of behaviour reduces the growth potential in people, stopping them from being truly themselves and living a life that's right for them. We'd even go so far as to say that what we have is a *myth of individuality* in our society because what's actually created is a bunch of people doing the same kinds of things as each other and being frightened to be truly individuals.

Following authority

Jack says: People usually sort themselves into a hierarchy where there are those who lead and those who follow - or they step outside of these roles. Personally, I've never felt comfortable in either of these roles and naturally gravitate to the world of freelance, self-employed work.

In Stanley Milgram's classic experiment (described in our chapter on *the Self*), he demonstrated the willingness for people to follow orders provided that those issuing the orders had *credibility*.

In order to follow authority, people have to stop trusting their own perception, their commonsense and generally stop thinking for themselves, or they have to shut themselves off from more critical people who do trust their perceptions and do think for themselves.

The important point is that in today's world, lots more of us need to be thinking for ourselves rather than following others' lead or leading blindly on the basis of traditional ideas. We need to be looking carefully at the source of what we're told.

Psychological and behavioural issues

- *denial* is a big problem because we fail to act – in our own interests and in the interests of the planet - and we add to the problems by compensatory overconsumption, passivity, inauthentic relating, 'partying', continuing exploitation of resources, and allowing problems to build up and get worse

- there are new challenges in *parenting* to face – we need to tap into psychological knowledge and support and agree

683

approaches with our children; motivating, preparing and encouraging our children to live in the world we're leaving them is no mean task. Post-second world war, however children felt individually, collectively there was a sense that the older generation had given something to society to make it a better, safer place – now there's a sense that the older generation have been greedy, corrupt and irresponsible, making it difficult to claim credibility with younger people and resulting in potential tensions between the generations

- we're not aiming for *maturity* when we *should* be; staying in infantile and childish stages of development (such as wanting immediate gratification) will not be helpful in facing the challenges ahead – politicians not just private individuals need to think about this for themselves – we need them to make wise choices that aren't based on emotive kneejerk reactions and we need to encourage a climate in which personal growth and wisdom is valued

- *psychopathology* is a problem in individuals and in organisations, often in the direction of narcissism (see our chapter on this) – we need to be aware of this and to encourage people (especially those in influential roles) to utilise their psychopathology for good rather than being unaware of it and making decisions steered by transient emotions and volatility or deeprooted personal fears and desires (for example, turning *paranoia* into helpful health and safety policies or *grandiosity* into positive ambitions for the future)

- *fear and conformity* are also big problems – we need to face up to what we're frightened of, create and link up with networks of support, increasing our understanding of the issues and dangers involved and take our own power, seeing ourselves as equal citizens with all others rather than being led by people in whom we have little confidence

- control and manipulation by large organisations set a dreadful model as does their anti-social behaviour – telephone 'menus', robotic call-centre procedures, conflictive and 'no can do' attitudes, insensitive and exploitative policies and wanton environmental damage - none of which do much to help us through troubled times, and much of which renders us helpless, frustrated, stressed and angry

- we believe in myths when we should be looking at the reality – facing up to reality will help us to 'grow up' and take responsibility for our own lives and for the life of the planet

- we have out-of-control addictive/compulsive consumerism which encourages ego and competition rather than sharing and cooperation

- we have an obsession with *status* such that people (particularly middle and upper class people) constantly need to throw away last year's fashions and consume the latest product, thus generating the need for more production and high levels of waste and feeding the capitalist machine instead of enjoying things for their intrinsic worth and keeping them going for as long as possible

- we don't question the 'heroes/heroines' and models in our society enough – this is necessary not just in terms of the values or lack of them that they promote, but also because some of them are not what they seem – witness recent claims against celebrities, police, social workers and politicians for a range of hidden behaviours including evading tax, fiddling expenses, having inappropriate relationships, making false claims, distorting evidence, and sexually abusing vulnerable people

- our *moral development* (see Lawrence Kohlberg) has been eroded by modern culture and having values should be thought of as something to be restored. (See also our *Values* chapter).

What can be done?

Assumptions

Most solutions proposed for the 'crisis we're in' assume for example that we'll have:

- *cooperation* when in fact there's competition and there are problems with leadership

- *equality and sensible behaviour from élites and individuals* (including philanthropy) when in fact people are generally individualistic and selfish

- *an eco-friendly position from everyone* when in fact countries and companies struggle to afford or choose this against their own self-interests and growth agendas

- *dissemination of wisdom* but in fact knowledge is usually coming from a compromised pool of experts following a non-holistic single scientific mind-set

- *a multi-factorial approach* rather than the myths of science prevailing (eg. we can overcome climate problems without political cooperation etc.)

- *a non-biased media* rather than a propaganda system

- *clear thinking, good-willed, principled people not tied into 'the system'* instead of power blocs and people who are very confused about their values

- *proper democracy in which the majority of the people determine policy and look after minorities* rather than a fairy-tale world of 'democracy' that isn't what it appears

- *trustworthy financial institutions* rather than organisations with endemic corruption and incompetence

- *policymaking that's rational* when it's actually riven with human factors such as psychopathology, greed, fear and social distance

- *general commitment to values* when there's no clear framework and an antipathy to spirituality

- *responsible government and societies* instead of chaos, autocracy and conflict around the globe

- **in fact *none of the above* can be guaranteed or assumed.**

Possible solutions

We view survival of the crisis as involving individual effort and wider society effort. We think survival needs to involve efforts at both levels and that they're inter-linked. We've covered individual effort in many of our chapters and particularly in our chapter on *Stress*. Here we focus on what needs to be done at the level of wider society.

The big features to pick out are needs to:

o clean up and change capitalism and make it *sustainable*

o recognise the true *interconnectedness* of countries and banking systems (for example, creditors and debtors need each other)

o stop the erosion of democracy, rights and values and enable a wide range of ideas and opinions to be heard and utilised

o develop a mature approach including *sensitivity to other cultures and between groups* in society

- o realise once and for all that even without pollution we're reaching a *serious resource depletion stage.*

- o be less consumerist and stop worrying about status – we can't afford it any more.

- o be less stuck in our egos and operating as stuck in our egos (the central axis of the problem): be more socially minded, humanistic and caring, whether we consider ourselves spiritual or secular.

- o although psychopathology has always been with us and there are numerous examples through history of celebrities and leaders who've been narcissistic, paranoid, psychopathic etc. we might expect by now to recognise them and not allow psychopathology to seem 'normal' or to allow it *as* normal.

- o drop our belief in policymaking as *rational* (– there are all sorts of circumstances that inform it) and question who's manipulating it - including academia.

- o look at creative and radical ideas like job-sharing, food banks, community housing, cooperatives etc. on a much wider scale than ever before so that work is shared out, and those who are working themselves into the ground are saved from stress-related ill-health and those who've lost self-esteem through unemployment can become stakeholders in society. Do something about the fact there's a significant proportion of people whose income even from working round-the-clock still doesn't meet the basic needs of their family. Cut the costs of living in so many individual households – sharing community resources (eg; washing machines, lawn-mowers, cars and bicycles, meals, energy sources etc)

- o look at new ways of living, tackling the atomised approach whereby so many people live alone (even when they don't want to), transforming the idea that our privacy doesn't matter (when it does) into new ways of giving people space while fostering positive and supportive connection, and doing something about our fears of losing autonomy by recognising the importance of solitude, ownership and voice – ideas that need to be reflected for example in the way we design buildings and living and working space

o   change mind-sets towards caring and cooperation, led by charismatic but responsible leaders; remember that we're all equal in human terms and look towards making this a life worth living for everyone as a top priority; consider the question of philanthropy more seriously – in particular whether it's a moral duty on all or some in society, and how it compares with alternative methods of redistribution such as direct taxation; also, consider philanthropy as an approach to general caring so that we give time or direct help (eg. offering our expertise) as well as (or instead of) money, to others; challenge ideas of selfishness and recognise that our own survival and growth depend on others surviving and growing as well

It's important too - when we know the worst and are not in denial - to have *time off*. We can go bonkers if we try to solve all the world's problems all the time.

Get clear about what you do to:

(a) make it worse
(b) make it better

and keep to what you *can* be in charge of so as not to feel powerless.

Basically:
—   be aware and have time off!
—   be in charge of what you can.

Guidelines for survival at the level of wider society

- define the role and shape of capitalism with clear limits on ambitions

- introduce regulation of corporations

- challenge corruption

- work on transparency and partnership (not top-down/manipulation or secrecy)

- humanise corporate life

- keep alert to psychopathology and its influence on society

- de-monopolise corporations

- go small and local

- clarify the job of governments and their relationship to big business, defining the nature of democracy (or non-democracy) in each case

- define role and rights of individuals ensuring that minorities have their stake in society recognised

- challenge trades in people that involve modern-day slavery and enforced labour and work to stop or ameliorate them

- put an end to predatory financial activity and judgemental approaches to debt which has been 'engineered' or bought and sold

- encourage re-distribution of economic resources such as philanthropic activity, particularly among those who have the most

- use 'perverse positivity'
  - accept that may need to get worse to get better
  - accept that less is more
  - accept that suffering *is* deepening of the self vs usual tosh reassurance

- recognise and stem the drift of democratic principles, insisting that 'healthy' democracy is maintained, including support for minority groups

- ensure that internet channels and communication systems remain open as a global resource

- challenge internet hacking and work to keep internet communications systems functional and 'clean'

- reduce blind faith in scientific community – see the 2012 *L'Aquila* case whereby scientists have been jailed for giving false reassurances over the likelihood of disaster, and consider the 'precautionary principle' which can be used to err on the side of caution

- get more social – can we afford to live in atomised individual units, should we be looking increasingly at collective living projects?

- stop the creation of inequality and work to address imbalances including job-sharing and 'giving'

- stop throwing out spirituality, caring etc. in favour of robotic and automated approaches

- try and understand fairness, love, humanity, spirituality etc. in a wide variety of domains of life. Unless we get to grips with this, we're finished

- work on psychological, physical and environmental *health* and create environments for real healing, not try to tackle everything with science and technology

- provide a range of sources of information and media and stop propaganda

- think longer-term and own up to our responsibility to future generations

We're in *'post post-modernism'* as a society and need to make capitalism:

- humane
- regulated
- eco-friendly

and stop erosion of:

- democracy
- rights
- values

We need to get back to basic job descriptions, redefining our roles and what society is about.

The crisis of trust

Sadly, although some things have got better, overall we've made our problems worse not better over last 40 years and there is now a need to 'clean up our act', not just the environment. The catalogue of scandals in the UK and elsewhere is a wakeup call to what people are doing in democracy. We need to stop corruption, illegality, manipulation, exploitation, and injustice. We need in short, a *mature* world.

The process of facing up to these problems is on the right path, and there's no doubt that advances in things like the internet, CCTV, forensic science and the huge profusion of data collection we have can help us to track wrongdoing. Nevertheless, we're now in an age where not only do people find it difficult to trust in God or a god, there's also been a huge breakdown in trust in professionals and experts. This means that the time is ripe for us to face life as *adults*, learning to trust ourselves and assuming responsibility for getting accurate information and effective skills ourselves or from those we commission to do jobs in our society. In this sense, we're getting wiser and less naïve.

Positive steps

Good work IS being done on the environment even if in a compromised way. It will depend on your view whether you think any of the following are a good thing or a bad thing.

Repair of the Ozone layer is an example where cooperation has worked well.

Anthony Giddens describes the movement to make things better through technology and people power *'ecological modernisation'*. *Ecological modernisation*, led by big business, is a challenge to *sustainable development*, which has global inequality at the forefront of its concerns. New developments under this banner include things like catalytic converters and emission controls on motor vehicles, innovations in waste recycling, and improvements in the field of energy such as wind turbines. It may be that some of these outcomes are positive contributions to tackling our ecological crisis.

But companies also take the risks to explore new parts of the globe for sources of fuel to keep the world going, such as drilling for oil in the Arctic or fracking shale rock to release gas. *Greenpeace* and others have raised questions about the safety risks of these processes and there are protests about these developments, representing as they often do the intention to keep going with a growth agenda. The questions we need to ask are about how much such developments are essential for our continuance as a human race and how much are they part of a push for growth and profit? Are the risks worth it, and what happens when even more of the earth has been plundered and there are no frontiers left to dig up, mine, or drill for? Are we setting ourselves up for even more ecological disaster, given the dangers of these processes? Or are we panicking – haven't all new explorations in the past been surrounded by cautions and anxieties, or are we really at a point of no return?

Hazel Barton at the University of Akron is one of the people who've brought to our attention the efforts being made to find new antibiotics through the combination of her scientific work and her long experience in caving. Many of the bacteria found at the bottom of Lechuguilla Cave in New Mexico resist our strongest antibiotics, and so are very interesting for us to study. There's hope that we can gain new learning from these millions of years' old closed, natural environments for the development of new drugs. However, apart from the risks taken by caving scientists to reach the material we need, there's always the risk of potential damage to the fragile environments in which the micro-bacterial material is found through tourism, mineral extraction and water contamination - conflicting and converging priorities increasingly have to be discussed and resolved.

About 70% of the earth's population depend on fish as their primary source of protein, yet world stocks of fish have *massively* depleted in recent years. The Marine Stewardship Council work to recognise and reward sustainable fishing and change consumer practice (eg. with MSC labelling). The World Wildlife Fund is working to reduce 'bycatch' – marine life which is accidentally caught along with targeted fish (around 40% of catch is like this on average).

What's sure is that there's now international concern and debate about keeping going under old models of exploiting the earth and its seas, informed by knowledge, data and research and scrutinised by international organisations and the media. This makes it more difficult (but not impossible) for anyone to hide, but the balance of decision-making still depends on negotiations and battles between powerful groups. One big problem is the impasse in the free market economic world where powerful players still resist change, but the good news is that there is much interest in sustainable economies.

It's beginning to feel that things are at last beginning to change.

Johnathan Bloom highlighted the 50% of food that's wasted in America in his 2010 book. The European Union is declaring 2014 a *Year Against Food Waste,* with a target of 50% reduction of food waste, two-thirds of which they reckon is edible. Current estimates put food and plant waste in Europe at 300kg per person per annum. Measures will range from rethinking supermarket packaging dates to encouraging local farming to meet local demands.

Governments are beginning to develop new systems to *improve regulation*. In the UK as we go to press, new ideas are being explored about greater safety in surgical operations, greater protection of whistle-blowers, better press regulation, more helplines etc. There's more recognition of the impact of *inter-dependence* as for example we recognise that imported goods such as cut flowers include water that's desperately needed in the source countries that export them.

New religious leaders such as the new Pope and the new Archbishop of Canterbury are making tackling poverty a central issue in their ministry.

Within the big banks, there are new moves to focus on ethical performance as well as financial outcomes, so it may be that after decades of bad behaviour, financial organisations *are* trying to clean up their act. The damage is so great that it's far too early for us to know how real these changes will be, how effective they will be in repairing things and whether they will be sustained.

Following protests in Rejkavik in 2009 against the way financial matters had been handled for the country, resulting in the toppling of the government and the indictment of the country's leader, the new Icelandic government listened to a Forum, grassroots think-tanks, and then a Constitutional Assembly which involved members of the public being selected at random from a national registry into debate, pioneering new forms of democratic involvement in state decision-making. It's been dubbed the first national 'revolution' to bring about the downfall of a government in relation to the financial crisis.

There are new developments in sexual politics and gender awareness and in disability rights and in age concern and in the acceptance of diversity, yet it's also clear that there's still a long way to go on these matters.

Grassroots actions, assisted by the internet - are on the up. There's a higher speed of change than ever before though whether speed of change is a good idea may be open to question. For example, the Arab Spring has already wrought big change in the Middle East (though it may yet be too early to evaluate the long-term outcomes) - often at the cost of agonising ongoing struggles in a number of countries. The energy for change and a new order is emerging. People are on the streets across Europe – times are hard but people are beginning to express themselves.

Social media like *Facebook*, *Twitter* and internet search engines are important tools for social action, providing a lot of hope for openness, fast communication and organising action from the 'bottom-up'. See for example Paul Mason's recent books about the development of social movements round the world. Some governments are therefore looking into ways of curtailing the use of social media, often under the guise of editing out opportunities for abuse.

Following the Julian Assange case and the fears that have emanated after the public release of sensitive documentation through *Wikileaks*, defending the right to free communication has become one of the next global battlegrounds. Internet hacking, malware, viruses etc. are now problems for all users of modern technology (including young people who also have their own special vulnerabilities to predators), generating new industries in protective systems which monitor the net, detect threats and block 'attacks'. It can be tempting therefore to support collective and governmental actions to make the worldwide web a safer place in which to do business but the negotiations around freedom of expression and association make this a complex arena.

Time for change?

We believe that in democratic societies the élites can only push and control the citizens so far before they react negatively. Governments now quite often construct policy by asking for feedback on policy in advance ('consultations') in order to gauge the level of potential resistance and deciding whether to push through reforms and innovations. Leaders and principled charismatic leaders can appear in this process and for 'followers', this can be helpful.

Stéphane Hessel's (2010) book *Time for Outrage!* inspired the Spanish street protests in 2011 and 2012 by *Los Indignasos (The Outraged)* which have mobilised thousands of the poor, vulnerable, unemployed, disabled, etc. into protesting not just about austerity measures but about the breakdown in effective responses by the financial and political power system to listen to and look after the populace – a breakdown in democracy effectively.

Katsuji Imata, the Acting Secretary General of CIVICUS (World Alliance for Global Participation) - an organisation that promotes civic participation and freedom of expression round the world, reckons that the world has gone past a 'tipping point' with the developments of people protest that we have seen since 2011.

There IS a lot of concern in the world about the crisis we're in and many initiatives, formal and informal - but not necessarily enough 'oomph' yet. The momentum for improving things has to grow, *is* growing, needs to grow more.

We think many people are still in a *contemplative* stage (see our chapter on *Dependencies*) but in the meantime we do have to do practical things ourselves like checking our own consumerism and materialism, being willing to job-share and make distribution of work and pay fairer, and consider radical options in our lives like living with other people and educating our children to look at the world differently.

Some people break out of the rigid structures they find themselves in and these are pathfinders – organic food producers, home educators, alternative health practitioners, people into eco-living, beekeepers and cheese-makers, co-housing communities, furniture-makers, spinners and weavers, herbalists, people who choose woodland burials, etc. and these alternatives can build into a critical mass that can ultimately challenge old consumerist patterns. Perhaps what's important here is that people **retain a sense of the radicalism of what they're doing**, of pioneering, conserving, reviving traditions, critiquing the mainstream etc. and not simply creating a new kind of élite materialism that ignores the needs of wider society. It will be important to think about how to disseminate new and old knowledge and to inspire a wider mass of people to look afresh at how they live.

We can't predict the future – charismatic personalities, spiritual approaches, creativity, and a universal 'unconscious' – are all 'out there' so that anything can happen and with speed. Nassim Nicholas Taleb tells us to be ready for uncertainty, to anticipate that *'black swans'*– unusual creatures - will come into our lives and have significant impacts, and to incorporate the idea of unpredictability into our calculations. Certainly, however much we try to plan and predict, we can be sure that something will happen that we hadn't quite counted on. Some of it could be good.

Incrementalism is now understood as a viable method for bringing about change - small, slow steps that can become contagious in a positive sense and add up to quite a lot in the end. Just like this book.

Summarising......from Jack

This section isn't about solutions which include 'clever' or expert quick fixes which are unworkable in practice at present, such as:

- a technological solution
- immediately stopping 'dependent' consumerism
- changing the belief that policymaking is 'rational'

As a population, we're worried about the future and we use all kinds of strategies to cope which include:

- burying our heads in the sand (ostrich method)

- making 'delinquent'-type responses

- 'carrying on as normal' (for example with 'negativity')

- being selfish/individualistic (more of the same)

- stopping real living (being more austere than say, government-imposed austerity)

- survivalism – some people for example are building bunkers to live in
- 'dog eat dog'-ism (competition)

- exploiting 'the system'

- partying

- finding our place in the control/conformity power structures and hoping for the best

- developing addictive or dependent behaviours including addiction to entertainment

- falling prey to illness, depression and passivity

- adopting pseudo-rational approaches eg. exclusive technical or unworkable policy solutions

- seeking out false hope eg. by turning to books on 'the crisis' – for example, ones that say a technological or economic fix will save the day.
-

Perhaps you can think of more to add or mix-and-match different approaches.

We need to avoid false hope, but remember that we seem to *need* real hope and we're writing this summary to emphasise that we need to construct a new, more mature normality for psychological, social and economic survival.

In developed countries, we can't easily understand the idea of suffering leading to growth or the deepening of people or society but there are plenty of examples of this throughout history.

It may be that it actually *has* to get worse in order to then get better. As we write, America is debating its gun laws after the shooting of 27 people in a primary school. Sadly, it often takes trauma to get people round the negotiating table. It's important that we listen to those who warn us about problems ahead rather than waiting for disaster to strike, yet we know that human beings have a tendency to leave things until the last moment.

In the UK, there's been scandal after scandal in the media, the care system, the healthcare system, the political system, the police and criminal justice system, the economic system, and in religious institutions. It's possible to 'reframe' the awfulness of all of this in terms of a process of *facing up to what has been going on* and a *renewal process* that has to be underpinned by an initial 'cleaning-up' and some honesty about the underlying issues and the barriers to change. We believe that this avalanche of revelations does represent a kind of turning-point – but as a world we'll all have to make sure that investigations and the reforms that follow are more than cosmetic and that real change does occur, particularly in the financial industry.

In human relations, there are signs that people are getting fed up with our narcissistic and celebrity culture, and that calls for more attention to be paid to the quieter, softer, less aggressive and less arrogant voices may hold the key to necessary shifts in our psychological landscape.

We've developed a simple, commonsense model - as a starting point whilst you're finding your own individual strategies - for finding meaning and hope, which consist of:

1. managing stress	2. looking after physical health
3. finding happiness and enjoyment in life	4. being increasingly active and productive not passively consuming

Notes:

All of these need awareness, action and detachment (not denial).
1 and 2 overlap as stress can affect physical health.

Finding happiness need not be complex or expensive – enjoying nature, music, loving relationships etc. work well.

We think ***finding hope and meaning*** in uncertain times is an individual matter to start with but will lead to social action. For me (Jack), *spirituality* is important - as is reducing *ego*. (See chapters on *Spirituality* and on *The Self*)

A leap of faith

There are stumbling blocks to sorting out the chaos of our times discussed in the book and part of the problem is the size and complexity of the problem. What works for us is constructing a leap of faith, built on basic positive core beliefs about human nature and society, which help in a time of flux and uncertainty.

These beliefs include ***the idea that people are basically 'good'*** and that ***society is basically social not anti-social*** and the logic of this comes ultimately from a will to survive and cooperate and grow and develop and that there is a push to develop individuals and society. If we don't have positive core beliefs about people/society, faith is harder to construct. If we need to increase positive beliefs, changing perception by ***looking for positives*** can make all the difference.

Another decision to make in a time of excess is to ***decide how much we need*** in terms of material goods, power, money etc. and the notion of *less is more* works well to counter for example, a dependency on materialism.

Facing the future for me is to operate ***as if there is a future***. Probably this also depends on a belief that people can solve problems and be creative. ***If we develop our capacity to solve problems and be creative, this belief will grow.*** We need too to actively look for the signs of hope in the future all around us.

701

Overview of way out – main dimensions

What we need to escape from	What we need to develop
Individual ego	The individual in context of society
Over consumption	Simplicity and frugality
Specialised knowledge (often science)	Holistic and natural wisdom
Policy as inhuman 'efficiency'	Policy - humane and democratic
Inequality	Equality
Corruption	Honesty and transparency
Manipulation by powerful	Partnership
Artificial novelty	Useful innovation and creativity
More	Less

Some final thoughts from Julia:

I think that our ability to go forward *as if there is a future* will have a strong relationship to what's going on in our own lives. If key people in our lives are dying or have died, for example, or we've become ill or financially bankrupt ourselves, this will affect our energy to think positively about the future of the world. Some of the more optimistic visions are in the sights of healthy young people whilst some older people believe the world will end because they themselves are 'leaving' this world. Believing in ourselves and in a future for the world is an expression of life energy; if ours is low, we need to see what we can do to cultivate it, and we hope this book is a contribution to knowing how to do that.

With regard to *suffering*, I do believe that we can develop from painful events and times and that we can find many new insights and find our relationships changing so that we learn much more about the bases on which they're built. If people abandon us, we have the opportunity to recognise the truth in relationships and to show kindness to those who struggle to find enough courage or stamina for the hard times. If we have to face physical or economic hardship, we learn a lot about others' willingness to share and help and about our own attachment to good things, and we can develop new skills in conserving, repairing, being creative, and spreading out the 'fishes and the loaves' to go farther. Hard

702

times prompt us to dig deeper, to understand more, to investigate so that we know why hard times have come about and to think about how to get through them or make better times come again (if that's possible), or how to see them as a new and meaningful reality. We learn to rely on ourselves and those we love and who love us and to find out what are the real priorities of our life. We can become wonderfully creative around new initiatives for our community and break out of the psychological atomisation that is so much a feature of modern life.

Our chapter *Finding our own direction* is intended to stimulate thinking around the question of assessing our personal resources and deciding how to live at any particular time in our lives. It may be that all of us return again and again to those questions, making different choices at a later point from the ones we're making now. Throughout the book we've worked with the idea of ***balancing the personal with the political, the individual with the social, showing how the way we're constructed has something to do with our context and history,*** as is the way we choose to relate to the world now. We've emphasised our belief that stepping out of blind conformity is important for the future of the world. ***Creative problem-solving and fluid styles of thinking, fresh communication approaches, being in touch with our feelings, our history, our bodies etc and being committed to positive values*** are all part of the toolkit we might need to go forward.

We've made the case that ***we're all uniquely responsible for how we live our lives***, once we've woken up to the pressures, systems, influences, hidden factors, corruption, psychopathology, emotions, motives, ambitions, values, hopes, myths, ignorance, lies, resource levels, dangers, habits etc. that beset us. We believe that this book offers insight into these aspects of life and the difficult times we're in and provides a 'road-map' for finding information resources which can guide us on the path to survival and growth.

We believe that 'survival' and 'growth' are concepts that need careful evaluation both in our personal lives and for the world as a whole, and that their meanings should include a compassionate awareness of one another as equal participants in the world.

References and books to follow up

We're not specialists in facts and figures so we suggest where you're interested in these (eg. international comparisons, costs of inquiries, scale of debt etc.) you follow up the ideas we've put forward with your own research. Data is changing all the time and different sources will often make different calculations etc. because they will include and exclude different factors. Our intention has been to highlight issues and raise questions rather than to grapple with numbers, so if you need real numbers, we encourage you to explore some of the sources we list below and find others of your own.

Vishal Arora (2012) *Bhutan Happiness Index: Country fails on its Gross National Happiness (GNH)* http://www.huffingtonpost.com/2012/03/06/bhutan-happiness-index-gnh-gross-national-happiness_n_1324918.html 03.06.12

BBC *Jimmy Savile estate frozen after abuse claims* 1st November 2012 http://www.bbc.co.uk/news /uk-20162980

Catherine Belsey (2002) *Post-structuralism: a very short introduction* Oxford

John Bird (2012) *The Necessity of Poverty* Charles Glass/Quartet Books

Johnathan Bloom (2010) *American Wasteland: How America Throws Away Nearly Half of Its Food (and What We Can Do About It)* Da Capo Books

Cathy Bolkavac (2011) *The Whistleblower: Sex Trafficking, Military Contractors and One Woman's Fight for Justice* Palgrave Macmillan

Beth Breeze (2012) *Coutts: The Million Pound Donors Report* University of Kent/CPHSJ

Ian Bremmer (2012) *Every Nation for Itself: Winners and Losers in a GZero World* Portfolio Penguin

Druin Burch (2009) *Taking the Medicine* London: Chatto and Windus

Andrew Carnegie *Wealth* North American Review Vol.148, Issue 391 pp. 653–665, June 1889. (Later published as Part I of *The Gospel of Wealth*)

Center on Philanthropy at Indiana University *HM Revenue and Customs 2006 and The 2010 Study of High Net Worth*

Philanthropy: Issues Driving Charitable Activities among Affluent Households (2010)
Center on Philanthropy at Indiana University *HM Revenue and Customs* 2006 *and Bank of America Study of High Net Worth Philanthropy* (2008)
Ha-Joon Chang (2010) *23 Things They Don't Tell You About Capitalism* Allen Lane
Charities Aid Foundation (2012) *World Giving Report: a global view of giving trends*
Philip Coggan (2011) *Paper Promises: Money, Debt and the New World Order* Penguin/Allen Lane
CIPFA (2011) *Smart Cuts? Public spending on children's social care* NSPCC
Defeat the Debt.com *HOW MANY MEMBERS OF CONGRESS COULD PASS ECON 101?*
G. William Domhoff (2012) *Wealth, Income, and Power* October 2012 http://whorulesamerica.net/ power/wealth.html
Mary Douglas and Aaron B Wildavsky (1982) *Risk and Culture: An essay on the selection of technical and environmental dangers* Berkeley: University of California Press
Keith Dowding *Can Populism Be Defended? William Riker, Gerry Mackie and the Interpretation of Democracy* Government and Opposition Volume 41, Issue 3, pages 327–346, June 2006
Ronald Dworkin (2011) *Justice for Hedgehogs* Harvard University Press
The Economist Global Public Debt Clock http://www.economist.com/content/global_debt_clock
Esmee Fairbairn Foundation http://esmeefairbairn.org.uk/
Charles Ferguson (2012) *Inside Job: the Financiers Who Pulled Off the Heist of the Century* Oneworld
Niall Ferguson (2012) *The Ascent of Money: A Financial History of the World* Penguin
Niall Ferguson (2012) *The Rule of Law and its Enemies* May-July 2012 http://www.bbc.co.uk/ podcasts/series/reith
Fukuyama, Francis. *The End of History and the Last Man.* Second Edition with a New Afterword. London and New York, 2006.
Susan George (1976) *How the Other Half Dies: The Real Reasons for World Hunger* Penguin
Susan George (2007) *Down the Great Financial Drain: How debt and the Washington Consensus destroy development and create*

poverty Development 50, 4–11. http://www.palgrave-journals.com/development/journal/v50/n2/full/1100356a.html

Anthony Giddens (2011) *The Politics of Climate Change* Polity Press

Stephen Glover *Masters of cover-up: How the Establishment closes ranks to protect its own and deny the people the truth* http://www.dailymail.co.uk/news/article-2203524/Hillsborough-disaster-cover-How-Establishment-closes-ranks-protect-own.html#ixzz Alny3xSe 14th September 2012

Ben Goldacre (2012) *Bad Pharma: How the Drug Companies Mislead Doctors and Harm Patients* Fourth Estate

Gary Gutting (2005) *Foucault: a very short introduction* Oxford

Paul Hackett and Paul Hunter *Who Governs Britain: a Profile of MPs in the New Parliament* Smith Institute www.smith-institute.org.uk/file/Who-Governs-Britain.pdf

Daryl Hannah (2012) *The battle against Big Energy's rush to ruin our planet* http://www.guardian.co.uk/commentisfree/2012/oct/31/battle-big-oil-rush-ruin-darylhannah 31st October 2012

Adam Harvey (2013) *Stealthwear: new designs for counter-surveillance* Exhibition at *Tank Magazine*, Portland Street, London 17 January 2013 http://ahprojects.com/projects/stealth-wear

Havocscope Black Market website http://www.havocscope.com/products/ranking/

Richard Heinberg (2011) *The End of Growth: Adapting to Our New Economic Reality* Forest Row: Clairview

Christopher Hope *Exclusive: Cabinet is worth £70million* Telegraph 27th May 2012 http://www.telegraph.co.uk/news/politics/9290520/Exclusive-Cabinet-is-worth-70million.html

Mike Hulme (2009) *Why We Disagree About Climate Change* Cambridge University Press

Human Trafficking Team, Organised and Financial Crime Unit, Home Office *First annual report of the Inter-Departmental Ministerial Group on Human Trafficking* October 2012

Samuel P Huntington (2002 edition) *The Clash of Civilisations and the New World Order* Free Press

International Labour Organization, *A Global Alliance against Forced Labour* (Geneva, International Labour Office, 2005).

Tim Jackson (2009) *Prosperity without Growth: Economics for a Finite Planet* London: Earthscan

Owen Jones (2012) *Chavs: The Demonisation of the Working Class* Verso Books

Jubilee Debt Campaign http://www.jubileedebtcampaign.org.uk

John Keane *A Proposal for Rethinking the Origins and Future of representative Government* European Science Foundation http://www.thefutureofrepresentativedemocracy.org/

John Keane (2008) *The Life and Death of Democracy*, London: Simon and Schuster

Steve Keen (2001) *Debunking Economics: The Naked Emperor of the Social Sciences* London: Zed Books

Patrick Kingsley (2012) *Kalle Lasn – the man who inspired the Occupy movement* http://www.guardian.co.uk/world/2012/nov/05/kalle-lasn-man-inspired-occupy 5th November, 2012

Laurence J. Kotlikoff (2013) *Fiscal Child Abuse American Style* The World Financial Review http://www.worldfinancial review.com/?p=2240

Laurence J. Kotlikoff and Scott Burns (2012) *The Clash of Generations: Saving Ourselves, Our Kids, and Our Economy* MIT Press 2012.

Thomas Kuhn (1962) *The Structure of Scientific Revolutions* University of Chicago Press

Kalle Lasn/Adbusters (2012) *Meme Wars: the Creative Destruction of Neo-Classical Economics (by M.Adbusters)* Penguin Books

Konrad Lorenz (1963) *On Aggression* Routledge

Simon Malpas (2003) *Jean-François Lyotard* London: Routledge

Paul Mason (2010) *Meltdown: The End of the Age of Greed* Verso Books

Paul Mason (2012) *Why It's Kicking Off Everywhere* Verso Books

Paul Mason (2013) *Why it's STILL Kicking Off Everywhere* Verso Books

Donella Meadows, Jorgen Randers and Dennis Meadows (2004) *Limits to Growth: the 30 year Update* London: Earthscan

Alice Miller (2008 3rd edition) *The Drama of the Gifted Child* Basic Books

Stanley Milgram – see under Zimbardo

Kieron O'Hara (2010) *The Enlightenment: A Beginner's Guide* One World

Jim O'Neill (2001) *Building Better Global Economic BRICs*. Global Economics Paper No. 66 (66). 30 November 2001 Goldman Sachs & Co.

Naomi Oreskes and Erik M Conway (2010) *Merchants of Doubt: How a Handful of Scientists Obscured the Truth on Issues from Tobacco Smoke to Global Warming* Bloomsbury Press

John Quiggin (2010) *Zombie Economics: How Dead Ideas Still Walk Among Us* Princeton University Press

Ayn Rand (1966) *Capitalism: The Unknown Ideal* New York: New American Library.

Martin Rees (2004) *Our Final Hour: A Scientist's Warning* Basic Books

Andrzej Sitkowski 2006   *UN Peacekeeping Myth and Reality* Praeger Press

Muriel Steffans *Philanthropy is big business – except in corporate Australia* Sydney Morning Herald June 4, 2011

Sutton Trust *The Educational Backgrounds of MPs in 2010*   May 2010 http://www.suttontrust.com/reports/ST_Milburn Submission. pdf

Nassim Nicholas Taleb (2012) *Antifragile: how to live in a world we don't understand* Allen Lane

The Center for Nanotechnology in Society http://www.cns.ucsb.edu/about/nanotechnology-society

Transform Drug Policy Foundation http://www.tdpf.org.uk/MediaNews_FactResearchGuide_Sizeof theDrugMarket.htm#_ftnref7

United Nations Office on Drugs and Crime UN.GIFT *Human trafficking: an overview* 2008

John T Wenders *Democracy would doom Hong Kong* The Freeman, January 1998 The Foundation for Economic Education. also online at http://www.independent.org/newsroom/article. asp?id=214

Joe Wiesenthal (2010) *The Next BRICs: Six Surging Countries You Must Pay Attention To This Decade* Money Game Jan 6 2010 http://www.businessinsider.com/the-next-10-brics-2010-1?op=1#ixzz2OT3kkWNR

Richard Wilkinson and Kate Pickett (2009,2010) *The Spirit Level: Why Equality is Better for Everyone* Penguin Books

E N Wolff (2007). *Recent trends in household wealth in the United States: Rising debt and the middle-class squeeze.* Working

Paper No. 502 Annandale-on-Hudson, NY: The Levy Economics Institute of Bard College.

David Wootton (2006, 2007) *Bad Medicine* Oxford University Press

Robert Ward *Economist Intelligence Unit* http://www.eiu.com/site_info.asp?info_name=presenters_robert_ward&page=noads

Philip Zimbardo and Stanley Milgram (2010) *Obedience to Authority: An Experimental View* Pinter and Martin Ltd.

Howard Zinn (2005) *A People's History of the United States 1492-present* Harper Perennials

Yaneer Bar-Yam (2005) *Making Things Work: Solving Complex Problems in a Complex World* Amazon.com

The Project on Emerging Nanotechnologies *Website*
http://www.nanotechproject.org/topics/nano101/ introduction_to_nanotechnology/

TV:

Young, Posh and Loaded (2003) ITV1 *Made in Chelsea* (2011) E4
Ian Hislop (2011) *When Bankers Were Good* BBC2

bibliography and references

Theodor W **Adorno**, Else Frenkel-Brunswik, Daniel Levinson, and Nevitt Sanford (1950) *The Authoritarian Personality* Harper and Row

John S **Allen** *Creativity: Adaptation or a by-product of increased intelligence?* April 29, 2010
http://www.psychologytoday.com/blog/lives-the-brain/201004/creativity-the-brain-and-evolution

Tsultrim **Allione** (2000) (2nd ed) *Women of Wisdom* Snow Lion Publications

Peter **Anderson** and Ben Baumberg *Alcohol in Europe: a public health perspective: a report for the European Commission* Institute of Alcohol Studies, UK June 2006

Sebastian **Anthony** *Just how big are porn sites?* Extreme Tech April 4, 2012 http://www.extremetech.com/computing/123929-just-how-big-are-porn-sites

Lisa **Appignanesi** (2008) *Mad, Bad or Sad: a history of women and the mind doctors from 1800 to the present* Virago

Lisa **Appignanesi** (2011) *All About Love* Virago

Michael **Argyle** and Peter Trower (1979) *Person to Person: Ways of Communicating* Harper and Row

Karen **Armstrong** (1981, 1995) *Through the Narrow Gate* Harper Collins/Flamingo

Karen **Armstrong** (1986) *The Gospel According to Woman* Harper Collins/Fount

Karen **Armstrong** (1993) *A History of God* London: Vintage Books (also later book in 2006)

Vishal **Arora** *Bhutan Happiness Index: Country fails on its Gross National Happiness (GNH)*
http://www.huffingtonpost.com/2012/03/06/bhutan-happiness-index-gnh-gross-national-happiness_n_1324918.html 03.06.12

Jane **Austen** (1811) (2011 ed) *Sense and Sensibility* Penguin Popular Classics

BBC *Jimmy Savile estate frozen after abuse claims* 1st November 2012 http://www.bbc.co.uk/news/uk-20162980

Paul **Babias** and Robert D Hare (2006) *Snakes in Suits: When Psychopaths Go to Work* Regan Books

Michael **Balint** (1986 ed) *Doctor, his patient and his illness* Churchill Livingstone

Yaneer **Bar-Yam** (2005) *Making Things Work: Solving Complex Problems in a Complex World* Amazon.com

Diana Butler **Bass** (2001) *A People's History of Christianity: The Other Side of the Story* HarperOne

Jean **Baudrillard** (1994) *The Illusion of the End* Polity Press

Martine **Batchelor** (2007) *Let go – a Buddhist Guide to Breaking Free of Habits* Wisdom Publications

Catherine **Belsey** (2002) *Post-structuralism: a very short introduction* Oxford

Helen **Benedict** (2009) *The Lonely Soldier: The Private War of Women Serving in Iraq* Beacon Press

Graceann **Bennett** and Freya Williams (2011) *Moving Sustainability from Niche to Normal* Mainstream Green: The Red Papers : Issue 4 Ogilvy and Mather

J G **Bennett** (1992) *The Way To Be Free* Maine: Samuel Weiser

Alexander **Beliaev** (22nd September 2003) *Gay Men and the Anima Function* www.cgjungpage.org

Eric **Berne** (1961) (2009 ed) *Transactional Analysis in Psychotherapy* Eigel Meirovich

John **Bird** (2012) *The Necessity of Poverty* Charles Glass/Quartet Books

Johnathan **Bloom** (2010) *American Wasteland: How America Throws Away Nearly Half of Its Food (and What We Can Do About It)* Da Capo Books

Cathy **Bolkavac** (2011) *The Whistleblower: Sex Trafficking, Military Contractors and One Woman's Fight for Justice* Palgrave Macmillan

George A **Bonnano** (2009) *The Other Side of Sadness: What the New Science of Bereavement Tells Us About Life After Loss* Basic Books

Sissela **Bok** (1999) *Lying: Moral Choice in Public and Private Life* Vintage

Sissela **Bok** (2010) *Exploring Happiness: From Aristotle to Brain Science* Yale University Press

Dietrich **Bonhoeffer** (2001 ed) *The Cost of Discipleship* SCM Classics

John **Bowlby** (1951) *Maternal Care and Mental Health* report for the World Health Organisation New York: Schocken

Beth **Breeze** (2012) *Coutts: The Million Pound Donors Report* University of Kent/CPHSJ

Ian **Bremmer** (2012) *Every Nation for Itself: Winners and Losers in a GZero World* Portfolio Penguin

Alain de **Botton** (2004) *Status Anxiety* London: Penguin Books

Phil **Brown** and Stephen Zavestoski (2005) *Social Movements in Health* Oxford: Blackwell

Rita Mae **Brown** (1973) (1994 ed) *Rubyfruit Jungle* Penguin Books

Adelaide **Bry** (1979) *Visualization: directing the movies of your mind* Harper Collins

Druin **Burch** (2009) *Taking the Medicine* London: Chatto and Windus

Oliver **Burkeman** (2012) *The Antidote* Canongate

Oliver **Burkeman** (2013) <u>7 Ways to Success</u> *Psychologies magazine* Kelsey Publishing January 2013

Tom **Burns** (2006) *Psychiatry: a very short introduction* Oxford

Judith **Butler** (2006) *Gender Trouble: Feminism and the Subversion of Identity* Routledge

Tony **Buzan** (2009) *The Mind-mapping Book: Unlock your Creativity, Boost Your Memory, Change Your Life* BBC Active

Susan **Cain** (2012) *Quiet: The Power of Introverts in a World that Can't Stop Talking* Viking

Julia **Cameron** (2011) (7th ed) *The Artist's Way: a course in discovering and recovering your creative self* Pan Books

Alistair V **Campbell** and Michaela Willis (2006) *Narratives of embodiment and loss* in Frances Rapport and Paul Wainwright (2006) *The Self in Health and Illness* Oxford: Radcliffe

Walter Bradford **Cannon** (1915) *Bodily Changes in Pain, Hunger, Fear and Rage: An Account of Recent Researches into the Function of Emotional Excitement* Appleton

Andrew **Carnegie** *Wealth* North American Review Vol.148, Issue 391 pp. 653–665, June 1889. (Later published as Part I of *The Gospel of Wealth*)

Dale **Carnegie** (1936) *How to Win Friends and Influence People* Simon and Schuster

Ha-Joon **Chang** (2010) *23 Things They Don't Tell You About Capitalism* Allen Lane

Charities Aid Foundation (2012) *World Giving Report: a global view of giving trends*

Gary **Chapman** (2010) *The Five Love Languages* Moody Publishing

Phyllis **Chesler** (1972) *Women and Madness* Allen Lane

Noam **Chomsky** (1998) *On Language* The New Press

Church of England http://www.churchofengland.org/about-us/facts-stats.aspx

CIPFA (2011) *Smart Cuts? Public spending on children's social care* NSPCC

Mike **Clayton** (2011) *Brilliant Stress Management* Harlow: Pearson Education

Hervey **Cleckley** (1941) (1988 5th ed) *The Mask of Sanity* William A Dolan

Club of Rome – see Donella Meadows

Philip **Coggan** (2011) *Paper Promises: Money, Debt and the New World Order* Penguin/Allen Lane

Colleen M **Connolly** (2004) *Clinical issues with same-sex couples* Journal of Couple and Relationship Therapy Vol 3 No 2/3 p.3-12 The Haworth Press

Charles A **Corr** (1999) *Enhancing the Concept of Disenfranchised Grief* Journal of Death and Dying vol 38 no 1/1998/99 pp 1-20

Don **Cupitt** (2003) (3rd revised edition) *The Sea of Faith* SCM Press

Mary **Daly** (1973) *Beyond God the Father* The Women's Press

Mary **Daly** (1984) *Pure Lust* The Women's Press

Defeat the Debt.com *How Many members of Congress Could Pass Econ 101?*

George C. **Denniston**, Frederick M. Hodges and Marilyn Fayre Milos, (eds) (2009) *Human Rights and Circumcision* Springer

Emmy van **Deurzen** (2012) *Existential Counselling and Psychotherapy* London: Sage

Jared **Diamond** (2011) *Collapse: How Societies Choose to Fail or Survive* Penguin Books

G. William **Domhoff** (2012) *Wealth, Income, and Power* October 2012 http://whorulesamerica.net/ power/wealth.html

Mary **Douglas** and Aaron B Wildavsky (1982) *Risk and Culture: An essay on the selection of technical and environmental dangers* Berkeley: University of California Press

Keith **Dowding** *Can Populism Be Defended? William Riker, Gerry Mackie and the Interpretation of Democracy* Government and Opposition Volume 41, Issue 3, pages 327–346, June 2006

Windy **Dryden** and Colin Feltham (1992) *Psychotherapy and its discontents* Open University Press

Barry L **Duncan**, Scott D Miller, Bruce Wampold and Marc A Hubble (eds) (2009) (2nd ed) *The Heart and Soul of Change* American Psychological Association

Jack **Dusay** (1972) *Egograms and the constancy hypothesis* Transactional Analysis Journal 2(3), 37-41.

Kevin **Dutton** *The Wisdom of Psychopaths -- What Saints, Spies, and Serial Killers Can Teach Us About Success* Scientific America/FSG

Kevin **Dutton** http://www.smithsonianmag.com/science-nature/The-Pros-to-Being-a-Psy-176019901.html#ixzz2Lw1mBYdv

Ronald **Dworkin** (2011) *Justice for Hedgehogs* Harvard University Press

The Economist Global Public Debt Clock http://www.economist.com/content/global_debt_clock

Ann **Edwards** (2010) *How to Nurture Spiritual Development* Blue Ocean Publishing

Luise **Eichenbaum** and Susie Orbach (2000) (revised edition) *What Do Women Want?* Harper Collins

Luise **Eichenbaum** and Susie Orbach (1992) *Understanding Women* London: Penguin

Barbara **Ehrenreich** (2009) *Bright-sided: how positive thinking is undermining America* Metropolitan Books

Barbara **Ehrenreich** (2010) *Smile Or Die: How Positive Thinking Fooled America And The World* Granta

Barbara **Ehrenreich** and Arlie Russell Hochschild (eds) (2003) *Global Woman: Nannies, Maids, and Sex Workers in the New Economy* Henry Holt and Co./ Metropolitan Books

Albert **Einstein** (1931) *Living Philosophies* New York: Simon and Schuster

Erik **Erikson** (1994 edition) *Identity and the Life Cycle* W W Norton

Eve **Esler** (2001) *The Vagina Monologues* Villard/Random House

Walter **Evans-Wentz** (1935) *Tibetan Yoga and Secret Doctrines* London: Oxford University Press

Hans J **Eysenck** (1971) *Readings in Extraversion-Introversion* New York: Wiley

Esmee **Fairbairn** Foundation http://esmeefairbairn.org.uk/

Ann **Faraday** (1972, 1997 edition) *Dream Power* Berkley Trade

Ann **Faraday** (1975, 1990 edition) *The Dream Game* Harper Collins

Melissa **Farley**, Julie Bindel and Jacqueline M. Golding *Men who buy sex: who they buy and what they know* December 2009 Eaves, London

Anne **Fausto-Sterling** (2000) *Sexing the Body* Basic Books/ Perseus

Otto **Fenichel** (1938) *The Drive to Amass Wealth* Psychoanalytic Quarterly **7**: 69–95

Charles **Ferguson** (2012) *Inside Job: the Financiers Who Pulled Off the Heist of the Century* Oneworld

Niall **Ferguson** (2012) *The Ascent of Money: A Financial History of the World* Penguin

Niall **Ferguson** (2012) *The Rule of Law and its Enemies* May-July 2012 http://www.bbc.co.uk/ podcasts/series/reith

Leon **Festinger** (1970) *A Theory of Cognitive Dissonance* Stanford University Press

Alice **Flaherty** (2005) *Fronto-temporal and dopaminergic control of idea generation and creative drive* Journal of Comparative Neurology 493:147-153

Alice **Flaherty** (2005) *The Midnight Disease: The Drive to Write, Writer's Block and the Creative Brain* Houghton Mifflin Harcourt

John-Paul **Flintoff** (2012) *How to Change the World* Basingstoke: Pan Macmillan

Victor **Frankl** (1946) (new ed 2004) *Man's Search for Meaning* Rider

Deborah **Franklin** (2012) *How Hospital Gardens Help Patients Heal* Scientific American 19 March 2012 http://www.scientificamerican.com/article.cfm?id=nature-that-nurtures

Sigmund **Freud** (1899) *The Interpretation of Dreams* (1980 version) Avon Books

Sigmund **Freud** and Joseph Breuer plus Adam Phillips, Nicola Luckhurst, and Rachel Bowlby (2004) *Studies in Hysteria* London: Penguin Books

Erich **Fromm** (1969) *To Have or To Be?* Abacus Books

Michel **Foucault** (1965) (2006 ed) *Madness and Civilization: A History of Insanity in the Age of reason* Vintage

Michel **Foucault** (1995) *Discipline and Punish: The Birth of the Prison* Vintage Books

715

Michel **Foucault** and Paul Rabinow (1991) *The Foucault Reader: An Introduction to Foucault's Thought* Penguin Books

James W **Fowler** (1981) *Stages of Faith* Harper and Row

Francis **Fukuyama** (2006) (2nd ed) *The End of History and the Last Man* Free Press

Frank **Furedi** (2003) *Therapy Culture: Cultivating Vulnerability in an Uncertain Age* Routledge

Frank **Furedi** (2006) (2nd ed) *Where Have All the Intellectuals Gone?* London: Continuum

Atul **Gawande** (2008) *Better: A Surgeon's Notes on Performance* Profile Books

Atul **Gawande** (2008 2nd ed) *Complications: A Surgeon's Notes on an Imperfect Science* Profile Books

Atul **Gawande** (2011) *The Checklist Manifesto: How to Get Things Right* Profile Books

Ina May **Gaskin** (2002)(4th ed) *Spiritual Midwifery* Book Publishing Co.

Susan **George** (1976) *How the Other Half Dies: The Real Reasons for World Hunger* Penguin

Susan **George** (2007) *Down the Great Financial Drain: How debt and the Washington Consensus destroy development and create poverty* Development 50, 4–11. http://www.palgrave-journals.com/development/journal/v50/n2/full/1100356a.html

Anthony **Giddens** (2011) *The Politics of Climate Change* Polity Press

Paul **Gilbert** (2010) *The Compassionate Mind: Compassion-focused therapy* Constable

Erving **Goffman** (1963) *Stigma: Notes on the Management of a Spoiled Identity* Prentice-Hall/Penguin Books

Stephen **Glover** *Masters of cover-up: How the Establishment closes ranks to protect its own and deny the people the truth* http://www.dailymail.co.uk/news/article-2203524/Hillsborough-disaster-cover-How-Establishment-closes-ranks-protect-own.html#ixzz2Alny3xSe 14th September

Ben **Goldacre** (2012) *Bad Pharma: How the Drug Companies Mislead Doctors and Harm Patients* Fourth Estate

Emma **Goldman** (1972 ed) *Red Emma Speaks: Selected Writings and Speeches* New York: Random House

Daniel **Goleman** (1996) *Emotional Intelligence* Bloomsbury

Erving **Goffman** (1963) *Stigma: Notes on the Management of a Spoiled Identity* Prentice-Hall/ Penguin Books

Erving **Goffman** (1968) *Asylums* Pelican

John **Gray** (1992) *Men from Mars, Women are from Venus* Harper Collins/Thorsons

John **Grinder** and Richard Bandler (1983) *Reframing: Neurolinguistic programming and the transformation of meaning.* Moab, UT: Real People Press..

Phyllis **Grosskurth** (1991) *The Secret Ring: Freud's Inner Circle and the Politics of Psychoanalysis* London: Johnathan Cape/Westview Press

T B **Gustafson** and D B Sarwer (2004) *Childhood sexual abuse and obesity* The International Association for the Study of Obesity Obesity Reviews **5** , 129–135

Gary **Gutting** (2005) *Foucault: a very short introduction* Oxford

Paul **Hackett** and Paul Hunter *Who Governs Britain: a Profile of MPs in the New Parliament* Smith Institute www.smith-institute.org.uk/file/Who-Governs-Britain.pdf

Johnathan **Haidt** (2001) *The Emotional Dog and its Rational Tail: A Social Intuitionist Approach to Moral Judgment* Psychological Review 2001. Vol.108. No. 4, 814-834 http://www.nd.edu/~wcarbona /Haidt%202001.pdf

Jay **Haley** (1993) *Uncommon Therapy: Psychiatric Techniques of Milton Erickson M.D.* W W Norton

Calvin S **Hall** (1953) (2012 ed) *The Meaning of Dreams: their symbolism and their sexual implications* Iconoclassic

Paul **Halmos** (1965) *The Faith of the Counsellors* Constable

Donna J **Haraway** (1991) *Simians, Cyborgs, and Women* London: Free Association Books

Chris **Harman** (2008) *A People's History of the World* London: Verso

Thomas **Harris** (1995) *I'm OK, You're OK* Arrow Books

Elaine **Hatfield** and Richard L Rapson (2005) *Passionate Love, Sexual Desire, and Mate Selection: Cross-Cultural and Historical Perspectives* Page 227 www.elainehatfield.com/ch80.pdf

Daryl **Hannah** (2012) *The battle against Big Energy's rush to ruin our planet* http://www.guardian.co.uk/commentisfree/2012/oct/31/battle-big-oil-rush-ruin-darylhannah 31st October 2012

Robert D **Hare** (1999) *Without Conscience* in: Thomas G Plante (2006) *Mental Disorders of the New Millennium* Vol 1 Behavioral Issues Westport: Praeger

Adam **Harvey** (2013) *Stealthwear: new designs for counter-surveillance* Exhibition at *Tank Magazine*, Portland Street, London 17 January 2013 http://ahprojects.com/projects/stealth-wear

Havocscope Black Market website http://www.havocscope.com/products/ranking/

Jeremy **Hazell** (1982) *The unconscious significance of some motivational blockages in students at university* British Journal of Guidance & Counselling Volume 10 Issue 1

Jeremy **Hazell** (1989) *Thoughts on the Pain of Self-Disclosure* Journal of the British Association of Psychotherapists no.20 July 1989

Louise **Hay** (1984, 2004 edition) *You Can Heal Your Life* Hay House http:// www. hayhouse. com/

Richard **Heinberg** (2011) *The End of Growth: Adapting to Our New Economic Reality* Forest Row: Clairview

Bert **Hellinger** – see Joy Manne

Cecil G **Helman** (2007) *Culture, Health and Illness* Hodder Arnold

Stéphane **Hessel** (2010) *Time for Outrage!* London: Charles Glass Books

Christopher **Hitchens** (2007) *God is Not Great* Atlantic Books

Eric **Hobsbawm** (1995 ed) *The Age of Extremes: The Short Twentieth Century 1914-1991* Abacus

Stephen A **Hoeller** (2002) *Gnosticism: New Light on the Ancient Tradition of Inner Knowing* Quest Books

Alan **Hollinghurst** (2005) *The Line of Beauty* Picador

Thomas H **Holmes** and Richard H Rahe (1967) *The Social Readjustment Rating Scale* J Psychosom Res **11** (2): 213–8

Robert H. **Hopcke**, Karin Lofthus Carrington, and Scott Wirth (eds) (1993) *Same-Sex Love and the Path to Wholeness* Shambhala

Christopher **Hope** *Exclusive: Cabinet is worth £70million* Telegraph 27th May 2012 http://www.telegraph.co.uk/news/politics/9290520/Exclusive-Cabinet-is-worth-70million.html

Linda **Hopkins** (2006) *False Self: A Life of Masud Khan* Karnac Books

Roger **Housden** (2003) *ten poems to set you free* New York: Random House Crown Publishing/ Harmony Books

Roger **Housden** (2001) *ten poems to change your life* Harmony

Mike **Hulme** (2009) *Why We Disagree About Climate Change* Cambridge University Press

Human Trafficking Team, Organised and Financial Crime Unit, Home Office *First annual report of the Inter-Departmental Ministerial Group on Human Trafficking* October 2012

Samuel P **Huntington** (2002 edition) *The Clash of Civilisations and the New World Order* Free Press

M H Van **Ijzendoorn**, F A Goossens and R Van Dee Veer *Klaus F Riegel and Dialectical Psycology [sic] in Search for the Changing Individual in a Changing Society* University of Leiden *https://openaccess.leidenuniv.nl/bitstream/handle/.../7-703-175.pdf*

Ivan **Illich** (1976) *Limits to Medicine: Medical Nemesis: The Expropriation of Health* London: Marion Boyars

Chrys **Ingraham** (2008) *White Weddings: romancing heterosexuality in popular culture* Taylor and Francis

International Labour Organization, *A Global Alliance against Forced Labour* Geneva, International Labour Office, 2005

Tim **Jackson** (2009) *Prosperity without Growth: Economics for a Finite Planet* London: Earthscan

Oliver **James** (2007) *Affluenza* Random House/Vermilion

Oliver **James** (1998, 2010) *Britain on the Couch* London Random House/Vermilion

Kay Redfield **Jamison** (1993) *Touched with Fire: Manic-Depressive Illness and the Artistic Temperament* New York: The Free Press.

Karl **Jaspers** and Michael Bullock (tr.) (1953) *The Origin and Goal of History* London: Routledge and Keegan Paul

Susan **Jeffers** (1987)(2012 25th anniversary edition) *Feel the Fear and Do It Anyway* Random House/Vermilion

Paul **Johnson** (2001) *A History of the Jews* Orion/Phoenix

Paul **Johnson** (1980 ed) *A History of Christianity* Pelican

W.D.K. **Johnson** *Predisposition to emotional distress and psychiatric illness amongst doctors: the role of unconscious and experiential factors* British Journal of Medical Psychology, 1991 Wiley Online Library

Paul **Johnson** (2001) *A History of the Jews* Orion/Phoenix

Adam **Jones** (2008) *Crimes Against Humanity: A Beginner's Guide* Oxford: One World

Owen **Jones** (2012) *Chavs: The Demonisation of the Working Class* Verso Books

Jenny **Joseph** (1997) *Warning: when I am old I shall wear purple* Souvenir Press Ltd.

Jubilee Debt Campaign http://www.jubileedebtcampaign.org.uk

Tony **Judt** (2006) *Post-war: A history of Europe since 1945* Penguin Books

Tony **Judt** (2011) *Ill Fares the Land* London: Penguin Books

Immanuel **Kant** (1781, 2007 translation) *Critique of Pure Reason* Penguin Classics

Martin **Kantor** (2006) *The Psychopathy of Everyday Life: How Antisocial Personality Disorder Affects All of Us* Praeger

John **Keane** *A Proposal for Rethinking the Origins and Future of representative Government* European Science Foundation http://www.thefutureofrepresentativedemocracy.org/

John **Keane** (2008) *The Life and Death of Democracy*, London: Simon and Schuster

Steve **Keen** (2001) *Debunking Economics: The Naked Emperor of the Social Sciences* London: Zed Books

Patrick **Kingsley** (2012) *Kalle Lasn – the man who inspired the Occupy movement* http://www.guardian.co.uk/world/2012/nov/05/kalle-lasn- man-inspired-occupy 5th November, 2012

Melanie **Klein** (1975) *Envy and Gratitude and Other Works 1946-1963 (The Writings of Melanie Klein, Volume 3)* Karnac Books / Vintage books

Nathaniel **Kleitman** and Eugene Aserinsky (1953) *Regularly Occurring Eye Periods of Motility and Other Phenomena, During Sleep* Science New series 18:3062 September 4, 1953 273-274

Eric **Klinenberg** (2013) *Going Solo* Gerald Duckworth & Co.Ltd

Suzanne C **Kobasa** (1979) *Stressful life events, Personality, and Health – Inquiry into Hardiness* Journal of Personality and Social Psychology **37** (1): 1–11.

Gregorio **Kohon** (1986) *The British School of Psychoanalysis: the Independent tradition* London: Free Association Books

Lawrence **Kohlberg** (1981) *Essays on Moral Development* Vol I: *The Philosophy of Moral Development* San Francisco: Harper & Row.

Heinz **Kohut** (1971). *The analysis of the self: A systematic approach to the psychoanalytic treatment of narcissistic personality disorders.* Perspectives.

Laurence J. **Kotlikoff** (2013) *Fiscal Child Abuse American Style* The World Financial Review http://www.worldfinancial review. com/?p=2240

Laurence J. **Kotlikoff** and Scott Burns (2012) *The Clash of Generations: Saving Ourselves, Our Kids, and Our Economy* MIT Press 2012.

Elisabeth **Kübler-Ross** (1973) *On Death and Dying* Routledge

Imre **Kurtész** (1990) (2004 English translation T. Wilkinson) *Kaddish for an Unborn Child* Vintage

Will **Kymlicka** (2012) *Multiculturalism: Success, Failure, and the Future* Queen's University, Canada February 2012 Migration Policy Institute of Europe

Joan **Lachkar** (2004) *The Narcissistic/Borderline Couple* New York: Brummer/Routledge

Joan **Lachkar** (2008) *How to Talk to a Narcissist* Routledge

Ronald D **Laing** (1960) *The Divided Self: An Existential Study in Sanity and Madness.* Harmondsworth: Penguin.

Christopher **Lasch** (1979) (1991) *The Culture of Narcissism* New York: W W Norton & Co.

Christopher **Lasch** (1995) *Revolt of the Elites and the Betrayal of Democracy* New York: W W Norton & Co

Scott **Lash** and John Ury (1987) *The End to Organised Capitalism* Oxford: Blackwell/Polity Press

Kalle **Lasn**/Adbusters (2012) *Meme Wars: the Creative Destruction of Neo-Classical Economics (by M.Adbusters)* Penguin Books

Brother **Lawrence** (1981) *The Practice of the Presence of God* Hodder and Stoughton

D H **Lawrence** (1913) (1992 ed) *Sons and Lovers* Wordsworth editions

Annette **Lawson** (1988) *Adultery* Basil Blackwell

Richard S **Lazarus** (1966) *Psychological Stress and the Coping Process* New York: McGraw-Hill Book Co.

Darian **Leader** and David Corfield (2007) *Why do people get ill?* London: Penguin Books

Darian **Leader** and Judy Groves (2010 revised ed) *Lacan: A Graphic Guide* Icon Books

Darian **Leader** (2011) *What is madness?* Penguin: Hamish Hamilton

Denise **Linn** http://www.deniselinn.com/index.htm

Sarah **Litvinoff** (1991) *Better relationships: practical ways to make your love last* Ebury Press/ Vermilion

D **Liu**, M L Ng, L P Zhou, and E J Haeberle *Sexual Behavior in Modern China: Report on the Nation-wide Survey of 20 000 Men and Women* New York: Continuum 1997, pp. 586 (Chinese edition: Joint Publishers, Shanghai 1992, pp. 866)

John **Locke** (1690) *An Essay Concerning Human(e) Understanding in Works, Vol 1.* London: Taylor 1722

Peter **Longerich** (2012) *Joseph Goebbels: Biographie* Pantheon Verlag (German version)

Audre **Lorde** (1984) *Sister Outsider* Crossing Press

Mary **Loudon** (1994) *Revelations: the Clergy Questioned* Penguin Books

Alexander **Lowen** (1984) (2004) *Narcissism: Denial of the True Self* Simon and Schuster

Diarmaid **MacCulloch** (2010) *A History of Christianity: The First Three Thousand Years* London: Penguin

Alistair **McGrath** (2011) *Why God Won't Go Away: Engaging with the New Atheism* SPCK Publishing

Alistair **McGrath** (2007) *The Dawkins Delusion: Atheist Fundamentalism and the Denial of the Divine* SPCK Publishing

Kristin **Madden** (2005) *Exploring the Pagan Path: Wisdom from the Elders* new Page Books/Career Press

Rachel P **Maines** (2001 edition) *The Technology of Orgasm: 'Hysteria', the Vibrator and Women's Sexual Satisfaction* John Hopkins University Press

Simon **Malpas** (2003) *Jean-François Lyotard* London: Routledge

Joy **Manne** and Bert Hellinger (2012) *Family Constellations: A Practical Guide to Uncovering the Origins of Family Conflict* North Atlantic Books

Abraham **Maslow** (1962) (2010 ed) *Toward a Psychology of Being* Martino Publishing

Paul **Mason** (2010) *Meltdown: The End of the Age of Greed* Verso Books

Paul **Mason** (2012) *Why It's Kicking Off Everywhere* Verso Books

Paul **Mason** (2013) *Why it's STILL Kicking Off Everywhere* Verso Books

Jeffrey **Masson** (1989) *Against Therapy* London: Collins

Jeffrey **Masson** (1984) (1992 edition) *The Assault on Truth: Freud and Child Sexual Abuse* London: Harper Collins/Fontana

James E **Masterson** (1988) *The Search for the Real Self: Unmasking the Personality Disorders of Our Age* Free Press/Simon and Schuster

Medline Plus – Intersex http://www.nlm.nih.gov/medlineplus/ency/article/001669.htm

Ken **Mellor** and Eric Schiff *Discounting* Transactional Analysis Journal V.5, No.3, July, 1975, p 295-302

Donella **Meadows**, Jorgen Randers and Dennis Meadows (2004) *Limits to Growth: the 30 year Update* London: Earthscan

Alice **Miller** (1990) *The Untouched Key: Tracing Childhood Trauma in Creativity and Destructiveness* Virago

Alice **Miller** (2005) *The Body Never Lies: The Lingering Effects of Cruel Parenting* Norton

Alice **Miller** (2008 3rd edition) *The Drama of the Gifted Child* Basic Books

Jean Baker **Miller** (1977) *Toward a new psychology of women* Beacon Press

Tariq **Modood** (2013) *Multiculturalism* Polity Press

Bel **Mooney** (2003) *Devout Sceptics: Conversations on Faith and Doubt* Hodder and Stoughton

Cole **Moreton** (2010) *Is God Still An Englishman?* Abacus

Polly **Morland** (2013) *The Society of Timid Souls* Profile

Veronique **Mottier** (2008) *Sexuality: a very short introduction* Oxford University Press

Robert F **Murphy** (1990) *The Body Silent: The Different World of the Disabled* New York: W W Norton

The Center for **Nanotechnology** in Society http://www.cns.ucsb.edu/about/nanotechnology-society

The Project on Emerging **Nanotechnologies** *Website* http://www.nanotechproject.org/topics/nano101/introduction_to_nanotechnology/

National Patient Safety Agency *Safety in Doses: improving the uses of medicines in the NHS* Learning from National Reporting in 2007

Vicente **Navarro** (1986) *Crisis, health and medicine: a social critique* Routledge

John **Newsinger** (2000) *The Blood Never Dried: A People's History of the British Empire* London: Bookmarks

Virginia **Nicholson** (2007) *Singled Out: How Two Million Women Survived Without Men after the First World War* London: Penguin Books

Frederic **Nietzsche** (2004 ed) *A Nietzsche Reader* Longman

Jennie G. **Noll**, Meg H. Zeller, Penelope K. Trickett and Frank W. Putnam (2007) *Obesity Risk for Female Victims of Childhood Sexual Abuse: A Prospective Study* Pediatrics Vol. 120 No. 1 July 1, 2007 http://pediatrics.aappublications.org/content/ 120/1/ e61. short

J C **Norcross** and M R Goldfried (eds) (2005) (2nd ed) *Handbook of psychotherapy integration* New York: Oxford University Press

Josef **Novak** and D B Gowin (1984) *Learning How to Learn* Cambridge University Press

Kieron **O'Hara** (2010) *The Enlightenment: A Beginner's Guide* One World

Jim **O'Neill** (2001) *Building Better Global Economic BRICs*. Global Economics Paper No. 66 (66). 30 November 2001 Goldman Sachs & Co.

Ogi **Ogas** and Sai Gaddam (2012) *A Billion Wicked Thoughts: What the Internet tells us about Sexual Relationships* Plume Books

Michael **Oliver** and Colin Barnes (2012) *The New Politics of Disablement* Palgrave/Macmillan

Susie **Orbach** (2002) *Susie Orbach on Eating* London: Penguin

Susie **Orbach** (1999) *The Impossibility of Sex* Allen Lane

Naomi **Oreskes** and Erik M Conway (2010) *Merchants of Doubt: How a Handful of Scientists Obscured the Truth on Issues from tobacco Smoke to Global Warming* London: Bloomsbury

David **Owen** (1987) *In Sickness and in Power: Illness in the Heads of Government during the last 100 years* Methuen

John **Quiggin** (2010) *Zombie Economics: How Dead Ideas Still Walk Among Us* Princeton University Press

Fritz **Perls** (1964) *Games People Play* New York: Grove Press

Robert **Peston** (2012) *How Do We Fix This Mess?: The Economic Price of Having it All, and the Route to Lasting Prosperity* Hodder and Stoughton

Philip **Pettit** (1997) *Republicanism: a theory of freedom and government* Oxford University Press

Philip Pettit (2001) *Deliberative democracy and the discursive dilemma* Philosophical Issues Volume 11: 1 268–299 October

Center on **Philanthropy** at Indiana University *HM Revenue and Customs 2006 and The 2010 Study of High Net Worth Philanthropy: Issues Driving Charitable Activities among Affluent Households* (2010)

Center on **Philanthropy** at Indiana University *HM Revenue and Customs* 2006 *and Bank of America Study of High Net Worth Philanthropy* (2008)

Adam **Phillips** (1997) *Winnicott* Fontana Modern Masters

Jean **Piaget** and B Inhelder (1962) *The Psychology of the Child* New York: Basic Books

Thomas G **Plante** (ed) (2006) *Mental disorders of the new millennium* Praeger Publishers Inc.

Sylvia **Plath** (1963) (2005 ed) *The Bell Jar* Faber and Faber

Sylvia **Plath** (1966) *Ariel* Harper and Row

Eleanor H **Porter** (1913) *Pollyanna* L C Page

James W **Prescott** (1975) *Body Pleasure and The Origins of Violence* The Futurist Bethesda, MD. reprinted in: *The Bulletin of Atomic Scientists*, November 1975, pp.10- 20

James O **Prochaska** and Carlo DiClemente (1986) *Toward a Comprehensive Model of Change in Treating Addictive Behaviours* in W R Miller and N Heather (eds) *Treating Addictive Behaviors* New York: Plenum Press pp.3-27

Ayn **Rand** (1966) *Capitalism:The Unknown Ideal* New York: New American Library.

Nigel **Rapport** (2008) *Of Orderlies and Men: Hospital Porters Achieving Wellness at Work* Carolina Academic

Harvey **Ratner**, Evan George and Chris Iveson (2012) *Solution-focused brief therapy: 100 key points and techniques* Routledge

Janice **Raymond** (1995) *Report to the United Nations Special Rapporteur on Violence Against Women: Prostitution and Trafficking* Coalition Against Trafficking in Women

Eric **Rayner** (1991) *The Independent Mind in British Psychoanalysis* London: Free Association Books

Martin **Rees** (2004) *Our Final Hour: A Scientist's Warning* Basic Books

Antti **Revonsuo** *The reinterpretation of dreams: an evolutionary hypothesis of the function of dreaming* Behavioral and Brain Sciences (2000) 23:pp 877-901 Cambridge University Press

John Steadman **Rice** (1998) *A Disease of One's Own: Psychotherapy, Addiction and the Emergence of Co-dependency*

Transaction Publishers
Paul **Ricoeur** (1970) *Freud and Philosophy: An Essay on Interpretation* New Haven: Yale University Press
Klaus F **Riegel** *The dialectics of human development* American Psychologist, Vol 31(10), Oct 1976, 689-700
Ken **Robinson** (2001) *Out of our Minds: Learning to be Creative* Capstone
Ken **Robinson** (2009) *The Element: How Finding Your Passion Changes Everything* Penguin/Viking
Carl **Rogers** (1961) (2004 ed) *On becoming a person* London: Constable and Robinson Ltd.
Richard **Rorty** (1989) *Contingency, Irony and Solidarity* Cambridge University Press
Richard **Rorty** (1999) *Philosophy and Social Hope* Penguin Books
Philip **Roth** (2007) *Everyman* Vintage
Susan **Rowland** (2001) *Jung: a Feminist Revision* Polity Press
Elisabetta **Ruspini**, Jeff Hearn, Bob Pease and Keith Pringle (eds.) (2011) *Men and Masculinities around the World: Transforming Men's Practices* Palgrave Macmillan
Michael **Rutter** (1981) *Maternal Deprivation Reassessed* Harmondsworth: Penguin
Julie **Ruvolo** *How Much of the Internet Is Actually For Porn?* Forbes http://www.forbes.com/sites/julieruvolo/2011/09/07/ how-much-of-the-internet-is-actually-for-porn/
Joseph **Sandler** (1991) *Freud's 'On Narcissism: an introduction'* Yale University Press
Jean-Paul **Sartre** (1944) *Huis Clos/No Exit* Vintage
Annette **Scambler**, Graham Scambler, and Donald Craig (1981) *Kinship and friendship networks and women's demand for primary care* J R Coll Gen Pract 1981 December: 31(233) 746–750.
Graham **Scambler** (2004) *Re-framing Stigma: Felt and Enacted Stigma and Challenges to the Sociology of Chronic and Disabling Conditions* Social Theory and Health (2) 29 - 46.
Graham **Scambler** and Annette Scambler *Underlying the Riots: The Invisible Politics of Class* Sociological Research Online 16 (4) 25 http://www.socresonline.org.uk/16/4/25.html 10.5153/sro.2556 30 Nov 2011
Maggie **Scarf** (1987) *Intimate Partners* Century
Nancy **Scheper-Hughes** (2000) *The Global Traffic in Human Organs* Current Anthropology 41:2 April 2000

Jacqui **Schiff** and Aaron Schiff (1971) *Passivity* Transactional Analysis Journal 1: 1 (Jan 1971) 71-78
Jacqui Lec **Schiff** and Beth Day (1970) (1974 ed) *All My Children* Pyramid Books
Lisa **Schlessinger** (2001) *Ten Stupid Things People Do to Mess Up Relationships* Harper Collins
Albert **Schweitzer** (1954) *The Problem of Peace* – speech delivered for the 1952 Nobel Peace Prize http://www.nobelprize.org/nobel_prizes/peace/laureates/1952/sch weitzer-lecture.html
Morgan **Scott Peck** (1978) *The Road Less Travelled* Arrow Books
Jeremy **Seabrook** (2009) *The Refuge and the Fortress: Britain and the flight from tyranny* Palgrave Macmillan
Ruth **Seifert** *Rape: the female body as symbol and sign* in Ilkka Taipale (2002) *War or health?* Cambridge, Mass: International Physicians for the Prevention of Nuclear War (IPPNW)/Zed Books
Martin **Seligman** (2011) *Flourish* London: Nicholas Brealey Publishing
Hans **Selye** (1974) *Stress Without Distress* Philadelphia: J B Lippincott
Anup **Shah** (2012) *Global Issues website* http://www. globalissues.org/
Soyen **Shaku** (tr. by Suzuki) *Zen for Americans: Sermons of a Buddhist Abbot* www. forgottenbooks.org
Jerrold Lee **Shapiro** and Susan Bernadett Shapiro *Narcissism: Greek Tragedy, Psychological Syndrome and Cultural Norm* in Thomas G Plante (2006) *Mental Disorders of the New Millennium* Vol 1 Behavioral Issues Westport: Praeger
Steve de **Shazer** (1985) *Keys to Solution in Brief Therapy.* New York: W W Norton & Company
Gail **Sheehy** (1976) *Passages: predictable crises of adult life* New York: Dutton
Gail **Sheehy** (1981) *Pathfinders: how to achieve happiness by conquering life's crises* London: Sidgwick and Jackson
Philip **Sheldrake** (2012) *Spirituality: A Very Short Introduction* Oxford
Peter **Singer** (2001) *Marx: A Very Short Introduction* Oxford Paperbacks

Darra **Singh** *Policing large scale disorder: lessons from the disturbances of August 2011* Parliament: House of Commons Home Affairs Committee

Andrzej **Sitkowski** (2006) *UN Peacekeeping Myth and Reality* Praeger Press

Peter K **Smith**, Helen Cowie and Mark Blades (2011) *Understanding Children's Development* John Wiley

Alexander **Solzhenitsyn** (1963) (*tr.* R Parker) *One Day in the life of Ivan Denisovich* Penguin Classics

Alexandr **Solzhenitsyn** (orig. 1973) (2007 abridged ed) *The Gulag Archipelago* Harper Perennial

Baruch **Spinoza** (tr. Edwin Curley) (1996) *Ethics* Penguin Books

Benjamin **Spock** (1946) Benjamin Spock and Steven Parker (1998) (7th ed) *The Common Sense Book of Baby and Child Care* Pocket Books

John Shelby **Spong** (2011) *Re-Claiming the Bible for Non-Religious World* HarperOne

St. John of the Cross (1972 ed) *The Poems of St John of the Cross* New Directions Publishing

Starhawk (1982) *Dreaming the Dark: magic, sex and politics* Boston: Beacon Press

Muriel **Steffans** *Philanthropy is big business – except in corporate Australia* Sydney Morning Herald June 4, 2011

Claude **Steiner** (1971) *The Stroke Economy* TAJ, 1(3), pp.9-15

Claude **Steiner** (1990) (2000 edition) *Scripts People Live* Grove Press

Richard **Stephens,** John Atkins, and Andrew Kingston (2009) *Swearing as a Response to Pain* Neuroreport **20** (12): 1056–60

Robert J **Sternberg** (1988) *The Triangle of Love: Intimacy, Passion, Commitment.* Basic Books

Robert J **Sternberg** (2013) *Searching for Love* The Psychologist vol 26:2 February 2013 98-101

Anthony **Stevens** (2001) *Jung: a very short introduction* Oxford Paperbacks

David **Stewart** 1989 *The Hermeneutics of Suspicion* Journal of Literature and Theology 3: 296-307.

Ian **Stewart** and Vann Joines (1987) *TA Today: A New Introduction to Transactional Analysis* Life Space Publishing

Anthony **Storr** (1988) *Solitude* Collins: Fontana Books/Flamingo

Anthony **Storr** (2001) *Freud: a very short introduction* Oxford paperbacks

Martha **Stout** (2007) *The Sociopath Next Door* Bantam/Doubleday/Dell

Margaret **Stroebe**, Robert O Hanson, Wolfgang Stroebe and Henk Schut (eds) (2001) Handbook of *Bereavement Research: Consequences, Coping and Care* Washington DC: American Psychological Association

Sutton Trust *The Educational Backgrounds of MPs in 2010* May 2010 http://www.suttontrust.com/reports/ST_Milburn Submission.pdf

Thomas **Szasz** (1961, 1977) *The Myth of Mental Illness: Foundations of a Theory of Personal Conduct.* Harper & Row

Thomas Stephen **Szasz** (2006) *"My Madness Saved Me":*
The Madness and Marriage of Virginia Woolf Transaction Publishers

Nassim Nicholas **Taleb** (2012) *Antifragile: how to live in a world we don't understand* Allen Lane

Richard **Tarnas** (1991) *The Passion of the Western Mind* Random House/Pimlico Books

Richard **Templar** (2009 and 2013) *The Rules of Love* Pearson

Studs **Terkel** (2003) *Hope Dies Last: Making a Difference in an Indifferent World* Granta Books

Toby **Thacker** (2009) *Joseph Goebbels: Life and Death* Palgrave Macmillan

Brian **Thorne** (2012) *Counselling and Spiritual Accompaniment: Bridging Faith and Person-centred Therapy* Wiley-Blackwell

Paul **Tillich** (1952) *The Courage To Be* Collins: Fount Paperbacks

Richard **Tillett** *The patient within – psychopathology in the helping professions* Adv.Psychiatr.Treat 2003, 9:272-279

Transform Drug Policy Foundation
http://www.tdpf.org.uk/MediaNews_FactResearchGuide_Size OfTheDrugMarket.htm#_ftnref7

Bryan **Turner** (1995 2nd ed) *Medical Power and Social Knowledge (A Handbook of Experimental Pharmacology)* Sage

Jean **Twenge** (2012)_*The Revenge of the Insulted Narcissist* Psychology Today 25 July, 2012 (online)
http://www.psychologytoday.com/blog/the-narcissism-epidemic/201207/the-revenge-the-insulted-narcissist

Jean M **Twenge** and W Keith Campbell (2009) *The Narcissism Epidemic: Living in the Age of Entitlement* Free Press/Simon and Schuster.

United Nations Office on Drugs and Crime UN.GIFT *Human trafficking: an overview* 2008

Suzanne **Vender** and Phyllis Schafly (2011) *The Flipside of Feminism: What Conservative Women Know – and Men Can't Say* WND Books

Marc **Vernon** *Carl Jung part 8: Religion and the search for meaning* Guardian.co.uk 18th July 2011

John **Vidal** *UK relies on virtual water from drought-prone countries, says report* The Guardian 17th April, 2010

Howard **Waitzkin**, Celia Iriart, Alfredo Estrada, and Silvia Lamadrid *Social Medicine Then and Now: Lessons From Latin America* Am J Public Health. 2001 October; 91(10): 1592–1601

Bruce **Wampold** (2001) *The Great Psychotherapy Debate: Models, Methods and Findings* Routledge

Jeanne **Ward** and Mendy Marsh (2006) *Sexual Violence Against Women and Girls in War and Its Aftermath: Realities, Responses, and Required Resources: A Briefing Paper* Prepared for: Symposium on Sexual Violence in Conflict and Beyond 21-23 June 2006 Brussels (Belgium) UNPFA

Robert **Ward** *Economist Intelligence Unit* http://www.eiu.com/site_info.asp?info_name=presenters_robert_ ward&page=noads

Paul **Ware** (1983) *Personality adaptations (doors to therapy)* Transactional Analysis Journal 13: 11-19.

Margaret **Warner** *Person-Centred Therapy at the Difficult Edge: a Developmentally based Model of Fragile and Dissociated Process* Chap 8 in Dave Mearns and Brian Thorne (2000) *Person-Centred Therapy Today, New Frontiers in Theory and Practice* Sage Publications

Ashley **Weinberg** and Cary Cooper (2012) *Stress in Turbulent Times* Palgrave Macmillan

Marjorie E **Weishaar** (1993) *Aaron T. Beck (Key Figures in Counselling and Psychotherapy)* Sage Publications Ltd

John T **Wenders** *Democracy would doom Hong Kong* The Freeman, January 1998 The Foundation for Economic Education. also online at http://www.independent.org/newsroom/article. asp?id=214

Andrew **Wheatcroft** (2004) *Infidels: A History of the Conflict between Christianity and Islam* London: Penguin Books

Joe **Wiesenthal** (2010) *The Next BRICs: Six Surging Countries You Must Pay Attention To This Decade* Money Game Jan 6 2010 http://www.businessinsider.com/the-next-10-brics-2010-1?op=1#ixzz2OT3kkWNR

Richard **Wilkinson** and Kate Pickett (2009,2010) *The Spirit Level: Why Equality is Better for Everyone* Penguin Books

Donald W **Winnicott** (1960) *Ego Distortion in Terms of True and False Self* in *The Maturational Process and the Facilitating Environment: Studies in the Theory of Emotional Development.* New York: International UP Inc., 1965, pp. 140-152.

Jessica **Wolfe**, Kiban Turner, et al. (2005) *Gender and Trauma as Predictors of Military Attrition: A Study of Marine Corps Recruits* Military Medicine 170(2005): 12, 1037

E N **Wolff** (2007). *Recent trends in household wealth in the United States: Rising debt and the middle-class squeeze.* Working Paper No. 502 Annandale-on-Hudson, NY: The Levy Economics Institute of Bard College.

David **Wootton** (2006, 2007) *Bad Medicine* Oxford University Press

Ian **Wylie** *Space Invaders* http://www.guardian.co.uk/money/2008/feb/16/workandcareers

Hogie **Wyckoff** (1971) *The Stroke Economy in Women's Scripts TAJ I*, 3 pp 16-30

Irvin **Yalom** (1992, 2005 ed) *When Nietzsche Wept* Harper Perennial

Irvin **Yalom** (2008) *Staring at the Sun: overcoming the dread of death* Piatkus

Irvin **Yalom** (2012) (2nd ed) *Love's Executioner* Basic Books

Bernie **Zilbergeld** (2004) *Better than ever: time for love and sex* Crown House Publishing

Philip **Zimbardo** and Stanley Milgram (2010) *Obedience to Authority: An Experimental View* Pinter and Martin Ltd.

Howard **Zinn** (2002) *You Can't Be Neutral on a Moving Train* Beacon Press

Howard **Zinn** (2005) *A People's History of the United States: 1492-present-day* Harper Perennial

Carl **Zimmer** *Meet your secret master* The Brain *Fall* 2010 pp. 47-49

Man, Myth and Magic - original journal contains many articles of interest.

Web material
Medline Plus – Intersex http://www.nlm.nih.gov/medlineplus/ency/article/001669.htm
http://www2.hu-berlin.de/sexology/GESUND/ARCHIV/ MAY_97.HTM
http://www.personneltoday.com/articles/2002/07/09/13721/web-porn-at-work-leads-to-high-number-of-dismissals.html
http://www.ethicaltrade.org/in-action/projects/kenya-flower-project
http://www.treehugger.com/natural-sciences/are-cut-flowers-killing-the-wildlife-in-kenyas-lake-naivasha.html
http://www.guardian.co.uk/environment/2010/apr/19/uk-virtual-water

TV:
Simon Cowell *The X-factor* SYCOtv
Ian Hislop (2011) *When Bankers Were Good* BBC
Made in Chelsea (2011) E4
Young, Posh and Loaded (2003) ITV
Wonderland Series 5: *Young, Bright and On the Right* (2012) BBC

Films:
Chris Columbus (1993) *Mrs Doubtfire*
David Cronenberg (2011) *A Dangerous Method*
Clint Eastwood (2008) *Changeling*
Pascale Ferran (2006) *Lady Chatterley*
Tom Hooper (2010) *The King's Speech*
Beeban Kidron (1989) *Oranges are Not the Only Fruit*
Larysa Kondracki (2010) *The Whistleblower*
Steve McQueen (2010) *Hunger*
Steve McQueen (2011) *Shame*
Michael Mann (1999) *Insider*
Mike Nichols (1983) *Silkwood*
Damien O'Donnell (2004) *Inside I'm Dancing*
Steven Soderbergh (2000) *Erin Brockovich*
Barbra Streisand (1983) *Yentl*
Tanya Wexler (2011) *Hysteria*
Edward Zwick (2008) *Defiance*
Documentary film: John Bowlby and James Robertson (1952) *A Two Year Old Goes to Hospital*

If you would like to come to one or more of our workshops, based on our thinking in this book and on new topics, please get in touch

web: www.skettybooksandworkshops.co.uk

email: skettybooksandworkshops@btconnect.com

post: PO Box 680, Swansea, SA1 9NU

social media:

      facebook.com/Sketty Books and Workshops

      http://twitter.com/Sketty Books

Details of workshops - topics, dates, and locations - are regularly updated on our website